CW01E53640

THOMAS JONES

(1742–1803)

AN ARTIST REDISCOVERED

Ann Sumner

29 May 2003

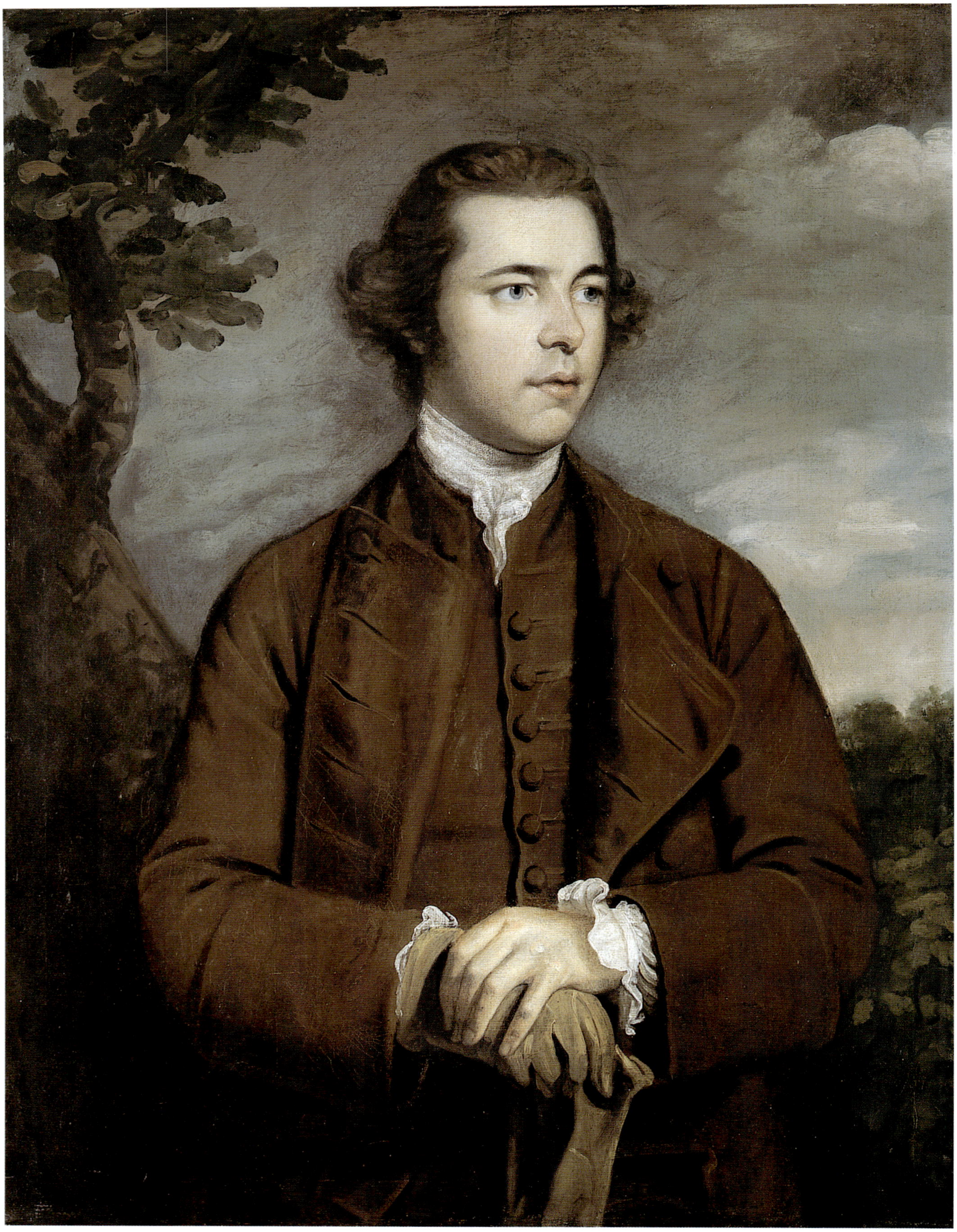

Giuseppe Marchi, *Thomas Jones*, 1768 (cat. no. 1).

THOMAS JONES

(1742–1803)

AN ARTIST REDISCOVERED

Edited by
ANN SUMNER *and* GREG SMITH

with contributions by
CHRISTOPHER RIOPELLE
CHARLES NUGENT
PETER BOWER
LINDSAY STAINTON
KATE LOWRY
BETHANY McINTYRE
and OLIVER FAIRCLOUGH

YALE UNIVERSITY PRESS
NEW HAVEN AND LONDON

in association with

NATIONAL MUSEUMS & GALLERIES OF WALES

AMGUEDDFEYDD AC ORIELAU CENEDLAETHOL CYMRU
NATIONAL MUSEUMS & GALLERIES OF WALES

Noddir gan
Lywodraeth Cynulliad Cymru
Sponsored by
Welsh Assembly Government

This catalogue was published in conjunction with the exhibition
Thomas Jones (1742–1803): An Artist Rediscovered at
National Museum & Gallery, Cardiff (21 May – 10 August 2003)
Whitworth Art Gallery, Manchester (22 August – 26 October 2003)
National Gallery, London (12 November 2003 – 15 February 2004)

First published in 2003 by National Museums & Galleries of Wales,
and Yale University Press, New Haven and London.

Design and production: Yale University Press
Printed and bound in Italy by Conti Tipocolor

Library of Congress Cataloging in Publication Data

Sumner, Ann.
Thomas Jones (1742-1803) : an artist rediscovered / Ann Sumner and Greg Smith.
p. cm.
Includes bibliographical references and index.
ISBN 0-300-09923-1 (cl : alk. paper)
ISBN 0-7200-0534-5
1. Jones, Thomas, 1742-1803–Catalogs. 2. Landscape painting, Welsh–18th century–Catalogs. I. Smith, Greg, 1958- II. Jones, Thomas, 1742-1803. III. Title.
ND497.J627 A4 2003
759.2'929--dc21
2002155408

A catalogue record for this book is available at The British Library

CONTENTS

SPONSOR'S FOREWORD

Sponsorship is one of the most exciting ventures any company undertakes. It rarely, however, allows for real discovery. This exhibition on Thomas Jones is the exception. Not only was he the author of one of the earliest autobiographies by a British artist, he was also creator of some of the most beautiful oil sketches of the eighteenth century, and yet, in spite of this, he remains unknown to many.

For a small and specialist art insurance company like AXA Art Insurance, this sponsorship has provided a unique opportunity to participate in this journey of discovery and to reveal the artist first in his native Wales and then to a wider public at both the Whitworth Art Gallery and the National Gallery, London.

AXA Art is the world's leading insurer dedicated to museums, galleries and private collectors. We are particularly committed to supporting museums in their mission both to educate and entertain. *Thomas Jones: An Artist Rediscovered* promises to fulfil both criteria and also to reshape our understanding of the origins of the British landscape tradition. The National Museums & Galleries of Wales are to be congratulated on this imaginative show, which has been undertaken with such enthusiasm by their committed and knowledgeable staff and their collaborators.

Adam Golder
CEO, AXA Art Insurance, London

AXA ART

DIRECTORS' FOREWORD

Thomas Jones, born at Trefonnen (Trevonen) in Radnorshire in 1742, was a pupil of the well-known Welsh landscape painter, Richard Wilson. Almost forgotten for a hundred and fifty years, Jones is now recognised as one of the most idiosyncratic and innovative of eighteenth-century British artists, and his richly anecdotal *Memoirs* are a fascinating window on his life in Wales, London and especially Italy. Nevertheless, his art, though increasingly admired for its clarity and a remarkable quality of timelessness, remains relatively little understood. This exhibition is the widest survey of his entire career. Incorporating much new research, it places his celebrated oil sketches of buildings in Naples and Rome in the wider context of his subject paintings, earlier oil sketches, drawings and watercolours. It also seeks to explain the social circumstances from which Jones's talents emerged and the family background to which he returned after the death of his elder brother in 1787. His posthumous reputation and the rediscovery of his art are also explored. The National Museums & Galleries of Wales long planned to celebrate the bicentenary of this Welsh artist, and this is the largest exhibition initiated at the National Museum & Gallery in Cardiff for many years. The occasion has also encouraged a rewarding working partnership among our three institutions, to highlight Jones's importance and bring his work to the attention of the widest possible audience.

The exhibition curator, Ann Sumner, Curator (Fine Art), National Museums & Galleries of Wales, had by happy co-incidence worked on the last major exhibition inspired by the art of Thomas Jones, *Travels in Italy*, held at the Whitworth Art Gallery, Manchester, in 1988. She devised the present exhibition, and has worked with great enthusiasm on it over a two-year period in collaboration with Charles Nugent at the Whitworth Art Gallery and Christopher Riopelle at the National Gallery, who has also made a major contribution to this catalogue. Ann has led the internal NMGW team, while bringing together an external advisory committee and an outstanding group of co-curators, including Greg Smith, Exhibition Researcher, who had also curated *Travels in Italy*, and Lindsay Stainton, whose experience of Jones stretches back to the only previous monographic exhibition of his work, held in London and Cardiff in 1970. Kate Lowry, Chief Conservation Officer (Fine Art) at the National Museums & Galleries of Wales, and Peter Bower publish groundbreaking studies of Jones's techniques. We are deeply grateful to the Advisory Committee, which has been a mainstay of support and a constant source of ideas and information. Particular gratitude must be extended to Brian Allen, Director of the Paul Mellon Centre for Studies in British Art. He has given wise and helpful counsel over a range of matters relating to the exhibition

After it closes in Cardiff, *Thomas Jones: An Artist Rediscovered* transfers, almost in its entirety, to the Whitworth Art Gallery, Manchester, where it takes its place in a distinguished sequence of exhibitions exploring British art of the eighteenth and nineteenth centuries. Such exhibitions include *John Robert Cozens* (1971), *Thomas Girtin* (1975) and *Travels in Italy* (1988). The Italian section of the exhibition then moves to the National Gallery, London, under the title *Thomas Jones in Italy*.

This exhibition is made possible through the generosity of many lenders, both individual and institutional, in Britain, Europe and the United States. We pay particular tribute to the many private lenders who have made their works available for long periods. Those who have agreed to be named are listed on page 280, but we are unable to acknowledge many others publicly. A number of private individuals have generously supported the exhibition team, providing new research leads and showing tremendous enthusiasm for the artist and his reputation. Certain public institutions have been particularly generous with loans, especially the British Museum, Tate and the Yale Center for British Art, New Haven. We are much in their debt. These loans, and especially that of *A Land Storm, with the Story of Dido and Aeneas* of 1769 from the State Hermitage Museum, St Petersburg, make this the most comprehensive survey of Jones's career. It has also been a particular pleasure to collaborate with John Nicoll and Gillian Malpass of Yale University Press on the catalogue.

Lastly, *Thomas Jones: An Artist Rediscovered* would not have been possible without the support of sponsors and donors. We would like to thank, in particular, AXA Art for their sponsorship of the exhibition at the National Museum & Gallery, Cardiff and the Heritage Lottery Museums and Galleries Access Fund for supporting the exhibition in Manchester. In addition, we thank Rocco Forte Hotels, The Thaw Charitable Trust, The Paul Mellon Centre for Studies in British Art and Arts & Business Cymru for their generous support of varying aspects of the exhibition. We are also grateful for the continued generosity of Christopher Gridley and his family.

We hope that you will share our delight and enthusiasm for this exhibition. Rediscovering a long-neglected artist is always a pleasure, and it has been our honour to facilitate the process.

Eurwyn Wiliam
Acting Director-General
National Museums & Galleries of Wales

Michael Tooby
Director
National Museum & Gallery, Cardiff

Charles Saumerez-Smith
Director
National Gallery, London

Alistair Smith
Director
Whitworth Art Gallery, University of Manchester

April 2003

EXHIBITION ADVISORY COMMITTEE

Brian Allen, Director of Studies, The Paul Mellon Centre for Studies in British Art, London
Andrew Clayton-Payne, Andrew Clayton-Payne Ltd, London
Mark Evans, Curator (Paintings & Drawings), Victoria and Albert Museum, London
Anne Lyles, Curator (British Art 1780–1860), Tate, London
Charles Nugent, Curator (Drawings and Watercolours), Whitworth Art Gallery, Manchester
Martin Postle, Senior Curator (British Art 1500–1780), Tate, London
Christopher Riopelle, Curator of Nineteenth-Century Paintings, National Gallery, London
Robin Simon, Editor, *British Art Journal*, London
Greg Smith, independent art historian
Lindsay Stainton, independent art historian
Ann Sumner, Curator (Fine Art), National Museums & Galleries of Wales (Chair person)
Ian Warrell, Curator (British Art 1780–1860), Tate, London
Timothy Wilcox, Acting Assistant Keeper, Prints and Drawings, British Museum
Andrew Wyld, Agnew's, London

Committee Secretary: **Bethany McIntyre**, Assistant Curator (Prints & Drawings), National Museums & Galleries of Wales

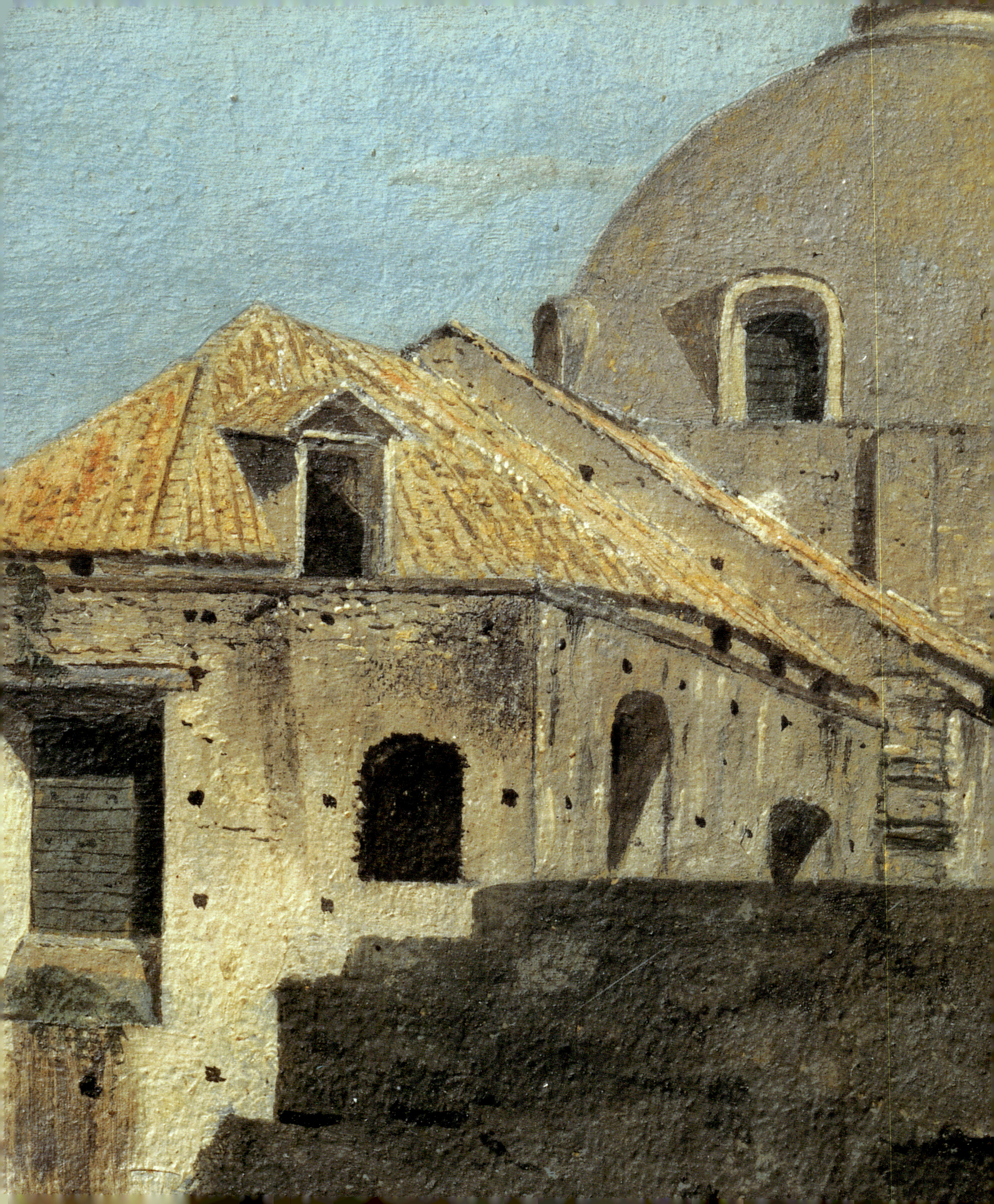

ACKNOWLEDGEMENTS

The National Museums & Galleries of Wales are much indebted to the members of the Thomas Jones bicentenary Advisory Committee who have met regularly at The Paul Mellon Centre for Studies in British Art and who have provided enthusiastic support for this exhibition. The exhibition has been the result of a successful collaboration between ourselves, the National Gallery in London and the Whitworth Art Gallery in Manchester. We have very much enjoyed working with our colleagues in both institutions and are grateful for the time and energy they have given to this project. We have also sought the help and advice of a wide range of scholars, researchers, curators, conservators and dealers within the United Kingdom, Europe and America, to whom we are deeply indebted. Many private collectors and owners have allowed us to view their works, contributing their individual knowledge and enthusiastically supporting the exhibition in many varied ways. We owe a great debt to the pioneering work of Ralph Edwards, who so championed the work of Jones in the first exhibition covering his entire career in 1970. Much research has been carried out over the past thirty-three years since that show, and we have built upon this to produce this exhibition and catalogue.

A group of Jones enthusiasts in Wales have particularly assisted the project from the outset, including Alwyn Batley, David Bellamy, Christine Churchill, Liz Fleming-Williams, Paul Joyner, Jenna Lindsay, Prys Morgan, Jeremy Rye and Denis Selwood. Joy Ashton has been a particular inspiration offering many leads for us to follow in the early stages of our research. Rachel Sholl of Radnorshire Museum and David Moore of Brecknock Museum have also been extremely supportive. It has been an enormous pleasure to work with these individuals and to share in their enthusiasm and dedication to the artist and his reputation. In addition, many other colleagues and scholars have given generously of their time and expertise. In particular, we would like to thank Philip Conisbee, Judy Egerton, Eric Forster, Adrian Le Harivel, Colin Harrison, John Hayes, Jenny and Christopher Newall, Anna Ottanni Cavina, Lucy Peltz, Lisa Renne, Jacqueline Ridge, David Scrase, Robin Simon, David Solkin, Kate Stuart, Sarah Taft, David Thomson, Joyce Townsend, Piers Townsend and Scott Wilcox. John Appleby, Tim Bathurst, Harriet Drummond, Ben Elwes, Martyn Gregory, Lowell Lisbon, James Mackinnon, Henry Wemyss and Andrew Wyld have particularly assisted with the tracing of works through the salerooms.

We should also like to thank all the institutions and private lenders to the exhibition and those who have helped to realize the project, including Geraldine Glynn, Nick Mayhew and Alex Newson (Ashmolean Museum, Oxford) Jane Farrington, Iain Harrison and Elizabeth Smallwood (Birmingham Museums and Art Gallery) Jon Finch and Jennifer Shaw (Bolton Museum and Art Gallery, Bolton MBC), Sheena Stoddard (Bristol Museum and Art Gallery), Anthony Griffiths, Janice Reading and Tim Wilcox (British Museum), Julia Blanks and Catherine Pütz (Courtauld Institute Gallery), Duncan Robinson and Thyrza Smith (Fitzwilliam Museum, Cambridge), Meg Anthony, Evelyn Smith and Jenni Spencer-Davies (Glynn Vivian Art Gallery, Swansea) Olga Ilmenkova and Mikhail Piotrovsky (State Hermitage Museum, St Petersburg), D. Michael Francis, Andrew Green, Ceridwen Lloyd-Morgan, Rhodri Morgan, and Gordon Reid (Llyfrgell Genedlaethol Cymru, National Library of Wales), Federica Pirani and Maria Elisa Tittoni (Musei d'Arte Medievale e Moderna, Roma), Meg Grasselli (National Gallery, Washington), Lucy R. Eldridge (The Pierpont Morgan Library, New York), Catherine Richards

FACING PAGE Detail of cat. no. 113.

(Radnorshire Society), Helen Dorey, Susan Palmer and Margaret Richardson (Sir John Soane's Museum, London) Tim Craven and Clare Mitchell (Southampton City Art Gallery), Stephen Deuchar, Lisa Hayes, Anne Lyles, Alison Miles, Martin Postle and Ian Warrell (Tate), Matthew Rowe (Towner Art Gallery, Eastbourne), Martin Durant, Miranda Percival and David Wright (Victoria and Albert Museum, London), Jonathan Jones, Glenda Lloyd Davies and David Peate (Wales Tourist Board), Melissa Gold Fournier and Timothy Goodhue (Yale Center for British Art, New Haven), Liz Hall, and Derrick and Doreen Smith.

The is the first time the National Museums & Galleries of Wales has collaborated with Yale University Press and we have much appreciated the support and dedication of John Nicoll, who has long appreciated the work of Thomas Jones and who was most encouraging at the outset of the project. We are especially grateful to Gillian Malpass for her catalogue design work, to Sarah Hulbert for copy-editing the English text, and to Jane Horton for the index.

All successful exhibitions are the result of teamwork and the National Museums & Galleries of Wales are a unique repository of knowledge about the history and landscape of Wales. We have also benefited greatly from the expertise of our colleagues in other departments, most particularly Richard Bevins (Geology), David Jenkins (Industry), John Kenyon (Library) and Kevin Thomas (Photography). Richard Tynen and Arabella Smith (Development), Robin Gwyn, Helen Talfryn Walters and Julie Richards (Strategic Communications) and Helen Jones and Nick Beasley (Marketing), Niclas Walker and Ray Woods (Museum of Welsh Life), and Sian Edwards (Visitor Services Department) have all worked with total dedication to support the exhibition and enhance awareness of it within Wales and beyond. Richard Bevins and Kevin Thomas have particularly assisted with the task of accurately locating many of Jones's Radnorshire views. Arwel Hughes and Mari Gordon (Publications & Design) have greatly assisted with the production of this catalogue. We are especially indebted to Martin Rees and Simon Tozzo (Publication & Design) for the design of the exhibition in Cardiff. Pip Diment and Jenny Thompson (Exhibitions) have been supportive with administration. We are also extremely grateful to the Friends of the National Museums & Galleries of Wales, for their support of this exhibition and most particularly to Eric Dover and his team of volunteer guides.

Within the Art Department itself, I am particularly grateful to Keith Bowen, Julia Carver, Hugh Chilcott, Carolyn Cheadle, Sandrine Decoux, Lyn Jarmen Davies, Mike Jones, Christine Mackay, Andrew Renton and Rachel Turnbull, who have all contributed greatly to the exhibition, and to Tim Egan who has skilfully organized the transport arrangements. The catalogue itself would not have been possible without the commitment of Bethany McIntyre (Assistant Curator, Prints & Drawings), who has acted as Committee Secretary and worked tirelessly and with great enthusiasm on the research and administration of the exhibition, as has Clare Smith (Collection Administrator). Clare has also, with Louisa Briggs (Assistant Curator, Modern & Contemporary Art), co-ordinated the photography for the catalogue illustrations. Our Keeper, Oliver Fairclough, who initiated the project, has provided support for all aspects of the exhibition, and it has been particularly rewarding to work closely with our Chief Conservation Officer, Kate Lowry. I also owe a great debt to my predecessor in the Art Department at the National Museum & Gallery, Mark Evans, with whom I have had many long and fruitful conversations about Jones.

We have found the collaboration with the Whitworth Art Gallery and the National Gallery, London beneficial and enjoyable. We are most grateful to Charles Nugent, Nicola Walker, Jennifer Harris, Penny Haworth, Catherine de Lisle, David Morris and Julian Tomlin at the Whitworth and Kate Bell, David Jaffé, Susan Foister, Christopher Riopelle, Denise King, Mary Hersov, Joanne Kent, Rosalie Cass, Sarah Walters, Michael Wilson and Xenia Corcoran at the National Gallery. We are especially grateful to Christopher Riopelle for his very considerable contribution to the catalogue.

The exhibition in Cardiff, and this catalogue, have been generously sponsored by AXA Art, and also generously supported by Rocco Forte Hotels, The Thaw Charitable Trust and Christopher Gridley and family. We are extremely pleased to be working with Clare Pardy (AXA Art Insurance) whose enthusiasm for

Jones is infectious, and Cindy Archer at the Thaw. Isabel Tapp and Tessa Gatti of Rocco Forte Hotels have worked closely with the transport of the St Petersburg picture.

The catalogue and academic conference have also been supported by The Paul Mellon Centre for Studies in British Art. We are particularly indebted to Brian Allen of the Paul Mellon Centre for all he has done to facilitate our committee meetings, and extend thanks also to Frank Salmon and Kasha Jenkinson.

Finally and by no means least, we would like to thank Greg Smith, Exhibition Researcher, for his dedicated scholarship and total commitment to the project. Greg worked on the *Travels in Italy* exhibition back in 1988 at the Whitworth and it has been a hugely rewarding experience to collaborate with him again on this redefinition of Jones's work.

Ann Sumner
Curator (Fine Art) and Exhibition Curator
National Museums & Galleries of Wales

April 2003

CHRONOLOGY

1742	26 September	Thomas Jones born at Trefonnen (Trevonen), second son of Thomas and Hannah Jones.
1749–50		Moves to Pencerrig, near Builth Wells.
1753–8		Educated at Christ College, Brecon.
1758–9		Pupil of Dr Jenkin Jenkins, distinguished classicist and Presbyterian minister.
1759	11 July	Attends Jesus College, University of Oxford, as a Commoner, until 1761. Leaves due to the death of his sponsor, his uncle.
1761	November	Enrols at William Shipley's Drawing School, London.
1762	October	Admitted as a member of the St Martin's Lane Academy.
1763	March	Begins two-year pupillage with Richard Wilson.
1764	June	Awarded Premium by the Royal Society of Arts for academic figure drawing.
1766		Elected Member of the Society of Artists. Shows two works.
1767	May	Wins First Premium for landscape painting from the Royal Society of Arts.
	October	Attends the meeting of the Society of Artists which leads to the secession of artists to found the Royal Academy.
1769		Shows *Dido and Aeneas* (cat. no. 20) at the Society of Artists.
1770		Visit to Gadbridge. First recorded oil sketches (cat. no. 39).
1772		Lengthy stay with Oldfield Bowles at North Aston, Oxfordshire. Again in 1773–4.
	July–August	Sketching in oils at Pencerrig.
1774		Exhibits *The Bard* (cat. no. 31). Paints *View of John Milton's Cottage at Chalfont St Giles* (cat. no. 33).
1775	September	Farewell visit to Pencerrig. Sketching in oils. Returns to London, September 1776.
1776	15 October	Departs for Italy, arriving in Rome, 27 November.
	December	First expedition to Lake Albano, Ariccia – the 'Magick Land'.
1777	April–May	Second trip to Albano and Nemi, partly in the company of William Pars.
	June	Begins *Lake Albano – Sunset* (cat. no. 56).
	November	Visits Tivoli.
1778	September	Journeys to Naples and stays until January 1779.
1779	April	Lists ten oil commissions that he is working on.
	July	First mention of Maria Moncke in *Memoirs*, initially as Jones's housekeeper.
1780	May	Leaves Rome for Naples.
	October	Expeditions along the Neapolitan coast.
		Daughter Anna Maria born.
1781	March	Francis Towne arrives from Rome. Sketching together until April.
	spring	Extensive sketching programme in the area of Santa Maria dei Monti.
		Daughter Elizabetha Francesca born.

1782	January	First of the small oil sketches on paper of Naples buildings.
	February	Begins *Lake Nemi* (cat. no. 58) a companion for *Lake Albano – Sunset* (cat. no. 56).
	October	Making studies for a major oil of the Campi Flegrei (untraced) for Sir William Hamilton.
	November	Death of father, Thomas Jones Senior.
1783	August	Departs Naples by ship with Maria Moncke and their two daughters, arriving in London in November.
1784	spring	Exhibits two works, including Hamilton's picture, at the Royal Academy.
	August	Spends two months at Pencerrig.
1785		Living in London Street, Tottenham Court Road.
1786	September–October	Sketching at Thomas Johnes's estate at Hafod.
1787		Inherits Pencerrig estate on death of brother John.
1789	May	Returns permanently to Wales.
		Marries Maria Moncke in London.
1791		High Sheriff of Radnorshire.
1797	July	Takes up painting again after a long break.
1798	spring	Exhibits for the final time at the Royal Academy.
	November	Completes his *Memoirs* (cat. no. 10).
1799		Death of Maria.
1803	29 April	Dies from 'Angina Pectoris'.

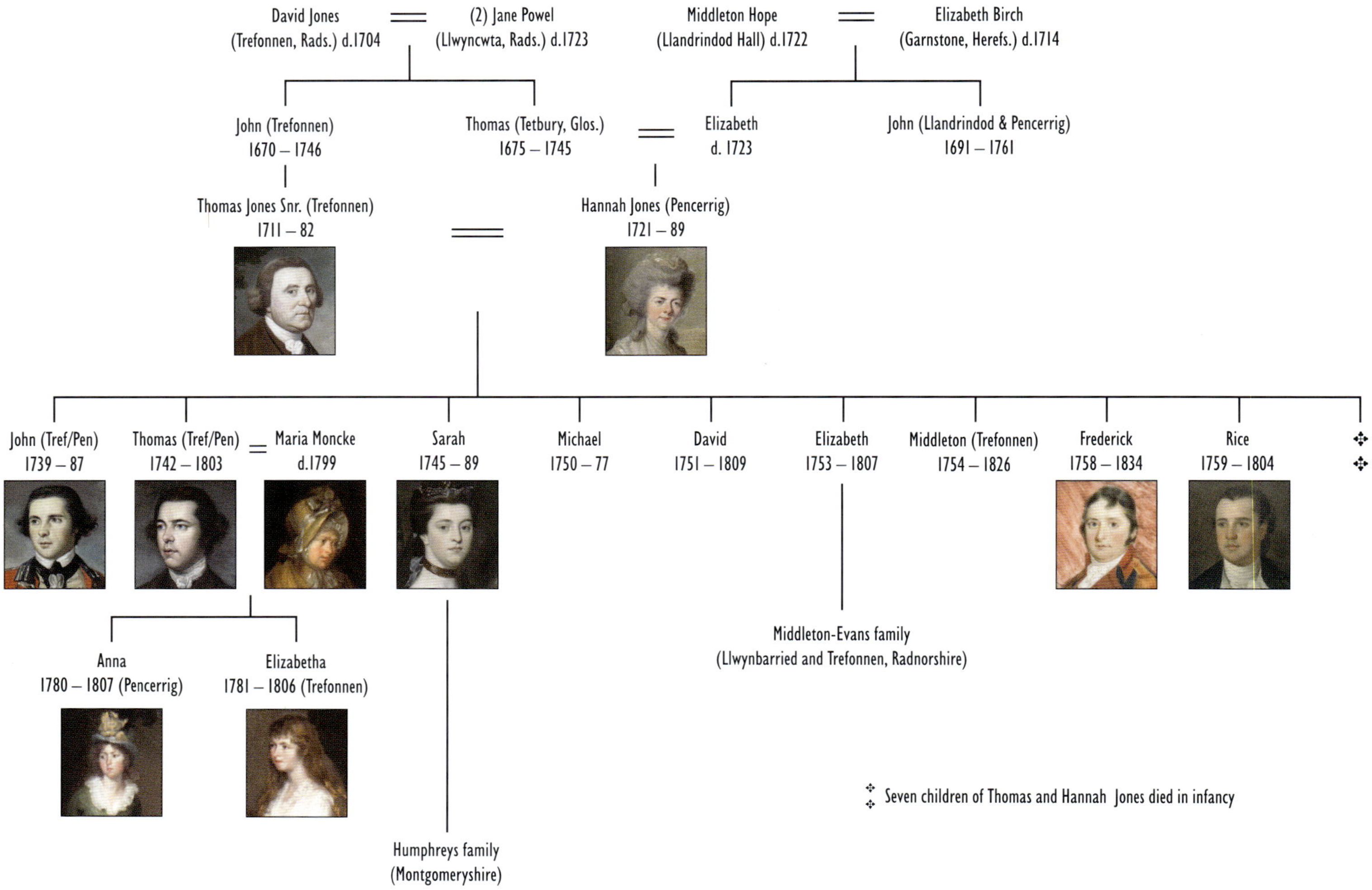

Fig. 1 Family tree of the Jones family of Trefonnen and Pencerrig.

WHO WAS THOMAS JONES? THE LIFE, DEATH AND POSTHUMOUS REPUTATION OF THOMAS JONES OF PENCERRIG

Ann Sumner

Thomas Jones (1742–1803) is one of a select group of eighteenth-century Welsh artists of international significance. Of these educated 'gentlemen' artists from Wales, the best known is Jones's master, Richard Wilson (1713–1782) (cat. no. 14), but the group includes less familiar contemporaries such as William Parry (1742–1791) and John Downman (1750–1824). Today, Thomas Jones is renowned as a painter of highly individual, small-scale oil studies depicting buildings in Naples and as the author of a vivid anecdotal account of his life in Italy. However, during his lifetime, his reputation was based instead upon a series of exhibited landscape paintings, mainly in the style of Richard Wilson. It was only when his *Memoirs* (cat. no. 10) were published in their entirety in 1951 that he was recognized as an important and amusing commentator on the eighteenth-century art world. Then, just a few years later, in 1954, a group of previously unknown oil sketches and unusual watercolours appeared on the art market, and his astonishingly personal and vibrant vision of the Welsh and Italian landscape was revealed to and appreciated by a small group of enthusiastic connoisseurs.

The small oil sketches of Naples, showing crumbling walls, shuttered windows, lines of washing and vegetation growing on brickwork, with their dusty blue and silvery grey tones, impressed art historians in the 1950s. These humble subjects and the compositional cropping he introduced gave his work a spontaneous, modern appearance. Thomas Jones's name was thus rescued from obscurity, and he was gradually recognized as one of the most original artists of the eighteenth century, championed initially by Ffransis Payne (fig. 8), Ralph Edwards (fig. 9), John Gere, Paul Oppé and R. C. B. Oliver, and later, in the 1980s, by Lawrence Gowing (fig. 11), Prys Morgan and Francis Hawcroft. Jones's oil sketches passed quickly into major British museums and were soon sought by American collections as well. This year, 2003, marks the bicentenary of Jones's death and provides the opportunity to consider the scope and character of his entire œuvre and the significance of the 'discovery' of his oil sketches, fifty years ago. So much is now known about Jones, his domestic arrangements, artistic training, working practices and friendships. The mounting of a major exhibition to celebrate his bicentenary provides the opportunity to consider a number of formative issues about him, such as his education and financial circumstances and whether his relative economic independence influenced his artistic development and his working practices. Was Jones really one of the first *plein-air* painters, as his champions in the 1950s thought, or are his oil sketches more planned and calculated than they appear at first sight? Could some of his Italian scenes which appear so spontaneous actually have been executed later in his career, from memory?

Recent art historical interest has focused almost entirely on Jones's oil sketches, which are extraordinarily contemporary in appearance, at the expense of the rest of his output. This introductory essay seeks to consider whether this focus on his oil sketches by modern critics is a valid one. The question of how they came to be overlooked for so long, and the initial reaction to them by a group of curators and connoisseurs in the mid-twentieth century, will be discussed. This exhibition, which is the largest ever to be devoted to Jones, seeks to assess his entire œuvre, particularly the work produced prior to his Italian sojourn, and loans include a number of important early subject paintings such as *A Land Storm, with the Story of Dido and Aeneas* (cat. no. 20) from The State Hermitage Museum, St Petersburg. A large selection of his oil sketches has been brought together, with particular emphasis given to his less well known Radnorshire studies, many of which have been topographically located and technically analysed for the first time. A study of the papers he employed for many of his oils and watercolours has also produced fascinating results, enabling the redating of some works. Through such new research and the display of paintings previously unseen, this exhibition seeks to lift the 'Cloud of Obscurity' in which Jones himself acknowledges that he 'has been so long enveloped'.[1]

The Life of the Artist

Jones was the second son of Thomas Jones (1711–1782) of Trefonnen (Trevonen) (cat. no. 2) and his wife Hannah (1721–1789, cat. no. 4), landowners in Radnorshire with strong dissenting beliefs. He was born on 26 September 1742 at his father's family home, Trefonnen (cat. no. 8) at Llandrindod Wells, the second of sixteen children, seven of whom died young. From 1750 he was brought up at Pencerrig, near Builth Wells (fig. 2), a house and estate inherited by his mother. He was educated at Christ College, Brecon, and Jesus College, Oxford, but a career in the Church did not materialize, owing to the death of his wealthy uncle John Hope, who had been financing his education. He rejected the offer of going to sea, an obvious choice of career for the younger sons of landed gentry. Instead, he persuaded his family to let him train as an artist, an unusual career for

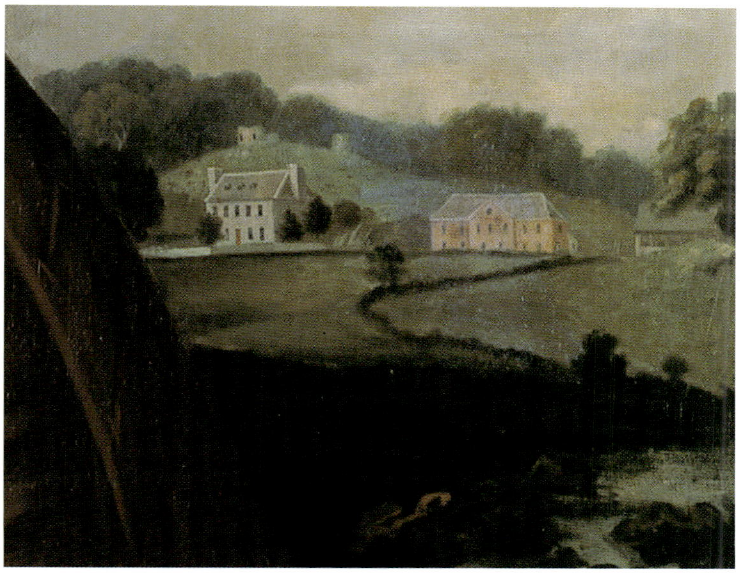

Fig. 2 Pencerrig. Detail from *Thomas Jones Senior*, *c.*1768 (cat. no. 2).

someone of his social standing. Jones went to Shipley's Drawing School and then joined his fellow Welshman, Richard Wilson, as a paying pupil for two years. In 1766 he was elected to the Society of Artists and for the next ten years pursued the career of a professional artist in London, returning to Wales in 1772 and 1775–6.

Jones was determined to follow in Wilson's footsteps and visit Italy, eventually setting off in the autumn of 1776, arriving in Rome after a month's journey. The arrival in Italy was a moment of great personal excitement for Jones. It seemed to him 'Magick Land . . . I had copied so many Studies of that great Man . . . Richard Wilson . . . that I insensibly became familiarized with Italian Scenes, and enamoured of Italian forms, and, I suppose, *injoyed pleasures unfelt by my Companions*'.[2] He remained in Rome for almost two years before his first visit to Naples. In both cities he came into contact with the British community of artists and patrons. His circle of friends soon included Francis Towne (1739–1816) (cat. nos 93–4), William Pars (1742–1782) (cat. nos 97–9), John 'Warwick' Smith (1749–1831) (cat. nos 100–01) and John Robert Cozens (1752–1797) (cat. nos 95–6), all of whom appear regularly in his *Memoirs*. Pars and Smith, for instance, 'privately celebrated St. Davids Day' with him in 1780, 'on board one of the Barques that trade in Spanish wine at the Ripa Grande'.[3]

After six years, Jones became increasingly restless and homesick and he decided to return to Britain from Naples on hearing of his beloved father's death in 1782. He and his lover, Maria Moncke, a Danish widow who had converted to Catholicism, set off by sea in a Swedish brig with their two young daughters in August 1783. His friend and fellow artist Joseph Farington (1747–1821) noted: 'He returned to England and brought with Him a person who went by the name of Mrs. Jones and two children, daughters, the issue of that connexion'.[4] Jones recognized the difficulties his relationship with Maria posed, referring to her as 'Miss Maria Moncke ... whom I afterwards married, th'g for family Reasons I did not think it prudent for some time to own the connexion'.[5] They settled into life in London and Jones struggled to revive his career, but financial matters were less pressing since they now had an income of £300 per annum, left to the artist by his father. A major disappointment for Jones was the discovery that most of the drawings and prints he had left behind had been ruined during his absence.[6]

In 1787 his elder brother, Major John Jones, a bachelor (cat. no. 6), also died and he found himself coming into 'possession of the whole of his Landed property'.[7] At the age of forty-five, Thomas Jones was now head of his family, with an annual income from his estates of some £4,000. The Jones lands extended between Penybont in the north and Builth in the south. Another property in north Breconshire, including Cribarth, came to the family through his mother. They also benefited financially from the popularity of Llandrindod Wells as a spa resort. They owned Llandrindod Hall, and rented it out as an hotel. His father's family home, Trefonnen, was also rented out to provide accommodation for visitors. After his bohemian lifestyle as an artist in London and Italy and liaison with Maria Moncke, Jones now transformed himself into a respectable country squire. His younger brother, Captain Frederick Jones of the East India Company (fig. 5), recorded in his diary in May 1789, 'Br Thomas from his house in London Street took Maria Moncke, his housekeeper and cook to Penkerrig',[8] where presumably her presence caused comment. Jones finally married Maria on 16 September 1789 at St Pancras Church, London, at the particular request of his devoutly religious mother,[9] who died shortly afterwards.[10]

Jones and Maria then settled into life at Pencerrig, leaving their daughters initially in London and later gradually introducing them to Radnorshire society. Jones's deep attachment to his native landscape is reflected in his early oil sketches of the area surrounding his family estate. In retirement, he continued to draw inspiration from the Radnorshire countryside; his sketchbooks often illustrate such agricultural developments as the new planting of trees and his watercolours record favourite trees or fields. His detailed accounts show that he delighted in the diligent management and improvement of his estates, as well as in his alterations to the garden and lake at Pencerrig and the upkeep of the water-pump at Llandrindod.[11] Jones became High Sheriff of Radnorshire in 1791 and a magistrate in 1792. He wrote a poem about the inspiration he drew from his native landscape in 1791, 'Petraeia', a classical reference to Cerrig in Pencerrig:[12]

> In these sweet shades kind nature did impart
> Her first choice lessons to my infant heart,
> Guided my youthful pencil not to stray
> From nature's laws, (and nature led the way);
> Nor let it wander wild in fancy's maze,
> But shew'd the beauties she herself displays.[13]

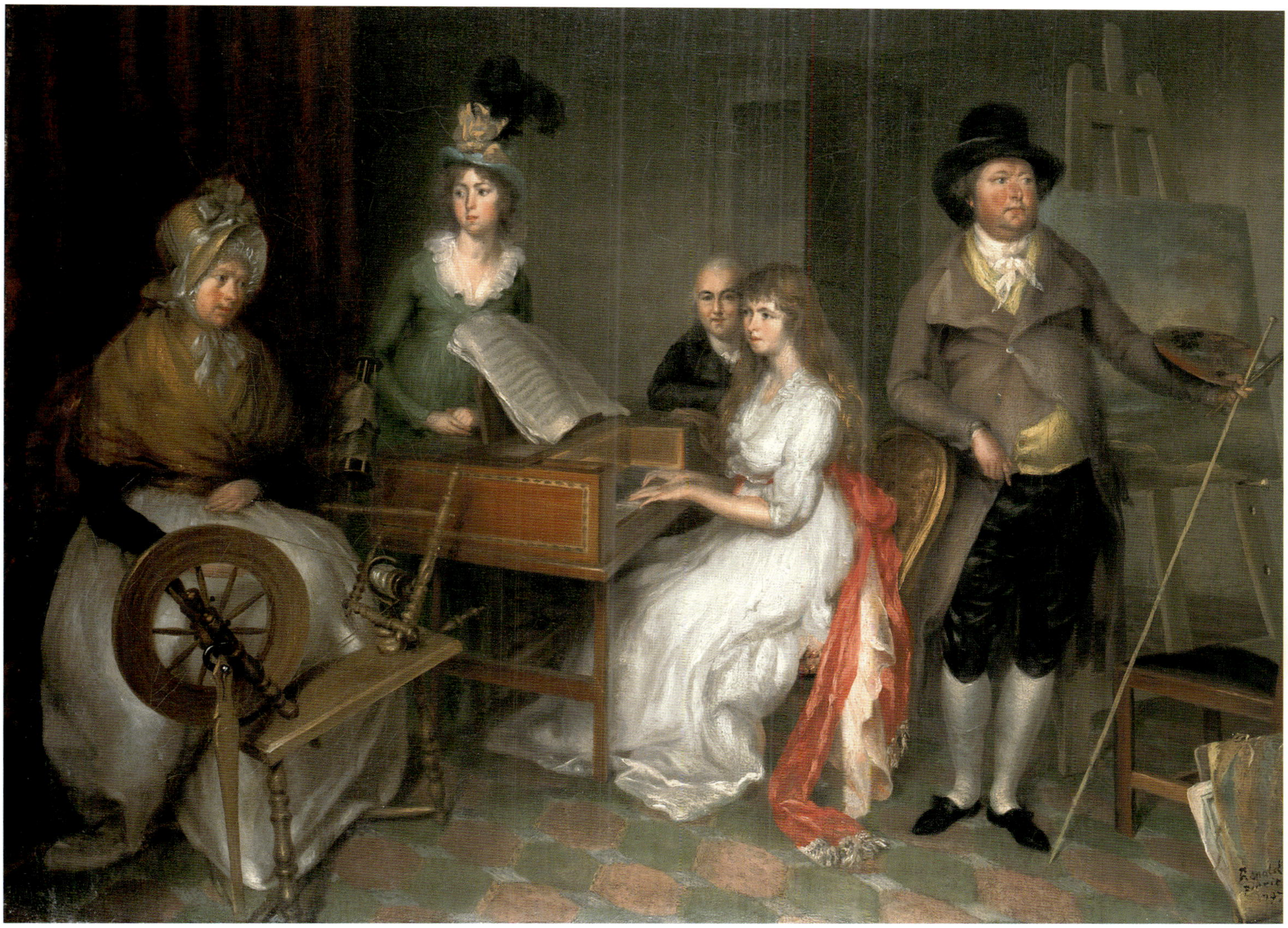

Fig. 3 Francesco Renaldi, *Thomas Jones and his Family*, 1797 (cat. no. 9).

Family life at Pencerrig was captured in the conversation piece painted by his old friend from Italy, Francesco Renaldi (1755–1798) in 1797 (fig. 3; cat. no. 9). This shows Jones as an artist by an easel with his palette, his wife and their two daughters and another as yet unidentified sitter, possibly one of his brothers or even Renaldi himself. Maria, shown at the spinning wheel, was probably already ill at the time this portrait was painted and Jones was deeply affected by her death two years later. He described her as 'an affectionate wife, a tender parent, a sincere friend', who had died after 'a lingering illness which she bore with Christian resignation'.[14] Despite his loss, Jones counted himself fortunate that he had his two daughters as 'some consolation to me'.[15]

Jones himself did not long outlive his wife, dying on 29 April 1803 at Pencerrig. The notice in the obituary columns of *The Gentleman's Magazine* ran 'In his 60th year, much regretted, Thomas Jones esq'.[16] He had suffered

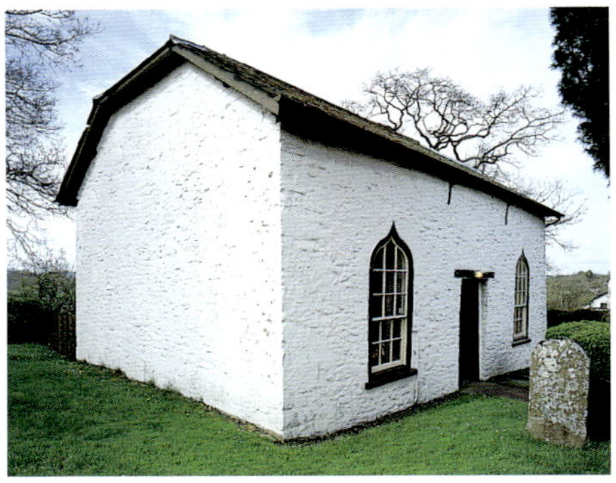

Fig. 4 Caebach Chapel at Llandrindod Wells, contemporary photograph.

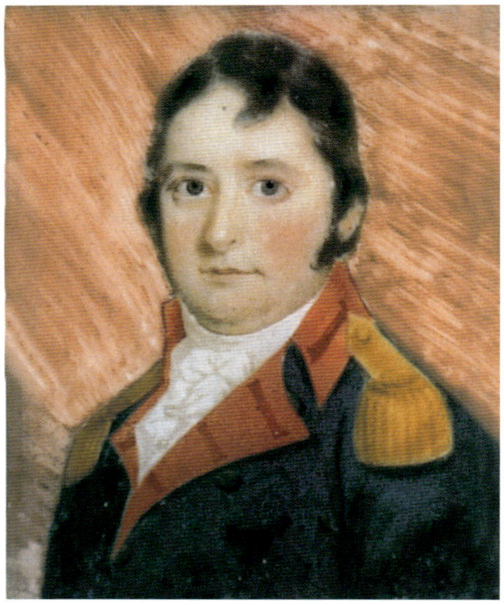

Fig. 5 Attributed to Edward Nash (1778–1821), *Captain Frederick Jones*, *c.*1810, watercolour on ivory, private collection.

ill health since 1801, including an apparent stroke in 1802. According to one of his daughters, he eventually died of 'Angina Pectoris'.[17] Descriptions of Jones suggest that he enjoyed his food and wine, the consumption of which is often detailed in his account books and his personal *Memoirs*. Even as a younger man, he was stout. He described himself while in Italy as 'Il Grasso' (the Fat One). The late conversation piece by Renaldi brings to mind the contemporary description by Uvedale Price of Foxley, Herefordshire, writing to Sir George Beaumont in June 1795, of Jones as 'a little stunted man, as round as a ball, the truest Welch runt, who was a pupil of . . . Wilson's and his face as red as his master's'.[18]

Despite the fact that after his mother's death the Nonconformism of the Jones family lapsed, they continued their association with the Caebach Chapel at Llandrindod Wells (fig. 4).[19] On 4 May 1803, Jones's body was carried in a funeral procession from Pencerrig to the small independent chapel[20] founded by his grandfather, a dissenting minister, in 1715. His mother had endowed the Caebach Chapel with the rent of a forty-acre farm in 1788 and his parents, elder brother, wife and many other family members were already buried in the family vault in the chapel. A marble plaque in the north-eastern corner (fig. 6), erected in 1810 by Captain Frederick Jones (fig. 5), commemorates the family members buried there.[21]

Jones retained many works which he brought back with him from Italy, including large-scale paintings, such as the view of Naples (cat. no. 106), and many oil sketches and watercolours, which then passed to his daughters, Anna Maria (1780–1807) and Elizabetha Francesca (1781–1806). On his death, each had £500 a year settled upon them.[22] Their uncle, Captain Frederick Jones, noted in his diary that the sisters were required to swear the Oath of Allegiance before they could inherit because they had been born abroad and their mother had been a foreigner.[23] Despite the legitimation of their parents' union, their right to inherit was questioned by one of their uncles.[24]

Jones did not live to see his beloved daughters married. Their joint weddings took place almost exactly a year after their father's death, on 11 April 1804, at their parish church in Llanelwedd. Anna Maria, the elder girl, then aged twenty-four, married the Glamorgan squire Thomas Thomas of Llanbradach and Elizabetha, by then twenty-three, married Captain John Dale of the East India Company. The service was performed by their uncle, David Jones, Rector of Gladestry in Radnorshire, before their other uncles, Frederick, Middleton and Rice. Anna Maria inherited Pencerrig and the surrounding estates while Elizabetha inherited Llandrindod Hall and the Trefonnen estate. Although both young women had children, they and their offspring had all died by 1810.

In 1813, Middleton Jones, a younger brother of Thomas, brought a lawsuit against the two widowers, centring on whether the two daughters of Jones had been legitimate.[25] Despite the efforts of Captain Dale, Middleton succeeded in obtaining the Trefonnen estate, but Anna Maria's estates, including Pencerrig and many of the paintings in the house, passed to her

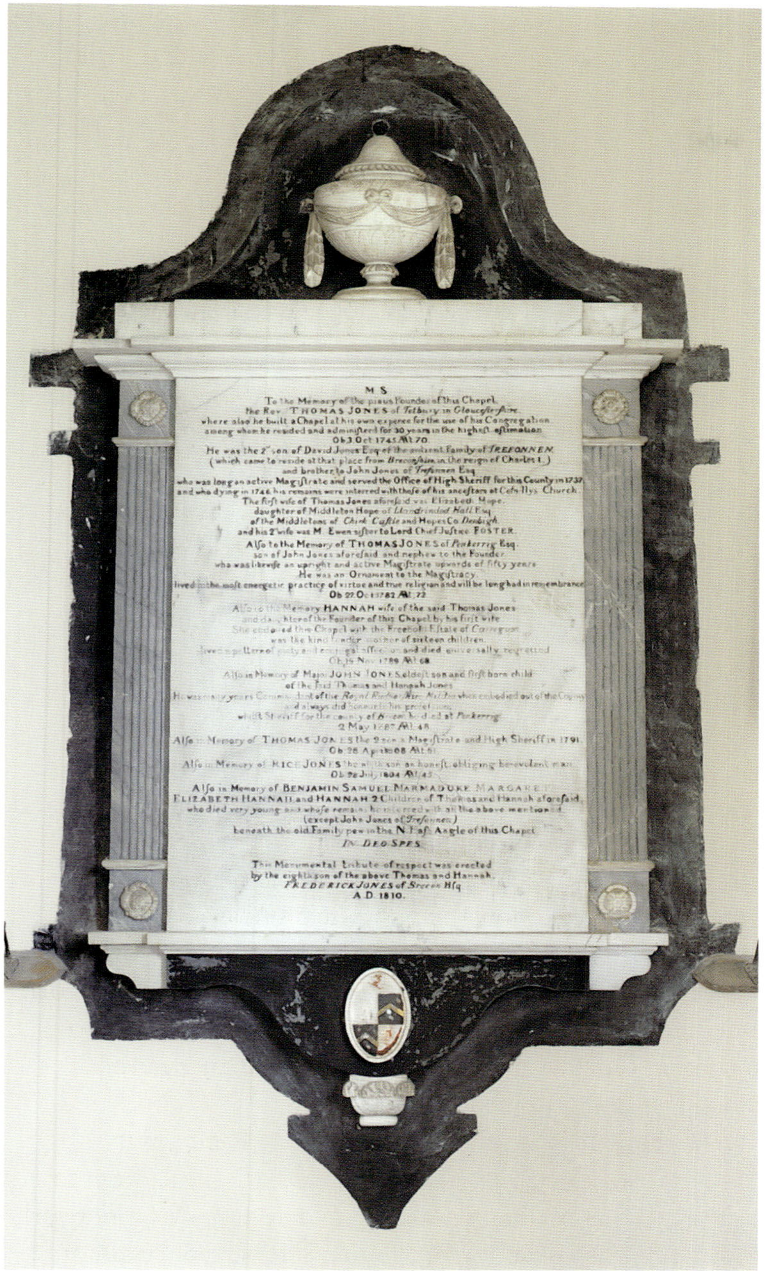

Fig. 6 Jones Family Memorial, Caebach Chapel, contemporary photograph.

husband, Thomas Thomas.[26] In June 1811, he took a second wife, Bridget Gwynne of Llanelwedd Hall, with whom he lived at Pencerrig.[27] Their daughter Clara inherited the house, the estates and the works of Jones surviving there. Through Clara's line, the Pencerrig estate and the paintings passed to the Lindsay family, who sold it in 1928 to a relative, Llewelyn Evan-Thomas. Works by Jones remained at Pencerrig until 1952 and Jane Evan-Thomas took a particular interest in them, and added to the collection. When the house was sold, she took the paintings with her. Pencerrig is now a country house hotel (see cat. no. 2, fig. 56). Captain Dale also remarried, and a substantial proportion of Jones's art, which had remained with him, passed down the family line.[28] Jones's art remained, for the most part, in these private family collections until the mid-twentieth century. The story of its emergence, its early champions and the considerable interest taken in Jones's approach to oil sketching in recent years is a fascinating one.

The Changing Fortunes of Jones's Artistic Reputation

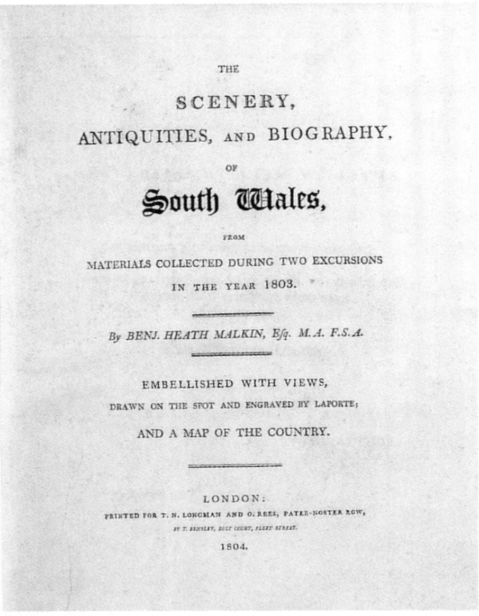
THE
SCENERY,
ANTIQUITIES, AND BIOGRAPHY,
OF
South Wales,
FROM
MATERIALS COLLECTED DURING TWO EXCURSIONS
IN THE YEAR 1803.

By BENJ. HEATH MALKIN, Esq. M.A. F.S.A.

EMBELLISHED WITH VIEWS,
DRAWN ON THE SPOT AND ENGRAVED BY LAPORTE;
AND A MAP OF THE COUNTRY.

LONDON:
PRINTED FOR T. N. LONGMAN AND O. REES, PATER-NOSTER ROW,
BY T. BENSLEY, BOLT COURT, FLEET STREET.
1804.

Fig. 7 Frontispiece to Benjamin Malkin, *The Scenery, Antiquities, and Biography, of South Wales*, 1804, National Museums & Galleries of Wales, Cardiff.

Jones's work was not entirely overlooked immediately after his death. Writing in 1804, in *The Scenery, Antiquities, and Biography, of South Wales* (fig. 7), Benjamin Malkin reminds his readers that when they visit Aberedw Rocks in Radnorshire, they should remember that the 'place derives an additional interest and importance, from having attracted and fixed the early studies of a painter, considerably approved in his department'.[29] That artist was of course 'Thomas Jones', described as 'a younger son of a gentleman, possessing a landed estate of some few hundreds a year in Radnorshire, near Aberedy'. Malkin outlines the early history of Jones's life and his apprenticeship to Richard Wilson, explaining that it 'is much to the credit of his memory, that he soon became a distinguished favourite of his ingenious and excellent master'. Malkin accurately reported his years in Rome and Naples and his artistic activity in London and Wales. He sensed, only a year after Jones's death, that the artist's reputation was diminishing: 'I cannot help thinking that the principality has some reason to be proud of him, though perhaps very few of its inhabitants are at all conscious of the honour . . . his talent was very considerable.'[30]

Following Jones's death, his friend and fellow artist Joseph Farington made a number of references to Jones's paintings in his diaries. In April 1808, he recorded being shown by Sir George Beaumont 'Jones's picture from "The Winters tale", the figures by Mortimer, & observed that it had more true merit than wd. be found in the pictures of the present day'.[31] On 9 August 1808, he writes that he was requested to go to a house in Portland Street to see 'two Landscapes said to be painted by *Wilson*. I found one of them a picture by Jones, the figures by Mortimer', indicating that Jones's paintings were already being confused with those of his master.[32] Farington was also approached in 1813 as a possible witness in the legal proceedings brought by Jones's brother Middleton against the husbands of Anna Maria and Elizabetha.[33]

Apart from these personal references, there is little or no evidence of interest in Jones as an artist throughout the nineteenth century. As Prys Morgan remarked in 1987, the 'Wilsonesque canvases he had painted sank into an art-historical compost'[34] and the oil sketches remained unseen, still in private hands. At the beginning of the twentieth century, there was a gradual recognition of his work, T. Mardy Rees noting in 1911: 'There seems to be a consensus of opinion regarding his remarkable ability as an artist'.[35] This was followed by W. Bowen Hamer's article, first published in June 1912 in *Wales*, a monthly magazine which appeared between 1911 and 1914. He refers to

Jones as a 'famous' artist but laments the fact that 'to-day – so ephemeral is Fame – even among cultured Welshmen the name and reputation of this talented Radnorian are practically unknown'. He also remarks that the largest collection of Jones's works was at Pencerrig and that 'the few in the possession of collectors are treasured as rarities'.[36] In 1925, W. S. Childe Pemberton in his biography of Frederick Augustus Hervey, 4th Earl of Bristol, Bishop of Derry and an important patron of Thomas Jones in Italy, quoted extensively from Jones's unpublished *Memoirs*.[37]

Revd D. Stedman Davies, a clergyman from Lincolnshire who retired to Llandrindod Wells, becoming one of the first Secretaries of the Radnorshire Society, edited extracts from the *Memoirs* and his *Account Book* and published them in 1942 in the *Transactions of the Radnorshire Society*. This article alerted Ffransis G. Payne of the Department of Folk Culture and Industries (fig. 8) to the delights of Jones and his paintings. Payne had been seconded to the Art Department at the National Museum for the duration of the Second World War, hence his interest in Jones. Writing in *Y Llenor* in 1944–5, he drew heavily upon the *Memoirs*, a typewritten copy of which he had borrowed from Llewelyn Evan-Thomas of Pencerrig. Payne produced an interesting assessment of Jones's life and work, illustrating his familiarity with the paintings remaining at Pencerrig. Also reflecting the period in which he was writing, Payne ponders the fate of Jones's famous work *A Land Storm, with the Story of Dido and Aeneas* (cat. no. 20) in the Hermitage, which he thought lost. A footnote reveals that he read in the *Museums Journal* that the painting was reported safe in Leningrad.[38] Writing in *Country Life* in 1945, Ralph Edwards (fig. 9), a keeper at the Victoria and Albert Museum and a member of the Council of the National Museum of Wales, acknowledges his debt to Payne for drawing his attention to the *Memoirs*. Although Edwards's article is titled 'Richard Wilson and his Pupil. Fresh Light from the Diary of Thomas Jones', it concentrates on Wilson. The opening statement that 'Richard Wilson, the first great English landscape-painter, is now amongst the cheapest and least regarded of "Old Masters"' reflects contemporary taste.[39] Jones's training in Wilson's studio is discussed in detail and the article is a significant commentary on the usefulness of the *Memoirs* in art-historical terms. Edwards, a patriotic Welshman with a forceful personality, became a pivotal figure in the re-emergence of Jones as an artist.

Ffransis Payne, meanwhile, writing later in a guidebook on Radnorshire, recalled:

> I was fortunate enough to visit Pencerrig before the coming of the evil days. It was towards the end of the Second World War, when I was looking for materials for articles on Thomas Jones which were later published in *Y Llenor*. Commander Llewelyn Evan-Thomas owned the house at the time and he was kind enough to let me study the diaries and the account books of the artist as well as the pictures and sketches of Jones's work which were in the house. Although Thomas Jones the artist had attracted me there, I could almost say that it was Thomas Jones the landowner who charmed me.[40]

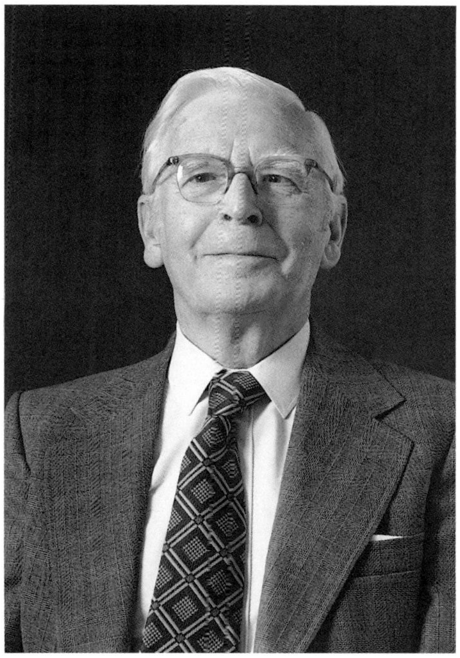

Fig. 8 Ffransis G. Payne, photograph, 1974.

Fig. 9 Ralph Edwards, re-photographed from *Apollo* magazine, 1977.

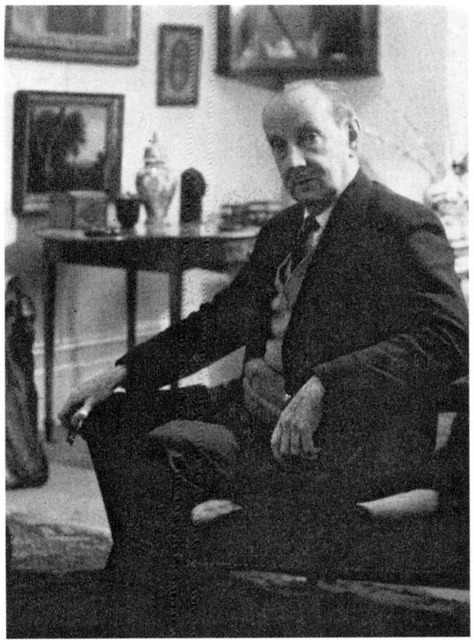

Despite this interest in Jones, in 1949 Professor Anthony Blunt turned down the proposal of an American student who wished to write a thesis on the subject at the Courtauld Institute of Art in London. Blunt considered him 'too obscure, his works (tucked away in remote Welsh houses) unworthy of the research necessary for a PhD thesis'. Later, Blunt himself came to appreciate the works of Jones.[41]

In 1951, the publication by the Walpole Society of Jones's entire *Memoirs* began a major resurgence of interest in him as an artist. The *Memoirs* were edited by Paul Oppé, the great collector of British and European drawings, and for a time Deputy Director of the Victoria and Albert Museum. He wrote an important introduction to his subject, putting this highly anecdotal, vivid and amusing account of the life of an artist into context by comparing it with the memoir of Reynolds's pupil Northcote and Jones's own fellow pupil of Wilson, Joseph Farington.[42] While Oppé was fascinated by Jones's relationships with other artists and his domestic circumstances, he had not yet come to fully appreciate his artistic achievements. He quotes Farington's description of Jones's art as 'very cold – like china' and commented on one painting he had seen on display in Birmingham in 1948,[43] thus: 'This coldness despite the hot colouring of the sunset is due to lack of inspiration and a hard exactness of detail.' He continued 'A large *Bay of Naples* and several small pictures of Italian, Swiss and local scenes which are still at Pencerrig are equally empty and uninspired and it is impossible not to sympathise with George Lord Herbert, later the 11th Earl of Pembroke, who visited Jones's studio in Rome in 1779 and found his work "in my opinion so-so".'[44]

The wider availability of the *Memoirs* meant that they became an obvious source for Wilson scholars. Brinsley Ford drew upon them in his assessment of Wilson's drawings in 1951,[45] and W. G. Constable in his monograph on the paintings of 1953[46] established Jones as an important source of information on his master's studio practice and as an early copyist and imitator of Wilson.

This perception of Jones as a mere imitator of Wilson was transformed on 2 July 1954 when fifty of his watercolours and oils of views in both Wales and Italy came on to the market at Christie's. They were described as 'The property of a lady whose husband was a descendant of Thomas Jones, a pupil of Richard Wilson, R. A.'. They had descended from the Captain Dale branch of the family.[47] Each lot contained a number of works, and many were purchased by the enthusiastic James Byam Shaw, working for Colnaghi, and Evelyn Joll, working for Agnews. The lots comprised between two and seven individual items and the highest bids were £33 12*s.* each on Lot 212 of three works, purchased by Ralph Edwards (fig. 9), and Lot 217, bought by Joll. Edwards was acting on behalf of the National Museum of Wales and his lot included *Buildings in Naples* (cat. no. 110) and *Buildings in Naples, with the North-East Side of the Castel Nuovo* (cat. no. 108).

Byam Shaw, a considerable art historian as well as a senior partner at Colnaghi, speedily drew the oil sketches to the attention of other discerning curators and private collectors. Karl Parker of the Ashmolean Museum selected *Rooftops in Naples* (cat. no. 111), one of Jones's most beautiful Neapolitan oil sketches, later that same year. The Fitzwilliam Museum also acquired a *Scene near Naples* (cat. no. 121) and Birmingham Museum and Art Gallery were particularly far sighted in acquiring both a view of *Pencerrig* of 1772 (cat. no. 40) and *The Hill of Vomero and the Dome of S. Caterina, Naples* (cat. no. 120). Oppé recognized the significance of these sketches and bought from Colnaghi (cat. nos 109 and 112), and John Gere of the British Museum purchased *Houses in Naples* (cat. no. 115) and later wished he had purchased directly from Christie's for his own collection as well. The Glynn Vivian Art Gallery in Swansea had the opportunity to buy *Ruined Buildings, Naples* (cat. no. 116). Thus a considerable number of works passed almost immediately into public collections. The response suggests that scholars were influenced by the recent rediscovery of oil sketches by Pierre-Henri de Valenciennes (1750–1819; figs. 23 and 25), a contemporary of Jones, although he does not appear to have come into direct contact with him. The exhibited works by Valenciennes were highly finished and a great contrast to a series of oil sketches, many showing humble Italian roof-tops, bequeathed to the Louvre in 1930.[48] Despite the obvious parallels between the two artists, Valenciennes had a far wider reputation than Jones before the discovery of his oil sketches in 1954–5. The arrival on the art market of these oil sketches, with their informality and directness of vision, transformed Jones's artistic reputation almost overnight.

Perhaps Jones's best-known work today, *A Wall in Naples* (fig. 10; cat. no. 114), which recently inspired a poem by the Poet Laureate, Andrew Motion, came on to the market the following year, 1955, at another Christie's sale. This time, it caught the keen eye of Evelyn Joll at Agnews, who purchased three works by Jones as part of Lot 6. He paid £14 14*s*. for all three.[49] But the work, which is extremely small in scale (11.2 × 15.8 cm) and depicts the rotting brickwork of a single wall in Naples, with the holes left by scaffolding, a decaying wooden door and small balcony with washing hanging upon it, did not immediately pass into a public collection. It was acquired from Agnews by Lady Ashton. Although it was seen by the public in exhibitions, it did not enter a public collection until 1995, when it was purchased from another private collection by the National Gallery in London, the first Jones they had acquired. One more sketch was sold at Sotheby's in 1956.[50]

Paul Oppé was another of those discerning collectors to buy from Colnaghi. He purchased the oil sketch of *Pencerrig* of 1772 (cat. no. 41) and it was displayed to the public as part of his collection at the Royal Academy in 1958.

Writing in 1959, John Gere noted that it was 'a pity that these oil-studies had not come to light before the publication of the *Memoirs*, since in this medium and on this intimate scale Jones rose to a height impossible to imagine from his large finished paintings'.[51] Gere makes the comparison for the first time between Jones's oil sketches and those of Valenciennes. He acknowledged that there was no evidence that they actually met in either

Fig. 10 Thomas Jones, *A Wall in Naples*, *c.*1782 (cat. no. 114).

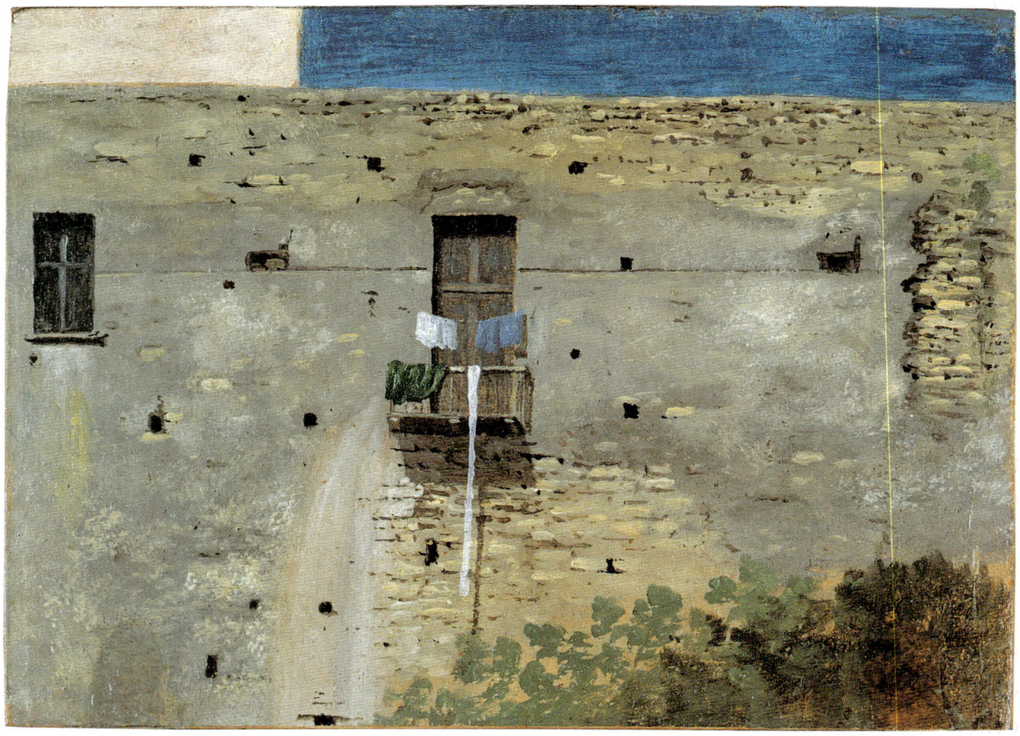

Rome or Naples, but observed that the 'oil sketches which the Frenchman likewise made for his own instruction and amusement are strikingly like Jones's in technique and spirit'.[52] Gere would go on to build up one of the most important collections of oil sketches ever assembled. Indeed, by the time he had written this article, he was already the owner of his first Jones, *The Grotto at Posillipo* (cat. no. 119), which he purchased from Colnaghi in 1956.

It was only in 1968, however, that Ralph Edwards attempted an extended assessment of Jones's career in *Connoisseur*. Edwards reminded his readers of such works as *The Bard* (cat. no. 31), which had been purchased by the National Museum of Wales in 1965, and Jones's early relationship with his patron Oldfield Bowles. He also considered his artistic debt to Wilson, publishing an early Italianate work by Jones, *On the Arno* of 1773 (cat. no. 26), and assessed the importance of the works which came on to the market in the 1950s, both oil studies and watercolours. Edwards closed his article with a plea for further work on Jones: 'It is surely time for a new and more favourable evaluation of Jones as an artist. His studies and little pictures in oil on paper are a distinguished and highly personal achievement; his watercolours in the sketch-books are spontaneous and charming in colour, and the charge of "very cold – like china" levelled against his pictures is of limited application.'[53]

In the same year as this article appeared, three works by Jones were selected by John Gage for the exhibition *A Decade of English Naturalism: 1810–1820* at the Castle Museum, Norwich and the Victoria and Albert

Museum, to illustrate the fact that landscape sketching in oil was established at the end of the eighteenth century. Edwards did not have to wait long, though, for the first exhibition devoted to Jones himself to materialize. His enthusiasm for the artist was infectious and Edwards was able to persuade John Jacob, Curator at Marble Hill, to organize an exhibition in collaboration with the National Museum of Wales. The show was opened at Marble Hill by the Marquess of Anglesey on 1 June 1970, exactly two years after Edwards's article appeared in *Connoisseur*, and transferred later that year to the National Museum in Cardiff.

The exhibition was arranged at extremely short notice, as the research assistant at the time of the exhibition, Lindsay Stainton, recalled, but with Edwards's determination a significant number of exhibits were drawn together, covering Jones's entire career. Edwards had clearly been viewing works during the latter half of 1969. Writing at the end of January 1970, John Jacob reveals that the selection process was not even complete for an exhibition that was due to open on 1 June the same year: 'Ralph Edwards and I have now almost an embarrassing wealth of material available, and we shall be making a final selection shortly'.[54] The works surviving in the collections of Captain Dale's descendants, the Evan-Thomas collections and other family collections were generously lent, as were those from the Paul Oppé Collection, although sadly he did not live to see the exhibition. The informative introductory essay was written by Edwards and surveyed Jones's entire artistic output. On 21 May 1970, John Jacob wrote to Rollo Charles, Keeper of Art at the National Museum of Wales, 'I have been arranging the Thomas Jones Exhibition at Marble Hill this week. Ralph Edwards has seen it and approved, and it certainly looks very well'.[55]

Writing in *Apollo* in June 1970, John Gere paid tribute to John Jacob and Ralph Edwards's 'research and enthusiasm' which 'have been largely responsible for the reappraisal of the artist'.[56] Gere selected two works for particular praise, the Glynn Vivian Art Gallery's *Ruined Buildings, Naples* (cat. no. 116) and the *Wall in Naples* (fig. 10; cat. no. 114), belonging then to Lady Ashton. On this particular work he comments that 'the beautifully calculated and near-abstract placing of the elements of the composition perhaps finds its closest analogy in a certain type of sophisticated modern architectural photography. If this sketch had been the only example of Jones's work to have survived, so that it had to be judged in isolation, it would not be easy to place: and would anyone have ventured to date it as early as 1782?'[57] The apparent modernity of such a work was clearly fascinating to scholars at the time and the general assumption was that Jones painted directly from nature in oil. Gere goes on to discuss the *Pencerrig* view of 1772, which shows the lake (cat. no. 41, then Oppé Collection) in the grounds, as an example of his mastering of *plein-air* sketching.

The impact of the 1970 exhibition was significant. As well as Gere's preview of the show in *Apollo*, Luke Herrmann reviewed it in the *Burlington Magazine*. John Jacob was disappointed with the contents, calling it a 'slightly luke warm review'.[58] Edwards himself was however thrilled with his considerable achievement in mounting the exhibition, as Rollo Charles recalls in July 1970, 'Ralph Edwards seems still very cock-a-hoop'.[59]

Herrmann's review in the *Burlington* is worth pausing to consider. He reviewed the Jones exhibition in conjunction with a George Lambert exhibition curated by Elizabeth Einberg at Kenwood showing at the same time, and he makes interesting comparisons between the two artists but does not share Edwards's enthusiasm for Jones. He commented:

> it is difficult to agree with Mr Ralph Edwards, who has contributed the vivacious Introduction to the Catalogue, that 'he ranks high in the category of British artists of considerable if secondary importance'. To art historians Thomas Jones is certainly important as the author of the invaluable Memoirs. He is of great interest as the artist of his unrivalled oil sketches, but, as this exhibition makes all too clear, the rest of his painting and most of his drawing would hardly justify the arrangement of such a splendid one-man exhibition. As it is the exhibition is thoroughly worthwhile, for it as last enables one to see Jones's by now well-known flashes of brilliance in their true context.[60]

While Edwards saw the importance of considering Jones in his entirety, Herrmann began the trend away from studying his career and towards a concentration upon the oil sketching, which has so obsessed recent scholars. In his 1974 *British Landscape Painting of the Eighteenth Century*, he devotes a number of pages to Jones but remains lukewarm in his praise for the artist. He concedes that his oil sketches

> can be considered as an outstanding personal achievement, though the temptation to make too much of them must be resisted. In the recent past their importance has been somewhat overemphasized, as, for instance, in the Introduction to the 1970 catalogue . . . In these oil sketches Thomas Jones was undoubtedly ahead of his time, but in his painting of finished landscape compositions he was very much of his time. Inside the very apartment from the roof of which he was making his vivid studies of the roof-tops of Naples, Jones was at work on his large *View of Lake Nemi* [cat. no. 58] . . . This, like the similar *Bay of Naples* [cat. no. 106] now at Cardiff, is formal and stiff, showing little sense of place or light.[61]

But Herrmann's voice was for the moment a lone one and the initial reaction to the 1970 exhibition was generally positive.

In August 1970, R. C. B. Oliver, an enthusiastic amateur historian and leading light in the Radnorshire Society, published his invaluable history of the Jones family.[62] Writing in his local newspaper immediately prior to the publication of his book, he stated, 'The current retrospective exhibition of his paintings and engravings in London, comes as the result solely of the persistent efforts of a few enthusiasts, mainly *London Welsh*, just over 200 years after Thomas Jones had shown in London at the Society of Artists in 1769 what he considered to be one of his best works, *Landscape with Dido and Aeneas*'.[63]

Anthony Blunt, although initially unimpressed by Jones, had by the 1970s reconsidered his art and devoted an article to him in 1973 in *Country Life*. Again, the theme was clear: while Jones's larger exhibited works were of interest, it was his oil sketches that were really appealing. Blunt commented: 'He also painted large landscapes in the manner of Claude to which he certainly attached great importance, but to us it is in the small studies that his sensitive observation of tones in the painting of trees, hills and buildings is most evident'.[64] Writing in *Art History* in 1979, on 'Pre-Romantic Plein-Air Painting', Philip Conisbee touches on Jones's oil sketching from nature, referring to it as 'an activity essentially different from the routines of the studio'. He points out that Jones was painting oil sketches prior to Valenciennes in 1770–2 and interprets them as a 'pure act of love and/or an additional appropriation of his family estates'.[65]

Jones's paintings were gradually included in more exhibitions throughout the 1970s[66] and 1980s, such as *Painting from Nature. The Tradition of Open-Air Oil Sketching from the 17th to 19th Centuries* at the Fitzwilliam Museum, Cambridge. Meanwhile, interest in Jones grew in America. Collectors such as Paul Mellon had been buying his work since the 1960s. Although Mellon initially favoured his finished paintings, such as *An Imaginary Coast Scene, with the Temple of Venus at Baia*, 1773 (cat. no. 28), which he purchased in 1963, he bought a Welsh oil sketch in 1965, *Pencerrig* of 1776 (cat. no. 43). Mellon's most significant purchase was *Lake Albano – Sunset* (cat. no. 56), which he acquired in 1971. In 1981, the now substantial Jones holdings of the Yale Center for British Art were included in an exhibition organized by Duncan Bull entitled *Classic Ground. British Artists and the Landscape of Italy, 1740–1830*. Jones's work was shown in two more Yale exhibitions in 1982 and 1986.[67]

Back in Britain, David Solkin's major Richard Wilson exhibition at the Tate and National Museum of Wales in 1982[68] did not concentrate upon his pupils. However, two lectures delivered in London, which were both later published, did make a considerable impact. On 2 May 1984, the historian Prys Morgan, of Swansea University, delivered a carefully researched, informative lecture to the Honourable Society of Cymmrodorion. The meeting was chaired by Nicholas Edwards, MP, Secretary of State for Wales and Ralph Edwards's son. Morgan outlined Jones's entire career in detail, emphasizing Jones's Welsh cultural heritage and literary achievements. Although Jones showed no knowledge of the Welsh language, he clearly met with fellow Welshmen such as William Parry in London. Morgan points out that the *Memoirs* contain a number of references to his Welsh background, such as paying with pictures for his fencing lessons from one Davies, 'a redhot Welshman',[69] in 1767. A close friend of his was the poet and critic Revd Evan Lloyd of Fronderw, Bala, through whom he met David Garrick (1717–1779) and with whom he enjoyed various escapades in London. On 1 March 1766, Jones served as steward of the 'Welsh Feast' and when he was in Rome in 1780 he organized a celebratory excursion for St David's Day on board a barque in the Tiber which traded in Spanish wine. Morgan wryly comments that 'one may assume that the ascetic's feast day was not toasted in water'. Morgan was also particularly impressed by the oil sketches and described them as having 'a freshness of colouring and a unity and immediacy of feeling that arise from being done all at one blow, as it were, in the open. They have a freedom from convention and a directness that seem to put them beyond any period.' Morgan felt that Jones had a breadth of appeal greater than his artistic career, commenting that 'the appraisal of Thomas Jones as a character in Welsh eighteenth-century history has hardly begun . . . if Thomas's papers, accounts, diaries, and so on were put together with his pictures and *Memoirs*, we might well find that we know more about him than almost any other eighteenth-century Welshman'.[70] He stressed Jones's achievements as a writer and acknowledged his debt in assessing Jones in art-historical terms to Lawrence Gowing.

In 1985, the seventeenth Walter Neurath Memorial Lecture was delivered by Gowing (fig. 11), Slade Professor of Fine Art at University College London. Entitled 'The Originality of Thomas Jones', it was later published by Thames and Hudson. Gowing saw Jones as 'this hero of mine'[71] and his vision of the artist is a highly romantic, personal response to the painter's life and work. He felt a personal bond with Jones partly because he claimed to have inherited Jones's studio off Warren Street. Gowing's lyrical responses to Jones's paintings are often quoted and he sometimes overstated the case. For instance, of the Gadbridge oil sketch which may not in fact have been sketched *en plein-air* (cat. no. 39) he writes:

> The bend and recoil of the trees before the wind was as solemnly observed as anything in eighteenth-century landscape. The passionate impetus with which Jones came to paint from nature in 1770, and the characterization of the ash trees, were both rare in the attenuated style of the time, and rarest in Sublime performances. The Gadbridge sketch recovered the force of first generation Rubenism; a seventeenth-century seriousness was reborn.[72]

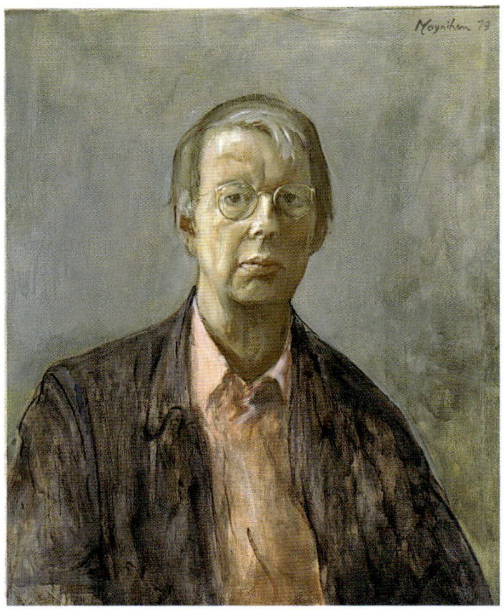

Fig. 11 Rodrigo Moynihan (1910–1990), *Lawrence Gowing*, 1979, oil on canvas, 76.2 × 63.5 (30 × 25), National Portrait Gallery, London.

Gowing responded particularly to the individuality and originality of the Naples oil sketches. Of the National Museum's *Buildings in Naples* (cat. no. 110) he commented:

> Once again an ordinary Italian building takes on a significance that transcends a given view. The simplicity of the thing in itself is rendered with unaccustomed, measured sharpness. It is just a white façade with a window and a door, which penetrate the radiant stucco with a clarity of other times. We notice a mathematic precision. The unshuttered window is four-sixths full of shadow. At the next recess in the surface the door faces us with seven-eighths of unyielding ochre.[73]

Gowing therefore, without the aid of any technical evidence, seems to sense that these sketches are perhaps far more ordered and less spontaneous than they at first appear.

Gowing's lecture and subsequent book drew attention to Jones once again and Francis Hawcroft, nearing retirement at the Whitworth Art Gallery in Manchester, decided to devote his last major exhibition to Jones, an artist in whom he had had a long-standing interest. Hawcroft worked closely with Brinsley Ford, whose knowledge of the life and work of British artists and their patrons in Rome was boundless, to produce an exhibition based upon the *Memoirs*, thereby limiting himself to Jones's Italian work. *Travels in Italy 1776–1783* opened in the autumn of 1988 and was organized topographically, with one section based on Rome and the other on Naples. It considered the artistic community in Italy at that time and the light Jones's *Memoirs* shed upon it, particularly the other artists working there, their patrons as well as the agents and dealers who controlled the market. Jones's watercolours, oil sketches and some larger paintings were placed in the context of other British artists, particularly the watercolourists Jonathan Skelton (*c.*1735–1759), John Robert Cozens (1752–1799), William Pars (1742–1782) and Francis Towne (1739–1816), but also the work of other artists, such as Joseph Wright of Derby (1734–1797) and Allan Ramsay (1713–1784) and the European artists Claude-Joseph Vernet (1714–1789), Giovanni Battista Lusieri (*c.*1755–1821) and Jakob Philipp Hackert (1737–1807). Sadly, Hawcroft died suddenly shortly before the exhibition was due to open and as a result the catalogue did not have the introduction he had planned to write.[74]

Art-historical interest in Jones increased dramatically after this exhibition. In 1991 Peter Galassi, then curator of photography at The Museum of Modern Art, New York published his *Corot in Italy*, and included a study of Jones's oil sketches in his introductory chapter entitled 'Painting from Nature', in which he considers the earlier *plein-air* painters working in oil. 'Jones in Naples', he wrote, 'turned away from the scenic motif of the bay to paint fragments of buildings, devoid of worldly consequence.'[75] He made particular comparison with Valenciennes. 'While Valenciennes was often hesitant and imprecise, Jones was confident and surehanded, achieving a palpable identity between subject and image that informs every stroke of the brush.'[76] Jones's work now began to appear in major international exhibitions such as *In the Light of Italy: Corot and Early Open-Air Painting* at the National Gallery of Art, Washington in 1996; *Grand Tour. The Lure of Italy in the Eighteenth Century* at the Tate Gallery, London in 1997; and *Paysages d'Italie. Les Peintres du Plein Air (1780–1830)* in Paris and Mantua in 2001. His works also appeared in major touring shows of established collectors such as *British Watercolours from the Oppé Collection* at the Tate Gallery in 1997 and *A Brush with Nature. The Gere Collection of Landscape Oil Sketches* at the National Gallery, London in 1999, thus confirming his new place in the history of British landscape painting.

One of the best assessments of Jones's art, to date, appeared in the *New York Review of Books* in March 1997. Accompanying the *In the Light of Italy* exhibition,[77] James Fenton introduced Jones's entire career to an

American audience. The title itself is significant: 'Who Was Thomas Jones?' While a circle of connoisseurs, art historians and Welsh cultural historians[78] are entirely familiar with the name, as an artist he has little reputation still with the public at large. Fenton in 1997 felt he had to ask the question 'Who Was Thomas Jones?' and that many would find his riveting account of the Welsh artist's life, accompanied by a colour photograph of *Wall in Naples* (fig. 10; cat. no. 114), a completely new subject.

Andrew Motion's poem, written in 2000 as part of the *Encounters* exhibition at the National Gallery in London, is an example of another way in which Jones's work is becoming more popular.

A Wall in Naples

I have forgotten whatever it was
I wanted to say. Also the way I wanted
to say it. Form and music.

Perhaps it had something to do with – no,
that's not it. More likely, I should just
look at whatever there is

and fix myself to the earth. This wall,
I mean, which faces me over the street
Smooth as a shaven chin

but pocked with the holes that the scaffolders left
and flicked with an overlow-flag. Which still
leaves pigeon-shit, rain-streaks, washing –

or maybe the whole thing's really a board
where tiny singing meteors strike.
How can we tell what is true? I rest my case.

I rest my case and I cannot imagine a hunger
greater than this. For marks.
For messages sent by hand. For signs of life.

In 2000, Peter Lord covered Jones's career in his *Imaging the Nation*, particularly concentrating on his relationship with Thomas Johnes of Hafod, which was also discussed by Roger Hallett in his 1992 article on the 'Hafod' sketchbook.[79] Of his later career, Lord comments: 'the paintings of his later years, many of them done around his estate in Radnorshire, manifested the naturalism to which his instincts had led him, years before it became the fashion'.[80]

It is the challenge of this exhibition and these bicentenary celebrations to transform the reputation of Thomas Jones the writer, Thomas Jones the eighteenth-century artist, Thomas Jones of Pencerrig, the Welsh landowner, into a name that is instantly recognizable amongst the wider public. The highlight of these celebrations is, of course, this exhibition itself, which sheds much new light on Jones and offers a major reassessment of his career.

Jones's art is now represented throughout British and American collections. The passage from almost complete obscurity, following his death 200 years ago, to being recognized by professional art historians as an artist whose approach to subject matter and composition was far ahead of his time was a dramatic one that has occurred only over the past fifty years.

Benjamin Malkin had, as we have seen, commented on Jones as an artist in 1804: 'the principality has some reason to be proud of him, though perhaps very few of its inhabitants are at all conscious of the honour.'[81] In one sense this situation has not changed. The vast majority of the public both in Wales and throughout the United Kingdom may understandably confuse Thomas Jones the artist with Welsh pop idol Tom Jones. This exhibition, which travels to Manchester and London, offers the opportunity to bring the unique observation of landscape and witty sense of humour, so obvious in his *Memoirs*, of this Welsh landscape painter to a whole new audience in Wales and beyond. Jones emerges from this exhibition as an artist with extraordinary vision, worthy of the term 'great Welsh artist', with his place in a European tradition.

Notes

1 *Memoirs*, p. 112.
2 Ibid., p. 55.
3 Ibid., p. 93.
4 Farington, *Diary*, vol. XII, 6 March 1813, p. 4310.
5 *Memoirs*, p. 89, n.
6 Ibid., p. 140.
7 Ibid., p. 141.
8 *Diary of Captain Frederick Jones*, Mss NLW 23794C, f. 29. Oliver does not transcribe this part of the diary (Oliver, 1983–4), National Library of Wales, Aberystwyth.
9 'T. Jones's marriage with Mary Moncke *in England* took place abt. Six years after He came from Italy, at St Pancrass's Church, at the particular desire of His Mother, who was the daughter of a Calvinist Clergyman of the name of *Hope*, & she inherited from Him very strict notions of religion' (Farington, *Diary*, vol. XII, 7 March 1813, p. 4312).
10 Jones explains that his mother fell ill at Brecon at her son Middleton's house and died 'in my Wife's Arms' (*Memoirs*, p. 141).
11 *Thos Jones's Book bought at Turin 8th Nov' 1776*, known as *The Account Book of Mr Thomas Jones* September 1788–April 1797, Radnorshire Society. Printed in *Transactions of the Radnorshire Society*, vol. LXX, 2000, pp. 104–10.
12 Pencerrig translates as 'the House at the Top of the Rocks'.
13 Baker, 1795, p. 226.
14 *The Gentleman's Magazine*, vol. LXIX, April 1799, p. 349.
15 Letter to Mrs Flowerdew quoted Oliver, 1970, p. 35.
16 *The Gentleman's Magazine*, vol LXXIIIL, May 1803, p. 484.
17 Farington, *Diary*, vol. VI, 27 June 1803, p. 2065.
18 Letter from Price to Sir George Beaumont, 3 June 1795, Mss MA 1581 (Price 4), Pierpont Morgan Library, New York, see Owen, 1988, p. 18.
19 'After the death of Mrs Hannah Jones of Pencerrig, Nonconformity lost its hold on this family' (Rees, 1872, vol. II, p. 535).
20 *Diary of Captain Frederick Jones*, 4 May 1803, Mss NLW 23794C, f. 39. Wrongly stated as being 6 May in Oliver, 1984, p. 52.
21 Two prominent family members' names who were buried there are missing – one was Maria, Thomas's wife, who may never have been fully accepted by his family due to her lowly birth and Roman Catholicism and the other was another brother, Middleton Jones, who

caused dissent in the family by challenging Thomas Jones's will (Oliver, 1970, p. 67).

22 Farington, *Diary*, vol. VI, 21 May 1803, p. 2034.

23 *Diary of Captain Frederick Jones*, 11 December 1801, see Oliver, 1984, p. 46.

24 See Oliver, 1970, pp. 55–7 for a discussion of the law suit.

25 Both Captain Frederick Jones's diaries and Farington's diaries give details of the law suit – *Diary of Captain Frederick Jones* 17, 24 March, 4, 19 August, 3, 24 November 1813 Mss NLW 23794C and Farington, *Diary*, vol. XII, 6 and 7 March 1813, pp. 4310–11.

26 Oliver assumes that the reason for this judgement must be that Trefonnen was entailed on legitimate heirs and the Pencerrig estates were not definitely so entailed. Oliver, 1970, p. 56. Farington's diary confirms this (vol. XII, 6 March 1813, p. 4310).

27 Oliver, 1970, p. 55.

28 Morgan, 1987, p. 60. It was the wife of a descendant of Captain Dale who decided to sell works in 1954.

29 Malkin, 1804, p. 282.

30 Ibid., p. 284.

31 Farington, *Diary*, vol. IX, 16 April 1808, p. 3260.

32 Ibid., 9 August 1808, p. 3327.

33 Ibid., vol. XII, 19 March, p. 4317.

34 Morgan, 1987, p. 60.

35 Rees, 1911, p. 95. There are some considerable inaccuracies in this text, however, such as referring to him as a native of Aberedw rather than Pencerrig, and some errors in the identification of prints after his work.

36 See Bowen Hamer, 1914, p. 84.

37 William Shakespear Childe Pemberton, *The Earl Bishop. The Life of Frederick Hervey, Bishop of Derry, Earl of Bristol*, London, 1925.

38 Payne, 1944–5, p. 65.

39 Edwards, 1945, p. 862.

40 Payne, 1966, pp. 123–4, translated from the Welsh and quoted by Prys Morgan in Morgan, 1984, p. 74.

41 Ashton, 2000 p. 123 and in conversation with the author.

42 *Memoirs*, pp. i–vi.

43 Birmingham, 1948, no. 164.

44 *Memoirs*, p. iv.

45 Brinsley Ford, *The Drawings of Richard Wilson*, London, 1951.

46 W. G. Constable, *Richard Wilson*, London, 1953.

47 Christie, Manson & Woods, 2 July 1954, Lots 212–23. Edwards erroneously refers to Lots 210–11, flower pictures in the same folio, as also being by Jones.

48 Bequest of Princess Louise de Cory, 1930.

49 Christie, Manson & Woods, 28 July 1955, Lots 1–6.

50 Sotheby's, 27 June 1956, Lot 47.

51 Gere, 1959, pp. 93–4.

52 Ibid, p. 93.

53 Edwards, 1968, p. 14.

54 Letter from John Jacob, Curator, Iveagh Bequest, Kenwood to Rollo Charles, Keeper, National Museum of Wales, 22 January 1970, National Museums & Galleries of Wales (archive).

55 Ibid., 21 May 1970.

56 Gere, 1970, p. 469.

57 Ibid.

58 Letter from John Jacob to Rollo Charles, 7 August 1970, National Museums & Galleries of Wales (archive).

59 Ibid., 9 July 1970.

60 Luke Herrmann, 'George Lambert and Thomas Jones: two London exhibitions', *Burlington Magazine*, vol. CXII, no. 809, August 1970, pp. 549–50.

61 Herrmann, 1974, pp. 68–9.

62 Oliver, 1970, reprinted with corrections and additions in 1987.

63 Oliver, 1970a, pt 5.

64 Blunt, 1973, p. 498.

65 Conisbee, 1979, p. 252 and p. 428, n.

66 *Landscape in Britain, c.1750–1850* Tate Gallery, London, 1973 and *British Artists in Rome 1700–1800*, Kenwood House, London, 1974.

67 *Presences of Nature. British Landscape 1780–1830*, New Haven, 1982 and *Oil on Water: Oil Sketches by British Watercolourists*, New Haven, 1986.

68 *Richard Wilson: The Landscape of Reaction*, Tate Gallery, London, and National Museum of Wales, 1982–3.

69 *Memoirs*, p. 11.

70 Morgan, 1984, p. 75. Morgan published a further paper on Jones expanding his research in *The Transactions of the Radnorshire Society*, vol. LVII, 1987, pp. 49–61.

71 Gowing, 1985, p. 7.

72 Ibid., pp. 17–18.

73 Ibid., p. 44.

74 *Travels in Italy 1776–1783 Based on the Memoirs of Thomas Jones*, Whitworth Art Gallery, Manchester, 1988.

75 Galassi, 1991, p. 31.
76 Clearly Galassi was unaware of Jones's extensive use of under-drawing.
77 Fenton, 1997, pp. 10–13, reviewing *In the Light of Italy: Corot and Early Open Air Painting*, National Gallery of Art, Washington, touring to Brooklyn Museum of Art and St Louis Art Museum 1996–7. The National Gallery of Art purchased its first work by Jones in 2002 (see cat. no. 81).
78 Paul Joyner produced a short but very informative entry for Jones in his *Artists in Wales* (pp. 66–7).
79 Roger Hallett, 'The "Hafod" Sketchbook of Thomas Jones' *Welsh Historic Gardens Trust Newsletter*, no. IV, August 1992, pp. 7–22.
80 Lord, 2000, p. 153.
81 Malkin, 1804. p. 284.

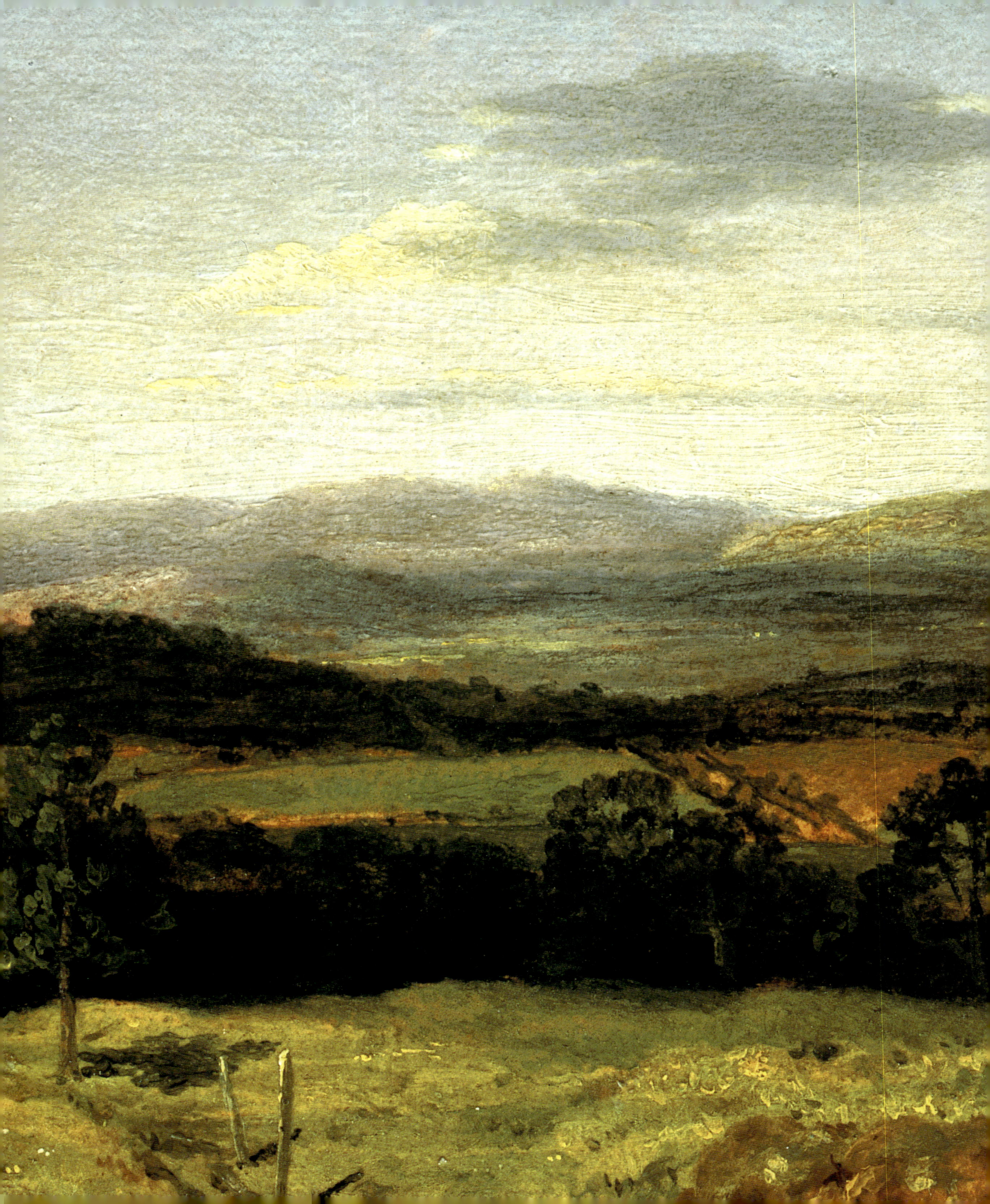

BEFORE ITALY: THE MAKING OF AN ARTIST

Lindsay Stainton

Towards the end of his life, Thomas Jones reflected on the origins of what he described as 'my beloved Art':[1] 'From my very Childhood, I was ever of rather a melancholy turn, and fond of Solitude, and very rarely joined in the Sports and Pastimes of the other boys. My greatest Amusement was in the looking at Prints and Pictures – Such exquisite Pleasure, indeed, have I often felt in contemplating a piece which struck my fancy at that time – that the finest works of Art have never been able since, to excite in me similar feelings'.[2] That he was able to translate this boyish passion into the reality of becoming a professional artist might initially have seemed improbable.

The Joneses of Trefonnen (Trevonen) were prosperous squires, their property extending to sixteen farms and a mill, but equally significant were Hannah Jones's connections (cat. no. 4). Her mother's family, the Hopes of Llandrindod Hall, were substantial landowners, and it became understood that the head of the family, her bachelor uncle John Hope – a successful lawyer in London – would leave his estate to her second son, Thomas Jones. In fact, ever since the marriage of Thomas Jones the elder and Hannah in 1738, the properties of the two families had been closely integrated, to their mutual benefit. By good fortune, Llandrindod had become a fashionable minor spa ('the Montpelier of Radnorshire'[3]), bringing a degree of prosperity to the area, not least to the Joneses, who owned two of the medicinal springs, and the Hopes, who leased out Llandrindod Hall as an hotel and informal assembly room. Indeed, as Thomas Jones later recorded, so popular was the spa, 'the influx of Visiters of all descriptions The infirm, the Rich, the Gay, the Idle and Dissolute . . . was so great, that it became an intollerable Nuisance to the Neighbourhood – On which Account, My father resolving to quit it, let Trevonen . . . as a Supplementary *Hotel*, and removed to Penkerrig',[4] a few miles away, near Builth. Pencerrig, the place Thomas Jones was always to regard as home, in fact belonged to John Hope and did not become the property of the Joneses until Hope's death in 1751.[5] As significant landowners, members of the family undertook various local civic responsibilities. As such, it is curious that Thomas Jones the elder never held such office, but the reason probably lay in his increasingly dissenting views,

FACING PAGE Detail of cat. no. 46.

in which he seems chiefly to have been influenced by his wife (and cousin) Hannah, the daughter of a dissenting minister, Revd Thomas Jones (1675–1745), who built a meeting house at Caebach near Trefonnen, later endowed by Hannah;[6] many members of the Jones family were in due course to be interred there. Yet this dissenting sympathy seems never to have stood in the way of their ambitions for their sons, at least three of whom were educated at Oxford, two being intended for the Established Church.[7]

Together with his eldest brother John, Thomas Jones was educated by tutors and at local schools, including Christ College, Brecon, where he was a pupil from 1753 to 1758 under the particular care of the local dissenting minister, presumably at the request of his parents, and from 1758 to 1759 at Llanfyllin, Montgomeryshire, where with the future Dr Abraham Rees he was a pupil of the distinguished classicist and Presbyterian minister Dr Jenkin Jenkins (d. 1780).[8] It was at Christ College that he first discovered his fondness for solitude – a theme that recurs throughout the *Memoirs* – as well as his interest in art, something encouraged both by a fellow pupil who seems to have taught Jones the rudiments of drawing, and by his father, who enabled him to buy prints, drawing materials and paints. It was also through his father that, while still at school in Brecon, Thomas Jones first met Charles Powell of Castlemadoc (1712–1796), who seems to have taken a quasi-paternal interest in him and was later to play a critical part in his decision to become an artist. At this stage, however, it is clear that art was simply a pleasant, harmless recreation. In 1756, his eldest brother John (cat. no. 6) went up to Merton College, Oxford (where he entered as a Commoner but was noted as being entitled to bear heraldic arms), apparently with the intention of preparing himself for a career at the Bar. For some unspecified reason, John did not graduate, returning instead to help run the family estate, joining the local militia, and becoming squire on his father's death in 1782;[9] it was his death, unmarried, in 1787 that resulted in Thomas Jones returning to Pencerrig as squire. But as a youth, Thomas Jones's prospects were more uncertain. He was the second son in a large family and thus had no such expectations, so it must have seemed providential when his maternal great-uncle proposed to pay for him to go up to Oxford and to make him his heir. There was, however, a proviso: he was to go into the Church. 'The Line my Uncle had plan'd out for me . . . was utterly contrary to my Inclinations – but I durst not hint at a disapprobation',[10] and in July 1759, following the well-established route for sons of Welsh gentry intending to take Holy Orders, he entered Jesus College (the first Protestant foundation at Oxford, the College had been established in 1571 by Dr Hugh Price of Brecon). The *Memoirs* recall his undergraduate experience in characteristically self-deprecating terms: 'except learning by rote a certain Latin formulary . . . I ever after rather lost, than acquired, any thing in Language or Science – for which I take Shame to myself', and, inevitably, he found himself in debt 'unless the young Student shd happen naturally to have by far a greater Share of Courage, Self-denial and Prudence than whatever I pretended to . . . I must own too that looking upon myself as Heir to a good Estate, I lanched into great excesses'.[11] As late as 1773–4, Jones found himself painting a small picture for the head cook at Jesus College as repayment for a debt allegedly outstanding since 1761.[12] It was in 1761 that Jones's life again took an unexpected turn: his great-uncle died intestate, and although one-third of his estate was in due course inherited by Thomas Jones the elder, 'all my Golden Dreams were at an End – Though this Event was an unspeakable Disappointment in one respect yet I declare it was a secret Consolation in another – I knew my father would not insist on continuing me in a Course, at so great an Expence, contrary to my Inclinations, and I had conceived a certain Antipathy to *taking Orders*'.[13] He had privately determined to be a painter.

Perhaps predictably, Thomas Jones's father was cautious about this proposal, but agreed to seek advice on his behalf. An old friend, a colonel in the Guards, consulted Richard Dalton (1713?–1791),[14] Librarian to the King, who had begun his career as a painter; his response was dispiriting: 'a friendly Advice not to enter upon a profession, by which [he] declared he never was able to *get Salt to his porridge*'.[15] For a time, other proposals were put forward by busybodying relations, notably that he should go to sea, a scheme that alarmed his father as much as himself: 'No – thought I – these [cousins] shall never . . . degrade me into a Cabin-boy, after having been a member of the University two years'.[16] It seemed that he would have to resign himself to a quiet life in Wales. At this point, fortuitously, the family's friend Charles Powell of Castlemadoc[17] provided the key introduction that would enable Thomas Jones to go to London in order to study art. Powell had become an early member of the Society for the Encouragement of the Arts, Sciences and Manufactures soon after its inception in 1754, and began a correspondence with the body's founder, William Shipley (1715–1803),[18] seeking advice on establishing an Agricultural Society in Breconshire. The aims of the Society of Arts were ambitious: 'To embolden enterprise, to enlarge Science, to refine Art, to improve our Manufactures and extend Commerce', and may be seen as a reflection of an increasingly self-confident bourgeoisie, keenly aware of the economic benefits of improvement in every aspect of life.

The Brecknockshire Agricultural Society was founded in 1755, the first of its kind and subsequently much copied;[19] Thomas Jones the elder became a member in 1758 and president in 1761. So successful was this society in improving local agricultural methods – and thus landlords' returns – that Shipley later claimed 'large tracts of land which before were only worth half-a-crown an acre are now let for twelve shillings'.[20] The range of Shipley's interests was remarkable: prison reform, poor relief, the teaching of modern languages and more besides, but he earned his living as a drawing master and it was on account of this that Charles Powell wrote to him about the young Thomas Jones, who received in return detailed advice and particulars of his drawing school. Reassured by the esteem in which Powell held Shipley, Thomas Jones's father agreed to let him go to London in November 1761, though almost certainly with some reservations.

The decision to become an artist was a far from conventional choice for the son of a well-established gentry family in the Welsh Marches, and throughout Jones's life one senses an ambiguity in how he himself, as well as others, perceived his status. He was later to observe that the Romans classified their English visitors into three groups, 'like the Positive, Comparative and Superlative of the Grammarians': 'Artists'; 'Mezzi Cavalieri . . . who lived genteely, independent of any profession'; and the 'true Cavalieri or Milordi Inglesi'.[21] Jones himself was to combine the 'Positive' with elements of the 'Comparative'. He was not, of course, the first Welshman to go to London to become an artist, and indeed his predecessors came from broadly similar backgrounds, but it was nevertheless unusual.

Some idea of the context in which Jones made his decision to become an artist can be gauged by looking briefly at three of these predecessors. John Dyer (1699–1757) – now better known as a poet than a painter – was the son of a lawyer in Carmarthenshire, who studied with his father before deciding in 1720 to become a pupil of Jonathan Richardson and then travelled to Italy in 1724–5, a generation before this became commonplace for aspiring artists; he subsequently became a clergyman (a richly varied career). His poems, 'Grongar Hill' (1726) and 'The Ruins of Rome' (1740), with their sensitivity to Welsh landscape and Celtic history, deserve recognition as precursors of a developing sense of national identity. It became the custom in the nineteenth century to write about Welsh art as if it had begun spontaneously and without precedent in the person of Richard Wilson (1713–1782). Edward Owen (d. 1740) of Penrhos, Anglesey made little impact in his short life, and almost none of his works has survived, but as Peter Lord has pointed out, he is of considerable interest for two reasons. First, his forgotten existence further undermines the myth of Wilson as a unique phenomenon in a nation without any prior interest in visual culture. Second, while he was at school in Oswestry – 'I draw picktures very much . . . [will you] alow somewhat to buy books to draw and engrediens to paint' – he began to write a series of letters to his family that give a rare insight for this date into the world of an apprentice artist, to some extent anticipating Jones's *Memoirs*. Like Jones, it was suggested that he become a clergyman, but he firmly expressed his preference: 'I like a limner best'. His sister concurred: since he knew his mind, 'it is best to let him follow it, & no doubt but with God's Grace he may make a competent honest livelyhood'.[22] This suggests that becoming a painter was not perhaps as controversial a choice as might be supposed. As an apprentice of the portraitist Thomas Gibson, he continued with his private studies in geometry and arithmetic, and took up French as well as drawing, complaining of the cost of materials. He reported that it was necessary to dress well, confirming other contemporary sources that suggest the increasing gentrification of artists as a group; a similar development may be seen with all the new professions gradually emerging from the anonymity of the middling ranks. The third Welsh artist to precede Jones to London was of course his future master, Richard Wilson (cat. no. 14). (It is worth noting, however, that in 1761, when Thomas

Jones's father was making enquiries in London about the art world, nobody seems to have recommended that he consult his fellow-countryman Wilson, by this stage well established.) It is arguable that Wilson came from a higher social echelon than Thomas Jones. Although his father was a clergyman who had been educated at Oxford, he could claim kinship with some of the greatest Welsh families through his mother. His first cousin became Lord Chancellor, and another close kinsman, Sir George Wynne, who funded his training with the portrait painter Thomas Wright, was for a time among the richest men in the country. Wilson was only about sixteen when he began his training, but he had apparently received a considerably more sophisticated education than was the norm for a young painter. So well grounded had he been in the classics that even towards the end of his life he could quote Horace extensively (in this he almost certainly bettered his Oxford-educated pupil Jones): he could therefore boast the education and connections of a gentleman.

Thomas Jones arrived in London in November 1761, 'to enter upon my Novitiate',[23] at a time of radical change in the art world. The challenge for artists was to transform an occupation hitherto considered artisanal into a modern profession, to develop a distinctive, national school of painting, to shape public taste for contemporary British art and to gain access to the new breed of patron that had emerged – the professional men: bankers, lawyers, clergymen and doctors, who were increasingly prosperous. Informal clubs, societies and academies for artists had existed since the end of the previous century, but by the 1750s there was an increasing need to establish a stronger sense of professional identity. Public exhibitions of modern British art were generally agreed to be a desirable way of educating the public and elevating the status of the participants. They demonstrated what British artists were capable of and gave a tangible form to the idea of a body of professional endeavour in place of an amorphous mass of individuals. Most straightforwardly, such exhibitions would provide a market-place, a means of reaching a large clientele without having to go through dealers. Despite these clearly perceived advantages, it took a considerable time for the artists to organize themselves well enough to put such ideas into effect. Hogarth's pioneering efforts at promoting British art at Vauxhall Gardens and the Foundling Hospital were not followed up until 1759, when a meeting of artists held at the hospital resolved to hold a public exhibition:[24] the first took place at the Society of Arts in 1760. As well as exhibitions to promote their work, the question of establishing professional art institutions was widely debated by artists and connoisseurs.

Proposals for a public academy under royal patronage had been put forward over the years, notably in 1755, but that scheme foundered chiefly because of disagreement over the hieratic structure envisaged by its proponents. A rival view opposed such an institution as the epitome of authoritarianism and intolerant classicism, favouring instead the kind of academy associated with Hogarth: democratic in organization, pragmatic in its aims. He wanted artistic standards to emerge from the practice of artists, not to be imposed by a privileged and selective body acting as an arbiter of taste. The tensions between these opposing views were to continue up to the eventual establishment of the Royal Academy in 1768, and indeed well beyond.[25]

Through his initial introduction to William Shipley, his subsequent training, his membership of the Society of Artists and the friendships he formed with particular fellow artists, Thomas Jones became associated from the outset with what might be described as the more pragmatic, 'Hogarthian' faction. From his *Memoirs* we have a vivid account of this period of upheaval, written from an insider's standpoint, tracing his development from student to independently established artist attempting to make a reputation and win commissions. Jones's account of his training begins with what he describes as the 'humiliating Situation of copying drawings of Ears, Eyes, mouths & Noses among a group of little boys of half my age who had the start of me by two or three years'; for a young man who had spent two years as an Oxford undergraduate, this must indeed have tested his resolve, but a certain doggedness that one notes throughout the *Memoirs* asserts itself here – 'This Spur'd me to greater Exertion'.[26] Shipley himself had recently retired from active management of the school, which had just moved to the 'Great Room' in the Strand, a relic of old Beaufort House,[27] and was now run by Henry Pars (1734–1806) and his brother William (1742–1782), one of Shipley's most talented pupils and a regular premium (prize) winner at the Society of Arts since 1756. Together with John Hamilton Mortimer (1740–1779) and James Gandon (1742–1823), both of whom he seems first to have met as fellow students at Shipley's, William Pars was among Jones's closest friends, first in London and later in Italy.[28] After a few months of drawing from standard exercise or pattern books, Jones was thought sufficiently competent to be introduced by Shipley to the Duke of Richmond's sculpture gallery, where carefully selected students had been allowed since 1758[29] to draw from the important collection of casts after the Antique, supervised at the outset by the sculptor Joseph Wilton (1722–1803) and the painter Giovanni Battista Cipriani (1727–1785), though they had both resigned by 1762. Among their first and most talented pupils had been Mortimer (winner of the first prize offered by the Society of Arts in 1759 for a drawing made in the gallery) (fig. 12). Wilton and Cipriani recommended the duke retain Mortimer in his household, but even at the outset of his career he characteristically valued his independence more than an attachment to a patron. No drawings by Jones survive from this period, and we therefore have to rely on his *Memoirs* for recollections of his activities and on studies by his contemporaries to gain some idea of what his work might have looked like. In October 1762, according to a cursory note in the *Memoirs*, he became a member of the St Martin's Lane Academy in order to learn life drawing; again, his fellow students included Mortimer and Pars and it may well have been here that he first met Giuseppe Marchi (*c.*1735–1808),[30] Reynolds's chief assistant since 1753, who was to remain a close friend until his death (cat. nos 1, 2, 5 and 6).

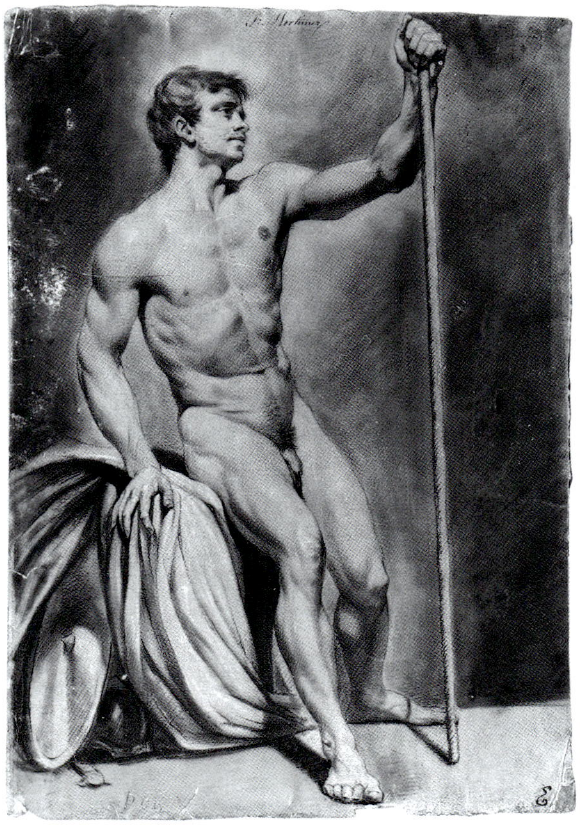

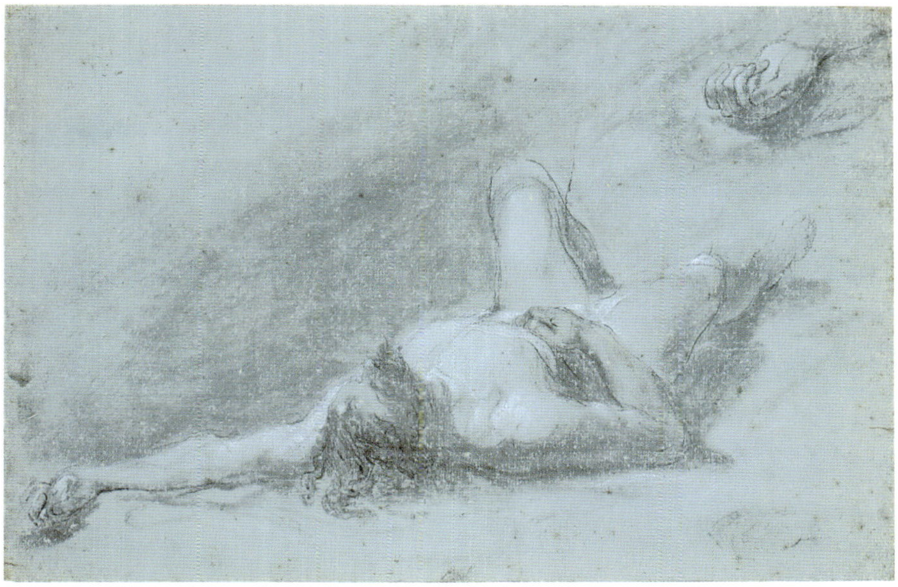

Fig. 13 Richard Wilson (1713–1782), *Figure Study for 'Niobe'*, c.1755–60, black chalk on prepared paper with white heightening, 33 × 51 (13 × 20), National Museums & Galleries of Wales, Cardiff.

Fig. 12 (LEFT) John Hamilton Mortimer (1740–1779), *Academy Study, Male Nude Seated on Drapery*, 1759, black chalk with white heightening, 53.6 × 39 (21⅛ × 15⅜), Royal Society of Arts, London.

The St Martin's Lane Academy had been revived by Hogarth in 1735[31] and was to continue until 1768. In the middle years of the century, it was more than an art school: it was at the centre of various initiatives and internal manœuvrings that were eventually to result in a mature institutional system for the arts. Not only students drew from the life at the academy; established artists including Cipriani, Francis Hayman (1708–1776) and Wilson attended. In Italy, while increasingly turning his attention to landscape painting, Wilson is known to have been a member of the Accademia del Nudo and seems, sporadically at least, to have continued to make such drawings after he returned to England; a study for one of the central figures in *The Destruction of the Children of Niobe* (Yale Center for British Art), exhibited 1760, was almost certainly made at the St Martin's Lane Academy (fig. 13). Close links with the newly formed Society of Arts led to a greater emphasis in the late 1750s on providing students with a sound theoretical training as well as establishing a more uniform academic style of life drawing; premiums were to be awarded each year for the best examples, as with drawings after the Antique in the Duke of Richmond's gallery. Thus in 1759, Mortimer not only won first prize for a study after Michelangelo's *Bacchus*, but also second prize for a life drawing (fig. 12). Stylistically, surviving examples of such drawings by Thomas Jones's contemporaries[32] are in the tradition established by the French Academy at the end of the previous century and introduced to

England by Louis Chéron (1660–1715) and John Vanderbank (1694–1739) in the 1720s. There is every reason to suppose that the life drawing for which Jones was awarded a premium in 1764 looked very similar to those by Mortimer and his contemporaries; so carried away was he by his success that he spent 'fifteen Shillings & 6 pence . . . [on] a new *gold lace* for my hat'.[33]

Jones began his relationship with Wilson almost by chance. He had intended to become a portrait painter, and a well-connected acquaintance, the amateur engraver and collector Captain William Baillie (1723–1810),[34] undertook to find him a suitable master, but the plan foundered because those he approached required either a very lengthy apprenticeship (in effect, cheap labour) or exorbitantly large fees. Almost casually, it seems, Baillie asked whether Jones had considered landscape painting: 'I told him my natural bias was to that branch of the Profession',[35] and in March 1763 Baillie introduced Jones to Wilson, the two quickly agreeing terms of pupillage – fifty guineas for two years.[36] It is interesting to note that despite the fact that both men were Welsh and Jones had asserted his preference for landscape painting, they had not met before. Jones readily admitted his ignorance 'of the true principles of the Art . . . I began to repent at having engaged my Self so precipitately – The characteristick Beauties of this great Master I was quite blind to – And I looked upon his pictures as coarse unfinished Sketches'.[37] Jones's initial reaction to his master's style gradually changed. His visual vocabulary was formed during the subsequent two years with Wilson, and one can trace the origins of much of his future practice to this period. It was also due to his experience as Wilson's pupil that he conceived a determination to go to Italy.

Though Jones's account of Wilson's studio practice is tantalizingly succinct, he describes his own initial training: for the first year he was confined to drawing in black and white chalk on tinted paper (Wilson's own favoured technique since his years in Rome, see cat. nos 17 and 19), copying his master's drawings and paintings, or drawing from nature, in order to ground him in the understanding of tonal values. This discipline of drawing in Wilson's manner seems to have been *de rigeur*; William Hodges (1744–1797), an apprentice from about 1758 until the mid-1760s, was certainly trained thus (cat. no. 13). Jones was soon joined as a fellow pupil (rather than apprentice) by Joseph Farington (1747–1821), who was also later to recall this period in his detailed diaries (cat. no. 11). The value of training in a studio depended not only on the pupil's skill but also on the attitude of the master. James Northcote was to comment rather bitterly on Reynolds's relationship with his pupil–assistants, 'he gave himself not the least trouble about them or their fate',[38] but the regime in Wilson's studio was a good deal more enlightened. His apprentices were expected to undertake much of the preparatory work 'by their assistance in dead Colouring and forwarding the Pictures'.[39] However, as pupils, Jones and Farington seem often to have been left to their own devices, wasting much of their time 'in idle Mirth & frolick' and receiving only the most laconic reprimand from Wilson: 'Gentlemen – this is not the way to rival Claude'.[40] But, unlike Reynolds, who was reluctant to impart technique to his pupils and always painted in a separate room, Wilson worked in front of his students and discussed his progress with them. He also took them on painting expeditions in the country, as recorded in a drawing by Farington showing Wilson painting from nature in Moor Park, dated 1765 (cat. no. 12). Like Thomas Jones, Farington also seems to have continued this practice, for the watercolourist Thomas Hearne made a drawing of him, with Sir George Beaumont, at work on easel pictures beside Lodore Falls in 1777 (The Wordsworth Trust), and this, as with Farington's drawing of his master, has all the characteristics of a documentary record, while also recalling Wilson's *Tivoli: the Cascatelli Grandi and the Villa of Maecenas*, 1752 (National Gallery of Ireland, Dublin), in which a painter is shown at his easel. Sketching of this sort certainly seems to have been a part of Wilson's teaching, despite his reservations about colouring from nature. Jones was to record his own experiments in painting *en plein-air* later in the decade.

During the time that Jones studied with Wilson, he would have been closely involved with the production of four important paintings of classical subjects commissioned by Henry Blundell of Ince Hall, Lancashire. Of these, *The Lake of Nemi with Dolbadarn Castle (Diana and Callisto)* (cat. no. 16), must have made a particular impression on Jones, so closely did Wilson intertwine Welsh and classical elements, identifying his native landscape – hitherto generally regarded as barbarous – with notions both of classical antiquity and ancient British history. Llyn Peris is transposed into Lake Nemi, while Dolbadarn Castle could be an ancient Roman monument: thus, perhaps, was Jones's nascent Welshness to be stirred. By disengaging himself from the constraints of topographical accuracy, Wilson separated himself from that class of painters who were expected only to imitate what was before them. Instead, he emphasized the selective and synthesizing role of the landscape painter, and would have subscribed to Reynolds's view that 'Claude Lorrain . . . was convinced, that taking nature as he found it seldom produced beauty'.[41] But besides classicizing landscapes such as these, in which Wilson symbolically equated antique Italy with ancient Britain (see also cat. no. 16), cast in the pictorial language of Dughet or Claude, two other Wilson prototypes were to be of considerable importance for Jones's future repertoire. First, the Sublime historical landscape, as exemplified in *The Destruction of the Children of Niobe* (Yale Center for British Art), shown at the first annual exhibition of the Society of Artists in 1760, which was to influence a significant number of Jones's exhibited paintings; and, second, a group of landscapes datable *c.*1765–75, painted in a significantly more naturalistic manner than his Grand Style compositions, in which Wilson set aside all classical, historical or literary allusions to paint simple rural scenes in a style more closely allied to the Dutch tradition of views of 'common nature'.

In March 1765, at the age of twenty-three, Jones left Wilson's studio to become an artist in his own right, exhibiting at the Society of Artists for the first time in that year. But the impression one receives from the *Memoirs* (which, of course, were written in the 1790s) is that he found considerable difficulty in establishing himself; much seems to have been left unsaid. What is certain is that, despite rebuffs and disappointments, he persisted in his determination to paint, 'fortified by the dignity of a reticent pride', as Lawrence Gowing described Jones's temperament.[42] There were moments of optimism, as in 1766 when he was elected a member of the Society of Artists, and in 1767 when he was awarded the first (and in 1768 the second) premium for landscape painting by the Society of Arts. His diffidence about his abilities led him to paint his 1767 submission in secret, 'so much afraid' was he 'of becoming an Object of Ridicule, even to my most intimate acquaintance'.[43] This disarming account, and other similar recollections throughout the *Memoirs*, anticipate the note he appended to the manuscript in 1798: 'With regard to *Egotism* – I have avoided it as much as a Man, who was writing of himself, could have possibly done – without Affectation – what render[s] that *Term* disgusting are Ostentation and vain boasting – the Offsprings of Vanity, with which, If I know my own heart, I am as little tainted as any One.'[44] Though we learn scarcely anything of the paintings on which he was working at this time, a few have survived, together with various leaves from a sketchbook he used sporadically between 1766 and 1774, and his earliest surviving oil sketches. Two canvases, *A View of a River on the Outskirts of a Town* and *A View of a Canal on the Outskirts of a Town* (figs 14 and 15), both dated 1768, perhaps show the outskirts of Walton on Thames,[45] and demonstrate Jones's early efforts to absorb Wilson's naturalistic manner, with their open, unconventional compositions and interest in the fall of light as a unifying element.

Woven in and out of Jones's narrative are the clues by which we may attempt, together with such studies as have survived from his pre-Italian years, to understand his development as a whole. It is fortunate that some works have survived, for Jones records that virtually all of his drawings and studies were destroyed by damp when they were stored in a cellar during his years in Italy.[46] The origins of oil sketching from nature have been much

Fig. 14 (BELOW LEFT) Thomas Jones, *View of a River on the Outskirts of a Town*, 1768, oil on canvas, 37.8 × 56.8 (14⅞ × 22⅜), present location unknown.

Fig. 15 (BELOW RIGHT) Thomas Jones, *View of a Canal on the Outskirts of a Town*, 1768, oil on canvas, 37.8 × 56.8 (14⅞ × 22⅜), present location unknown.

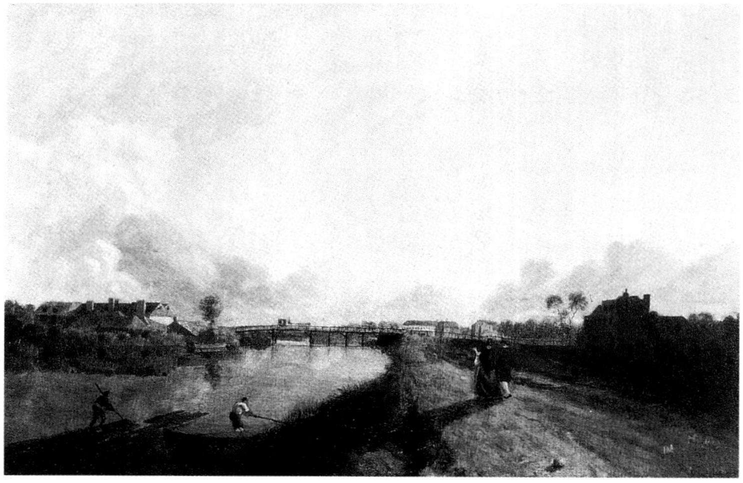

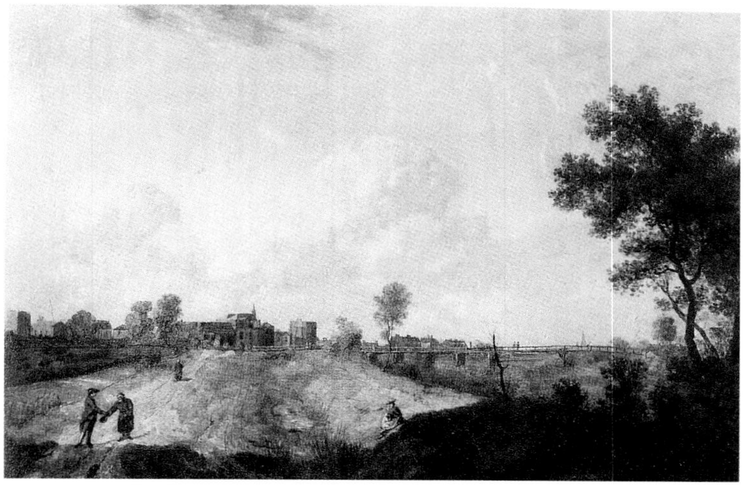

discussed in the past twenty years, and Jones's idiosyncratic contribution has long been acknowledged, but it has perhaps been too tempting to look at these expressions of what Gowing describes as Jones's 'sporadic genius' in aesthetic isolation, faintly embarrassed and puzzled as commentators have been that the same artist could be responsible for such works of unaffected directness as his Pencerrig oil studies (cat. nos 40 and 46), as for those classicizing and sometimes heavy-handed historical landscapes that he was concurrently exhibiting. In order to reconcile these apparently contradictory impulses, it is necessary to attempt some understanding of the immediate context in which he was working.

From his years in Wilson's studio, and from his knowledge of seventeenth-century landscape painting, Jones's aspiration was to work in the same ideal mode, estimating his own success, as his contemporaries inevitably judged him, by those criteria. 'Composing landscapes . . . is not the art of imitating individual nature; it is more; it is forming artificial representations of landscape on the general principles of nature'[47] – a sentiment with which Jones would have agreed. Yet he had also learned from Wilson that there was something to be derived from the practice of painting outdoors, providing the process was subjected to synthesis and adaptation in the studio. When did he begin to make such studies? The first specific reference in his *Memoirs* is in the summer of 1770, when he was staying with his cousin Rice James at Gadbridge, although it is possible that earlier references to 'Studies after Nature' also refer to sketching in oils. His earliest known oil on paper, *Gadbridge, Hertfordshire* (cat. no. 39), a study of storm-tossed trees, immediately prompts questions as to whether or not it was painted outdoors. In fact, despite its powerfully naturalistic character, it is possible that it was painted away from the motif. Here, Jones seems to anticipate the ambiguity of John Sell Cotman's struggle with 'Nature . . . that fickle Dame' thirty-five years later.[48] At the time that Jones painted this – and other, now lost studies – at Gadbridge, he was also working on his exhibited landscape compositions in the Grand Style, and must surely have had those in mind as he made such informal studies. A tantalizing reference in the *Memoirs* suggests that Jones may have made a series of oil sketches at Eastbourne, in the company of Mortimer. In 1769, an old mill overlooking the sea, which belonged to Mortimer's family, had been converted by James Gandon into 'Commodious Appartments for two small families to reside in during the Bathing Season – One of the rooms . . . was made use of as a Study to paint Scenes after nature as Cliffs, Waves, Shipping &c'.[49] Jones's studies must have perished, and the only tangible reminder of his visits is his painting *Coast Scene near Eastbourne with Approaching Storm* of 1771 (cat. no. 23). Mortimer, too, seems to have dabbled in landscape during his visits home, perhaps encouraged by Jones. *The West Gate of Pevensey Castle* (fig. 16), exhibited at the Society of Artists in 1774, is surprisingly sketch-like in character.

In 1772, Jones spent four months in Wales, when he notes that he made 'a good many Studies in Oil on paper';[50] of these, a small group survive and must be counted among his most beautiful and remarkable works (see cat.

Fig. 16 John Hamilton Mortimer (1740–1779), *The West Gate of Pevensey Castle, Sussex*, *c.*1774, oil on canvas, 70.8 × 90.8 (27⅞ × 35¾), Yale Center for British Art, New Haven.

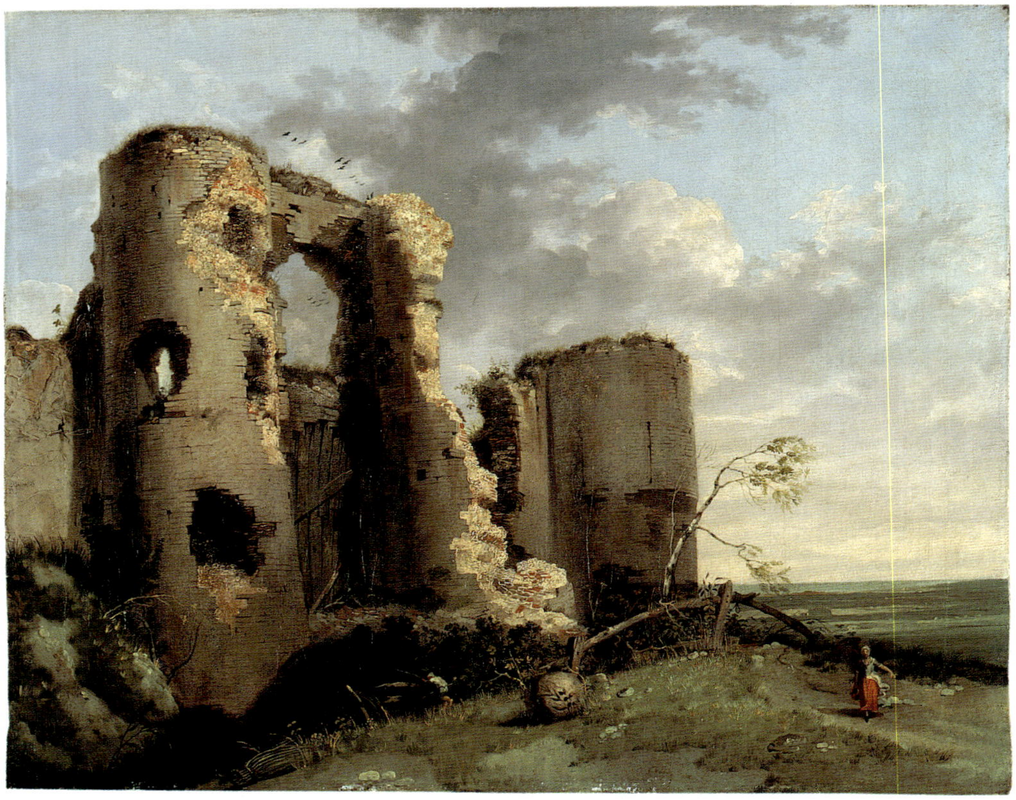

nos 40 and 41). It was while painting these that Jones formulated the compositional structure that characterizes nearly all his subsequent oil studies, namely the decision to omit any distinction between foreground and middle ground, to take away the conventional props that gradually lead the eye into the landscape. It would be a mistake, however, to think of these as simple transcriptions of nature. On the contrary, these compositions are carefully calculated, the sweeping shapes of the hilly landscape around Pencerrig emphasized by the distribution of light and shade, which cut across the lie of ground, casting bands of shadow here and there, and highlighting details such as the carefully placed farmhouse in the centre of catalogue number 40. The sky also plays an essential part in the total effect, now reflected in the water (cat. no. 41), now spanning the hillside in a vast silver-grey arc. For a moment, in catalogue number 41, with its golden glimmer of a harvest field, it is as if one has stepped into a corner of an early Gainsborough landscape, but Jones's genius lay in making a self-sufficient image from such a motif.

Back in London, as he continued with his efforts to establish himself in the artistic community, Jones sustained his contact with Welsh friends, acting as a steward at the 'Welch feast' on St David's Day in 1766 (perhaps one organized by the Society of Cymmrodorion, founded in 1751 to preserve Welsh language and customs, and to encourage bardic literature); he became a Freemason at the behest of his fencing master, 'the little . . . redhot Welshman' Davies, and developed a friendship with Revd Evan Lloyd

(1734–1776),[51] through whom he met David Garrick. Lloyd was an absentee cleric, who devoted himself to satiric verse to the extent that he was briefly imprisoned for libelling a neighbouring Welsh squire. A friend and patron of Mortimer, Evan Lloyd, would collaborate with Jones in a puff for the Society of Artists' exhibition in 1772, held in their new (and as it turned out, ruinously expensive) premises. Jones also describes an informal club, the Howdalian Society (named in honour of Captain Howdall, 'an enthusiast for the Arts')[52] chiefly consisting of members of the Society of Artists, including Mortimer, who was President, James Gandon and Joseph Wright of Derby, as well as himself. But besides details of his social activities, Jones's *Memoirs* for this period give us a first-hand account of the split within the Society of Artists, which came to a head in October 1768 and led directly to the formation of the Royal Academy. The central issue seems to have been the resentment felt by the younger members against their elders, who had established a stranglehold over the affairs of the Society. Jones himself was present at an acrimonious meeting, and describes the origin of the schism as 'the private feud of two rival Individuals . . . which insensibly involving the whole Society within its Vortex', that is to say, the rivalry between two architects, Sir William Chambers and James Paine.[53] Chambers and his supporters seceded, and through his astute use of his connections at court – he was the king's architect – the Royal Academy was established before the end of the year.

A majority of the best-established artists inevitably gravitated to the new academy, though the Society of Artists attempted to fight back. Mortimer, who was elected a director on 18 October 1768, was a supporter of Paine, and until 1775 was at the heart of the Society's deliberations, eventually serving as president. Jones himself was elected a fellow in 1771 and a director in 1773, but although the records show that he was assiduous in attending meetings,[54] and played a considerable part in arranging the inaugural celebrations for the Society's first exhibition in its splendid new premises in 1772, he came to realize that they had overreached themselves in building the largest and grandest exhibition space in London – designed by Paine – in an attempt to outdo the Academy. At Jones's request, Revd Evan Lloyd wrote an ode for the opening of the new rooms, set to music by Mr Hooke; not, it must be said, a work of any distinction, indeed its banality may be gauged from the concluding lines: 'Behold the Arts around us bloom / And its Muse–devoted Dome / Rivals the works of Athens and of Rome'.[55] To accompany the exhibition, Mortimer and Jones jointly wrote a guide, with a preface by Lloyd, *Candid Observations on the Principal Performances now Exhibiting at the New Room of the Society of Artists . . . Intended as a Vade Mecum to that Exhibition*, a bland effort, although notable for Mortimer's coupling of his own name with that of Salvator Rosa in connection with his exhibits of two *banditti* subjects, new to his repertoire. The Society became virtually bankrupt through financial mismanagement and its ill-advised development foray. In 1774, Jones noted that he was approached by various members of the Academy with the idea that he should

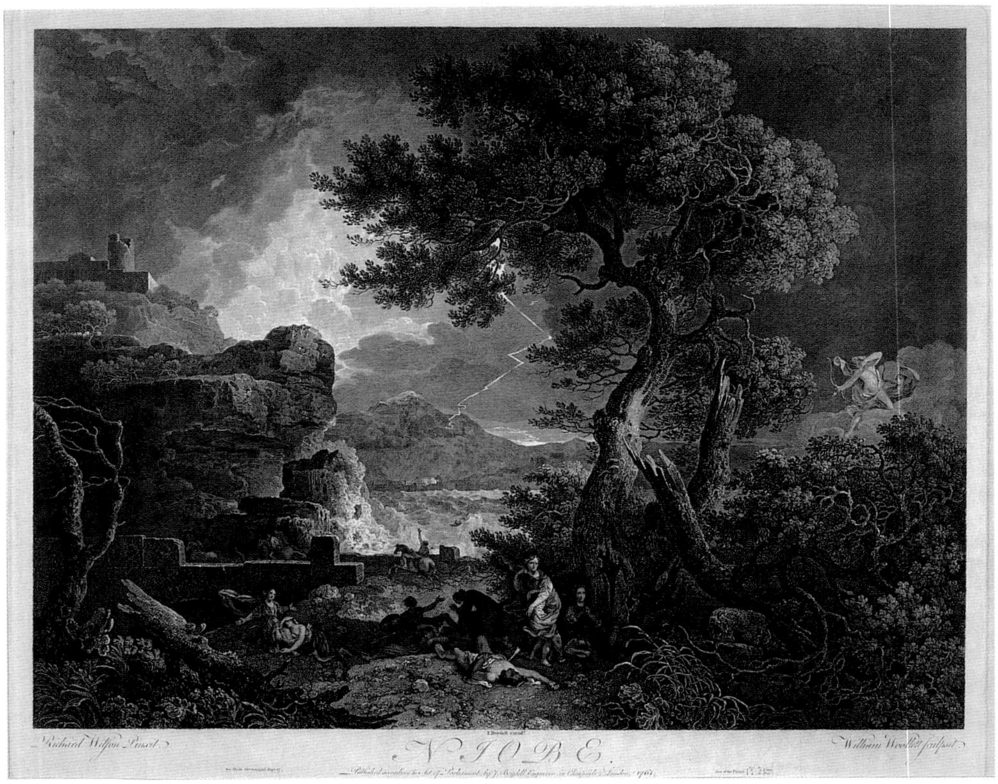

Fig. 17 William Woollett (1735–1785) after Richard Wilson (1713–1782), *The Destruction of the Children of Niobe*, 1761, engraving and etching, 48.5 × 61 (19⅛ × 24), National Museums & Galleries of Wales, Cardiff.

become a member, 'but as I had vowed a kind of fealty to the old *incorporated* Society, I resisted the temptation, at the same time I was aware of their ascending, and our descending progression'.[56]

By the early 1770s, the *Memoirs* record Jones working in a variety of styles and media: painting country-house views from drawings made at Fulke Greville's house, Wilbury near Andover; painting backgrounds for Nathaniel Hone (1718–1784) and for marine subjects by Richard Paton (1717–1791) (see cat. no. 23) – Mortimer was also recruited to paint figures for him, experimenting with pastels – so successfully in fact that, to his horror, he nearly found himself engaged as a drawing master for young ladies. Most importantly, however, he had exhibited his first attempt at painting an historical landscape in the manner established by Wilson with his *The Destruction of the Children of Niobe*, 1759–60 (fig. 17). This was *A Land Storm, with the Story of Dido and Aeneas* (cat. no. 20), in which Mortimer painted the figures. Like Wilson, Jones chose to set a dramatic episode from classical literature in an appropriately turbulent landscape, the inspiration for which must be the storm landscapes of Gaspard Dughet. The background emphasizes and complements the tragic narrative, just as the figures personify the elemental forces of nature. Jones proudly recalled it as 'one of the best I ever painted'; it must have seemed to augur the transformation of his reputation, especially when his friend, the celebrated engraver William Woollett (1735–1785), who had spread Wilson's name throughout Europe with the success of his print after *Niobe* (fig. 17), suggested engraving *Dido*

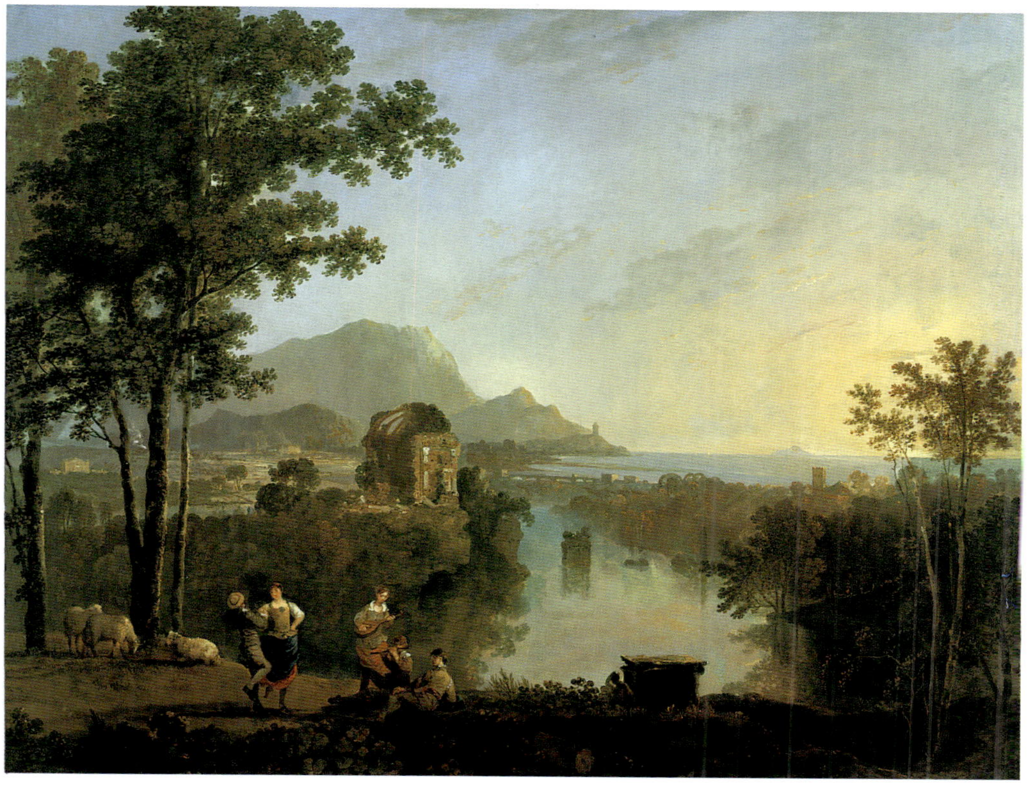

Fig. 18 Richard Wilson (1713–1782), *River Mouth with Peasants Dancing*, early 1770s, oil on canvas, 139.6 × 184.3 (55 × 72½), Bayerische Staatsgemäldesammlungen, Munich.

and Aeneas. Although Woollett began the engraving and exhibited an early state at the Society of Artists in 1773, he set it aside, to Jones's bitter disappointment. He seems never to have known that the engraving was completed after Woollett's death by Bartolozzi, and dedicated in 1787 by Elizabeth Woollett to the Empress Catherine, who – again unknown to poor Jones – had acquired the painting itself. Storm scenes of this type seem to have fascinated Jones, who exhibited one or two such subjects each year between 1769 and 1772.

To judge from the number of classical landscapes in the manner of Wilson that have survived, Jones must have found – for a time at least – a reasonable market.[57] While Jones's version of the Italianate idyll may lack Wilson's sophistication of design, complex use of allusion and luminosity of atmosphere, these pictures have undoubted charm. His favourite compositional device is a stretch of winding river in the middle distance, reminiscent of the Wye, with hills beyond, perhaps with a suggestion of a classical ruin; in the foreground are a rutted track and a group of rustic figures – a decidedly un-Italian touch (cat. nos 26 and 27). On several occasions, Jones noted making copies after Wilson; catalogue number 29 may well be such a picture, perhaps painted when Jones stayed with Oldfield Bowles in 1773–4, for it resembles a *Scene on the Coast of Baia* by Wilson, a version of which may by this date have been in a collection well known to them both, at nearby Rousham (fig. 18).[58]

Encouraged by the success of *Dido and Aeneas* in 1769, Jones decided to continue painting large landscapes with figures taken from classical or literary sources. Of those recorded as having been exhibited at the Society of Artists – where he was a prolific exhibitor until 1780 – only a few have as yet been identified. His chief submission for the 1770 exhibition, *A Landscape with the Death of Orpheus; the Figures by Mr Mortimer*, on which he worked for just under a year, was described by him as '8 feet by 6 with figures from 12 to 18 inches high by Mortimer'; considerably cut down, this is now in a private collection,[59] but an autograph reduced version (cat. no. 22) well represents the complete composition, in which Mortimer's figure group is set in an extensive landscape, far more self-consciously Romantic in mood, with its heavily wooded, naturalistic setting, than Wilson would ever have painted. Could Jones have referred to studies 'in Oil . . . of Trees &c after nature,' such as he possibly made that summer at Gadbridge (cat. no. 39), while working on such landscapes? His collaboration with Mortimer continued in the following year with a storm scene from *The Winter's Tale*, now untraced, which was to be bought by their mutual patron Sir George Beaumont in 1775, who showed it many years later with considerable pride to their old friend Joseph Farington;[60] again, Woollett expressed an interest in engraving the subject, though as Jones wryly noted, 'but this like many other projects of his – *dyed away in* thinking'.[61]

From *c.*1770 to 1773, Mortimer was involved with a very different project, in which Jones was to assist in a subsidiary capacity, the decoration of the saloon at Brocket Hall, Hertfordshire (fig. 19), a commission that almost

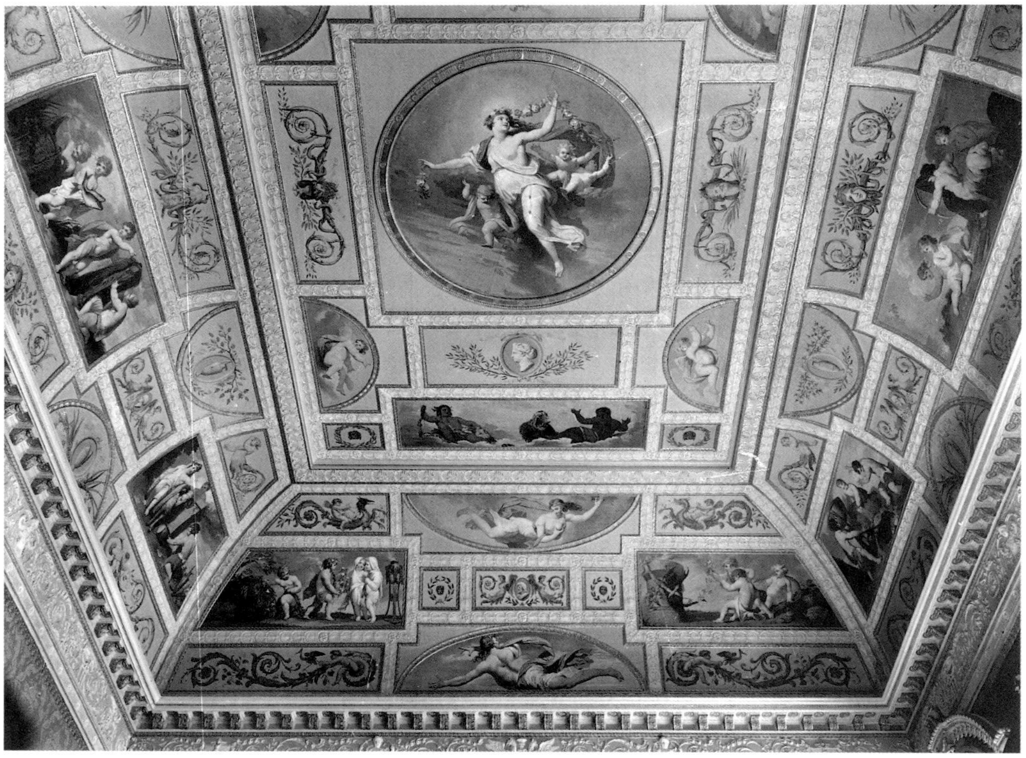

Fig. 19 John Hamilton Mortimer (1740–1779) with the assistance of others including Thomas Jones, part of the Saloon ceiling, Brocket Hall, Hertfordshire, *c.*1770–3.

certainly came through the architect of the house, James Paine (1717?–1789), an old friend and colleague of both Mortimer and Jones through their membership of the Society of Artists. Paine seems to have been responsible for the overall design of the ceiling, while Mortimer supervised a team of assistants in the execution of the painted decoration, which illustrated the theme of Love, Time and Fecundity;[62] early ideas for the project may be dated *c.*1770, but work on the ceiling seems to have been delayed for a time. From Jones's *Memoirs*,[63] we know that it was well under way in June 1772, when he visited Brocket Hall with Paine, and in January 1773 he joined Mortimer's team for just over a month, working with Francis Wheatley (1747–1801), James Durno (*c.*1745–1795) and Burnaby Mayor (*fl.*1767–1774). Whether Jones was paid is not specified; perhaps it was a similar arrangement to that he noted in May 1771, when he helped Wheatley 'in painting the large Cascade Scene in Vauxhall Gardens . . . all I got by this business was a good dinner every day'.[64]

Of Jones's exhibited pictures, *The Bard* (cat. no. 31), Society of Artists 1774, which was painted during a year-long stay with his pupil and friend Oldfield Bowles, is his most ambitious and in some respects his most original historical landscape composition, its dramatic character unparalleled in his work. Jones's source was Thomas Gray's poem of the same title, published in 1757, which was to be the chief literary text of the nascent Celtic Revival[65] and inspired several artists, but it was Jones who merged the image of the mediaeval bard with that of the ancient Druids. To underline this allusion, he included a stone circle and cromlech in the middle distance, unaware that these were monuments of a yet more ancient past. Stylistically, the influence of Gaspard Dughet (1615–1675) and Salvator Rosa (1615–1673) is clearly apparent, that of Wilson only in the detail of the corpses, inspired by similar figures in *The Death of the Children of Niobe*. The figure of the stricken bard – 'Robed in the sable garb of woe . . . Loose his beard, and hoary hair' – seems to have been Jones's own invention, for there is no reference to Mortimer as collaborator, though it is worth noting the close likeness between Jones's *Bard* and Mortimer's print of *Lear* of 1775–6.[66] According to the *Memoirs*, Jones painted *The Bard* during his second extended stay with Oldfield Bowles of North Aston, Oxfordshire, from March 1773 to March 1774. They had first met at the end of 1771, when Jones became Bowles's painting tutor, and the following year he spent three months with his pupil, who, given 'some cooperation and assistance' made such progress that – slightly to Jones's chagrin – he was judged by a critic to have 'surpassed his Master' in paintings exhibited at the Society of Artists in 1773.[67] Jones gives a lively description of life at North Aston, which chiefly revolved around the painting room, the hunting field and the private theatre set up by Bowles: reluctantly sent out to follow the hounds, Jones was then almost asphyxiated by the fumes from the paints he used for the theatre sets. Yet it seems to have been both a happy and productive time for Jones, who gave Bowles *The Bard* in thanks for his hospitality and in 1795 recalled his stay with obvious pleasure to Uvedale Price. Writing to Sir George Beaumont, who had been a participant in Bowles's amateur theatricals, Price reminded him of his old acquaintance, 'a little stunted man, as round as a ball, the truest Welch runt . . . his face as red as his master's'.[68]

In the summer of 1774, Jones went to stay with another patron, Dr Benjamin Bates (1736–1828) of Little Missenden, Buckinghamshire, whom he must have met through Mortimer.[69] Bates was a successful physician, an example of the new middle-class collectors who were beginning to emerge as patrons of young British artists; he bought Joseph Wright of Derby's *An Experiment on a Bird in an Air Pump* (National Gallery, London) and was one of Mortimer's most loyal friends and patrons, introducing him – and Jones – to other local collectors. Through Bates, Jones was taken to see the paintings by Claude-Joseph Vernet belonging to William Drake of Shardeloes, which he much admired, and during the two months he stayed at Little Missenden, he began work on a commission to paint a view of Milton's cottage at Chalfont St Giles (cat. no. 33), in which Mortimer was to paint figures illustrating a scene from *L'Allegro*. Bates soon decided to commission a pendant, a scene from *Il Penseroso*, again with figures by Mortimer, but Jones had to paint this from his imagination, since he 'could find no Scene in this beautiful Country, suitable to the Subject'.[70] The pair was exhibited at the Society of Artists in 1775. This was to be his last collaboration with Mortimer, who died in 1779, when Jones was in Italy.

By 1775, Jones had two loyal patrons, Oldfield Bowles and Dr Bates, a developing friendship with Sir George Beaumont and a respectable standing among his peers as a painter of historical and classicizing landscapes. He could reasonably have continued to follow the pattern he had developed, dividing his time between working on exhibition pictures in London and making extended visits to friends and patrons in the country. But he had by now decided to make a fundamental change to his life. In August, his former fellow pupil in Wilson's studio, William Hodges, returned from a voyage to the South Seas as draughtsman to Captain Cook's expedition, and some weeks later, Jones was approached by the architect 'Mr Stewart' (James 'Athenian' Stuart, 1713–1788) on behalf of the Society of Dilettanti to determine whether he would join Cook's next voyage in the same capacity. Jones, however, had a different plan in mind. Ever since his days in Wilson's studio, the idea of going to Italy had haunted him; 'I had seen and Copyed so many Studies of that great Artist . . . and was so familiarized with, & enamoured of *Italian* forms'.[71] The time had come for him actively to pursue this 'favourite project that had been in agitation for some Years, and on which my heart was fixed', and at the end of August he sent off his pictures and baggage to William Woollett for safekeeping and left for Wales: 'I had now, in a manner, taken leave of London, and was on a farewell visit, to my Parents, Relations and friends in the Country, previous to my departure for Italy'. But, as he noted, there were various practicalities to be overcome; 'some pecuniary Difficulties' had meant the postponement of this journey on previous occasions, and he now resolved to paint sufficient pictures while

FACING PAGE detail of cat. no. 33.

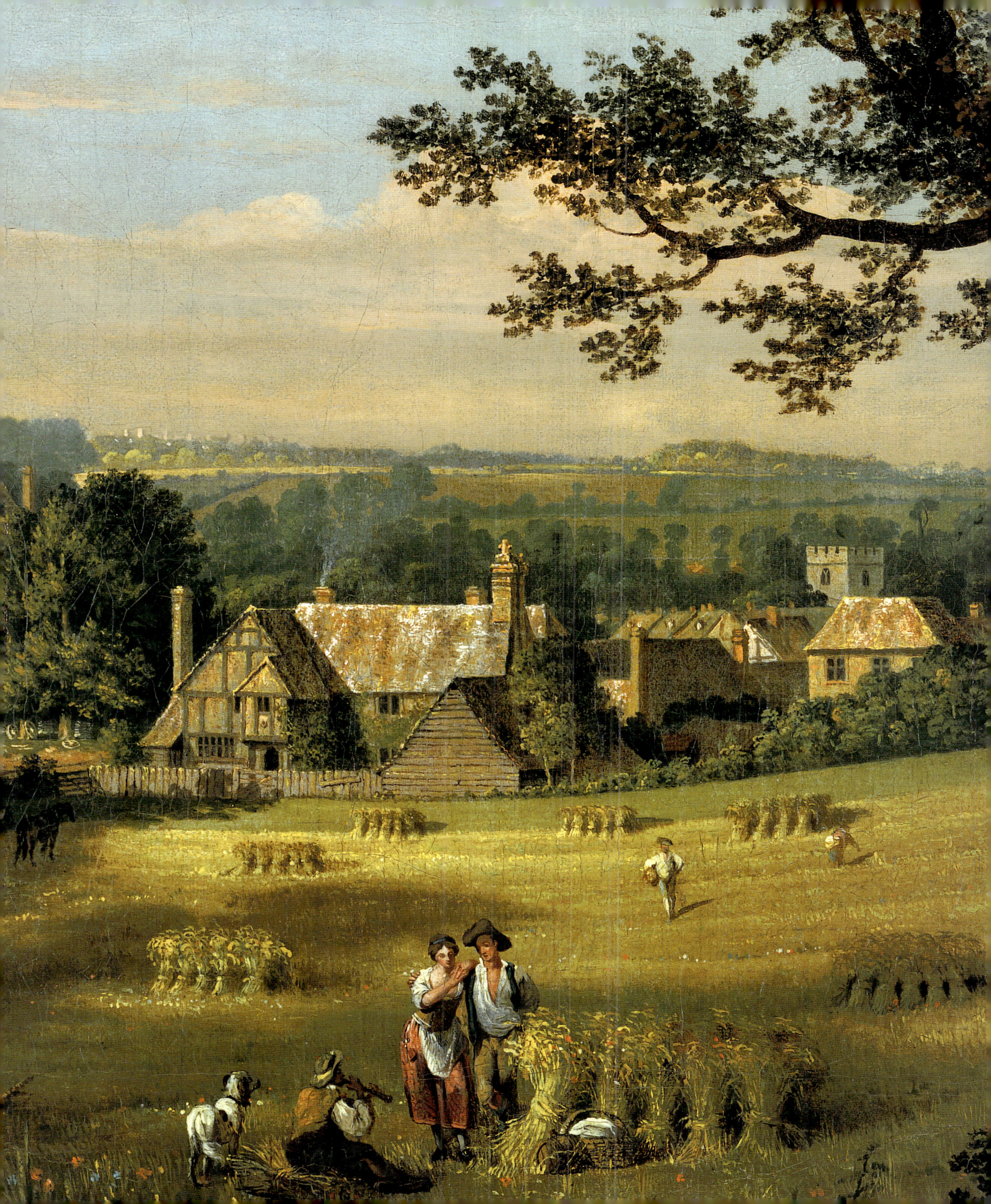

staying with his family to discharge 'all Demands, and leave a few Guineas' to supplement the allowance he hoped his father would make him. There was also the question of obtaining his parents' consent 'to set out forthwith on my Travells and which was a Circumstance, I knew, they were very Averse to – But . . . They preferr'd sending me to Italy than to the South Seas'.[72]

Jones recorded in his *Memoirs* the finished pictures he painted while at Pencerrig in the year prior to his departure for Italy and the prices he charged: the grand total came to 107 guineas, or £112.7.0. Stylistically, this year's work may be considered in three categories: topographical commissions, ideal landscapes and the studies in oil from nature that he also notes working on at intervals between his studio pictures. To these must be added a number of drawings and watercolours as well as a group of topographical prints not mentioned in the *Memoirs*, which may be dated around 1775–6, *Six Views in South Wales, Drawn after Nature* (cat. no. 55). They appeared at much the same time as Paul Sandby's more sophisticated aquatints. The topographical paintings, mostly views of country houses belonging to relations or friends of Jones (cat. no. 37), were predictably the most handsomely paid, but do not necessarily show the artist at his best, being characterized by a slightly naïve and old-fashioned literalness – though such exactness was probably what his clientele wanted.

The view of *Maeslough House* (cat. no. 37), painted for a local nabob, Walter Wilkins, shows him and his future wife proudly overseeing the landscaping of their estate; they seem to have been pleased with Jones's painting (which cost 30 guineas), allowing it to be exhibited at the Society of Artists in 1777. Besides formal commissioned views, Jones also made a number of landscape paintings and drawings during this year in Wales. Those that survive were mostly inspired by views along the Wye (cat. no. 35), conceived in a romantic-picturesque style that emphasizes the grandeur of the landscape. Another painting evocative of the Wye, *River Landscape with Figures Beside a Weir*, dated 1775 (cat. no. 34), is perhaps the picture listed by Jones as having been painted for 'Taylor' – possibly the Mr Taylor he had met at North Aston,[73] or, less probably, Isaac Taylor, the engraver and Secretary of the Society of Artists – for which he charged the modest sum of eight guineas. In Jones's fascination with the varied landscape of the Wye, perhaps one may sense an anticipation of William Gilpin's notion of the Picturesque as expressed in his *Observations on the River Wye . . . Relative Chiefly to Picturesque Beauty*, first published in 1782.

The classicizing landscapes Jones painted at this time are on the whole more sophisticated variants of those he had painted during the preceding ten years or so; there seems to be a new refinement and delicacy in the *Classical Landscape with Figures and Cattle* (private collection), 1776, perhaps the 'Oval within a 3 quarters sold in the Exhibition 12 Gs' or 'D'o its Companion' in Jones's list.[74] He was to abandon the large historical landscapes for which he had established a reputation at the Society of Artists' exhibitions, partly, one suspects, because they were not particularly easy to sell; and on his return to England in 1783 he was to find that idealizing landscapes in the manner of Wilson had also lost the appeal they had for patrons in earlier decades. Jones's repertoire was to seem painfully old-fashioned.

Yet while he clung to the kind of formal landscape he admired, his private painting was developing in a remarkable way; fortunately, a significant group of oil sketches survives from this period. In place of the absolute clarity that characterizes those dating from 1772 (cat. nos 40 and 41), a new sense of atmosphere pervades those painted during his 1775–6 visit to Pencerrig. There is a numinous quality and a sense of the fleeting, changeable aspects of nature, as hilltops are wreathed in mist (cat. no. 42), or clouds seem to drift through a vast sky (cat. no. 46).

Besides airy, panoramic sketches (cat. nos 44 and 45), Jones turned his attention also to the details of nature: the edge of a wood (cat. no. 47); a fallen tree (cat. no. 48); a field with late spring flowers (cat. no. 49). Looking at such studies, one is reminded of Turner's remarks in a lecture of 1811, when he sought to analyse Claude's method: 'we must consider how he could have attained such powers but by continual study of parts of nature. Parts, for, had he not so studied, we should have found him sooner pleased with simple subjects of nature, and [would] not [have], as we now have, pictures made up of bits, but pictures of bits.'[75] While Turner himself preferred the former, 'pictures of bits' have their own merit and appeal, as Jones realized. Although a number of the studies are dated 1776, others are undated, including *Carneddau, from Pencerrig* (cat. no. 42), a view taken from below the house, looking south-east on an autumn day, the air palpably damp and the bracken on the hillside turning brown, which can probably be dated to October or early November 1775, since Jones had left Wales by mid-September 1776. Careful examination reveals extensive underdrawing in several of these studies (for instance, cat. nos 45 and 49), which suggests that they were much more carefully considered compositions than might be thought, and were almost certainly not painted outdoors.

By mid-September 1776, Jones was at last ready to realize his 'favourite project that had been in agitation for some Years'; he made farewells[76] to his family and friends in Wales, and then, after visiting his patrons, Oldfield Bowles and Benjamin Bates, returned to London to make the final arrangements for his journey to Italy. He had intended to take the sea route, but an introduction by his old friend and fellow Welsh artist William Parry to the antiquarian Christopher Norton[77] led to a change of plan. Early on 15 October, after a last-minute panic in which he managed to forget all the letters of introduction he had carefully assembled, Jones set off with Norton for Brighthelmstone. The next morning, they embarked on the packet boat to France. 'Wind against us – did not lose sight of Beachy head till dark'.[78] On 27 November, after a carefully chronicled journey, Jones arrived in Rome. His initial excitement waned. It was a cold, wet, early winter, and after huddling round a brazier in the English Coffee House, he retreated to his 'melancholy Chamber' hung with 'dirty dismal pictures of Weeping Magdalens, bloody *Ecce homos*, dead-Christs and fainting Madonas . . . lulled to sleep by the pattering of the rain against the windows, [I] sometimes dreamt of the many Enjoyments I had left behind me in London'.[79] What was Italy to offer?

NOTES

1 *Memoirs*, p. 142.
2 Ibid., pp. 4–5.
3 Williams, 1859, p. 272.
4 *Memoirs*, p. 3.
5 Oliver, 1970, p. 16.
6 Williams 1859, p. 274.
7 The brothers John, Thomas and David Jones were all educated at Oxford; Thomas was intended for Holy Orders, and his younger brother, Revd David Jones, became the incumbent of Llandrindod in 1776 (*Memoirs*, p. 37), the very benefice in which the Caebach meeting house was situated.
8 As a pastor, Dr Jenkin Jenkins seems to have advocated unorthodox theological views, but was widely regarded as an outstanding classical teacher (see *The Dictionary of Welsh Biography*, 1959).
9 *Memoirs*, p. 118. See also Oliver, 1970, who notes that as well as being able to leave each of his five surviving sons at least two farms each, and make generous provision for his widow and unmarried daughter, Thomas Jones the elder could also bequeath to his eldest son a considerable estate extending through five parishes as well as significant property in north Brecknockshire (p. 19).
10 Ibid., p. 5.
11 Ibid., pp. 5–6.
12 Ibid., p. 33.
13 Ibid., p. 6.
14 Dalton subsidized his early artistic career by dealing.
15 *Memoirs*, p. 6.
16 Ibid., p. 7.
17 Charles Powell (1712–1796) of Castlemadoc established a reputation as an antiquarian, but his chief interest lay in agricultural improvement; see note 20.
18 Allan, 1968 (reprint with amendments, 1979), is the fullest account of Shipley's life.
19 See Allan, 1968, pp. 61–2, 64–7 and Edmunds, 1956.
20 Ibid., pp. 201–2.
21 *Memoirs*, pp. 70–1.
22 Lord, 1994, pp. 164–7 and Lord, 2000, pp. 75–80.
23 *Memoirs*, p. 8.
24 Jones refers to this, *Memoirs*, p. 8.
25 Bignamini, 1988.
26 *Memoirs*, p. 8.
27 Allan, 1968, p. 85.
28 Mulvany, 1846, p. 202.
29 Contemporary press reports praised the liberality of the duke in opening his gallery to young artists.
30 Marchi is recorded as a subscriber to the St Martin's Lane Academy (Bignamini, 1988, p. 116). Marchi remained a friend until Jones's death, Joseph Farington noting that he last visited Jones in Wales in the summer of 1802, following two bouts of illness.
31 Bignamini, 1988, pp. 95–124.
32 An album belonging to the Royal Society of Arts (RSA, vol. C) includes life drawings and drawings from casts in the Duke of Richmond's gallery by James Gandon, John Hamilton Mortimer, William Pars, John Smart and William Woollett among others, giving a good idea of the prevailing style.
33 *Memoirs*, p. 10.
34 Jones may have been introduced to Captain Baillie by Mortimer, who seems to have been a good friend.
35 *Memoirs*, p. 9.
36 This compares with £100 paid by Mortimer's father six years earlier for three years' study with Hudson.
37 *Memoirs*, p. 9.
38 Northcote, 1818, vol. II, p. 180.
39 *Memoirs*, p. 9.
39 Ibid., p. 10; p. 9.
40 Ibid., p. 10.
41 Wark, 1975, pp. 69–70. On 27 May 1801, in the course of a rare visit to London, Thomas Jones dined at Joseph Farington's house, when he 'observed that Claude & Nicolo Poussin never painted views of places. They collected their materials from nature and

combined them according to their fancy' (Farington, *Diary*, vol. IV, p. 1554).

42 Gowing, 1985, p. 29.

42 *Memoirs*, p. 12.

42 Ibid., pp. 140–1.

42 Gowing, 1985, p. 29.

43 *Memoirs*, p. 12.

44 Ibid., pp. 140–1.

45 Gowing, 1985, p. 14.

46 Jones described the bitter disappointment he felt when he went to recover his books, papers and drawings on his return to England, and found that nearly all were irretrievably damaged (*Memoirs*, p. 140), but did not identify the 'Gentleman' at whose house they had been left. A note in the small sketchbook which he used as a diary between 1783 and 1791 suggests that it was 'Mr James', presumably his cousin Rice James.

47 Cozens, 1786, p. 2.

48 Kitson, 1937, p. 80.

49 *Memoirs*, p. 23.

50 Ibid, p. 27.

51 For Lloyd's friendship with Mortimer, see Sunderland, 1986, p. 3, pp. 85–6, p. 7, p. 127, p. 152; see also Price, 1953–4, pp. 264–305, pp. 426–48.

52 *Memoirs*, p. 11. A slightly different account is given in Mulvany, 1846, pp. 211–12.

53 *Memoirs*, p. 14. Jones perhaps over-personalizes the rift.

54 The minutes of the Society of Artists, now in the library of the Royal Academy, note who were present at meetings. The last meeting Jones attended was on 13 April 1775. In October 1775, Mortimer resigned as president, perhaps alarmed by the crisis in the Society's finances.

55 Published in *The Annual Register*, vol. XV, 1772, pp. 206–8.

56 *Memoirs*, p. 33.

57 London, 1982, p. 21.

58 Ibid., p. 244. Joseph Farington noted seeing a landscape by Wilson at Rousham on 15 December 1808, 'the scene represented (I understood) "somewhere near Naples"' (*Diary*, vol. IX, p. 3382).

59 Sunderland, 1986, cat. no. 35.

60 Farington notes that Beaumont showed him the painting on 16 April 1808. Jones and Beaumont first met in 1772, when Beaumont 'bespoke a picture of me' (*Memoirs*, p. 26), his earliest purchase from a living artist. In 1773 they were both guests of Oldfield Bowles, Beaumont taking an active part in the amateur theatricals at North Aston; see Owen, 1988, pp. 15–17.

61 *Memoirs*, p. 23.

62 Sunderland, 1986, pp. 40–3.

63 *Memoirs*, p. 26.

64 Ibid., p. 24.

65 See Hinnant, 1974.

66 Mortimer exhibited 'Twelve Heads, from Characters in Shakespeare' at the Society of Artists in 1775. That of *Lear* was among the second group to be published as etchings in 1776.

67 *Memoirs*, p. 32.

68 Uvedale Price to Sir George Beaumont, 3 June 1795. Pierpont Morgan Library, New York, Mss MA 1581 (Price 4). See Owen, 1988, p. 18.

69 Bates had known Mortimer since 1770, when he bought *St Paul Preaching to the Ancient Britons*, Sunderland, 1986, cat. no. 13.

70 *Memoirs*, p. 35.

71 Ibid., p. 60.

72 Ibid., p. 37.

73 Ibid., p. 31.

74 Ibid., p. 38. The pair were nos 47 and 48 in the Society of Artists' exhibition of 1776.

75 Ziff, 1963, p. 144.

76 His father was to die in October 1782; Jones heard the news in Naples.

77 Christopher Norton (*c.*1740–1799) became the partner of James Byres (1734–1817), one of the leading antiquarians and art dealers in Rome.

78 *Memoirs*, p. 39.

79 Ibid., p. 54.

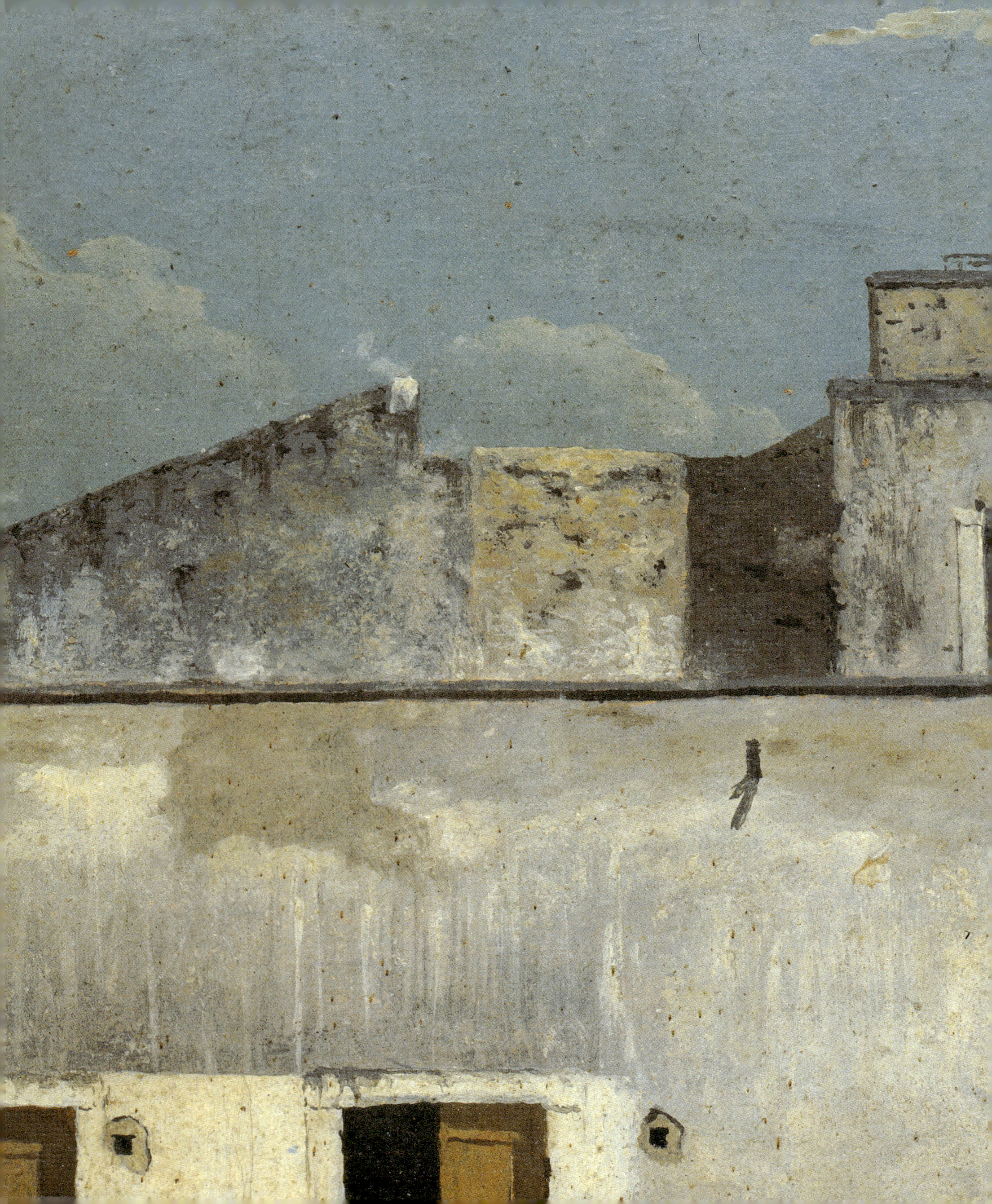

THOMAS JONES IN ITALY

Christopher Riopelle

Thomas Jones had long intended to travel to Italy. It was 'a favourite project that had been in agitation for some Years, and on which my heart was fixed'.[1] Outstanding debts and his parents' disapproval of the plan had kept him in Britain. By September 1775, however, he was determined to overcome these obstacles. He left London for his father and mother's home in Radnorshire, where he painted pictures 'sufficient to clear all Demands, and leave a few Guineas in my pocket'.[2] A fortuitous invitation to join Captain Cook on a voyage to the South Seas soon reconciled his parents to Italy as by far the safer alternative. It would be October 1776, however, before Jones's affairs were in order and he finally saw the coast of England drop below the horizon, from the deck of a packet ship bound for the Continent. Jones was nearing his thirty-fourth birthday and his life was more than half over, but the most significant chapter of his artistic career was now set to begin. He would not see Britain again for seven years.

It is not surprising that a young British landscape painter, attempting to establish a career in the final quarter of the eighteenth century, should have set his sights on Italy. Jones's teacher, Richard Wilson (1713–1782), had spent some six years there in the 1750s and enjoyed his first success as a landscape painter with his Italian scenes. Back in England, Wilson continued to consult the studies he had made in Italy, and his admiring student Jones copied them; thus, 'insensibly', the latter had become 'familiarized with Italian Scenes, and enamoured of Italian forms'.[3] Travel to Italy would allow him to build up his own stock of studies, which he too could consult for years to come. As Jones also knew, contemporary artist friends in London like John Robert Cozens (1752–1797) and Francis Towne (1739–1816) felt the same craving to make the journey south.

Jones also would have known that artists from across Europe – in addition to the British, they included Frenchmen, Germans and Scandinavians – were congregating there in increasing numbers. Italy, Rome in particular, was the world's academy, the place where the arts of antiquity, and of the High Renaissance of Raphael and Michelangelo, were to be studied. Young artists drew the ancient marbles and copied the masterpieces of painting in princely and papal collections. Landscape painters sought out the same timeless views

FACING PAGE Detail of cat. no. 111.

and limpid light that had transfixed Claude Lorraine and Salvator Rosa more than a century before. Contemporary artists ventured out into the Roman Campagna as their seventeenth-century predecessors had done, to paint and draw the famously picturesque ruins and natural wonders. Italy tested artists' skills against the ages and gave the final polish to their training.

By the time Jones set out for the south, Italy was emerging as the vital centre of an increasingly important artistic activity, the painting of landscape oil sketches out of doors in nature. Artists had painted such casual sketches, usually on paper or small canvasses, since the seventeenth century at least. By the late eighteenth century, the activity was coming to be recognized as a staple of artistic pedagogy. The ability to record humble motifs and fleeting effects of light rapidly in oil paint was increasingly seen as a necessary test of the artist's hand and eye. These works were rarely intended for public exhibition, but were skilled exercises in the observation and transcription of natural phenomena. Along with sketching in pencil and painting in watercolour, the oil sketch was a third weapon in the landscape painter's arsenal. From such unassuming beginnings, he could work his way towards the large-scale, composed landscape paintings, completed in the studio, which were recognized at the time as the final measure of an artist's achievement.[4]

Artists in Britain also painted landscape oil sketches, Jones among them.[5] He would continue to do so in Italy. Word of the increasing importance of the activity there had been filtering back to Britain for years. Even though Jones's master, Wilson, is not known to have made such sketches, both he and Sir Joshua Reynolds (1723–1792) were acquainted with the French painter Claude-Joseph Vernet (1714–1789), long resident in Rome, who was an enthusiastic exponent.[6] Arriving in Rome for a second time at almost the same moment as Jones, in 1777, Pierre-Henri de Valenciennes (1750–1819) soon became an important practitioner, teacher and theorist of the oil sketch. Indeed, between them, in the years around 1780, the outdoor works of Jones and Valenciennes 'mark[ed] the beginning of a continuous tradition, the importance of which continued throughout the nineteenth century'.[7]

Ever since Jones's landscape oil sketches first came to light in 1954, he has been recognized as a highly original practitioner of the genre, indeed one of its most accomplished masters. So great has the fame of Jones's oil sketches become that it has eclipsed his overall reputation as an artist. In fact, Jones's oil sketches are far fewer in number than the pencil and chalk drawings with which he filled sketchbooks, and the watercolours and classical landscape paintings he also produced. Moreover, Jones sometimes studied the same motifs in pencil and oil sketches, and in watercolour too. Some of his oil sketches began as, or are based on, pencil and chalk sketches and all these works are otherwise intricately interrelated. Any full account of Jones's Italian sojourn must take into account his artistic production in all media, the complex ways in which they depend on one another, and the importance that Jones himself ascribed to his various artistic activities. In this way, a truer estimation of his Italian achievement can be reached.

Landing at Dieppe on 17 October 1776, Jones and a few companions began their journey south, through Paris – where Jones was 'much disappointed and disgusted with the filth and narrowness of the Streets'[8] – to Châlons and Tournus; there at last he 'began to observe the buildings assume an Italian air – The Roofs flattish and not high and steep as at Paris'.[9] As he made his tedious, lurching way by coach, Jones worked at his art, remarking that only fear of the police at Lyon – foreign travellers always faced the risk of being taken for spies – prevented him from making 'several Studies'.[10] He added jealously that the landscape painter William Marlow (1740–1813) executed many such studies there, 'but by what licence or under what protection I know not'.[11] At Lyon, Jones did stock up on artists' supplies, for which the city was famous, and, thus prepared, on Friday, 1 November he crossed the frontier at Pont de Beauvoisin and entered Savoy.

The following day, 2 November, Jones passed through the town of Montmélian. Nearby, he made a sketch of the town and of other sites along the way, remarking enthusiastically, 'Some effects of Light & Shade from broken Clouds & rugged Mountains were wonderfully fine'.[12] An oil on paper, small in scale but panoramic in conception, and probably based on sketches made that day, shows Montmélian from afar (cat. no. 67). The town stretches along the meandering Isère river while jagged hills, a fortress dominating one hilltop, rise all around. Towering Alps disappear into the clouds above, and vivid shadow patterns play across the hills and valley floor. Jones was also fascinated by the human presence at this site. Minuscule farmers and their mules till the fields, a tiny figure emerges at a cottage door and others stroll along the riverbank. Detailed and densely worked, the sheet registers the artist's awakening delight at the complexity and animation of a sublime mountain landscape of a kind and on a scale he could not have found in his native Wales. It marks a milestone in his conception of the expressive possibilities of landscape.

Jones continued to make sketches as he journeyed south. At Turin on 8 November, he bought a blank book, inscribing it with his name and the date; three years later, it became the Account Book in which he recorded his Neapolitan expenses (cat. no. 73). Seventeen swift and linear pencil sketches, some showing the hilly north Italian countryside through which he was travelling in November 1776, and many inscribed with dates and locations, were bound into this book at a later date. Two drawings, on pages 75 and 76, were made on 19 November, on a road some nineteen miles from Florence. The latter drawing shows a single-span stone bridge traversing a placid river; seated on its parapet, a solitary traveller, his back to the viewer, surveys the scene (fig. 20; cat. no. 73). The drawing is typical of many of the small-scale works Jones made in Italy. At the centre of the sheet the artist records a simple, architectonic form, worn by time and use, embedded in nature, almost a part of it. Over and again, in both cities and countryside, Jones sought out such humble man-made motifs, evidence of the ways in which the Italian environment had been tempered by centuries of habitation and use.

Fig. 20 Thomas Jones, *Bridge near Florence*, from the Account Book, 1776 (cat. no. 73).

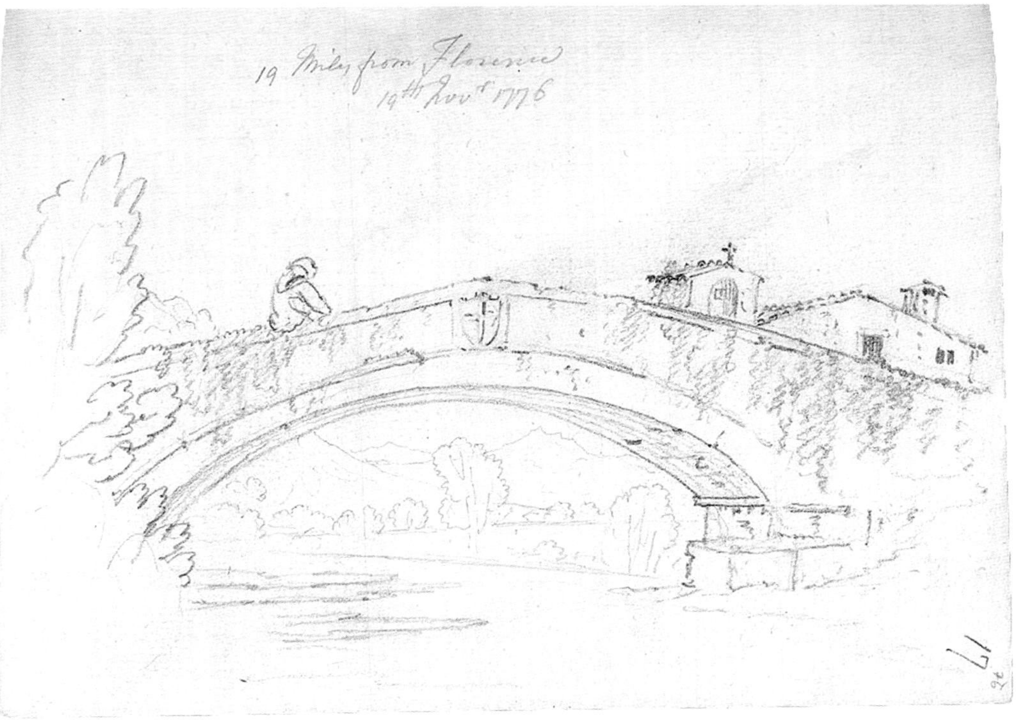

Some time after making this pencil sketch – perhaps soon after, perhaps years later – Jones used it as the basis for a small oil painting on paper in which he repeated every detail of the drawing, adding figures to further animate the scene (cat. no. 68). This is not a true landscape oil sketch, executed in a single sitting in front of the motif, but a 'finished' painting which retains the immediacy of such a sketch; the distinction is vital. At almost the same moment, probably in 1777, a French painter, probably Jean-Antoine Constantin (1756–1844), known as Constantin d'Aix, was painting a similar single-arched stone bridge at Subiaco, east of Rome, also on a sheet of paper and in a similarly austere manner (fig. 21). It is not the only case of similarities between a work by Jones and one by a contemporary artist in Italy very probably unknown to him. Such coincidences suggest the increasing ubiquity of this kind of painting, and that almost inevitably it came to share a relatively restricted repertory of motifs.

On Wednesday, 27 November 1776, Jones arrived at last at 'the *Metropolis of the Christian World* as 'tis called'.[13] With only about 150,000 people, Rome was not the largest city in Italy, nor the most powerful politically. Large stretches within its ancient walls remained uninhabited, and thieves, confidence men, cutthroats and prostitutes plied their trade in its streets in startling numbers. It was, however, the seat of the Pope and his *curia*. Pius VI Braschi (1717–1799) had been elected the previous year, beginning what would turn out to be the longest pontificate since St Peter himself, and a particularly corrupt and disastrous one.[14] Several princely courts, one more splendid than the next, animated the social scene, while churches, confraternities and convents continued to fill up with art. Painters, sculptors, architects and printmakers from across Europe, vastly disproportionate in numbers to the population of the town, vied for patronage, but riches and an international reputation could be made here as nowhere else. Two painters, Pompeo Batoni (1708–1787) and the German Anton Raphael Mengs (1728–1779) dominated the artistic scene. The young Frenchman Jacques-Louis David (1748–1825) was forging his revolutionary neo-classical painting style in a studio at the Académie de France in Palazzo Mancini on the Corso. Forward-looking young artists found themselves drawn to the dark and hallucinatory images of ancient Rome that the Venetian-born engraver and designer Giovanni Battista Piranesi (1720–1788) was publishing. These admirers helped to spread his fame and influence across Europe. Finally, the city was the destination for a steady stream of distinguished and noble visitors, some travelling on diplomatic missions – and sumptuous diplomatic receptions were among the most colourful public spectacles the town had to offer – many more making the Grand Tour.[15] On only his second day in Rome, Jones met the Duke of Gloucester, brother of George III himself. It

Fig. 21 (BELOW) Jean-Antoine Constantin (1756–1844), *Bridge at Subiaco*, *c.*1777, oil on paper, 28.7 × 38.4 (11¼ × 15⅛) (irreg.), the Gere Collection, on long-term loan to the National Gallery, London.

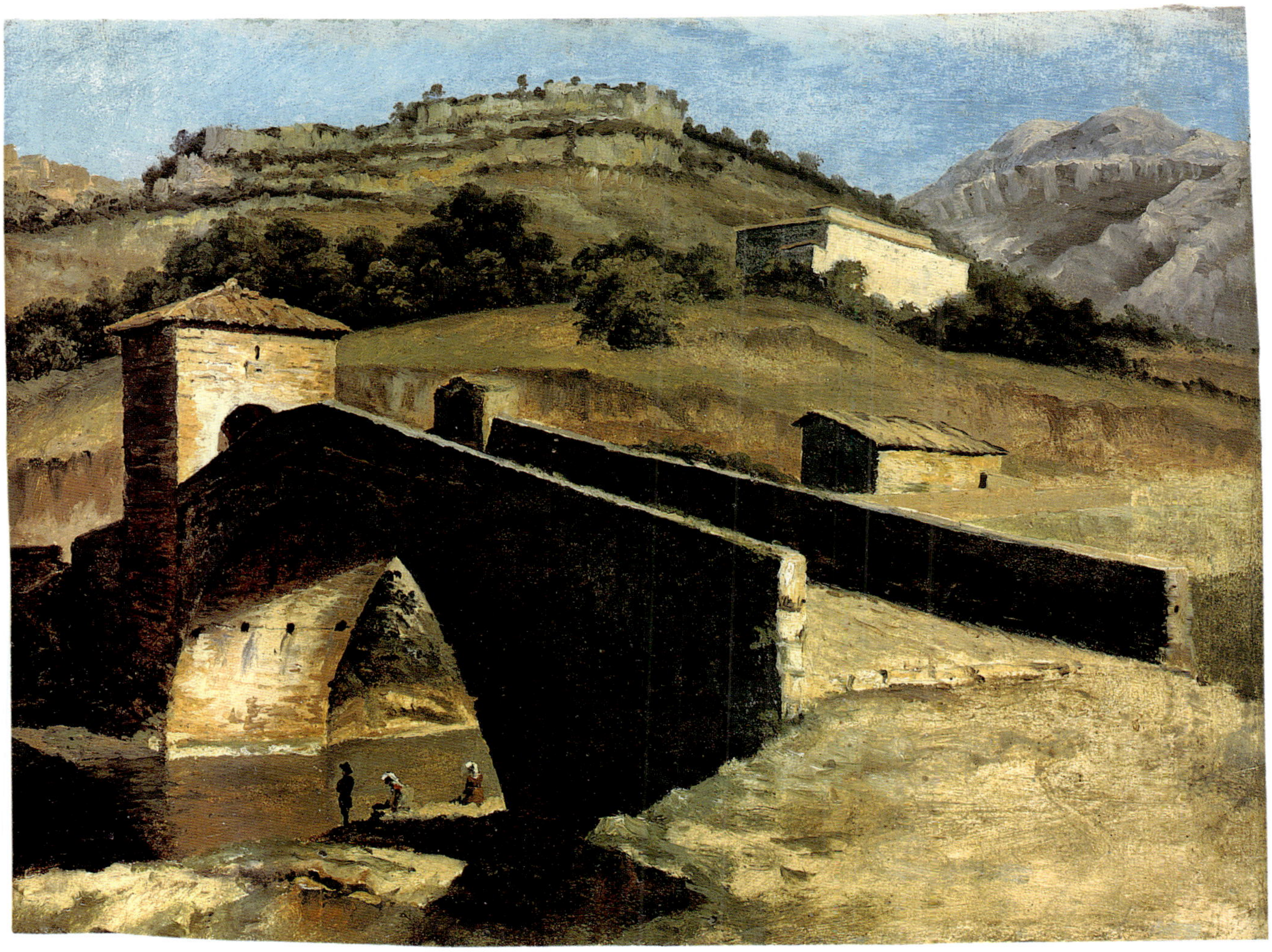

must have seemed like an omen of future success. That same day, Jones visited St Peter's, dryly conceding that, 'taken in every respect, [it] is I suppose the grandest effort of human art in the world'.[16] Jones was not about to let himself be overwhelmed too quickly by the wonders that now surrounded him.

Practical considerations regarding the advancement of his career marked Jones's attitude from the beginning. His first call, immediately upon arrival in the city, was on the Scottish-born Catholic, James Byres (1734–1817), an antiquarian, guide and leader of the British artistic community in Rome. Jones had travelled with a letter of introduction to Byres,[17] and was taken to meet him by the engraver Christopher Norton (*c.*1740–1799), an associate of Byres with whom Jones had journeyed to Rome. As Norton would have explained, wealthy British patrons passing through the Eternal City often sought Byres's advice on what to do, or see, or buy there. When these visitors wished to acquire works of art, Byres could direct their attention to struggling British painters like Jones, should they have found their way into his favour. Leaving Byres's house, Jones moved on to the Caffè degli Inglesi, or English Coffee House, in the Piazza di Spagna at the foot of the Pincian Hill. This was the meeting place *par excellence* of the community of British artists in Rome. There, he met up with his 'Old London Acquaintance', including the painters William Pars (1742–1782) and Jacob More (1740–1793), and was introduced to other artists whom he had not known in London, not least Henry Fuseli (1741–1825).[18] Upon arrival in Rome, then, Jones's priority was to make immediate contact with the British expatriate community there; it would prove to be an important lifeline during the years he spent in the city.

Not long afterwards, Jones met another important figure in Rome's British community, 'the great Mr Jenkins'.[19] Like Byres, Thomas Jenkins (1721–1798), a painter and dealer in antiquities who, despite his Welsh-sounding name, was born in Rome of Devonshire parentage, was an important rallying point for British artists and a source of commissions and sales for their works. In earlier decades he had proved instrumental in introducing British patrons to the art of Mengs and was a great friend of Batoni's.[20] Moreover, he was an old acquaintance of Richard Wilson's, which may have drawn Jones to him. Jones's relationship with Byres and Jenkins was primarily financial. Like other British artists, he was expected to present examples of his work to both men. 'These Specimens were hung up in their respective Rooms of Audience for the inspection of the Cavaliers who came.'[21] If the visiting *milordi* liked what they saw, then they might be expected to call on the artist in his studio and to commission paintings. Money for such works was not paid to the artist directly but through Byres or Jenkins as agent. Jenkins and Byres ruled competing 'courts', however. On Christmas Day 1776, Jones dined with Jenkins, noting that 'there had been a kind of Schism in the body of Students in late Years, on Account of Mr Byres giving a dinner on the same day'. By accepting Jenkins's invitation, Jones discovered that he had 'imperceptibly enlisted under his Banner'.[22]

Soon, Jones was painting pictures for Jenkins.[23] He came to rely more and more on the older man's kindnesses and deep pockets. None the less, he remained friendly with Byres, and availed himself of his services as well.

Installed in lodgings near the Spanish Steps – the first of several sets of Roman rooms he would occupy over the next three years, some splendid, some grim – Jones was soon exploring the sights of the city with the enthusiasm of an eager tourist. He made his forays 'sometimes in Company and sometimes alone', he reported, 'for I could not always persuade my Country men to attend me to see Sights with which they had already been glutted'.[24] In addition to St Peter's, he went to see the Villa Medici, the Pantheon, the Forum Romanum, the Colosseum and the Piazza Navona, the latter flooded with water 'and all the Carriages of the Nobility parading in it – an Annual Ceremony'.[25] The excavation of antiquities attracted his particular attention, and he attended an execution in the Piazza del Popolo.[26] Such sites were on every visitor's itinerary, and the grander ones among them had been depicted by the leading Roman view painter of the eighteenth century, Giovanni Paolo Panini (1691–1765). Indeed, that artist's meticulous paintings provide us with the best visual record of the Eternal City – or at least its monumental face – during the years that Jones explored its streets.

Unusually, Jones early on showed a predilection for little-known and little-populated corners of the city, away from the grand piazzas and palazzi. Masonry walls, characterful and pitted with age, particularly caught his eye. Sketches in his Account Book (cat. no. 73) include some showing dusty Roman lanes and once elegant but now neglected gateways leading into private gardens. He made a pencil sketch and later painted one such deserted gateway, the Porta de' Cavalleggeri near St Peter's, most of the image consisting of blank walls (cat. no. 70). More striking, in December 1776 he sketched in pencil humble Roman houses and roof-tops (fig. 22); the sheet anticipates the oil sketches of Neapolitan walls and roofscapes he would paint six years later (cat. no. 110). It anticipates also Valenciennes's *View of the Porta del Popolo, Rome* (fig. 23), a roofscape the French painter made in about 1782–3. Even as he explored the tourist's Rome, Jones was defining and refining his idiosyncratic perception of the place.

By mid-December, Jones was making his first foray outside Rome, walking to Frascati in the company of the painters Robert Home (1752–1834) and William Miller (1740–1810), and moving on from there to Genzano, Lake Albano, Castel Gandolfo and other well-known destinations. 'And here I can not help observing with what new and uncommon Sensations I was filled on my first traversing this beautiful and picturesque Country – Every scene seemed anticipated in some dream – It appeared Magick Land'.[27] The Italian scenes he had studied in the sketches of Richard Wilson back in London were now coming alive in front of his eyes, and Jones no longer masked that he was thrilled to the quick. During his first months in Rome, however, it seems that he remained more the avid sightseer than an artist greedy for new motifs, for he tells the story against himself that, some time after his arrival, he was visited by two English connoisseurs who were disappointed to find

Fig. 22 Thomas Jones, *View of Houses, Rome,* from the Account Book, 1776 (see cat. no. 73).

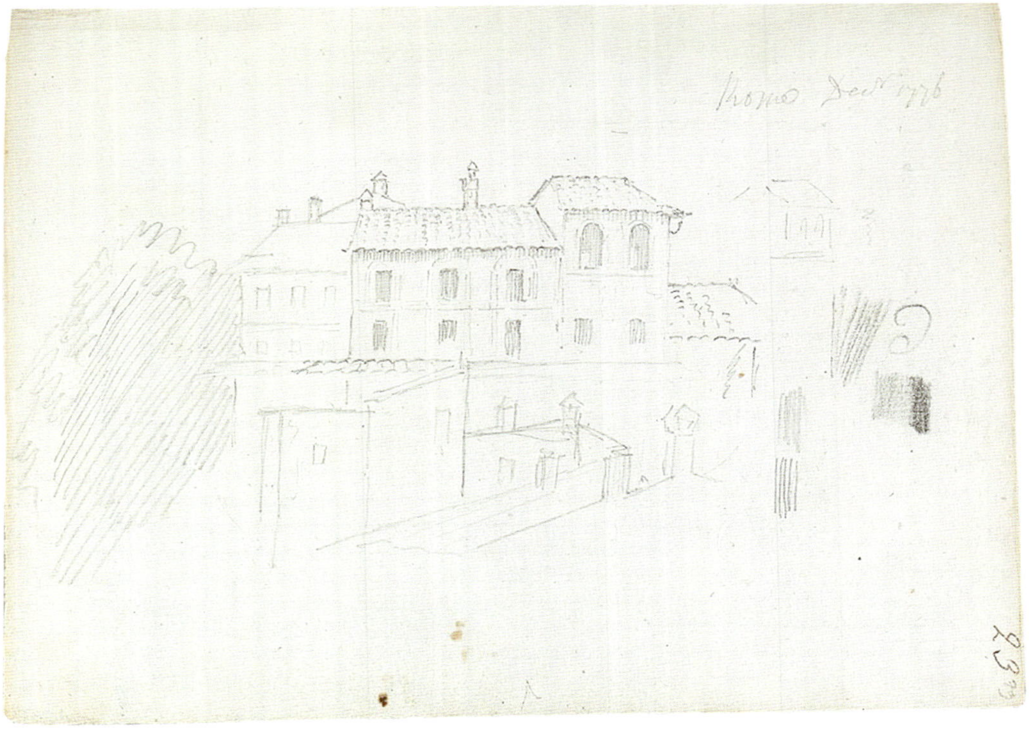

that he had no portfolio of Roman studies to show them; 'concluding, I suppose, that I was a very idle fellow, [they] never called upon me afterward'.[28]

Several sketching trips into the Roman Campagna, to Tivoli and to Lake Albano and Lake Nemi followed. On such excursions, Jones henceforth was assiduous in making pencil sketches. On 1 May 1777, for example, he and friends came upon the ancient Roman bridge known as the Ponte Loreto, on the road to Ostia, which they both sketched and measured.[29] A small, highly finished and carefully composed oil painting on paper derives from the observations made on that day (cat. no. 151). It is probable, however, that Jones executed the painting several years later, back in London, in preparation for an exhibition at the Royal Academy in 1787. Like his master Wilson, the stock of images Jones assembled in Italy would be available for his consultation long after he returned home.

Jones's sketching trips outside Rome were often made in the company of fellow British artists, including William Pars and John Robert Cozens, whom Jones always called 'little Cousins'. The history painter Henry Tresham (1751–1814) was also a favourite companion. Jones often travelled by donkey or pony, and was away from Rome for days at a time, staying at favourite country inns. He and Cozens also stayed at the villa of a mutual friend at St Agnese, beyond the Porta Pia, a major city gate, sketching in the surrounding countryside. Jones's *Memoirs* are filled with vivid accounts of these journeys, and of encounters with the sometimes colourful, sometimes dangerous locals they encountered along the way. Of one such rural excursion Jones rapturously remarked: 'This Country . . . seems formed in a peculiar manner by Nature for the Study of the Landscape-Painter.'[30]

In addition to pencil sketches, oil sketches and watercolours, Jones also worked on large-scale landscape paintings in a classical mode. They were meant to attract the approbation of connoisseurs, who for the most part would only ever consider acquiring such highly finished works. He began one such painting in his studio on 12 June 1777, on a canvas measuring five and a half feet by four. It was based on sketches of Lake Albano and was meant to show 'a Sun set' (cat. no. 56).[31] Rome was experiencing a heat wave that summer, and 'I was kept in a gentle perspiration', he reported, 'sitting in my Shirt & thin linen Drawers without Stockens – with the Windows open – and in this dress I sat down to paint'.[32] Jones worked on the painting for a total of forty-one days, finishing it on 21 August. 'This was the first Picture I finished, and it attracted a good deal of Notice not only from My brother artists & English Cavaliers but from the foreign Artists & Cavaliers, of all nations.'[33]

Indeed, the success of Jones's Roman sojourn depended upon his ability to attract patrons for such grandly ambitious evocations of an ideal Italian landscape. In the spring of 1778, there 'was at Rome . . . a great Concourse of the English Nobility & Gentry, male & female'.[34] Jones records a long list of *milordi*, including Russians, Germans and a French general, who made their way to his studio that spring, 'and some became Purchasers'.[35] Chief among them was Frederick Augustus Hervey (1730–1803), the 4th Earl of Bristol and Bishop of Derry, who visited Jones's studio frequently and in May of that year acquired from him the *Lake Albano – Sunset* on which he had worked so hard the summer before (cat. no. 56). He paid £40 for the painting. It was the first of five purchases the Earl–Bishop, a strange and eccentric collector long resident in Italy, made from Jones, becoming his most important patron. A few years later, in Naples, he commissioned a pendant

Fig. 23 Pierre-Henri de Valenciennes (1750–1819), *View of the Porta del Popolo, Rome*, c.1782–3, oil on paper, 15.5 × 41.5 (6 × 16⅜), Musée du Louvre, Paris.

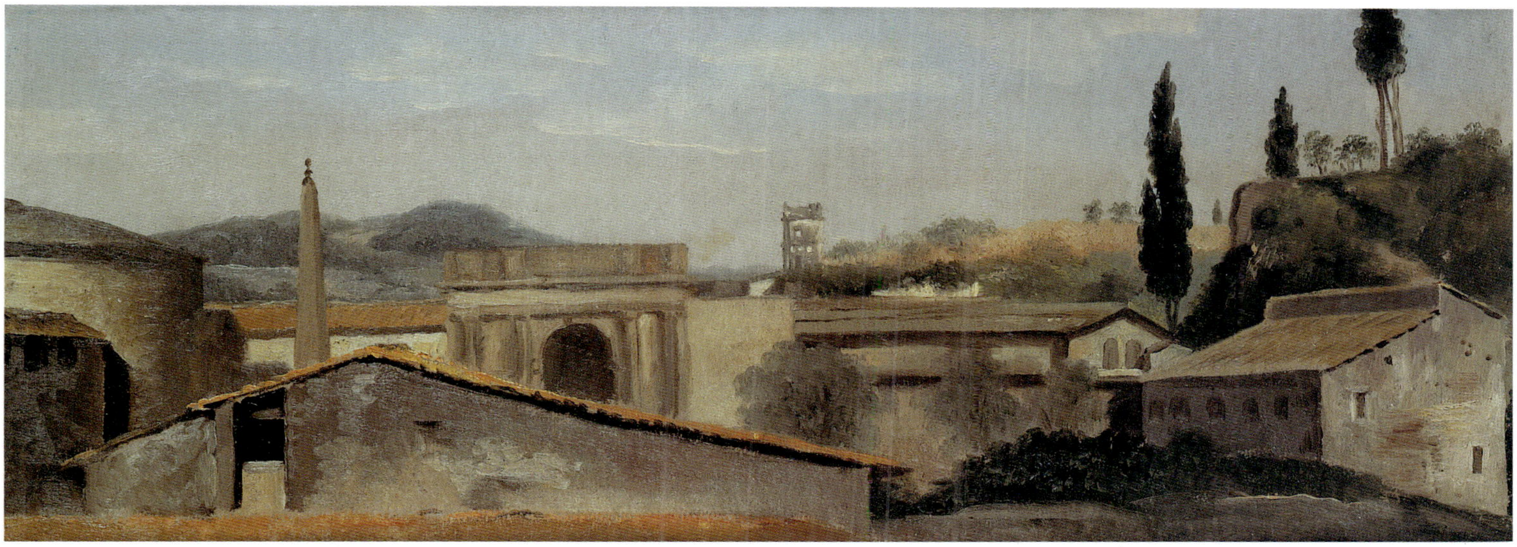

to the Albano, *Lake Nemi* (cat. no. 58). Both are Wilson-like evocations of a calm and ordered Italy, bathed in limpid light. They are carefully balanced compositions, one with the other. The conventions of staffage and framing are carefully observed, and the finish is high. Tall trees dominate each picture, while peasants in colourful garb disport themselves in their shade. It was on the strength of such works that Jones intended to secure his reputation at home.

Life was not always easy in Rome. Jones was robbed more than once.[36] Death stalked the small British community, as when the wife of his great friend Pars died in June 1778. It was with the eye of a painter, attuned to unusual and emotive light effects, that he recorded her night-time funeral in the Protestant Cemetery beyond the walls of the city: 'At the funeral all the English Artists who were then at *Rome* walk'd in procession with torches to the number of 18 or 20 . . . The Scene was grand & striking – The Moon, just hid behind the tomb of *Caio Sesto* [Caius Sestius], cast her Silvery Tints on all the Objects around, save where that large dark Piramid threw its broad Shadow over the Place in which the Solemn Ceremony was performing by the dusky Light of Torches'.[37] The dominant note of the *Memoirs*, however, is one of camaraderie and good fellowship. Even when there was little bread on the table, Jones enjoyed Rome and his companions there, and described it with an amused and sardonic eye. His *Memoirs* are the most complete, and entertaining, literary record that has survived of a British artist's life in eighteenth-century Rome.

In September 1778, Jones expanded his Italian horizons, travelling south to Naples for the first time, in the company of Giuseppe Plura (*fl.*1777–1786), son of the sculptor of the same name established in Bath. Jones gave no reason for making the journey. None was needed. Naples was an important destination for foreign visitors to Italy, the city and surrounding countryside full of motifs and vistas to delight a landscape painter's eye. A lively market existed for images of Mount Vesuvius, preferably in eruption, and Jones was not the first British artist to climb and sketch it (fig. 24). As at Rome, he made frequent excursions into the country, and to islands lying offshore, sketching as he went. On one such trip, on 1 October, 'to view the Curiosities at Pompaej',[38] Jones's travelling companions included the Scottish landscape painter Jacob More (1740–1793), one of the most highly regarded British artists in Italy; he was held in esteem not only by his countrymen, but by such international figures as Goethe and Canova.[39] Jones and his companions admired More for their own reasons: 'during the last excursion we were amused with More's flying Sketches as he call'd them – for tho' none of the Company waited a moment for him, he contrived to keep up with the party & brought back a dozen Views & these were to pass as *portraits*

Fig. 24 Joseph Wright of Derby (1734–1797), *Vesuvius in Eruption*, *c.*1774, gouache on paper, 32.4 × 46.7 (12¾ × 18⅜), Derby Museums and Art Gallery.

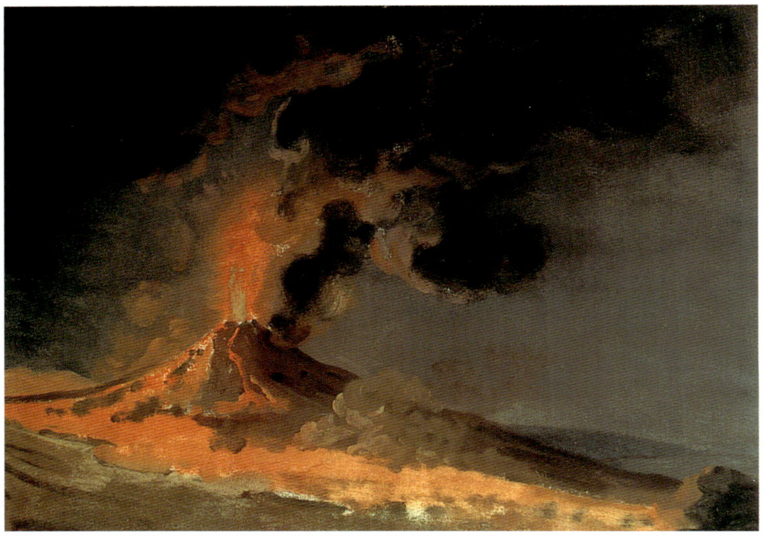

of the respective Scenes'.[40] The comment indicates how the ability to work speedily in front of a landscape motif, and to invest it with individual character, were particularly appreciated among artists. No doubt Jones wished to emulate such virtuosity in his own sketches.

Naples agreed with Jones. He stayed for five months, made friends, and seemed to enjoy the colourful, confusing city itself. He also met with some success there. In December, the Earl–Bishop of Derry arrived from Rome, accompanied by the architect John Soane (1753–1837), and commissioned two large paintings from him, 'and the Example was followed by some other English Gentlemen then at Naples'.[41] Jones had less luck with another British visitor who proposed to commission pictures but then questioned him on his use of materials and techniques, comparing them unfavourably with those employed by the rising star of landscape painting in Italy, the German-born Jakob Philipp Hackert (1737–1807), then active in Rome. No commission was forthcoming.[42] Nor would it be the last time Jones found himself in unwitting opposition to the German painter. By late January 1779, however, it was time to return to Rome. 'The few remaining days I spent in making little solitary Excursions about the City & its Environs, sketching Views, & taking leave of my friends'.[43]

Returning to Rome, Jones moved into a house built by Salvator Rosa in the previous century near Trinità dei Monti on the Pincian Hill with his friend Pars. On 8 April, Jones drew up an account of the commissioned paintings on which he was then at work, numbering ten. The prices he was expecting for them rose to the not inconsiderable sum of £347.[44] Three of the paintings were to go to Byres, one to Jenkins. Two months later, when Pars moved to grander apartments elsewhere in the city and Jones relocated to more modest quarters a floor below their former rooms, the latter were taken by Anton Raphael Mengs and his family. 'Pars & my self on his arrival, waited to receive him at the Gate with all ye Defference due to so respected a Character, and assisted in Conveying him up stairs – for the last time'.[45] The great master died there two weeks later, on 29 June 1779.

Jones's kindly show of respect for Mengs points to an intriguing aspect of his character, his openness and willingness to engage with the foreign artists from across Europe whom he met in Italy. On one occasion, he enjoyed a smoky feast with Scandinavian, Russian and German artists, 'a very loud & unintelligible jargon of Northern Dialects, of which I could not understand a single Word'.[46] On another, he made a point of visiting an exhibition of Mengs's monumental *Perseus and Andromeda* of 1777 (The State Hermitage Museum, St Petersburg), destined for a Welsh patron, although he was not impressed.[47] He showed his own 'finished' paintings to foreign artists and noted their comments. And his unpublished Account Book contains curious recipes he collected among the artists he met. On 21 November 1782, 'Sre Luigi Michilli came to me this morning to make a varnish which was communicated to him by a German artist'.[48] Some time later, 'Mr Rinaldi recommends a size made of boiled Rice'.[49] Among the Italians, he also came to know Piranesi well (see below), and at Naples formed a close friendship

Fig. 25 Pierre-Henri de Valenciennes (1750–1819), *Two Poplars at the Villa Farnese*, *c.*1782–3, oil on paper, 25.3 × 37.8 (10 × 14⅞), Musée du Louvre, Paris.

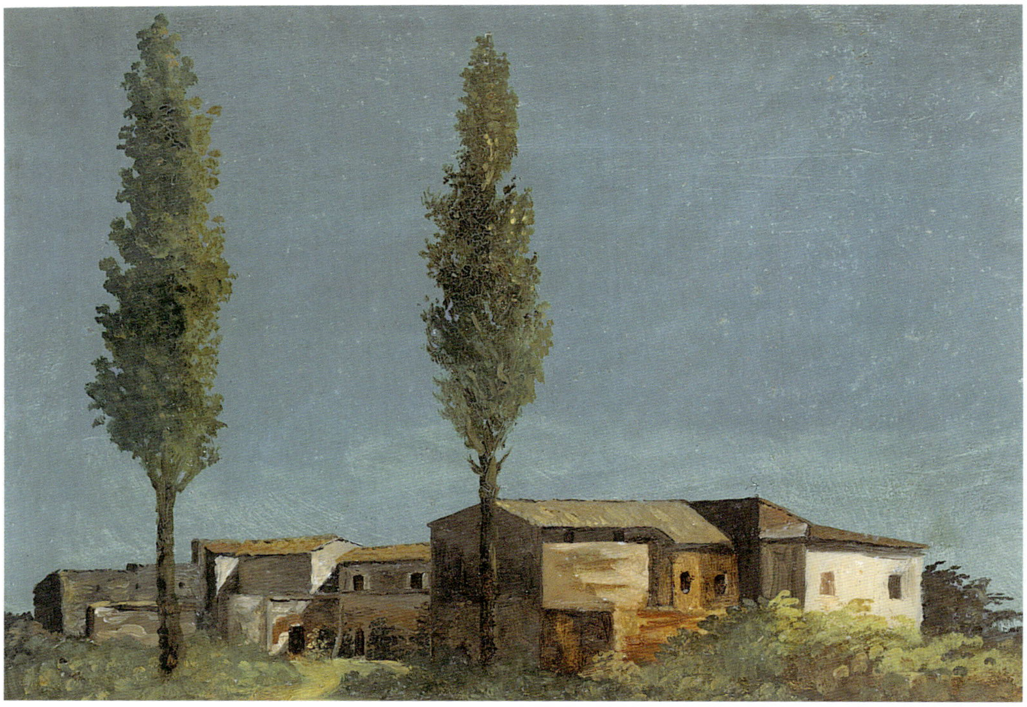

with the landscape painter Giovanni Battista Lusieri (*c.*1755–1821; cat. nos 102 and 103). Jones's was a warm and open personality, and it seems he had trouble only with the French who 'form as mark'd a Character in Italy as in England, and are, I believe, as distinct from the rest of mankind as the Chinese'.[50]

And yet it is particularly about Jones's relations with French artists in Rome that one wants to know more, specifically whether he met Valenciennes, who had arrived in the city less than a year after Jones, on 10 October 1777. Valenciennes went on to paint remarkably open and limpid landscape oil sketches. Like Jones, he focused on informal and humble aspects of the scene, roof-tops with laundry drying in the breeze, scudding clouds, ancient ruins overgrown with tumbledown modern accretions (fig. 25). Valenciennes's treatise, *Elémens de perspective pratique*, published in 1800, contains a famous chapter on the oil sketch. It is acknowledged to record what he and fellow painters were saying about the oil sketch some twenty years earlier in Rome, and gives advice on how to choose motifs and how to go about painting them. Did Jones participate in these conversations? He nowhere mentions Valenciennes, nor does the French painter mention him. Probably the answer will never be known.

Recently, Anna Ottani Cavina has concluded that the two artists did not need to meet. While their oil sketches resemble one another, sometimes in choice of motifs, sometimes in manner of paint handling, at another level they are very different things. Whereas Valenciennes, influenced by the classical aspirations of David and his circle, sought an architectonic rigour and sense of order in his sketches, Jones was intrigued by the mute specificity of the objects, natural and man-made, on which he trained his eye. His sketches emerge from a specifically British tradition of empirical observation of phenomena. It is a case, she concludes, of two artists finding a singular mode of expression more or less simultaneously.[51]

Equally frustrating is the little we know about Jones's relationship with the greatest artistic genius of eighteenth-century Rome. The English Coffee House, where the Welshman spent so many convivial hours, had been decorated in 1767 in a fantastic and complex neo-Egyptian style by Piranesi himself. Jones's first impressions of the place were not favourable. He described it as 'a filthy vaulted room, the walls of which were painted with Sphinxes, Obelisks and Pyramids . . . fitter to adorn the inside of an Egyptian-Sepulchre, than a room of social conversation'.[52] As Jones spent more time at the café, however, and as he saw more of the ancient Roman ruins that were the principal subject of Piranesi's art, his opinion shifted. Several months later, in August 1777, he boasted: 'About this time I was introduced and got intimate with that great but excentric genius Piranesi.'[53]

Piranesi's richly imaginative engravings of the ruins of ancient Rome are remarkable for their intricacy, with spaces opening into spaces beyond; for the profusion of minutely detailed architectural and sculptural forms they contain; and for the sensuous play of inky light they suggest (fig. 26). For Piranesi, the city was a vast palimpsest, where the detritus of the ancient past piled up around the visitor, or lay just beneath his feet, waiting to be unearthed. Each new revelation was a confirmation of the terrifying grandeur that had been Rome. Piranesi's hypnotic images influenced generations of Italian and foreign artists, writers and critics who came to see the city through his eyes. Some of Jones's Roman paintings reveal that he, too, fell under the spell. On 5 July 1777, he visited an archetypal Piranesian site – and one that was attracting considerable attention that summer – the excavation of an ancient Roman house, grandly decorated with frescoes, at the Villa Montalto Negroni on the outskirts of the city. 'The Reds, purples, Blues & Yellows [of the frescoes] very bright – but had a dark & heavy effect,'[54] Jones remarked, as if he were contemplating a particularly gloomy Piranesi print. He went on to paint the excavation site (cat. no. 65). Here, the viewer's eye is drawn down into the murky depths of the buried rooms, caught by the colours, and then, as if to underscore the contrast with the subterranean depths, upwards across the tree-tops and into the brilliant sunlit distance. Similarly, when he painted the Roman Colosseum, as in catalogue number 59, Jones entered into the middle of the ruins themselves, looking up from an oppressive arched space to other arched spaces beyond, and only then out into sunlight. Both paintings, little anticipated by Jones's earlier works, are distinctly Piranesian in their delight in spatial complexity and evident awe at the all-encompassing allure of antiquity.

By early 1780, Jones's opportunities in Rome seem to have been dwindling as fewer commissions came his way. Moreover, he had managed to alienate both of his agents. After falling out early in 1778 with Jenkins's sly and insinuating servant, a man named Franceschini, and after reporting

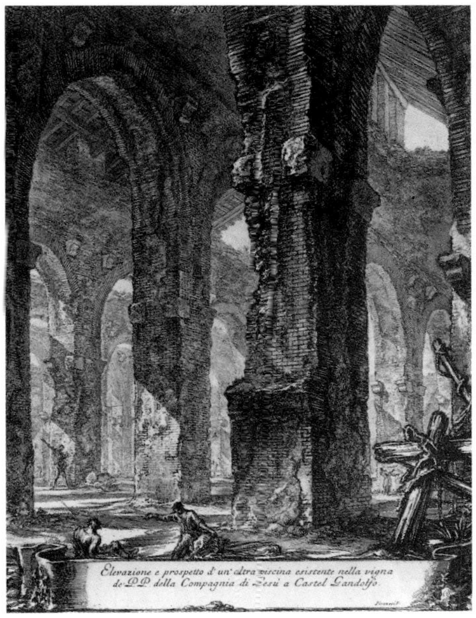

Fig. 26 Giovanni Battista Piranesi (1720–1778), *Elevation and View of an Underground Reservoir in the Vineyard of the Jesuit Order at Castel Gandolfo* (detail), from *The Antiquities of Albano and Castel Gandolfo*, 1764, etching, engraving and drypoint, The Whitworth Art Gallery, University of Manchester.

Francheschini's unscrupulous behaviour to Jenkins himself, from 'this time I found myself declining more & more every Day, as far as decorum would permit, in Mr J—'s favour'.[55] As for Byres, Jones came to suspect, with an almost Proustian appreciation for nuance, that a chill had entered their relationship – 'his reception of me whenever I waited upon him, particularly of late', he fretted, 'was polite in the *extreme*'[56] – but it was Jones's old friend Norton who finally had to tell him how he had in fact offended the powerful agent. It was in his wallet, of course, as Jones had received money for a commission directly and not through Byres (cat. no. 104).[57] Jones protested that the commission had not in fact come through Byres and that the agent was not entitled to profit from it, but Byres did not see it that way and the break was made. Thus, in the face of dwindling opportunities, in early 1780 Jones determined to leave Rome. He would establish himself in Naples.

Jones would have found several excellent reasons for relocating to Naples. A return to Britain was out of the question. He had recently entered into an amorous relationship with Maria Moncke, a highly capable maidservant whom he had hired in July 1779, and with whom he would later have children and marry, but he did not want to make the union known to his family quite yet. He had discovered the appeal of the southern metropolis during his five-month-long visit the previous year and knew that it offered opportunities for an ambitious young painter. Indeed, most of the commissioned pictures on which he was at work in his final months in Rome were Neapolitan views. With some 350,000 residents, it was a far larger city than Rome; indeed, the largest in Italy. It was a lively intellectual centre and the site of a rich and ostentatious Bourbon royal court. A vast, new royal palace at Caserta needed decorating and the royal family seemed to favour landscape painters. (They would eventually settle on Hackert not Jones.) The city and its surroundings offered novel and appealing motifs for painters, including Vesuvius, frequently in eruption in those years, the limpidly beautiful Bay of Naples and nearby islands, and man-made wonders too, like the Grotto of Posillipo. The queen, the shrewd Austrian Maria Carolina, wife of the dim-witted, hunt-obsessed Ferdinand IV, was an ardent Anglophile and anti-French – Marie-Antoinette was her sister, but so what? – while her closest confidant in prosecuting a pro-British politics, John Acton, was of English descent. While there had been no British envoy at Rome to protect the interests of his countrymen there, at Naples, however, the English ambassador was the famous Sir William Hamilton (1730–1803), a noted natural scientist, antiquarian, collector and patron of art. Moreover, Hamilton's first wife, Catherine, was Welsh like Jones. Wealthy visitors repeatedly came to see and stay with this gracious and hospitable couple. Jones made sure he left Rome armed with a letter of recommendation to Hamilton, from whom he hoped to receive lucrative commissions.[58] Finally, the cost of living was cheaper in Naples, artists fewer, British artists fewer still, and competition among them was likely to be less onerous than in the Eternal City.

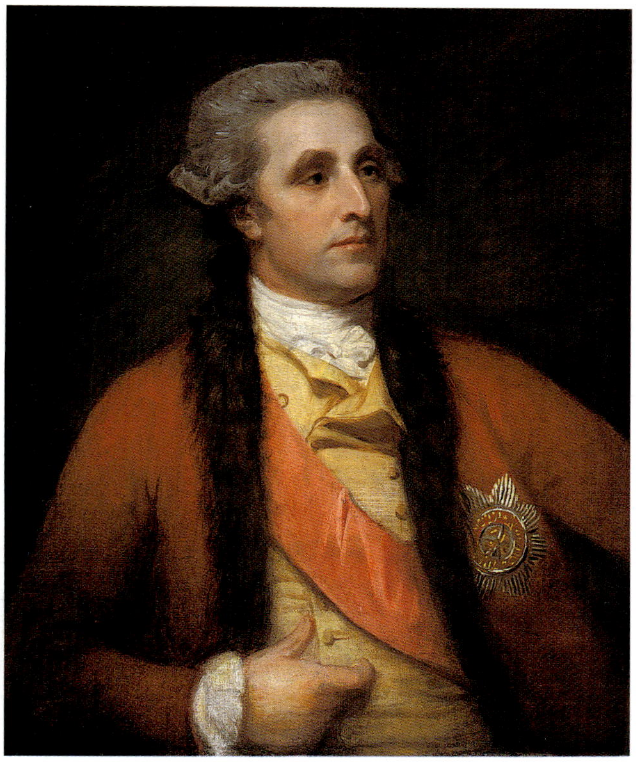

Fig. 27 George Romney (1734–1802), *Sir William Hamilton*, c.1783–4, oil on canvas, 76.8 × 65.1 (30¼ × 25⅝), National Gallery of Art, Washington.

On 1 April 1780, Jones sent Maria on before him to find lodgings. On 20 May, he began to keep scrupulous financial accounts in the book he had bought at Turin on first entering Italy in 1776, with the entry: 'set off from Rome by Procaccio and arrived at Mrs Sherry's Locanda [or hotel] in Naples on Wednesday the 24th by 11 o'clock in the forenoon'.[59] Auspiciously, he and Maria soon found ample quarters in 'a large new built house or Palace if you please', which included a painting studio and came with the use of a roof terrace, opposite the Dogana del Sale, or salt customs house, near Naples's teeming harbour.[60] Although the area was somewhat insalubrious, and he was unlikely to attract clients there to look at his paintings, Jones remained in the house for two years. The second phase of his Italian sojourn had begun. It would last three years, but would provide him with only about as much success as he had found in Rome. During those years, however, he would paint the group of small-scale oil sketches on which his subsequent renown principally rests today.

As in Rome, Jones's first considerations in Naples were practical ones. Almost immediately, he called upon Sir William Hamilton (fig. 27), and was greeted with politeness. He attended Hamilton's *levées* frequently after that. No return visit to Jones's studio was made by the august gentleman, however, nor were commissions forthcoming from that quarter. Equally disappointing, Jones met with rude and dismissive treatment from British residents of Naples whom he had come to know on his earlier sojourn in the city. Naples was a much more insular milieu than Rome, he discovered, one more given to petty jealousies than the jolly English Coffee House by the Spanish Steps. 'Looking upon my self as deserted by my Countrymen – the depression of my Spirits was such, that I endeavoured avoiding as much as possible those places where I was most likely to meet them.'[61] One small, perhaps unconscious, sign of the alienation from the British community that Jones felt early in his stay in Naples was that on 19 June, for the first time, he began entering dates in his Account Book in Italian rather than English.[62]

A realist, with responsibilities for a partner, and a child on the way – the first of two daughters was born in Naples in 1780, the second a year later – Jones methodically assessed his flimsy prospects, balanced them against the income he could expect to receive for completing commissions already on his easel, and concluded that, if the family continued to live frugally, he had the financial resources to remain in Italy for a further three years. This he determined to do and the decision constituted a kind of liberation: 'a calm resignation ensued – which brightened up by degrees into a Gleam of Happiness I was utterly a Stranger to, during the heavy load of Suspense and Chagrin I laboured under – Blessed thought I, are those who have nothing to expect – for they shall not be disappointed.'[63]

Jones was soon back exploring the city and its environs, very often in solitude, sketching as he went. 'The various picturesque Scenes of Nature had still their Charms,' he reported, '& I made Studies of them with ye same Ardour as ever.'[64] Even more so than at Rome, Jones took delight in searching out unlikely sites from which to sketch, and vistas that had not been rendered stale by too-frequent depiction. When Towne arrived from Rome in March 1781, 'I was able to conduct him to many picturesque Scenes of my Own discovery, entirely out of the common road of occasional Visiters, either Cavaliers or Artists, from Rome.'[65] Another time, near Santa Maria dei Monti, a monastery to the east of the city, he was pleased to come upon 'a most beautiful Series of picturesque Objects, which I discovered by Accident in one of my perambulations'.[66] By April 1781 he was painting 'several Studies upon paper in oil' and in May he even painted 'a View of my Kitchen . . . The Subject was prosecuted and finished *con Amore*.'[67] (When bad weather kept him indoors, Jones's chief occupation was 'touching on my sketches',[68] an indication that such works were not necessarily created in single sessions.) Convinced that he was unlikely to receive new commissions, Jones felt himself freer to explore original motifs and unexpected subjects of a kind that, in any case, were not likely to appeal to patrons. More than any time previously, he was painting for himself.

Even when he did depict well-known landmarks, the results could be unexpected, as in *The Bay of Naples and the Mole Lighthouse* (cat. no. 109). Here, the lighthouse, a strong vertical accent at the left of the sheet, is the one clearly articulated form in a richly atmospheric blend of sky, water and distant mountains disappearing into haze. Another favoured site was the Grotto of Posillipo, a man-made passageway cut through the rock by the ancient Romans to link Naples with Pozzuoli, further west along the coast. Jones often used the route to take himself into the countryside, no doubt stopping to contemplate Virgil's tomb at its exit. Countless artists painted the grotto, including Jones's friends Pars and Towne, who executed watercolours during visits to Naples (cat. no. 98).[69] Jones, too, made a detailed watercolour of the site (cat. no. 139). In August 1782 he painted an oil sketch of the same motif over a pencil sketch, traces of which can be seen on the left side of the sheet (cat. no. 119). The effect is entirely different. Jones seeks to capture not topographical detail but the contrasting play of light and shade across the bare rock face, and the even stronger contrast between brilliant blue sky above and, at the centre of the sheet, the ebony depth of the entrance. Here, he exploited the opacity and tonal density of oil paint with verve and a new pictorial concision.

Even earlier that same year, Jones had begun to paint a group of small oil sketches on paper, most likely from the roof terrace of the house opposite the Dogana del Sale which he had occupied since arriving in Naples, and which he was soon to vacate. From this elevated vantage point, the artist looked around at the roof-tops and walls of neighbouring buildings, the bases of which were invisible to him. He filled small sheets with the details, mostly mundane, of what lay before him. On one sheet, the medieval Castel Nuovo and the balustrade of the Palazzo Reale loom on the skyline, but more prominent in the foreground are far humbler buildings closer to hand (cat. no. 108). On another sheet, the roofs of the vast city, punctuated by domes, can be made out at a distance beyond the crumbling wall of an adjacent house occupying the foreground plane (fig. 10; cat. no. 110). In one remarkable painting, an old wall, pitted by time and wear, is rendered with a meticulous eye for such details as laundry hanging to dry, and with the sense that, beyond the dark windows, life goes abundantly on (cat. no. 114). Later, in May 1782, Jones found a studio on the ground floor of a convent in the suburb of Chiaja where, for two weeks, he continued to paint oil sketches. Here, he looked through the studio window upwards to the surrounding buildings, masses of masonry towering over him, their sun-drenched, pock-marked surfaces full of incident (cat. no. 115). The choice of a low viewpoint and the complex play of rectilinear and rounded architectonic forms, including the dome of a church, are strikingly similar to elements of a sketch by the Welsh-born artist John Downman (1750–1824) showing roof-tops at Nice which dates from as early as 1773 (fig. 28). One wonders if Jones had prior knowledge of this remarkable image when he began to paint at Chiaja. Downman's sheet is a reminder that innovations in depicting visual phenomena are not found in oil sketches alone.

Jones's sketches are of an immediacy and directness almost unprecedented in the history of European painting, and of a proto-photographic presence that has rendered them central to any discussion of the rise of the oil sketch tradition. From the moment of his arrival in Italy, in 1776, the artist had gravitated to humble, time-worn architectonic motifs in which a single masonry mass predominated. He had shown a predilection for unassuming objects, perhaps in out-of-the-way corners of the city, or down unexplored country lanes. Such motifs had been overlooked by traditional view painters. Therefore there was little precedent for depicting them. By choosing them, Jones created for himself the freedom to paint in a new way. He also seems to have understood the implications of Piranesi's odd perspectives and perhaps Downman's unusual viewpoint as well. Jones explored ways of painting in which he could dispense with foreground detail, or in which he sketched from below looking upwards, through and around complex spaces

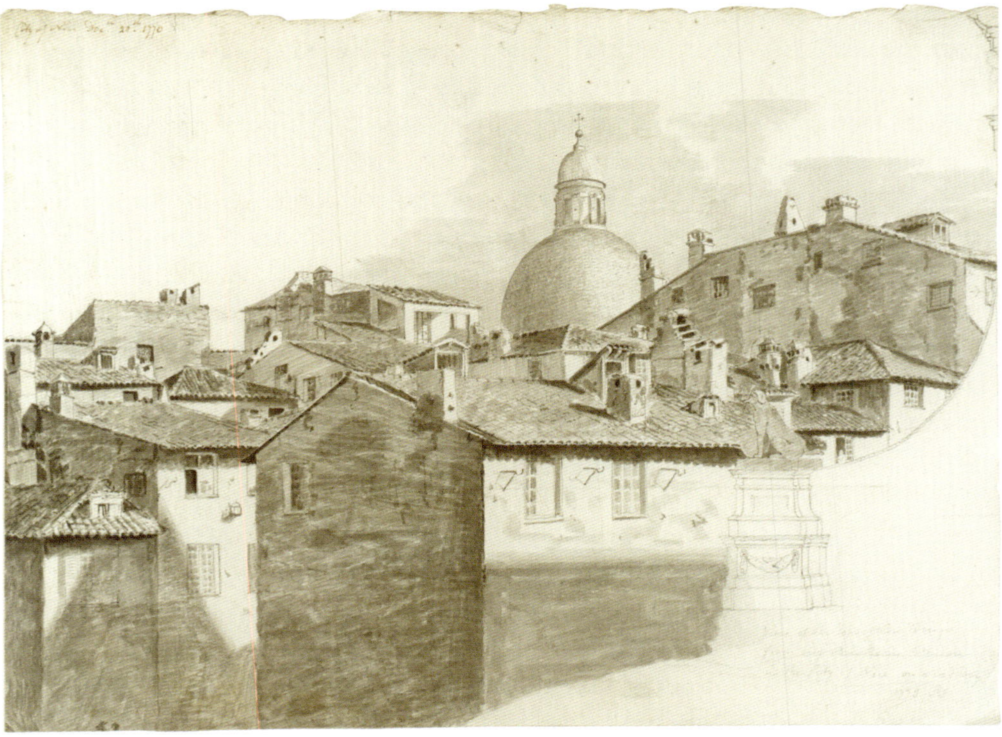

Fig. 28 John Downman (1750–1824), *View of Roof Tops, Nice*, 1773, pencil, watercolour, pen and ink on laid paper, 26.5 × 36.7 (10⅜ × 14½), Tate, London.

and forms, as in his early representations of the Colosseum (cat. nos 59 and 60).

In many sheets, such as the view of Montmélian (cat. no. 67), Jones also explored the depiction of panoramic views on a small scale. In Italy, he knew two highly original painters of large-scale panoramic works, Jacob More and Lusieri. The latter, particularly, became a close friend in Naples; Jones affectionately called him Don Titta, and his last journey to Vesuvius, before departing for Britain in July 1783, was in Lusieri's company. The latter's panoramic watercolour depiction of Naples from a window in Hamilton's house is a vital record of the city in the 1790s (fig. 29). Full of myriad details, in which modest and grand motifs jostle one another, such works were, for Jones, 'deservedly admired for their Correctness and strict attention to Nature'.[70] In their impeccable attention to detail, and to the abrupt transitions in scale between near and far, Jones's own oil sketches of Neapolitan walls resemble nothing so much as details of the city panoramas on which Lusieri was at work more or less simultaneously. Is there an affinity between the large works of one artist and the small ones of the other, a shared aspiration to truth to visual phenomena under the Neapolitan sun?

As time went on, English friends visited from Rome. In addition to Towne, Pars made the journey south in both 1780 and 1781. In June 1781, even the agent Byres stopped by to see Jones, 'to my great surprise'.[71] In 1782, Cozens came, in the retinue of the connoisseur and collector William Beckford (1759–1844). (The latter called at Jones's studio, but the painter was away and no sale was made.) With each welcome visitor, sketching expeditions were organized. At the same time, Jones cultivated friendships with Italian and foreign artists, for the most part landscape painters like himself. In addition to Lusieri, he came to know the Austrian Michael Wutky (1739–1822), patronized by the Austrian Ambassador. He also met the French painter Pierre-Jacques-Antoine Volaire (1729–1792 or 1802), famous for his depictions of Vesuvius in eruption. One morning in December 1782, Hackert himself, recently arrived in Naples, called on Jones. While Jones was scathing about the self-importance of the German artist, this may well have had to do with pique at Hackert's considerable worldly success at a moment when Jones had none whatever. In fact, Hackert seems to have done Jones a favour by reporting to the Earl–Bishop of Derry on his visit, and on improvements he noted in Jones's art, in the most flattering terms.[72] It is unlikely Jones showed Hackert his recent oil sketches. Hackert, whose chilly and conventional landscapes found favour at the Neapolitan royal court, most likely would have been unmoved by their wilful insignificance (fig. 30).

At least the Earl–Bishop of Derry remained a loyal patron of Jones's 'finished' landscapes. On 31 December 1781, Jones delivered to him two large pictures, a 'View of the *Coast of Baja*' and a 'View of *Terracina*'.[73] The following February, he began work on the large *Lake Nemi* (cat. no. 58), which was to be the pendant to *Lake Albano – Sunset* (cat. no. 56) which he had painted for the same patron in Rome (see above).[74] A year later, as Jones began to plan for a return to Britain, the Earl–Bishop wrote to him once more, suggesting that he might be able to sell all his pictures that were unspoken for in Ireland, and indeed offering him 'an Establishment under the Roof of his own palace at *Londonderry*'.[75] Had Jones been able to find one or two more patrons as generous as the Earl–Bishop, his fortunes in Italy might have been different.

Despite previous disappointments, in the final months of his stay in Naples Jones renewed his hopes for patronage from Hamilton. In December 1782,

Fig. 29 Giovanni Battista Lusieri (1755–1821), *View of the Bay of Naples from the Palazzo Sessa*, 1791, watercolour, pen and ink on paper, 102 × 272 (40⅛ × 107), The J. Paul Getty Museum, Malibu, California.

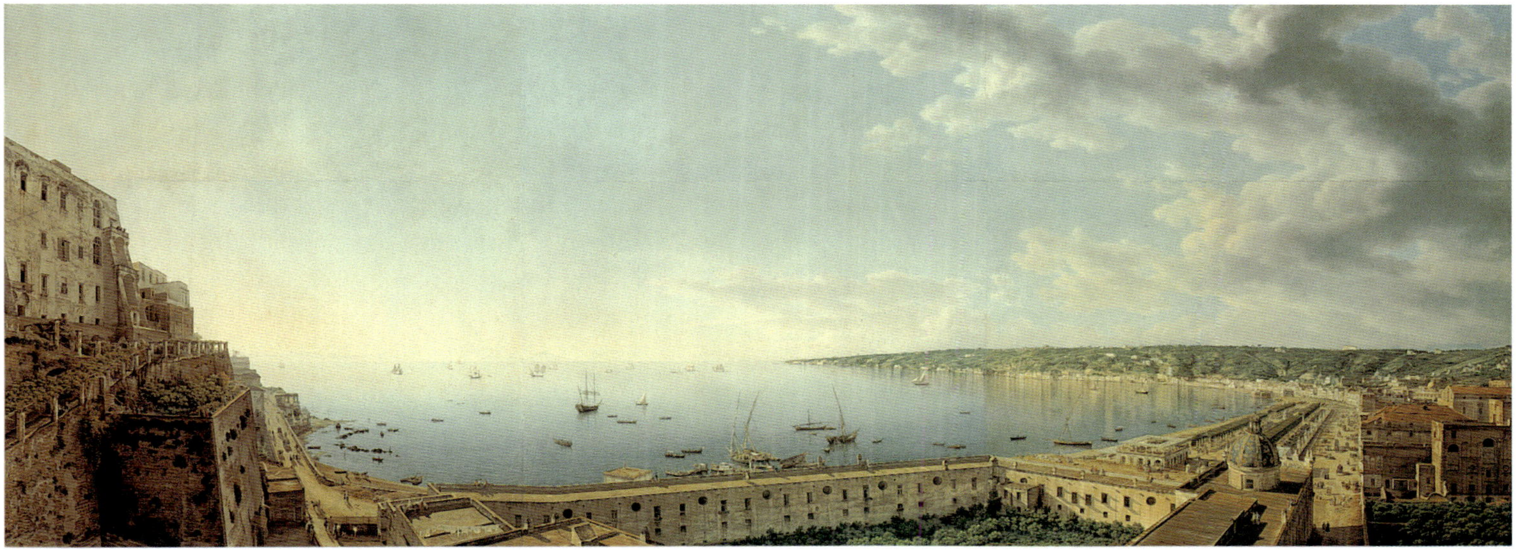

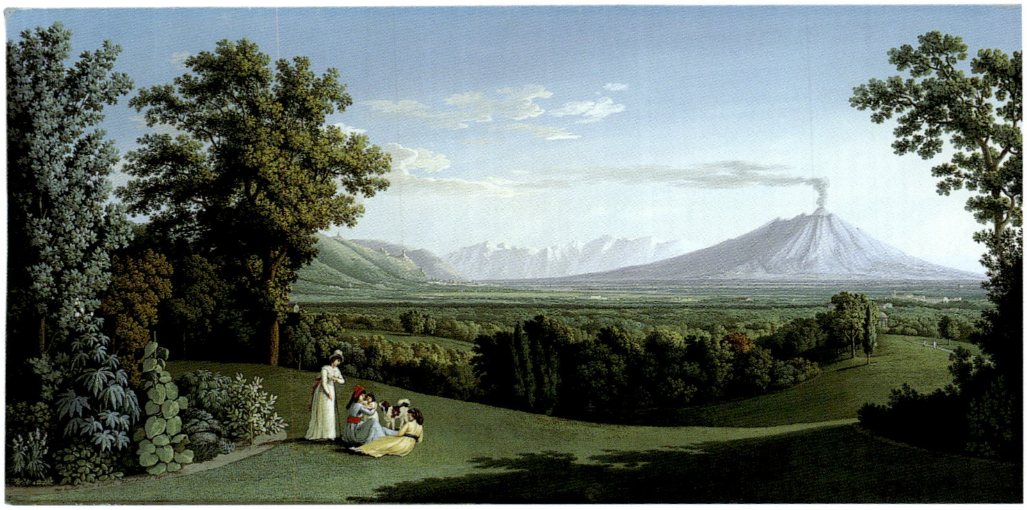

Fig. 30 Jakob Philipp Hackert (1737–1807), *The English Garden, Palazzo Reale, Caserta*, 1792, tempera on paper, 46.5 × 96.5 (18¼ × 38), Palazzo Reale, Caserta.

he moved to new quarters 'at the *Court End* of the Town – where I might paint, and exhibit my Pictures within the *Reach* of Visiters'.[76] A few months earlier, he had made an excursion to Campi Flegrei, or the volcanic landscape west of Vesuvius, where he made 'a large and correct Sketch of the whole, with an idea of painting it on a grand Scale'.[77] No subject would be more likely to appeal to Hamilton, both as an antiquarian and a natural scientist. As Hamilton would have appreciated, the area had been much discussed by the great writers of antiquity, and in 1776 he himself had penned a treatise on the area, *Campi Phlegraei: Observations on the Volcanos of the Two Sicilies*. In 1782, Jones's friend Wutky depicted the same monumental and eerie landscape (private collection) and it may have been this painting, 'a very large View of the Solfatara', that Jones saw when he visited the Austrian on 25 January 1783.[78] By April, Jones himself had almost completed his own large-scale depiction of the site, now lost, and indeed it was duly purchased by Hamilton that same year, for fifty guineas.[79] Later still, Hamilton allowed Jones to use the billiard room of his Naples home for a few weeks before the artist departed for Britain. Better late than never, Jones had finally secured the patronage of the influential figure he had most avidly pursued when he first came to Naples. He would pin his hopes for success on Hamilton upon his return to Britain. The time was now propitious for that return.

On 3 August, Jones and his family sailed from Naples on a Swedish ship. After a harrowing journey, including a stop at Gibraltar and quarantine at Dover, 'we had our promise of liberty of coming ashore', only thirteen weeks later.[80] If the experience of his teacher Wilson and of other artists whom Italy had helped to form were repeated, and if Hamilton did indeed lead new clients to Jones, then he was set to launch a prosperous and successful new career back in Britain.

Notes

1 *Memoirs*, p. 37.
2 Ibid.
3 Ibid., p. 55.
4 On the landscape oil sketch tradition, see Washington, 1996.
5 See cat. nos 39–50.
6 Galassi, 1991, p. 18.
7 Ibid., p. 37.
8 *Memoirs*, p. 40.
9 Ibid., p. 41.
10 When Jones mentions 'studies' and 'sketches' in his *Memoirs*, it is rarely immediately evident to which medium he is referring.
11 *Memoirs*, p. 43. Jones must have seen those sketches earlier, in London, or later, on his return there, as Marlow had passed though Lyon a decade earlier, in 1765.
12 Ibid., p. 44.
13 Ibid., p. 94.
14 Philadelphia, 2000, p. 31.
15 On Rome in the eighteenth century, see most recently the indispensable Philadelphia, 2000.
16 *Memoirs*, p. 53.
17 Ibid., p. 56.
18 Ibid., p. 53.
19 Ibid., p. 56.
20 London, 1993b, pp. 13–14.
21 *Memoirs*, p. 94.
22 Ibid., p. 56.
23 Ibid., p. 63.
24 Ibid., p. 53.
25 Ibid., p. 62.
26 Ibid., p. 63.
27 Ibid., p. 55.
28 Ibid., p. 56.
29 Ibid., p. 59.
30 Ibid., p. 66.
31 Ibid., p. 62.
32 Ibid., p. 63.
33 Ibid., p. 62.
34 Ibid., p. 70.
35 Ibid.
36 Ibid., pp. 63, 67.
37 Ibid., p. 73.
38 Ibid., p. 79.
39 Paris, 2001, p. 5.
40 *Memoirs*, pp. 79–80.
41 Ibid., p. 83.
42 Ibid., p. 84.
43 Ibid.
44 Ibid., pp. 87–8.
45 Ibid., p. 89.
46 Ibid., p. 92.
47 Ibid., pp. 69–70.
48 Account Book, cat. no. 73, p. 146. Michilli was probably the Roman painter Luigi Micheli whom Jones knew at Naples.
49 Ibid., p. 58.
50 *Memoirs*, p. 53.
51 Ottani Cavina, 2001, pp. 296–7.
52 *Memoirs*, p. 54.
53 Ibid., p. 63.
54 Ibid., p. 62.
55 Ibid., pp. 69–70.
56 Ibid., p. 94.
57 Ibid.
58 Ibid., p. 95.
59 Account Book, p. 6.
60 *Memoirs*, p. 95.
61 Ibid., p. 97.
62 Account Book, p. 13.
63 *Memoirs*, p. 97.
64 Ibid.
65 Ibid., p. 102.
66 Ibid., p. 104.
67 Ibid., p. 103.
68 Ibid., p. 100.
69 On which, see Paris, 2001, cat. nos 39 and 40.
70 *Memoirs*, p. 112.
71 Ibid., p. 105.
72 Ibid., p. 117.
73 Ibid., p. 109.
74 Ibid., p. 110.
75 Ibid., p. 121.
76 Ibid., p. 118.
77 Ibid., p. 115.
78 Ibid., p. 119. Wutky's painting is illustrated in Milan, 2002, cat. no. II.10.
79 Ibid., p. 122.
80 Account Book, p. 124.

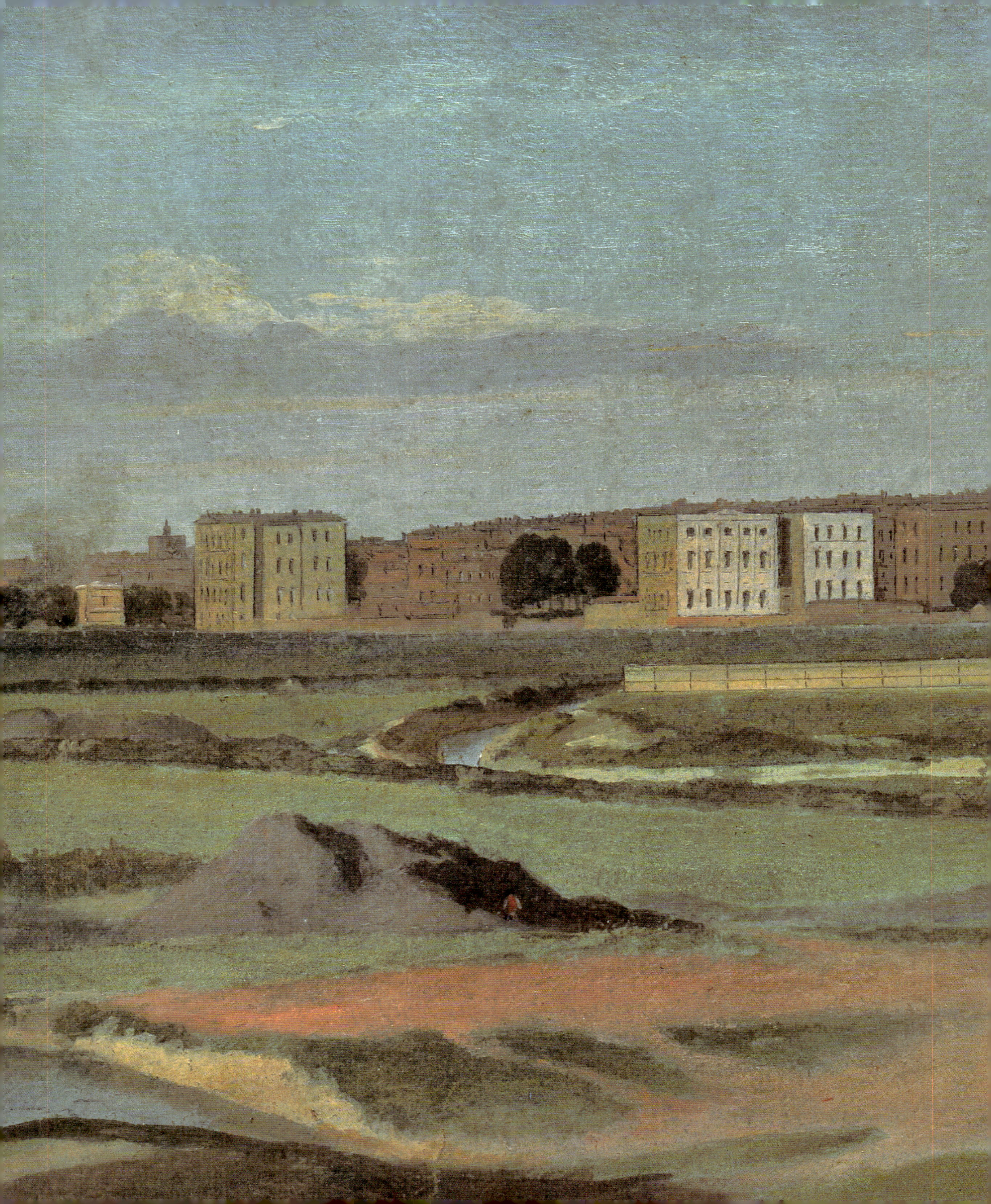

PAINTING 'FOR MY OWN AMUSEMENT': FROM PROFESSIONAL ARTIST TO AMATEUR, 1783–1803

Greg Smith

A successful landscape artist returning from Italy brought back two things that were crucial to his career. First, a stock of sketches and studies meant that he could subsequently supply a wide range of subjects; and, second, contacts with British tourists might be cultivated to form a supportive network of patrons. There is no doubt that Thomas Jones returned with the former, but the poor fortunes he enjoyed with patrons in Italy intensified on his return. Within a year, Jones was noting gloomily that 'my professional Career was at an End' and that earnings from his art provided only a small supplement to the income he received from the estate left to him by his father.[1] With the death of his brother in 1787, and his inheritance of the Pencerrig estate, Jones became financially independent, and, in a move that signalled that he was cutting himself off from the artistic community, he 'quitted London, as a place of Constant Residence'.[2] The trajectory of Jones's career was an unusual one, since economic failure as an artist usually meant penury, but in Jones's case it coincided with a substantial inheritance and so he became an amateur artist in all but name. His fate was in some respects an enviable one, therefore. Thus, although his responsibilities as a landowner and public figure limited his opportunities for painting, the change in Jones's status meant he was able to paint exclusively for his 'own Amusement' and this had a profound effect on his work.[3]

Perhaps because the period from 1783 onwards did not see Jones's best work, it has not been accorded the careful consideration it deserves. In fact, not only did he produce many fascinating views of Welsh scenery which extended the range of his landscapes, but he also used his free time to revisit his Italian sketches. Jones continued to paint Italian scenes in London and later in Wales, including many works which have often been assumed to have been made on the spot in Italy. It is crucial, therefore, if we are fully to appreciate the scale of Jones's achievement in his Italian sketches – which must remain the cornerstone of his reputation – that we also understand the character of his work during the last twenty years of his life, and, in particular, the influence of his amateur status.

FACING PAGE Detail of cat. no. 153.

One of the reasons for the relative lack of interest in Jones's later artistic career lies in the fact that his candid *Memoirs* – a key to his current standing – effectively end with his return to England in November 1783. He details the problems he had with customs officials and sadly relates the fate of his 'Books, Prints Drawings and other papers' which had rotted in his absence, but concluded the text by summarizing his disappointments in a few lines. It is not surprising that Jones omitted the various stages of his professional disappointment, but at least he had the consolation of knowing that the odds were stacked against him in a London art world that had changed considerably whilst he was away. Jones had previously been a loyal supporter of the Society of Artists, but the body had declined to such a degree in his absence that it had lost many of its most important members and failed to organize exhibitions in 1779, 1781–2 and again in 1784. Jones was aware that he had chosen the wrong side in the factional struggles that dominated the art world at the outset of his career, noting that the Royal Academy was 'ascending' just as the Society of Artists was 'descending', but this left him exposed when he sought to advertise his abilities on his return.[4] Jones showed two works at the Academy in 1784 and 1785, but he was at the mercy of the hanging committee, who may have rejected other paintings brought back from Italy. It is noticeable, too, that although he called on the president of the Royal Academy, Sir Joshua Reynolds, the artists he met on his return to England were lesser lights in the art world such as John Robert Cozens, John 'Warwick' Smith and Giuseppe Marchi, who were not in a position to lobby for his interests. It is telling that by 1785 one of Jones's submissions had been relegated to the less important Ante-Room and it is possible that he entered works in 1786 but had them rejected.

The *Memoirs* do not give many details, but they leave little doubt that the collapse of Jones's professional career stemmed from an over-reliance on the one important connection that he made towards the end of his time in Italy,

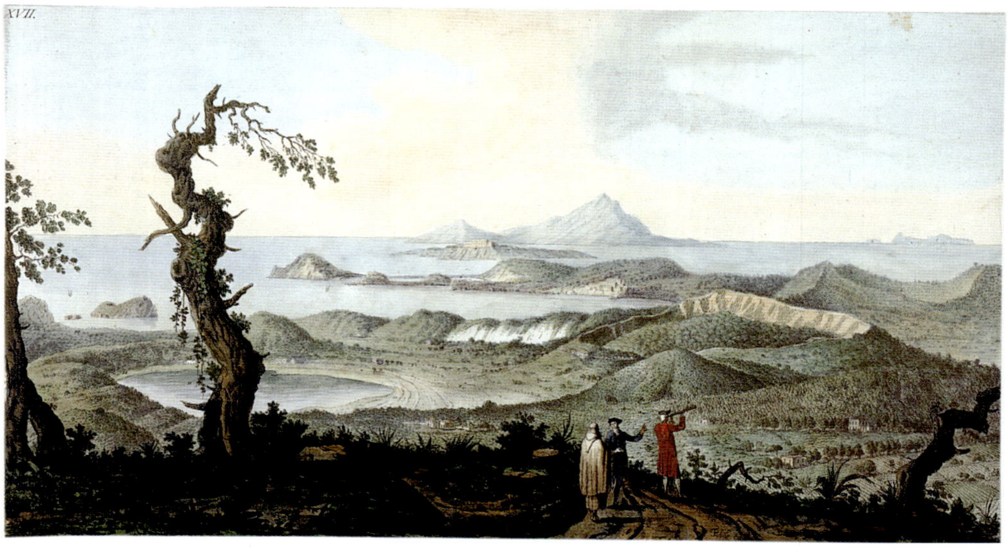

Fig. 31 Pietro Fabris (fl. 1756–1784), *View of the Isle of Ischia from the Convent of the Camaldoli of Naples [View of the Campi Phlegraei] from 'The Campi Phlegraei'*, 1776, hand-coloured etching, *c.*39 × 21.5 (15¼ × 8½), The British Library, London.

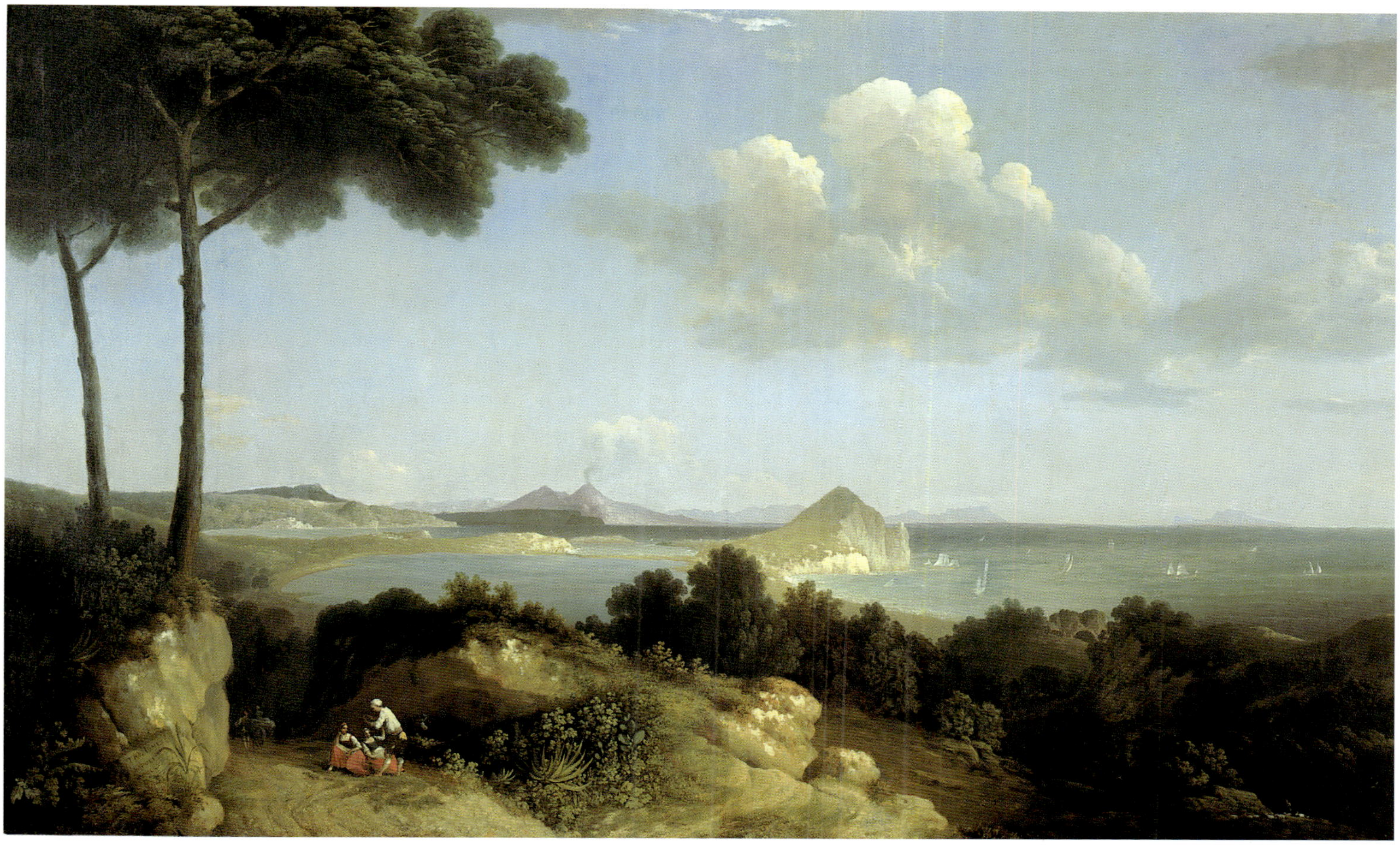

Sir William Hamilton. He records meeting him for the first time in August 1782, when the patron praised his works and lent him 'his Treatise on Volcanoes with the Prints highly colored by his favourite painter M. Fabris' (fig. 31).[5] In October 1782, Jones said that he visited 'the Convent of Camaldole which is the highest Situation near Naples' specifically to study the 'Campi Flegrei . . . which Sr W'm Hamilton has Discussed in his Treatise', and he 'made a large and correct Sketch of the whole, with an idea of painting it on a grand Scale'.[6] By April 1783, Jones had nearly finished the work and he succeeded in securing a promise of fifty guineas from Hamilton, who was pleased that the painting was 'rather explanatory of his description of the Scene'.[7] Hamilton left the work in Jones's hands to transport back to England and the task of framing it subsequently took up much of his time.[8] More importantly from the artist's point of view, the patron allowed Jones to show it at the forthcoming exhibition at the Academy, and *View of the Campi Flegrei from the Camaldolise Convent near Naples* duly appeared as testimony to his best efforts and evidence of Hamilton's support.

Sadly, the work has been lost, but we can get an idea of its appearance from the plate in Hamilton's *Campi Phlegraei* that Jones studied; furthermore, there is an earlier oil from 1780 which probably shows a

Fig. 32 Thomas Jones, *Naples from the Campi Flegrei*, 1780, oil on canvas, 76.2 × 128.3 (30 × 50½), private collection, Rome.

similar view (fig. 32). The exhibition piece was clearly a major statement and, with the benefit of novelty, it attracted at least four reviews, two of which were complimentary. The *Morning Chronicle* thought that the work 'shows a great deal of merit . . . learning, taste', adding, on another occasion, that the choice of subject is 'fine, his execution masterly, and his effect charming'.[9] Perhaps Jones had a friend in the press – he himself wrote a flattering review of the Society of Artists' exhibition in 1772 – since the *Morning Chronicle's* praise was not repeated.[10] The *St James's Chronicle*, for instance, complained that the middle ground was too 'distinct' so that 'the Leaves may be counted', whilst the 'distant Prospect' was 'similar to that of the Whole'.[11] As the *Morning Post* similarly noticed, Jones's works were deficient in 'that aerial perspective' that is essential to animate 'works of this class'.[12] A similar pattern emerges in comments about his other exhibit in 1784, *Morning View of Naples*, which was said to have had 'several of the same Faults', though 'considerably better'.[13] This can be identified as *The Bay of Naples* from 1782 (cat. no. 106). It must have been a blow to Jones to find that not only were his works subject to censure, but that it was generally agreed that he had regressed during his absence. Even more damaging, however, was the silence that greeted his two exhibits a year later; furthermore, to add insult to injury, when he did once again attract notice, in 1787, with his only exhibit, *View of the Ponte Loreto* (cat. no. 151), the sole critic to notice the work attacked his unconventional 'Choice of Nature' and a composition in which the 'Lines are petite, or frittered into small bits'.[14]

All of this would have mattered less had Jones attracted commissions, but, although Hamilton 'had used all his Interest' the artist was sadly forced to conclude that it was 'without Effect', the patron 'could be of no Service' in England, unlike Italy.[15] Jones attributed his failure to overestimating the 'Influence' of his patron, but the newspaper reviews suggest more fundamental problems. As the *Morning Chronicle* noted, the 'artist is not alone in this branch of painting', so that although Jones might have felt that the death of his master, Richard Wilson, in 1782, paved the way for him, there was too much competition already.[16] The other point that emerges from the reviews is that Jones was found wanting in an area in which Wilson was said to have consistently triumphed: aerial perspective. Wilson's critical standing was in any case low in comparison with earlier in his career, so to be found wanting at this time and in this way was especially damning. Jones's relationship with Wilson was also problematic, since he admitted to 'a few innocent Impostures – by making Imitations of my old Master'. These, he said, 'passed among Our Connoisseurs at some of the public Sales for Originals' before he was exposed by someone whose trade in forgeries was 'infringed upon'.[17] Jones's claim that his pastiches of Wilson were 'innocent' and his anger that this source of income was ended by the 'jealousy' of another artist underlines his frustrations and the lengths to which he was prepared to go to survive as a professional.

Jones believed that the engraving of his works would boost his standing. In 1784, John Boydell published an engraving by James Peak titled

The Travellers' Repose (cat. no. 145). The print states that this was from 'the Original Picture Painted by Thomas Jones', though the source has not been identified and it may have been produced earlier. As Jones noted, Wilson's reputation had been 'spread abroad through the Medium' of engraving and Boydell's print reintroduced the artist's name to the public.[18] Jones was referring to William Woollett, who had originally undertaken to produce a print after *Dido and Aeneas* (cat. no. 21) only to abandon the plate. Woollett died in 1785 and his widow employed another engraver to finish the plate, which was finally published in 1787. By that time, the work was owned by Catherine the Great of Russia, though this did not help Jones. He remained unaware that one of his most important works had entered the collection of a patron who was the epitome of liberal generosity and whose support of other artists he envied.[19]

There was, however, a category of patron who continued to support Jones, his 'friends'; though this also points to his changing status. One of the 'three or four [anonymous] friends' Jones referred to was Thomas Johnes of Hafod.[20] Johnes had moved to his newly inherited estate in Cardiganshire, some seventy miles from Pencerrig, in 1783 and had begun an extensive and ambitious programme of improvements that was to make the estate one of the most celebrated in Britain. We do not know when Jones first visited, but since he showed *Waterfall in the Garden of Thomas Johnes, Esq., at Havod, Cardiganshire* at the Royal Academy in 1786, it was presumably some time in 1785. Jones was certainly there the following year, in the middle of September and again in early October, because there are drawings of the estate in the last of his surviving sketchbooks (cat. no. 154), including a series of studies of trees such as this made on 16 September (fig. 33). Sadly, Hafod was damaged in a fire in 1807 and Jones's estate views were lost. These included the 1786 Academy exhibit, another of a *Scene in the grounds* shown in 1788, 'four coloured drawings of scenes within the precincts of Havod', which were hung over the doors in the 'winter dining-room', 'Four small Views' shown in a passage, and, most intriguingly, a 'large port-folio, full of paintings (on paper) of a variety of views'.[21] This latter information came from William Gilpin, who was shown the views in April 1787, as well as others at a later date. An echo of what must have been an extensive survey of the estate is provided by an unusual source. The 'Hafod' service, produced for Johnes by the Derby Porcelain factory in 1787, is decorated with a large number of landscape views (fig. 34; cat. no. 155). It seems that Johnes passed on Jones's paintings and drawings of the estate to the factory for them to work from. A scene such as *The Entrance to the Ladies Walk*, which is painted on to an oval dish, probably records one of Jones's lost views.[22]

Fig. 33 Thomas Jones, *Tree Study at Hafod*, from a sketchbook, 16 September 1786 (see cat. no. 154).

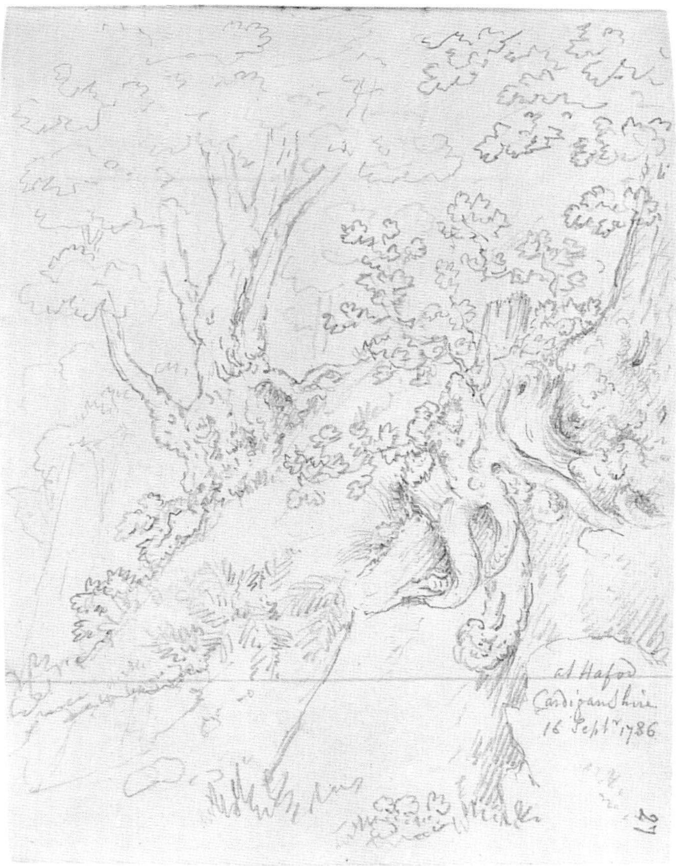

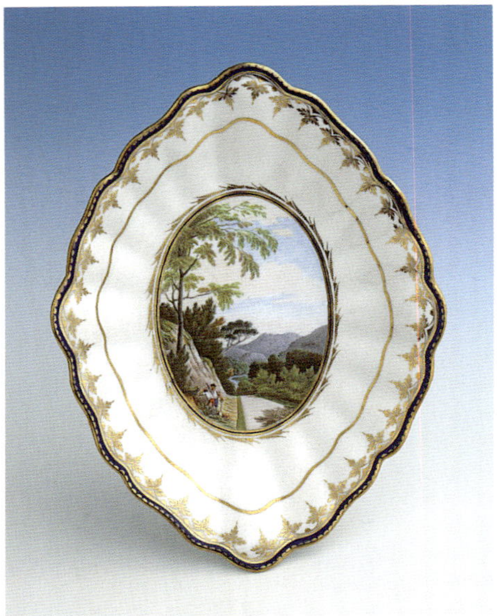

Fig. 34 Derby Porcelain Factory, dessert dish from the 'Hafod' service, decorated with a view of the entrance to the Ladies' Walk, 1787 (see cat. no. 155).

Jones's work at Hafod may have been lost, but it is still significant for a number of reasons. Firstly, the fact that he undertook work portraying the house and grounds of a fellow landowner in Wales underlines the fact that Jones had reverted to a similar pattern of employment to the period before he travelled abroad. In other words, he continued to depend on personal connections, as in the case of his work at Maeslough House (cat. no. 37) and Llwynmadoc (cat. no. 25). Secondly, Gilpin's assertion that Jones produced 'paintings (on paper)' suggests that there was a substantial body of oil sketches post-dating his return from Italy and that *The Outskirts of London* (cat. no. 153) was not a one-off. And finally, the works, or the reaction they prompted, indicate another reason why Jones struggled to attract patrons. Gilpin thought Jones was 'one of your *religious copyists*', by which he meant that his adherence to a broadly empirical tradition put him at odds with the contemporary interest in the picturesque, with its concern with generalized effects.[23] Jones's commitment to the depiction of the ordinary, something which we welcome today as an antidote to stale pictorial conventions, was a source of suspicion in some quarters.

The second commission from a friend came from James Baker, whose *Picturesque Guide Through Wales and the Marches* contains five aquatints after works by Jones. Again, the original drawings have been lost, but they may have been small in scale and in monochrome.[24] It is clear from the text that Baker worked closely with Jones, since, in addition to the images, which include favourite views along the River Wye at Aberedw and near Builth, and a scene showing the 'artificial lake' that Jones had had constructed at Pencerrig (fig. 35), the text also contains information that he supplied to Baker. The author was thus familiar with Jones's birthplace at Trefonnen (cat. no. 9) and the estate at Pencerrig and he talks about seeing the 'highly finished coloured drawings' on view at the latter.[25] More interestingly, Jones also contributed a poem, 'Petraeia' – a Latinized version of Pencerrig. This describes some of the scenes around Pencerrig, concentrating in particular on the melancholy loss of its 'native forests' of 'graceful flowing ash' and 'sturdy knotted oak'.[26] This was poignant, Jones continued, because it was here that he felt his first calling as an artist:

> In these sweet shades kind nature did impart
> Her first choice lessons to my infant heart,
> Guided my youthful pencil not to stray
> From nature's laws, (and nature led the way)[27]

The combination of a personal testament with images of favoured scenes emphasizes Jones's strong feeling for his native place, something that does not shine through the *Memoirs*.

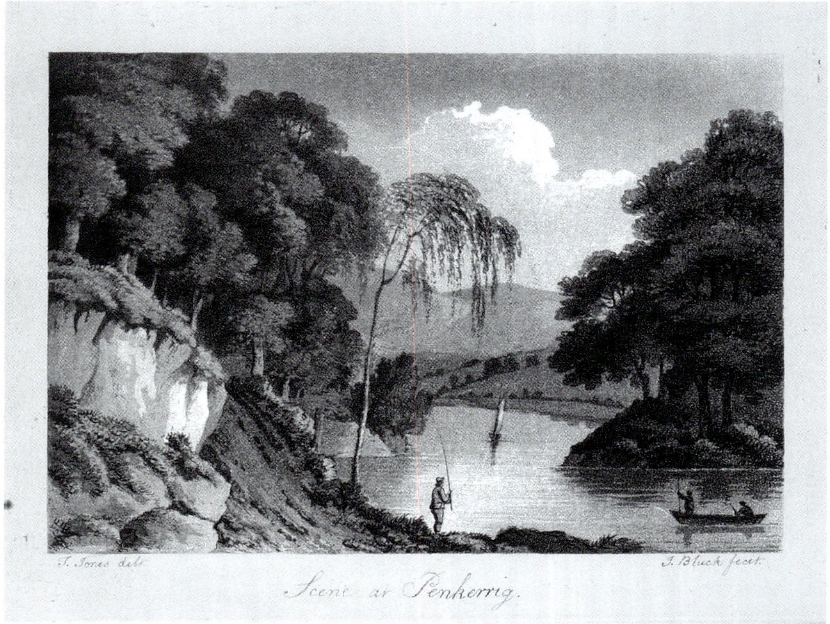

Fig. 35 J. Bluck (exhibited 1791–1819), after Thomas Jones, *Scene at Pencerrig*, illustration to James Baker's *A Picturesque Guide Through Wales and the Marches*, 2nd edn, 1795, aquatint, 13.8 × 19 (5⅜ × 7½), National Museums & Galleries of Wales, Cardiff.

It is possible that one further group of works, five oil paintings produced between 1790 and 1797, was commissioned. Works that Jones painted for his own amusement invariably remained in the possession of his family, but these paintings have not survived. Jones greatly valued them because he recorded their production in detail in a section of his diary for the 1790s which is preserved in the Account Book (cat. no. 73). Two, possibly three, of the paintings were shown at the Royal Academy in 1798, marking Jones's return to the exhibition after ten years. *A View of Sorrento*, a sunrise, is the work he called 'N°4' and the *View from above Sorrento, looking over the Bay of Naples* was probably 'N°5', whilst one of the other three paintings he detailed may have been the *Winter Scene in Italy*.

It is not clear why Jones chose to return to the public fray, and the question certainly exercised Joseph Farington, who was sufficiently surprised to note the fact in his diary.[28] Jones's decision to return to the Italian scenes that he had begun work on in 1790 is less surprising since he often revisited the subjects he had sketched there. The process of writing the *Memoirs*, completed in 1797, may have inspired him, as might the arrival of his old colleague Francesco Renaldi, who spent two months at Pencerrig at the end of the same year, painting the portrait of Jones and his family (cat. no. 9). Jones is shown with palette, marl stick and brushes in hand, taking a break from painting an upright landscape in oils – a coastal view? This was presumably one of the paintings he describes in his diary, so that the portrait records Jones's resumption of painting after having 'not once touch[ed] a Pencil in *Oil* Colors' since 1791.[29] The point would have been reinforced when the portrait was exhibited at the Royal Academy in 1798 along with Jones's three oils; indeed, one of them would have hung close to Renaldi's work in the Ante Room.[30] Sadly for Jones, his efforts were not universally welcomed. His old student colleague, Farington, thought that 'Jones's landscapes [are] very cold – like China', whilst the *Whitehall Evening Post* complained that the *View from Above Sorrento* was an 'execrable performance' and wondered how it 'could ever attain a place in the Exhibition'.[31] Such an adverse reaction presumably persuaded Jones not to risk the exposure to public opinion again and it was perhaps at this point that he added the brief appendix to the *Memoirs* summarizing his disappointments.

It is difficult not to attribute Jones's reticence about this period to a sense of insecurity about his identity as an artist. Jones admitted as much in the *Memoirs* when he said that his 'professional Career was at an End', but quickly added that although he primarily worked for his own pleasure, he still took 'Commissions' from friends.[32] Interestingly, Jones used the word 'profession' in its modern sense of a remunerative career, rather than the older meaning of a calling or vocation. The key point, however, is that he did not claim the status of amateur on achieving financial independence. The 1780s saw the beginning of a shift away from the older, more deferential, attitude towards amateur practice, with many critics ridiculing the efforts of honorary exhibitors, arguing that, without 'the motive power of interest', the non-professional inevitably lacks the serious commitment needed to excel.[33] Jones was also presumably aware of the opprobrium which had recently been levelled at Nathaniel Dance (1735–1811). He had ceased to exhibit at the Academy in the mid-1770s on acquiring an independent fortune and had compounded this slight to his former profession in 1790 by resigning his membership and showing as an 'honorary exhibitor'. As Anthony Pasquin later noted, he 'ungenerously turned his back upon the Muses, as not fit company for the aristocracy of England'.[34] Renaldi's portrait of Jones and his family (cat. no. 9) illustrates the ambiguity of his position. Jones is not shown working in a studio. Instead, he inhabits the same domestic interior as his daughters, who are engaged in music-making, and his wife, who spins, both suitable activities for the genteel. Jones is shown engaged in painting in oils and not, as with the majority of depictions of amateur artists, working in watercolours or pencil on a smaller scale. Moreover, he is detached from the family group in a relatively plain setting with the simplest of chairs to sit on, so that if we ignore the rest of the painting it is still possible to imagine him as a working professional in his studio.

Whatever the ambiguities of his position, Jones had the consolation of working for his own pleasure, a liberty granted to the amateur, but with a professional's skill. This meant that he was able to continue his earlier practice of portraying the family estate at Pencerrig, as well as the surrounding countryside. This had to wait initially until August 1784, when Jones felt able to be away from London. During his stay in September and October, he completed at least five watercolours, each of which is carefully finished and dated. These represent a major departure for Jones on two counts. Firstly, unlike the earlier sketches he made around Pencerrig in 1772 and 1775–6, they were in watercolours rather than in oils. He did not cease to use oils entirely – the Hafod group, for instance, appear to have been in this medium – but there was a double shift in his practice which saw him recording the scenery at Pencerrig and its surrounds in a different medium and as finished views, rather than sketches.[35] This constitutes a significant change in his use of the medium, so that instead of adding colour to an outline drawing, often at a later date, such works as *A Barn at Pencerrig* (fig. 36; cat. no. 144) were conceived as watercolours from the beginning. Jones's use of watercolour in Italy was ancillary to the production of oil paintings, but now he regarded the medium as suitable for independent finished works. The second perceptible shift in the scenes painted in 1784 lies in the type of composition Jones adopted. In contrast to the earlier oil sketches, which predominantly show wide-open views, often with low horizons, Jones turned to more occluded scenes, with dominant trees, buildings and rocks bursting out of the composition. Two of the watercolours (fig. 36; cat. nos 144 and 143) actually show humble buildings – a barn and a hut – cut in a seemingly random way, whilst the most unconventional composition, *The Knoll in the Grounds of Pencerrig* (fig.37) shows a close-up view of a tree-topped mound, again cropped arbitrarily. In this respect,

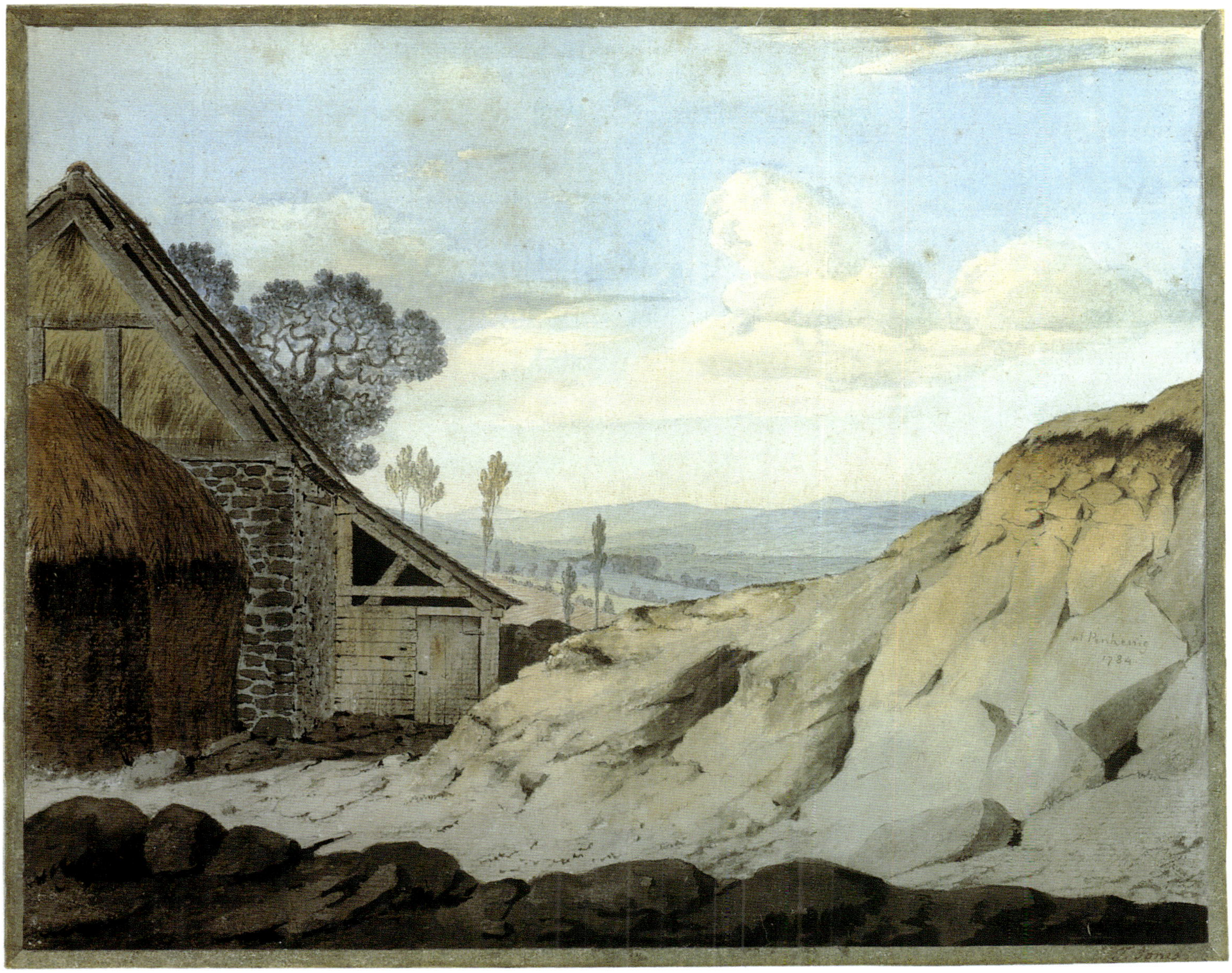

Fig. 36 Thomas Jones, *A Barn at Pencerrig*, 1784 (cat. no. 144).

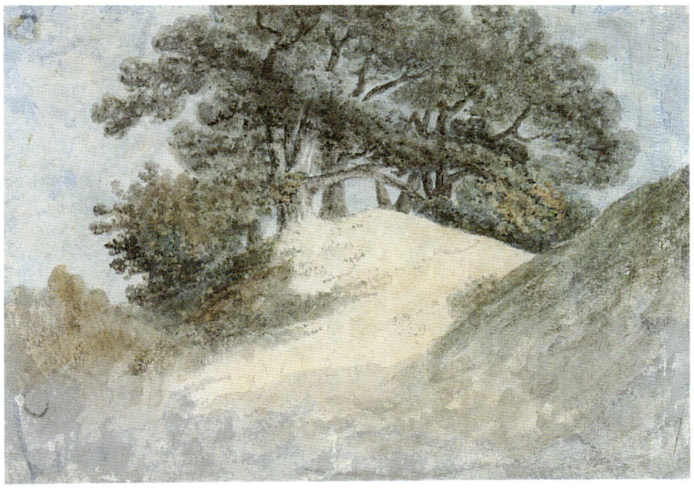

Fig. 37 Thomas Jones, *The Knoll in the Grounds of Pencerrig*, 1784, watercolour, 19.1 × 27.3 (7½ × 10¾), private collection.

therefore, Jones translated the experience of sketching in oils from the windows of his studio in Naples to his finished watercolours of the Welsh countryside, and this was helped by the fact that the Pencerrig estate and its surrounds had numerous rocky corners similar to those that had so entranced him in the shady roads above that city.

There was, however, a significant continuity between Jones's views of Wales from before and after his Italian trip; namely, that he continued to depict only his immediate locality in Radnorshire. There is little evidence that he went in search of views further afield – certainly he did not visit the northern mountains – and Jones's was a parochial vision of the country. It focused on scenes associated with his early life (cat. no. 8) and on views of sites which belonged to his family or were visible from 'my Paternal Estate' and its vicinity.[36] After 1787, these paintings gained an added resonance when the artist inherited Pencerrig, so that in his later years he exercised the ultimate prerogative of the amateur: the chance to portray and fashion an image of his own land. The strength of Jones's feeling for his native place comes across strongly in the information he communicated to the author Benjamin Malkin and is a presiding theme of his poem 'Petraeia'. The title refers to 'the comely height that rises above Penkerrig' and the poem itself is an extended hymn to the beauty of the surrounding countryside and the glories of the 'sturdy knotted oak'.[37] According to Malkin, there 'are no estates in all these parts where the native oak groves, &c. are more carefully preserved', and he enthused about the manner in which they blend 'with the majestic rocks and romantic hills'.[38] Watercolours such as *An Oak Tree with a Distant View near Pencerrig* (cat. no. 142) show some of the antique specimens which had survived the depredations Jones mourned in his poem. More than that, though, Jones threw himself wholeheartedly into the business of land management. The abundant evidence of Jones's extensive planting campaigns in the estate records is matched by the watercolours of this later period, which often illustrate Jones's efforts at woodland management.[39] *A Barn at Pencerrig* (fig. 36; cat. no. 144), for instance, shows a row of saplings and, like many of the sketches in his last surviving sketchbook, it records the well-tended fences and farm buildings found on the estate (cat. no. 154).[40] This is a particularly interesting image for it includes a glimpse of the house shown at an oblique angle. This was the closest Jones came to showing Pencerrig in any of his works, despite the fact that he painted other people's homes in the vicinity. As a landscape painter who had thrown himself into his role as a landowner, it was the surrounding estate and the views from it that were of interest and not the building.

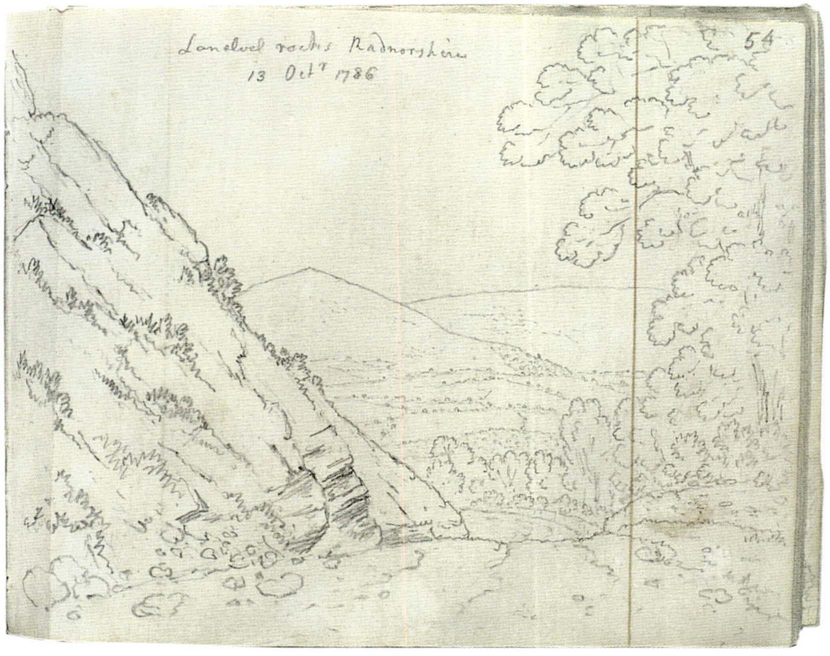

Fig. 38 Thomas Jones, *Garth from Llanelwedd, from a Sketchbook*, 1786 (cat. no. 154).

Jones produced a further group of watercolours of Pencerrig subjects in 1794 and 1795 which were again presumably personal in their motivation. The six highly finished works are all mounted with the same washline border and each has a descriptive title inscribed at the bottom. The works were possibly designed by Jones to be shown in frames, and they certainly appear to have been conceived as a group since they offer a systematic survey of the Carneddau hills to the east of Pencerrig. In 'Petraeia', Jones describes a scene he must have witnessed many times:

See, see the wide horizon's glorious blaze!
The setting sun descending low,
Beyond the fervid mountain's brow.
And high *Carnedda's* top reflects the ling'ring rays[41]

The watercolours (cat. nos 157–9) have faded a little and some of their subtly has been lost, but they could never have captured the type of light effect Jones describes. The mid-1790s saw a new sophistication in the use of watercolours for the depiction of landscape effects, and the pioneering works of J. M. W. Turner and Thomas Girtin took the art to new heights. Jones's finished watercolours, with their muted range of colours, strong pen and ink outlines and disregard for atmospheric effects would have appeared old-fashioned to contemporaries. It was one thing to use a few washes of colour to transform an outline drawing, but Jones lacked the increasingly specialized skills associated with the modern art of 'paintings in water colours'.[42] It would be wrong, however, to say that watercolours such as *The Northern Extremity of Carneddau* (cat. no. 158) reflect a falling off in artistic ability, but rather that Jones sought to produce a new type of work for which he was not technically equipped. This is certainly the implication to be derived from the few sketches in watercolours he produced in the 1790s, such as the two studies of rocks near Pencerrig from 1796 (fig. 39 and cat. no. 162; cat. no. 163). As so often with Jones, the adoption of a less formal composition was accompanied by a simpler use of materials – a few washes of flat colour and no dominating line – which is highly effective.

The surviving works from the latter part of Jones's life do not add up to a considerable body of work: one sketchbook, a dozen or so watercolours, one oil painting and a single oil sketch. Much is known to have been lost, including a large number of views of Hafod and at least five major oils, but even making allowances for this, it is clear that there were long periods during the course of the almost twenty years left to Jones after his return from Italy when he did not paint. There is, however, another category of material that occupied his attention: Italian subjects painted in Britain and works begun in Italy but subsequently altered in some way. Exactly how much time Jones spent revisiting his sketches and working up compositions is not entirely clear; however, careful consideration of the archive and the physical evidence provided by the works suggests that it is dangerous to assume that any undated Italian view was wholly or partly done prior to 1783. Indeed, there is a symmetry here between the way that Jones explored

Fig. 39 Thomas Jones, *A Rocky Outcrop at Pencerrig*, 1796 (cat. no. 163).

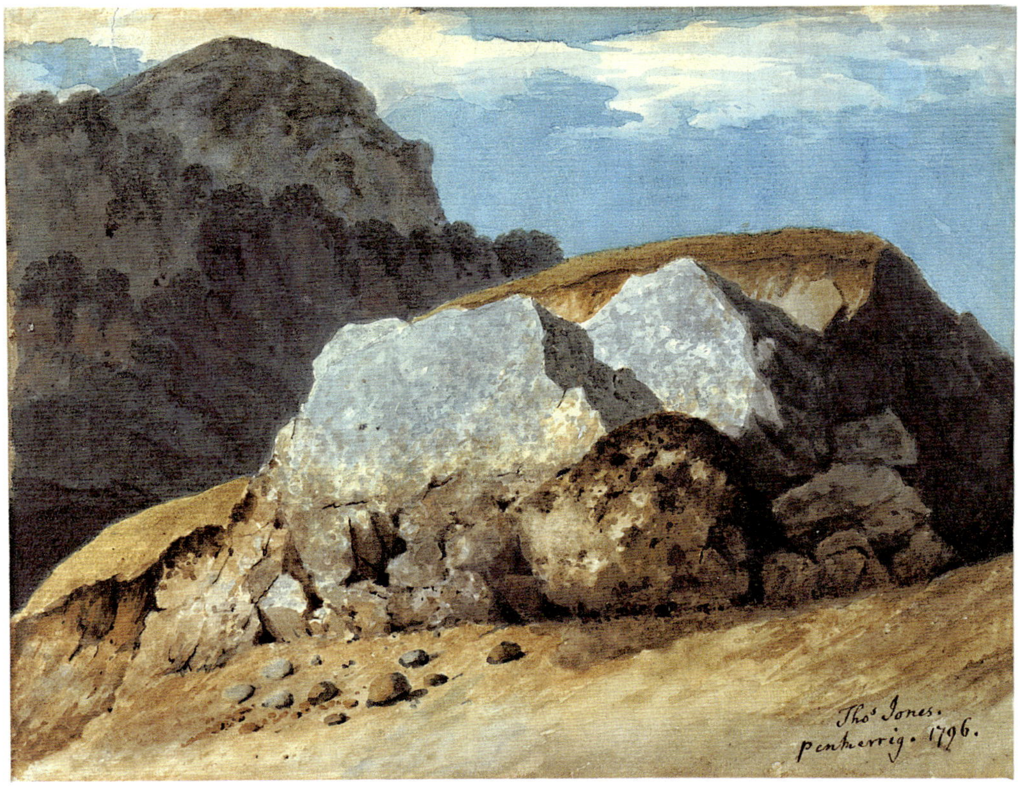

images of Italy at second hand before he travelled to the country and the manner in which he reworked his sketches after he returned.

There are two types of evidence which help to determine the extent to which Jones's Italian subjects were produced back in Britain. Firstly, and most obviously, there are a small number of Italian subjects that are dated 1784 and later. Examples include *View of the Temple of Diana at Nemi* (fig. 41; cat. no. 146) and *Monte Compatri, near Frascati* (cat. no. 147), both from 1785. Secondly, there is the evidence provided by the materials Jones used, particularly the papers he employed. The paper on which he painted *Gaiola on the Coast of Posillipo, near Naples* (fig. 40; cat. no. 164) is a Whatman wove which must date from the 1790s and this is confirmed by a second date on the drawing – 1796. The other date, 1778, presumably refers to the sketch on which it is based. The view of *Terracina* (cat. no. 166) can also be dated to the 1790s because of the support it is painted on and a fuller survey of Jones's papers would presumably throw up more examples. Two other types of evidence help to build up a picture of an artist who compulsively revisited and reworked the images he had sketched during his travels. In the first instance, the presentation of finished studio watercolours such as *On the Road to Civita Castellana* (cat. no. 149), which is dated 1785, suggests that it is part of a group. *Houses on the Road from Rome to Civita Castellana* (cat. no. 150), for example, is identical in size and is mounted in exactly the same way. In the second instance, the fact that so

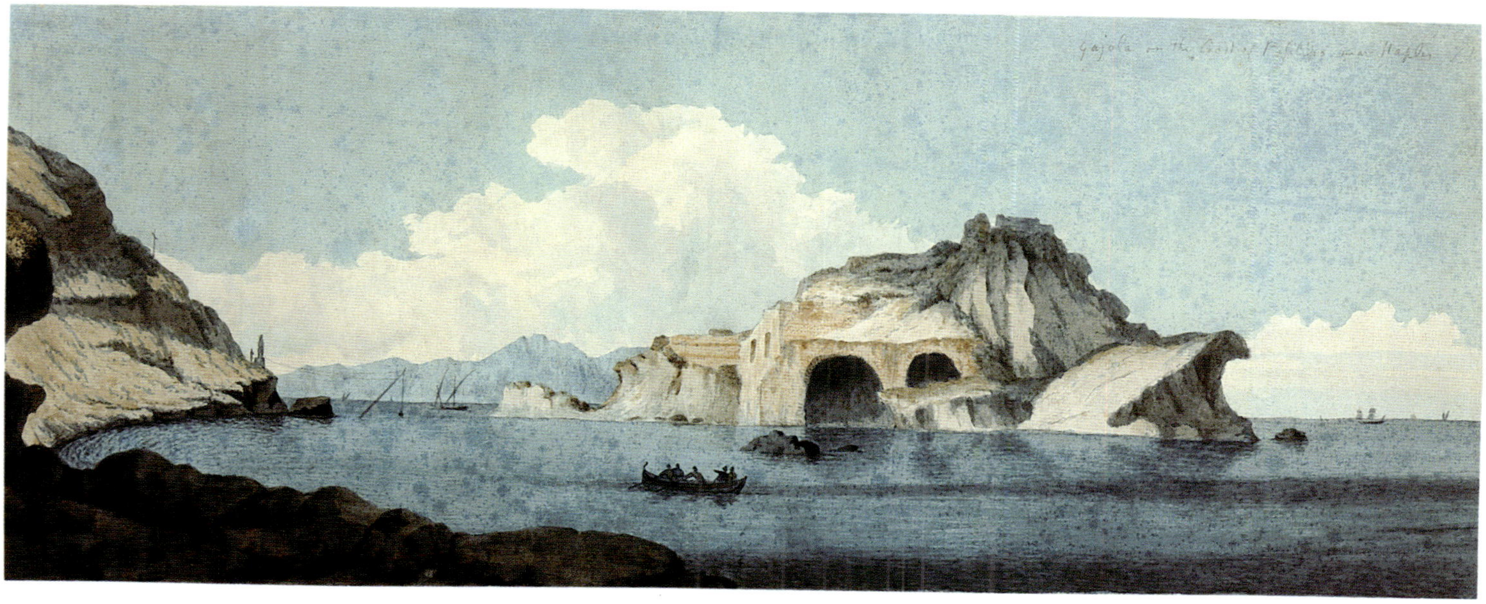

Fig. 40 Thomas Jones, *Gaiola on the Coast of Posillipo, near Naples*, 1796 (cat. no. 164).

many of the Italian scenes that are dated after 1783 are of the same characteristic type of oil painted on paper – larger and more finished than the studies made from Jones's apartments in Naples in 1782–3 – suggests that at least some of the undated examples were also produced in Britain. A closer look at this group is particularly revealing. The character, function and date of the works helps to add a more nuanced gloss to the often repeated idea that there is a gulf between the spontaneous expression of the small oil sketches and the laboured conventionalism of Jones's large finished oil paintings.

The Temple of Diana at Nemi (fig. 41), dated 1785, is a characteristic example of this type of oil painted on paper. At 36 × 52 cm ($14\frac{1}{4} \times 20\frac{1}{2}$ inches), it is bigger than works such as *Buildings in Naples* (cat. no. 110) and typically it has an elaborate and prominent title which forms part of the work, rather than the inscription of information on the back for future reference – as is normally the case with the oil sketches made on the spot. In addition to the title and signature, there is also a number, in this case '29'. Many of these larger oils on paper have numbers, and though there are many questions to be answered about their function, it seems more likely that they refer to their position in a sequence rather than their source material. There are only two examples of sketchbook drawings (cat. nos 68 and 70) which relate directly to oils on paper and their numbers do not tally.[43] The fact that only two of the numbered larger oils on paper are after known pencil sketches might lead one to conclude that at least some of the others were painted on the spot if there was not further evidence that they were carefully finished studio works.[44] The figures that populate the works, in distinction to the deserted architectural studies made in Naples, are also carefully considered as part of the composition, and they are redolent of studio production. And then there are two works, *Near Chambéry* (cat. no. 66) and

Fig. 41 Thomas Jones, *View of the Temple of Diana at Nemi*, 1785 (cat. no. 146).

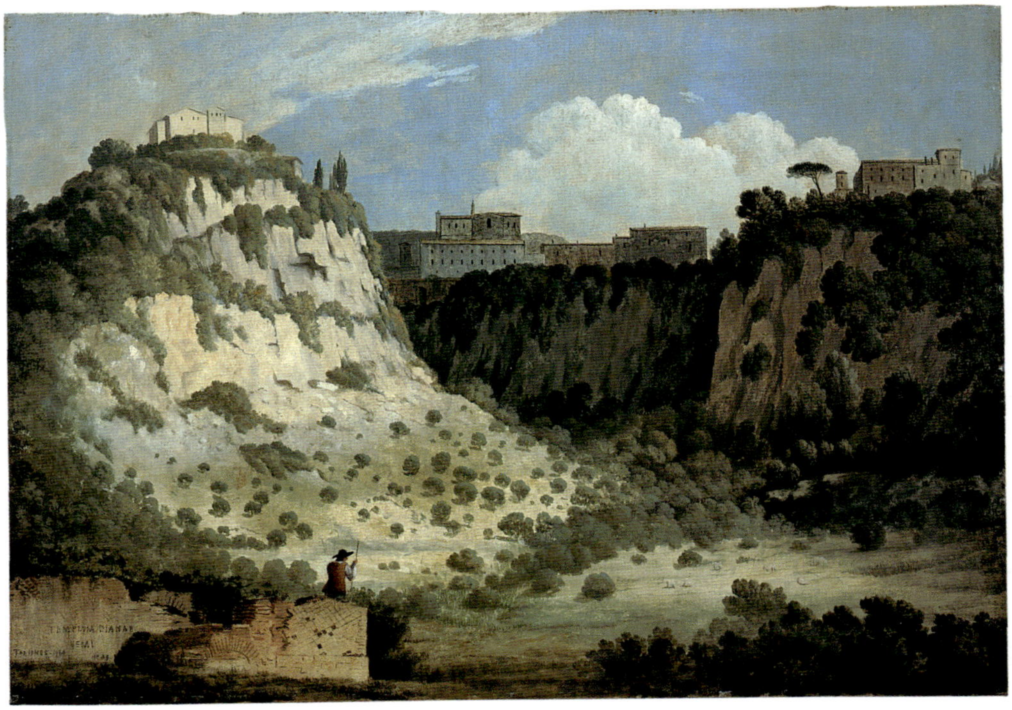

Montmélian (cat. no. 67), each measuring approximately 33 × 52cm, which cannot have been executed on the spot. During Jones's journey to Italy in 1776, he would only have had time to take a swift pencil sketch and the oils are clearly the result of careful preparation. They, together with *The Villa of Maecenas, Tivoli* (cat. no. 152), may date from around 1787 because of their close resemblance to the view of Ponte Loreto (cat. no. 151) which was presumably the 'Ponte Loreto near Nettuno' that Jones showed at the Academy in that year. The evidence to say that any of the undated larger oils on paper was executed after 1783 is rarely conclusive, but where there is an elaborate inscription, carefully worked out figures and stylistic similarities with dated works such as *Monte Compatri* (cat. no. 147), a later date must be a possibility.[45]

The other feature that is common to this group of larger oils on paper is that they remained in the hands of Jones's family after his death, underlining the fact that they were not commissions and were executed for his own pleasure. Even before his return to Britain, Jones noted that a still life 'was prosecuted and finished con Amore' and that he painted on it 'by way of Relaxation', and his professional failure gave him even more opportunities to paint 'for my own Amusement'.[46] Jones continued that he still kept 'this picture by me as a pleasant remembrance of Times past' and it was presumably as a pleasing 'remembrance' that he chose to work up many of his Italian pencil sketches as oils on paper. Moreover, as the client as well as the artist, Jones had nobody to please but himself and it would be surprising if he were not to invest his subjects with personal memories. Indeed, the choice of subject was presumably governed as much by recollections of the circumstances in which it was originally sketched as the scene's formal qualities. *Piperno* (cat. no. 126), for which there is some inconclusive technical evidence to suggest that it was painted after his return, is one of the more explicit examples of the artist painting 'a pleasant remembrance'.[47] Jones records how his party was met by 'some peasants with Buffaloes, who had come to meet us to drag up our chaises with those Animals to Piperno', and these are shown in the work; it may be that he painted it at the same time as he was transcribing passages from his diary.[48] In other cases, it was the ordinariness of a scene which possibly attracted the artist's attention. Thus, whilst the oil sketches focus on intimate corners of the landscape and the large commissions depict broader views of well-known spots, the larger oils on paper time and again show the everyday scenes that greeted him as he travelled. It is the road and means of conveyancing that predominate, so that works such as *Monte Compatri* (cat. no. 147) or *On the Tiber* (cat. no. 71) form a narrative of a journey that takes in a different Italy from the picturesque or historical sites frequented by tourists.

The larger oil on paper is a hybrid which reflects the uncertainty of Jones's position somewhere between amateur and professional. In scale, works such as *Walls of Rome* (cat. no. 70) have some of the intimacy of the sketches made on the spot, but more of the finish associated with commissioned oil paintings. They may be studio works, but they also retain enough of the immediacy of the sketches to have persuaded many writers that they, too, were made from nature. The larger oils on canvas may not convince as works of art, but this does not mean that it is only as a sketcher that Jones is deserving of acclaim. He did know how to preserve in studio works some of the spontaneity of his sketches, but we need to look away from his canvases for the evidence. The key point is that whilst Jones may have sketched in oils on paper, many of his oils on paper were painted in the studio.

The uncertainty over the dating of the larger oils on paper is matched by a similar set of issues relating to Jones's watercolours. The problem is not with finished watercolours such as *On the Road to Civita Castellana* (cat. no. 149) which are dated after the return to Britain and are based on earlier drawings. Rather, it is sketches such as *In the Bay of Salerno* (cat. no. 127), with their prominent inscriptions, that create difficulties. This example was no doubt begun on the spot as an outline drawing, but one wonders how many of this type were actually redrawn at a later date, as in the case of *Gaiola* (fig. 40; cat. no. 164). The paper historian Peter Bower has confirmed that the second date of 1796 does not record when the artist added colour to a drawing begun in 1778 – the paper dates from the 1790s – but when he copied a lost sketch from the earlier date. Crucially, Jones employs in *Gaiola* an identical palette to other drawings which are dated from the period of his stay in Italy, and there is the same relationship between the dominant outline and the limited washes of colour. In other words, there is no stylistic change that indicates that *Gaiola* was coloured twenty years later than *The Grand Cascatelle at Tivoli* (cat. no. 84). The similarity of the works suggests another possibility, however; namely, that whilst a drawing may have been outlined on the spot and be inscribed and dated to the period of Jones's stay, the colouring, or at least some of it, was added much later.

The drawings Jones made on the road to Santa Maria dei Monti (cat. nos 131–4) are instructive of his practice in this respect. Nine of them were made on the same day, 10 May 1781, in which case he would have had time only to make a pencil outline and perhaps add a few monochrome washes. Two, more richly coloured, works, which were begun on 6 May (cat. nos 131 and 132), have the word 'October' written over 'May', indicating later work, and on another occasion Jones went further in the process of transforming his original drawing. *In the Road to Santa Maria dei Monti, near Naples* (cat. no. 133) is inscribed '2d April 1781', but it is clearly the work of more than one day, and the application of multiple washes and gum arabic must have resulted from considerable work in the studio, even though its origin in an outline drawing with prominent inscriptions is not entirely obscured.[49] Jones mentions in 1778 that I 'touched on my Sketches for amusement' and again in October 1780 that he was forced by bad weather to abandon sketching from nature and took the opportunity of 'touching on the Sketches I had made', but there is every chance that the fundamental transformation involved in this case, as with *Gaiola*, may have taken place much later.[50] Certainly, the uniformity of many of these hybrid watercolours, which show a level of finish associated with studio works even as the pencil inscriptions and strong outlines show through, suggests that this was part of a more general pattern which saw the artist constantly revisiting and revising his sketches. Other than working for personal pleasure, fuelled by the desire to recreate fond memories, it is difficult to conceive of a motive for what remains an unusual practice and one that has no commercial rationale.[51]

The pattern of working that is here proposed for Jones's Italian oils and watercolours also lay at the heart of the composition and preparation of the *Memoirs*, and there is much to be gained from considering this text as the natural corollary to his artistic achievements in the latter part of his life. In the first part of the appendix, the author explains the *ad hoc* principles of its composition: it is a 'journal', he claims, which was assembled 'from short hints and Memoranda of a Diary' that he had kept for many years. The scarcity of dates and the more discursive style of the text for the period up to his departure for Italy suggests that this portion was composed from memory sparked by whatever memoranda came to hand, perhaps a day book for the dates; thereafter, he had a complete diary to take 'Extracts from', as he put it. This has been lost, but if it was anything like the short sequence of entries that are included in the Account Book for parts of 1783–4, 1790–1 and 1797, it means that we have been deprived of a considerable amount of extra detail by the editorial process. The 'Memoranda' Jones refers to presumably included items such as the thinly fictionalized account of a trip undertaken with Joseph Farington in 1767, and there are other places in the *Memoirs* where general recollections are punctuated with extensive details.[52] When we come to the Italian trip, however, the narrative takes on a different tone. The dates now refer to actual diary entries, so that the impact of the reportage is heightened. At the same time, Jones frequently introduces commentaries and longer digressions which act as a gloss on the action as it is related by the diary entries, only to break off the reflection with a comment such as 'but to resume my journal'.[53] The cumulative effect is a series of slightly disorientating shifts of perspective and tense which move us rapidly from events recorded in the present to more polished reflections presented with the benefit of hindsight. The point is that the shifts from swiftly noted reportage to more finished prose in the *Memoirs* have close structural parallels with the range of works he produced both in Italy and of Italian scenes on his return. Like his sketches, Jones revisited his diary notes to rework them in some cases, and in others to quote from them in a raw state.

Jones's motive in writing the *Memoirs* was no doubt the same that prompted the production of his retrospective views of Italy. The 'original Intention . . . was only for the Amusement of vacant hours in my present Retirement, and the Perusal of a Few', he wrote.[54] In a revealing passage, Jones talks of the triple pleasure he derived from his engagement with Italian scenery. The countryside was appreciated in advance through the process of copying, its pleasures were enhanced by sketching on the spot, and finally there was the joy of recollection that comes from perusing his studies. Now 'at this day', he wrote, I 'a third time enjoy those delightful Scenes, whenever I look over the Sketches I made on the spot, of such interesting Objects'.[55] To this list we might add the further satisfaction that came from reworking his sketches, making selections from his diaries and tidying up his memories and words into a more polished form. In the case of the text of the *Memoirs*, the process seems to have occupied Jones over a long period. The manuscript is dated November 1798 at the end, but at an earlier point in the narrative he refers to some 'painting Tools . . . many of which . . . I have still by me in the Year 1794', so there must have been a period when he was both writing and painting his memories of Italy.[56] It may be that he began the text earlier; certainly he was still revising it much later. Many passages are scored through – they have been deciphered and appear in the published version in brackets – and some were reworked. As Paul Oppé, the editor of the *Memoirs*, noted, Jones was partly concerned with matters of propriety since he went to some lengths to mask the nature of his irregular relationship with Maria Moncke, but in other cases it is a matter of adding new material and rewording, as well as editing.[57] The point about the amateur, though, is that without the end point of a sale or commission there is no way that one can ever be sure about the status of a work – finished, in progress, or incomplete. This is true of the *Memoirs*, just as with many of the views of Italy he worked up for his own amusement. Any drawing or painting by an amateur can be reworked and, given Jones's interest in returning to his sketches, it is not inconceivable that even the oil sketches of Rome and Naples, which are always thought to epitomize a direct response to nature, were touched up later. Sadly, Jones's reticence about his later career means that we shall never be able to say for certain whether this was the case, but an amateur artist, like the unpublished author, has the rare privilege of always being able to return to a work.

Jones was, of course, a very particular type of amateur artist by virtue of also having once been a struggling professional, and in many ways it was a lack of success that made possible his unique achievement. It was the artist's failure to play the market effectively in Rome and Naples that gave him the time to produce oil sketches for his own pleasure as well as begin the process of transforming his utilitarian drawings into independent watercolours. In an important sense, then, Jones's journey from professional artist to amateur began earlier than 1787 with his inheritance of Pencerrig. Jones, as a professional artist with some money, acted for much of his time as an amateur who followed his calling and worked for pleasure or at least outside the cash nexus. Actual financial independence merely confirmed a way of working that marked him out from fellow professionals.

Jones's finest works may well be marked with 'originality', but it was the singularity of his position, shifting between amateur and professional, that actually made his achievements possible. And it was this, too, that meant that his works remained hidden for so long. His best paintings were not produced to be sold and he bequeathed to his family the financial means to make their sale unnecessary so that our rediscovery of Jones's work follows the typical trajectory of amateur artists.

Notes

1 *Memoirs*, p. 141.
2 Ibid.
3 Ibid.
4 Ibid., p. 33.
5 Ibid., p. 114.
6 Ibid., p. 115.
7 Ibid., p. 122.
8 Jones records the details in the Account Book (cat. no. 73).
9 *Morning Chronicle*, 13 May, 1784; 29 April, 1784.
10 *Memoirs*, p. 26.
11 *St James's Chronicle*, 4–6 May 1784.
12 *Morning Post*, 1 May 1784.
13 *St James's Chronicle*, 4–6 May 1784. As a result of recent conservation it is now clear that the view of the Bay of Pozzuoli (cat. no. 107) dates from 1786. This discovery was made too late for the implications of this to be discussed here other than to note that it underlines the way Jones continued to explore Italian subjects back in England.
14 Ibid., 12–15 May 1787.
15 *Memoirs*, p. 141.
16 Jones argued in 1769 that when the competition for patronage is strong 'talent' and 'great Exertions' are less important than 'great Interest' (*Memoirs*, p. 20).
17 *Memoirs*, p. 141. This was presumably Joseph Farington.
18 Ibid., p. 19.
19 Ibid., p. 118.
20 Ibid., p. 141.
21 Malkin, 1804, p. 357; Hallett, 1991, p. 10; Barbier, 1963, pp. 71–2.
22 Ledger, 1992, pp. 13–14.
23 Barbier, 1963, pp. 71–2.
24 Jones refers to another set of '6 small Drawings in Chiaro Scuro for a publication of Baker' in the portion of the diary bound with the Account Book (cat. no. 73). Entry for the '30th to the 5 November' 1797.
25 Baker, 1795, p. 224.
26 Ibid., p. 225.
27 The perpetrator of this crime against Jones's youthful inspiration was identified by Baker as the 'last possessor

of the estate', his brother, though the writer might have meant his father, in which case the artist's impassioned attack could be interpreted as a complaint against paternal oppression.

28 Farington, *Diary*, vol. III, 28 February 1798, p. 986.

29 Portion of diary bound with the Account Book (cat. no. 73). Entry for '28th of July 1797'. This was not strictly true, since *Classical Landscape* (cat. no. 156) is dated 1794.

30 It was described in the catalogue as 'Portrait of his own family and Mr Jones'.

31 Farington, *Diary*, vol. III, 1 April 1798, p. 996; *Whitehall Evening Post*, 5–8 May 1798. The *Winter Scene in Italy* was better received by the *London Packet*, however (4–6 May 1798).

32 *Memoirs*, p. 141.

33 For this issue, see Smith, 2002, pp. 99–103.

34 *Morning Herald*, 4 May 1809.

35 Two other oil sketches painted in 1797 on 'light brown Cartridge paper' do not seem to have survived (diary entry for 28 July in the Account Book; cat. no. 73).

36 *Memoirs*, p. 141.

37 Malkin, 1804, p. 225.

38 Ibid., p. 224. For a spirited discussion of the oak as a national symbol and much more, see Coventry, 1987.

39 Oliver, 1970, p. 30.

40 An earlier oil sketch, *Field near Pencerrig* (cat. no. 49), also shows a young plantation.

41 Baker, 1795, p. 217.

42 See Smith, 2002, pp. 141–2 for this issue.

43 The highest number is forty-two and so far only eleven numbered works have been traced, which suggests either a painfully high rate of attrition or perhaps that the sequence refers to a list of possible subjects.

44 The corollary to this argument is that there must be a number of missing sketchbooks and the fact that the existing books only cover a part of the Italian trip certainly supports this conclusion.

45 Perhaps as many as a dozen examples in this exhibition were painted in Britain.

46 *Memoirs*, p. 103; p. 139.

47 The paper on which it is painted is possibly an English grey wrapping.

48 *Memoirs*, p. 77.

49 The larger sketchbook (cat. no. 75) also contains later reworking in pen and ink dating from May 1802.

50 *Memoirs*, p. 83, p. 100.

51 Francis Towne's outlines also underwent a similar process of transformation and many of the arguments put forward by Timothy Wilcox for Towne hold true for Jones (Wilcox, 1997, pp. 9–13). The two artists were friends, though on balance it is unlikely that there was a direct influence either way since the crucial factor in both cases was that they had sufficient financial independence to invest time in working for their own satisfaction.

52 This is deposited at the National Library of Wales.

53 *Memoirs*, p. 56.

54 Ibid., p. 140.

55 Ibid., p. 60.

56 Ibid., p. 43.

57 What appears to be a fair copy of the *Memoirs* remains in the possession of the family. This was possibly made for Elizabetha Dale, the artist's youngest daughter, to compensate for the fact that she did not inherit the original manuscript.

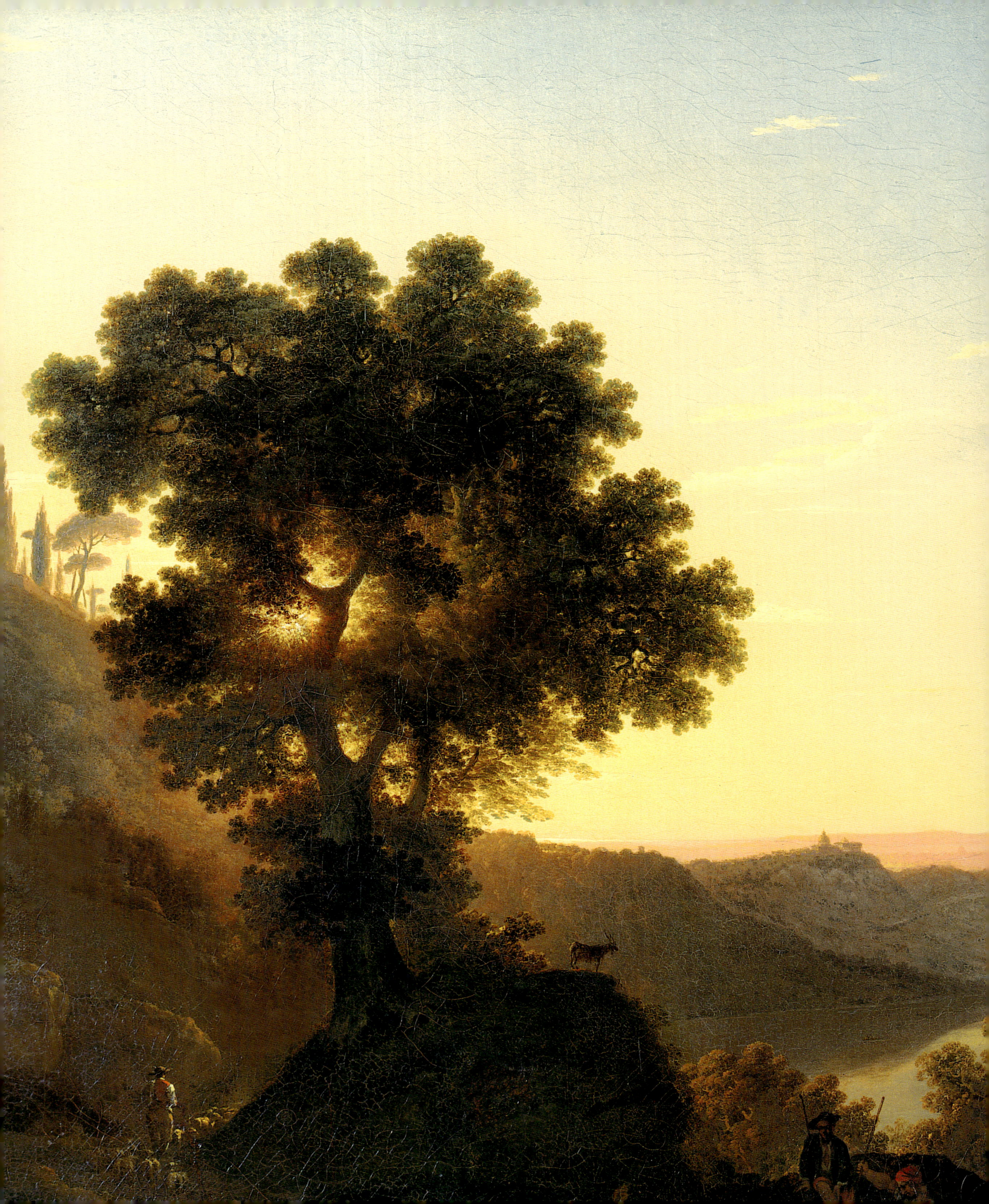

THOMAS JONES: A TECHNICAL STUDY OF HIS OIL PAINTINGS

Kate Lowry

Hitherto, there have been few investigations of Thomas Jones's materials and painting technique and little has been published.[1] The collecting together of such a large number of his oil paintings, both on canvas and on paper, and from all periods of his life for this exhibition has provided an ideal opportunity to carry out technical examinations, using standard investigative techniques such as microscopy, infra-red imaging and X-radiography. Information collected in this way, combined with evidence derived from the surviving documentation of Jones's *Memoirs* and Account Book, has enabled us to gain a far greater understanding of his output than was previously possible. This research, following a two-year investigation of the materials and techniques employed by Thomas Jones's teacher, the landscape painter Richard Wilson (1713–1782), funded by the Getty Grant Program,[2] has also allowed us to make comparisons between Wilson's working practice and that of his pupil. This essay contains a summary of our findings.

Thomas Jones became a paying pupil of Wilson at his studio in Covent Garden in London in 1763. He paid Wilson fifty guineas for his two-year pupillage, the first year of which was to be devoted entirely to drawing in black and white chalks on paper of a middle tint, working either from Wilson's drawings and paintings or from nature. Wilson believed this would give his pupil a good grounding 'in the Principles of Light & Shade, without being dazzled and misled by the flutter of Colours'.[3] In the process of learning to draw, Jones would also have learned the art of composition from Wilson, who was adept at producing idealized landscape views derived from a combination of his studies from nature and his imaginary arrangements of forms and effects of light. The second year of Jones's training was presumably devoted to painting. Jones's *Memoirs* do not give much detail as to what form Wilson's teaching of the art of landscape painting took, but the pupils observed him at work,[4] made painted copies after his compositions and may also have assisted with the early stages of Wilson's paintings known as deadcolouring and forwarding.

FACING PAGE Detail of cat. no. 56.

Oil paint dries relatively slowly and must be applied in layers, each being allowed to dry before the next is added, to avoid the paint cracking. Once the master had brushed in the main lines of the composition, using a red-brown or grey-brown paint, a thin underpainting or deadcolouring was laid in by the apprentices. After the deadcolouring had dried thoroughly, it was rubbed over with oil and Wilson made two or more further applications of paint to complete the work.[5]

Earlier generations of painters had relied on apprentices for the preparation of their materials in the studio. However, by this period, artists could buy primed canvases and oil paints from the colourmen who had been established in London since the beginning of the eighteenth century. There was now little need for the studio apprentices and pupils to prepare supports or grind pigments in oil. As there is no mention of such activities being carried out in Wilson's studio, it can be assumed that he used commercially prepared materials. Examples of paintings by Jones and Wilson from the 1760s and 1770s show that both artists commonly used a medium-weight linen canvas with a simple weave. However, twill weave is occasionally found, as in Wilson's *Dinas Bran* (National Museums & Galleries of Wales) and Jones's *The Bard* (cat. no. 31), both dating from the 1770s. The wooden stretcher on which the canvas was strained had relatively narrow outer members with square morticed joints, and those of a larger size also had diagonal corner braces. Though few of these stretchers survive, their outline can often be observed in the lines of cracklure present in the paintings themselves. Outlines of a similar stretcher can be seen in Jones's *Lake Nemi* (cat. no. 58). These canvases also came in standard sizes, as is evidenced by an entry around 1776 in one of Jones's notebooks, which contains a list of canvas sizes together with prices for finished paintings.[6]

Before the canvases were stretched up, the colourman coated a length of the cloth with an oil ground, usually consisting of two layers of lead white and chalk bound in linseed oil, sometimes separated by an intermediate application of size or glue. This was then cut to the required dimensions and attached to the stretcher. Examination of Wilson's paintings has shown that such commercially prepared double grounds are very common. Further investigation of Thomas Jones's early works reveals the occurrence of both commercial and the artist's own grounds. *The Bard*, 1774 (cat. no. 31), is on a commercially prepared canvas with unpainted ground visible on the surviving original turnover edges, whilst *Classical Landscape*, 1772 (cat. no. 24), and *Italian View: On the Arno*, 1773 (cat. no. 26), are probably on the artist's own preparation applied after stretching, as bare canvas is visible beyond the edge of the ground where some original turnover survives.

There are also indications in Thomas Jones's writings that he occasionally prepared his canvases himself. A diary entry made by Jones in late 1776 in Rome describes a size recommended by Francesco Renaldi, made of boiled rice, applied in two coats and then smoothed with a pumice stone before priming the canvas. This, he declared, was preferable to any other for preparing canvases, as it was not so apt to crack or peel off as the common pastes were inclined to.[7] Much later, in 1791, he described two landscapes painted on ticking cloth, 33 × 25 inches, prepared by himself at Pencerrig in 1776 and given a coat of Spanish Brown after his return from Italy in 1783.[8]

The ground itself provides the artist with a relatively smooth, non-absorbent surface on which to paint. The colour of the ground can be varied by the inclusion of pigments in addition to the normal lead white and chalk content. The ground colour is a matter of the artist's personal choice and affects the final appearance of the painting wherever it is left exposed or only thinly overpainted. Early on in his career, Wilson used either a grey or red ground and his later landscapes have grey or white grounds. Thomas Jones preferred to use a grey ground for most of his early landscapes, as in *Garthmyl Hall*, 1771–2 (private collection), *Classical Landscape*, 1772 (cat. no. 24), *Italian View: On the Arno*, 1773 (cat. no. 26), *The Bard*, 1774 (cat. no. 31) and *Maeslough House*, 1776 (cat. no. 37) although white grounds occur occasionally, as in *River Landscape with Figures Beside a Weir*, 1775 (cat. no. 34).

Thomas Jones's Account Book (cat. no. 73) gives us some information about the supports he purchased later on in Rome and Naples, and his entries suggest that he was buying standard sizes of ready-stretched and prepared canvas.[9] However, the origin and quality of the linen is hardly mentioned and only rarely does he note the purchase of canvas from France or Holland or specify a fine or smooth cloth,[10] so we can only assume that most of the canvases that he purchased were of a standard weave and of local origin.

The canvases Jones used in Italy usually have a rough, open weave. One of his first large-scale Italian paintings, *A Storm – Prospero, Miranda and Caliban Spying the Shipwrecked Ferdinand* (cat. no. 57), painted in Rome in 1778, has a very coarse, simple-weave linen support, similar to that of Wilson's *Banditti Around a Tent* (National Museums & Galleries of Wales), painted in Rome in 1752. Both *View of Lake Avernus*, *c.*1779 (cat. no. 104) and *Lake Nemi*, 1782 (cat. no. 58) have similar coarse-weave supports. The standard size canvases he bought in Italy were usually measured in *palmi*.[11] However, Jones sometimes bought a long length of canvas measured in *canne*,[12] which suggests that he may occasionally have stretched up his own cloth. His normal practice in Italy, however, seems to have been to purchase his canvases ready primed.[13]

Thomas Jones only once mentions the precise colour of an oil ground on canvas, in connection with *Campi Flegrei* of 1783, a painting which is untraced. This was apparently painted on a white ground, though few other cases have so far been detected in this period. *A Storm – Prospero, Miranda and Caliban*, 1778 (cat. no. 57), has a grey ground,[14] whilst *The Bay of Naples*, 1782 (cat. no. 106), has a coarse-textured light red ground and *Lake Nemi*, 1782 (cat. no. 58), a coarse dark red ground. In the latter painting, the ground is used to great effect as a foil to the foliage of the tree against the sky wherever it is left unpainted. Leaving parts of the ground exposed to play a part in the final appearance of the painting in this way is characteristic of Wilson's practice, but is rare for Jones, whose grounds are usually completely hidden by the subsequent paint layers.

In addition to prepared canvases, Thomas Jones recorded the purchase of colours in his Italian Account Book. These ready-made oil paints were supplied to the artist by the colourmen in pigs' bladders. Unfortunately, Jones rarely specifies which colours he bought. However, analysis carried out so far on his paintings,[15] together with the few available indications of specific pigments purchased in Italy, shows that the content of his palette coincided largely with that of his master Wilson. Jones used the common red, yellow and brown earths, Prussian blue, Naples yellow, vermilion, lead white and ivory black as well as red and yellow lakes. In addition, Jones mentions the purchase of Cologne earth[16] and in his late diary entries he describes the use of asphaltum and Cologne earth to add modifying glazes in the final stages of painting.[17] There is no record that Wilson used these organic tarry browns in his paintings and it would appear from this and other comments in his *Memoirs* that Jones relied more heavily on the use of transparent colours than did Wilson.[18]

Jones also adopted two unusual pigments, orange orpiment and Patent yellow. His diary entries in the early 1790s describe their frequent use to achieve sunlit effects.[19] Orange orpiment, better known as realgar, is a naturally occurring sulphide of arsenic with a long history of use in European painting until the end of the seventeenth century. It makes a rare reappearance in Jones's paintings. This pigment has been firmly identified in his *Classical Landscape* of 1772 (cat. no. 24), which suggests that he used it throughout his career, not just in his later paintings.[20] Patent yellow, lead oxy-chloride, on the other hand, which was patented in England in 1780, could only have been available to Jones after this date and has been found in his *Classical Landscape with a River* of 1794 (cat. no. 156).[21] The addition of these bright orange and yellow pigments to his palette enabled Jones to produce much warmer effects of sunlight than any found in Wilson's paintings (figs 42 and 43).

Fig. 42 (BELOW LEFT) Cross section showing the use of orange orpiment in Thomas Jones's *Classical Landscape*, 1772 (cat. no. 24).

Fig. 43 (BELOW RIGHT) Cross section showing the use of Patent yellow in Thomas Jones's *Classical Landscape with a River*, 1794 (cat. no. 156).

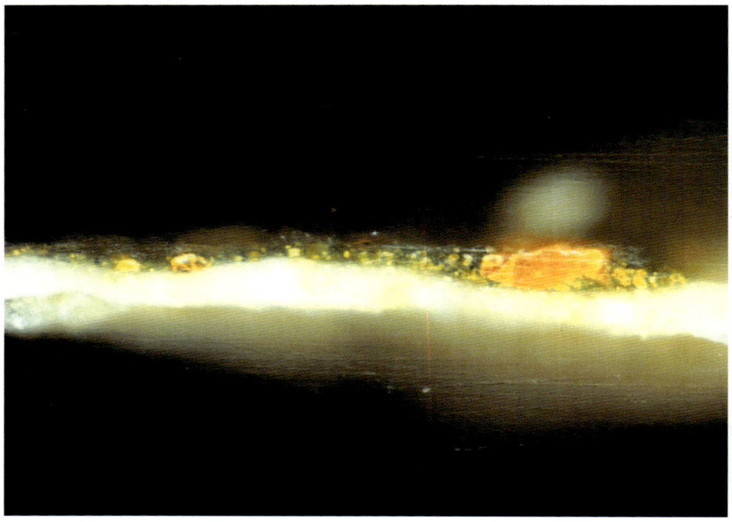

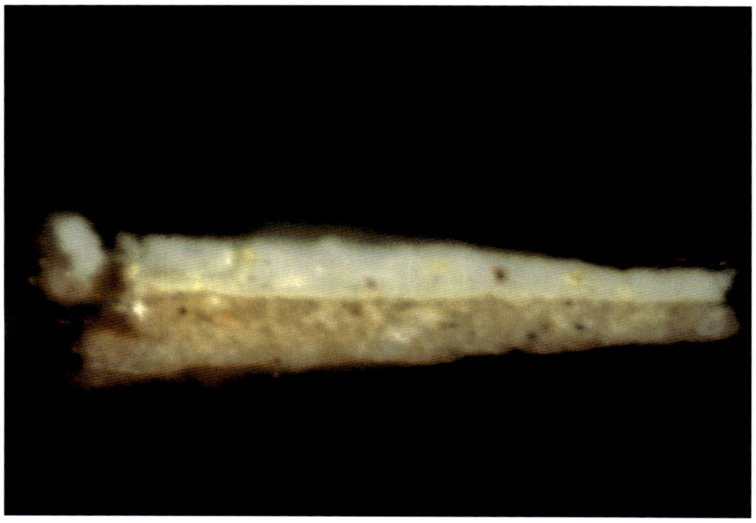

The binding medium used by the colourmen in preparing paints for sale was generally linseed oil, although nut oil was sometimes used for white and blue pigments, being less prone to yellowing. Samples analysed from Wilson's paintings have shown additional traces of resin which may indicate the artist's use of megilp,[22] an oil–resin medium consisting of linseed oil and mastic resin varnish added to the paint on the palette to improve handling and to produce transparent effects. In his Account Book, Thomas Jones gives a recipe for a white drying oil containing nut oil, mastic resin and sugar of lead, which he believed was used by Wilson in Rome.[23] It is therefore likely that Jones first learned to use oil–resin media in Wilson's studio and that he used them throughout his career, although it is only in Jones's late diary entries from the 1790s that we find direct evidence of his use of megilp or a mixture of megilp and white drying oil for glazing and retouching his paintings, some of which he had begun a decade earlier.[24]

It was Wilson's practice to place the main lines of the composition over the ground using a red-brown or grey-brown paint before painting proper began.[25] For this reason, underdrawing is rarely detected in his work. Similarly, few signs of underdrawing are visible in Thomas Jones's oil paintings on canvas. Notable exceptions are *The Bard* (cat. no. 31), where the artist has altered the outlines of the stones and *Lake Nemi* (cat. no. 58), where the clouds have been placed with a pencilled outline. More extensive drawing may be present in this latter painting, but the red ground may prevent its detection with the infra-red camera. Once established in Italy, we know that Jones made detailed sketches on paper, in the field, of views he wanted to reproduce later in oil.[26] It is highly likely, therefore, that he would have copied at least some of their detail on to his canvas before painting (fig. 44).

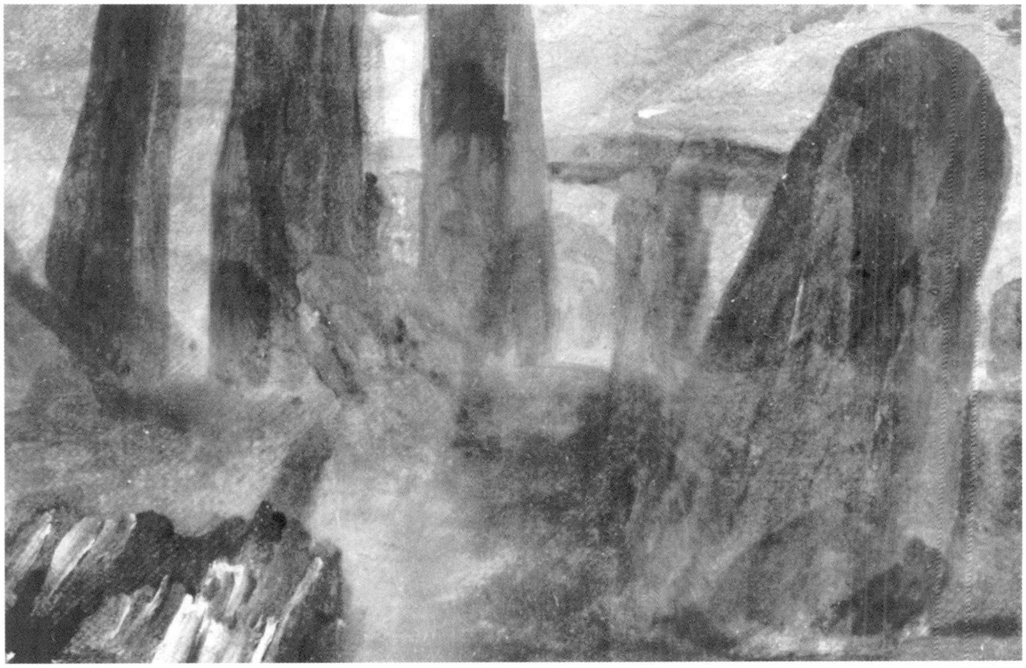

Fig. 44 Infra-red image of the underdrawing of Thomas Jones's *The Bard*, 1774, showing a detail of the stones (cat. no. 31).

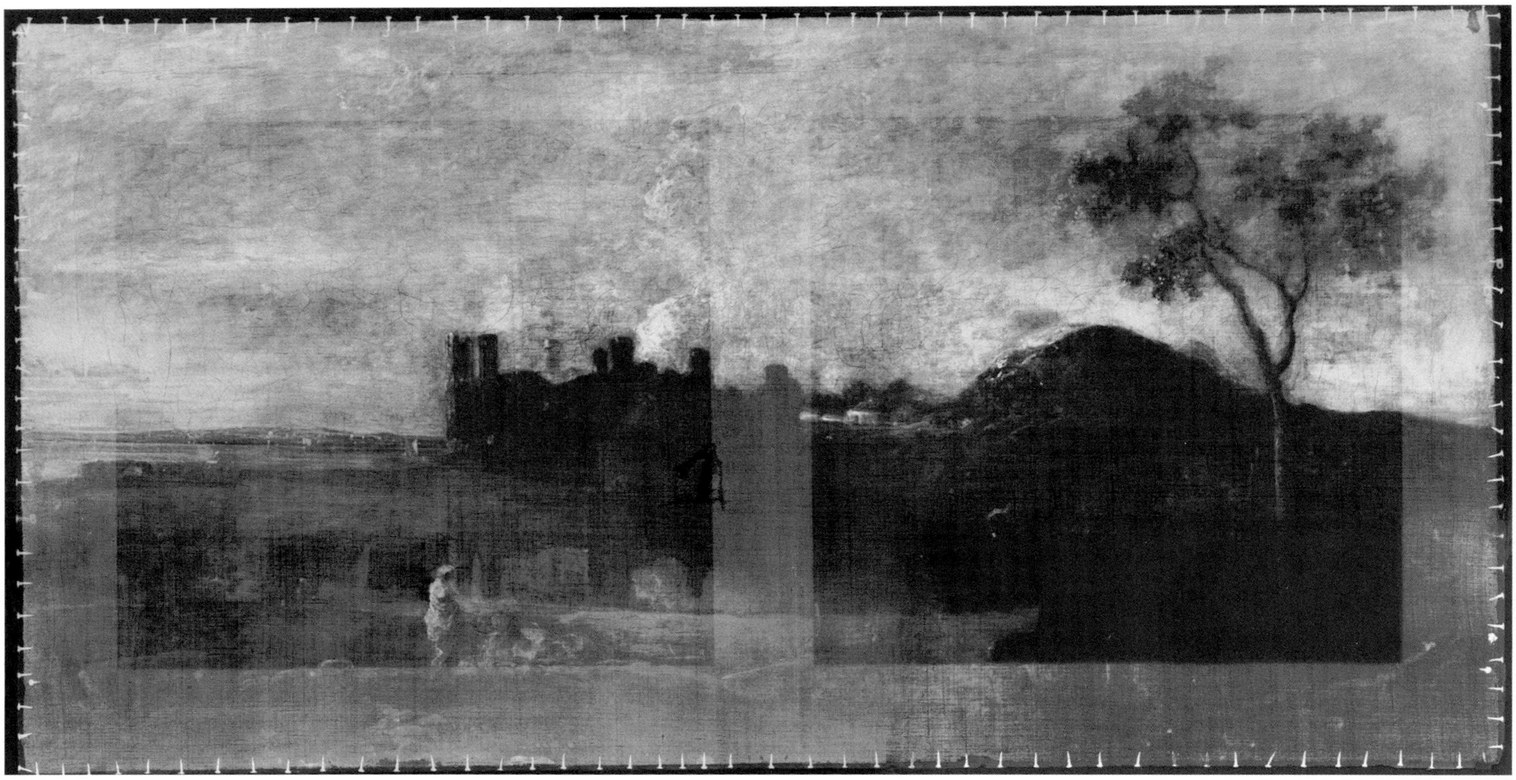

Fig. 45 X-ray image of Richard Wilson's *Caernarfon Castle*, National Museums & Galleries of Wales, Cardiff.

While the materials employed by Jones were generally similar to those of his master, Wilson, his painting technique was very different. In Wilson's practice, the deadcolouring consisted of a thin wash of blue for the sky and another for the 'air tint', and Prussian blue and a red earth for the landscape. In the second painting, he placed the half-tints and shadows and for the third painting he deepened the darks and placed the final highlights.[27] Comparison of the X-ray images of Wilson's and Jones's landscapes shows the difference in their styles of underpainting and forwarding. Wilson always made a bold distinction between the sky and landscape areas. This is evidenced by the strong tonal contrast in the X-radiograph. He reserved areas of foliage and buildings to be outlined against the sky from the outset and made changes to these later when necessary (fig. 45).

Several entries in his *Memoirs* show that Jones followed a procedure of deadcolouring and forwarding,[28] but his late method, outlined in his diary of 1791, shows that the deadcolouring of his skies now differed from Wilson's simple thin wash of blue. Jones describes how he employed warm yellows and oranges to establish the lightest areas of sunlight he required, before merging them with the surrounding blue tones.[29] Jones's approach to the laying in of the main features of his composition was much more cautious than that of his master. As a result, his reserved areas appear less distinct in the X-ray image and few clear changes of mind are visible (fig. 46).

The two artists also differed in their handling of paint, and this is seen particularly in their depiction of foliage and vegetation. Wilson's brushwork

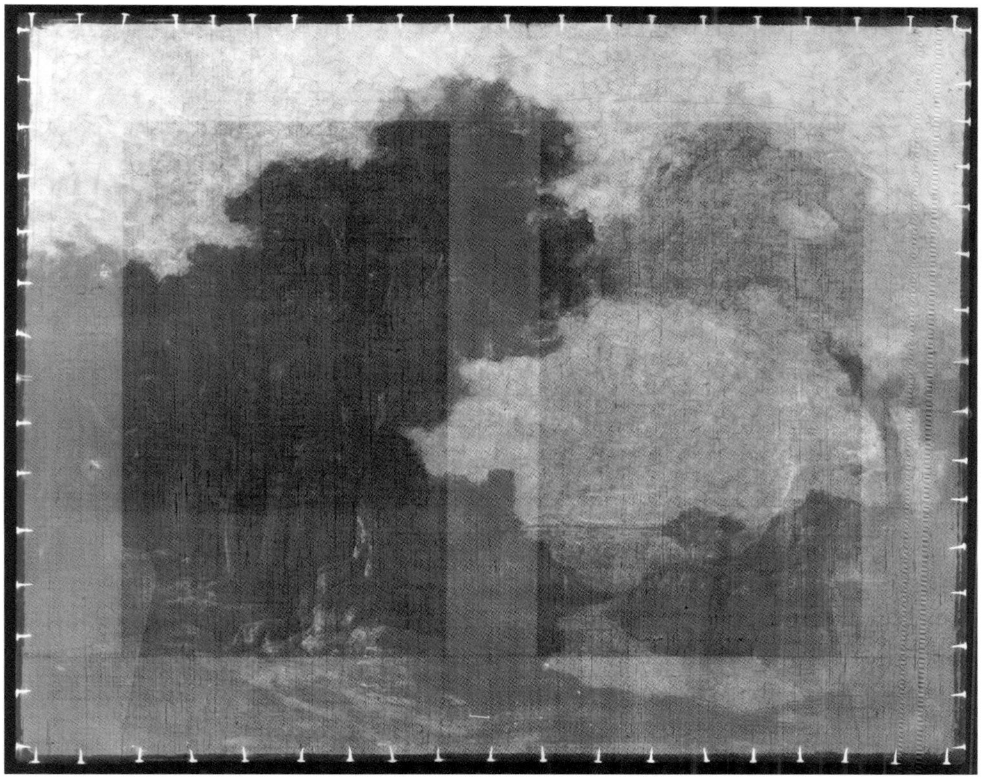

Fig. 46 X-ray image of Thomas Jones's *Classical Landscape*, 1772 (cat. no. 24).

is always bold, whilst Jones uses fine brushstrokes both for the leaves on his distant trees and to produce a smoothly detailed enamel-like finish for foreground plants. Jones's late accounts of his landscape painting also show that he relied heavily on repeated final glazing to increase the depths of his darks and the warmth of his sunlit effects, as well as scumbling with cooler, more opaque colours in order to reduce the warmth of his initial tones.[30]

Their handling of skies and the far distance is also quite different. Wilson frequently worked wet-in-wet, applying new paint before an earlier application had dried. This permitted him to blend his sky tones and clouds more smoothly and allowed him to establish his horizons with especial brilliance. This all contributed to the illusion of aerial recession. Jones, on the other hand, rarely worked wet-in-wet. The horizon lines in *Field near Pencerrig*, *c.*1776 (cat. no. 49) and *Pencerrig*, 1772 (cat. no. 41), are notable exceptions. In his later diaries, he describes how he built up his layers methodically, always allowing them to dry fully between sessions.[31] The result is a rather precise and mechanical handling of spatial effects, typified by the way he drew the clouds in over the sky in *Lake Nemi* (cat. no. 58) and painted them separately. Perhaps it is not surprising that contemporary critics bemoaned his lack of aerial perspective.[32]

In modern times, interest in Thomas Jones's paintings has centred not so much on his canvas paintings, but on his oils on paper. The use of oil on paper was not unique to Jones. However, it was a departure from the practice of Wilson's studio. Although the best-known examples of this type of work are those produced during his time in Italy, Jones was already using the technique prior to 1776 to record the Welsh countryside.[33] He always refers to them as studies, suggesting that he produced them to capture particular views in a finished form for his own satisfaction, rather than regarding them as a marketable product.

The papers used for these works are varied in type and colour. He used a coarse white wrapping paper containing pieces of animal hair and hemp for his landscape painted at *Gadbridge* (cat. no. 39). *A View in Radnorshire* (cat. no. 45) and *Pencerrig, 1776* (cat. no. 44), are both painted on a dark brown wrapping. *Pencerrig* (cat. no. 41), is on a lighter-weight, coarse-textured pale brown wrapping paper which was folded and creased to wrap an object prior to its use as a painting support. A heavy white paper, Italian in origin, with a rough textured surface is often found in his Italian oil sketches, as in the two works entitled *Buildings in Naples* (cat. nos 108 and 110). Another Italian paper with strongly marked laid lines is found in *A Cavern near S. Agnese Outside the Porta Pia at Rome* (cat. no. 61) and *Suburbs of Naples with Figures and Bridge* (private collection).

Jones's Account Book for his second visit to Naples indicates that he bought a good deal of paper during his stay, most of which he describes as Dutch,[34] although Genoese and Roman (tinted) papers are also mentioned.[35] He also used coloured papers: *Piperno* (cat. no. 126) is painted on a grey paper and both *Monte Compatri* (cat. no. 147) and *Italian Landscape at Sunset* (cat. no. 123) have a blue wrapping paper support. For some of his late Welsh studies in this medium, Jones recorded the use of a light brown cartridge paper, although no examples of this have yet been found.[36]

In his *Memoirs* and later diary, Jones mentions working in oil on paper which had first been prepared with a priming or ground.[37] Priming gives a smooth surface upon which to paint, eliminating the fibrous texture of the paper and its colour. The colour and extent of the priming varies as much as his choice of paper. Although some of his papers are primed, others are not. *A View in Radnorshire* (cat. no. 45), *Gadbridge* (cat. no. 39), *Pencerrig* (cat. no. 44) and *Pencerrig* (cat. no. 41), and *Field near Pencerrig* (cat. no. 49) for example, are painted directly on to the paper. In the first three of these, the paper is almost entirely hidden by the paint layer, whilst in the latter two, areas of the support are left exposed to form the lightest tones of the composition. Some of his papers are only partly primed, as in *Buildings in Naples* (cat. no. 110), where only the buildings have a white underpaint layer, whilst in *River Scene, on the Wye* (cat. no. 35) only the landscape is underpainted a pale yellow-brown. The view of *Piperno* (cat. no. 126) has a partial white ground thickly applied beneath the sky and distant mountains, effectively hiding the grey of the underlying paper in these areas.

In his late diary, Jones describes a priming for paper made of whiting or chalk and a weak size.[38] Analysis of the orange priming of *The Capella Nuova Outside the Porta di Chiaia* (cat. no. 113), has shown it contains chalk, kaolin and red earth bound with animal glue.[39] In the foreground of

Piperno (cat. no. 126), Jones has written in pencil at the lower edge, 'starch'. The evident softness of this ground, now damaged by small scratches, may indicate that he used this material as the binding medium. It is possible that he also used oil for some of his primings, but this has not yet been investigated.

The colour of the priming of Jones's oils on paper ranges from the pale grey of *Buildings in Naples, with the North-East Side of the Castel Nuovo* (cat. no. 108), *A Cavern near S. Agnese* (cat. no. 61), *The Villa of Maecenas, Tivoli* (cat. no. 152) and *Tivoli* (cat. no. 64), to the pale yellow-brown of *Suburbs of Naples with Figures and Bridge* (private collection) and the white ground of *House and Tree with Vesuvius in the Background* (cat. no. 118), *Monte Compatri* (cat. no. 147) and *Italian Landscape at Sunset* (cat. no. 123). In the case of the last two works, this is used to hide the blue of the paper completely.

In many of these works, underdrawing is clearly visible when viewed with infra-red light. The type of underdrawing varies from the fluid lines found in *Field near Pencerrig* (cat. no. 49), *Cavern near S. Agnese* (cat. no. 61) and *Tivoli* (cat. no. 64), which is reminiscent of Wilson's drawing style, to the tight, detailed drawing of *Suburbs of Naples with Figures and Bridge* (private collection) and *Capella Nuova* (cat. no. 113), which is more like the style of Jones's Italian drawings produced in pencil and ink during his sketching tours. Although Jones may have made some of these underdrawings in the field or from a window, he also copied some of them in the studio from drawings made outdoors. This is obvious from the dating of *Monte Compatri* (cat. no. 147) to 1785, after his return from Italy. In some instances, Jones drew details in pencil over the painted surface, as in *Suburbs of Naples* (private collection) and *House and Tree with Vesuvius in the Background* (cat. no. 118). Furthermore, features present in the underdrawing are not always realized in the subsequent painting. The underdrawing for *Monte Compatri* includes a donkey, subsequently left unpainted, whilst that of *House and Tree with Vesuvius in the Background* contains alterations to the buildings and a woman's figure painted out in the lower left foreground. Such evidence again suggests works produced or at least reworked in the studio. Even in the more spontaneous-looking early oil studies such as *Pencerrig*, 1772 (cat. no. 41), and *Field near Pencerrig*, *c.*1776 (cat. no. 49), the underdrawings show that Jones added features such as trees at the painting stage which were not present in the initial drawing, suggesting that he inserted these later for compositional reasons (see fig. 47).

The high tone, crisp brushwork and simplicity of composition found in the best of Jones's oils on paper has drawn comparison with the *plein-air* painters of the nineteenth century. There is no doubt that both his master Wilson and Jones's contemporaries occasionally painted in oil outdoors,[40] but it is not clear from his *Memoirs* whether, or how frequently, Jones actually did so.[41] From his writings, we know that several of the oil studies were done from his window both in Naples[42] and at Pencerrig.[43] Other oil studies

Fig. 47 The underdrawing of *Field near Pencerrig* c.1776 (cat. no. 49).

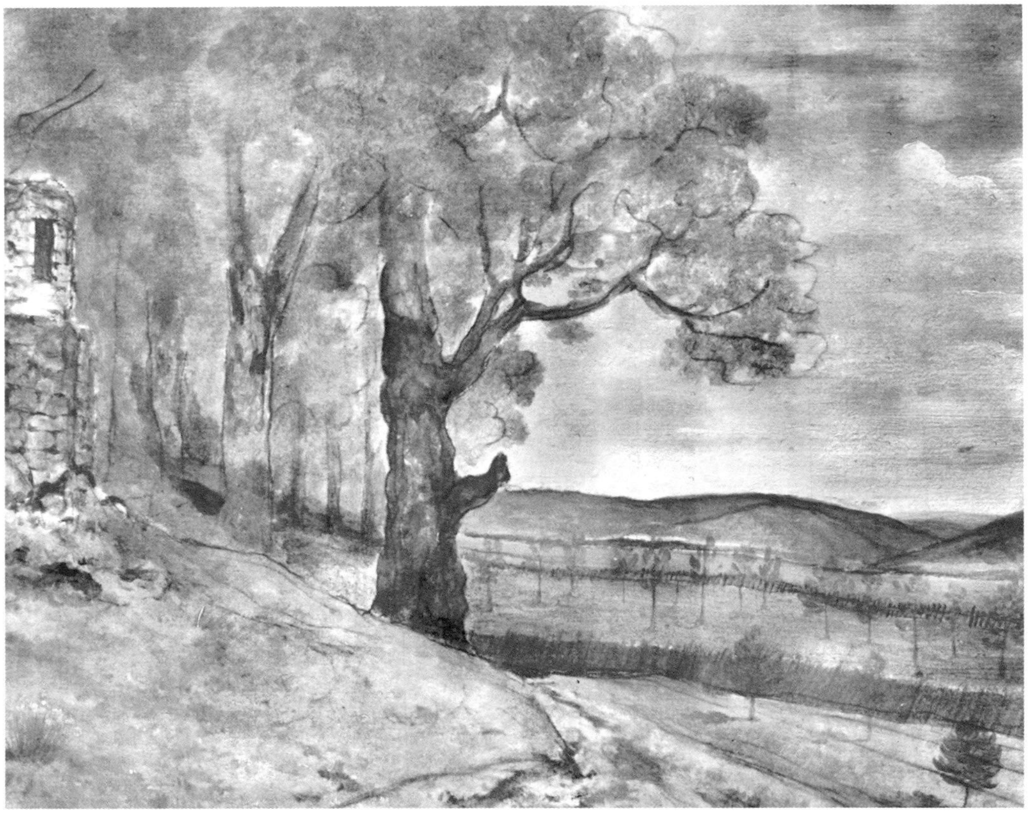

were worked up from drawings done on the spot, either on return to his lodgings when in Italy, as in *Suburbs of Naples* (private collection), or after his return home, as in *Monte Compatri*, 1785 (cat. no. 147).

The commonly held assumption that Jones was a forerunner of the French *plein-air* painters has been based on a small number of his Italian views executed in Naples which he drew and painted from his window. The clarity of light and high tone of these paintings is largely due to the absorbent quality of their priming and supports. Without the yellowing effect of excess linseed oil, now absorbed by the paper, the colours still appear remarkably bright and clean. In addition, as these studies were not intended for sale or display, they have not suffered the usual saturation or discolouration from the application of varnish. Where varnishing has subsequently taken place, as in *Tivoli* (cat. no. 64) and *Cavern near S. Agnese* (cat. no. 61), this characteristic brightness has been lost. It is clear from this study of a larger group of oils on paper that Jones used the medium to produce small studies which were partly or wholly completed in his studio, rather than in the field.

In conclusion, it may be said that whether working on a small scale in oil on paper or painting on a larger scale in oil on canvas, Jones based his mature compositions closely on drawings made from nature. Apart from a few small additions of figures, trees or plants to enliven the overall effect on the viewer, his paintings are much nearer to the original views which inspired them than Wilson's idealized landscapes. In addition, whilst his actual painting materials were similar to those of his master, Jones's large Italian landscapes are characterized by fine brushwork and a warm tonal range very different from Wilson's bold handling of paint and rather blue, limpid light effects.

Notes

1 The exception is an essay by Jacqueline Ridge in Hackney, 1999.
2 NMGW Getty-funded Wilson Project carried out by Kate Lowry and Rachel Turnbull, 2000–2 (unpublished).
3 *Memoirs*, p. 9.
4 Ibid., p. 10.
5 Wright, 1824, pp. 19–20.
6 Account Book, second page after frontispiece, dated November 1776.
7 Ibid., Rome, late 1776.
8 Ibid., 24 January 1791.
9 *Memoirs*, p. 62.
10 Account Book, 6 May 1783 and 7 June 1783.
11 One palmo is equal to approximately 25 cm or 10 inches.
12 One canna is equal to 2–3 metres.
13 'On his arrival . . . Sr *Thomas* examined & crossexamined me with respect to the Cloths & Colors I made use of – Whether I prepared the Canvasses myself? & whether my Colors were all Minerals? – I innocently told him that I bought my Cloths & Colors ready prepared at the Colorshops, & were the same that all other Painters used' (*Memoirs*, p. 84).
14 A cross-section sample revealed two layers of grey ground with an intervening size.
15 Hackney, 1999, p. 193.
16 An entry in the Account Book in 1783 includes a list of pigments to be purchased before leaving Naples (cat. no. 73).
17 Ibid., 23 December 1790 and 5 January 1791.
18 *Memoirs*, p. 84.
19 Account Book, 12–14, 17, 26 and 28 January 1791.
20 SEM analysis carried out by Joyce Townsend at Tate Britain.
21 SEM analysis carried out by Joyce Townsend at Tate Britain.
22 Baxter, 1986, p. 18.
23 Account Book, p. 10 of a later diary, *c.*1797.
24 Ibid., 6 January 1791 and October 1797.
25 Wright, 1824, pp. 19–20.
26 *Memoirs*, p. 115, and p. 121.
27 Wright, 1824, pp. 19–20.
28 *Memoirs*, p. 62 and p. 94.
29 Account Book, 26–27 January 1791.
30 Ibid., 2 February 1791.
31 Ibid., 12–21 January 1791.
32 *Morning Post*, 1 May 1784.
33 *Memoirs*, p. 38.
34 Account Book, 13 October 1780, 21 August 1781, 10 August 1782, 15 October 1782, 15 November 1782, 9 December 1782 and 17 April 1783.
35 Ibid., 21 August 1781 and 11 September 1781.
36 Ibid., 28 and 31 July and 3 August 1797.
37 *Memoirs*, p. 38 and p. 111.
38 Account Book, 1797.
39 Hackney, 1999, p. 193.
40 Conisbee, 1979, pp. 424–6.
41 *Memoirs*, p. 103.
42 Ibid., p. 119.
43 Account Book, 28 and 31 July and 3 August 1797.

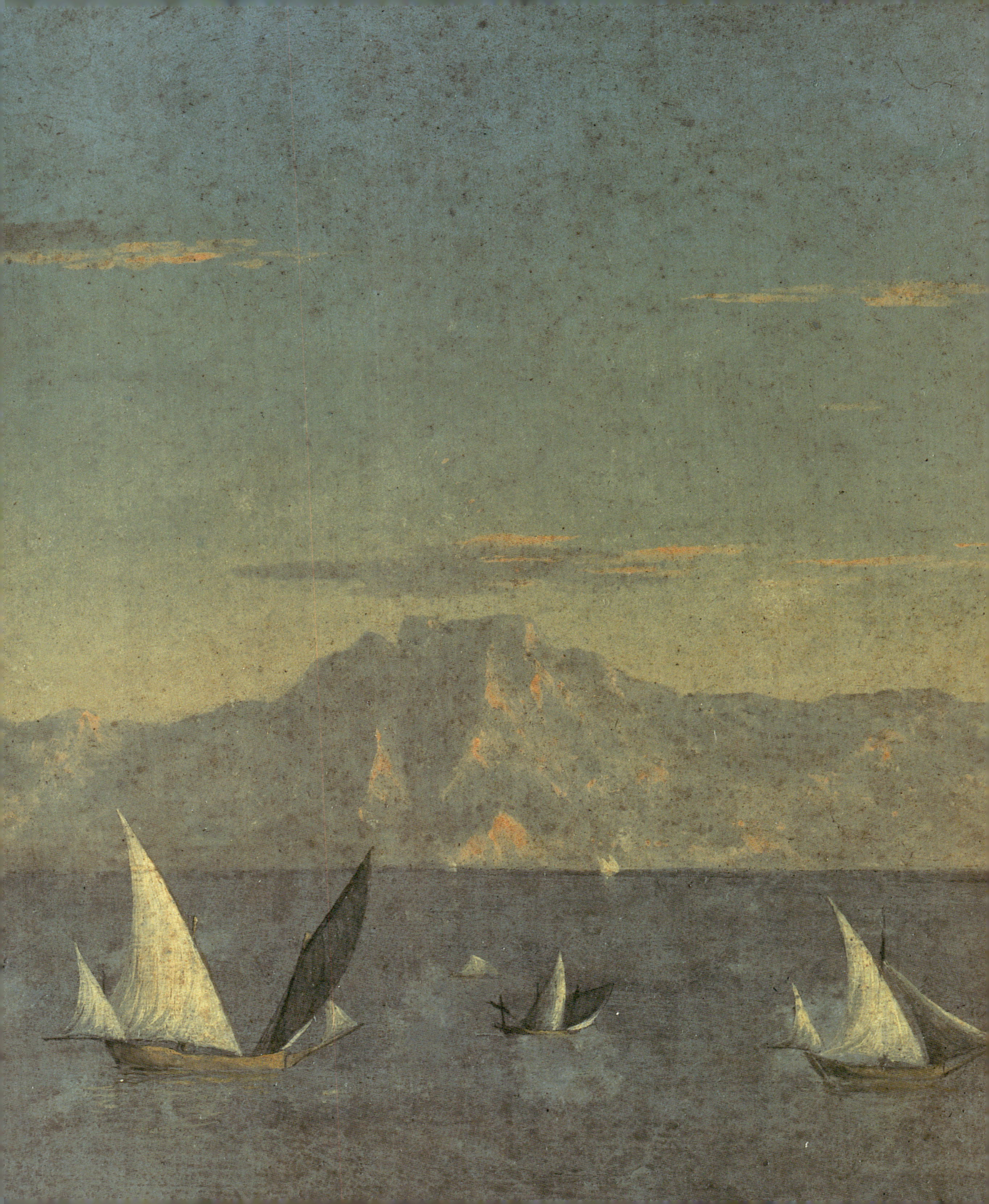

CAREFUL AND CONSIDERED CHOICE: THOMAS JONES'S USE OF PAPER

Peter Bower

An artist's choice of papers tells us much about their practice. The different working methods of individual artists contribute much to their choice of paper. Thomas Jones's landscapes appear to have begun almost by accident and on paper selected at random: 'About the beginning of the Year 1768 – happening accidentally to be on a morning lounge at a Crayon painter's – to pass the time, I took up his Crayons, and on a Scrap of Paper, made a Sketch of a Landscape, which pleased beyond Expectation'.[1] However, analysis of the papers used later in his career shows that Jones chose his papers with care, rarely working on whatever was to hand. Comparisons between his choice of papers and that of his contemporaries illustrate that, out of the hundreds of different examples available to him in both Italy and Britain, he utilized a relatively limited range of writing and wrapping paper from a small number of sources. What these papers have in common, despite their differences, are similar surface strengths. Their subtle variety of tone and texture stem from the small-scale handmade production of batches of individual sheets. Local and regional variations in papermaking practice, particularly in the choice and preparation of the rags used and the sizing of the sheets, led to the availability of a rich variety of different papers. Jones's work can be divided into different categories – watercolours and drawings, oils on paper, works in Italy, works in Wales – but his paper usage often crosses these categories and the same support is employed for both watercolour and oil.

Unlike many artists, who leave few clues as to where and when they acquired their materials, Jones provides us with information in his sketchbooks and notebooks. His Account Book (cat. no. 73) is inscribed 'Thos Jones'^{s} Book / bought at Turin / 8th Novr 1776' and the sketchbooks bought in Rome are similarly dated '2^{d} December 1776', '17 February / 1777' and '29th March 1777'. His Account Book, kept in Italy from 20 May 1780 until his departure for England on 9 September 1783, details several purchases of paper, generally in small amounts. Some of these papers were Italian but most of the references are to '*carta d'olanda*', Dutch writing

FACING PAGE Detail of cat. no. 109.

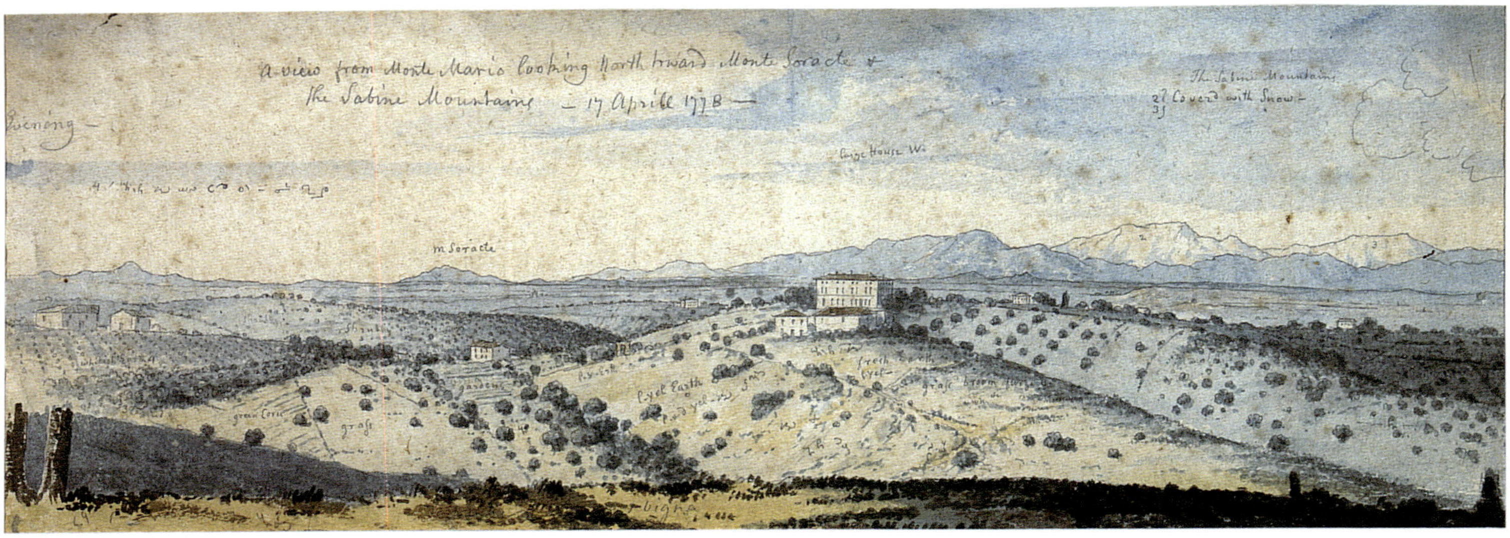

Fig. 48 Thomas Jones, *View from Monte Mario Looking Towards Monte Soracti*, 1778, pencil, watercolour on laid paper, 13.8 × 39.8 (5½ × 15¾), private collection.

paper. French, Dutch and English papers were all available in Italy, particularly in Rome, Florence, Venice and Naples, during this period.[2]

Some of the entries refer to sizes of paper such as '*posta*', literally Post paper (a size of paper designed for writing and available as Thick or Thin and in variants such as Large Post). Others describe qualities, such as '*Carta Straccia*' (linen paper)[3] or '*Carta tinta Romana*' (coloured Roman paper).[4] Analysis of the quantities and the amounts paid for the paper suggests that most of them were writing papers, bought in small amounts, much of it probably used for his correspondence. The most he spent on Dutch paper, using Jones's own conversion tables (also in the Account Book), was 4s. 6d. for six sheets of Dutch Imperial (30 × 22 inch). This is not a letter paper size and it was probably bought for drawing.[5]

The use of the word '*foglie*' (folio) in several of these references is not to a size but to the traditional practice of selling paper folded, either in quires or in groups of sheets. This practice had developed throughout Western Europe as a result of the method of drying paper, where the sheets were hung over ropes. As the sheets dried, the area across the centre of the sheet, which was in contact with the rope, shrunk at a different rate, producing wrinkles and creases, known as the 'back'. Several of Jones's works, such as *View from Monte Mario Looking Towards Monte Soracti* (fig. 48) show just such wrinkles and allow us, by their position in the sheet, to determine to some extent the original size of the paper.

The internal evidence of the papers, their laid and chain line alignments[6] and the position of watermarks within the trimmed sheets, show that most of Jones's works were executed on half or quarter sheets. So the six sheets of Dutch Imperial referred to above would have provided him with enough paper for between twelve and twenty-four works.

The physical structure of several of the sheets of paper that Jones used in Italy shows that although he often thought he was buying Dutch paper, not all of these sheets were actually of Dutch manufacture. Italian and Dutch mouldmakers constructed their paper moulds differently: in particular, the way the chain wires were arranged and their spacing varied. Recent research has shown that some of the supposed '*carta d'olanda*' available to Jones and his contemporaries was produced by Italian makers. In the 1770s, Valentino Galvani, whose mill was at Pordenon in the Veneto, was producing paper watermarked D & C BLAUW, and Domenico Vezzoli at Govardo used two versions of the I HONIG / & / ZOON mark.[7]

The combination of wire gauges, chain-line construction and above all, the felt impression visible in the surface of the sheet, especially under ×10 magnification, suggest that, despite their apparent Dutch origin, some of Jones's papers were Italian versions of '*carta d'olanda*'. Examples of such papers include those used for *Tivoli* (cat. no. 64) and two studies of buildings in Naples (cat. nos 108 and 110). Genuine Dutch writing paper, from at least two different makers, was used for *From Santa Maria dei Monti*, 1781 (fig. 49), which has a Vryheyt watermark, probably made by Cornelis and Jan Honig at the Herderskind (Shepherdess) mill, Zaandyk, Holland. Another Honig paper, watermarked C & I HONIG, from a different batch, was employed for *View from Chiaja to Pizzofalcone, Naples* (cat. no. 138). The second Dutch maker who has been identified is Lubertus van Gerrevinck, who operated the Phoenix Mill at Egmond an der Hoef. His paper was used by Jones for *The Coast near Vietri* (cat. no. 128).[8]

The origins of many of Jones's papers can also be determined, not just through the watermarks, but also sometimes by a combination of the colour and tone of the paper, the fibre blends used, the wire profiles of the laid and chain lines (visible in transmitted light) and the surface textures, particularly the impression left by the felt during its manufacture.[9] All papers, by the nature of their manufacture, are two-sided: the side next to the wire during the formation of the sheet (the wireside) is different from the other, which is pressed down on to a felt when it is transferred from the papermaking mould (the feltside). Many artists have a preference for working on one side, and in Jones's case, where the surface can be identified, he usually chose the wireside (see fig. 52). Approximately seventy per cent of the works examined appear to be on the wireside and thirty per cent on the feltside. Neither the type of paper, the maker, nor the origin of the sheet, Italy, Holland or England, appears to play much part in this choice.

Perhaps the most typical of Jones's papers for watercolour and drawings are the Italian-made, stamper-beaten[10] white laid writing papers manufactured by many of the small provincial mills around Fabriano, or further south at Amalfi and Vietri, such as that made by Antonini used for the 1782 *Suburbs of Naples* (cat. no. 136; see figs 50 and 51). Although the Account Book shows Jones regularly buying small amounts of paper, it is obvious that he did not necessarily use all his paper before he bought more. For example, *Ariccia: Buildings on the Edge of the Town,* 1777 (cat. no. 80), *The Villa of Maecenas, Tivoli*, 1780s (cat. no. 152) and *Houses in Naples*, 1782 (cat. no. 115), all of different dates and locations, are on the same batch of Italian white laid writing paper, watermarked with a fleur-de-lys in a double circle with the initials 'CB'.

Fig. 49 (RIGHT) Part of a Vryheyt watermark found in Thomas Jones's *From Santa Maria dei Monti*, 1781 (private collection). The Tree of Liberty above the crown is typical of Vryheyt watermarks used by Cornelis and Jan Honig at the Herderskind (Shepherdess) Mill, Zaandyk, Holland. Compare the laid and chain-line structures and the quality of the pulp with the detail seen in fig. 50 (this image has been reversed so that the watermark reads correctly).

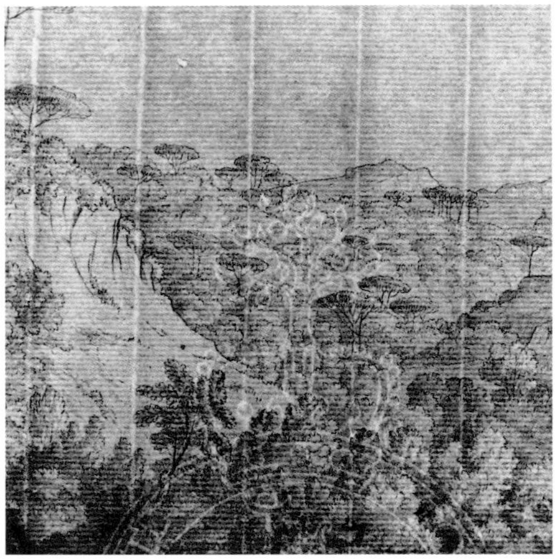

Fig. 50 (FAR RIGHT) An Italian B / fleur-de-lys in a single circle / V watermark found in Thomas Jones's *Villa at Frascati*, 1777 (cat. no. 77). Compare the laid and chain-line structures with those seen in fig. 49. The specks and flecks seen within the sheet are typical of stamper-beaten pulp (this image has been reversed so that the watermark reads correctly).

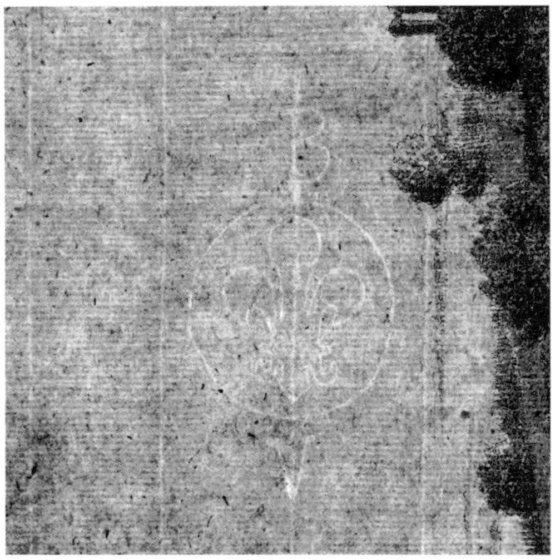

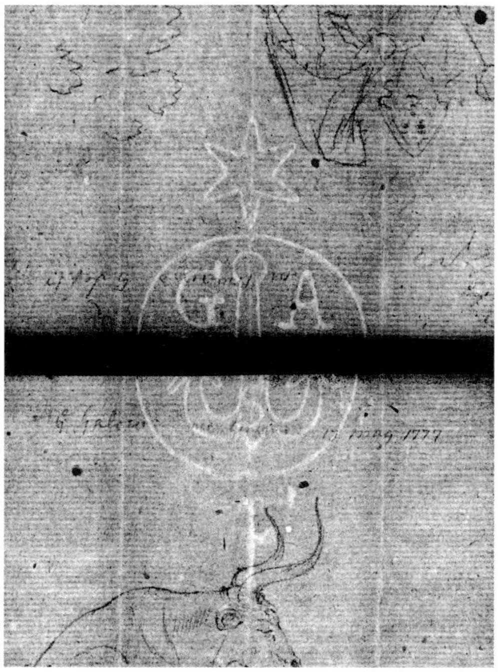

Fig. 51 (RIGHT) Composite image of the Star / Anchor GAS / F watermark found in the pages of Thomas Jones's sketchbook 'bought at / Rome 29 March 1777' (cat. no. 76).

This paper was probably made by Bracciano at Fabriano. Paper from the same source also makes up the large sketchbook in the British Museum (cat. no. 75). Slight differences in the wire profiles of the different examples are the product of the fact that the moulds were used in pairs and the two watermarks would have had slight differences. Watermarks also vary slightly in size and shape, depending upon the action of the coucher, who transfers the wet sheet from the mould to the felt, and also during drying, when differences in temperature and humidity can lead to more or less shrinkage of the sheet (fig. 51).

Comparisons between the papers Jones used for his oil studies, whether in Wales or Italy, show that they came from a variety of sources. Like many artists, he appears to have simply worked on whatever was to hand, sometimes preparing the sheets before applying the ground and at other times not. What attracted Jones to paper for oil sketching was its easy portability and, depending on how it was prepared, its relative absorbency: an absorbent ground allowed the artist to work faster. One of his studies of Pencerrig from 1772 (cat. no. 41) is on low-grade, laid wrapping from an unknown maker, probably English but possibly Welsh. The presence of many specks, shives and process dirt in this paper suggest it was made as a wrapping from a blend of very dirty, low-grade linen and old hemp rope, as was typical with many small rural mills in Britain that served a mostly local market.

In contrast, *The Bay of Naples and the Mole Lighthouse* (cat. no. 109) is on a fine, white laid paper. As with *Pencerrig* (cat. no. 41), the oils from the paint have discoloured the paper considerably. The presence of knots and lumps in the sheet (cat. no. 109), visible from the verso, shows that the paper was stamper-beaten rather than hollander-beaten. Together with the thickness of the wire used for the laid lines and a chain-line width of 30mm, this suggests an Italian origin for the paper. Despite the similarities in tone and, to some extent, texture between this sheet and that used for *Pencerrig*, they are completely different papers, one made as a cheap brown wrapping, the other as a writing paper. Amongst the oil sketches, some of what appear to be brown papers are, in fact, blue wrappings now discoloured by the oils and grounds applied to them. One such work is *Monte Compatri, near Frascati*, 1785 (cat. no. 147). It is likely that this is an English blue wrapping paper.

A later Account Book reference to a different kind of paper occurs in a series of journal entries after Jones's return to Britain: 'When I began dead Colouring in oil on paper a Study of the Trees . . . in the Entrance of the Walk leading to the house by the Garden fishpool . . . the above Study is on a half Sheet of light brown Cartridge paper prepared with a slight ground of Whiting & weak size – This I finish[d] – as like wise a Companion to it on ye Same kind of Paper'.[11] Unfortunately, Jones does not tell us what kind of cartridge paper he was using. By 1797, both Dutch and English cartridges,

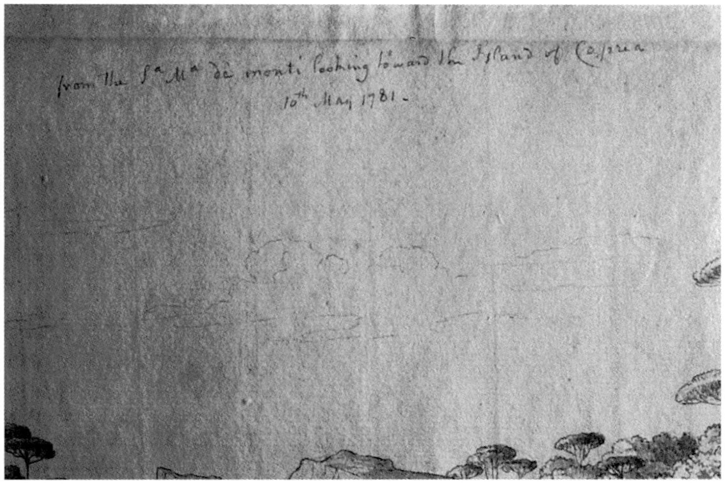

Fig. 52 (BELOW LEFT) Raking light detail of Thomas Jones's *From Santa Maria dei Monti*, 1781 (private collection) showing the wireside of the sheet. Compare this with the surface seen in fig. 53.

Fig. 53 (BELOW RIGHT) Raking light image of the feltside surface of Thomas Jones's *Villa at Frascati*, 1777 (cat. no. 77). Compare this with the surface of the Dutch paper in fig. 52.

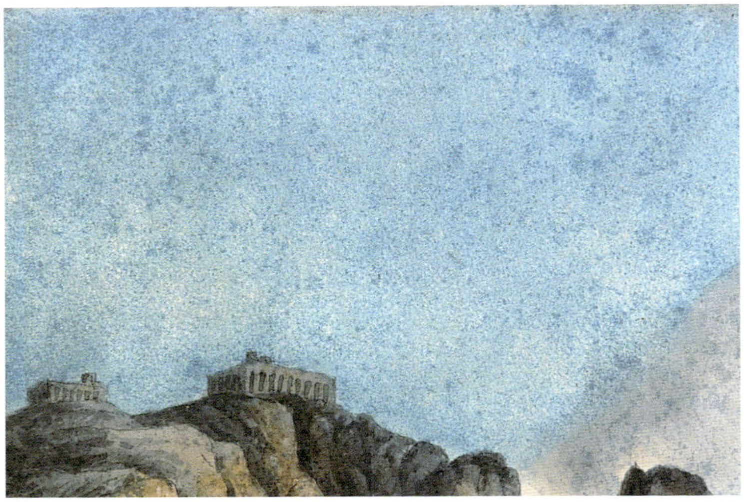

Fig. 54 Detail of the sky in Thomas Jones's *At Terracina*, 1790s (cat. no. 166), showing the uneven sizing of a white wove paper made by William Balston and the Hollingworth brothers at Turkey Mill, Kent.

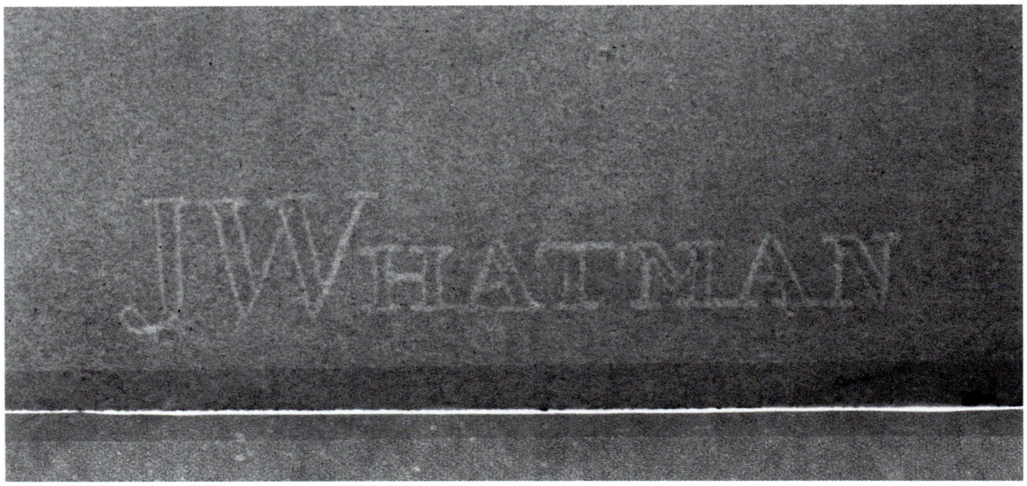

Fig. 55 J Whatman watermark from the white wove paper made by James Whatman the younger at Turkey Mill, Kent that Thomas Jones used for several works in the 1790s, including *Lake Nemi* (cat. no. 165).

designed for wrapping powder, were available, as were newly developed Drawing Cartridges, particularly from the Kent manufacturers, Robert Edmeads and John Pine.[12] This was not the first time that Jones had used cartridge paper: *Carneddau, from Pencerrig, c.*1775 (cat. no. 42) is also on an English cartridge support.

Despite living in remote rural Radnorshire after his return to Britain, Jones kept up with developments in the papers available to artists. A Whatman white wove writing paper made by William Balston and the Hollingworth Brothers, the sucessors to James Whatman at Turkey Mill, Kent, was used for *At Terracina* (cat. no. 166) and *Gaiola* (cat. no. 164). Balston was beginning to experiment with white wove papers made specifically for watercolour and some of these sheets have a characteristic feature, typical of several batches of this paper, which was also used by Turner and Girtin. In some areas of the paper, the gelatine sizing is uneven, leading to a mottling in the paint, particularly visible in the sky of *Terracina* (cat. no. 166). The form of J WHATMAN watermark found in *Lake Nemi* (cat. no. 165) shows that this sheet is an earlier paper, made before 1794 when James Whatman the younger retired (figs 54 and 55).

Despite the occasional flaw in some of the sheets, Jones's choice of paper confirms his care, interest and understanding of the qualities of his supports in every aspect of his practice. His focused and specific use of paper had more in common with artists of a slightly later generation than with his own contemporaries. He demanded much of his paper, particularly in watercolour, not merely that it could carry an image, but that it would behave in a manner that allowed him to express his vision.

Notes

1 *Memoirs*, p. 15.
2 See Bower, 1996, pp. 7–15, for a discussion of Dutch papers available in mid- to late eighteenth-century Italy.
3 Account Book, 27 December 1781.
4 Ibid., 11 September 1781.
5 Ibid., 21 October 1782.
6 Laid and chain lines are visible within the sheet in transmitted light and are formed by the wires used to make the surface of the papermaking mould.
7 Marrozzi, 1996, p. 317 and p. 321.
8 A sheet of imported white laid writing paper watermarked L V GERREVINCK. Although van Gerrevinck's initials LVG were appropriated by several papermakers, including English makers, as a sign of quality, the use of the whole name and the particular style of the letter forms show this to have been produced by the Gerrevincks rather than by one of their imitators.
9 The felt is a woven woollen blanket onto which the newly formed wet sheet is transferred. The wool leaves an impression in the surface of the paper when the sheets are pressed. Italian felts were generally much coarser than Dutch or English examples.
10 Stampers are a series of water-powered hammers used to pulp the rags by pounding them in a trough. These continued to be used in Italy long after they were superseded by the hollander beater in Holland and England. The hollander worked by crushing and grinding the rags as they passed between a very heavy barred roller and a bedplate located in a large oval trough.
11 Account Book, 28 July 1797.
12 The great user of cartridge papers for watercolour was Thomas Girtin. See Bower, 2002, pp. 136–141.

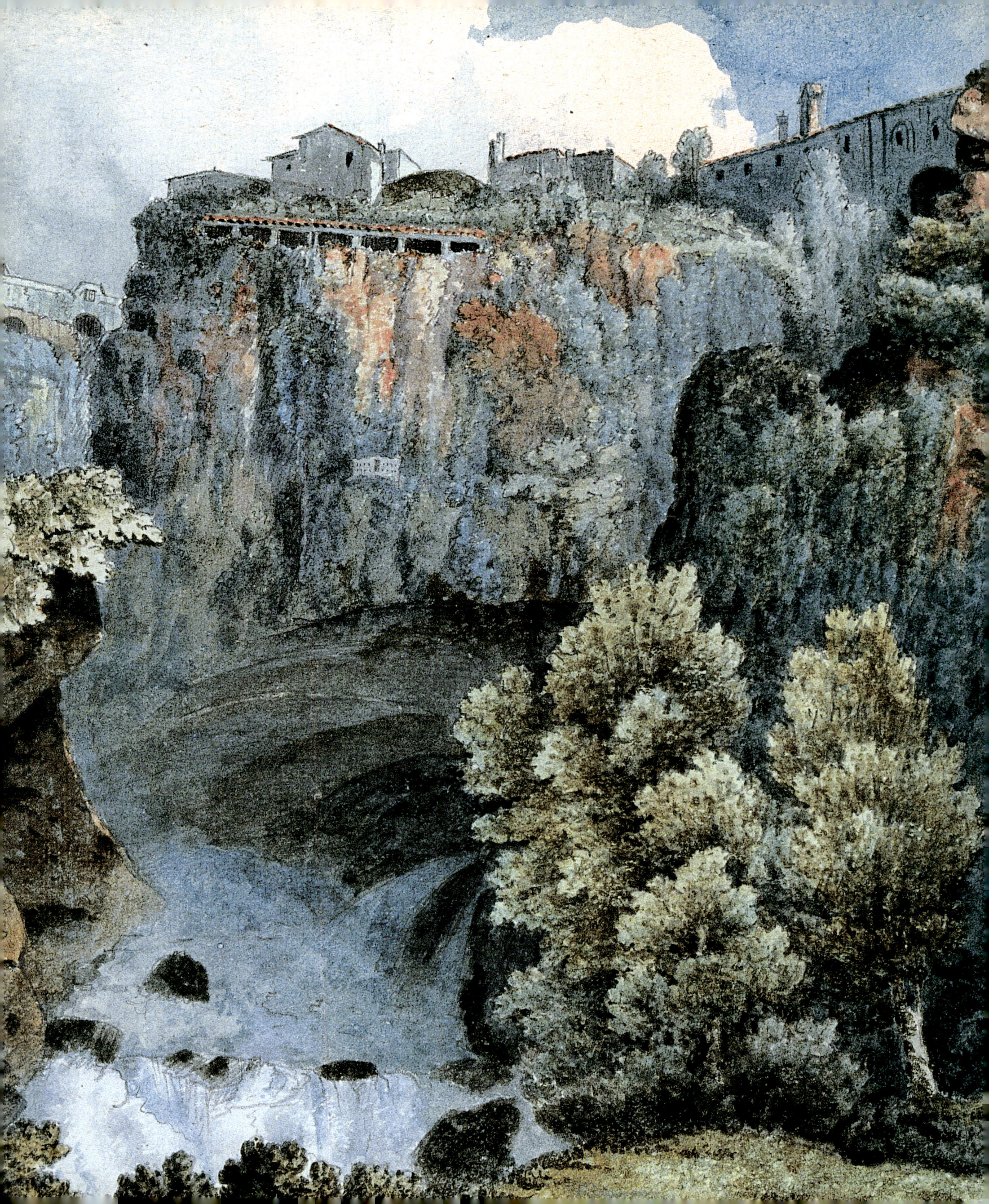

CATALOGUE

NOTES ON THE CATALOGUE

All references are in the format of 'Author, date' or, if exhibition catalogues, as 'Location, date'. They are given in full in the bibliography, which is split into two sections. Two further references are given. '*Memoirs*' refers to Paul Oppé's edition ('Memoirs of Thomas Jones, Penkerrig, Radnorshire, 1803', *The Thirty-Second Volume of the Walpole Society*, 1946–8 and 'Farington, *Diary*' refers to the Yale edition (Garlick, Kenneth, Mackintyre, Angus, Cave, Kathryn, and Newby, Evelyn, eds, *The Diary of Joseph Farington*, New Haven and London, 17 vols, 1978–98).

An asterix, '*', after the media means that the paper has been inspected by Peter Bower. The provenance for the works, as long as they remained in the possession of Jones's family, is given in an abbreviated form. After the artist's death, his works were inherited by his two daughters, Anna Maria Thomas (1780–1807) and Elizabetha Dale (1781–1806). On their deaths – both childless – their portions were inherited by their husbands, Thomas Thomas and Captain John Dale respectively. Thereafter, the collections were passed on by family descent, though those which remained at Pencerrig were sold by the Lindsay family to Llewelyn Evan-Thomas, still a relative, in 1928.

The titles, where they indicate locations, are given in modern usage and these therefore sometimes differ from Jones's often idiosyncratic spelling.

The catalogue entries have been written by the following:

Oliver Fairclough (ONF)
Bethany McIntyre (BM)
Charles Nugent (CN)
Christopher Riopelle (CR)
Greg Smith (GS)
Ann Sumner (ABS)

FACING PAGE Detail of fig. 87; FOLLOWING PAGES Detail of cat. no. 9

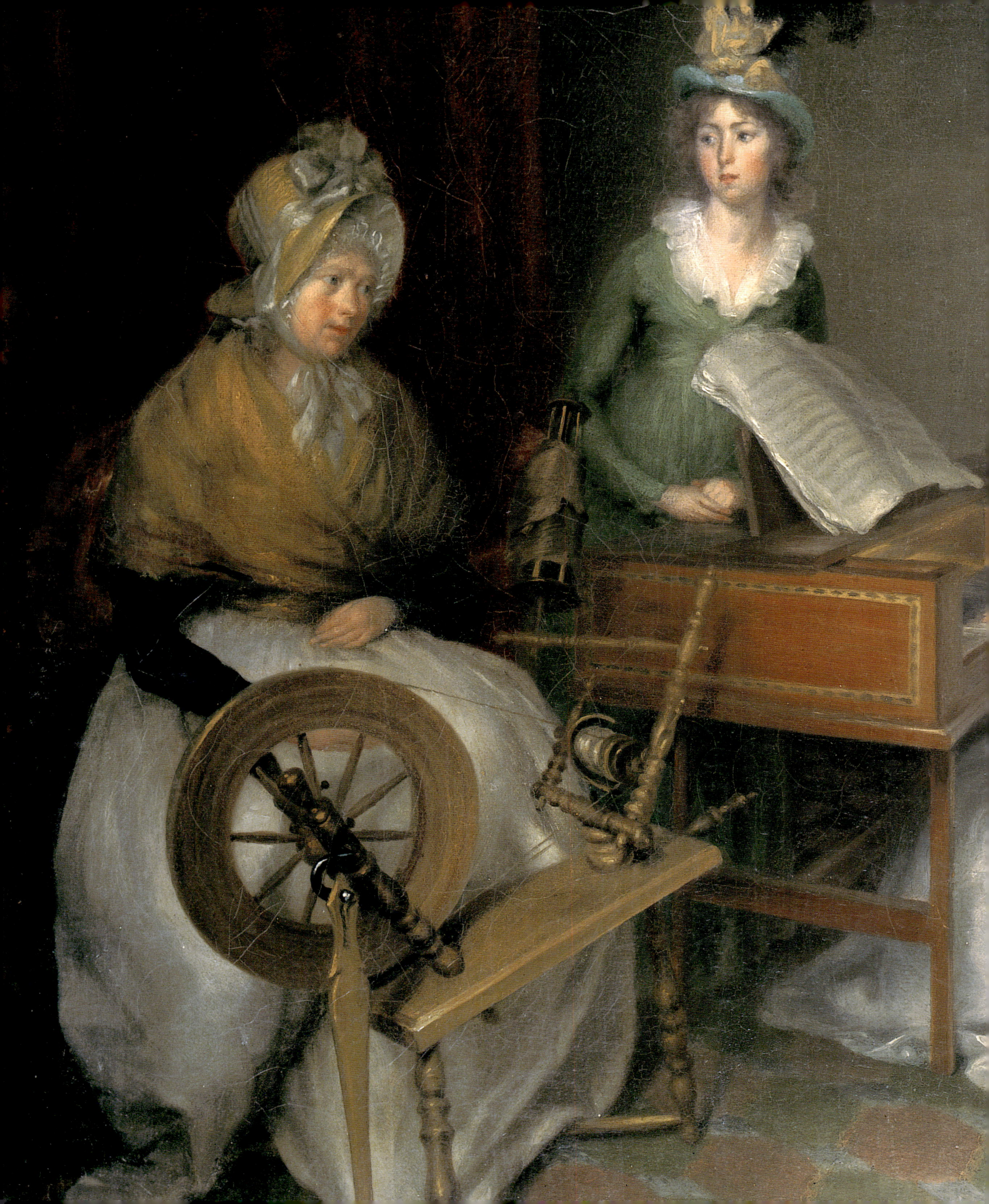

FAMILY BACKGROUND

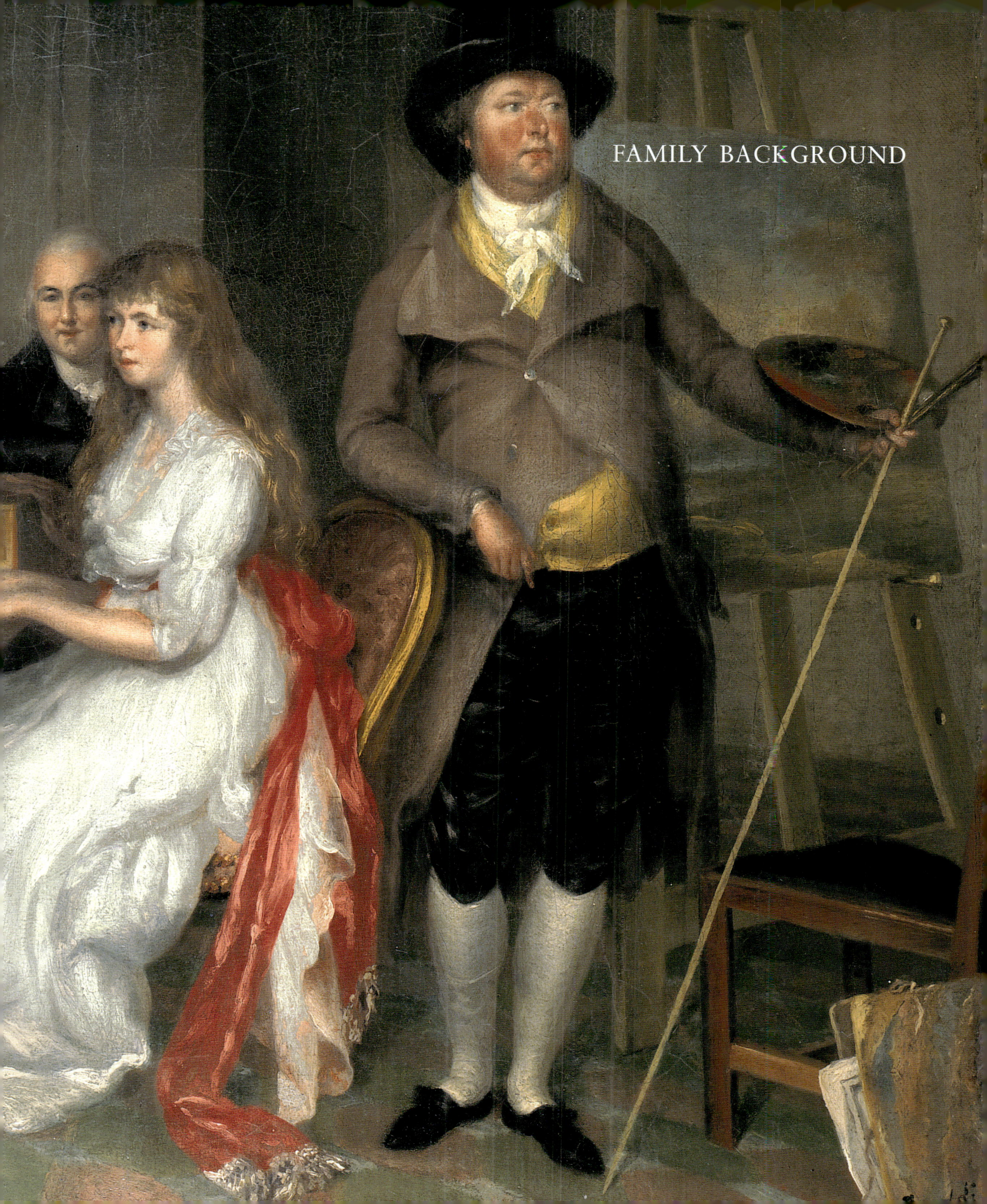

1

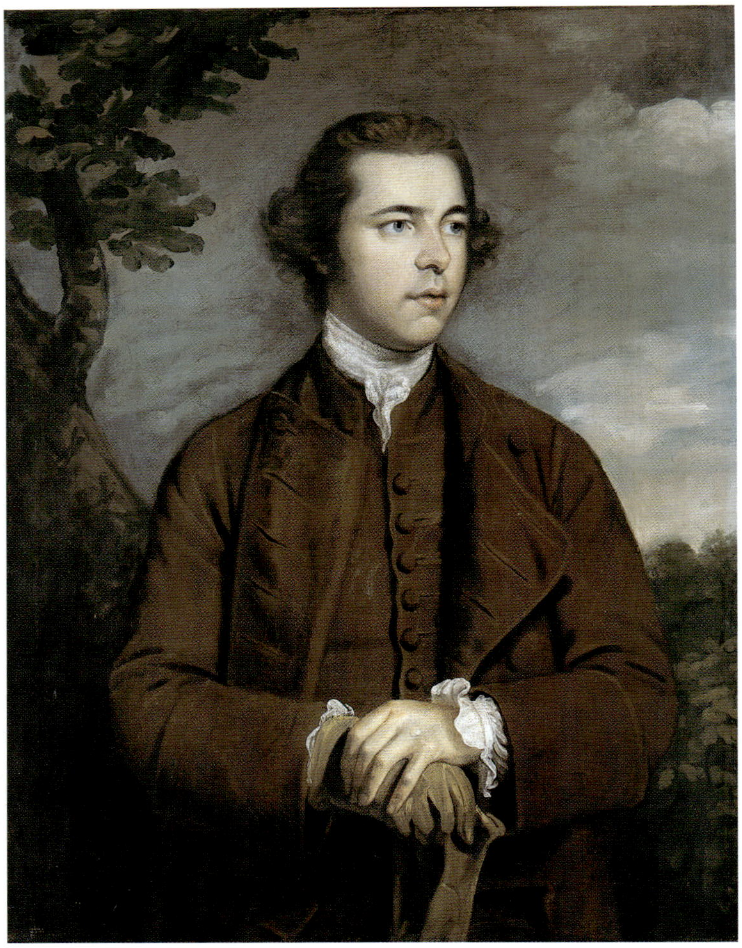

2

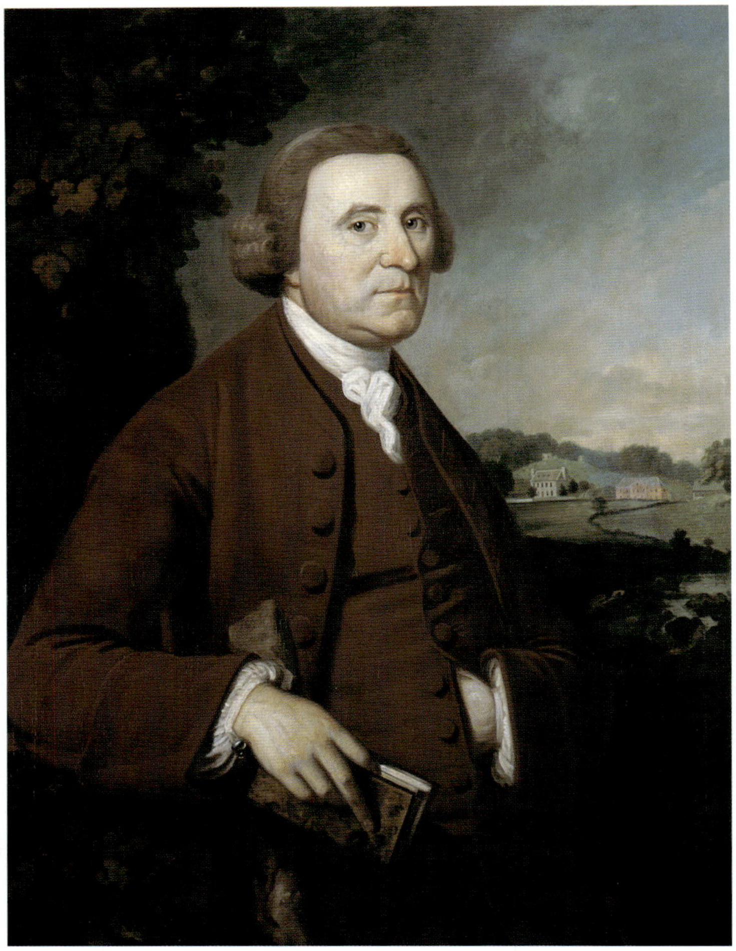

1

GIUSEPPE MARCHI (*c.*1735–1808)

Thomas Jones 1768

Oil on canvas, 92 × 72 ($36\frac{1}{4} \times 28\frac{3}{8}$)

Ins.: 'M-Thos Jones son of Thomas Jones Esq. 1768' in ink on the stretcher
Prov.: Sotheby's, 24 November 1965, no. 84; presented by the Friends of the National Museum of Wales, 1965
Exh.: London, 1970, no. 93; Aberystwyth, 1971, no. 22
Lit.: Joyner, 1997, pp. 77–9, fig. 59; Lord, 2000, pp. 17–18; fig. 196

National Museums & Galleries of Wales (NMW A 82)

Cardiff and Manchester only

Illustrated on p. ii, frontispiece

This portrait shows Jones, aged twenty-six, at the beginning of his career. He spent time sketching in the summer of 1768 at Gadbridge in Hertfordshire and then on 14 September 'set off with my old friend *Gioseppe Marchi* for Wales . . . During Marchi's stay', Jones continued, 'he painted Portraits of many of the family, and some few friends' (*Memoirs*, p. 15). The Italian painter Marchi had returned to England with Joshua Reynolds in 1752 and became his chief studio assistant, painting draperies and copying portraits. However, for a short period between 1768 and 1769 he attempted to set up as an independent portraitist, first in London and then at Swansea. The group of Jones family portraits are therefore key examples of his independent work, though paintings such as this are still much indebted to Reynolds. Two other portraits said to represent Jones as a young man are recorded, a chalk drawing by John Russell (untraced) and a miniature by John Smart (untraced). He is shown in later life in the well-known conversation piece by Renaldi (cat. no. 9). (ABS)

2

Giuseppe Marchi (*c.*1735–1808)

Thomas Jones Senior *c.*1768

Oil on canvas, 90 × 71 (35⅜ × 28)

Prov.: Sarah Humphreys, then by descent
Lit.: Lord, 2000, pp. 127–8, fig. 198

Private collection, family of the sitter

Cardiff only

Thomas Jones Senior (1711–1782) was the only son of John Jones of Trefonnen. Marchi shows him as a successful Welsh squire in his mid-fifties, with the family home, Pencerrig, near Builth Wells, in the background (fig. 2). In 1738 he married his first cousin, Hannah Jones (cat. no. 4), who brought with her the Pencerrig estate. They lived initially at Trefonnen, moving to Pencerrig in the winter of 1749–50, although Hannah did not inherit the house until 1761. Jones Senior was a respected landowner, president of the Brecknockshire Agricultural Society – the first of its type in Wales. He was an affectionate father and Jones refers to him as a man of 'firm mind, equal temper and cheerful disposition' (*Memoirs*, p. 7), and on receiving the news of his death in 1782 acclaimed him as 'One of the best of Men in every Respect!' (ibid., p. 118). Presumably it was Jones Senior who commissioned Marchi to paint the family portraits at Pencerrig in 1768.

Fig. 56 Pencerrig Gardens Hotel, contemporary photograph.

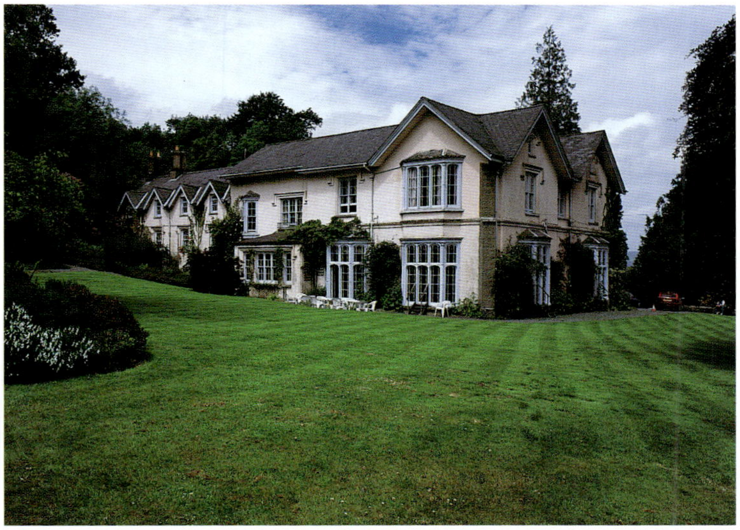

The depiction of Pencerrig is particularly significant since it shows the house, below its sheltering rocky hill, in its original form as a five-bay, hipped-roofed, eighteenth-century building. Since 1831 it has been engulfed by Gothic additions, transforming its appearance, as a contemporary photograph shows (fig. 56). (ABS)

3

Attributed to Francesco Renaldi (1755–1798)

Thomas Jones Senior *c.*1782

Oil on panel, 46 × 34 (18⅛ × 13⅜)

Prov.: Thomas Thomas, then by descent

Private collection

Cardiff only

This small-scale work is a pair with cat. no. 4 and shows the artist's father seated in a relaxed pose in his study. The interior has elaborate panelling and a rich Turkey carpet, but there is no way of knowing if this was an interior at Pencerrig. The elderly squire is portrayed in a grey jacket, presumably in his study, and is quite different from the sombre, somewhat austere figure seen in the earlier portrait (cat. no. 2). The features are clearly discernible, however, and suggest the passage of some fifteen years, thus confirming the later dating of this portrait. If the attribution to Renaldi is accepted, then the work was probably painted in the year of the sitter's death, since Renaldi was still in Rome in October 1781 but was back in London by 1783, being one of the first people Thomas Jones the artist encountered on his return to Britain in November that year. (ABS)

4 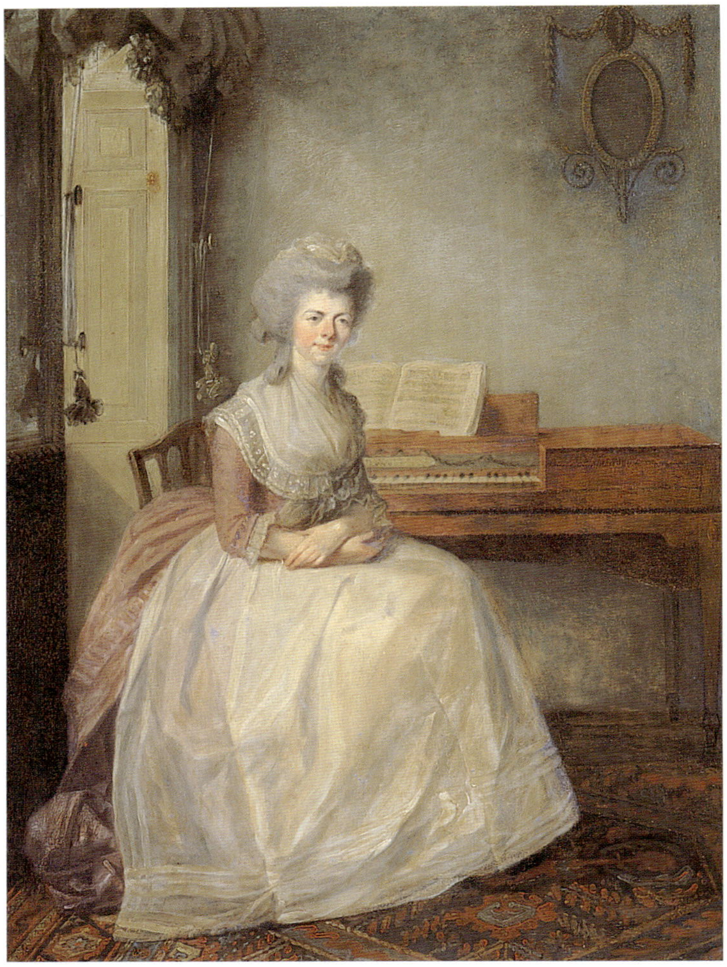

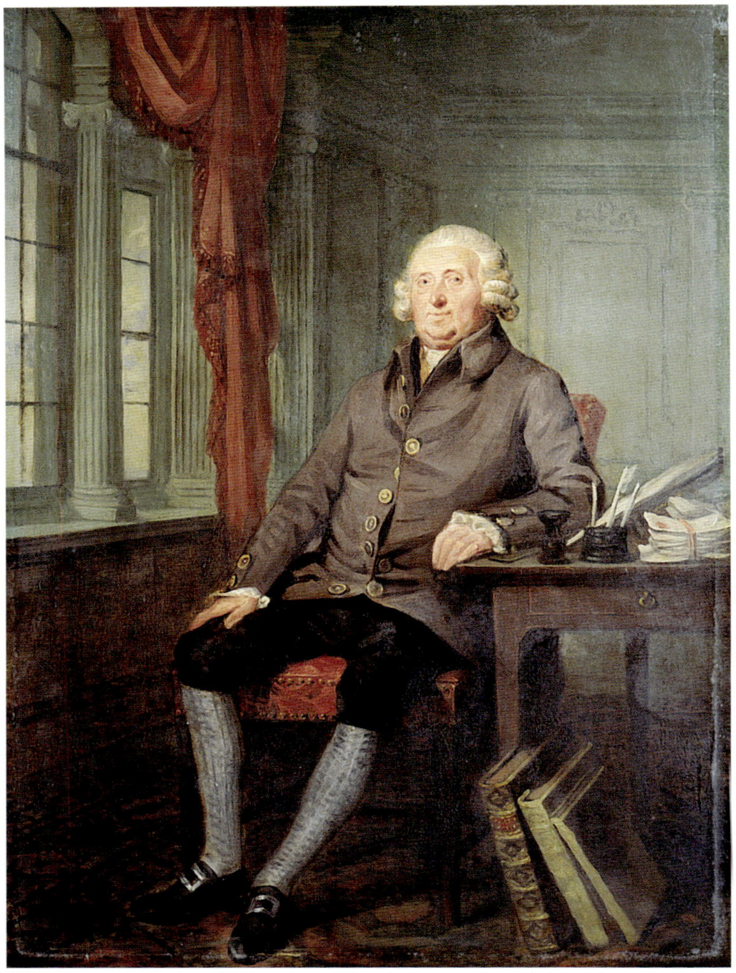 3

4

Attributed to Francesco Renaldi (1755–1798)

Hannah Jones *c.*1782

Oil on panel, 46 × 34 (18⅛ × 13⅜)

Prov.: Sarah Humphreys, then by descent
Lit.: Oliver, 1970, p. 41, p. 74

Private collection, family of the sitter

Cardiff only

Hannah Jones (1721–1789) was the daughter of Thomas Jones, younger son of David Jones of Trefonnen, who settled in Tetbury, Gloucestershire, and Elizabeth Middleton Hope of Llandrindod Hall. In 1715 her father founded the Caebach Chapel which contains the Jones family memorial (fig. 4). At the age of seventeen, she married her first cousin Thomas Jones Senior (cat. no. 2). They went on to have sixteen children, nine of whom survived childhood. Hannah brought to the marriage not only a strong Nonconformist tradition, but also a considerable inheritance from her mother's family, including the house and estate at Pencerrig. Hannah outlived her husband by seven years, staying on at Pencerrig with her eldest son John. In the sermon delivered at her funeral the Revd John Thomas said 'She is no more at Penkerrig, with an open house, an open heart, to receive the poor, to feed the hungry & clothe the naked. She is gone to her reward' (Oliver, 1970a).

This intimate, small-scale portrait, showing Hannah in her informal day wear, is a pair with cat. no. 3. It is possible that Jones recommended Renaldi to his parents. Renaldi was in Naples and Rome with Jones in 1781, but on his return to London he could have painted these companion portraits in the year of Thomas Jones Senior's death in 1782, though there is no record of a visit to Pencerrig. An earlier date in the 1770s is implausible, given the age of the sitters. (ABS)

5

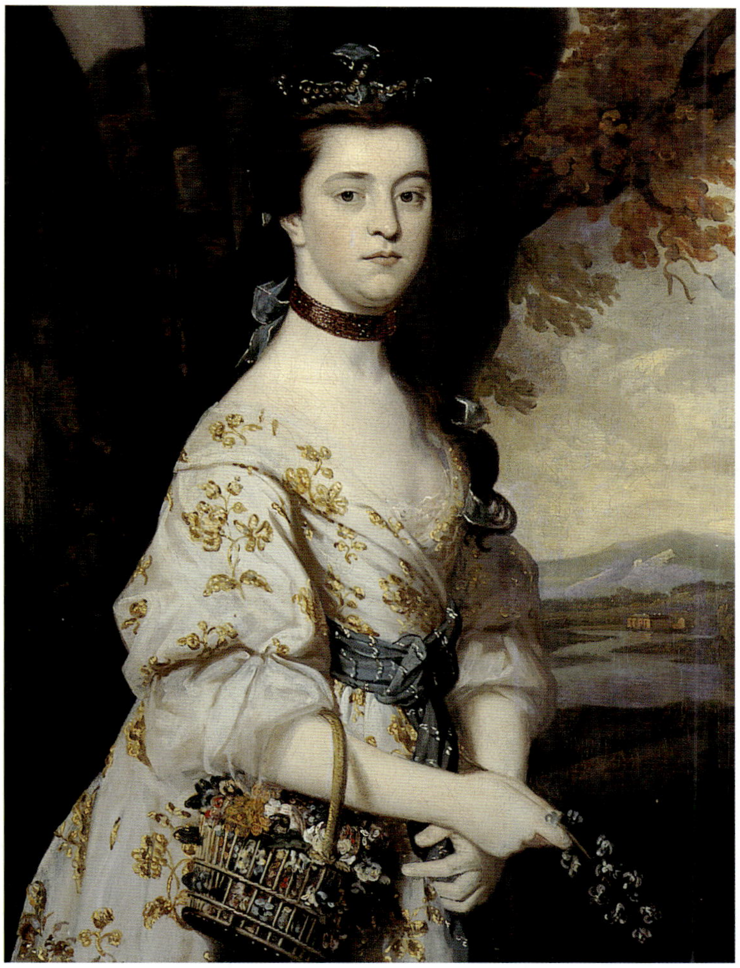

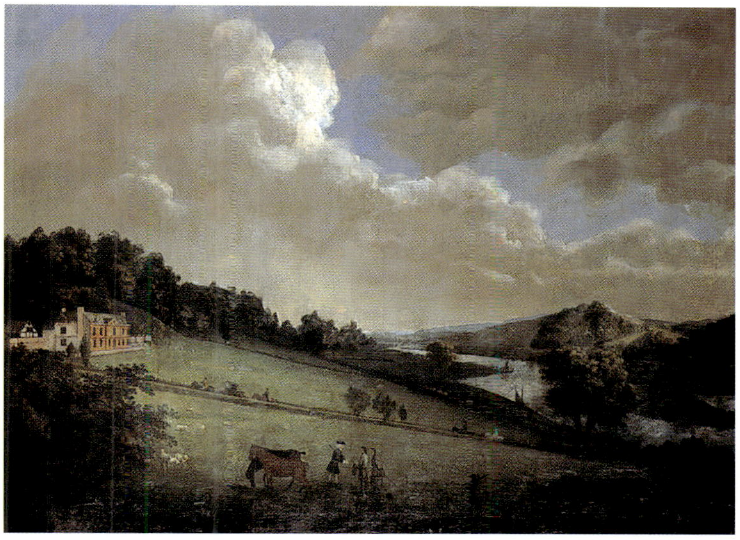

Fig. 57 Thomas Jones, *View of Pennant Hall*, *c.*1772, oil on canvas, 92 × 127 (36¼ × 50) (private collection).

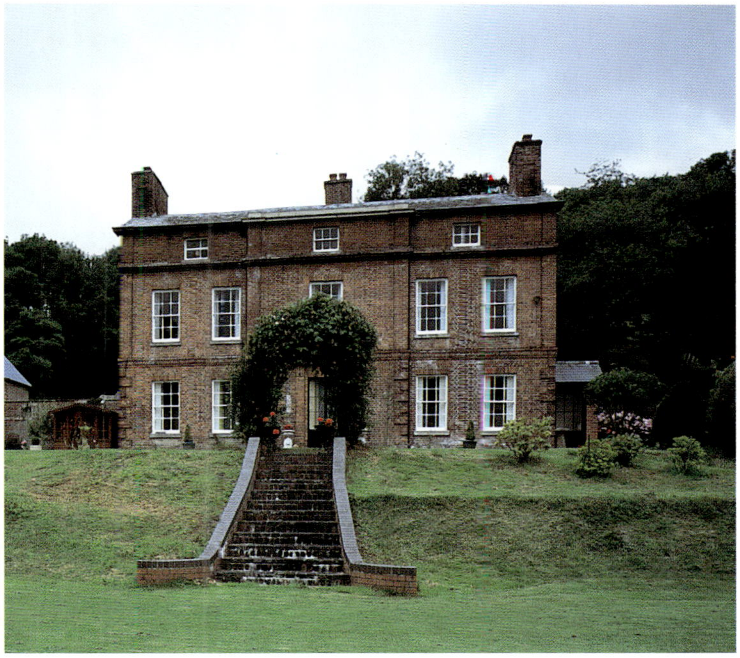

Fig. 58 Pennant Hall, contemporary photograph.

5

GIUSEPPE MARCHI (*c.*1735–1808)

Sarah Humphreys *c.*1768

Oil on canvas, 90 × 71 (35⅜ × 28)

Prov.: Sarah Humphreys, then by descent
Lit.: Oliver, 1970, pp. 39–40; Lord, 2000, pp. 127–8, fig. 197

Private collection, family of sitter

Cardiff only

Sarah Humphreys (1745–1789) was the older of Thomas Jones's two sisters to survive childhood. In 1768 she married a lawyer, Humphrey Humphreys (1742–1781), only son of Charles Humphreys, who had rebuilt Pennant Hall in 1755. Thomas Jones recalls that after he and Giuseppe Marchi had stayed at Pencerrig in 1768, they went to 'my brother in law (Humphrey)'s at Pennant in Montgomeryshire', *en route* to London. It was presumably on this occasion that Marchi made portrait studies of the recently married Sarah. Marchi, whose expertise was in drapery painting, typically concentrates on the elaborate floral dress. Pennant Hall still stands

6

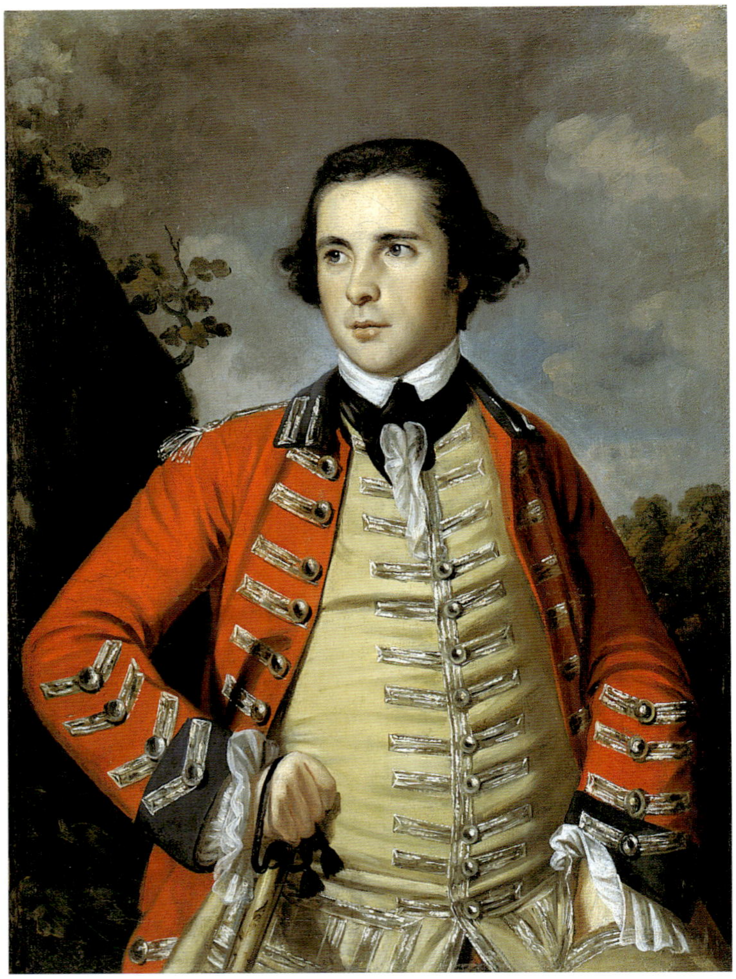

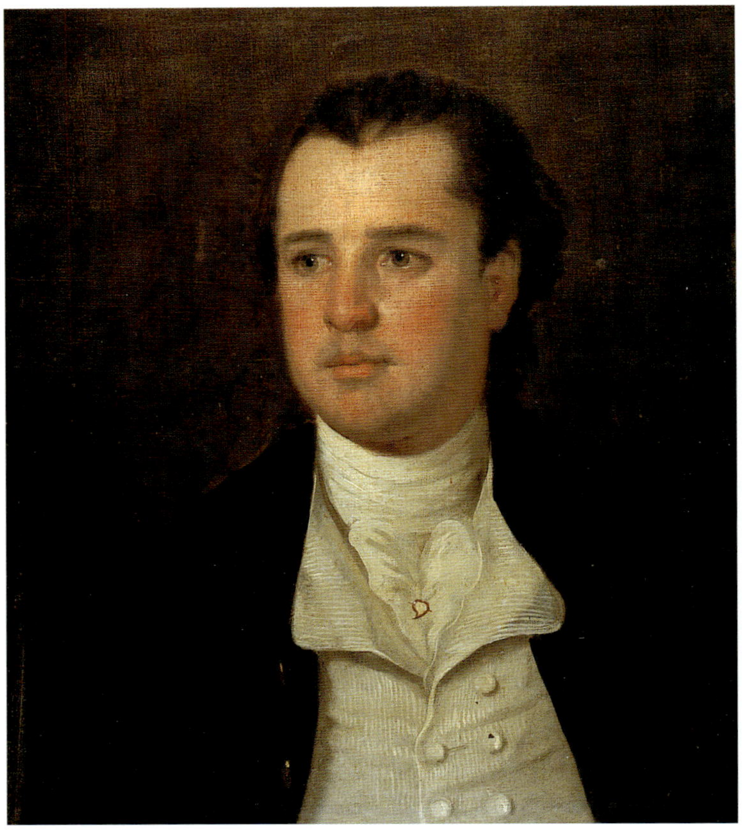

7

today, little altered (fig. 58), off the road between Newtown and Berriew. Jones himself painted the house, probably in 1772 (fig. 57) when he visited again (*Memoirs*, p. 27).

Humphrey died in 1781 and Sarah was left with five young children all under the age of twelve and debts of £3,000. The widow and her children continued to live at Pennant, but let out part of the house. She died in 1789, the same year as her mother (ibid., p. 141). (ABS)

6

GIUSEPPE MARCHI (*c.*1735–1808)

John Jones 1768

Oil on canvas, 92 × 72 ($36\frac{1}{4} \times 28\frac{3}{8}$)

Prov.: Sotheby's, 24 November 1965, no. 85; Agnew's; Phillips, 19 June 1981, no. 26; purchased 1981

Lit.: Oliver, 1970, pp. 20–1; Waterhouse, 1981, p. 231

National Museums & Galleries of Wales (NMW A 83)

Cardiff only

John Jones (1739–1787), the elder brother of Thomas Jones the artist, was educated with him at Christ College, Brecon. He went on to Oxford, matriculating in 1756. Although intended for the Bar, he seems to have returned home to run the family estates. The portrait, presumably painted when Marchi visited Pencerrig in 1768 (see cat. no. 1), shows him in the uniform of the Radnorshire Militia. He attained the rank of Major Commandant by 1779, but resigned his commission in 1782 when he inherited the estates from his father. He became High Sheriff of Breconshire in 1787, the year of his death. As a bachelor, his death had a profound impact on Thomas Jones's life. He records in his *Memoirs*, 'My eldest Brother dying, I came into possession of the whole of his Landed property' (p. 141). (ABS)

7

Attributed to Giuseppe Marchi (*c.*1735–1808)

Rice Jones *c.*1785

Oil on canvas, 54 × 48 (21¼ × 18⅞)

Prov.: Thomas Thomas, then by descent

Mrs George Lindsay

Cardiff only

Rice Jones (1759–1804) was the youngest of Thomas and Hannah's seven sons, though he survived his elder brother Thomas by only one year. Unlike his brothers, he does not appear to have followed a professional career. Instead, he remained at home to run the Pencerrig estates. On the death of his father, he received £800 and the annual rent from two farms, and in September 1787 he was described as 'gamekeeper to Thomas Jones, esq' in the *Hereford Journal*. Subsequently, Rice is often mentioned in Thomas Jones's Account Book (cat. no. 73), attending meetings on estate business. This portrait is traditionally attributed to Giuseppe Marchi and considered to have been painted in London nearly twenty years after the Pencerrig group (cat. nos 1–2, and 5–6). In style and size it is quite different and the attribution consequently remains uncertain. However, Thomas Jones recorded in his daybook for 3 November 1789 that he 'paid Marchi for my wife's portrait £3–5'. This painting is now lost, but the entry indicates that there was contact with Marchi and a further portrait of Rice might have been commissioned. (AB3)

8

Thomas Jones (1742–1803)

Trevonen, from a Sketch Made in the Year 1775 *c.*1795

Pencil, watercolour, pen and ink on laid paper on original mount, 24.6 × 38.4 (9¾ × 15¹⁄₁₆)

Ins.: 'T. Jones' l.r. on the original mount; 'Trevoner Radnorshire from a Sketch made in the year 1775' on the mount
Prov.: Thomas Thomas, then by descent to Jane Evan-Thomas; bequeathed 2000
Lit.: Oliver, 1970, pp. 14–15

Llyfrgell Genedlaethol Cymru, The National Library of Wales (P2000108444)

Cardiff and Manchester only

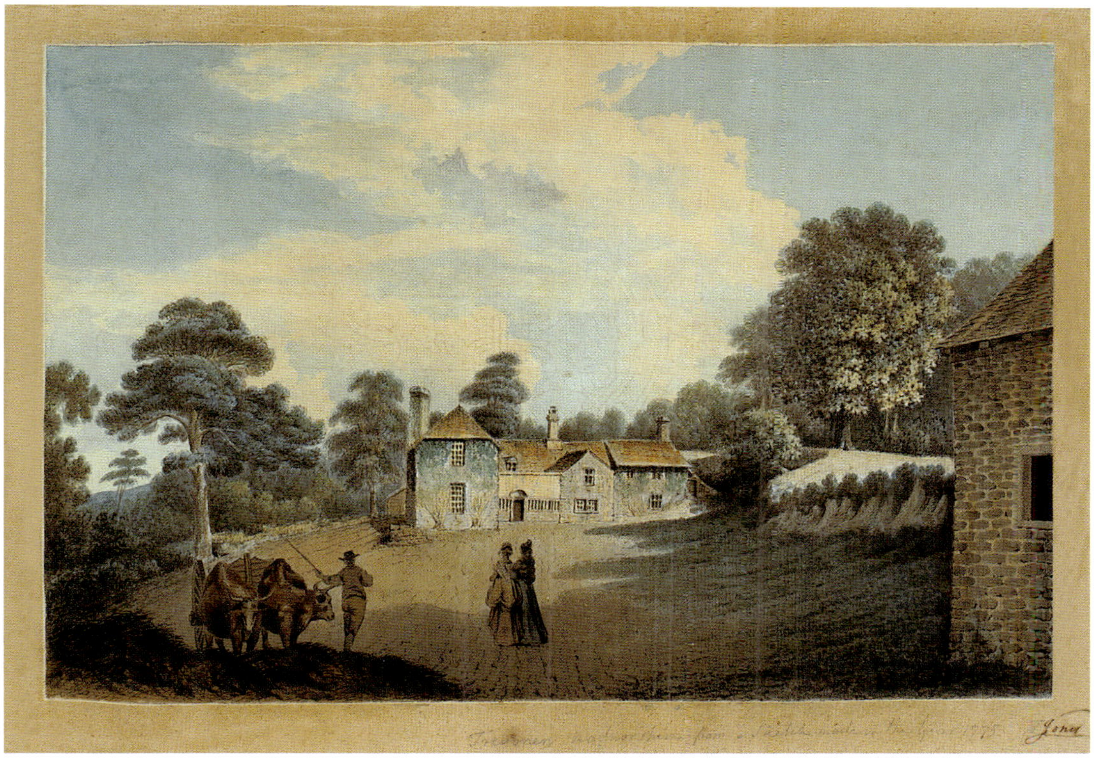

8

Jones travelled to Pencerrig in September 1775 to take his leave of his family, and at some time during that year, according to the inscription on the mount of this watercolour, he made a sketch of Trefonnen (Trevonen), his father's family home since the mid-seventeenth century. It was here that Jones was born in 1742 and lived until the winter of 1749–50, when the family moved to Pencerrig. This watercolour dates from about 1795, when he produced other local views on the same size paper (*c*.24 × 38 cm) with similar mounts (cat. nos 157–9). This is a late example, therefore, of Jones looking back to an earlier sketch in order to make a finished drawing. The figures, which have not been identified, may have had a personal, possibly family, significance, though the house was tenanted in 1775. The house had fallen into disrepair by the 1970s and has now been demolished. (GS)

9

FRANCESCO RENALDI (1755–1798)

Thomas Jones and his Family 1797

Oil on canvas, 74.9 × 101.6 (29½ × 40)

Ins.: 'Renaldi Pinxit 1797' l.r. on the portfolio; 'Thomas Jones artist and sq of Pencerig with his wife Rachel, his two daughters, Mrs Thomas of Pencerig and Mrs Dale & Mr Dale' verso
Prov.: Thomas Thomas, then by descent to Clara Thomas; D. E. T. Lindsay; Sotheby's, 22 November 1961, no. 189; Colnaghi's; purchased 1961 with the assistance of the National Art Collections Fund
Exh.: Royal Academy, 1798, no. 304 as 'Portrait of his own family and Mr Jones'; Swansea, 1964, no. 151; London, 1970, no. 95; Manchester, 1988, no. 2
Lit.: *Memoirs*, pp. ii–iii; Edwards, 1968, p. 14; Oliver, 1969, p. 42; Oliver, 1970, pp. 33–4; Lord, 2000, fig. 238

National Museums & Galleries of Wales (NMW A 92)

Cardiff and Manchester only

Illustrated on p. 5, fig. 3

Thomas Jones is shown as a middle-aged country squire, with his Danish-born wife Maria and their two daughters, Anna Maria (born 1780), on the left, and Elizabetha (born 1781) playing the spinet. The identification of the fifth figure remains uncertain, however. It could be either of Jones's younger brothers, Revd David

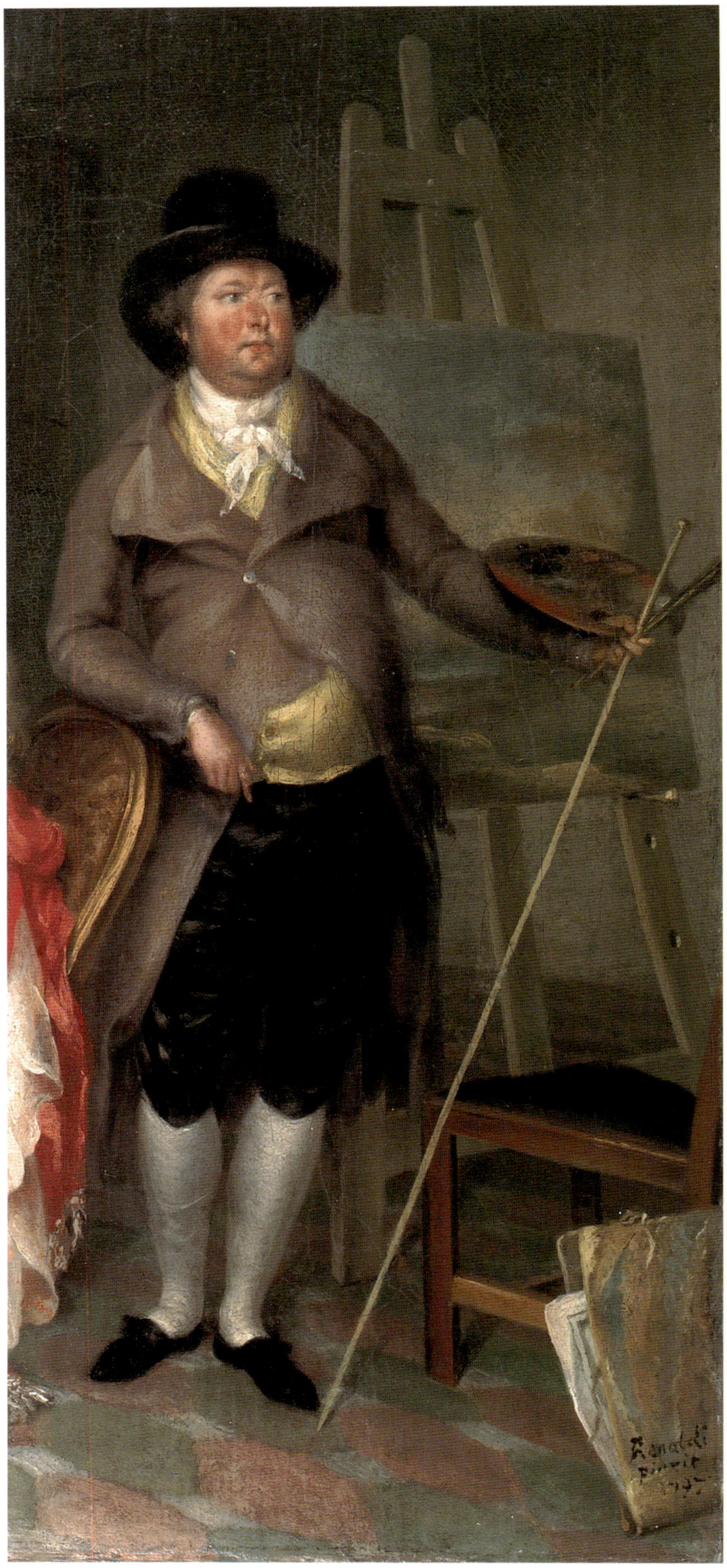

Detail of cat. no. 9, showing Thomas Jones.

Jones (1751–1809) or Rice Jones (cat. no. 7), or even the artist himself, though not Captain John Dale, as suggested in an inscription, since Elizabetha did not marry him until 1804. Jones's full figure recalls a description of him by his friend Uvedale Price in 1795, as 'a little stunted man, as round as a ball, the truest Welsh runt' (Oliver, 1970, p. 34). Jones is shown as a painter with his palette and brushes before an easel. His wife is seated at the spinning-wheel, looking frail – she died two years later. Joseph Farington recorded details of Francesco Renaldi's visit to Pencerrig, noting on 28 February 1798 that he had 'been with Jones 2 months' painting '2 pictures for Exhibition' (*Diary*, vol. III, p. 986). The present work was exhibited in that year and is Renaldi's last known painting. No payment for the painting is recorded in Jones's Account Book (cat. no. 73), suggesting that it was a gift. (ABS)

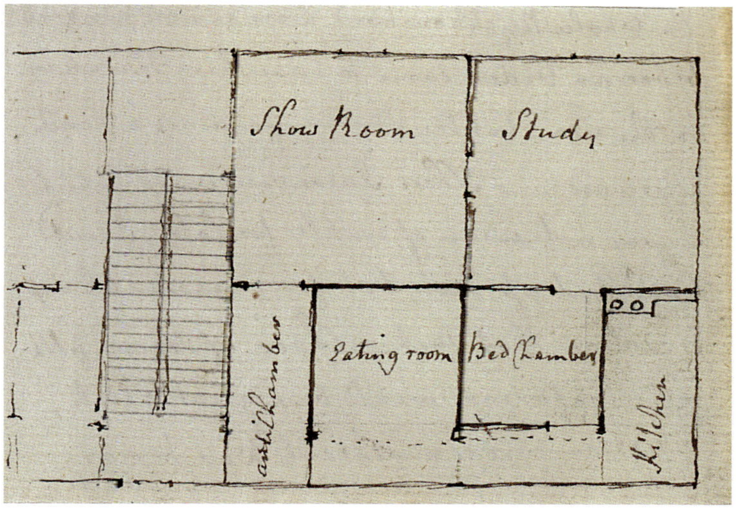

10

10

THOMAS JONES (1742–1803)

The Memoirs of Thomas Jones of Pencerrig

1798

Bound volume (225 sheets), 33 × 13 (13 × 5⅛)

Ins.: 'Memoirs &c / Thos Jones Penkerrig / Radnorshire 1803' inside cover; 'Thos Jones / Penkerrig Radnorshire. Nov[r] 1798 – / Finis' conclusion of the text (p. 436)
Prov.: Thomas Thomas, then by descent to Clara Thomas; D. E. T. Lindsay; sold *c.*1961; Jane Evan-Thomas; bequeathed 2001

Llyfrgell Genedlaethol Cymru, The National Library of Wales (NLW M 23812D)

Cardiff and Manchester only

The growing popularity of Jones has been helped by his achievement as the writer of some of the most vivid and revealing memoirs of any artist. Even if they did not contain an unparalleled wealth of material on British artists and their patrons in Italy and a fund of information on painting practice, Jones's text would be of paramount importance for historians in many fields, ranging from the grand tour to the Welsh landed gentry. It is also important that we do not also lose sight of the personal qualities of a text which is at times highly confessional. Jones perhaps reveals more about his character than he intended, as he details his disappointments, periods of depression and his illicit union with Maria Moncke with its disruptive consequences for his family. Consequently, we should probably take his statement that he did not intend his text for publication at face value. Certainly, it is not a highly polished piece of writing, since it incorporates transcriptions of large sections of his diaries, interspersed with more reflective commentaries. This, however, only gives the *Memoirs* a greater immediacy and freshness, with the unconventional charm of the finest of his oil sketches. Occasional illustrations include a plan of his studio in Naples – as shown here (May 1780) – and an image of Vesuvius. (GS)

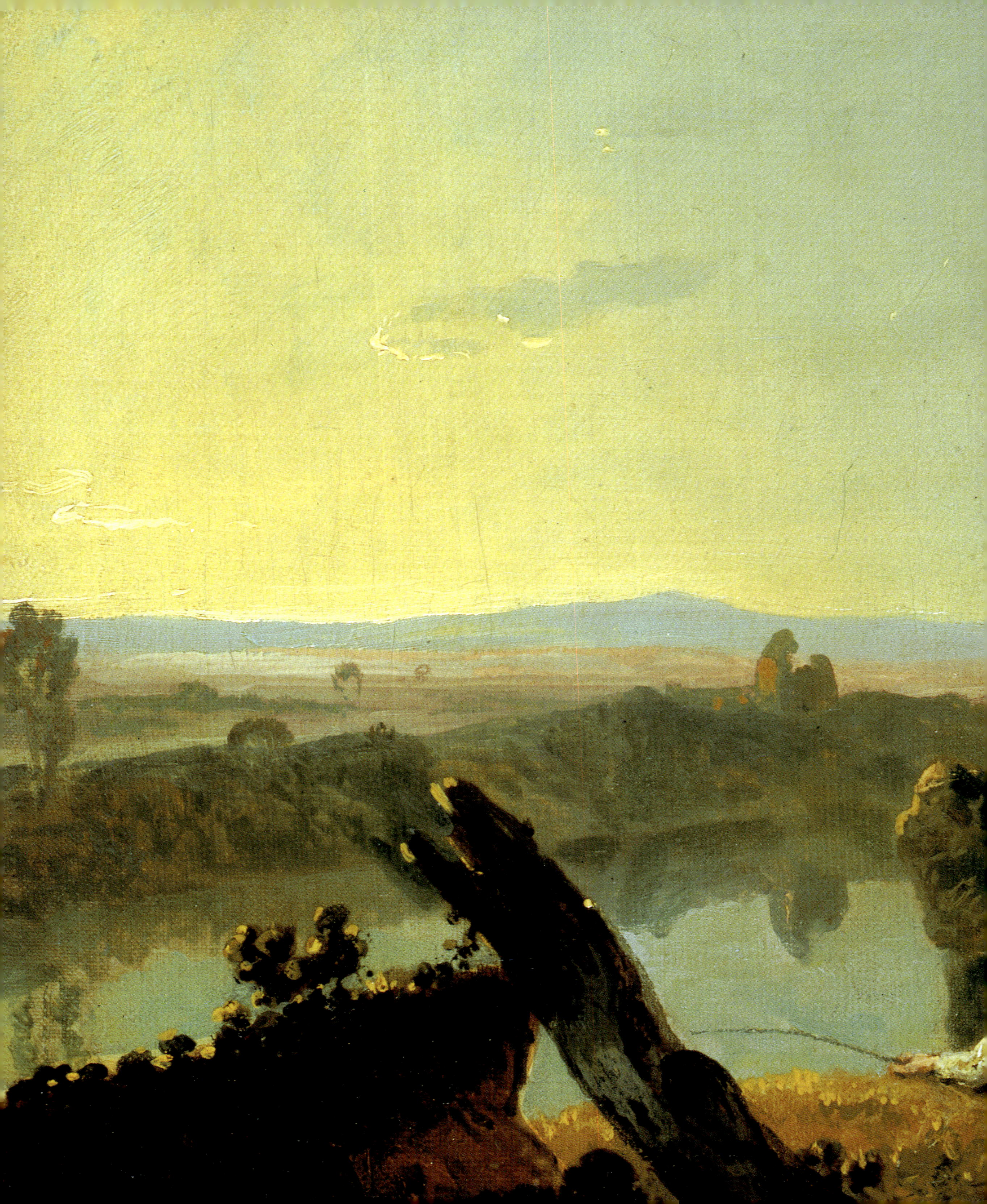

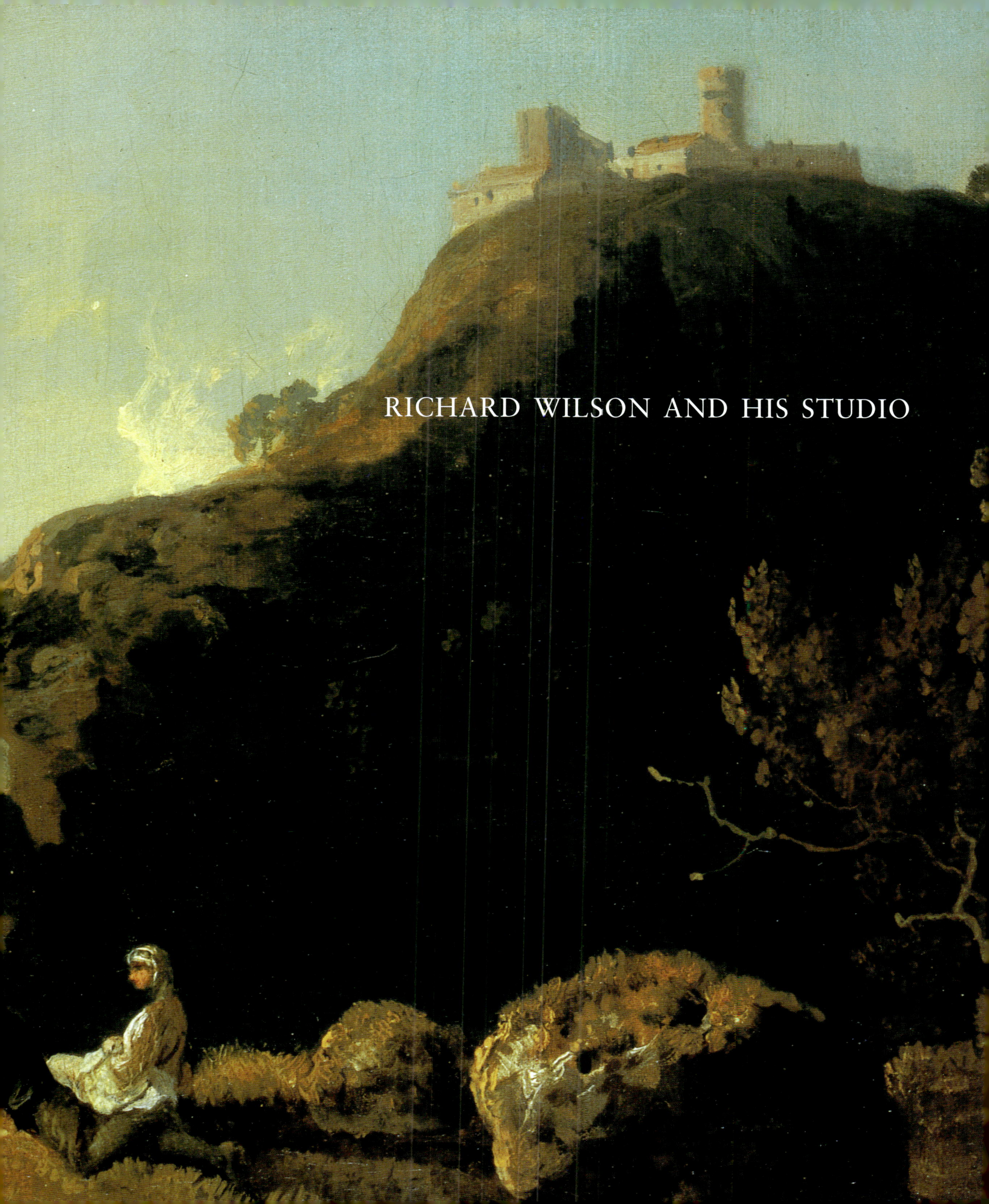
RICHARD WILSON AND HIS STUDIO

11

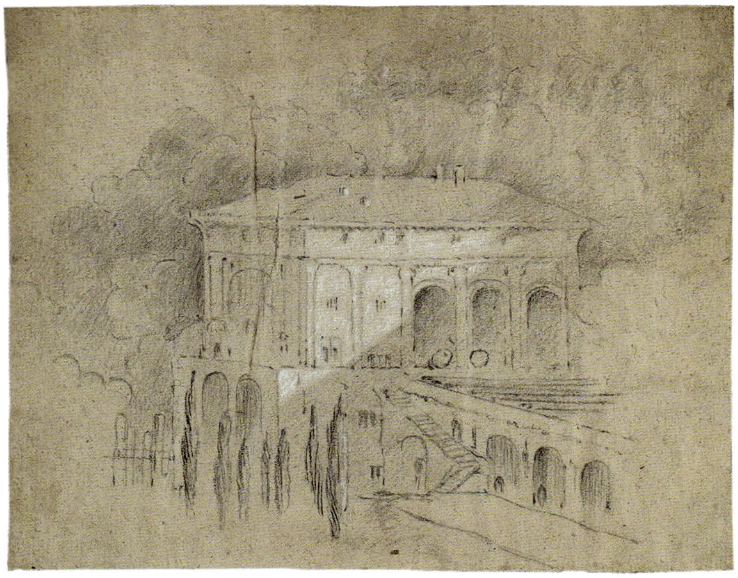

12

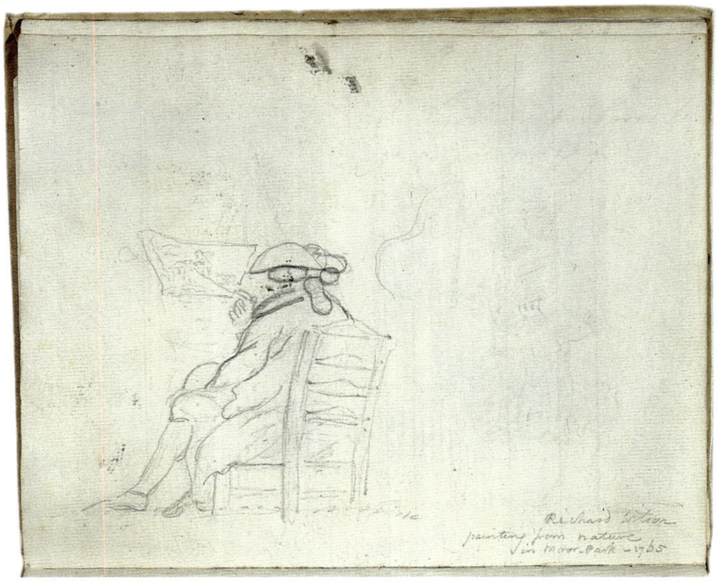

11

JOSEPH FARINGTON (1747–1821)

Sketchbook, Showing 'The Villa Madama, Rome, after Richard Wilson' 1763

Black chalk heightened with white on laid paper, 13.6 × 17.5 (5⅜ × 6⅞)

Ins.: 'This Book belongs to / Jos. Farington / at / Mr Richd Wilson's / Landscape painter / in the / Great-piazza / Covent-Garden / London / Decr.2 / 1763' in the inner side of the front cover; 'Villa Madama after Mr. W' on the exhibited page (f. 7)
Prov.: The artist, then by descent; Puttick & Simpson, London; purchased 1921
Exh.: Bolton, 1977, no. 5

Victoria and Albert Museum, London (P72-1921)

Cardiff and Manchester only

Jones began his pupillage with Richard Wilson in 1763 and Joseph Farington joined him soon after. Jones recalled how the two men were set to 'making Drawings with black and white Chalks on paper of a Middle Tint, either from his Studies and Pictures, or from Nature' (*Memoirs*, p. 9). Sadly, none of Jones's drawings from this period survive, but we can get some idea of his practice from Farington's sketchbooks. They contain copies of Wilson's sketches, including this view of the Villa Madama made from a drawing of around 1753 (London, 1982, no. 37). The process of copying monochrome sketches, Wilson told Jones, was to 'ground me in the Principles of Light & Shade, without being dazzled and misled by the flutter of Colours' (ibid.), but it had another result. 'I had copied so many Studies' of Italian scenery by Wilson, he noted of his first experience in that country, that 'I insensibly became familiarized with Italian Scenes, and enamoured of Italian forms' (ibid., p. 55). (GS)

12

JOSEPH FARINGTON (1747–1821)

Sketchbook, Showing 'Richard Wilson Painting from Nature' 1765

Pencil on paper, 16.5 × 21.1 (6½ × 8¼)

Ins.: 'Sketch Book Number 4 / Hertfordshire &c / 1765' on the inner side of the front cover; 'Richard Wilson / painting from nature / in Moor-Park-1765' l.r. on the exhibited page
Prov.: The artist, then by descent; Puttick & Simpson, London; purchased 1921
Exh.: Bolton, 1977, no. 7

Victoria and Albert Museum, London (P75-1921)

Cardiff and Manchester only

Jones's period of study with Wilson terminated in March 1765 and he may not have accompanied Joseph Farington and his master on

13

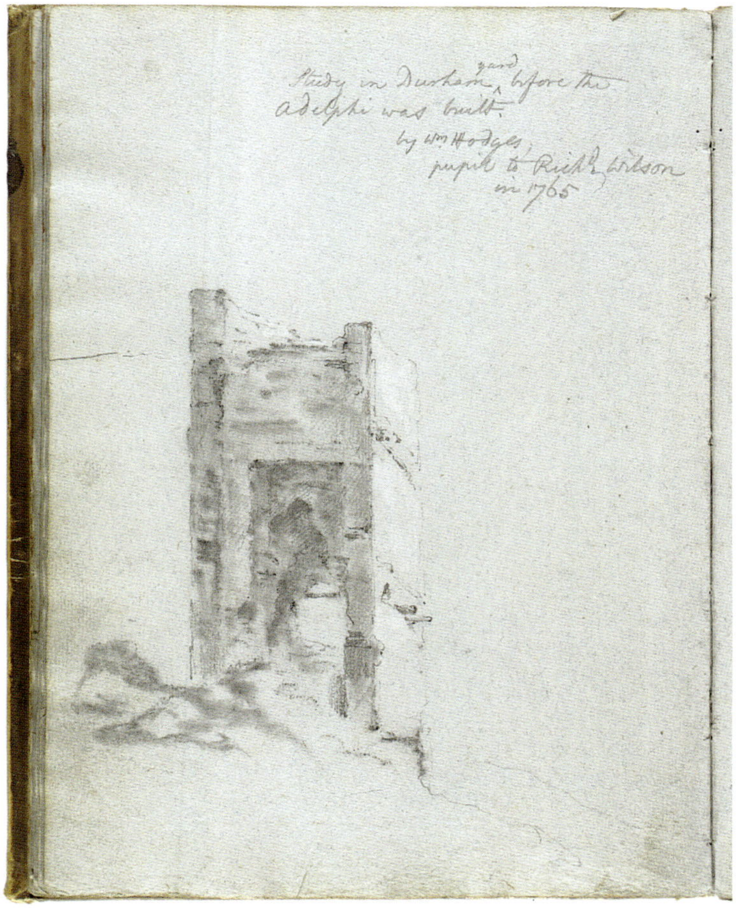

the expedition to Moor Park in Hertfordshire that is recorded here. That said, the image is still of great significance for Jones, since it suggests that 'painting from nature' was both an integral part of Wilson's teaching and a feature of his practice. Jones's own first dated oil sketch, cat. no. 39, comes from 1770, but it may be that the 'Studies . . . from Nature' that were lost in 1783 included earlier efforts inspired by Wilson's example (*Memoirs*, p. 140). Even though no examples of Wilson's oil sketches from nature have come to light, and it is difficult to say for sure which paintings he produced on the spot (London, 1982, pp. 182–3), it is possible that Jones's lifelong commitment to the former practice stemmed from the years he spent with his master. (GS)

13

WILLIAM HODGES (1744–1797)

Richard Wilson's Italian Sketchbook, Showing William Hodges' 'A Tower in Durham Yard'

1765

Black chalk with stump, heightened with white on paper, 28.6 × 21 ($11\frac{1}{4}$ × $8\frac{1}{4}$)

Ins.: 'Study in Durham[yard] before the / Adelphi was built / by Wm. Hodges. / pupil to Rich[d] Wilson / in 1765' t.l. on the exhibited page (p. 23v)
Prov.: Oldfield Bowles; Sir George Beaumont; purchased by Paul Mellon, 1963
Exh.: Oxford, 1937, no. 64; New Haven, 1977, no. 15; New Haven, 1981, no. 90; London, 1982, no. 39
Lit.: Constable, 1954, p. 143; Sutton and Clements, 1968, I, pp. 43–4, II, p. 23v; Stuebe, 1979, pp. 8–9, pp. 301–2

Yale Center for British Art, Paul Mellon Collection (B1977.14.359)

Cardiff and Manchester only

William Hodges, who achieved considerable success following his travels with Captain Cook, joined Richard Wilson as an apprentice in about 1758. According to the *Memoirs*, his lively character contributed to the light-hearted atmosphere in Wilson's studio during the period of Jones's pupillage (p. 9). By the date of this study, Hodges was quite adept at copying his master's drawings, in this case a slight study which is in the same sketchbook (p. 25v). Another drawing of the tower by Joseph Farington also exists (sketchbook in the Victoria and Albert Museum, dated 1765, p. 3), suggesting that Wilson set the subject as an exercise. This amounted to more than simply copying the work, since the original is very slight and Farington's version has an invented landscape setting and signs that he sought to shape his material into an oval composition. Jones may have left Wilson's studio by this date, but this is presumably the sort of exercise that he also undertook. (GS)

14

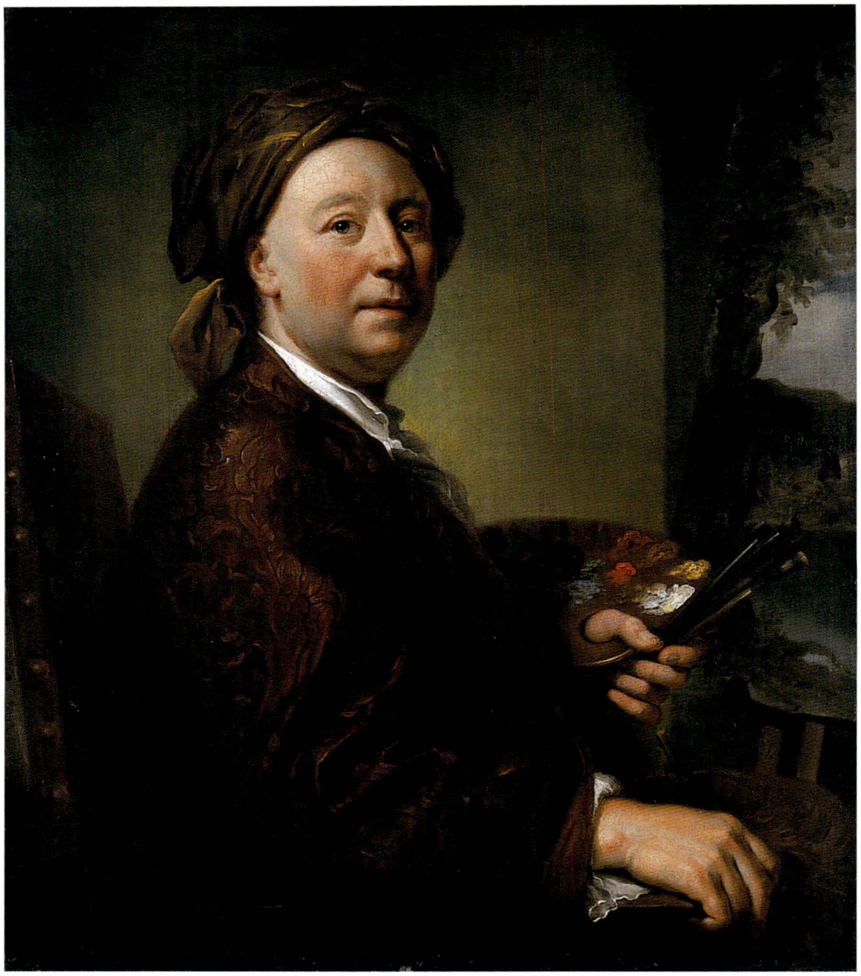

14

Anton Raphael Mengs (1728–1779)

Richard Wilson 1752

Oil on canvas, 84.6 × 75.2 ($33\frac{1}{4} \times 29\frac{5}{8}$)

Prov.: Exchanged by the artist for a work by Richard Wilson; Sir Watkin Williams Wynn; Sotheby's, 5 February 1947, no. 45; purchased by Renwick; purchased with the assistance of the National Art Collections Fund, 1947
Exh.: Cardiff, 1969, no. 1; London, 1993b, no. 18
Lit.: Granville, 1948, pp. 67–8; Constable, 1953, pp. 67–8
Eng.: W. Bromley (1785 and 1790) and W. Bond (1812 and 1824)

National Museums & Galleries of Wales (NMW A 113)

Cardiff only

This portrait of Wilson, shown seated before an easel on which a landscape is displayed, was painted in Rome in 1752. Wilson was in close contact with the artist Anton Raphael Mengs, one of the leading artists of the neo-Classical school, at this date and he is said to have painted either one or two landscapes in return for this work. This image of a personal friend and fellow artist at work has an intimate quality which is sometimes lacking in Mengs's later portraits. There is no evidence as to how the work entered the collection of Sir Watkin Williams Wynn (1749–1789), but it was hanging in the Stone Parlour at Wynnstay in 1790. Jones was aware of the friendship between Wilson and Mengs and observed the latter's *Perseus and Andromeda* at his studio in Rome (*Memoirs*, p. 68). Intended for Sir Watkin Williams Wynn, this famous painting was lost to French pirates *en route* back to Britain. According to Farington, 'Jones told me that Mengs, the German Painter . . . said that He never met with but 2 English Artists of superior genius, they were R. Wilson, – and Athenian Stuart' (*Diary*, vol. IV, 27 May 1801, p. 1554). (ABS)

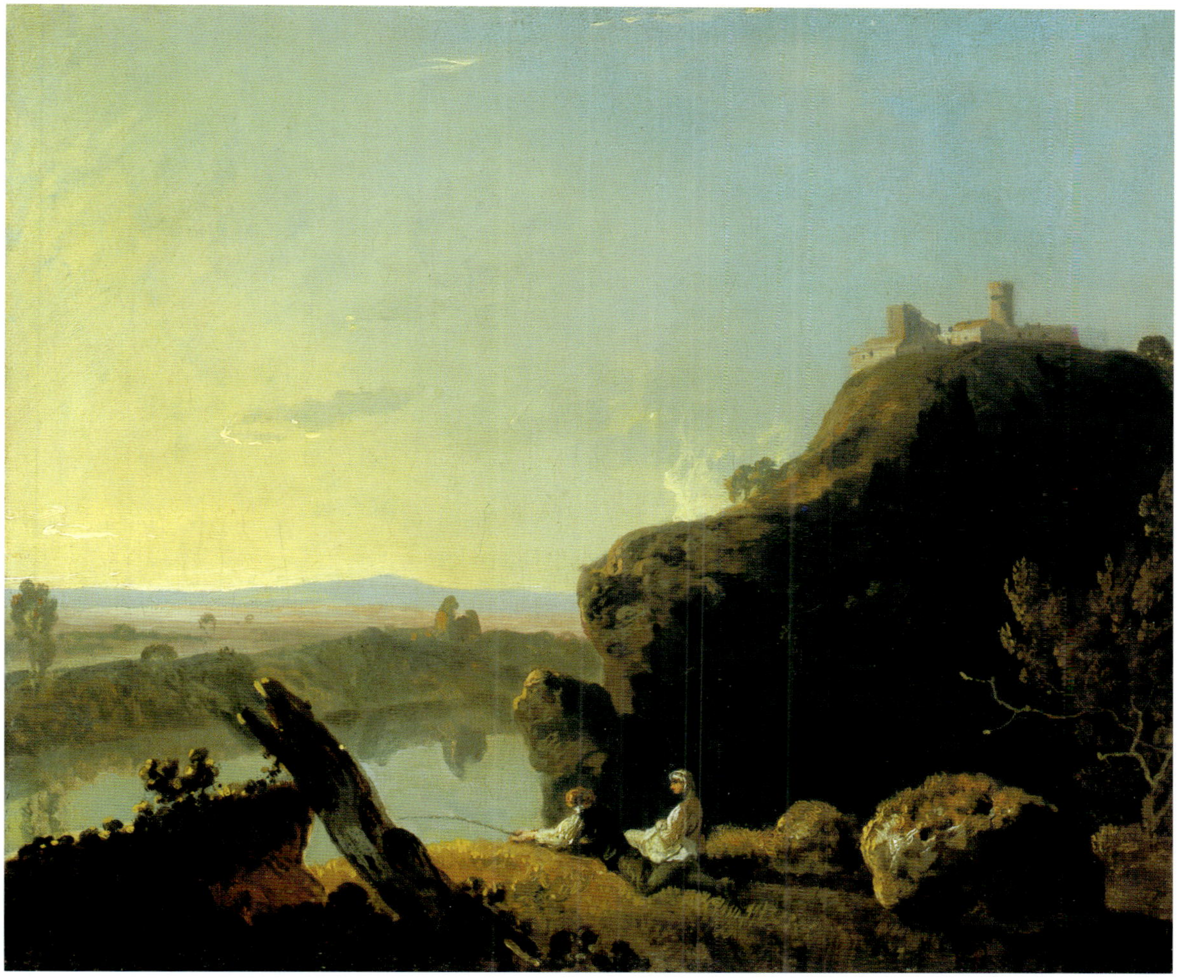

15

15

Richard Wilson (1713–1782)

River View, On the Arno *c.*1760–5

Oil on canvas, 44.5 × 54.6 (17½ × 21½)

Prov.: Bequeathed by George Salting to the National Gallery in 1910; transferred to the Tate in 1919
Lit.: Constable, 1953, pp. 213–14; London, 1982, pp. 221–3

Tate. Bequeathed by George Salting, 1910 (N02647)

Cardiff and Manchester only

Wilson painted over thirty works, varying in size, with a composition similar to this. They are traditionally said to represent a view on the River Arno in Italy. Wilson and his studio habitually repeated compositions and it is possible that Jones copied his master's works, even if he did not contribute to their production. As he noted in his *Memoirs*, this was the task of Wilson's apprentices (p. 9). Martin Postle has pointed out that the title *On the Arno* derives from the etchings made after Wilson by Thomas Hastings in 1825. Wilson himself described a version of the subject (Manchester City Art Gallery) as simply *A Summer Evening* and claimed that the picture was 'Esteemed by the first painters here to be my very best performance'. Wilson continued that he 'kept a Drawing of it in order to do another for our next exhibition' (London, 1982, p. 222). This version was doubted by W. G. Constable, but, following conservation in 1994, the sensitive treatment of light and dextrous handling of pigment suggest that it is by Wilson. (ABS)

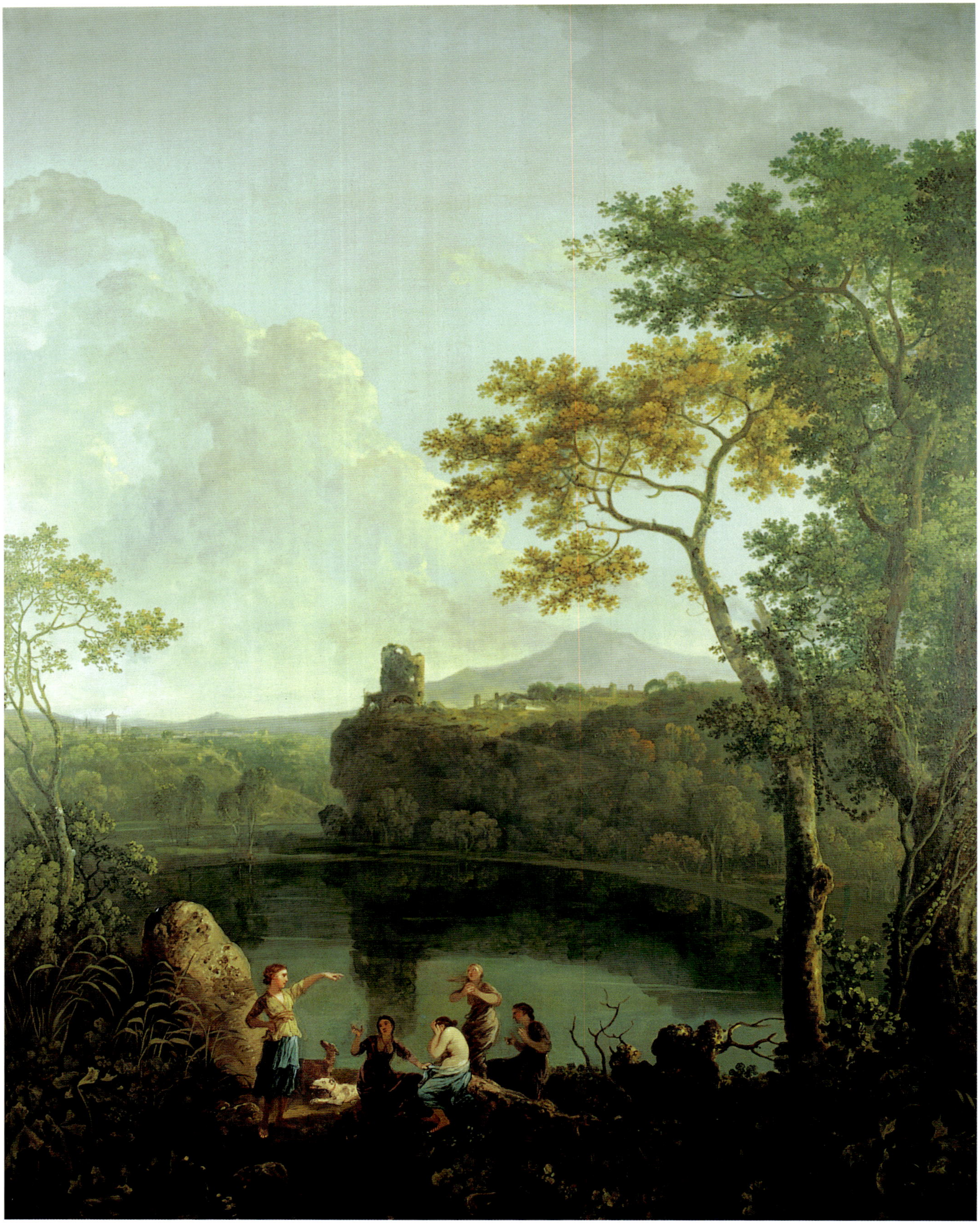

16

Richard Wilson (1713–1782)

The Lake of Nemi with Dolbadarn Castle (Diana and Callisto) *c.*1764–5

Oil on canvas, 229.2 × 183 ($90\frac{1}{4} \times 72$)

Prov.: Henry Blundell; given by Charles Blundell to John Gladstone of Fasque; by descent to Mrs Geoffrey Parsons; Sotheby's, 20 April 1955, no. 106; Agnew's; purchased 1955
Exh.: Cardiff, 1969, no. 40; London, 1982, no. 106
Lit.: Constable, 1953, pp. 164–5; Solkin, 1981, p. 413

Bristol Museum and Art Gallery

Cardiff only

This painting is one of four large canvases that Wilson and his studio executed for Henry Blundell of Ince Hall in Lancashire. Joseph Farington, who was a pupil with Wilson from 1763 to 1767, mentions that the 'pictures were painted while I was with Him, were prepared and far advanced towards finishing by his pupils, but Wilson went over and regulated them' (*Diary*, vol. VII, 26 June 1806, p. 2797). Stylistically, it seems likely that they were painted around 1763–4 and therefore Jones, as well as Farington, might have had a role in their production, or at least witnessed the process.

In the foreground, Diana is shown chastizing the errant nymph Callisto (Ovid, *Metamorphoses*, II 441–5). This was a suitable subject for a view of the Lake of Nemi which was otherwise known as the Speculum Dianae, or mirror of Diana. The composition is basically a repetition of the *The Lake of Nemi, or the Speculum Dianae* (National Trust, Stourhead), but there are significant alterations. Most obviously, Wilson has introduced Dolbadarn Castle into the distant landscape, thus associating his native Welsh landscape with one of the most significant classical sites, a gesture that cannot have been lost upon his young pupil. (ABS)

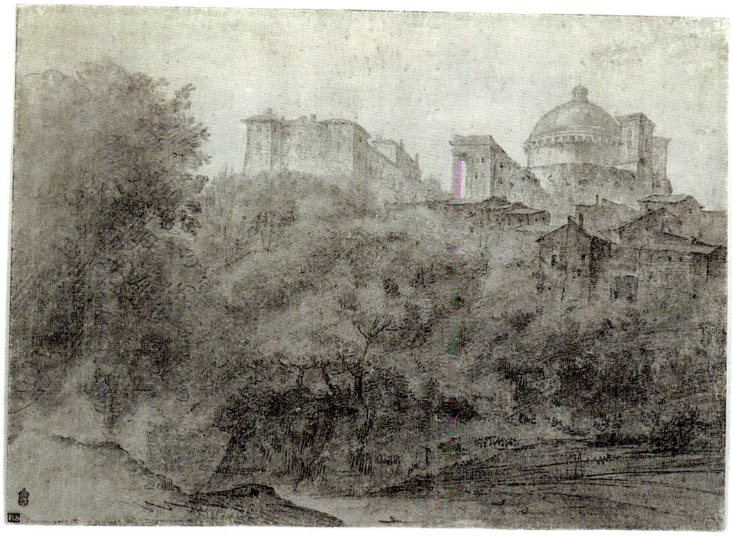

17

17

Richard Wilson (1713–1782)

Ariccia *c.*1754–6

Black chalk and stump on laid paper with grey preparation, 32.2 × 44.7 ($12\frac{5}{8} \times 17\frac{5}{8}$)

Prov.: Paul Sandby; A. G. B. Russell; Paul Oppé, 1948; Armide Oppé; purchased 1996
Exh.: Birmingham, 1948, no. 127; Sheffield, 1952, no. 77; London, 1958, no. 12; London, 1982, no. 55; London, 1997, no. 13
Lit.: Ford, 1951, no. 65

Tate. Purchased as part of the Oppé Collection with assistance from the National Lottery through the Heritage Lottery Fund 1996 (T08164)

Cardiff and Manchester only

This drawing, from the latter part of Wilson's Italian stay, shows the Chigi Palace and Bernini's church of Santa Maria dell' Assunzione at Ariccia. Wilson employed his favourite drawing medium of black chalk and stump (a roll of paper used to smudge the chalk), working on a paper prepared with a grey wash. It was this type of drawing that Jones produced during his first year of study, though none of his student drawings survive. They included views of Ariccia, since Jones noted that he had 'copied some views' that Wilson had made in the Chigi Park many years earlier (*Memoirs*, p. 61). Jones may even have had this drawing in mind when he sketched there in 1777, since his view on the edge of the

18

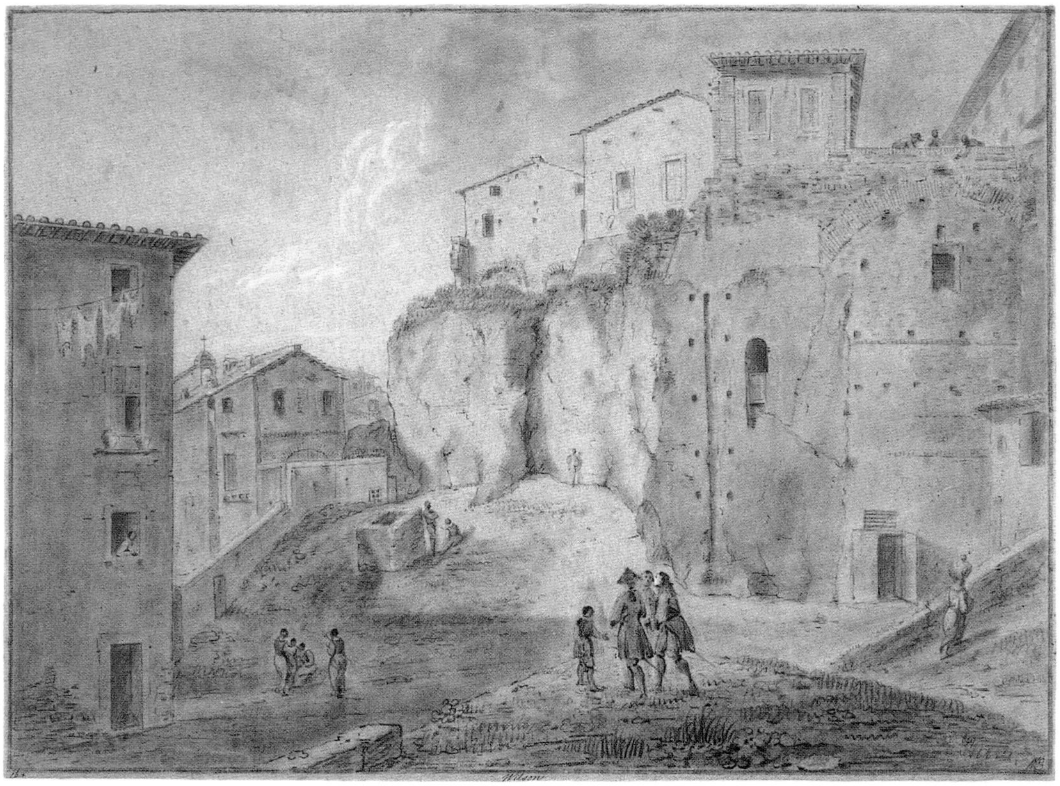

town (cat. no. 80) employs a similar composition, with a series of buildings stretched out along the horizon with a clump of trees to the left. (GS)

18

ATTRIBUTED TO RICHARD WILSON (1713–1782)

The Tarpeian Rock, Rome *c.*1754–6

Black chalk with stump, heightened with white, on paper, 31.4 × 42.7 (12⅜ × 16¾)

Prov.: Thomas Monro; William Esdaile; Alexander Dyce; bequeathed 1869
Lit.: Ford, 1951, no. 87, pp. 40–1

Victoria and Albert Museum, London, Dyce Collection (Dyce 649)

Cardiff and Manchester only

The Tarpeian Rock – the part of the Capotoline Hill from which condemned criminals were flung in ancient Rome – was a popular site with grand tourists and was depicted by many artists. The interest in this drawing, however, lies in its similarities with later works by Jones in which he indulged his fascination with the interplay of surface and void in walls and rock faces. Copying similar drawings in Wilson's studio may have been one of the factors which encouraged Jones's interest in such subjects when he arrived in Italy. Intriguingly, Richard Wilson's Italian *Sketchbook* (cat. no. 13, p. 17) contains a roof-top view Jones's master made from the window of his Roman lodgings.

The fact that this drawing might have been produced by one of Wilson's many pupils – Brinsley Ford attributed it to J. Plimer – does not invalidate the argument. Indeed, the difficulty in discriminating between master and pupils, and between individual students, is indicative of the free exchange of ideas in Wilson's studio. In the absence of a signature, moreover, there is no way of knowing for certain if this drawing is not even by Jones himself. (GS)

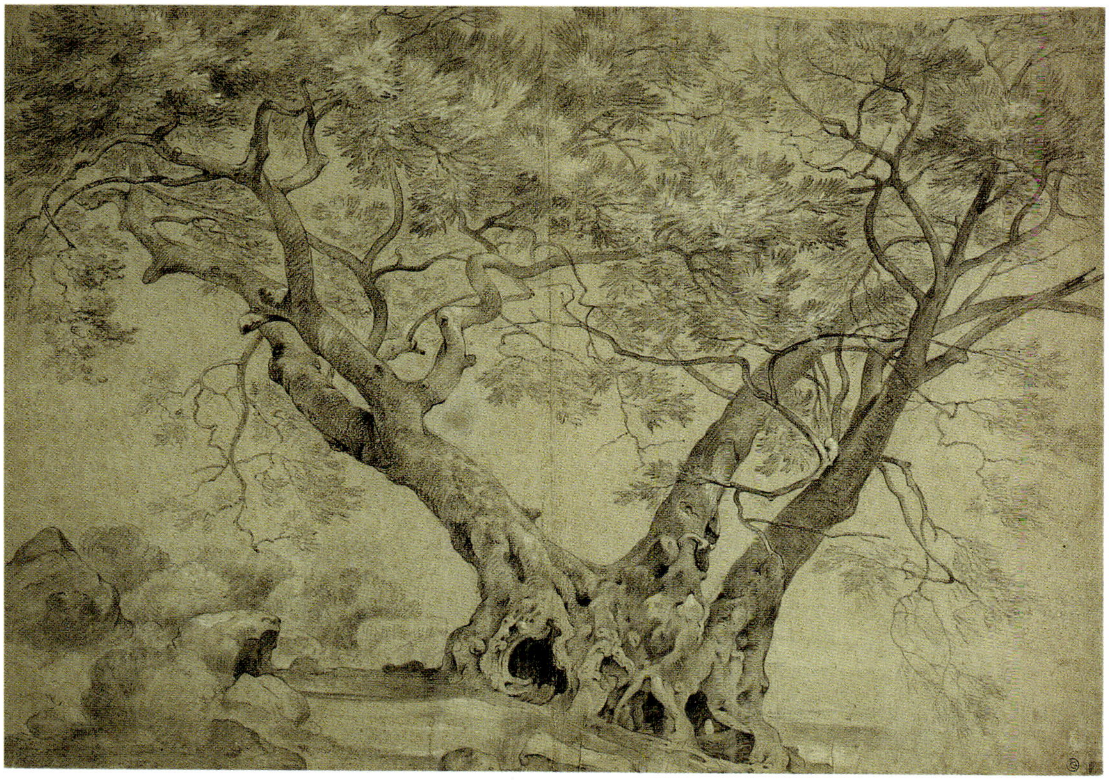

19

19

Richard Wilson (1713–1782)

The 'Arbra Santa' on the Banks of Lake Nemi

*c.*1754–6

Black chalk, heightened with white on grey laid paper, 38.5 × 55.5 (15⅛ × 21⅞)

Prov.: Paul Sandby; Christie's, 3 May 1811, no. 101; Mrs Arthur Clifton; Agnew's, 1964
Exh.: New York, 1972, no. 26; New Haven, 1977, no. 18; London, 1982, no. 52

Yale Center for British Art, Paul Mellon Collection (B1977.14.4655)

Cardiff and Manchester only

Jones noted during a second trip to the lakes of Nemi and Albano to the south-east of Rome in April 1778 that his party 'went to make Sketches . . . particularly a large *Plane* tree on the edge of the Water call'd the *Arbor Santa*'. It 'has a hollow within that I believe w'd contain a dozen persons', and, he continued, my 'Old Master *Wilson* when in this Country made use of it as a Study to Paint in' (*Memoirs*, p. 58). Although Jones's drawing does not survive, we can assume that it did not resemble Wilson's imposing and detailed record of the characterful tree. There is just the one instance of Jones producing a large presentation drawing of this type – cat. no. 130 – and he was not influenced by this important aspect of Wilson's practice. (GS)

FOLLOWING PAGES Detail of cat. no. 40.

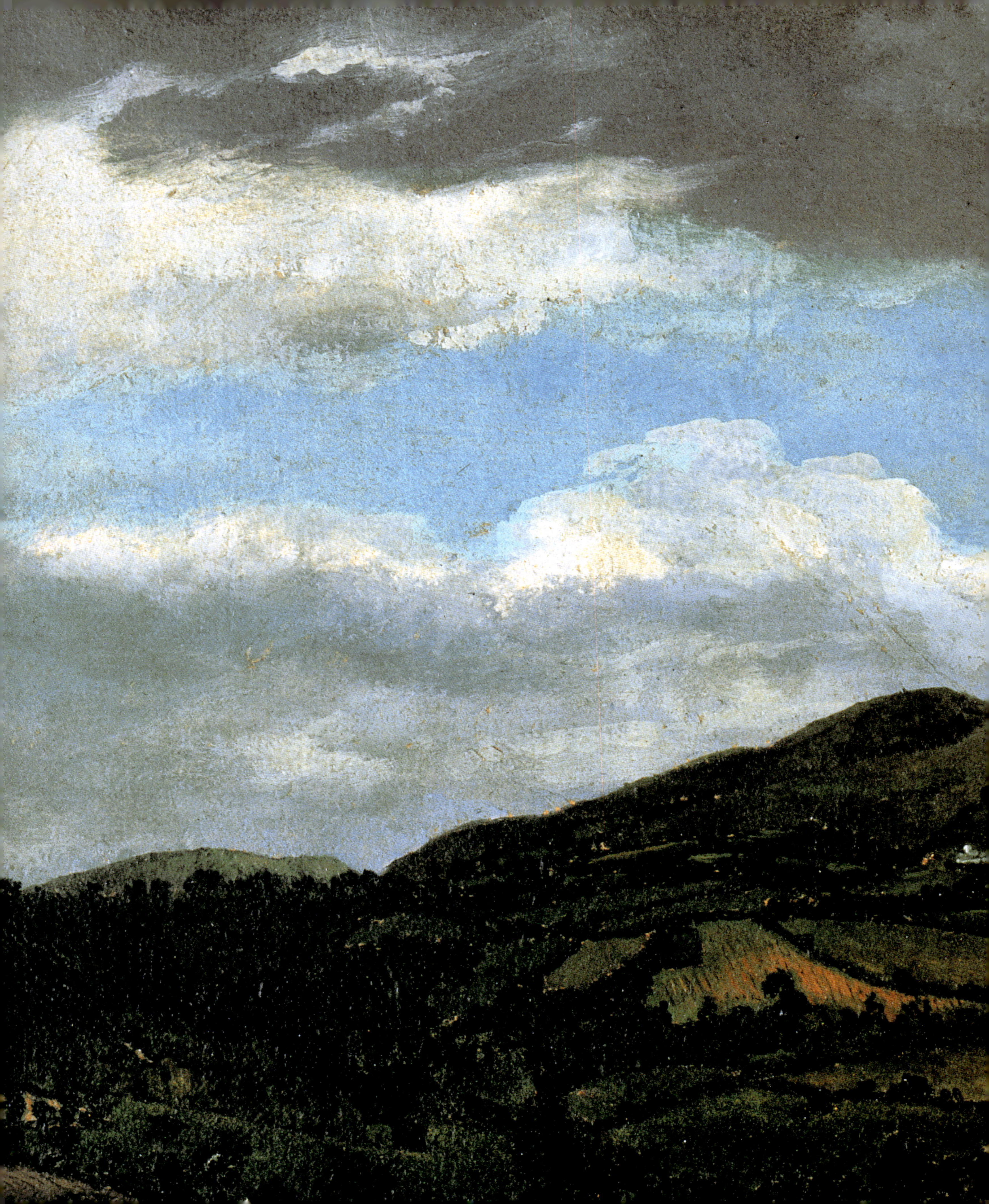

EARLY CAREER PRIOR TO ITALY

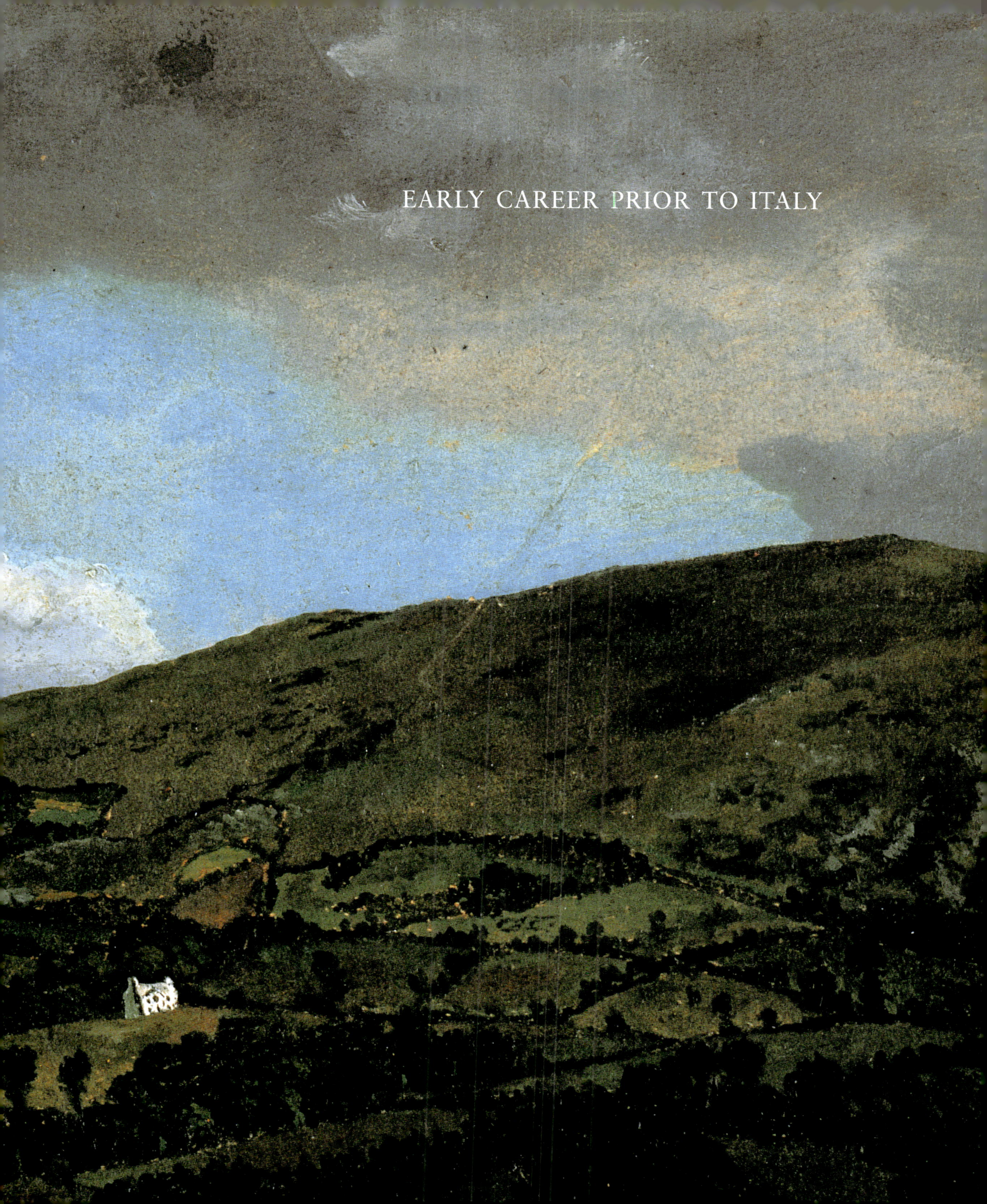

20

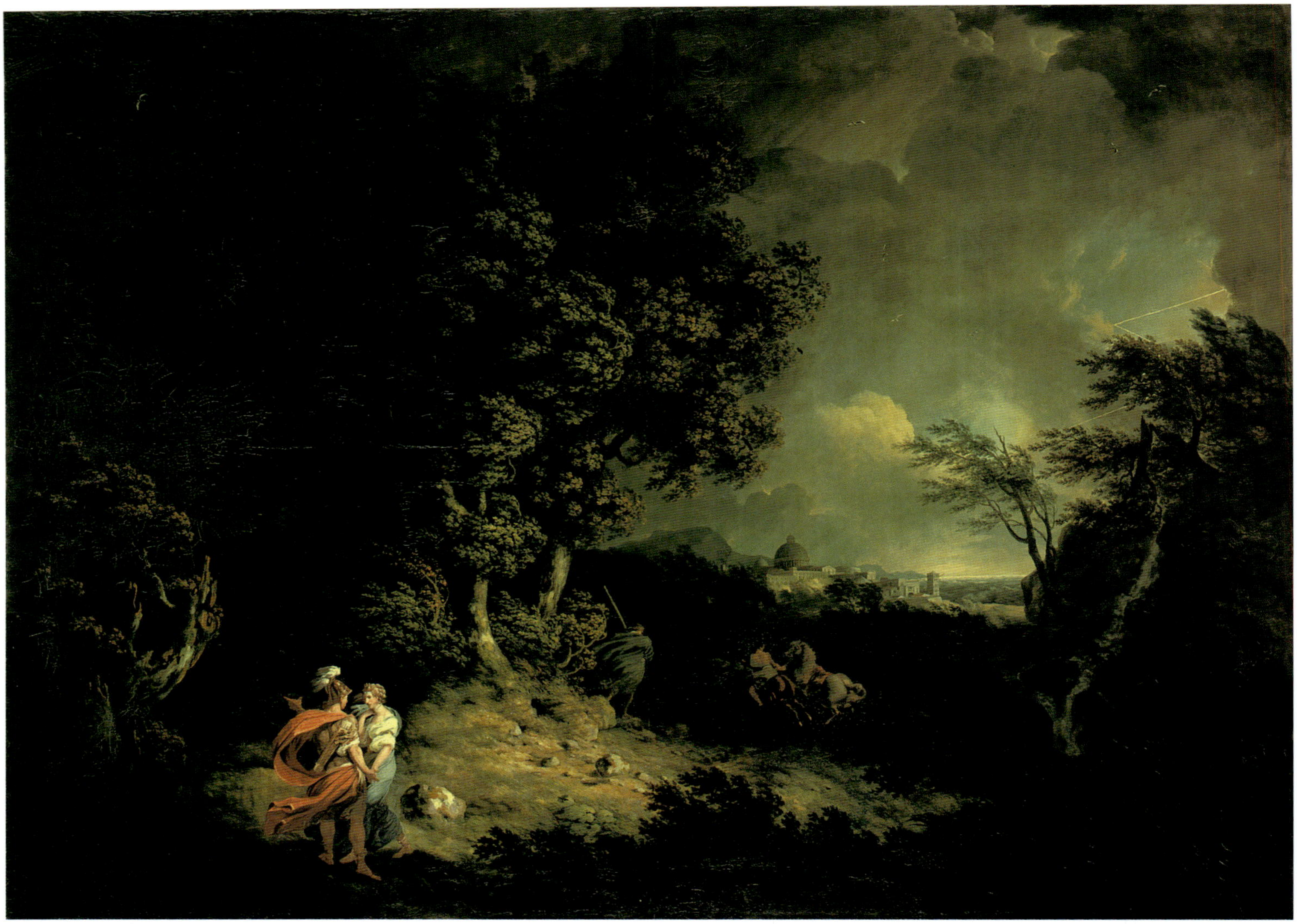

20

THOMAS JONES (1742–1803) AND JOHN HAMILTON MORTIMER (1740–1779)

A Land Storm, with the Story of Dido and Aeneas
1769

Oil on canvas, 137.5 × 193.5 ($54\frac{1}{8}$ × $76\frac{3}{16}$)

Ins.: 'Tho Jones pt 1769' l.r.
Prov.: Lord Grosvenor; Baronet Watson, 1772; Christie's, 24 June 1772, no. 80; Catherine II, St Petersburg; Prince Grigory Potemkin, St Petersburg; from 1792 in the Winter Palace; 1799, transferred to Gatchina Palace; returned to the Hermitage no later than 1821
Exh.: Society of Artists, 1769, no. 74; New Haven, 1996, no. 11; Frankfurt, 1999, no. 150
Lit.: Kroll, 1961, pp. 14–15, p. 81; Gowing, 1985, p. 15; Sunderland, 1986, p. 46, cat. no. 24
Eng.: William Woollett and Francesco Bartolozzi, 1769

The State Hermitage Museum, St Petersburg

Cardiff and Manchester only

This was one of Jones's best-known paintings during his lifetime, after being successfully exhibited in 1769 at the Society of Artists. The story is taken from Virgil's *Aeneid* and tells of the love affair between Dido, first Queen of Carthage, and Aeneas, the legendary founder of Rome. While out hunting, the couple took shelter in a cave during a violent storm and consummated their relationship. Jones recalled that he 'began the Picture (a Storm)' in March 1769 'in which my friend Mortimer had introduced the Story of Dido and Aeneas retiring to the Cave'. Jones thought that it 'was one of the best Pictures I ever painted' and that William Woollett's offer to 'engrave a Print' would help establish his reputation (*Memoirs*, p. 19). The painting was probably acquired by Catherine the Great between 1785 and August 1786, when William Woollett's widow received permission to dedicate the print to her. Jones seems to have been unaware that his work had entered one of the greatest art collections of the day. (ABS)

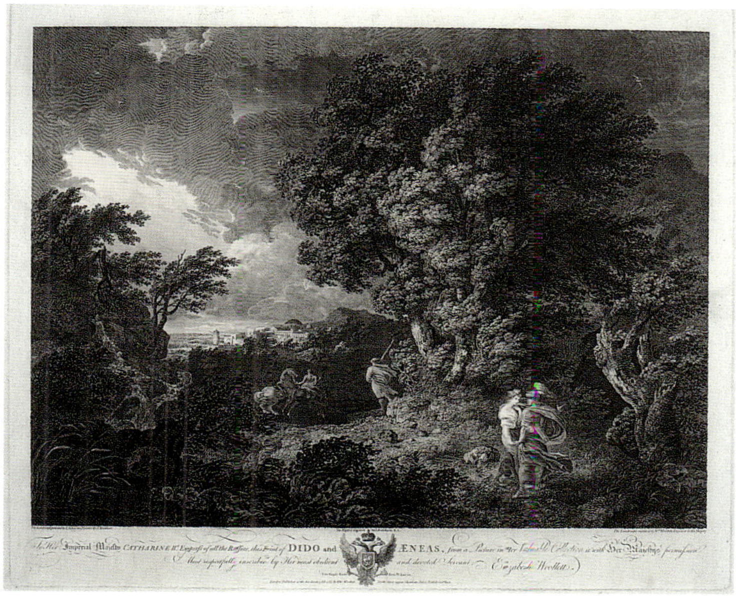

21

21

WILLIAM WOOLLETT (1735–1785) AND
FRANCESCO BARTOLOZZI (1725–1815),
AFTER THOMAS JONES (1742–1803) AND
JOHN HAMILTON MORTIMER (1740–1779)

Landscape with Dido and Aeneas 1769–87

Engraving and etching, 45.6 × 56.6 (18 × 22¼)

Ins.: 'The Landscape painted by T. Jones, the Figures by J. Mortimer' l.l.; 'To Her Imperial Majesty CATHARINE IId Empress of all the Russias, this Print of DIDO and AENEAS, from a picture in Her Valuable Collection is with Her Majesty's Permission / Most respectfully inscribed by Her Most obedient . . . and devoted Servant, / Elizabeth Woollett' l.c.; 'The Landscape engraved by Wm Woollett Engraver to His Majesty' l.r.
Exh.: Society of Artists, 1773, no. 408

National Museums & Galleries of Wales (NMW A 22878)

Cardiff and Manchester only

The plate for this print was begun by William Woollett in 1769. Jones wrote that he hoped that his 'Reputation would be established, and spread abroad through the Medium of that celebrated Engraver' (*Memoirs*, p. 19). Woollett, a friend to Jones, had had great success, particularly with his print of Richard Wilson's *The Destruction of the Children of Niobe* (1761), which helped to spread Wilson's fame and was one of the first English engravings to gain notice on the Continent. Woollett excelled at engraving landscapes, and was particularly successful at capturing different textures. Bartolozzi, another renowned engraver, was responsible for the figures. Jones records that Woollett abandoned the plate and that it 'remained locked up and forgotten during the remainder of his Days' (ibid., p. 20). This, however, was not the case, as the engraving was exhibited at the Society of Artists in 1773 and a new edition was produced in 1787 after Woollett's death by his widow, with the additional inscription seen in this print to Catherine II, who had acquired the original painting. (BM)

22

THOMAS JONES (1742–1803) AND
JOHN HAMILTON MORTIMER (1740–1779)

The Death of Orpheus c.1770

Oil on canvas, 95.2 × 129.5 (37½ × 51)

Prov.: Jane Mortimer?; Christie's, 25 March 1808, no. 63, unsold; Christie's, 10 December 1864, no. 136, unsold; H. L. Mortimer, 1865; Gerald Fulthorpe; Christie's, 24 June 1960, no. 122; Agnew's; purchased by Paul Mellon, 1960; presented 1981
Exh.: Society of Arts, 1770, no. 61?; The British School, London, 1803, no. 408; British Institution, London, 1806, no. 80; Richmond, 1963, no. 378
Lit.: Cormack, 1985, p. 130; Sunderland, 1986, p. 46, no. 35a

Yale Center for British Art, Paul Mellon Collection (B1981.25.458)

Cardiff and Manchester only

22

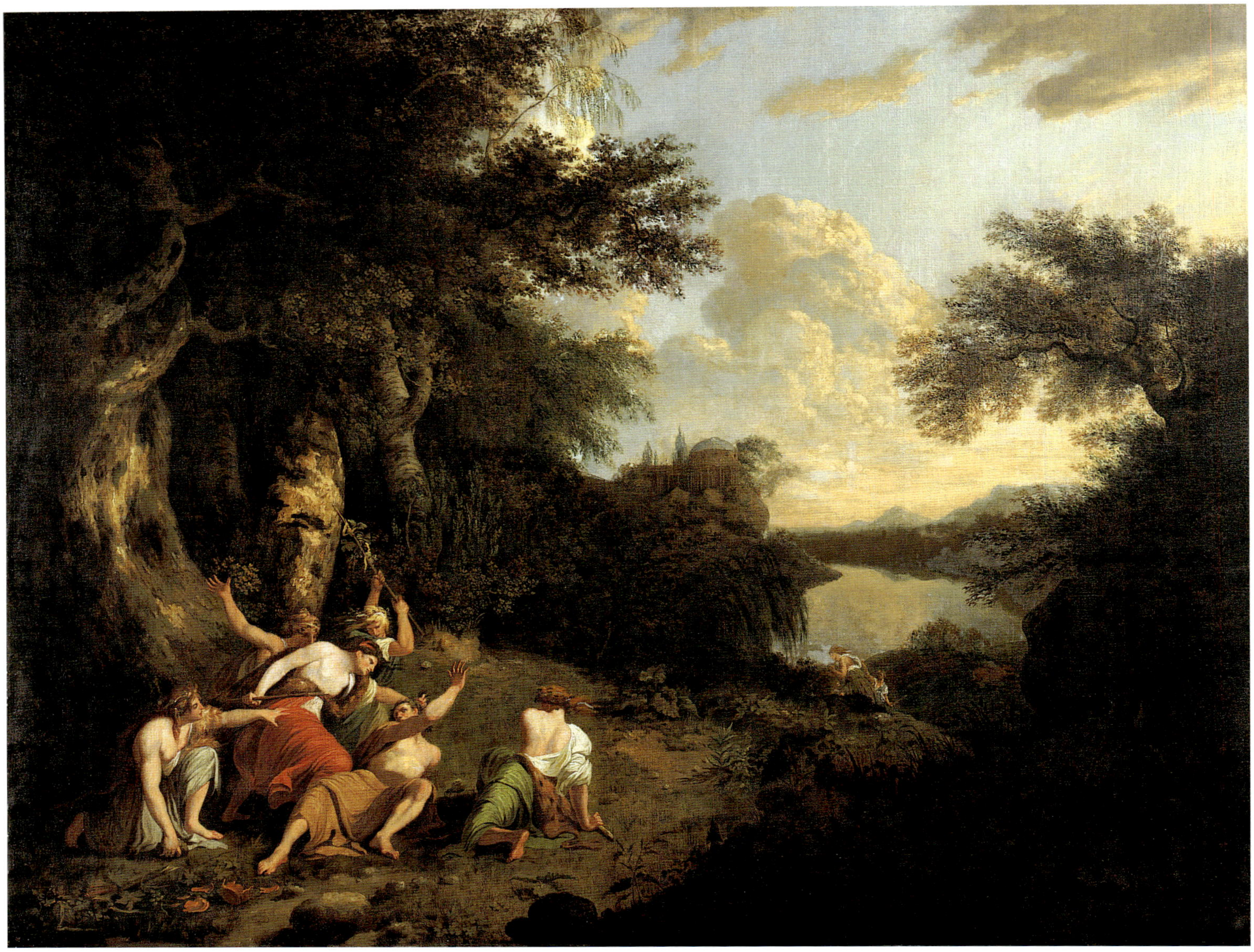

The story of how Orpheus descended into Hades to bring back his beautiful wife, Eurydice, only to lose her for a second time, has always been popular with artists, but Jones chose to illustrate the tragic sequel. In desperate grief, Orpheus developed a hatred of all women, turning to the company of men. During a frenzied orgy, he spurned the amorous advances of the Thracian Maenads and they tore him to pieces in revenge.

Jones records that in 1770 he began a large picture '8 feet by 6 with figures from 12 to 18 inches high by Mortimer', and in November he wrote that 'I finished the large landscape . . . in which the death of Orpheus was introduced' (*Memoirs*, p. 22). John Sunderland has pointed out that this picture is a reduced version after the original painting, now in a private collection, and considerably cut down. This variant copy appears to have been produced by Mortimer and Jones together and shows the entire composition, though it is not clear if it was the work exhibited at the Society of Artists. (ABS)

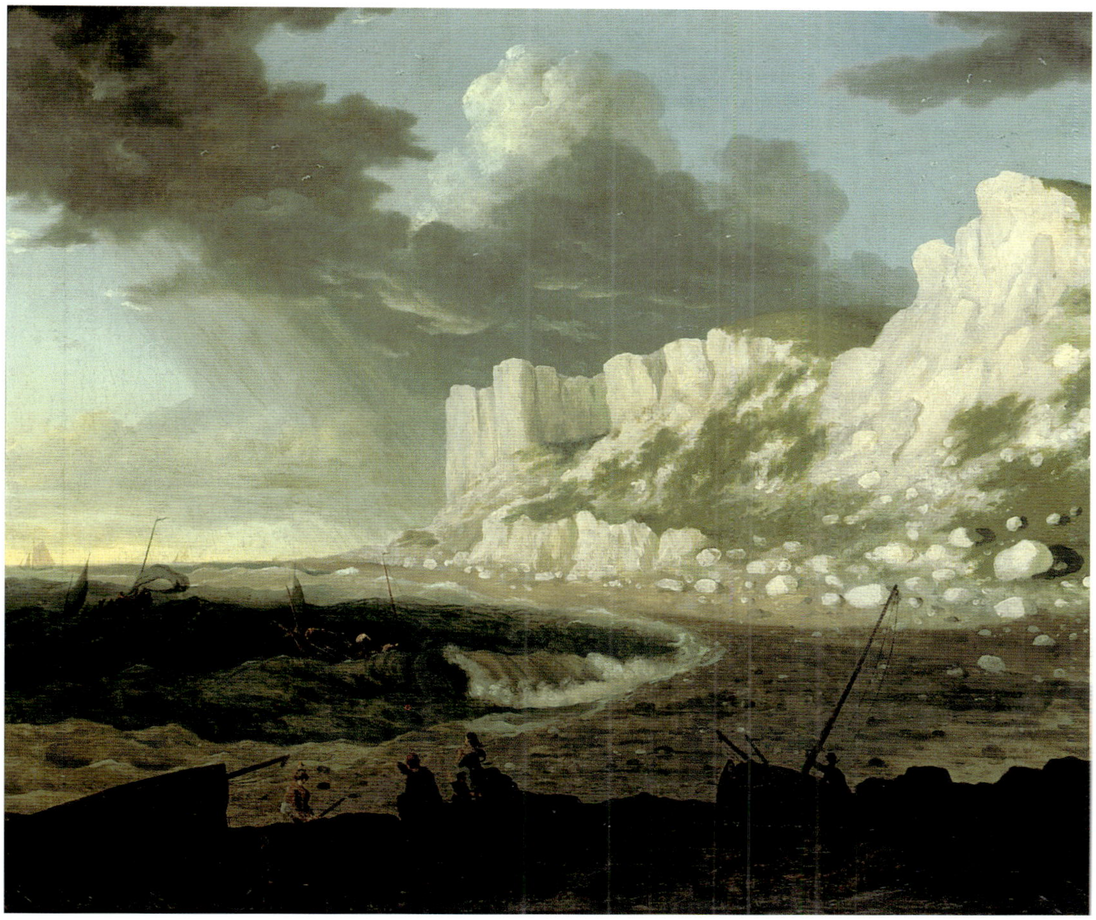

23

23

THOMAS JONES (1742–1803)

Coast Scene near Eastbourne with Approaching Storm 1771

Oil on canvas, 61.5 × 74.5 (24¼ × 29¼)

Ins.: 'T. Jones pt / 1771' l.l.
Prov.: Sotheby's, Margam, 19 October 1999, no. 85, (unsold); Sotheby's, 22 March 2000, no. 6; acquired with the assistance of the National Art Collections Fund, Resource / V&A Purchase Grant Fund and the Friends of the Towner Art Gallery
Lit.: National Art Collections Fund, 2000 Review, p. 123

Towner Art Gallery, Eastbourne (EASTG2218)

Cardiff and Manchester only

On 21 December 1770, Jones went to Eastbourne to celebrate Christmas with his friends John Hamilton Mortimer, the figure painter, and the architect James Gandon. This was Mortimer's home town, where his father was a dealer in flour and the owner of several mills. One such circular mill had been converted by Gandon into a beach house. 'One of the rooms', Jones recalls, 'was made use of as a Study to paint Scenes after nature as Cliffs, Waves, Shipping &c' (*Memoirs*, p. 23). The present picture, which depicts the white chalk cliffs at Eastbourne and fishing vessels struggling in a storm, was inspired by the observation of winter storms during his stay. Jones also describes numerous sailing expeditions in his *Memoirs*, including one to Calais in 1767 with Joseph Farington, when he endured a gale (ibid., p. 13), and another storm in May 1769 off the Essex coast (ibid., pp. 16–17). Jones also worked for Richard Paton, the ship painter (see cat. no. 32), and so it is only to be expected that he should attempt his own coastal scene. (ABS)

24

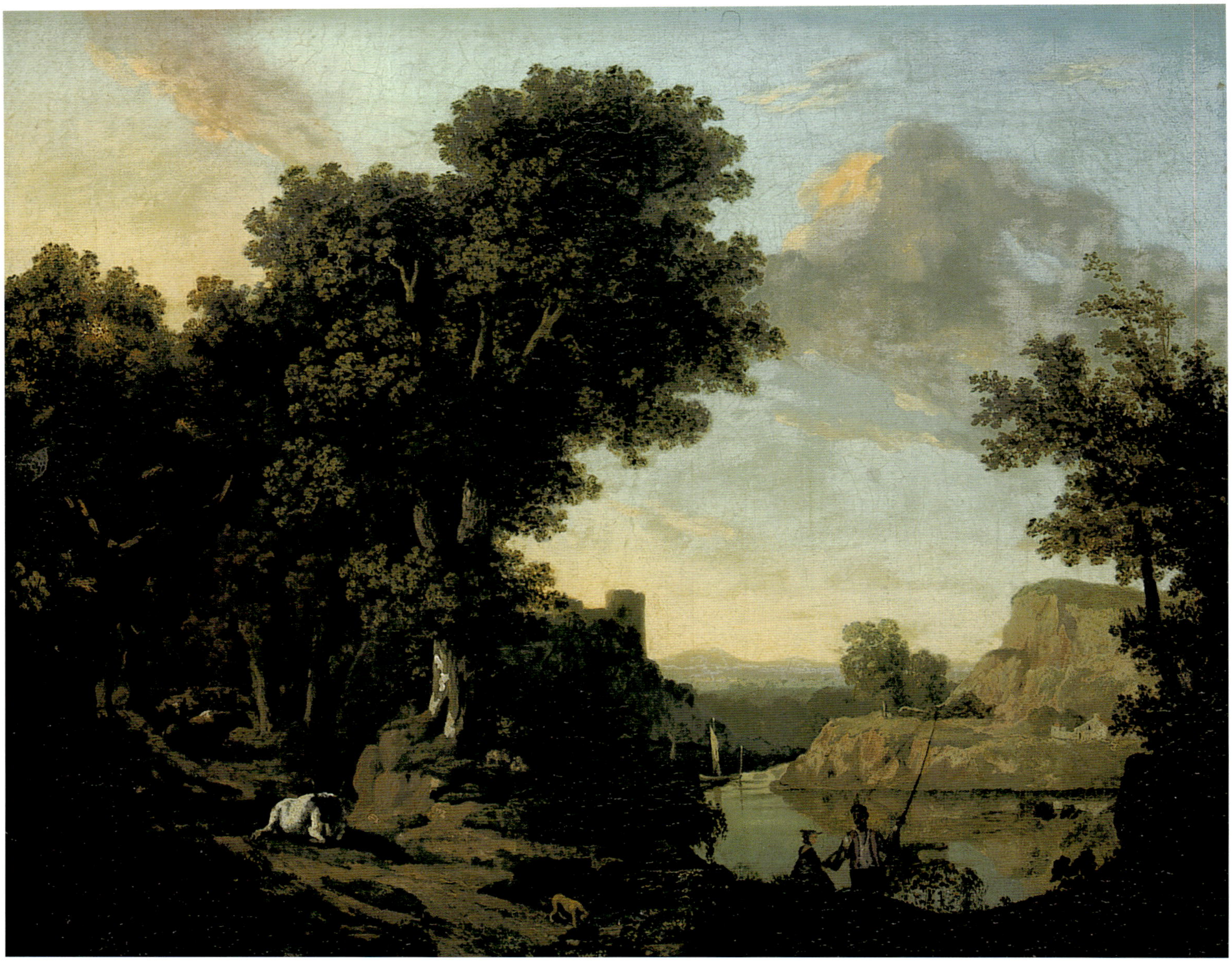

24

THOMAS JONES (1742–1803)

Classical Landscape 1772

Oil on canvas, 45.7 × 59.6 (18 × 23½)

Ins.: 'THO JONES 1772' l.r.
Prov.: Duke of Connaught; Fine Arts Society; purchased 1952
Exh.: Norwich, 1969, no. 28; London, 1970, no. 3
Lit.: Gowing, 1985, p. 18, pl. 8

National Museums & Galleries of Wales (NMW A 84)

Cardiff and Manchester only

This small classicizing landscape again owes much to Jones's master Wilson. Unlike cat. nos 26 and 28, however, it was not intended to evoke a sense of Italy. The trees and cows to the left are indebted to Thomas Gainsborough and Dutch seventeenth-century artists such as Jacob Ruisdael, whilst the castle, winding river and rock formations on the opposite bank evoke a sense of Jones's native landscape. Lawrence Gowing observed that this work 'had more identification with a real subject than anything in existing British landscape but early Gainsborough and the best of Wilson himself' (Gowing, 1985, p. 18). (ABS)

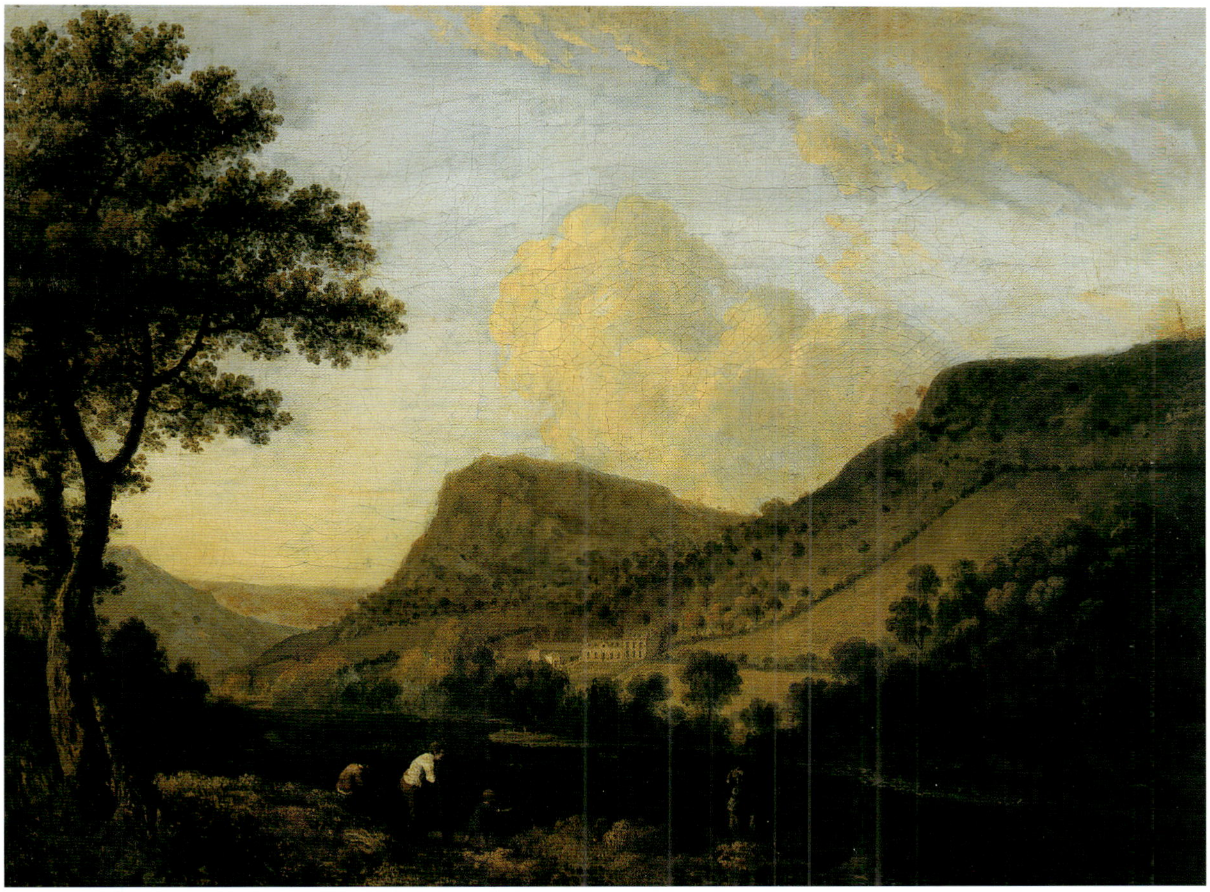

25

25

THOMAS JONES (1742–1803)

View of Llwynmadoc c.1772

Oil on canvas, 55.6 × 74.6 (22 × 29½)

Prov.: Thomas Thomas, then by descent
Exh.: London, 1970, ex. cat.

Private collection

Cardiff and Manchester only

During the year Jones spent at Pencerrig in 1775–6, he carried out a number of topographical commissions, including views of 'Castelhowell' and 'Maeslough' (*Memoirs*, p. 38). The views of Pennant, his sister Sarah's home (fig. 57, p. 115), and Llwynmadoc, the home of the neighbouring Thomas family, also relations by marriage, are not mentioned in the list in the *Memoirs* and the present work may date from Jones's 1772 visit. Llwynmadoc was built for Evan Thomas in 1747 and had nine bays, two storeys and a tall pedimented gable, though it has since been altered. Although not in prime condition, with some retouchings in the figures, this work reflects Richard Wilson's influence in the foliage and clouds. It is an autumnal scene, with three generations of a family depicted in the foreground. The difficulties Jones appears to have experienced in working out the spatial relationships and the balance between the sky and the light source, as well as the clumsy painting of the hill, indicate the earlier date of 1772. (ABS)

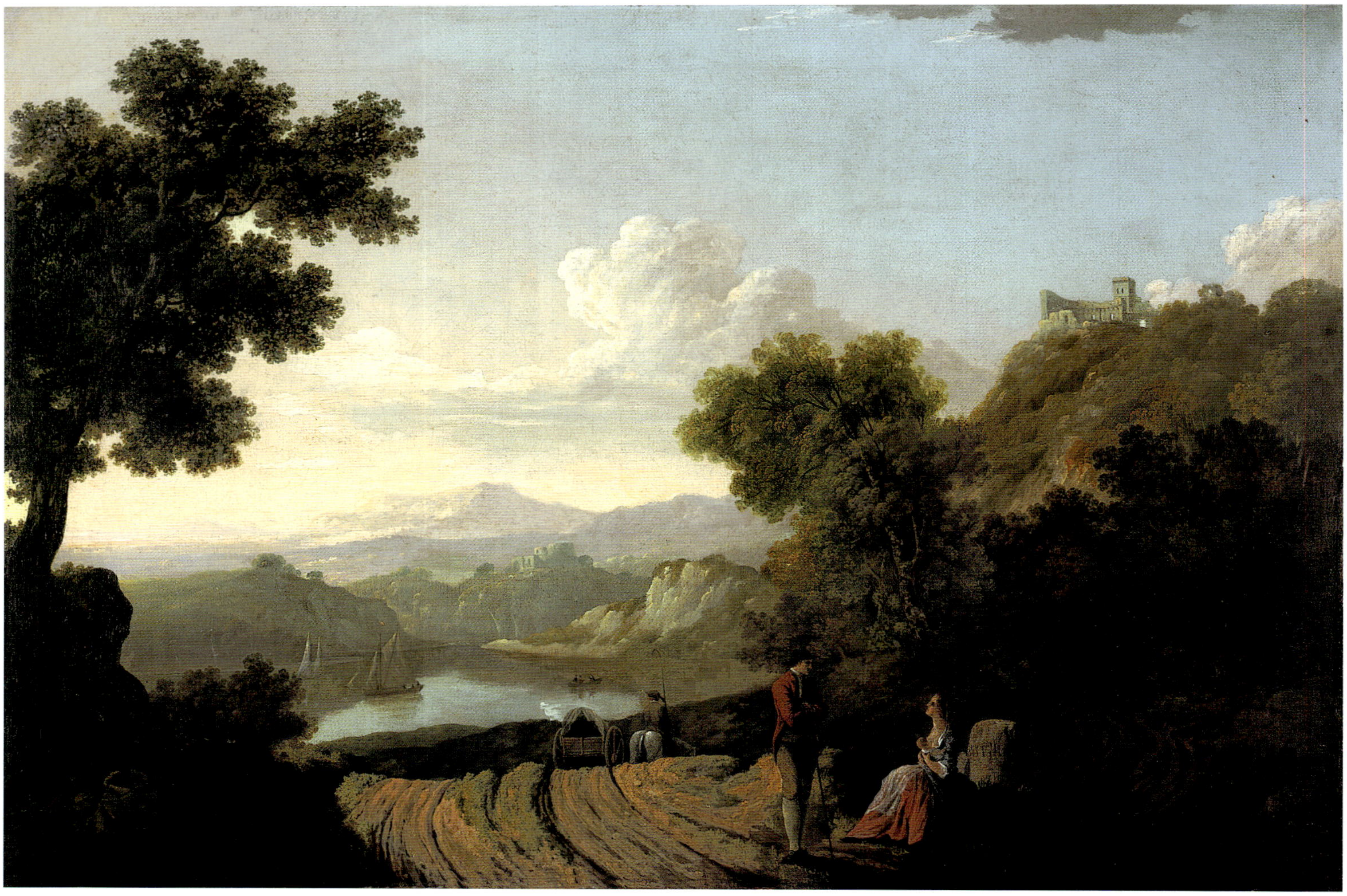

26

Thomas Jones (1742–1803)

Italian View: On the Arno 1773

Oil on canvas, 96.5 × 109.2 (38 × 43)

Ins.: 'xxxviii mil' on the milestone; 'Tho Jones / 1773' l.r.
Prov.: Ralph Edwards, then by descent
Exh.: London, 1970, no. 7, p. 7
Lit.: Edwards, 1968, pp. 10–11

Private collection

Cardiff and Manchester only

There are clear compositional similarities between this work and cat. no. 15 and Ralph Edwards (London, 1970, p. 7) tentatively suggested that it can be identified with 'a copy after Wilson for myself' that Jones included in a list of works he produced whilst staying with Oldfield Bowles at North Aston in 1773–4 (*Memoirs*, pp. 32–3). No dimensions are given and there are other candidates, including two imaginary landscapes also dated 1773 (cat. nos 28 and 29). The palette employed by Jones in the present work, the large boulder to the right, the positioning of the river and hilltop fortress and the distant mountainscape are all reminiscent of Wilson's composition, from which it also takes its title (cat. no. 15). However, the lush vegetation and the rutted road owe a debt to Thomas Gainsborough.

Edwards attributes the softly painted elongated figures to John Hamilton Mortimer. Similar figures appear in cat. nos 27 and 29. The thinly painted boats may have been late additions and X-radiography reveals that the male figure in the foreground was possibly an afterthought as well. The largest vessel has a spritsailrig, which is more typical of the barges Jones observed on the Thames in 1769 than of any Italian vessels. (abs)

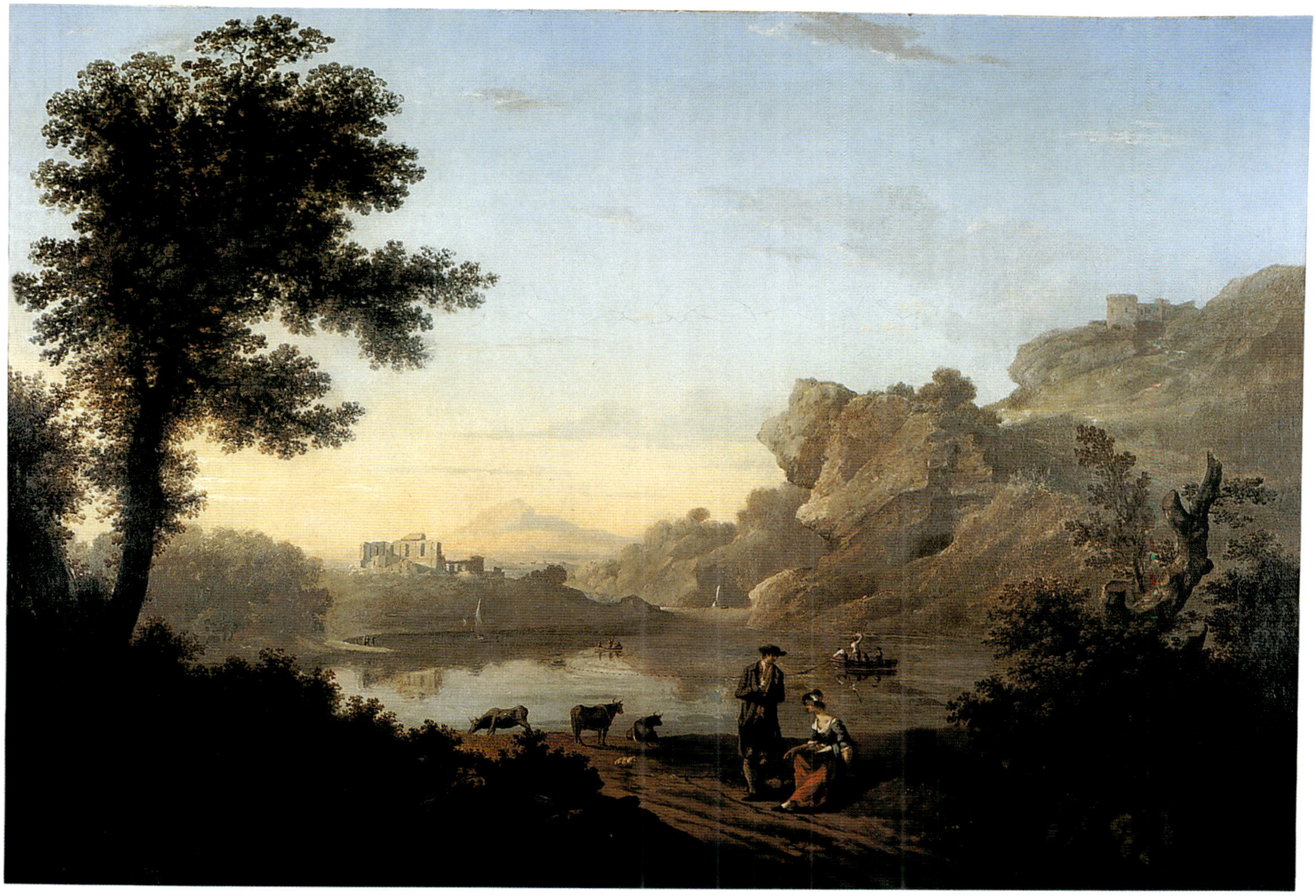

27

27

THOMAS JONES (1742–1803)

Lake Avernus 1774

Oil on canvas, 81 × 118 ($31\frac{7}{8} \times 46\frac{1}{2}$)

Ins.: 'T. Jones / 1774' l.l.
Exh.: Milan, 2002, no. II.5, illustrated in reverse

Private collection, Italy

Not in exhibition

This work is close in composition to cat. no. 26 with a similar rutted pathway and elongated figures, possibly attributable to John Hamilton Mortimer. It is still much influenced by Wilson, so much so that despite being signed, it has been attributed to him in the past. Although the date has been read as 1779 (Milan, 2002), it is much more likely, on stylistic grounds, to predate his Italian trip and it is significant that the inscription has also been recorded as 1774. The painting is traditionally said to represent Lake Avernus, west of Naples, but it is greatly at variance with Jones's depiction of the subject for Philip Yorke around 1779 (cat. no. 104). This is presumably because it was painted from another source prior to Jones's visit to Italy, and this was also the case in his depiction of the River Arno in cat. no. 26. (ABS)

28

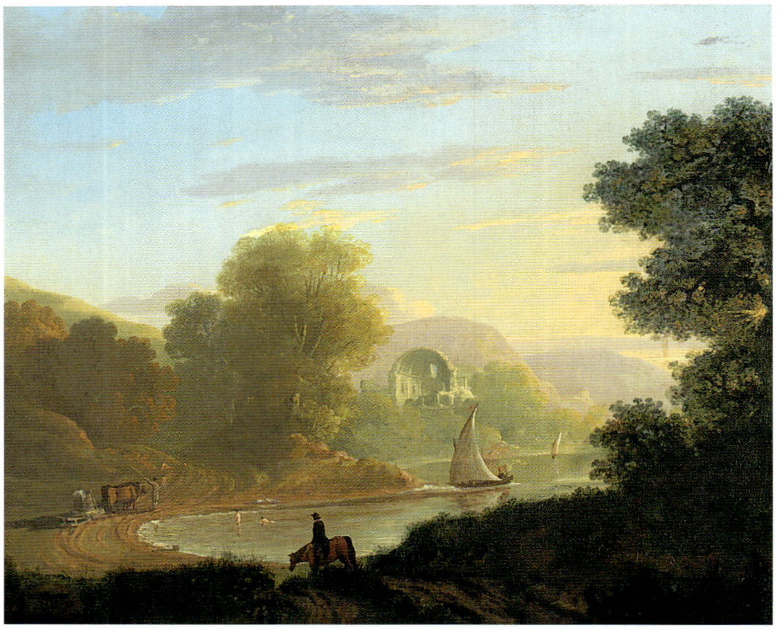

29

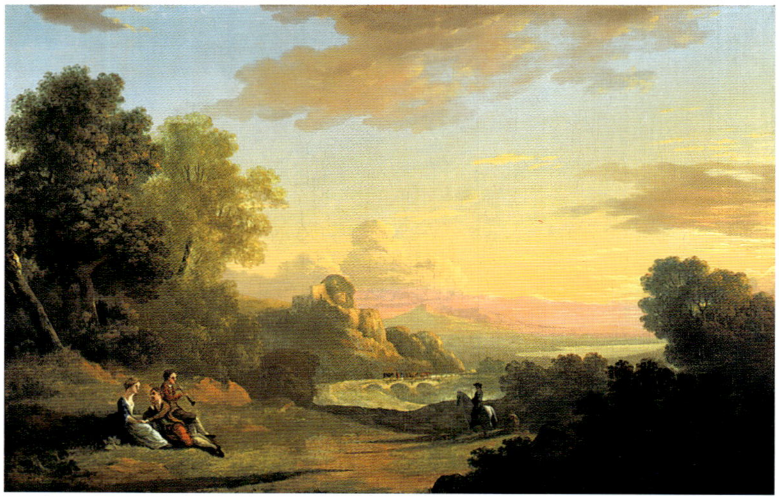

30

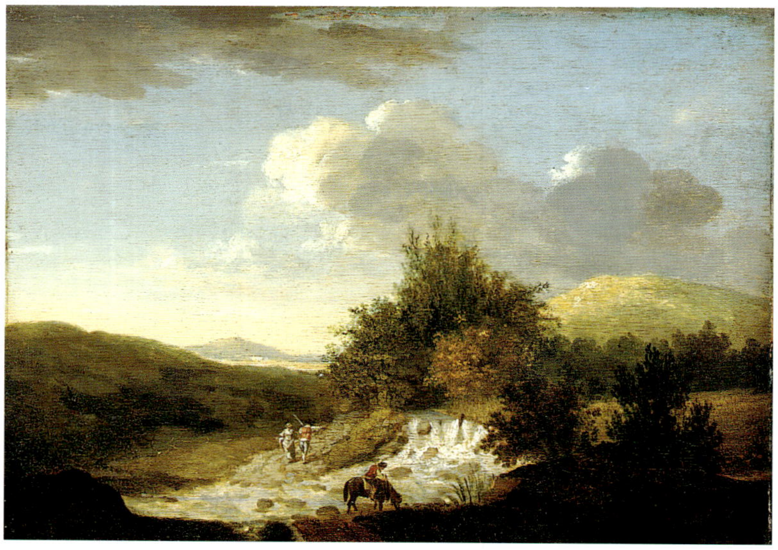

28

Thomas Jones (1742–1803)

An Imaginary Coast Scene, with the Temple of Venus at Baia 1773

Oil on canvas, 48.2 × 60.9 (19 × 24)

Ins.: 'T. Jones / 1773' l.l.
Prov.: Mitchell and Sons; purchased by Paul Mellon, 1963; presented 1981
Exh.: New Haven, 1981, no. 44
Lit.: Cormack, 1985, p. 130

Yale Center for British Art, Paul Mellon Collection (B1981.25.380)

Cardiff and Manchester only

This painting and cat. no. 26 were produced in the same year as cat. no. 29 and are close in style and palette. The elongated horseman is similar in proportion to the man in the foreground of cat. no. 26 and features such as the deeply rutted road and the flimsy boats are very close. All three could have been the work referred to as being after Wilson, cited by Jones in the list of paintings executed during 1773–4. Duncan Bull puts the Yale paintings forward as possible candidates (New Haven, 1981, p. 40). While neither can be securely identified with the listed work, they nevertheless illustrate Wilson's influence. Although painted with no direct knowledge of the Italian location – Jones was not to visit Italy for another three years – the distinctive landscape and placement of the circular temple recall the example in the Bay of Baia, near Naples, which Jones would have known from the drawings and paintings of his master. The temple also bears a resemblance to that of Minerva Medica, near Rome, also painted by Wilson. (ABS)

29

Thomas Jones (1742–1803)

An Imaginary Landscape with a Traveller and Figures Overlooking the Bay of Baia 1773

Oil on canvas, 48.4 × 74.6 (19 1/16 × 29 7/16)

Ins.: 'T. Jones / 1773' l.r. (indistinct)
Prov.: Thomas Jones, then by descent; Sotheby's, 4 April 1973, no. 35; purchased by Paul Mellon, 1973; presented 1973
Exh.: New Haven, 1981, no. 43
Lit.: Cormack, 1985, p. 130

Yale Center for British Art, Paul Mellon Collection (B1973.1.29)

Cardiff and Manchester only

This view is again very Wilsonian in style and colouring, but though it is a variation upon a number of his compositions, the ruined temple might be more strictly seen as a generic type. The figure of the horseman in the middle distance is similar to the elongated types in cat. nos 26 and 27, but those in the foreground, which were revealed during recent conservation, are quite different in feeling and execution, suggesting that two hands may have been at work. The provenance is also significant in this case, since the painting stayed in the family and was not therefore a commission. This helps to make a case for the present work being the 'Copy after Wilson' that Jones said he did 'for myself' (*Memoirs*, p. 32). (ABS)

30

Thomas Jones (1742–1803)

A Wooded River Landscape with Figures by a Ford 1775

Oil on panel, 29 × 40.2 (11 3/8 × 17 7/8)

Ins.: 'T. Jones p^{t} 1775' l.r.
Prov.: By descent from the family; Sotheby's, 28 October 1988, no. 294; purchased by the present owner

Private collection

Cardiff and Manchester only

This small cabinet-sized work, showing two figures on a path beside a stream with a horse and rider in the foreground, is painted on an unprepared panel. Such works are unusual in Jones's oeuvre. The sky and cloud formations are thinly painted in an accomplished manner. The stream with the rushing water over small boulders, painted with heavy impasto, is also successfully presented. However, there is an unresolved area to the left where Jones's attempt at aerial perspective is not entirely successful. Although signed, the date of the work is difficult to decipher. A later date of 1775 seems more likely, since the landscape, although clearly not an accurate topographical Welsh view, is inspired by the countryside around Pencerrig in more general terms. (ABS)

31

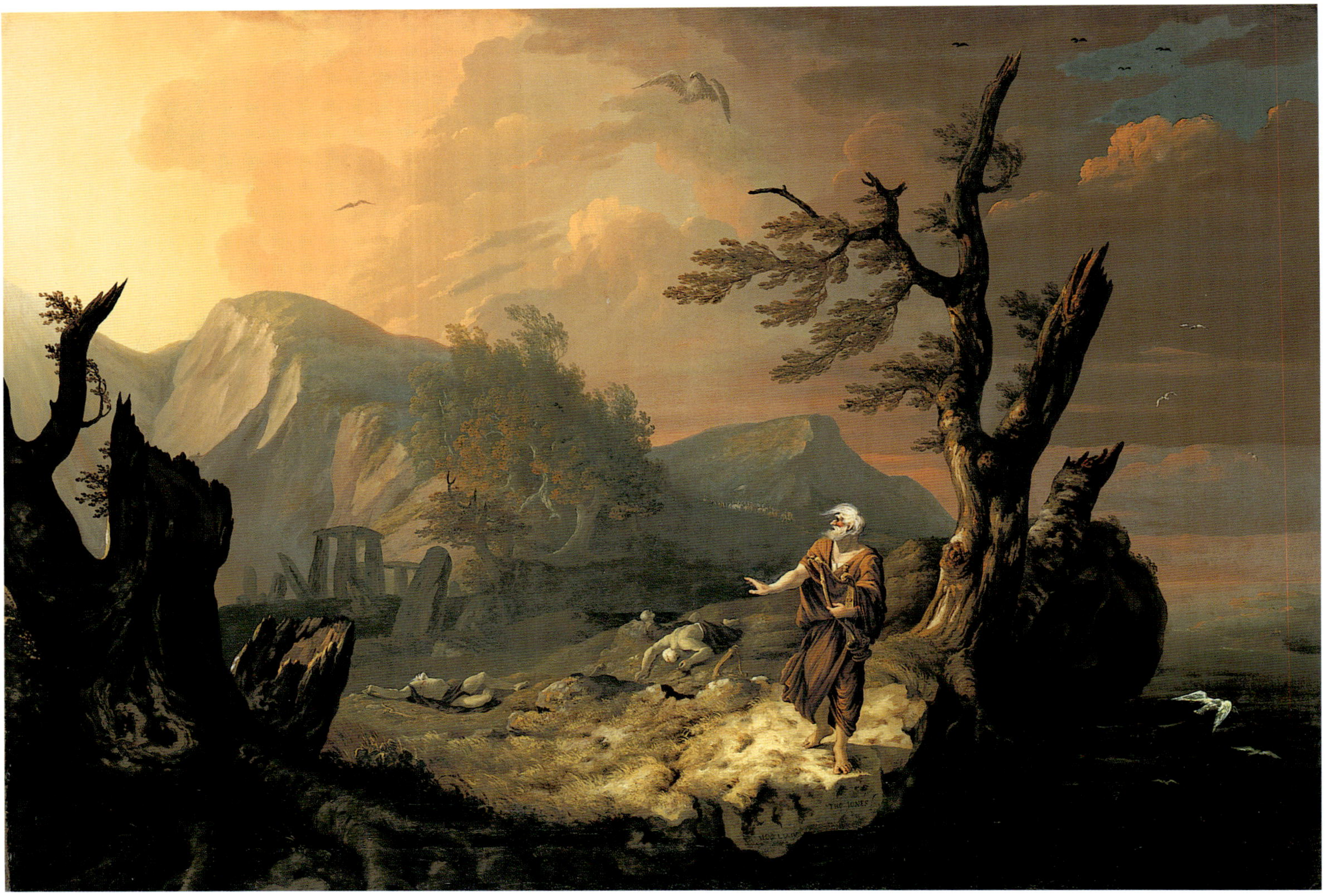

31

Thomas Jones (1742–1803)

The Bard 1774

Oil on canvas, 115.5 × 167.7 (45½ × 66)

Ins.: 'Tho Jones P MDCCLXXIV' l.c.
Prov.: Oldfield Bowles, 1775; Cardiff sale room, 1915; Revd Williams, then by descent to Mrs M. Vosper; purchased 1965
Exh.: Society of Artists, 1774, no. 123; Swansea, 1964, no. 213; London, 1970, no. 8; Aberystwyth, 1971, no. 24; York, 1973, no. 65; London, 1973a, no. 94; Southampton, 1987
Lit.: Edwards, 1968, pp. 9–10; Gowing, 1985, p. 7; pp. 20–1, pl. 1; Morgan, 1984, pp. 59–60; Owen, 1988, pp. 17–18; Smiles, 1994, pp. 53–4; p. 100; p. 180; p. 185; Lord, 1994, p. 113; Lord 2000, p. 115, fig. 173
Eng.: Mezzotint by John Raphael Smith, published by John Boydell, 1773. Proof exhibited at the Society of Artists, 1775, no. 222

National Museums & Galleries of Wales (NMW A 85)

Cardiff and Manchester only

This important historical work is based on Thomas Gray's dramatic poem *The Bard* (1757). It recounts the legendary tale of Edward I's massacre of the Welsh bards and the curse of the last survivor, who hurled himself from a cliff-top to his death. In the background can be seen the bodies of the bards, with Edward's cavalcade visible beyond. The circle of stones is inspired by Stonehenge, which Jones visited in 1769. He believed that this 'Stupendous Monument of remote Antiquity' was Druidic and he transplanted it to a windswept mountain (*Memoirs*, p. 21).

Many artists were inspired by Gray's poem, including Paul Sandby and Benjamin West, but few linked the medieval bard with

32

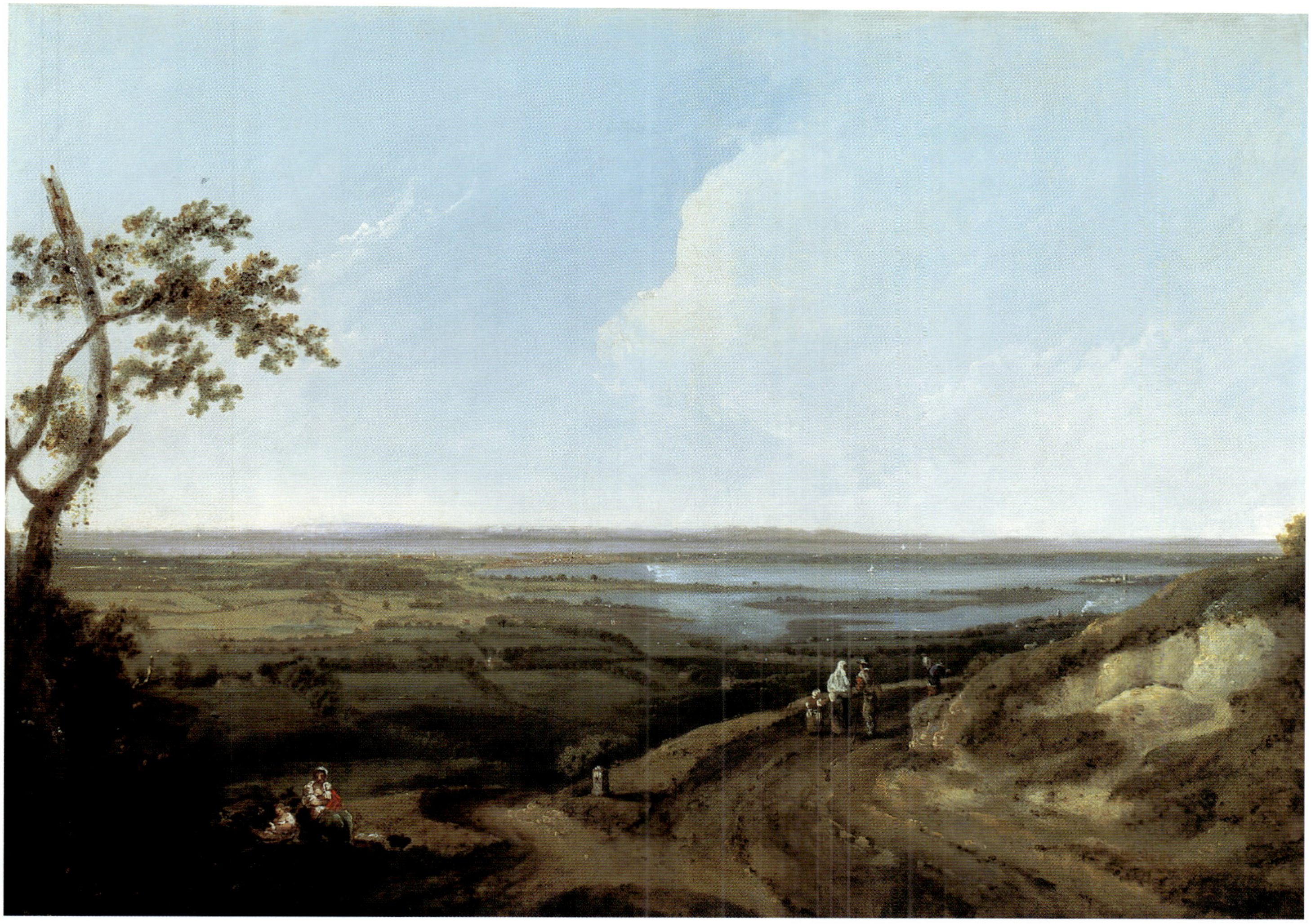

the ancient figure of the Druid. The influence of the seventeenth-century artist Salvator Rosa was more common, though. The composition follows *Augures*, probably known to Jones as an etching. This very Welsh subject was presented to his English patron Oldfield Bowles. Jones believed that it was one of his 'best' paintings (ibid., p. 33) and this opinion was shared by the *Middlesex Journal*, which proclaimed it 'finely romantic . . . a most capital piece' when it was exhibited in 1774 (30 April–3 May). (ABS)

32

THOMAS JONES (1742–1803)

View of Portsmouth from Portsdown Hill *c.*1774

Oil on canvas, 101.7 × 142.2 (40 × 56)

Ins.: 'Portsmouth' l.l. (not Jones?)
Prov.: 'Paton, the Shippainter'; Tollemache Estates Sale, 15 May 1953, no. 60 as Richard Wilson; Messrs Edward Speelman Ltd; purchased 1955
Lit.: Edwards, 1968, p. 1[illegible]

Southampton Art Gallery (Acc. no. 1469)

Cardiff and Manchester only

This work is presumably the 'View from Portsdown, looking over Portsmouth and the Isle of White for Paton the Shippainter' which Jones began in July 1774 (*Memoirs*, p. 33). Jones's association with Richard Paton (1717–1791) went back to 1769, when he painted the landscape backgrounds for coastal views of 'Cuba and Hispaniola' and he also assisted with 'some large Pictures of the defeat of the Turkish fleet – for the Empress of Russia' (ibid., p. 15, p. 24). This appears to have been a commission, however, and Jones was able to make use of material he had gathered on a trip to Portsmouth in the previous year. The panoramic view is relieved by a foreground with the same type of curving road that features in *Italian View: On the Arno* (cat. no. 26). The influence of Richard Wilson is still apparent at this date, and it is therefore not surprising that this work was wrongly attributed to Jones's master until comparatively recently. (GS)

33

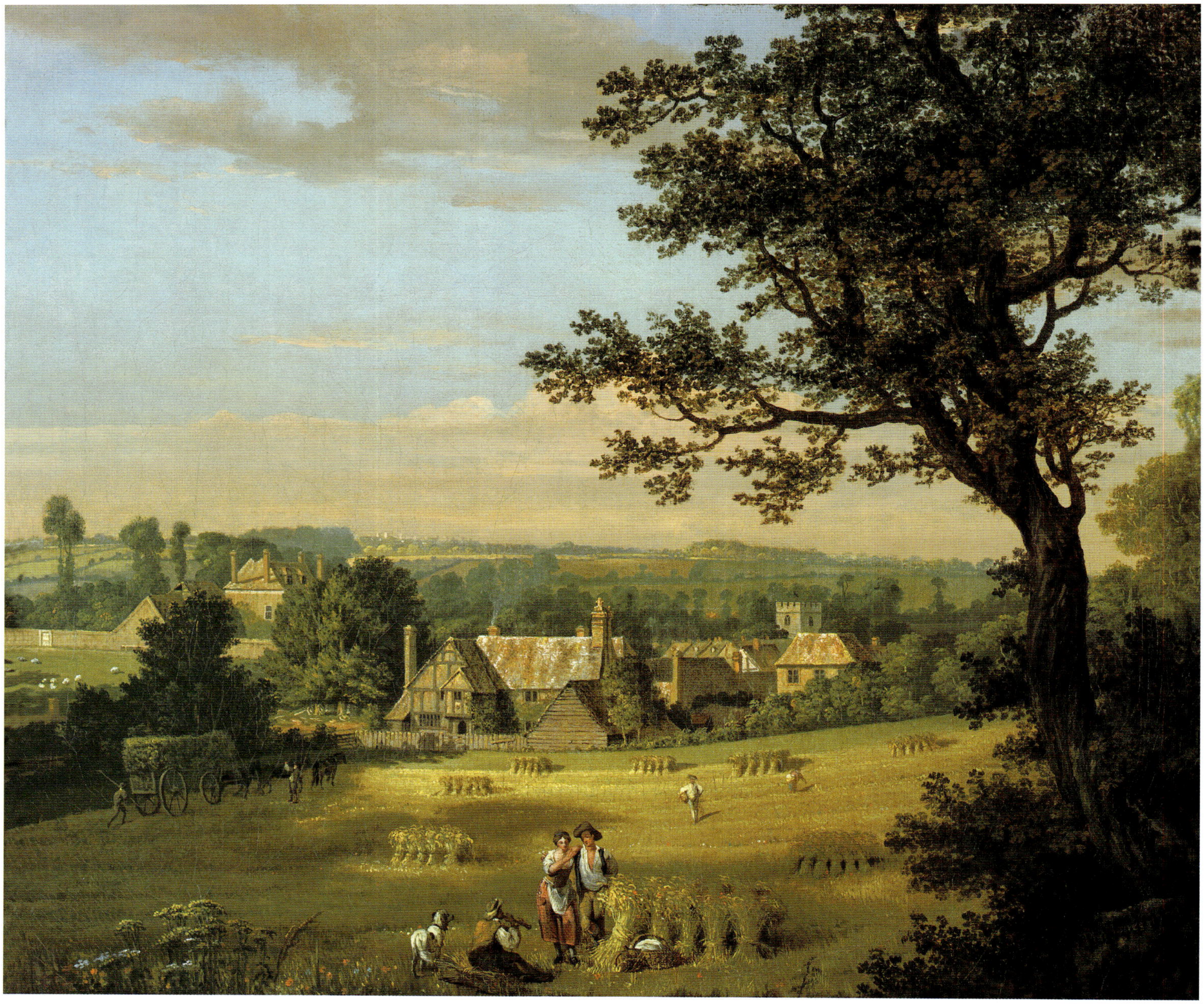

33

THOMAS JONES (1742–1803) AND
JOHN HAMILTON MORTIMER (1740–1799)

A View of John Milton's Cottage at Chalfont St Giles 1774

Oil on canvas, 42.6 × 50.8 (16¾ × 20)

Prov.: Dr Benjamin Bates; Phillips, 27 April 1993, no. 37; Leger
Exh.: Society of Artists, 1775, no. 119 as 'A View of the House in Chaffant, St. Gile's, Bucks, where Milton resided during the Plague of London, and where he wrote his L'Allegro'; London, 1994, no. 19
Lit.: Sunderland, 1986, p. 47, p. 90; Everett, 1994, p. 69

Private collection

Cardiff and Manchester only

This work was one of Jones's most important early commissions. The patron was Dr Benjamin Bates (*c.*1736–1828), a physician who lived in Buckinghamshire. Jones records that on 1 August 1774 'I packed up a few painting utensils and went . . . with my friend Dr *Bates*' to Buckinghamshire in order 'to paint . . . a view of the house at Chalfont St Giles, whither, according to tradition, the Poet *Milton* . . . wrote his L'Allegro & Il Penseroso' (*Memoirs*, p. 33). On 5 August, Jones proceeded to 'make a Sketch of the Aforementioned house' and he returned on 9 August (ibid., pp. 33–4). Four drawings survive in the partially split-up sketchbook (see cat. nos 51–54, private collection), including a detailed study of the house (p. 19 verso) and a view overlooking the village (p. 33 verso). Mortimer was persuaded to add rural figures from *L'Allegro* suited to its theme of 'mirth'. Jones also painted a companion piece to illustrate *Il Penseroso* (untraced). However, despite the fact that Jones 'searched the most Solitary places near Chalfont', he could find nothing suited to the contrasting theme of melancholy, and 'so was obliged to paint an ideal one – more sequestered and wild'. (ABS)

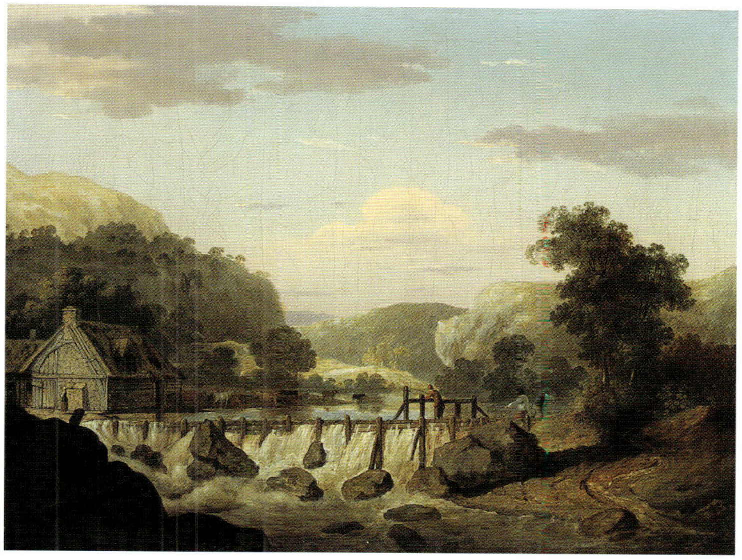

34

34

THOMAS JONES (1742–1803)

River Landscape with Figures Beside a Weir 1775

Oil on canvas, 43 × 59 (16⅞ × 23¼)

Ins.: 'THO: JONES PT. / 1775' l.l. on rock in foreground
Prov.: Lord Magheramorne; Sotheby's, 11 March 1987, no. 66; Sotheby's, Margam, 19 September 1999, no. 86
Lit.: Lord, 2000, fig. 235

Private collection

Cardiff and Manchester only

Jones returned to Pencerrig in September 1775 for a 'farewell visit, to my Parents, Relations and friends in the Country, previous to my departure for Italy' (*Memoirs*, p. 37). He remained there for the year, painting both oil sketches and commissions, in order to discharge certain debts. This signed picture, painted on a simple weave canvas with a white ground, is a strong candidate for the work he described as 'An Idea taken from ye Wye, for Taylor . . . 8Gs' (ibid., p. 38). The compositions of the present work and cat. no. 35 seem to show the same weir and mill and both views look upriver. The character of the hills is reminiscent of the upper reaches of the Wye, while the tranquil riverside scenery is more in keeping with the lower stretch, where there are weirs (for example, Brockweir). However, the large boulders are not typical of scenery so far downriver. Jones's use of the word 'Idea' suggests that in any

35

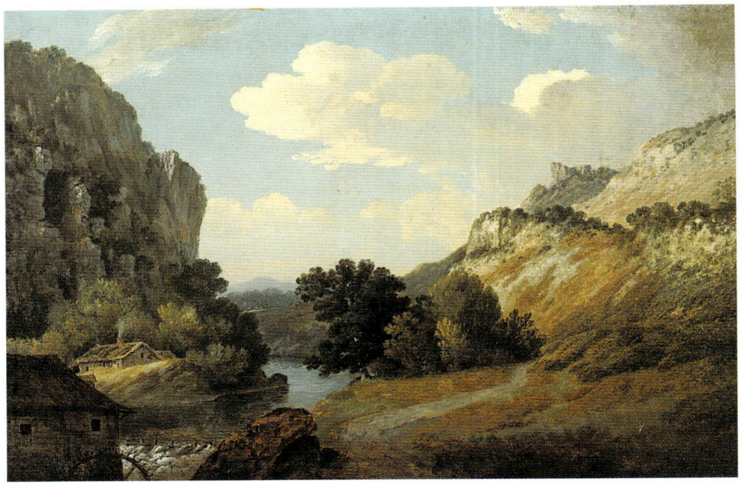

that the work shows an imaginary scene inspired by the Wye (see cat. no. 34). (ABS)

36

Thomas Jones (1742–1803)

River Scene, on the Wye 1776

Oil on paper, 18.8 × 29.8 (7½ × 11⅝)

Ins.: '1776' l.c.
Prov.: Sotheby's, 2 June 1965, no. 121; Jane Evan-Thomas; given to the present owner
Exh.: London, 1970, no. 16

Judy Egerton

Cardiff and Manchester only

This scene tallies with Benjamin Malkin's lyrical description of the river scenery at Aberedw, one of the most spectacular stretches of the Wye in this part of Wales. Malkin's assertion that Jones had made the 'romantic scenery' at this spot the focus of his 'early studies' is confirmed by his autobiographical poem 'Petraeia', which dedicates a stanza to the pictorial delights of '*Vaga*' – the Wye (Malkin, 1804, p. 280).

> Clear *Vaga*, whose meand'ring floods
> Embrace fair Lechria's fields and woods,
> Here gently gliding o'er the plain,
> There foaming like the angry main;
> Rushing through rock with horrid sweep,
> Or whirling down the giddy deep (Baker, 1795, p. 226).

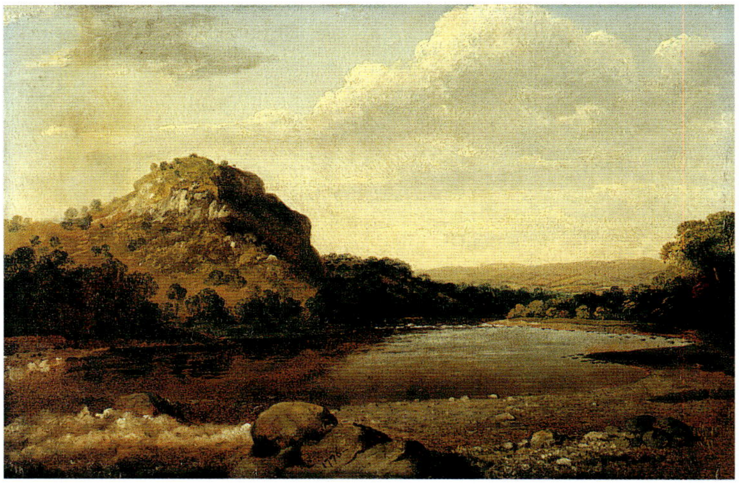

36

case, this and cat. no. 35 are not intended to be topographically accurate representations, but images inspired by the Wye. (ABS)

35

Thomas Jones (1742–1803)

River Scene, on the Wye *c.*1775–6

Oil on laid paper later lined on to canvas, 34 × 52 (13⅜ × 20½)

Prov.: Agnew's, 1958; Appleby's, 1964; Jane Evan-Thomas; presented by her about 1987
Exh.: London, 1970, no. 17
Lit.: Gowing, 1985, p. 26, pl. 16

Brecknock Museum & Art Gallery, Brecon (BRCNM 85–24)

Cardiff and Manchester only

This view, looking upstream, shows a bend in a river, possibly on the Wye. Jones made a list of the works he completed whilst staying at Pencerrig in 1775–6, including 'An Idea taken from ye Wye, for Taylor' (*Memoirs*, p. 38). This could refer either to this work, or to cat. no. 34, though the fact that it is painted on white paper with no ground suggests that in this case Jones was painting for personal pleasure rather than as a commission, when he tended to use canvas.

Jones's paintings of river views that have been associated with the Wye do not appear to depict specific geographical locations and it has not been possible to identify a comparable weir and mill with limestone rocks on the river, though there are some downstream between Monmouth and Chepstow. It appears likely, therefore,

Jones may have generally resisted the attractions of continental sublime scenery – and the mountains of North Wales – but the 'Alpine majesty' of the Wye proved a fruitful exception (Malkin, 1804, p. 280). (GS)

37

THOMAS JONES (1742–1803)

Maeslough House 1776

Oil on canvas, 74 × 110 (29⅛ × 43¼)

Ins.: 'Jones 76' l.l. below the watering can
Exh.: Society of Artists, 1777, no. 52

Private collection

Cardiff and Manchester only

Maeslough House was built *c.*1715 by Humphrey Howarth, though he went bankrupt in the mid-eighteenth century and the estate was purchased by John Wilkins (1713–1784), a wealthy Brecon judge. His son, Walter Wilkins (1741–1828), made his fortune in the East India Company and returned to Wales in 1773 to find his father owned the estate, and it was he who commissioned this work, paying thirty guineas for it (*Memoirs*, p. 38). The patron can be seen proudly surveying the newly laid-out gardens with his future wife, Catherine Hayward. The figures are unusually prominent and they include the head gardener and two workers rolling the grass. The long shadows cast by the figures suggests late afternoon and the presence of a madonna lily in flower and a larch fully leafed point to the months of June or July. The 'up-river trows' (the traditional barge of the Severn and Wye) seen in the distance here reflect an experiment in navigation of the Wye initiated by Walter Wilkins. The typical square main and topsail rig that these vessels would have carried at that time is accurately portrayed by

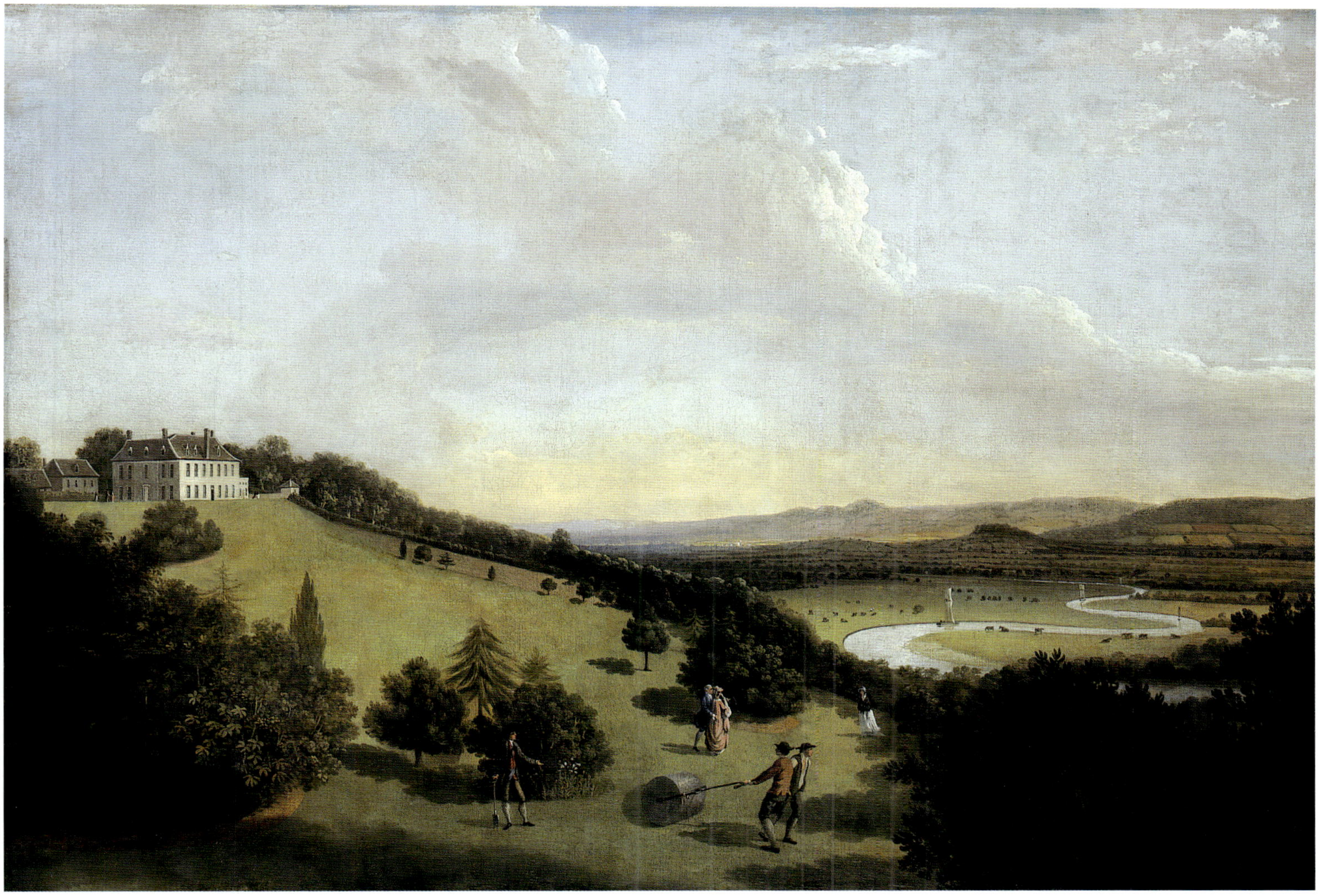
37

38

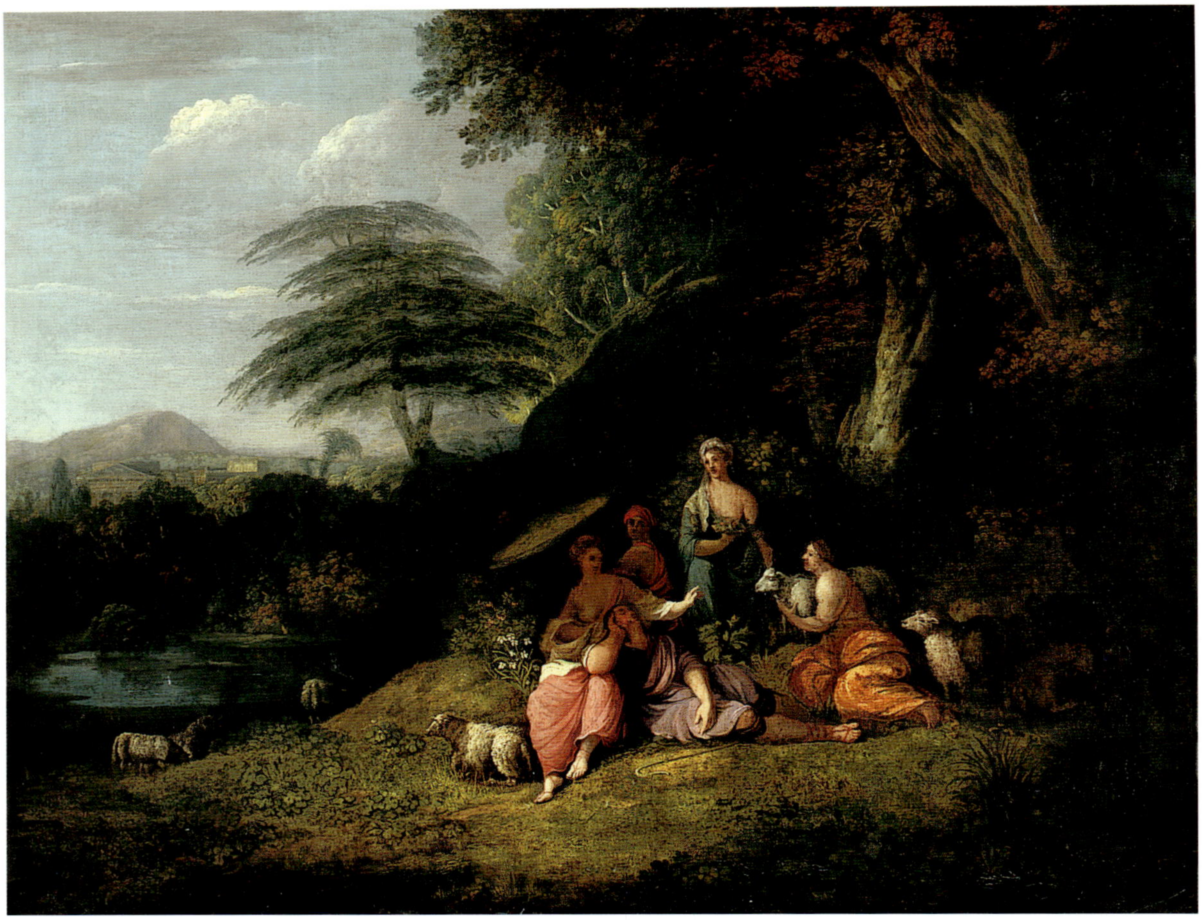

Jones. After Wilkins's death, following a long period as MP for Radnorshire (1796–1828), the house was demolished. Walter sponsored Jones's younger brother Frederick as a cadet in the East India Company army. (ABS)

38

THOMAS JONES (1742–1803)

A Shepherd Sleeping with his Flock 1776

Oil on canvas, 70 × 91 ($27\frac{1}{2} \times 35\frac{7}{8}$)

Ins.: 'Thos Jones: pt / 1776' l.r.
Prov.: Sotheby's, 9 April 1997, no. 56

Private collection

Cardiff and Manchester only

This unusual landscape, painted on the eve of Jones's departure to Italy, includes a distant mountainscape reminiscent of Wales, though a prominent palm and a large cedar tree give it a Mediterranean feel. The figures have previously been identified as a shepherd and his flock, but this is clearly an inadequate interpretation of the subject and given the scale of the work it is tempting to look at the subjects he exhibited at the Society of Artists in 1776, such as *A Landscape: the Evening, with the Story of Callisto*. Another suggestion is that it might represent Lot and his daughters. Lot was a shepherd and the fact that this figure is sleeping surrounded by women makes this a credible suggestion, though Jones is not known to have painted the subject. The figures in this work, which include an African holding a sun parasol over the sleeping man, are quite different in proportion and execution from those in other historical works by Jones and paradoxically they may actually be by the artist himself rather than by another hand. The figures are, however, so subordinate to the landscape that uncertainty about the exact subject has inevitably arisen. (ABS)

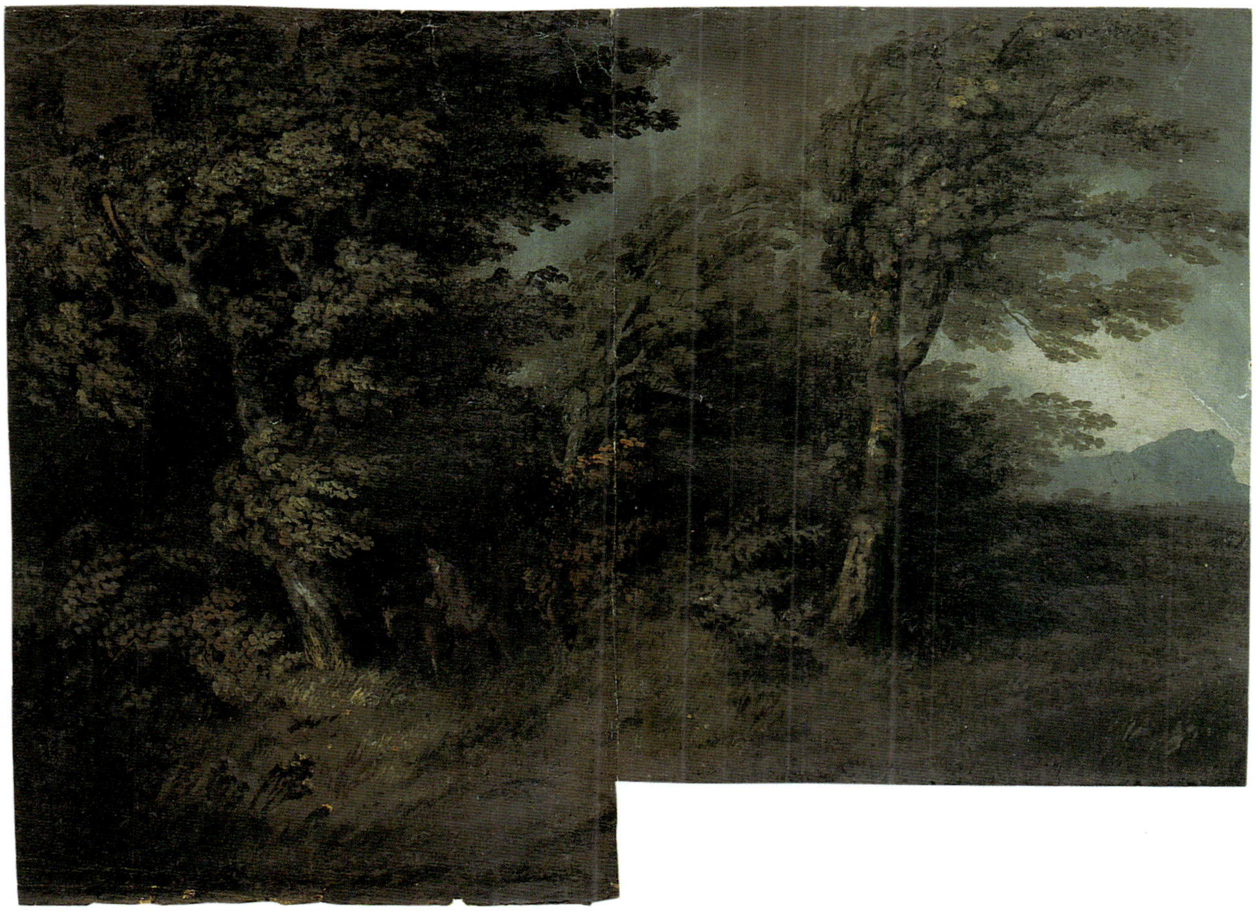

39

39

THOMAS JONES (1742–1803)

Gadbridge, Hertfordshire 1770 and 1771

Oil on two pieces of off-white wrapping paper*, 30.5 × 20.6 (12 × 8⅛) and 26.6 × 21.3 (10½ × 8⅜)

Ins.: 'Gadbridge Hertfordshire / 1770 & 1771' verso of both pieces of paper and unclear shorthand; left-hand sheet numbered '14' on verso; right-hand sheet numbered '15' on verso
Prov.: Captain John Dale, then by descent
Exh.: London, 1970, no. 1; Cambridge, 1980, no. 16
Lit.: Gowing, 1985, pp. 17–18, pl. 7

Private collection

Cardiff and Manchester only

During the summer of 1770, Jones suffered an attack of 'nervous fever' and he travelled to his cousin Rice James's house at Gadbridge in Hertfordshire to recuperate. Here he made a 'number of Sketches from the little picturesque Bits round about . . . and painted in Oil some Studies of Trees &c after nature' (*Memoirs*, p. 22); this is the only work that survives, however. It is painted on two pieces of off-white wrapping paper, taped together on the reverse, though one of them was cut at some stage. They are two pages of a book, since they are numbered '14' and '15' on the back and one has holes from a sewn binding. The second date of 1771 on the reverse presumably refers to a subsequent trip to Hertfordshire.

The inscription possibly refers to where the work was painted rather than its location, so it was probably not sketched on the spot. Certainly, it shows the influence of Thomas Gainsborough in its treatment of the trees and the horseman. Moreover, the distant hill is more reminiscent of Wales than Hertfordshire, whilst the windswept trees recall those in *Dido and Aeneas* (cat. no. 20) painted the previous year. (ABS)

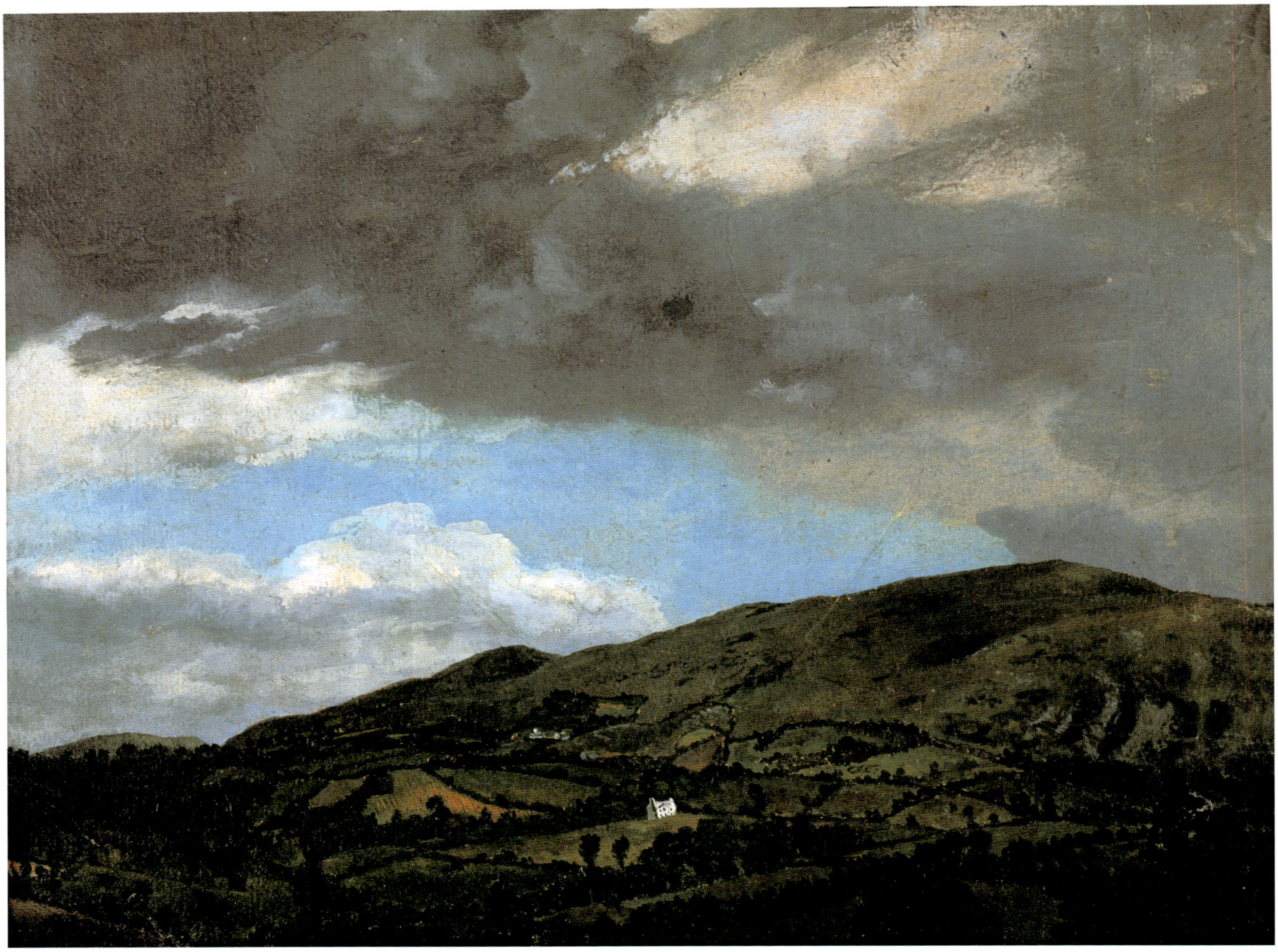

40

Thomas Jones (1742–1803)

Pencerrig 1772

Oil on paper, 22.8 × 30.5 (9 × 12)

Ins.: 'Penkerrig 1772' verso
Prov.: Captain John Dale, then by descent; Christie's, 2 July 1954, no. 218; Colnaghi's; purchased 1954
Exh.: London, 1970, no. 4; London, 1973, no. 95; Milan, 1975, no. 53; Cambridge, 1980, no. 17
Lit.: Gowing, 1985, pp. 18–19, pl. 9; Smith, 1983, p. 144

Birmingham Museums & Art Gallery (1954P56)

Cardiff and Manchester only

Jones arrived at Pencerrig in 1772 on 30 July, remaining in Wales until early December. During his stay, he records making a 'good many Studies in Oil on paper' (*Memoirs*, p. 27). A number of sketches survive from this visit, including cat. no. 41. This view is taken from the house at Pencerrig, looking north-east towards Newmead Farm, which is situated in the centre of the composition. The hill in the background is part of the Carneddau. It is underlain by ancient volcanic rocks which are more resistant to erosion than the softer shales found around Pencerrig, hence the prominent ridge.

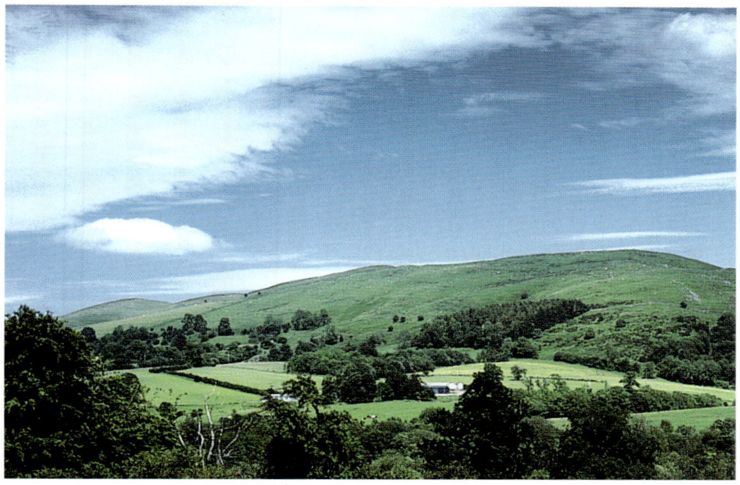

Fig. 59 View near Pencerrig, contemporary photograph.

Jones painted this work prior to the enclosure of the countryside, but the carefully observed field boundaries have remained essentially unchanged (fig. 59). The sky is a dominant feature of the composition, with carefully observed cloud formations. (ABS)

41

THOMAS JONES (1742–1803)

Pencerrig 1772

Oil on laid wrapping paper*, 31.8 × 22.2 (12½ × 8¾)

Ins.: 'ptd in 1772' verso
Prov.: Captain John Dale, then by descent; Christie's, 2 July 1954, no. 218; Colnaghi's; purchased by Paul Oppé, 1954; Armide Oppé; purchased 1996
Exh.: London, 1958, no. 295; London, 1970, no. 5; Cambridge, 1980, no. 18; London, 1997, no. 43
Lit.: Gowing, 1985, pp. 9–12; pp. 18–20, pl. 3

Tate. Purchased as part of the Oppé Collection with assistance from the National Lottery through the Heritage Lottery Fund 1996 (T08247)

Cardiff and Manchester only

This view appears to show a possibly natural, smaller lake than that found at Pencerrig today, which was expanded and improved when Jones inherited the estate (Baker, 1795, p. 224). Jones recalls in October 1795 in his Account Book (cat. no. 73): 'This evening I let down the Plug or Bolt of the Pool which the men began to clear out the mud and marl of, and likewise to cut and sink deeper in particular places the 15th of June last'. Jones appears to have taken this view from a field east of the main house, looking north across the original lake or pond, during his return in 1772, and the carefully noted field patterns are still recognizable. Like cat no. 40, it is dated on the verso. Technical analysis has revealed extensive underdrawing beneath the landscape, though not under the sky. The three trees are all painted without prior underdrawing, suggesting that they might have been added later in the studio, as compositional devices. The corn stooks indicate a date of late summer, so it is possible that Jones painted this work in late August, following his return on 30 July 1772 to Pencerrig. (ABS)

42

THOMAS JONES (1742–1803)

Carneddau, from Pencerrig *c.*1775

Oil on laid paper laid down on panel*, 29.5 × 51 (11½ × 19½)

Prov.: Appleby's, 1962; Jane Evan-Thomas; bequeathed 2000
Exh.: London, 1970, no. 85; London, 1973, no. 96; Madrid, 1992, no. 35
Lit.: Gowing, 1985, p. 26, pl. 17

National Museums & Galleries of Wales (NMW A 17645)

Cardiff and Manchester only

This view is taken from below the house at Pencerrig, close to the clump of oak trees looking south-east towards Carneddau, and was presumably painted in the autumn of 1775. The execution of the foreground is somewhat crude and schematic, but the mist on the hilltops and the sunlight on the fields to the right are skilfully and atmospherically observed. Bracken appears to be turning brown on the hills. The photograph published by Gowing (1985, p. 26) is misleading, as it shows a part of the ridge of the Carneddau slightly to the north of the area that Jones painted, as the contemporary photograph illustrates (fig. 60). Towards the right are two farms owned by the Jones family. (ABS)

41

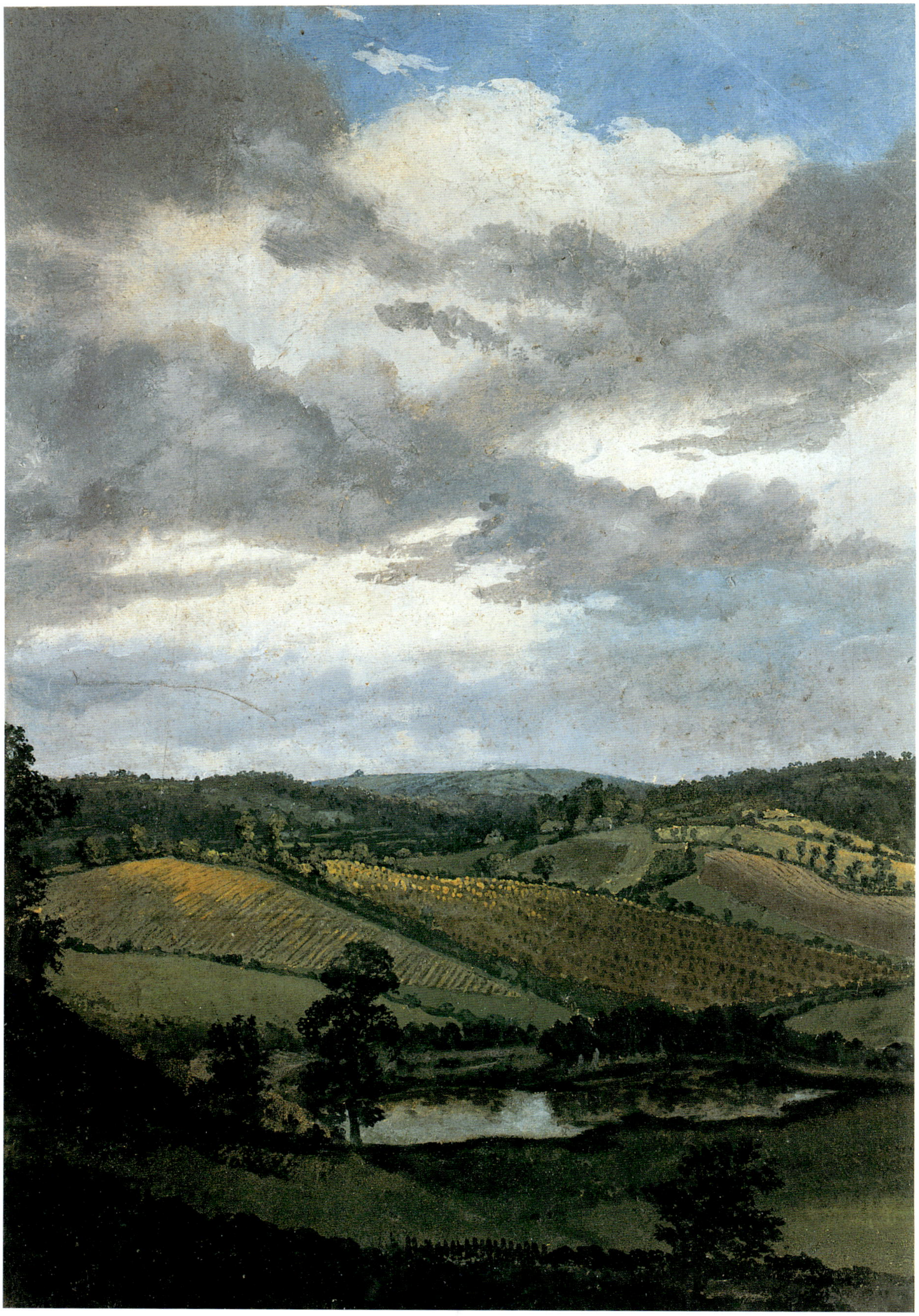

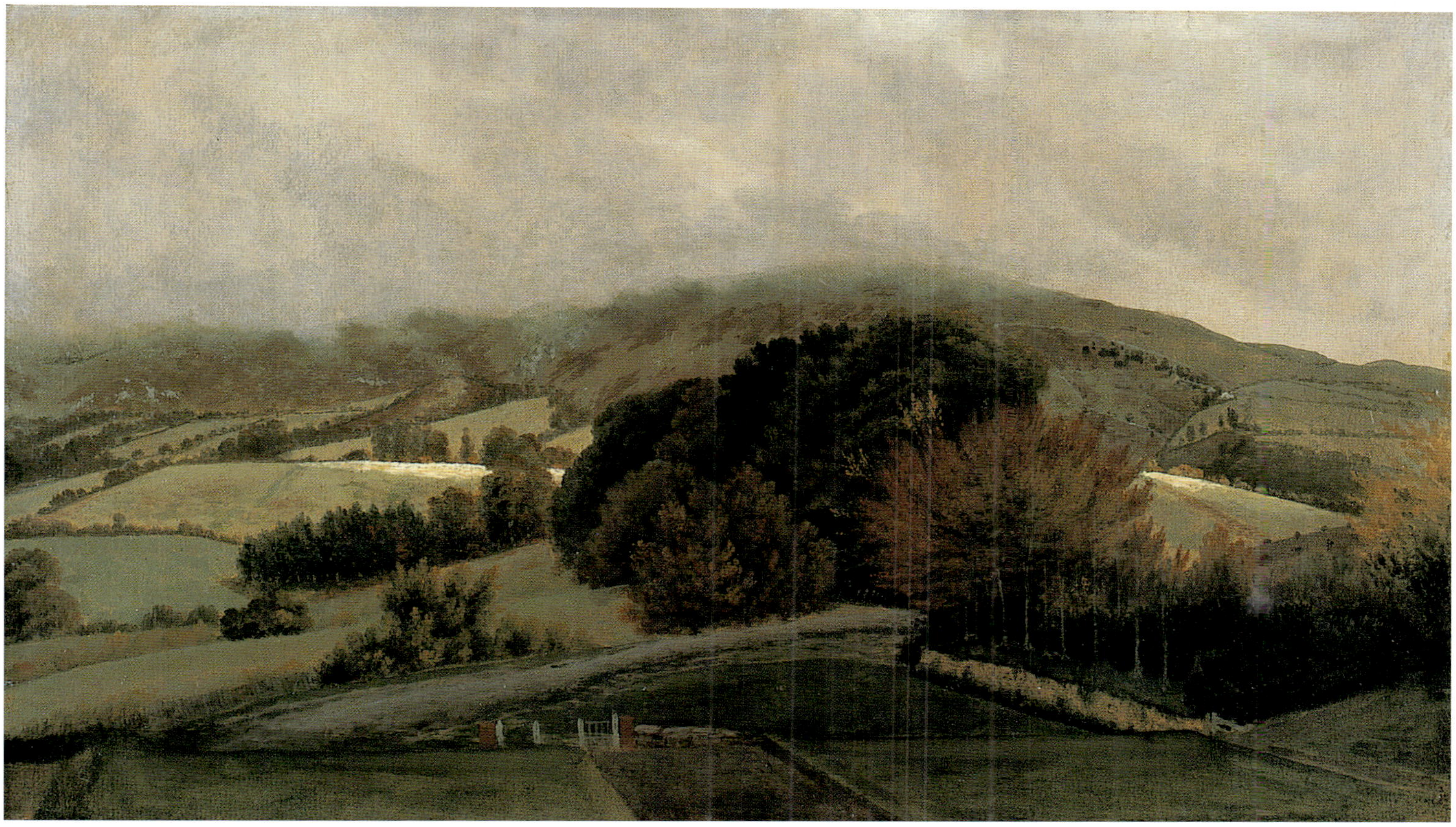

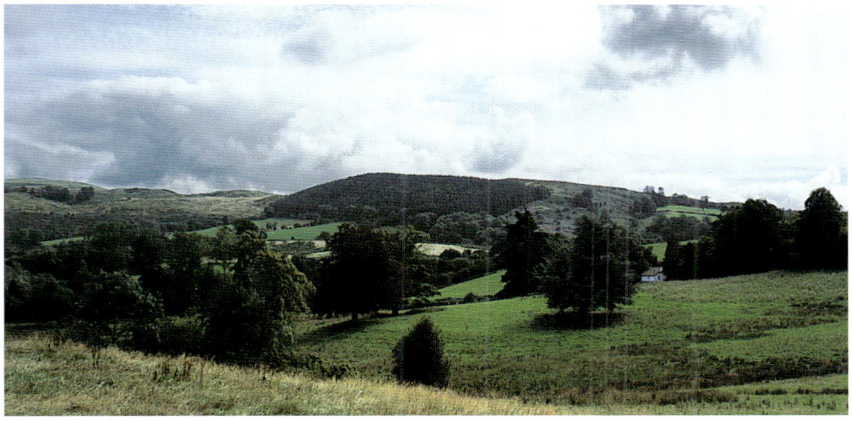

Fig. 60 Carneddau, from Pencerrig, contemporary photograph.

43

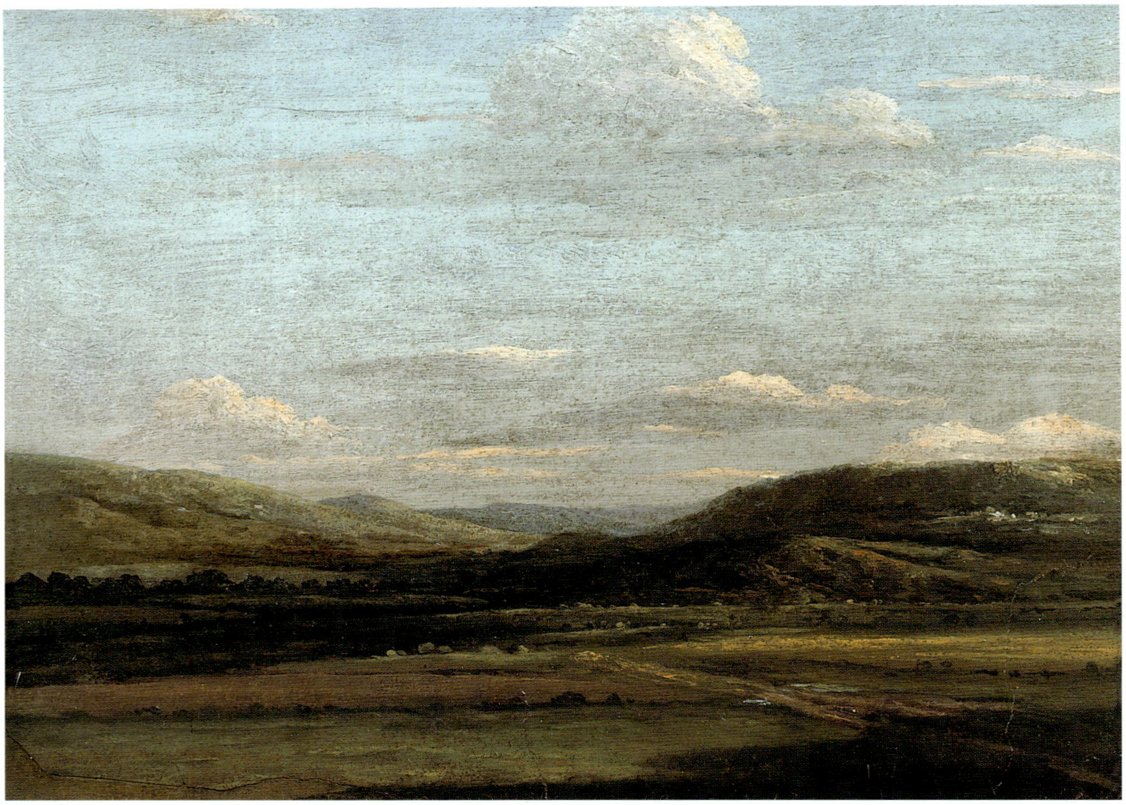

43

THOMAS JONES (1742–1803)

Pencerrig 1776

Oil on paper laid on panel, 23.5 × 32.5 (9¼ × 12¾)

Ins.: '1776' l.r.
Prov.: Captain John Dale, then by descent; Christie's, 2 July 1954, no. 214; Colnaghi's; purchased by Captain G. Crawshay, 1954; purchased by Paul Mellon, 1965; presented 1981
Exh.: New Haven, 1982, no. IV.1; New Haven, 1986, no. 34

Yale Center for British Art, Paul Mellon Collection (B1981.25.381)

Cardiff and Manchester only

This work dates from Jones's year-long visit to Pencerrig, prior to his departure for Italy in the autumn of 1776. With its vast expanse of sky and distant mountain range, it is clearly related to cat. nos 44 and 45. The traditional title, *Vale of Pencerrig*, is not in current use. (ABS)

44

THOMAS JONES (1742–1803)

Pencerrig 1776

Oil on low-grade wrapping paper*, 23.2 × 31.7 (9⅛ × 12½)

Ins.: '1776' l.l.
Prov.: Captain John Dale, then by descent; Christie's, 2 July 1954, no. 214; Colnaghi's; Paul Oppé; Armide Oppé; purchased 1996
Exh.: London, 1958, no. 298; London, 1970, no. 13
Lit.: Gowing, 1985, p. 23, pl. 15

Tate. Purchased as part of the Oppé Collection with assistance from the National Lottery through the Heritage Lottery Fund 1996 (T08243)

Cardiff and Manchester only

This distant view of rolling hills and expansive sky is similar in style and subject matter to *A View in Radnorshire* (cat. no. 45) and *Pencerrig*, also inscribed 1776 (cat. no. 43). Even though there is a distant farm in the centre, it has not been possible to identify the location more precisely, and, despite the specific titles of all three

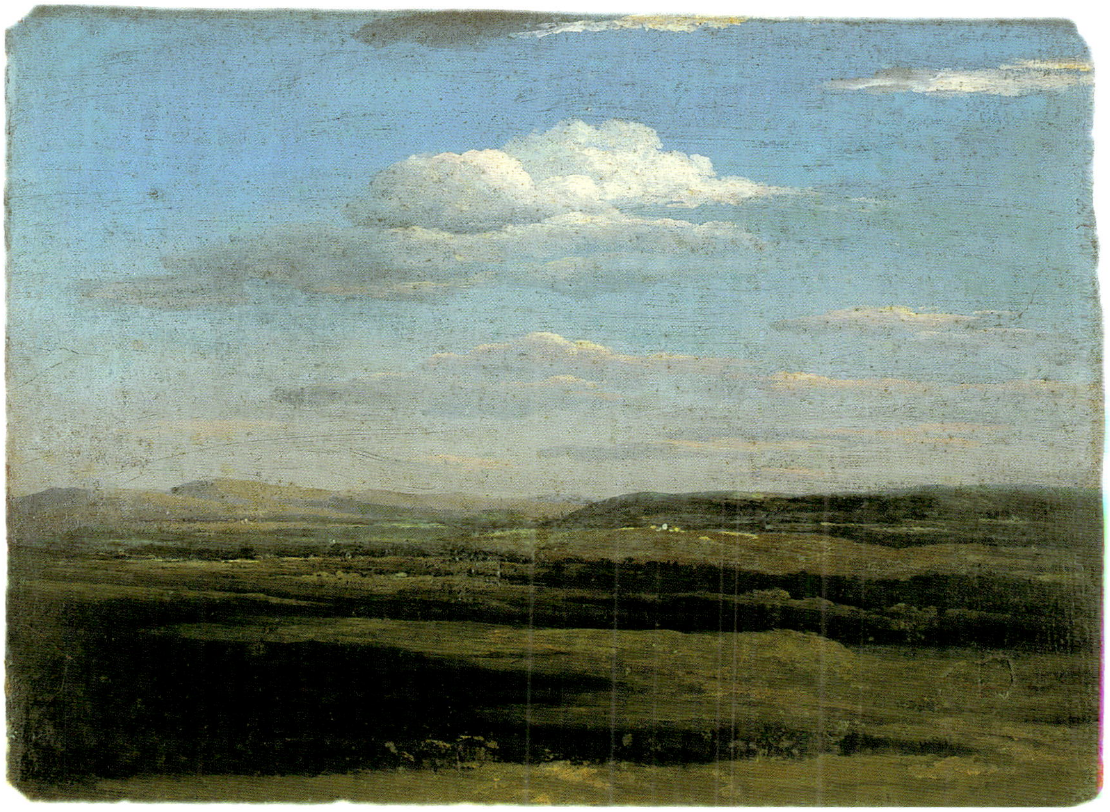

44

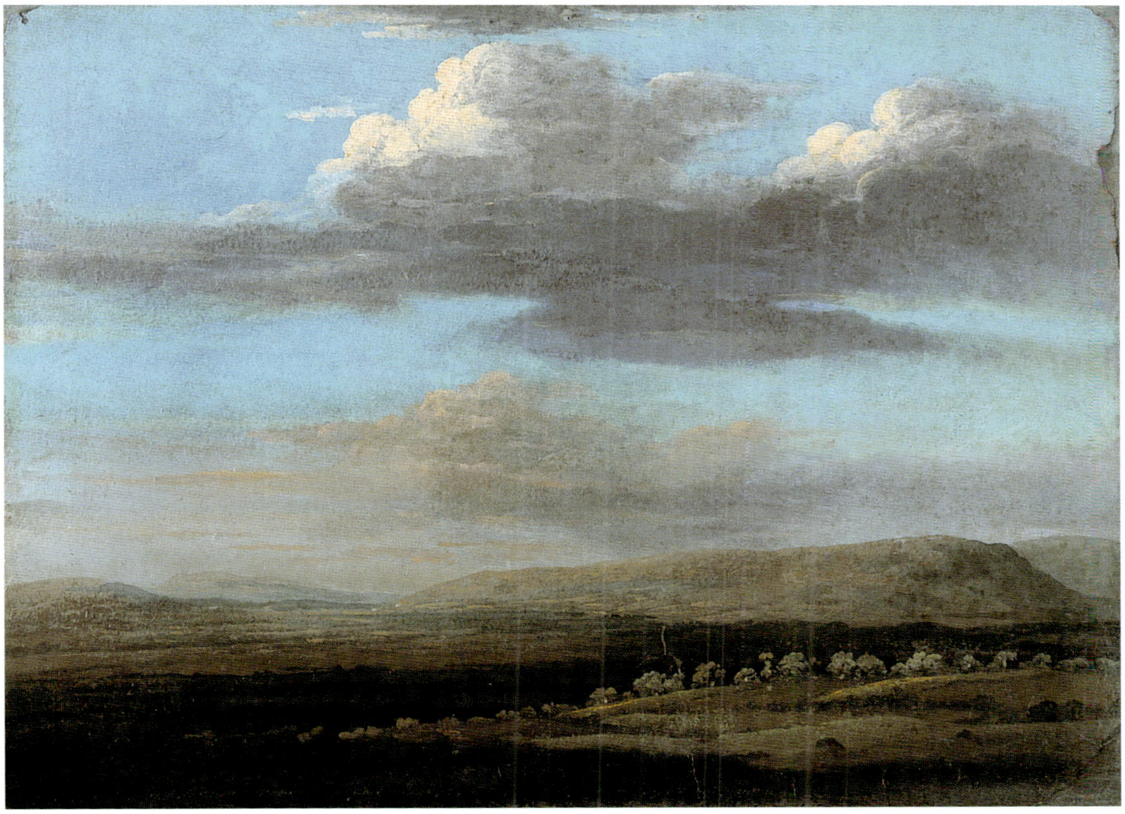

45

works, it is perhaps better to regard them as being idealized views. Under ultraviolet light, a small pond appears at the right edge of the middle ground. Jones was particularly observant of the cloud formations he witnessed in the skies above his native Radnorshire. Benjamin Malkin, when describing this area of Wales in 1804, wrote that 'Radnorshire is generally considered, in a picturesque point of view, as the least interesting of the Welsh counties' but it 'has isolated scenes which vie with anything in the whole compass of the district that surrounds it' (Malkin, 1804, p. 262), a view that Jones presumably shared. (ABS)

45

THOMAS JONES (1742–1803)

A View in Radnorshire c.1776

Oil on a brown wrapping paper*, 22.8 × 32.1 (9 × 12⅝)

Prov.: Captain John Dale, then by descent; Christie's, 2 July 1954, no. 214; Colnaghi's; purchased 1954
Exh.: London, 1970, no. 84; Aberystwyth, 1971, no. 27; Japan, 1986, no. 12
Lit.: Gowing, 1985, p. 23, pl. 14; Lord, 2000, fig. 237

National Museums & Galleries of Wales (NMW A 86)

Cardiff and Manchester only

The prominent whale-back ridge to the right somewhat resembles the Carneddau hills viewed from the west. However, it is difficult to reconcile the rather flat, featureless topography of the foreground with this location. Underdrawing is visible in the sky and on the horizon in this work, which is executed on a brown wrapping paper similar to that used in the 1776 sketch of Pencerrig (cat. no. 44). (ABS)

46

THOMAS JONES (1742–1803)

Landscape, Wales 1776

Oil on paper, 21.6 × 25.4 (8½ × 10)

Ins.: '1776' l.r.
Prov.: Captain John Dale, then by descent; Christie's, 28 July 1955, no. 6; Agnew's, 1956; John Higginson; Rossi's, Ballymead Lodge, Co. Down, 19 May 2001, no. 80

David W. Posnett

Cardiff and Manchester only

This oil sketch has not been precisely located, but it may have been painted at Dollynwydd looking north towards Garth, immediately to the south of Builth Wells. The conical hill in the centre left of the picture would then be Garth, with Carneddau behind and Aberedw to the right. The other possibility is that it was observed from above Newmead Farm (see cat. no. 40), looking towards Garth Bank, another conical hill, but located to the west of Builth Wells (fig. 61). The short shadows suggest midday and the season appears to be late spring, with green grass in the foreground, daffodils still flowering and the trees coming into full leaf. (ABS)

Fig. 61 View from above Newmead Farm Towards Garth Bank, contemporary photograph.

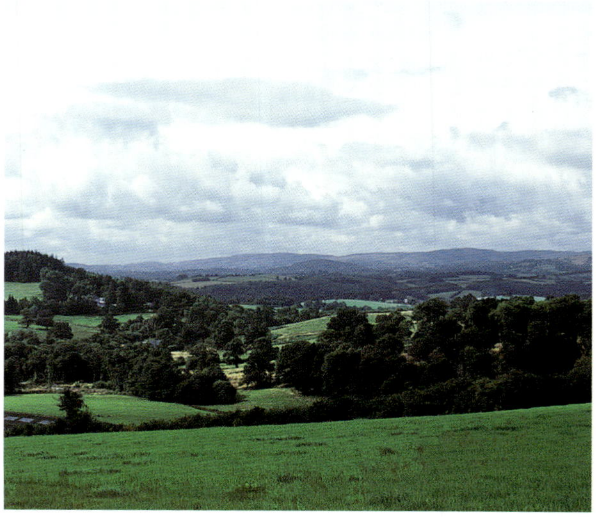

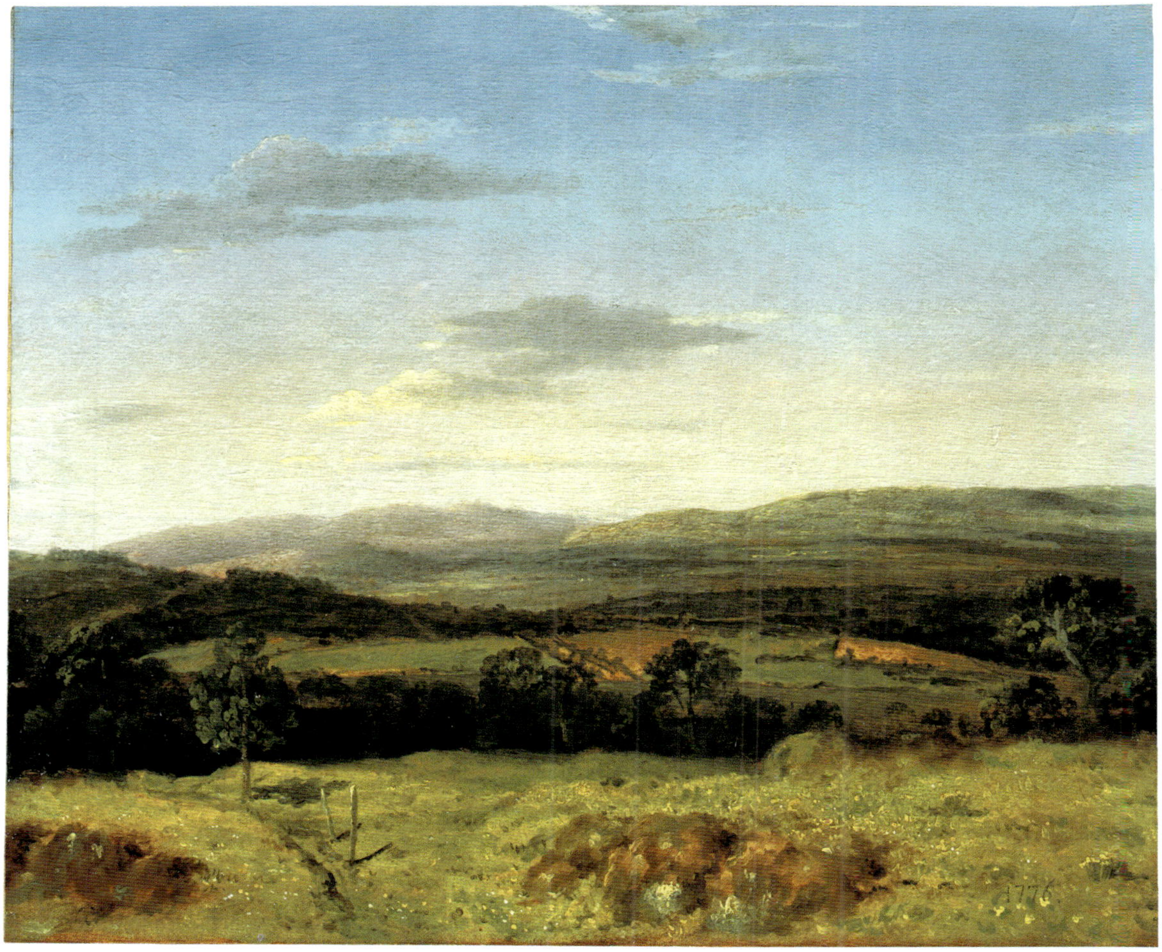

46

47

THOMAS JONES (1742–1803)

Sketch in Wales, Pencerrig 1776

Oil on laid paper, 22.4 × 31.8 (8⅞ × 12½)

Ins.: ‘1776’ l.r.
Prov.: Colnaghi’s; Benedict Nicolson; bequeathed to present owner
Exh.: Norwich, 1969, no. 26; London, 1970, no. 12; Sudbury, 1991, no. 13
Lit.: Gowing, 1985, pp. 22–3, pl. 12

Lady Ginette Darwin

Cardiff and Manchester only

This view is uncharacteristic of the oil sketches that Jones produced in 1776, since it avoids the broad open view and low horizon typically seen in *Pencerrig* (cat. no. 44). Instead, the artist reverts to a closer viewpoint to produce a more enclosed vision of nature as he had done in *Gadbridge* (cat. no. 39), though this is relieved by the field to the left. This is the first time that Jones introduced a

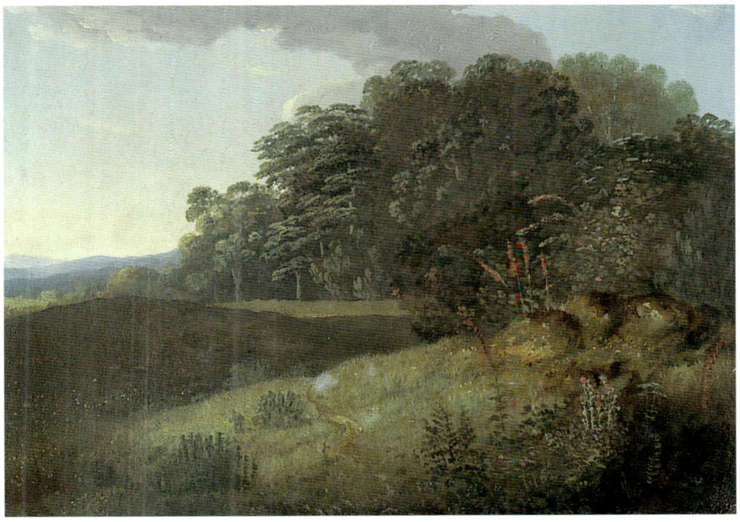

47

48

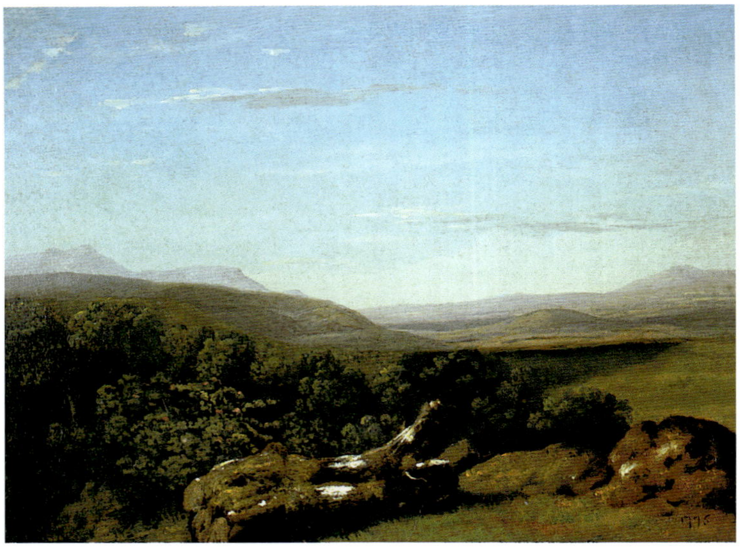

characteristic feature of later studies: a prominent rock or mound placed close to the viewer. In this case, it is covered with late-summer wild flowers such as foxglove and thistle. This view has in common with the other oil sketches a rejection of landscape conventions and a focus on an unexceptional stretch of landscape, presumably at Pencerrig. (GS)

48

THOMAS JONES (1742–1803)

View near Pencerrig? 1776

Oil on paper laid on panel, 24 × 31.5 $(9\frac{1}{2} \times 12\frac{1}{2})$

Ins.: '1776' l.r.
Prov.: Agnew's, 1960; Sir Hugo Boothby by descent; Sotheby's, 9 April 1997, no. 53
Exh.: London, 1970, no. 11

Private collection

Cardiff and Manchester only

This oil sketch concentrates upon the fallen tree in the foreground and a shrubby hedge in flower, possibly with dog rose. In the background are unidentified sizeable peaks which are more reminiscent of the mountains of the Brecon Beacons than the hills around Pencerrig. Jones depicts the fallen tree, especially the bark formations, in considerable detail. (ABS)

49

THOMAS JONES (1742–1803)

Field near Pencerrig *c.*1776

Oil on paper, 23 × 30.3 $(9 \times 11\frac{7}{8})$

Prov.: Captain John Dale, then by descent; Christie's, 2 July 1954, no. 223; purchased by D. L. Corkery, 1954; Agnew's; James Mackinnon, from whom purchased by the National Museums & Galleries of Wales, 2002
Exh.: London, 1970, no. 14
Lit.: Gowing, 1985, p. 23, pl. 13

National Museums & Galleries of Wales (NMW A 23200)

Cardiff and Manchester only

This scene shows a stone building, perhaps a folly, to the left, a central tree which appears to be an English elm, and an area of line-planted saplings, possibly apple trees, beyond. It was painted on the Pencerrig estate, south-west of the house, looking north-west to Gorllwyn, a prominent mountain which has a cairn on its summit. A contemporary photograph (fig. 62) shows that the view is little changed today. The direction and warmth of the light suggest an early evening scene, the sun appearing to have just set. It was probably painted in late April or early May 1776, as suggested by the single clump of daffodils in full flower and the partial leafing of the trees.

Technical analysis has revealed extensive underdrawing (fig. 47, p. 98), with the details of the tree trunks and the distant hills carefully outlined. Jones also extended the folly and altered the branch above it. Such details reveal that this was less of a swift response to nature than initially appears. No traces of dust, pollen or sand particles were found within the paint surface, making it unlikely that the study was actually made on the spot. (ABS)

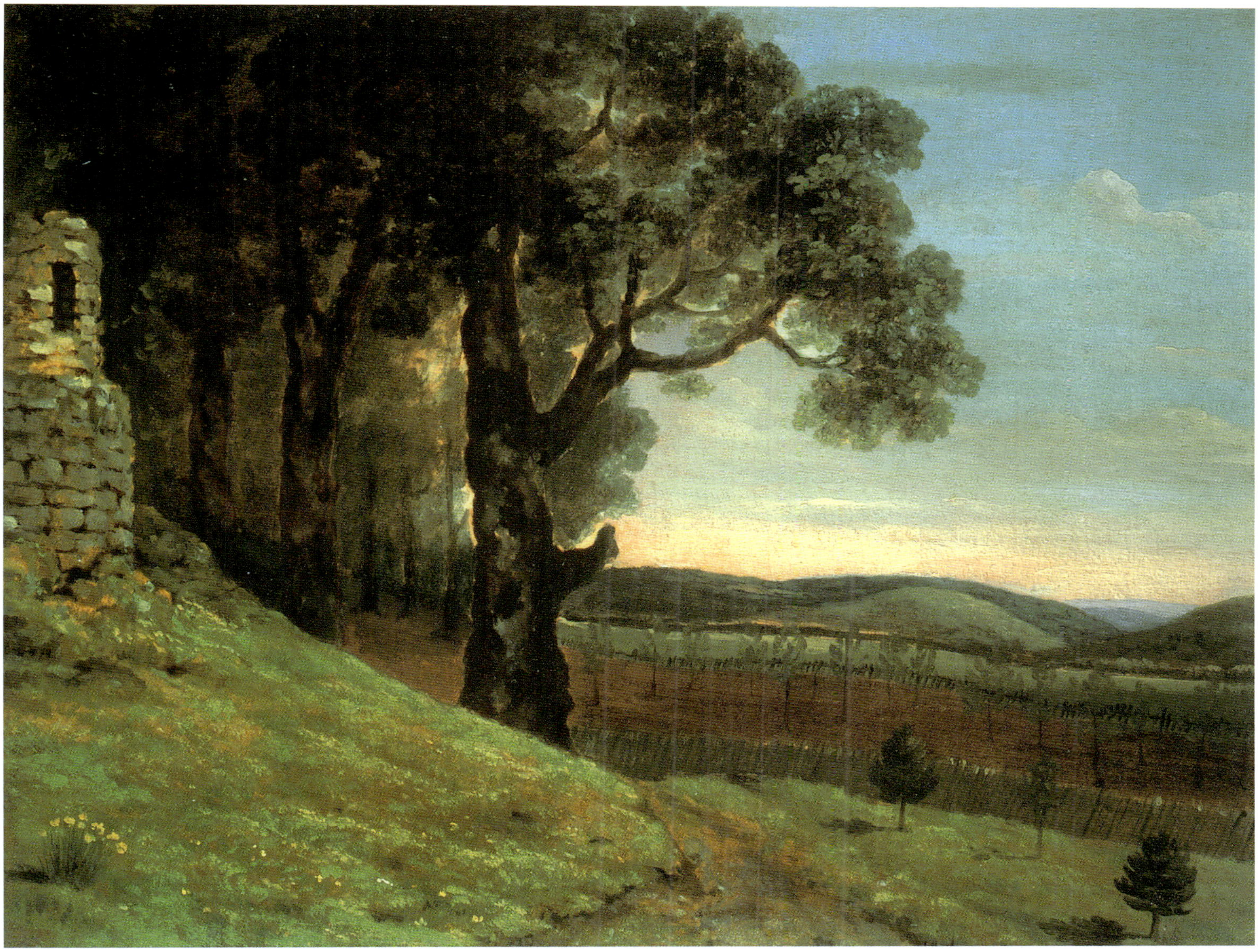

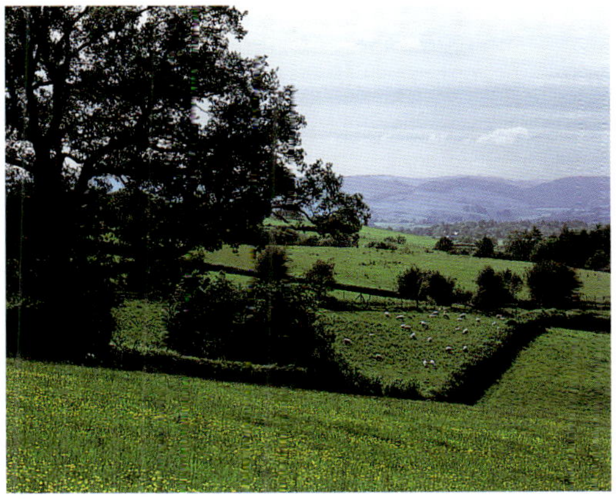

Fig. 62 View from Pencerrig Towards Gorllwyn, contemporary photograph.

50

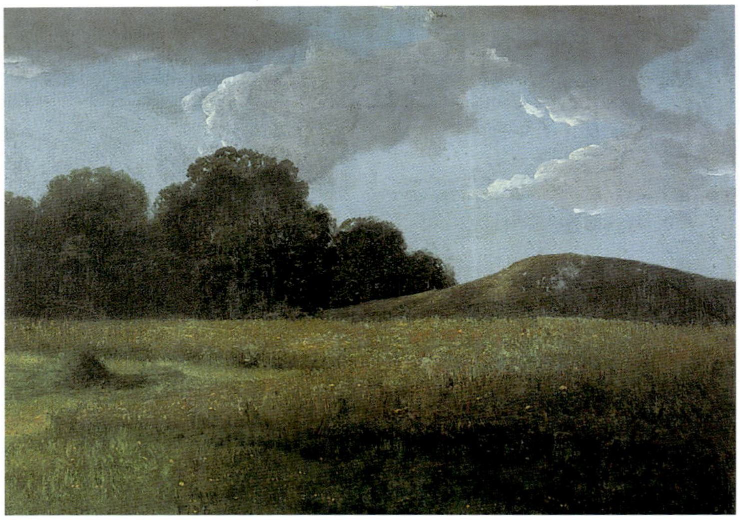

to Pencerrig and is therefore more likely to date to 1775–6. This is one of Jones's freshest and apparently most spontaneous works. It was presumably painted in high summer. (ABS)

50

THOMAS JONES (1742–1803)

Welsh Landscape with Cornfield *c.*1776

Oil on paper, 22 × 31 (8⅝ × 12¼)

Prov.: Purchased 1950s, then by descent

Mrs George Lindsay

Cardiff and Manchester only

This work is painted on thick rough textured paper and is laid on to a backing card with lines drawn around it to form a mount; presumably this was done by Jones himself. It has not been possible to locate the hill, or the distant oak trees, but it is presumably close

51

THOMAS JONES (1742–1803)

A Bend in a Road: An Unidentified View in the Chilterns 1771

Watercolour on laid paper (watermark: crown over GR and HONI SOIT QUI MAL Y PENSE), 16.5 × 29 (6½ × 11⅜) image size; 35.5 × 29.4 (14 × 11⅝) page size

Ins.: 'August 24 1771' l.l.
Prov.: Thomas Thomas, then by descent to Jane Evan-Thomas; given to R. C. B. Oliver; presented by him, 1989

The Whitworth Art Gallery, The University of Manchester (D.1989.2)

Cardiff and Manchester only

This, and the following two watercolour sketches, come from the only surviving sketchbook that dates from prior to Jones's trip to Italy. It has not been possible to identify the views, but it is likely that they were painted on one of the 'excursions' Jones said that he made during the summer of 1771 (*Memoirs*, p. 24). Jones did not specify where he went, but he often visited his cousin at Gadbridge in Hertfordshire and the scenery shown in the four sketches that have survived is in keeping with the characteristic chalk landscape of the Chilterns. (GS)

51

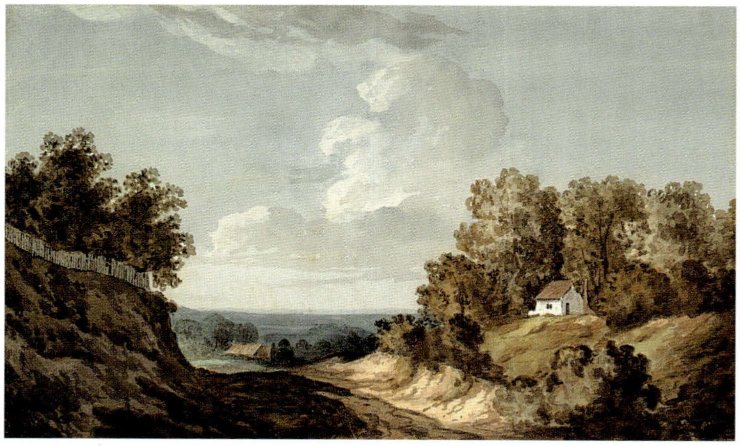

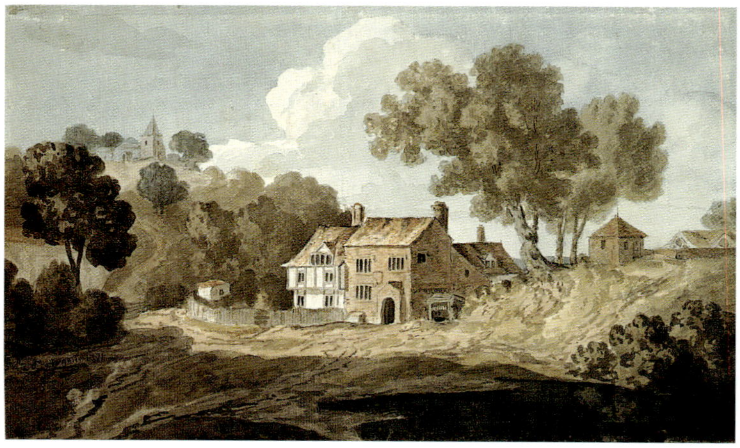

52

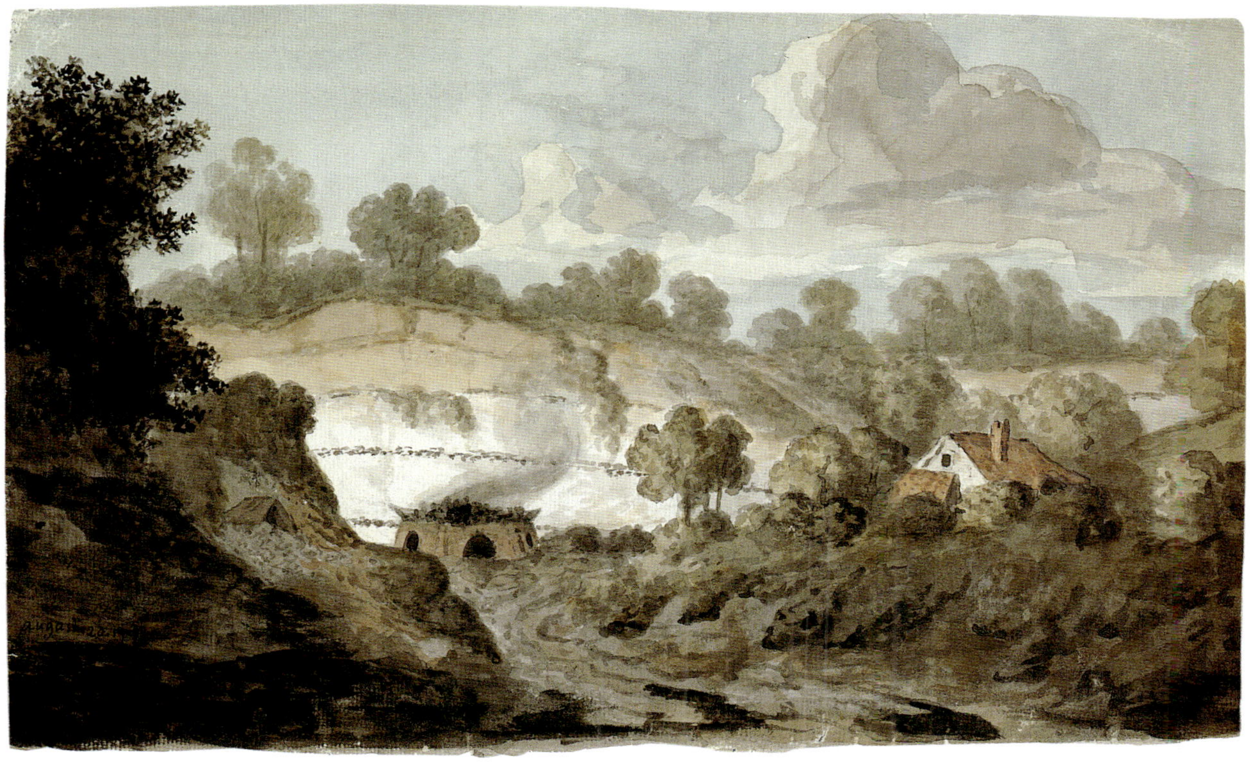

53

52

THOMAS JONES (1742–1803)

A House by a Road: Unidentified View in the Chilterns 1771

Watercolour, pen and ink on laid paper, 17.8 × 29.2 (6½ × 11¼) image size; 35.5 × 29.4 (14 × 11⅝) page size

Ins.: '26 August 1771' l.l.
Prov.: Thomas Thomas, then by descent to Jane Evan-Thomas; bequeathed 2000
Exh.: London, 1970, no. 2

The Whitworth Art Gallery, The University of Manchester (D.2000.6)

Cardiff and Manchester only

The sketchbook from which this work was detached was in use from 1766, soon after Jones left Richard Wilson's studio, to 1774. The book has been partially split up, but it is known to have contained a mix of early pencil studies 'from different Masters', as Jones expressed it, and later landscape sketches 'from Nature' such as this and cat. nos 53 and 54, made in 1771 (*Memoirs*, p. 140). The latest drawings were made on an excursion in 1774 to Milton's cottage at Chalfont St Giles in Buckinghamshire in connection with a major commission (cat. no. 33). There is no evidence, however, that these three unspectacular views of Chiltern scenery were anything other than on-the-spot sketches of subjects that attracted Jones's attention. (GS)

53

THOMAS JONES (1742–1803)

A Chalk Pit with Lime Kiln: Unidentified View in the Chilterns 1771

Watercolour, pen and ink on laid paper (watermark: crown over GR and HONI SOIT QUI MAL Y PENSE), 17.8 × 29.2 (6½ × 11¼) image size; 35.5 × 29.4 (14 × 11⅝) page size

Ins.: 'august 20 1771' l.l.
Prov.: Thomas Thomas, then by descent to Jane Evan-Thomas; bequeathed 2000

The Whitworth Art Gallery, The University of Manchester (D.2000.7)

Cardiff and Manchester only

54

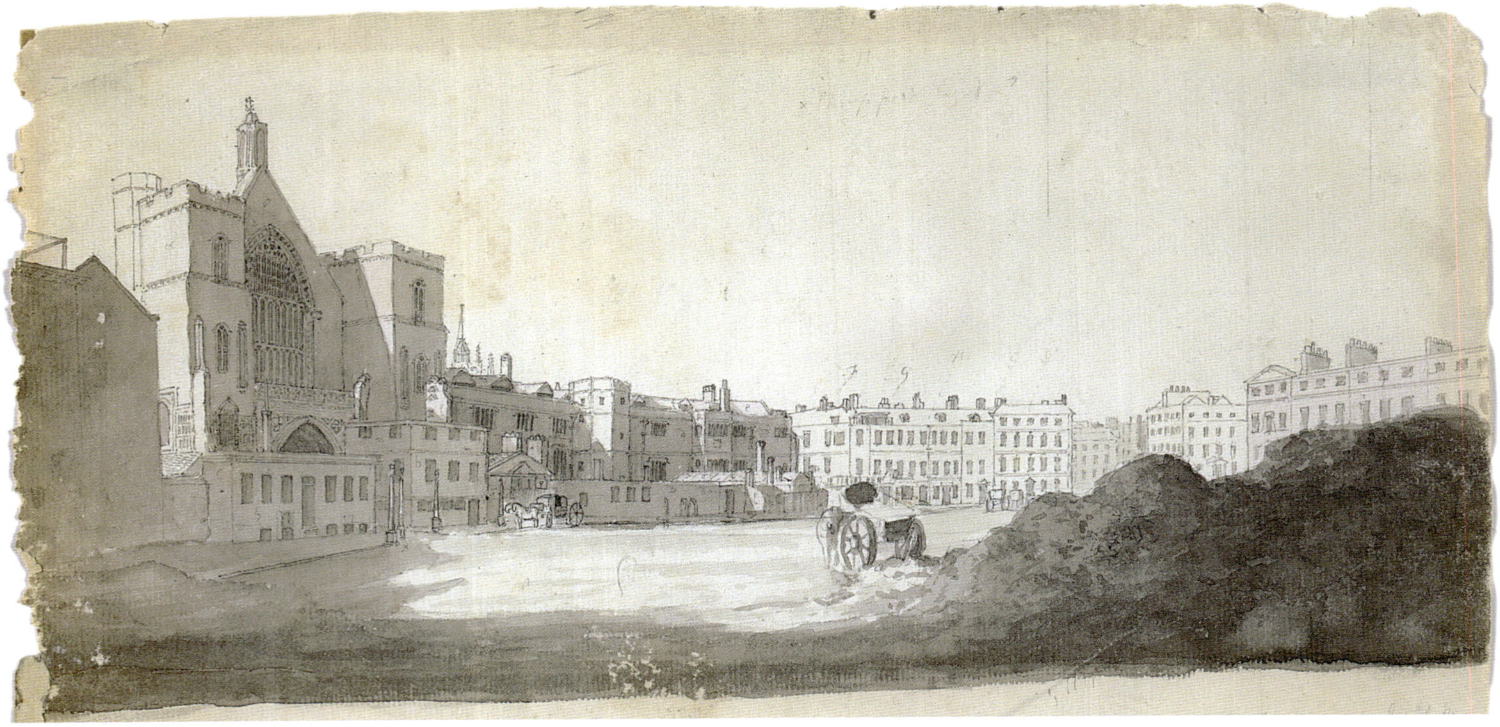

On his return from Italy, Jones recorded how he found that his earliest drawings and sketches, which he had consigned to the care of a friend, had been left in a 'damp Dungeon' and had turned into 'one undistinguished heap of Rubbish' (*Memoirs*, p. 140). The volume from which this drawing was extracted appears to have been a unique survivor. It was inscribed 'A Book of Sketches after Nature belonging to Thomas Jones Landskip Painter' and the three landscapes from it (cat. nos 51–3) certainly appear to have been coloured on the spot. Given the losses suffered amongst his early works, it is impossible to say whether Jones's use of watercolour as a sketching medium at this date was a regular part of his practice. (GS)

54

THOMAS JONES (1742–1803)

New Palace Yard, Westminster, with the Façade of Westminster Hall *c.*1766–74

Pencil, watercolour on laid paper, 11.9 × 27.7 (4⅝ × 10⅞) (sight)

Ins.: 'Thomas Jones – Palace Yard' below image (hidden)
Prov.: Thomas Thomas, then by descent to Jane Evan-Thomas; given to present owner

Lit.: Morgan, 1984, p. 75

Private collection

Cardiff and Manchester only

This sketch shows the façade of Westminster Hall and part of the old Palace of Westminster from New Palace Yard. Unlike the standard topographical prints and drawings of the time, Jones adopts an idiosyncratic viewpoint at an oblique angle to the façade, so that the towers of Westminster Abbey are obscured – part of St Margaret's is just visible – and much of the foreground is taken up by a large mound of what appears be builder's rubble. Thus, whilst other artists show an elegant town square, Jones's image is a less flattering snapshot of city life. Like cat. nos 51–3, this drawing was removed from the sketchbook Jones used from 1766 to 1774. The loss of almost all of his early sketches means that we cannot say whether this type of view was a one-off or formed a significant part of his early artistic development. (GS)

55

Thomas Jones (1742–1803)

Six Views in South Wales, Drawn after Nature

*c.*1775–6

Six engravings bound in a volume with historical notes, 22.7 × 29.9 (8⅞ × 11¾)

Lit.: Morgan, 1984, pl. 2a–b; Joyner, 1997, pp. 66–7

Llyfrgell Genedlaethol Cymru, The National Library of Wales (PD308, BV202)

Cardiff and Manchester only

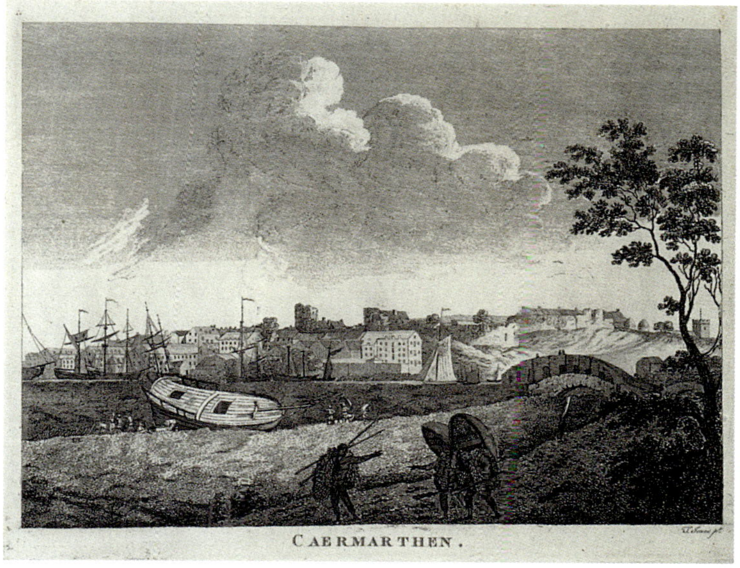

55

The engravings include views of Brecon Castle, Brecon Mere, Carmarthen, Careg-Cennen Castle, Kidwelly Castle and Pembroke. The prints are undated, but they are all inscribed with Jones's name, indicating that he was the artist of the original views, whilst two of them, *Kidwely Castle* and *Pembroke*, are also marked 'sculp', identifying Jones as the engraver as well. The volume includes an impressive list of sixty-five Welsh subscribers, including many members of his family, and twenty-seven English. Interestingly, Richard Wilson's name is present as a subscriber for seven sets, possibly to sell in London on Jones's behalf. The volume is open at the view of Carmarthen town quay, showing the ruins of the castle to the right and trading vessels in the background, including two smacks, two brigs and a fully rigged ship. There is a vessel probably undergoing repair at the water's edge and a number of coracle fishermen in the foreground, a tradition which continues today. (ABS)

FOLLOWING PAGES Detail of cat. no. 69.

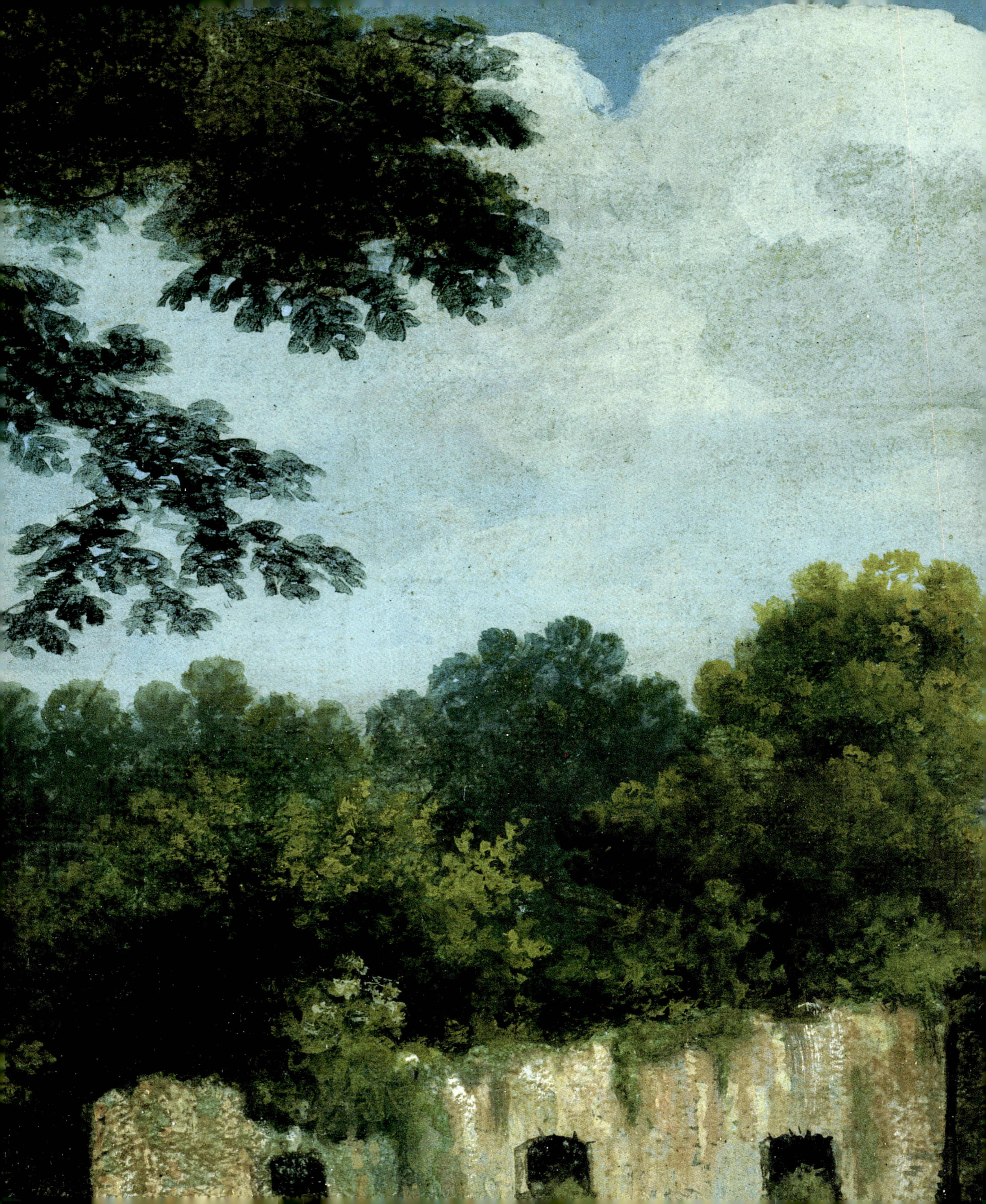

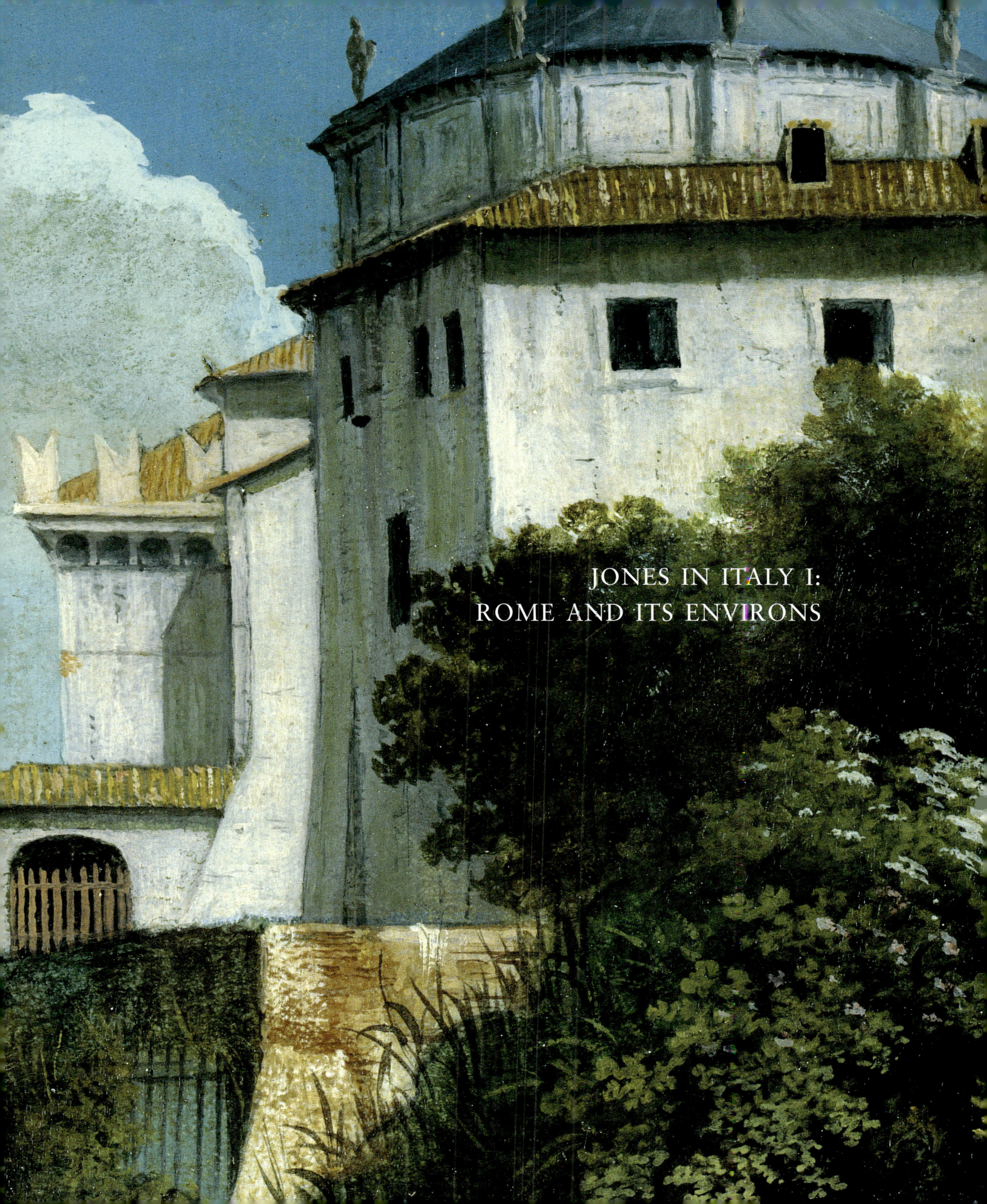

JONES IN ITALY I:
ROME AND ITS ENVIRONS

56

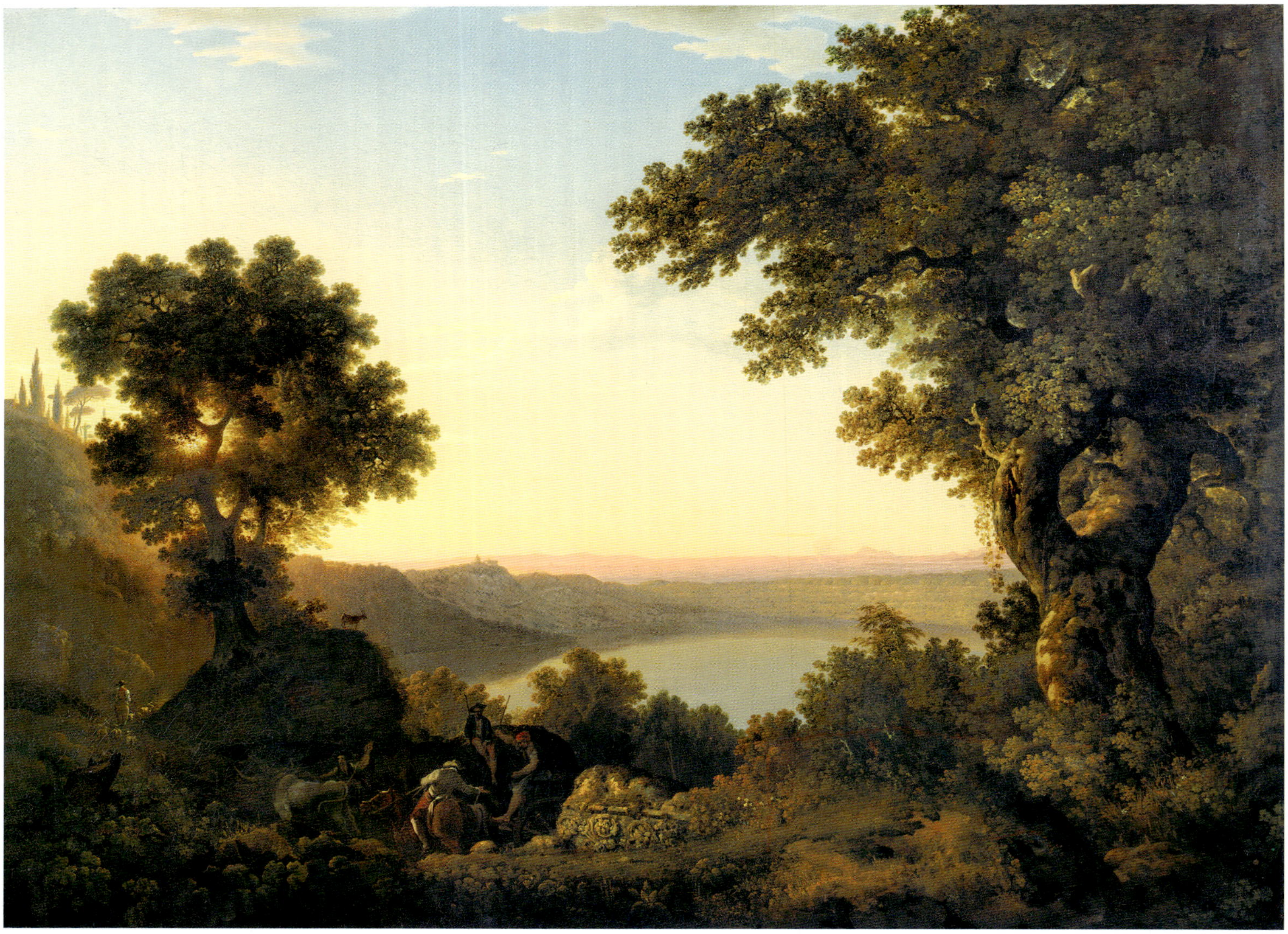

56

THOMAS JONES (1742–1803)

Lake Albano – Sunset 1777

Oil on canvas, 119.7 × 165.8 (47⅛ × 65¼)

Ins.: 'THO JONES: / MDCCLXXVII / ROMAE' l.r.
Prov.: 4th Earl of Bristol and Bishop of Derry; Agnew's; purchased by Paul Mellon, 1971; presented 1973
Exh.: Agnew's, 1971, no. 40; New Haven, 1981, no. 14

Yale Center for British Art, Paul Mellon Collection (B1973.1.30)

Jones visited Lake Albano in December 1776 and May 1777, though no drawing survives for this view. It was the first canvas Jones completed in Italy and it is well documented. Jones began work on 12 June 1777, describing it as '(a Sun set) on a large Cloth 5 feet 6 Inches by 4 feet' (*Memoirs*, p. 62). By 17 June he had 'painted the Sky & distance a second time', noting that he 'took half an Ounce of Ultramarine in the Middle Distance – used no Blue – only black Italian chalk ground, White Naples Yellow & Vermilion' (ibid.). In all, the painting took '41 Days' and it was complete by August. According to the artist, 'it attracted a

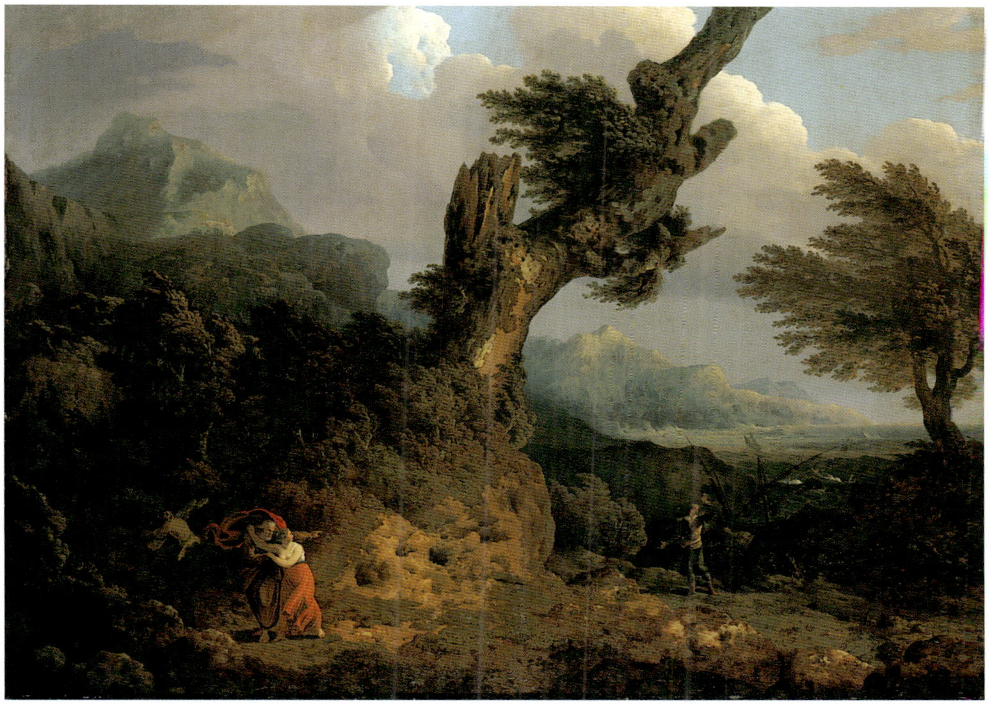

57

good deal of Notice not only from My brother artists & English Cavaliers but from the foreign Artists & Cavaliers' (ibid., pp. 62–3). Frederick Hervey, Bishop of Derry and later 4th Earl of Bristol, regularly visited his studio and Jones eventually persuaded him to buy the painting in May 1778 for '40£ Sterling' (ibid., p. 71). This proved a significant sale, for Hervey's support helped to establish Jones's position and in 1782 he commissioned a companion to this work, *Lake Nemi* (cat. no. 58). (ABS)

57

THOMAS JONES (1742–1803)

A Storm – Prospero, Miranda and Caliban Spying the Shipwrecked Ferdinand 1778

Oil on canvas, 123.2 × 155 (48½ × 61)

Ins.: 'Tho: Jones. P. / Romae MDCCLXXVIII' l.l.
Prov.: Lord Donoughmore; Sotheby's, 7 July 1982, no. 44; purchased by the National Museum of Wales, 1982

National Museums & Galleries of Wales (NMW A 91)

Cardiff and Manchester only

Jones takes as his subject the second scene of Shakespeare's *The Tempest*, where Prospero and his daughter Miranda catch sight of her future lover, the shipwrecked Ferdinand, who is entranced by the singing of the spirit Ariel. Jones's composition is influenced by the wild landscapes of Salvator Rosa, with a dramatic mountainous coastal scene in the distance, though details such as the leaves are minutely observed. Jones had previously used stormy landscapes as the basis for literary subjects in *Dido and Aeneas* (cat. no. 20) and a scene from Shakespeare's *Winter's Tale* (untraced). This appears to be the first subject painting Jones produced in Italy, though. On 31 July 1777, he recalls that he 'began a Storm Scene on a Cloth 5 feet by 4 – in which is to be introduced the Story of *Prospero & Miranda*' (*Memoirs*, p. 62). Then, in March 1778, he states that he 'finished the large Storm of Prospero & Calliban, begun the 26th of July last' (ibid., p. 70). This presumably refers to the same painting, suggesting that the subject may have changed during the intervening months. (ABS)

58 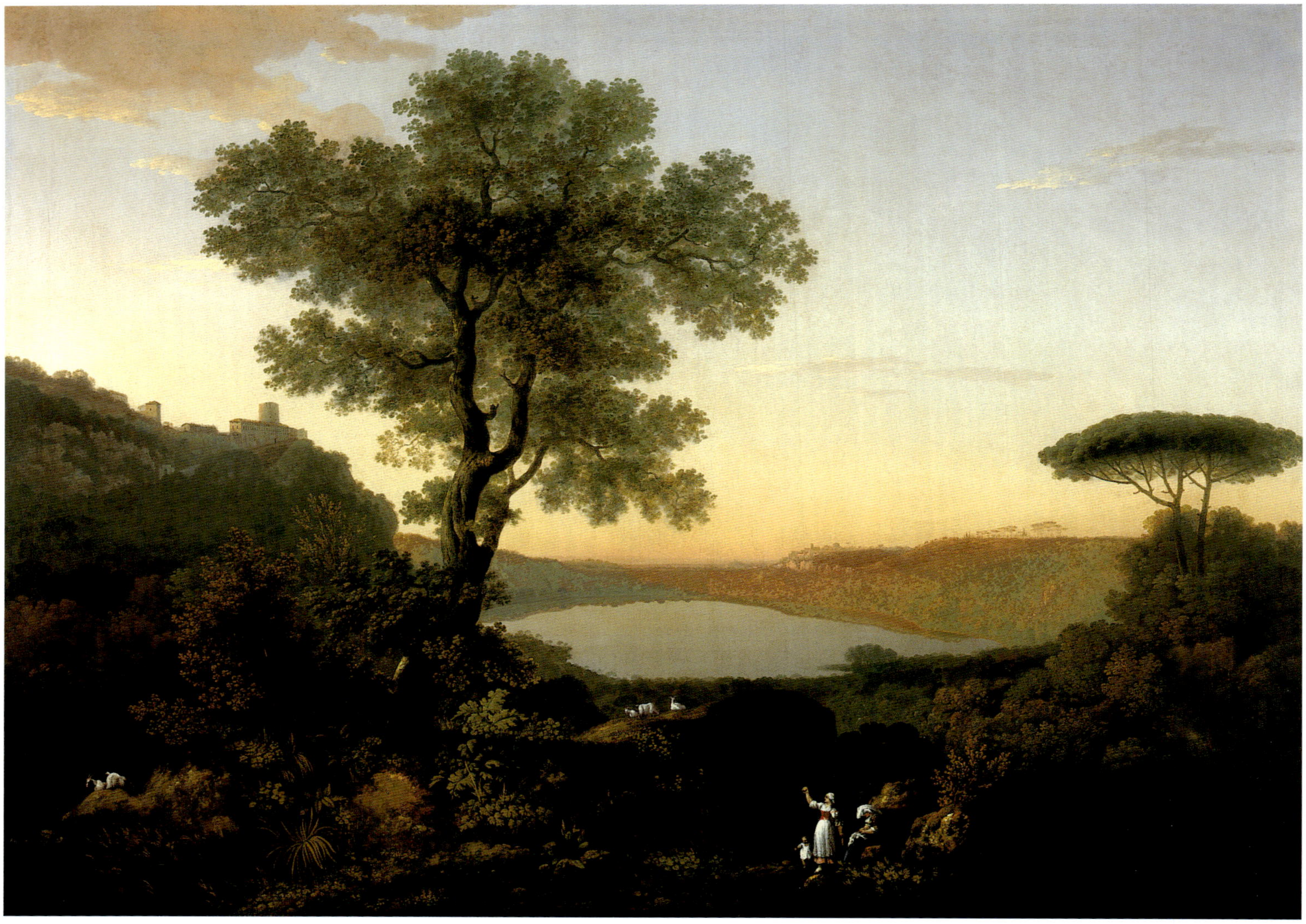

58

THOMAS JONES (1742–1803)

Lake Nemi 1782

Oil on canvas, 124.4 × 177.8 (49 × 70)

Ins.: 'THO. JONES. pinxt NEAPOLI / MDCCLXXXII' l.r.
Prov.: Commissioned by the 4th Earl of Bristol and Bishop of Derry, then by descent; E. Holland Martin, then by descent
Exh.: Birmingham, 1948, no. 164; London, 1970, no. 58
Lit.: Apollo, June 1966, p. 445

Private collection

The 4th Earl of Bristol and Bishop of Derry (1730–1803) was Jones's most assiduous patron in Italy, acquiring five of his highly finished classical landscape paintings. They included this large work, showing the lake, south of Rome, which, along with nearby Lake Albano, was a favourite motif with artists and their patrons. Jones had sketched Lake Nemi on 30 April 1777 (*Memoirs*, p. 58). He began the painting in Naples in February 1780, describing it as 'a morning Scene, which was bespoke by the Earl of Bristol as a Companion to the Lake of Albano, Evening Scene, which his Lordship bought of me at Rome' (ibid., p. 110). He finished and dated the canvas two years later. The companion piece is cat. no. 56. (CR)

59

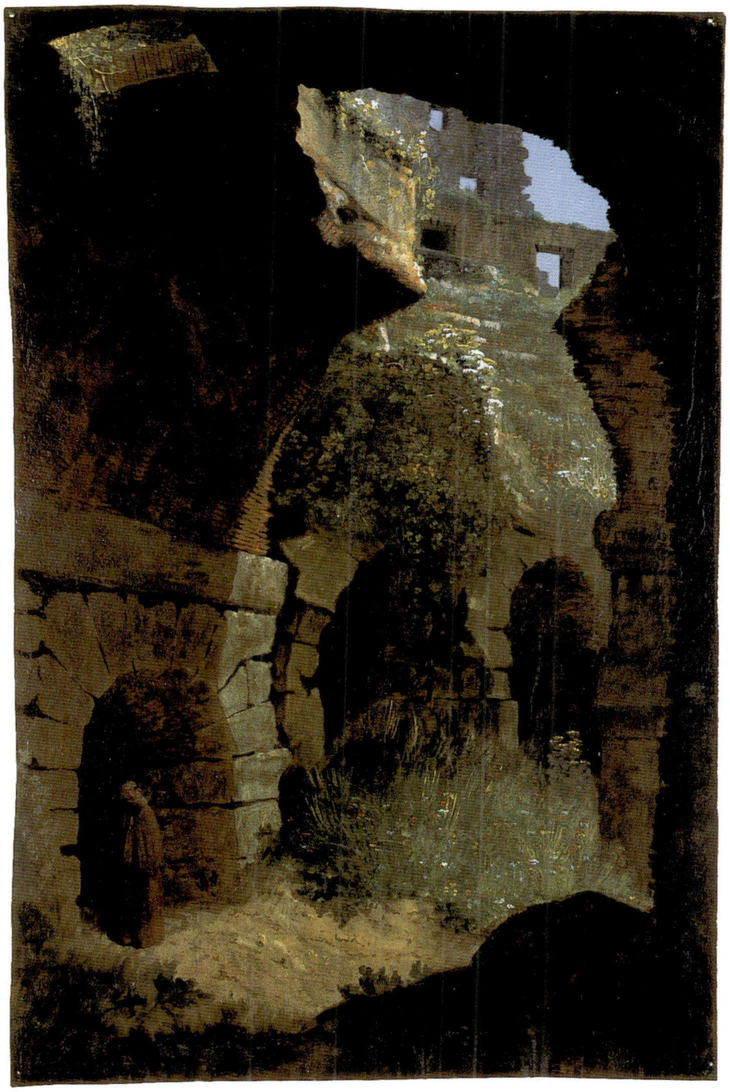

59

Thomas Jones (1742–1803)

In the Colosseum, Rome *c.*1777

Oil on paper, 43.2 × 28.9 (17 × 11⅜)

Ins.: 'No7 / A Scene in the Collosseo at Rome / T Jones' verso
Prov.: Captain John Dale, then by descent to Canon J. H. Adams; presented 1983
Exh.: London, 1970, no. 32; Cambridge, 1980, no. 20; Stockholm, 1982, no. 124; Manchester, 1988, no. 36
Lit.: Gowing, 1985, p. 33, pl. 26

Tate. Presented by Canon J. H. Adams 1983 (T03546)

Jones began visiting the antiquities of Rome almost immediately upon his arrival in late November 1776. No doubt he made his way to the Colosseum, the most prominent work of ancient architecture in the city, on several occasions, although only one such visit is recorded, on 9 April 1777, when he painted and inscribed a watercolour study in the large British Museum sketchbook (cat. no. 75, p. 20). Here, he looks through a broken arch upwards to the sky and brilliant sunlight beyond. The spatial complexity of the scene suggests the influence of the engravings of Piranesi, whom Jones came to know and admire in Rome. (CR)

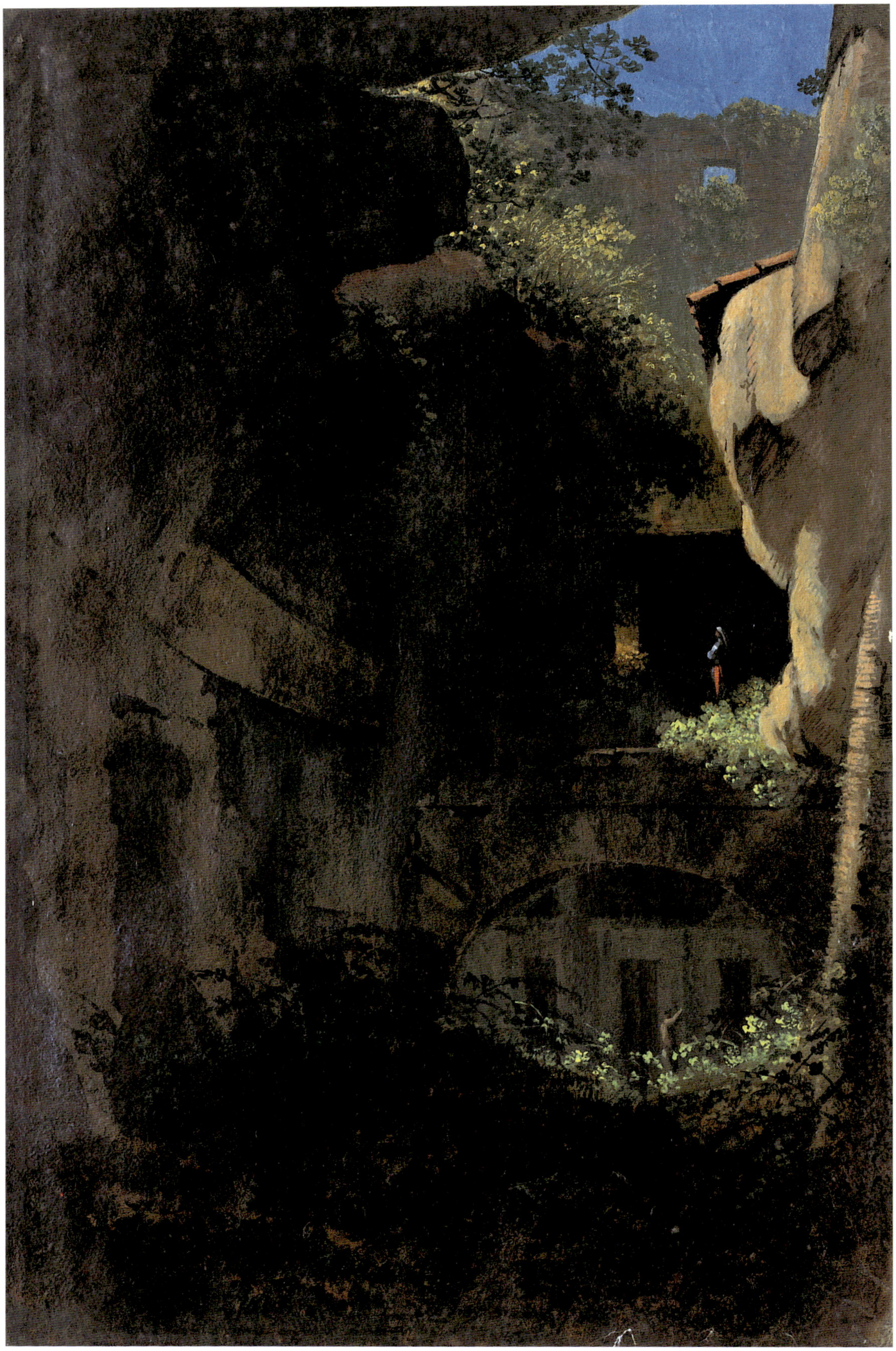

60

THOMAS JONES (1742–1803)

Scene in the Colosseum, Rome *c.*1777

Oil on laid paper, 41 × 28 ($16\frac{1}{8} \times 11\frac{1}{16}$)

Ins.: 'No. 6 / A Scene in the Colloseo at Rome / T Jones' verso
Prov.: Colnaghi's, 1958; W. A. Brandt, then by descent
Exh.: Ickworth, 1969, no. 19; London, 1970, no. 31

Private collection

This oil possibly dates from 1777, and, like cat. no. 61, it may have been sketched on the spot. The inscription on the back suggests that it was part of a sequence, though numbers '1' to '5' are untraced. Like numerous other artists visiting Rome, Jones was fascinated by the ruined galleries and the dramatic forms they assume, as well as the contrasts of light and shade that envelop the monument. In these respects, the overgrown monument resembled the grottoes and caves he also sketched at this time (cat. nos 61 and 62).

The two figures add to the work's mysterious atmosphere. A clue to their identity is provided by cat. no. 59, where a monk stands in one of the arches. The lower arch at the back of this view, together with the door and the line of projecting tiles at the top right, are actually part of the small chapel that was built within the amphitheatre following the consecration of the structure in 1750. This can be seen in John 'Warwick' Smith's general view (Manchester, 1988, no. 41). (GS)

61

THOMAS JONES (1742–1803)

A Cavern near S. Agnese Outside the Porta Pia at Rome *c.*1778

Oil on Italian laid writing paper, varnished*, 28 × 32 ($11 \times 12\frac{1}{2}$)

Ins.: 'No. 9 A cavern near Sant' Agnese without the Porta Pia at Rome T. Jones' verso
Prov.: Captain John Dale, then by descent to Canon J. H. Adams; Sotheby's, 27 November 1975, no. 91 – bought in; W. W. Jones; Christie's, 16 November 1982, no. 91 – bought in; presented by Jane Evan-Thomas, 1985

National Museums & Galleries of Wales (NMW A 88)

For several months in the spring and summer of 1778, Jones spent time with his friend John Robert Cozens at a villa near S. Agnese outside the walls of Rome. 'Here I made some Studies in Oil of the surrounding Scenery and was accommodated with a nice Poney whenever I pleased to take an Airing with little Cousins and his jackAss' (*Memoirs*, p. 73). This oil sketch no doubt dates, or derives, from one such excursion. It resembles other Roman sketches, such as *In the Colosseum* (cat. no. 59), in the artist's choice of a sheltered location from the shade of which he could look outward into the sunlit distance – though in this case he shows a sunset or sunrise. There is evidence of some underdrawing around the opening of the cave. (CR)

62

THOMAS JONES (1742–1803)

A Cavern near Rome *c.*1778

Oil on paper, 27.4 × 39 ($10\frac{3}{4} \times 15\frac{3}{8}$) (sight)

Ins.: 'No. 8 / A Cavern near Roma / T Jones' on a piece of paper on the back of the frame. Not Jones, but an early hand
Prov.: Captain John Dale, then by descent

Private collection

This presumably shows the same cavern near S. Agnese outside the Porta Pia as cat. no. 61, which is inscribed 'No. 9' whilst this is 'No. 8'. *Porta Pia, Rome* (private collection) is possibly one of the 'Studies in Oil' Jones produced at this time and both cavern views are candidates for being amongst the first of the Italian oil sketches made on the spot (*Memoirs*, p. 73). The evidence is not, however, clear cut. There is no debris on the paint surface, as is often the case with oils worked from nature, and the two red-coated figures, introduced to vary the palette of muddy browns, ochres and dark olives, are more indicative of studio practice. Jones travelled around the Campagna with John Robert Cozens who, like many artists at this time, was fascinated by the dramatic potential of cave scenery (see cat. no. 96). (GS)

61

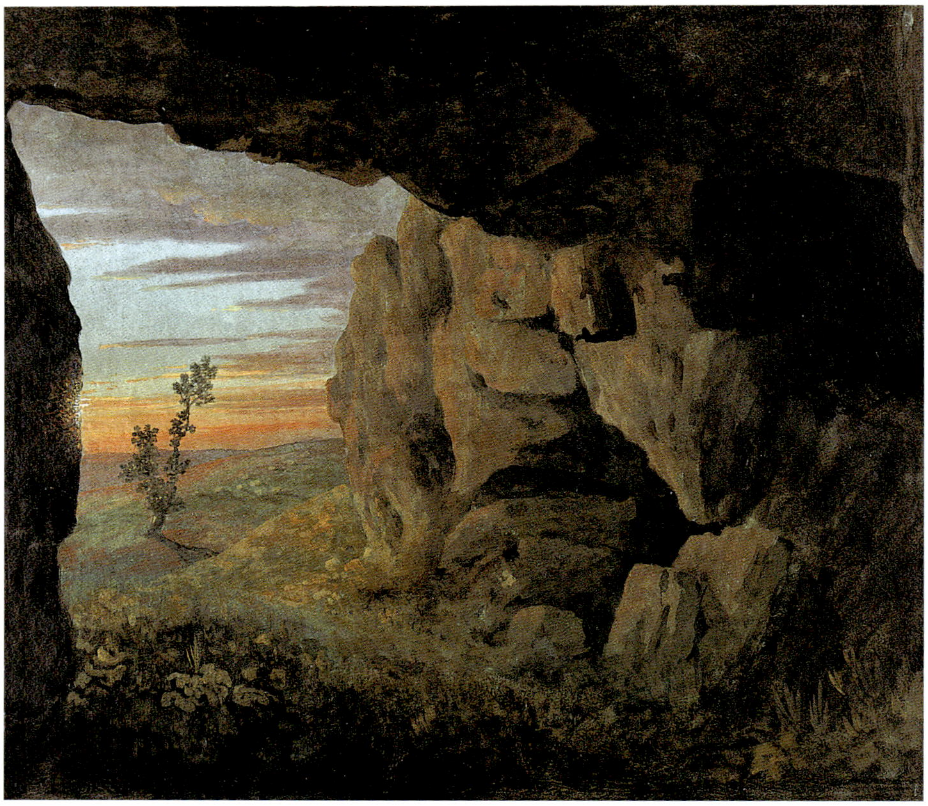

62

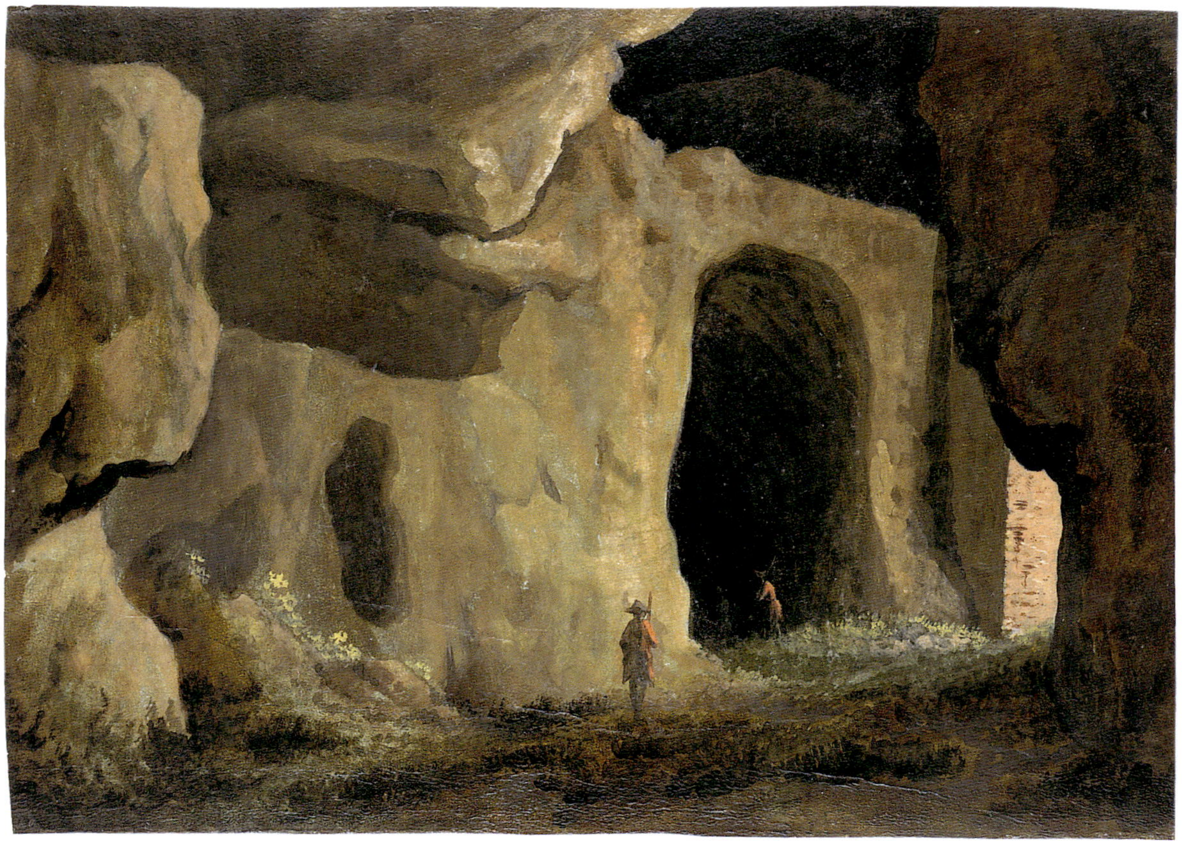

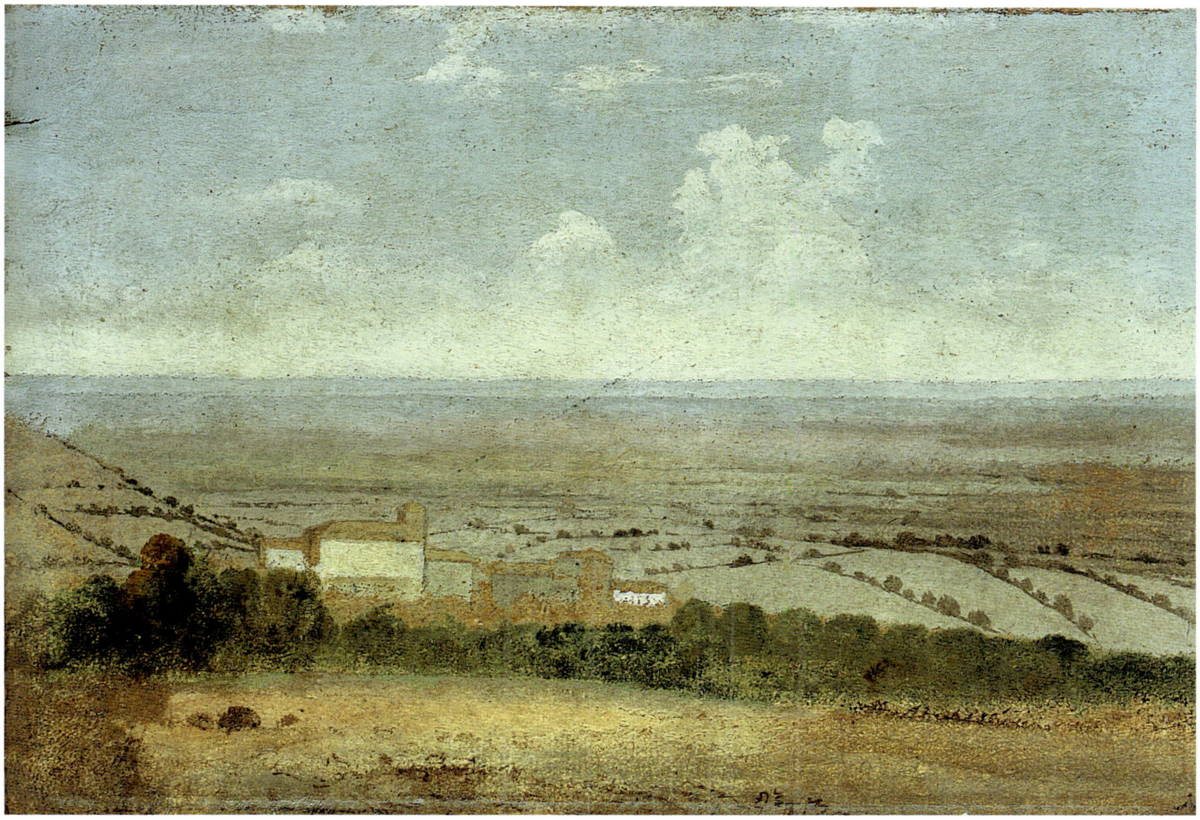

63

63

THOMAS JONES (1742–1803)

Landscape with a Distant View of the Sea

late 1770s?

Oil on laid paper mounted on board*, 14.7 × 22.1 (5¾ × 8⅝)

Prov.: F. R. Meatyard; John Gere; Charlotte Gere
Exh.: London, 1970, no. 18; London, 1999, no. 44
Lit.: Gowing, 1985, pp. 29–30, pl. 20

The Gere Collection, on long-term loan to the National Gallery, London (L841)

The sheet is not dated, nor is the site identified. Gowing thought that it represented Wales and predated the Italian journey. Comparisons can be made with landscapes made early in his Italian stay, however. Though small in scale, the panoramic sweep of the view suggests Montmélian in Savoy (cat. no. 67) and *The Ponte Loreto Close to Lake Nemi* (cat. no. 151). The distinctive use of clusters of hedges to show the crisp divisions of the distant fields is like that in the latter painting and in a watercolour, *View of Ariccia* (Manchester, 1988, no. 72). If painted in Italy, then the site is most likely the Roman Campagna, south of Rome, looking west toward the sea. (CR)

64

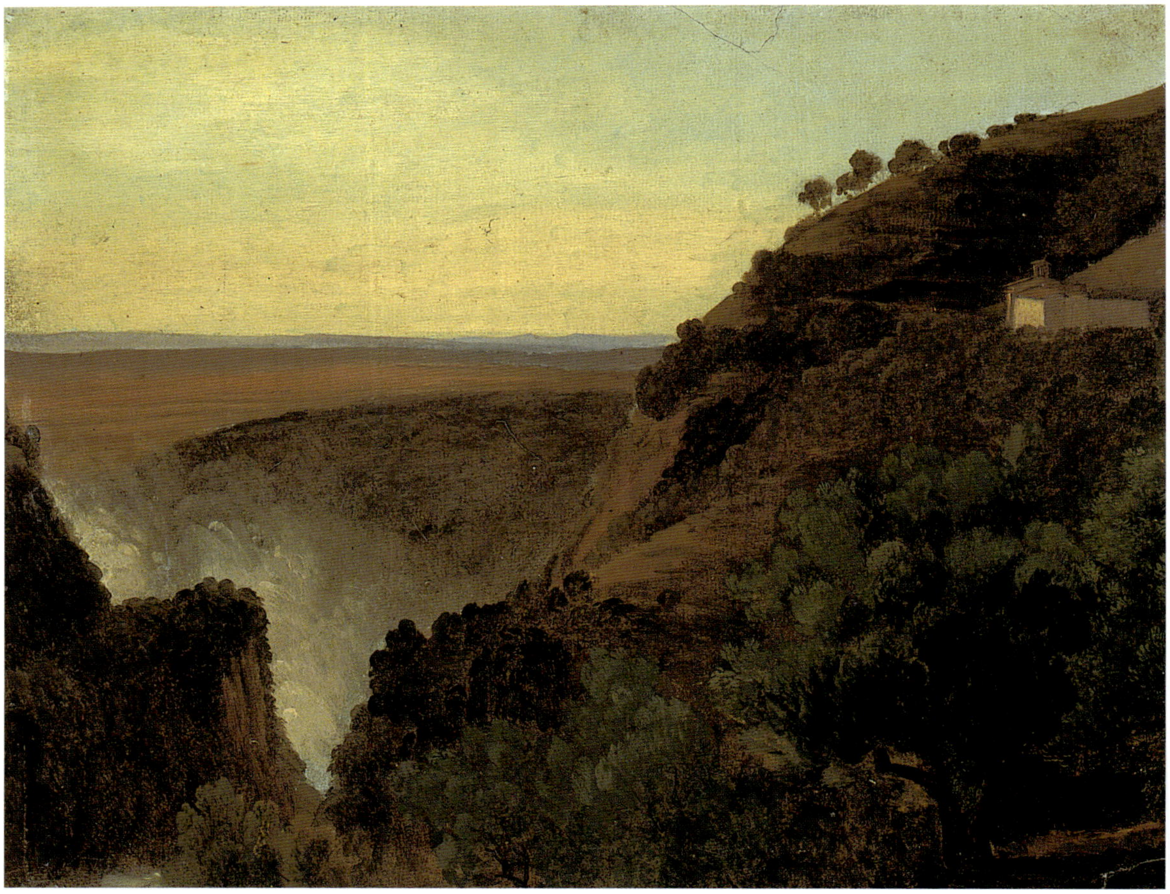

64

THOMAS JONES (1742–1803)

Tivoli *c.*1777

Oil on paper, varnished (possibly Italian-made 'Dutch' writing paper)*, 26.3 × 34.5 ($10\frac{3}{8} \times 13\frac{5}{8}$)

Ins.: 'Tivoli' t.c. verso
Prov.: Ralph Edwards, then by descent
Exh.: London, 1970, no. 33; London, 1974a, no. 33
Lit.: Gowing, 1985, p. 36, pl. 28

Private collection

Jones did not record sketching in oils on his trip to Tivoli in November 1777, but this may have been coloured on the spot. On the back is a rough sketch showing a view over the Campagna, which suggests that he took up a convenient piece of paper and worked on it rather than carefully selecting a sheet in his studio. However, a full underdrawing is visible under infra-red illumination – there are two extra buildings on the skyline and at least two alterations to other buildings – suggesting that this is probably a studio work. The view over the distant landscape, with a watery mist rising from an unseen fall in between, may mean that the view from above the Grand Cascade is depicted. Therefore, Jones is looking in the opposite direction from cat. no. 86. Jones worked here on 15 November and the colouration, especially in the woodland in the foreground, indicates an autumn scene. (GS)

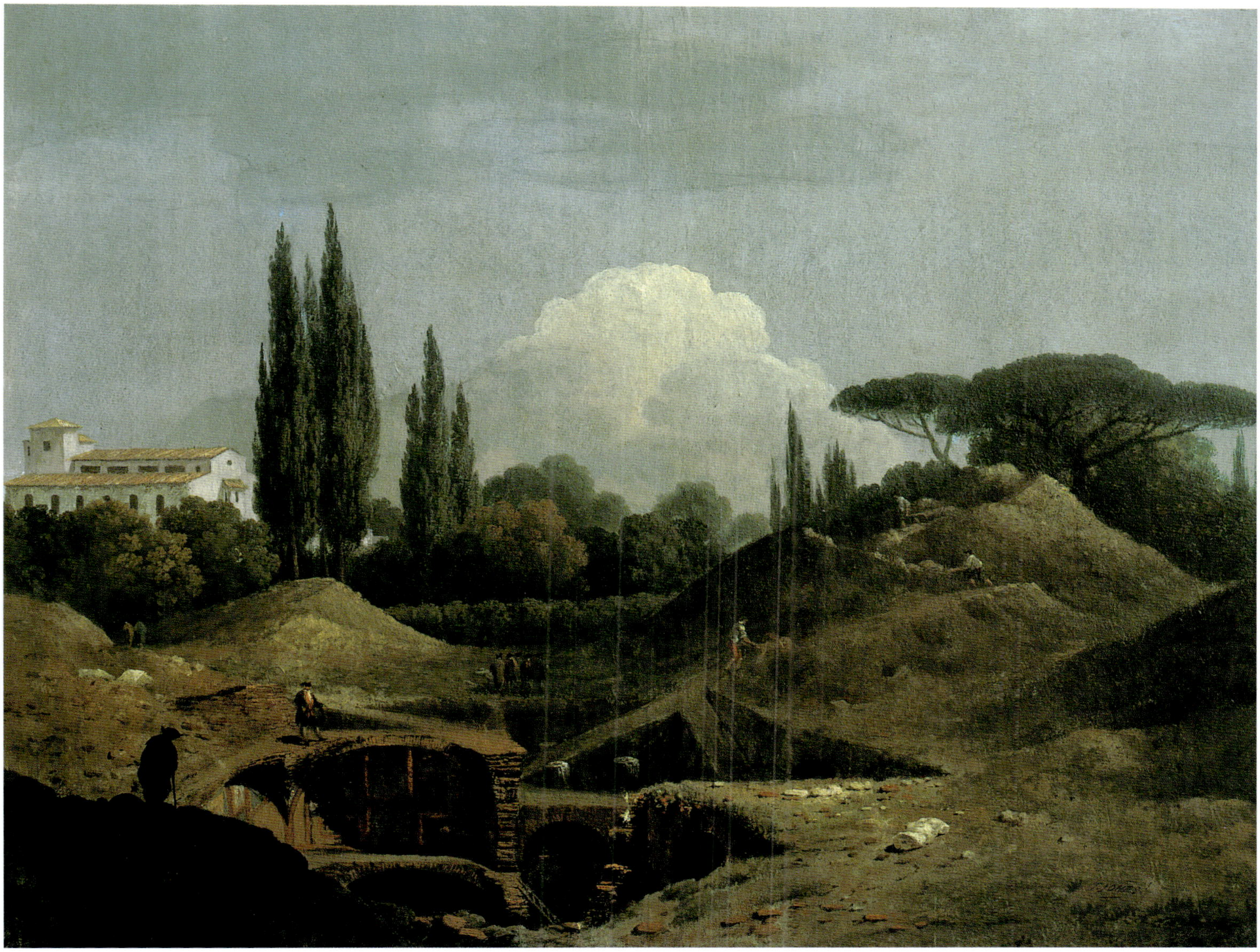

65

65

Thomas Jones (1742–1803)

An Excavation of an Antique Building Discovered in a Cava in the Villa Negroni at Rome 1780s?

Oil, pencil on paper, 40.7 × 55.2 (16 × 21¾)

Ins.: 'T. JONES' l.l.; 'N°.2 An Antique Building discovered in a Cava / in the Villa Negroni at Rome in ye Year 1779 / T Jones' verso
Prov.: Captain John Dale, then by descent to Canon J. H. Adams; presented 1983
Exh.: London, 1970, no. 30; London, 1974a, no. 9; Munich, 1979, no. 97; Cambridge, 1980, no. 19; Stockholm, 1982, no. 146; Manchester, 1988, no. 48; London, 1991, no. 2; London, 1997a, no. 173; Paris, 2001, no. 60
Lit.: Gere, 1970, pp. 469–70; Gowing, 1985, p. 33, pl. 27; Tate, 1986, p. 36

Tate. Presented by Canon J. H. Adams 1983 (T03544)

Jones, accompanied by Henry Tresham, visited the recent excavations of an ancient residence in the grounds of the Villa Negroni, Rome on 5 July 1777, describing the frescoes they saw there as 'painted Ornaments much in the Chinese taste' (*Memoirs*, p. 62). Tresham purchased the paintings, later selling them to the 4th Earl of Bristol. Whether Jones painted this sketch on site or

66

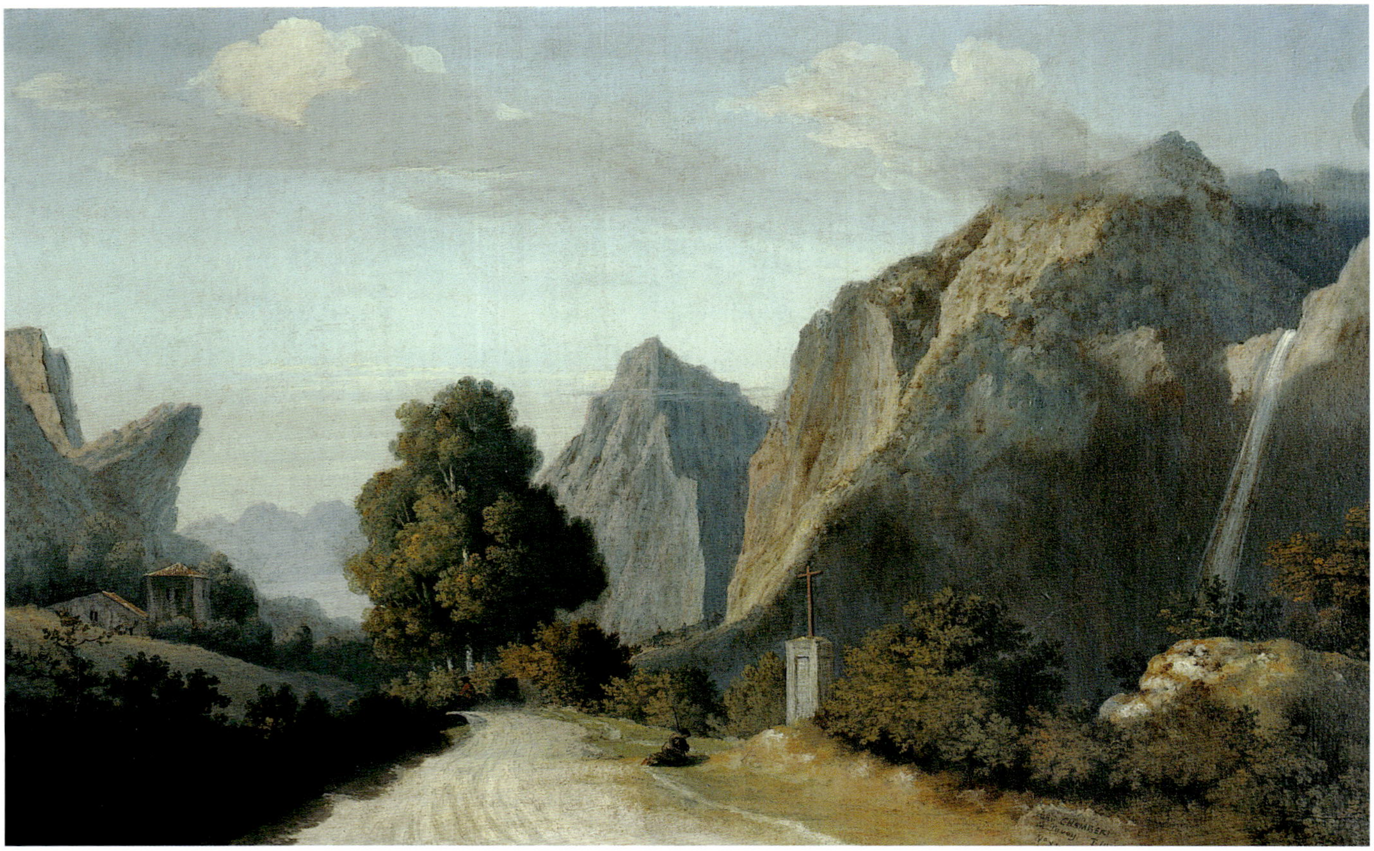

some time later is unknown. It is one of the most spatially complex sketches of his Roman years, however, with the viewer's eye drawn downwards into the shaded excavation and upwards into the sunlit distance, where the convent of S. Eusebio stands. When he came to date the sketch, Jones misremembered the year of the excavation. (CR)

66

THOMAS JONES (1742–1803)

Near Chambéry in the Savoy late 1770s, 1780s?

Oil on paper laid on canvas*, 32.8 × 54.2 (13 × 21⅜)

Ins.: 'near CHAMBERI / in Savoy. T. JONES / NoXVI' l.r. cut by frame
Prov.: Thomas Thomas, then by descent to Jane Evan-Thomas; Sotheby's, 12 March 1986, no. 87; unsold; given to present owner
Lit.: Gowing, 1985, p. 30, pl. 21

Judy Egerton

Cardiff and Manchester only

Jones stayed at Chambéry in Savoy on 1 November 1776 on his way to Rome and he presumably made the lost sketch on which this painting is based during the day (*Memoirs*, pp. 43–4). The work forms a pair with *Montmélian* (cat. no. 67); it is the same size and has a similar inscription in the right hand corner which also includes a number. In this case it is 'XVI', whilst *Montmélian* is 'XVIII'. This possibly refers to the page number of a missing sketchbook. It is not known when this work was painted, though it might have been much later, as it is the same size as *Ponte Loreto* (cat. no. 151), which Jones exhibited in 1787; certainly, he would not have had the time on his journey to colour it on the spot. The devout peasant shown praying at a wayside shrine is a common motif in Jones's finished oils and watercolours. More unusual is the mountain terrain, since Jones rarely depicted such obviously Sublime motifs. (GS)

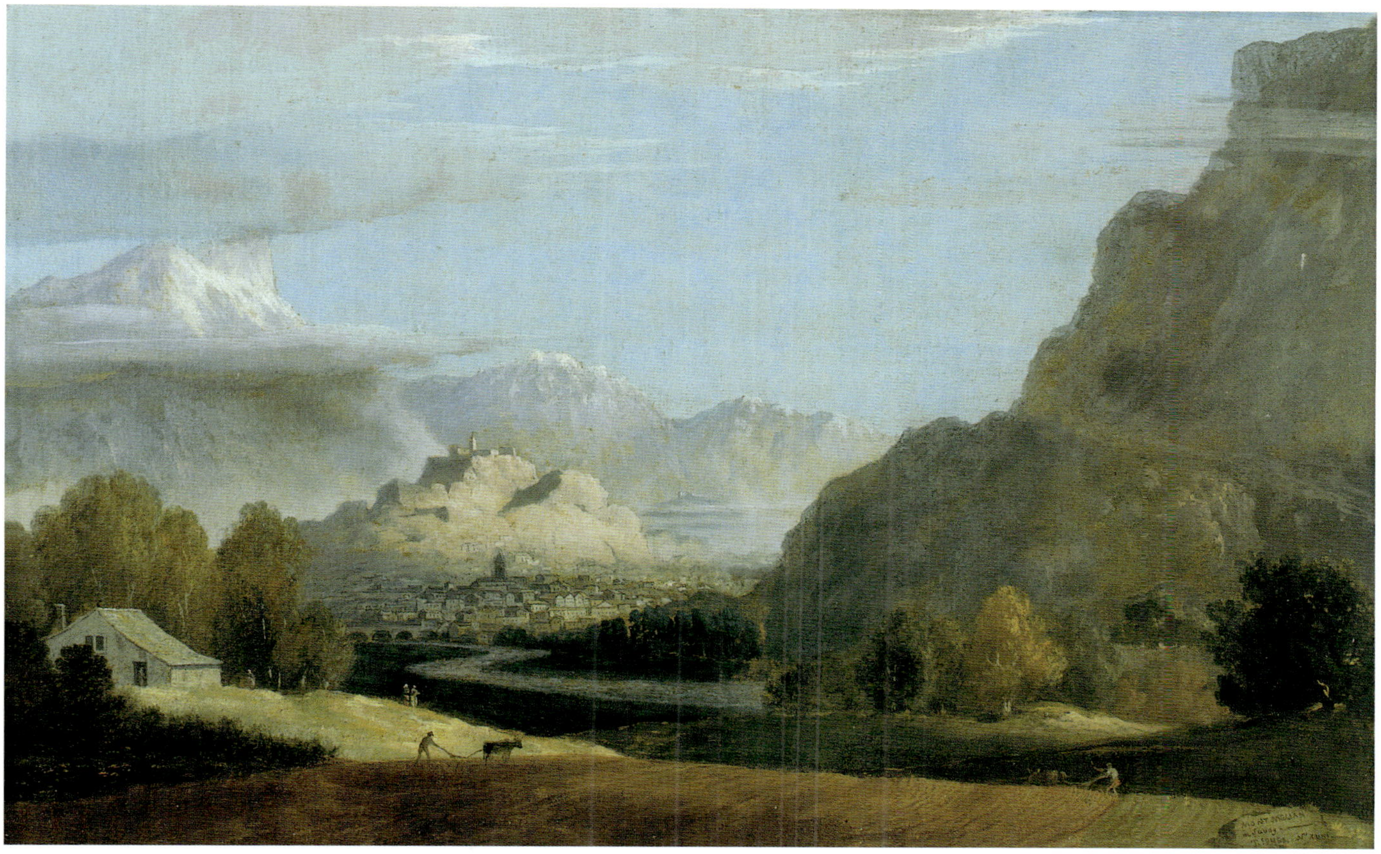
67

67

THOMAS JONES (1742–1803)

Montmélian in Savoy late 1770s, 1780s?

Oil on paper laid down on canvas, 34.3 × 52.7 ($13\frac{1}{2} \times 21\frac{3}{4}$)

Ins.: 'MONT MELIAN / in Savoy / T. JONES No.XVIII' l.r.
Prov.: Thomas Thomas, then by descent to Jane Evan-Thomas; given to a private collector; Phillips, 3 November 1986, no. 24; Elwes & Hanham Ltd

Private collection

Dating from the twelfth century, Montmélian is a fortified town on the river Isère in Savoy, south-eastern France. On his way to Italy, Jones passed through the town on 2 November 1776, pausing to sketch it from a high vantage point at a site he identified as '*Planese* a lone house' (*Memoirs*, p. 44). 'Some effects of Light & Shade from broken Clouds & rugged Mountains were wonderfully fine', he noted. The panoramic format and careful workmanship of the sheet suggest that it was painted at a later date, after drawings made *in situ* which have not survived. (CR)

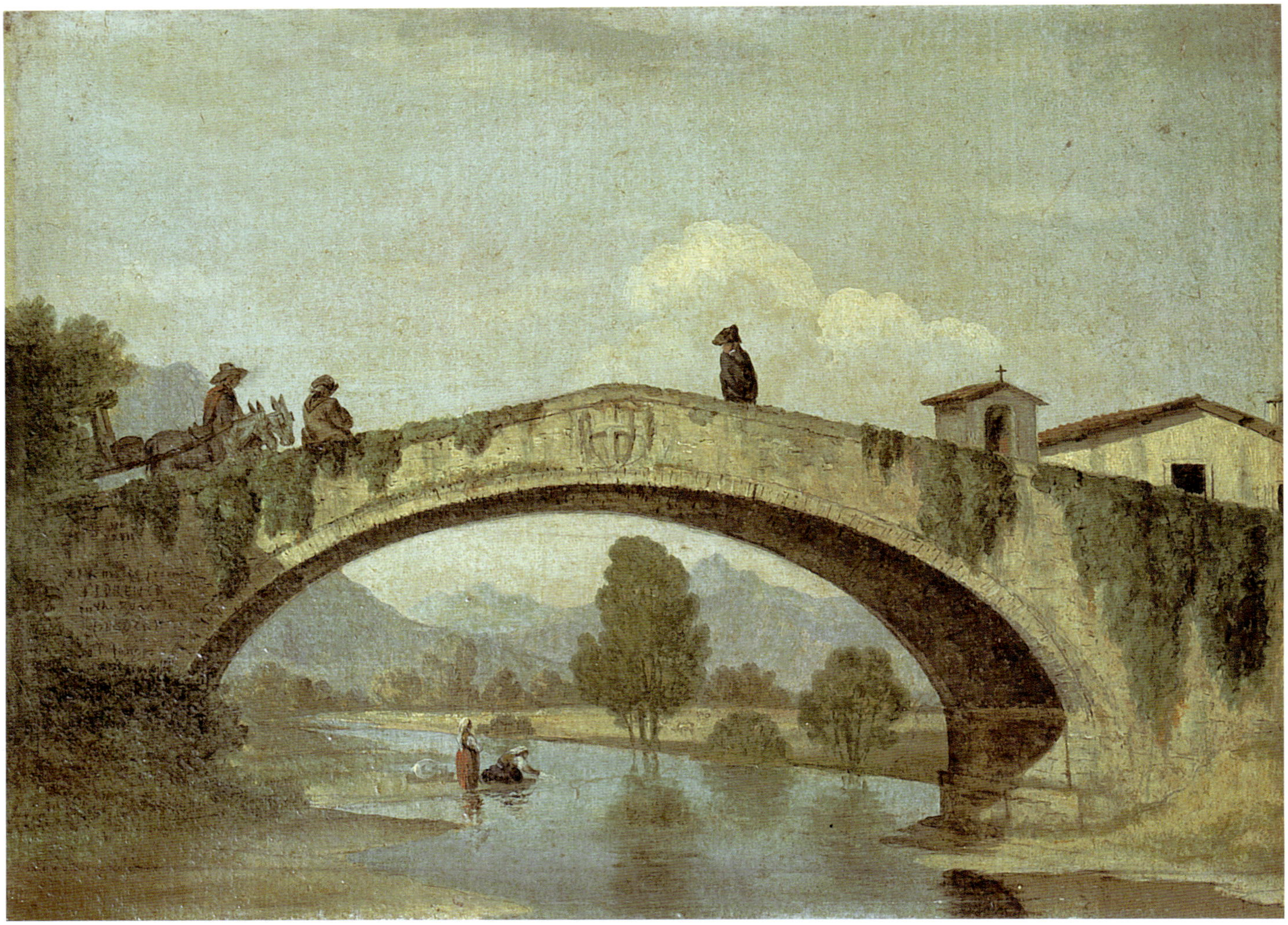

68

THOMAS JONES (1742–1803)

A Bridge near Florence late 1770s, 1780s?

Pencil, oil on paper laid down on canvas*, 23.4 × 34 (10¼ × 14)

Ins.: 'noxxvii / XIX miles from / FLORENCE / in the Road To BOLOGNA / T. Jones' l.l.
Prov.: Thomas Thomas, then by descent

Private collection

On 19 November 1776, as he journeyed towards Rome, Jones made a pencil sketch of the single-span bridge seen here, on page 17 of a gathering of sheets which were later bound with his Neapolitan account book (cat. no. 73, fig. 20, p. 50). He annotated the sheet to indicate that the bridge stood '19 Miles from Florence'. At a later date, Jones used the drawing as the basis for the present oil painting on paper, adding more figures on the bridge and numbering and annotating the painting in turn. Both the drawing and painting announce Jones's predilection in Italy for simple architectonic motifs and characterful masonry surfaces weathered by time and use. The same bridge appears in a drawing by Francis Towne (Yale Center for British Art) dating from 1781 and his return trip to England; Jones may have shown him his sketch, therefore. This work has not previously been published. (CR)

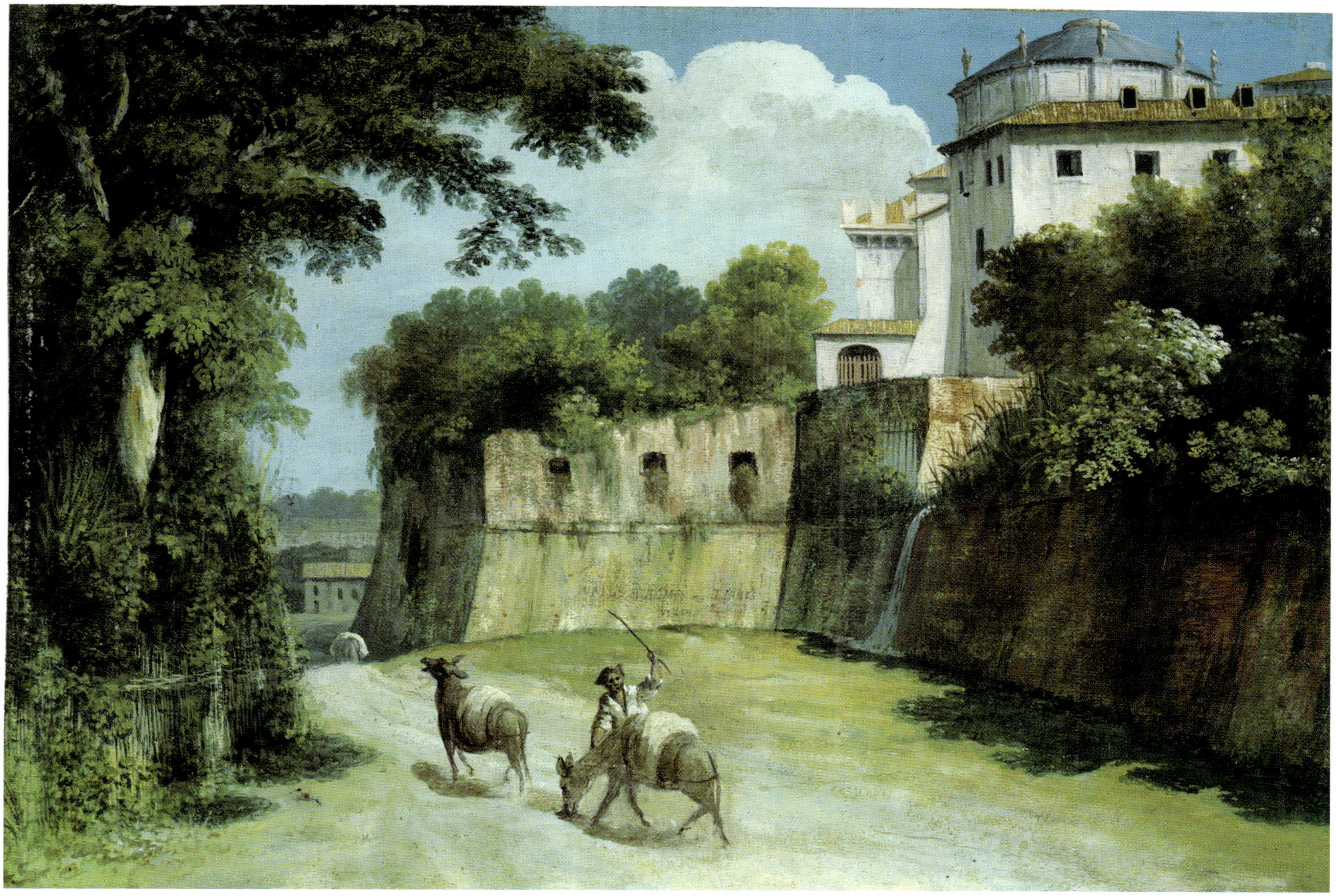

69

69

THOMAS JONES (1742–1803)

The Walls of the Vatican, Rome

late 1770s, 1780s?

Oil on paper, 29 × 44 (11⅜ × 17⅜)

Ins.: 'WALLS of ROME – T. JONES / N° XIII' on the wall
Prov.: Eugenio di Castro; presented
Exh.: London, 1970, no. 22
Lit.: Gowing, 1985, p. 32, pl. 23

Museo di Roma, Palazzo Braschi

Cardiff and Manchester only

The two Roman sketchbooks (cat. nos 74 and 75) contain numerous studies of the walls and gates of the city from early 1777. One of these was later worked up into cat. no. 70 and this view was presumably based on a similar sketch, perhaps from the same time as the two pencil and wash studies of the Vatican dated 23 January 1777 (Phillips, 18 April 1988, no. 10). The conclusion that this oil was not made on the spot is partly based on its similarity with cat. no. 70. They are, for instance, on paper of similar size and their subjects make them effectively a pair. There is also a marked similarity in the form of the inscriptions and their prominent position on the walls. Unlike the oil sketches from nature, which are generally inscribed on the verso, the larger oils on paper often have bold lettering which function as decorative titles rather than a record of information for later reference. (GS)

70

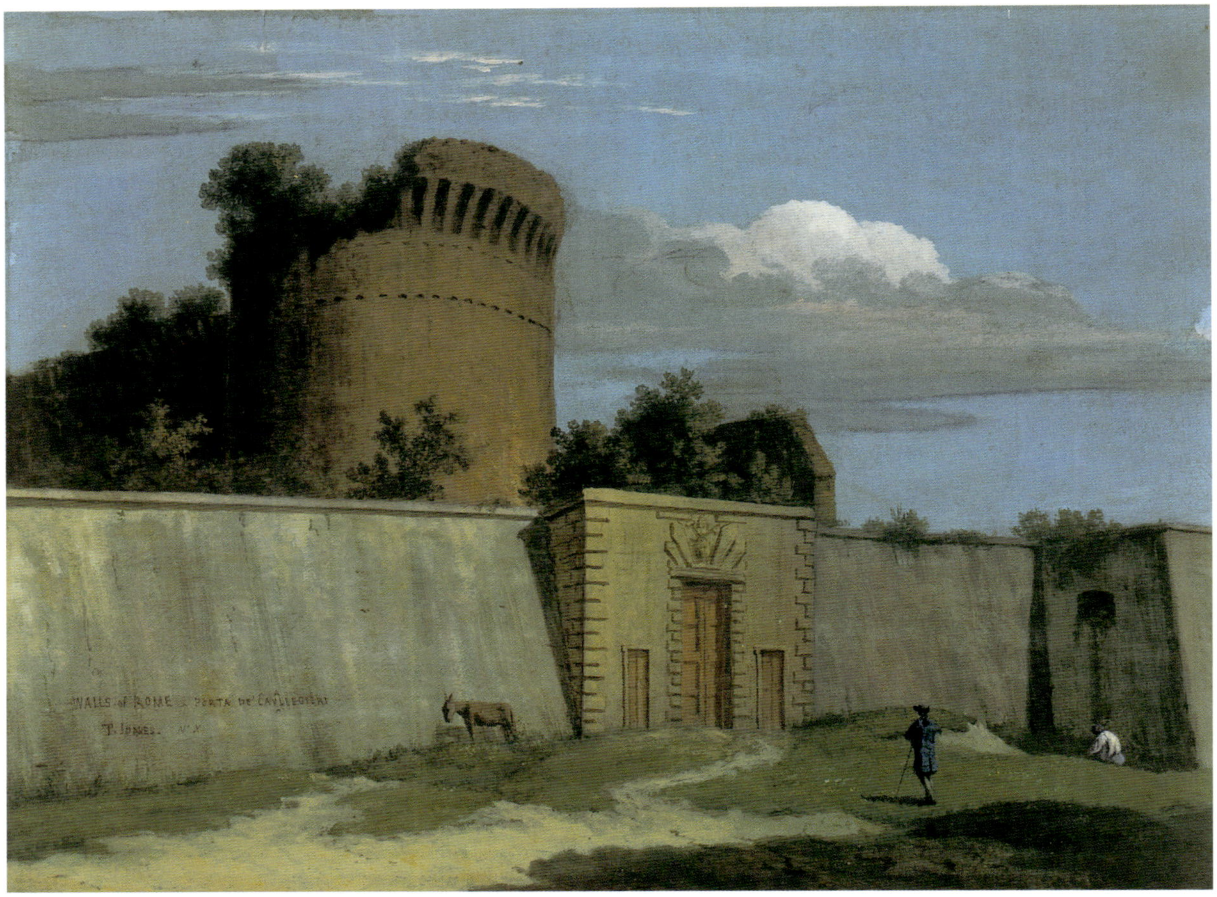

70

THOMAS JONES (1742–1803)

Walls of Rome – Porta Cavalleggeri late 1770s, 1780s?

Oil on Italian writing paper*, 28.3 × 39 ($11\frac{3}{16} \times 15\frac{3}{8}$)

Ins.: 'WALLS OF ROME – PORTA DE' CAV^{A}LLEGIERI / T. JONES. N°x' l.l.
Prov.: Thomas Thomas, then by descent
Exh.: London, 1970, no. 23
Lit.: Gowing, 1985, p. 33, pl. 24

Private collection

This painting is closely based on a pencil sketch in the small British Museum sketchbook (cat. no. 74, p. 39) inscribed 'Walls of Rome near St Peter's / 12 Feb – 1777'. The previous day had seen the end of Carnival, in which Jones had participated enthusiastically, and the beginning of good weather after a long, dreary spell (*Memoirs*, p. 57). Now, it seems, the artist returned to sketching the sites of the city and especially its little-populated outskirts. Here, as often, Jones was drawn to large, blank masonry forms, around which foliage is clustered, in this case the Porta Cavalleggeri. He would have worked up the pencil sketch into this painting at a later date. (CR)

71

THOMAS JONES (1742–1803)

On the Tiber, Rome late 1770s, 1780s?

Oil on paper laid down on board*, 22.4 × 31 ($8\frac{5}{8} \times 12\frac{1}{4}$) oval

Ins.: 'on the / TIBER / 41' l.c. on the rock
Prov.: Thomas Thomas, then by descent to Jane Evan-Thomas; given to present owner
Lit.: Gowing, 1985, p. 40, pl. 34

Judy Egerton

71

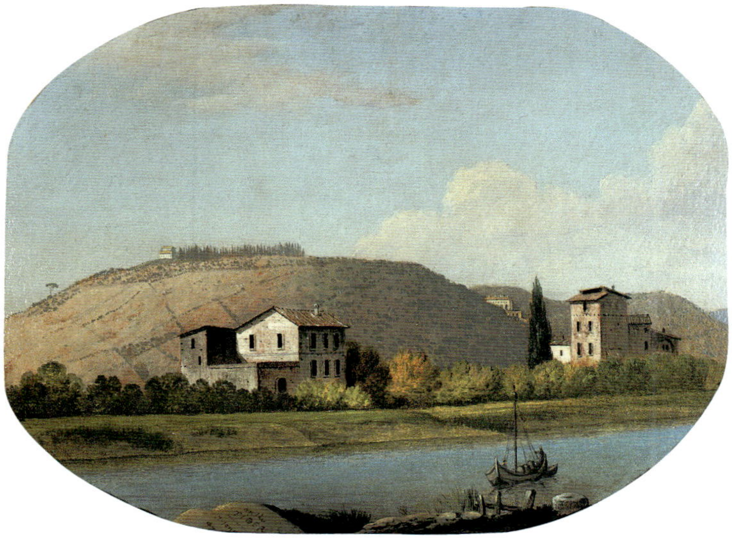

This small oil is not an on-the-spot sketch, but was made from a pencil drawing in the smaller of the Roman sketchbooks (cat. no. 74, p. 43). The sketch is inscribed 'between the Ripetta & the Ponte Mole / looking up the River' and it identifies the more distant of the buildings to the right as the 'villa Madama'. It was made on 15 February 1777 on an excursion to the north of Rome which resulted in two other sketches along the road to Civita Castellana from which Jones produced finished watercolours (cat. nos 149 and 150). There is no evidence to say that Jones painted this oil in Italy and it may have been produced later as a recollection of his first exploration of Rome and its environs. The work remained with his family, indicating that it was not a commission. (CS)

72

THOMAS JONES (1742–1803)

View of Lake Albano Looking Towards Castel Gandolfo late 1770s, 1780s?

Oil on paper laid down on canvas, 33.5 × 44 ($13\frac{1}{4} \times 17\frac{1}{4}$)

Ins.: 'Near / ALBANO' l.l.
Prov.: Captain John Dale, then by descent to Canon J. H. Adams; Sotheby's, 27 November 1975, no. 93; Spink's; Jane Evan-Thomas; Sotheby's, 20 November 1985, no. 78; unsold; given to present owner, 1986
Exh.: Manchester, 1988, no. 62

Private collection

Cardiff and Manchester only

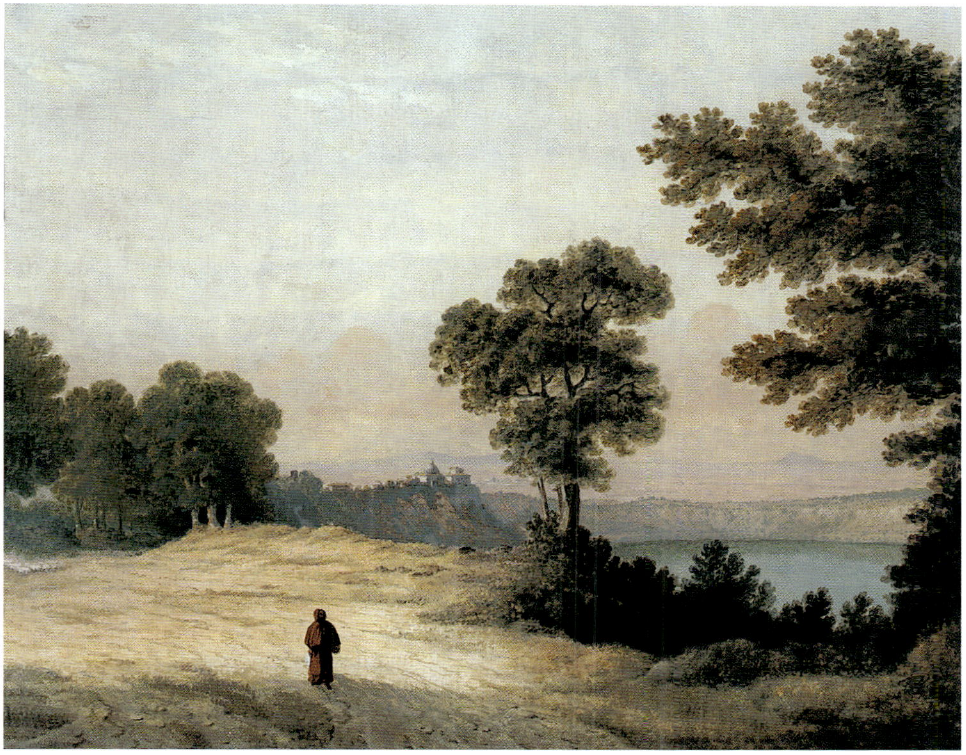

72

The work shows the south side of Lake Albano close to the Galleria di Sopra, with Castel Gandolfo beyond. This is a similar view to the large oil Jones began in 1777 (cat. no. 56), but it is probably not a study for it, as the viewpoint is slightly different. A watercolour showing the same view (Pittsburgh Museum of Art), inscribed 'A View from a Capuchin convent at Albano looking over Castello Gandolfo', identifies the figure in this work. However, it appears to be dated 11 November 1774, which has led one writer to conclude that it was copied from a 'print' (Gowing, 1985, pp. 21–2). In fact, it resembles the coloured pencil sketches that Jones made in the area in May 1777 and it may be wrongly dated. On balance, it is likely that this oil was painted later in the studio, possibly using the watercolour as a guide. (GS)

73

THOMAS JONES (1742–1803)

Account Book with Notes and Sketches, Showing 'A Bridge near Florence' 1776–97

Pencil, pen and ink on paper, 20 × 14.8 ($7\frac{7}{8} \times 5\frac{7}{8}$)

Ins.: 'Thos Jones'^{s} Book / bought at Turin / 8th Novr 1776' on the title page; 'within 19 Miles of Florence / 19th Novr 1776' on the exhibited page (p. 76)
Prov.: Thomas Thomas, then by descent to Jane Evan-Thomas; given to present owner
Exh.: Manchester, 1988, no. 139
Lit.: Ashton, 2000, pp. 104–10

Joy Ashton, on behalf of the Radnorshire Society

Pages illustrated on p. 50, fig. 20, and p. 54, fig. 22

At some stage, Jones gathered together a group of notebooks covering a range of functions – accounts, pencil sketches and diary entries – each of which are numbered separately. The longest part comprises a detailed set of accounts from 26 May 1780 and the artist's move to Naples, to his subsequent departure in September 1783; they provide an insight into Jones's domestic arrangements and record the purchase of artist's materials. The pencil sketches were made on the journey from Turin to Rome in 1776. One of these, showing a bridge near Florence (p. 76), was used for a small oil (cat. no. 68) and is exhibited here. The diary sections cover periods from December 1783 to January 1784, December 1790 to February 1791 and parts of July and December 1797. None of these periods is covered by the *Memoirs*, and the entries gain additional value because they are the type of raw material from which Jones compiled his recollections. On the back of the pencil sketches there is also a series of notes on artistic techniques and recipes which provide more details of Jones's working methods. (GS)

74

THOMAS JONES (1742–1803)

Small Sketchbook, Showing 'On the Tiber'

1776–7

Pencil, pen and ink, watercolour on Italian laid writing paper (watermark: star over circled anchor/F)(187 sheets)*, 12.8 × 18.2 ($5 \times 7\frac{1}{8}$)

Ins.: '2^{d} December 1776 – 6 May 1777' on cover; 'Thomas Jones^{s} Book / bought at Rome / 2^{d} December 1776' on inside cover; 'between the Ripetta & the Ponte Mole / looking up the River'; '15 Feby 1777; 'villa velini'; 'villa Madama'; 'Tiber' on the exhibited page (p. 41)
Prov.: Thomas Thomas, then by descent to Jane Evan-Thomas; purchased 1981
Exh.: London, 1970, no. 20; Manchester, 1988, no. 140

British Museum, London (1981-5-16-17)

Jones bought this book shortly after his arrival in Rome in November 1776 and he used it on his earliest explorations of the city and the surrounding countryside. It therefore contains the artist's first impressions of Lakes Albano and Nemi, the 'Magick

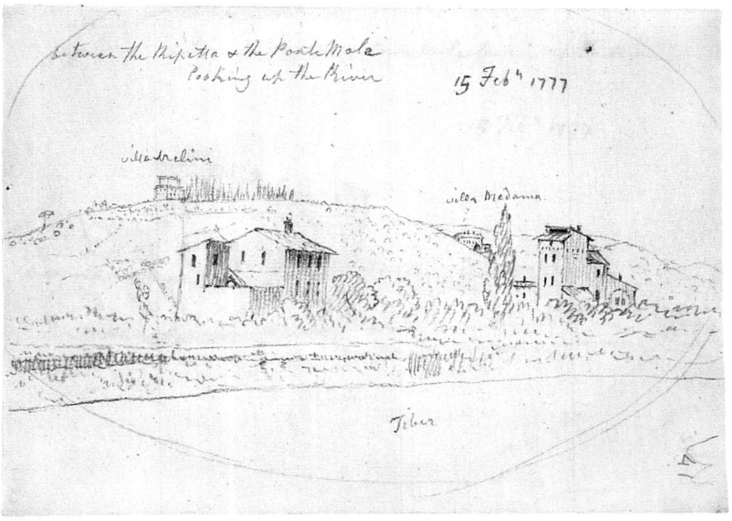

74

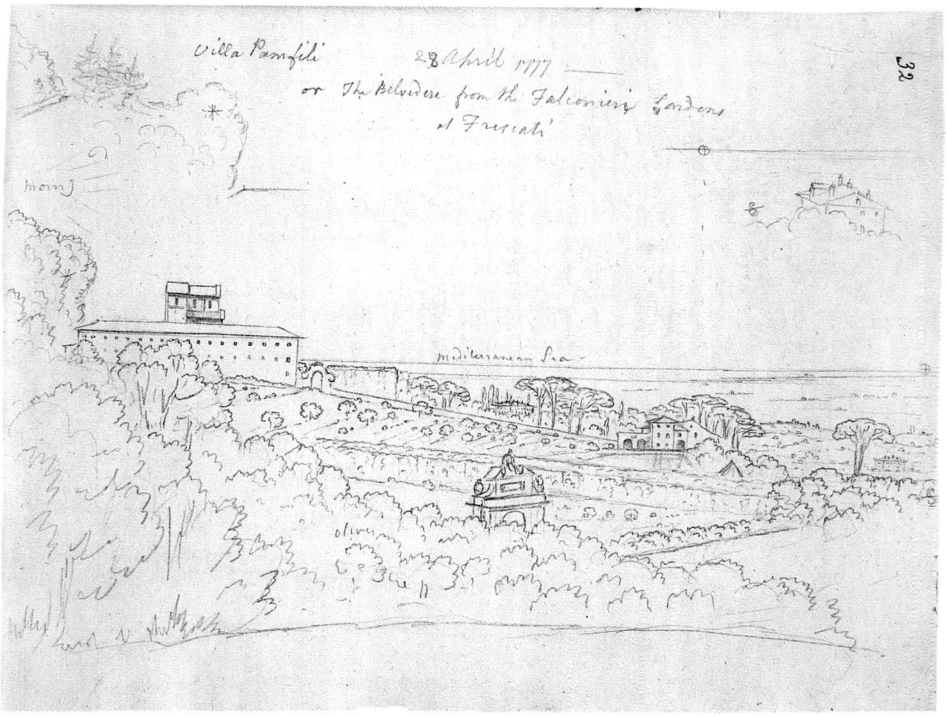

75

Land' he knew from Richard Wilson's studies. These were made on visits to the area in December 1776 and the following spring.

Jones used a number of sketches for finished works. Studies made in and around Rome in early 1777 provided the raw material for the *Walls of Rome* (cat. no. 70), whilst he used views on the road to Civita Castellana for a pair of watercolours (cat. nos 149 and 150). The book is opened at page 41 to show the sketch he used for a small oil painting, *On the Tiber* (cat. no. 71). The artist tried out the effect of an oval composition, adding a pencil line around the drawing. The finished work is inscribed '41', presumably referring to the page number, suggesting that the numbering on at least some of his finished works relates to their source material. (GS)

75

THOMAS JONES (1742–1803)

Large Sketchbook, Showing 'The Villa Pamphili'

1777

Pencil, pen and ink, watercolour on Italian laid writing paper (watermark: fleur-de-lys in a double circle/CB monogram) (36 sheets)*, 21.3 × 27.7 ($8\frac{3}{8}$ × $10\frac{7}{8}$)

Ins.: 'Thomas Jones's / bought at Rome / 17 February / 1777' on inside cover; 'Villa Pamfili 28 April 1777 – / or The Belvedere from the Falconieri Gardens / at Frascati' on the exhibited page (p. 32)
Prov.: Thomas Thomas, then by descent to Jane Evan-Thomas; purchased 1981
Exh.: London, 1970, no. 21; Manchester, 1988, no. 141

British Museum, London (1981-5-16-18)

Jones bought the larger of the Roman sketchbooks in February 1777 and used it in tandem with cat. no. 74. Working on a larger scale, he added watercolour washes to his drawings, though much of this was done at a later date. There are no less than nine drawings made on 4 March in the area of the Arco Scuro and he clearly could not have coloured them all on the spot. A drawing of the 'palace of Card' York at Frascati' is also definitely reworked. It is inscribed '26 April 1777' and 'May 1802', when he presumably added the pen work, and he followed this practice elsewhere, either over existing pencil work or on top of watercolour washes. The exhibited drawing of the Villa Pamphili (p. 32) was one of eleven completed during an excursion with William Pars to the 'picturesque country' around Frascati in April 1777. Only one of the drawings, a view of the Aventine Hill overlooking the Tiber (p. 12), was used for a finished composition (cat. no. 91). (GS)

76

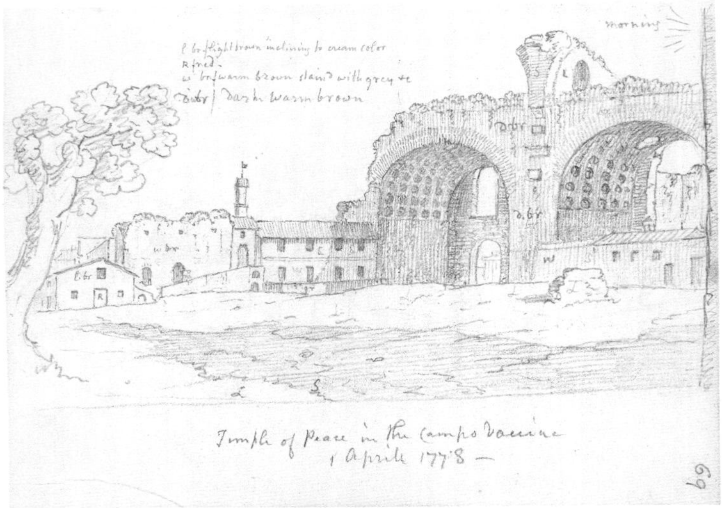

77

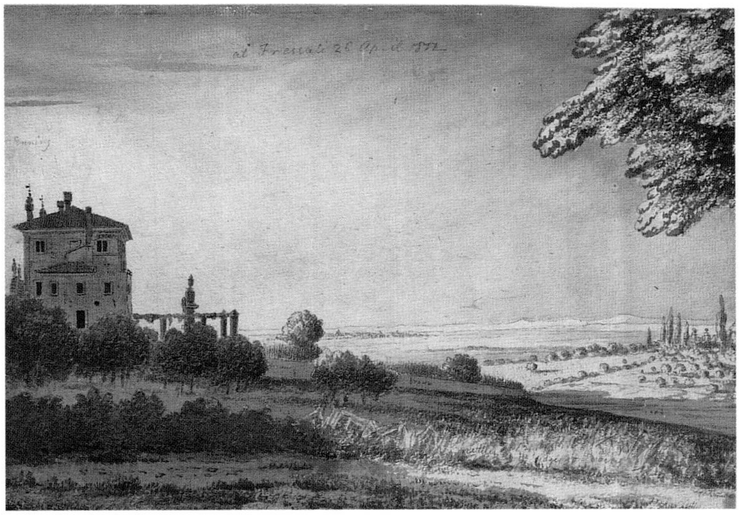

76

THOMAS JONES (1742–1803)

Sketchbook, Showing 'The Temple of Peace in the Campo Vaccino' 1777–8

Pencil on Italian writing paper (watermark: star over circled anchor GAS/F) (186 sheets)*, 13.5 × 18.4 (5⅜ × 7¼)

Ins.: 29th March 1777 – 9th December 1778' on the cover; 'Thomas Jones's bought at / Rome 29 March 1777 –' on inside cover; 'Temple of Peace in the Campo Vaccina / 1 April 1778' on the exhibited page (p. 69)
Prov.: J. H. Kenshole; purchased 1948
Exh.: Manchester, 1988, no. 142
Lit.: Edwards, 1968, p. 14

National Museums & Galleries of Wales (NMW A 2528)

Jones began using this book in May 1777 on excursions in and around Rome, including Ariccia and the lakes of Nemi and Albano, as well as to Tivoli. He also used it in Naples in 1778, when he made figure drawings and studies of shipping. Only one of the drawings was used as the basis for a finished composition (cat. no. 130). The reason for this perhaps lay in the fact that he started to produce a different kind of sketch at this date, working on meticulous pencil drawings on larger sheets of paper (*c.*27.9 × 40.6cm, *c.*11 × 16 inches), often with detailed notes. It seems that Jones adopted this larger format for subjects he hoped to paint and it is probably not a coincidence that he began his first large Italian commission, *Lake Albano* (cat. no. 56), in June 1777.

The book is opened at *The Temple of Peace in the Campo Vaccino* (p. 69). It shows Jones's key for the colour of the stones, as well as the way he often indicated the direction of the sun and the time of day. (GS and BM)

77

THOMAS JONES (1742–1803)

View of a Villa at Frascati 1777

Pencil, watercolour, scratching out on Italian writing paper (watermark: B circled fleur-de-lys/V)*, 19.5 × 29.5 (7⅝ × 11⅝)

Ins.: 'at Frescate 26 April 1777' l.c.; 'Evening' t.l.; 'Rome' on the horizon; 'nettles sedges & docks' foreground
Prov.: Thomas Thomas, then by descent

Private collection

Cardiff and Manchester only

Jones spent five days in late April 1777 in the company of William Pars, 'Agreeably rambling about and making a Number of Views and Sketches' in the 'most picturesque Country' around Frascati, south of Rome (*Memoirs*, p. 58). Jones completed three other sketches on 26 April in the small sketchbook (cat. no. 74) and one in the larger (cat. no. 75). The artist often inscribed his sketches with the time of day, and the inscription of the word 'Evening' here suggests that this was the last completed on a busy day. The choice of a larger piece of paper to work on, rather than a sketchbook page, suggests that Jones had a finished work in mind, though

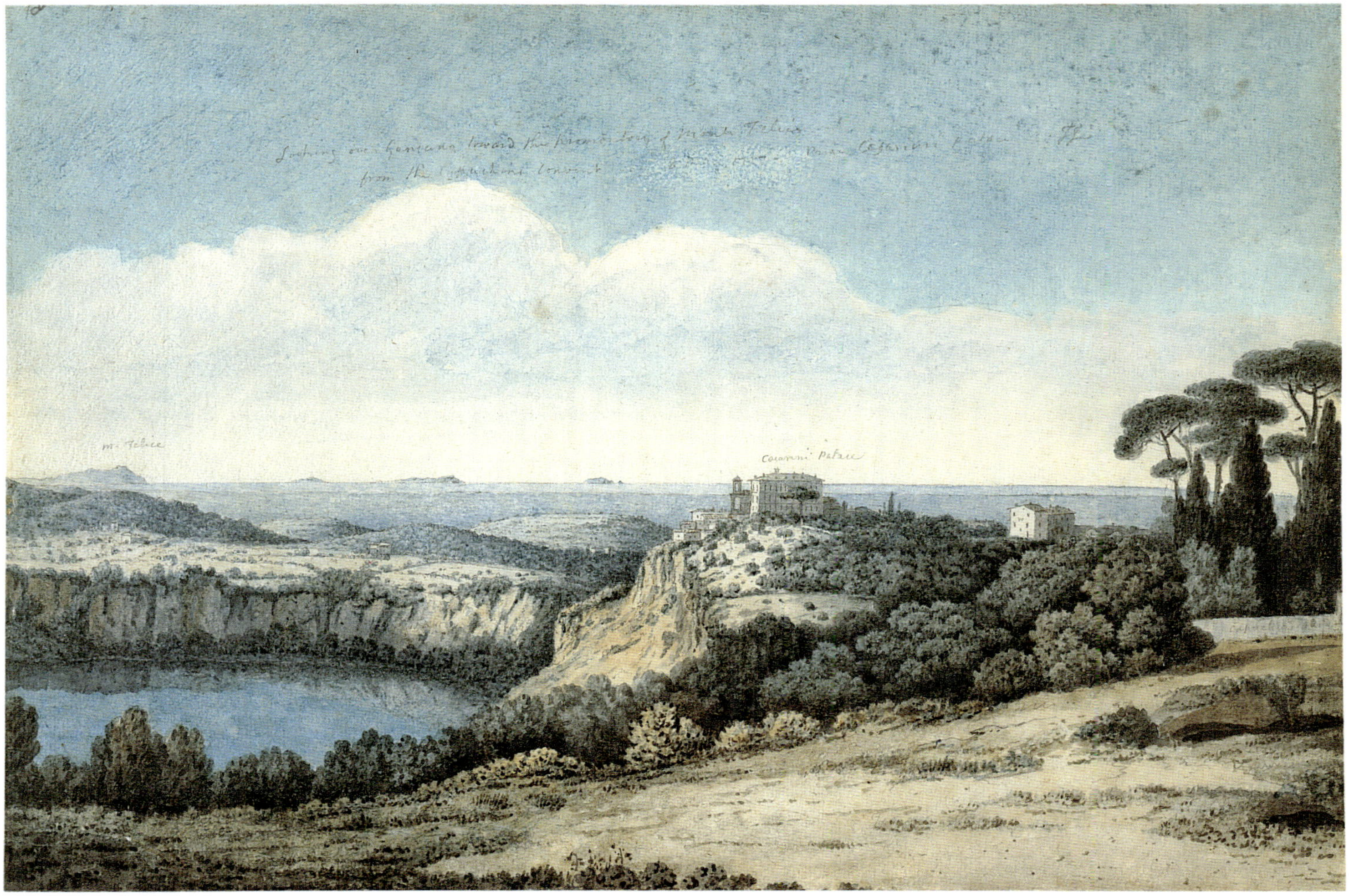

78

none has come to light. The watercolour was presumably added later when, unusually for Jones, he varied the textures of the monochrome wash by scratching out areas of the foreground and using a dry brush for the foliage to the right. (GS)

78

THOMAS JONES (1742–1803)

Lake Nemi Looking Towards Genzano 1777

Pencil, watercolour on laid paper, 27.4 × 41.3 ($10\frac{3}{4} \times 16\frac{1}{4}$)

Ins.: 'Looking over Gensano toward the promontory of Monte Felice / from the Capuchin Convent 8 May 1777 Prince Cesarini's Palace T. J.' t.c.; 'M Felice', 'Cesarini Palace', 'Capachini' on the drawing

Prov.: Captain John Dale, then by descent; Sotheby's, 26 July 1961, no. 59; Agnew's; presented by Lady Chorley through the Friends of the Whitworth, 1961

Exh.: London, 1968a, no. 24; London, 1974a, no. 124; Nottingham, 1981, no. 67; Manchester, 1988, no. 66; Manchester, 1993, no. 45

Lit.: Reynolds, 1971, pl. 51

The Whitworth Art Gallery, The University of Manchester (D.1961.15)

Jones first visited Lake Nemi in December 1776, shortly after his arrival in Rome, and he returned in April 1777 with William Pars. He records a sustained campaign of sketching around '*Gensano, Nemi, Larici, Albano* &c', both in company, and, by the date of this sketch on 8 May, alone (*Memoirs*, p. 59). There are a number of pencil studies in his sketchbooks (cat. nos 74 and 75), but he

79

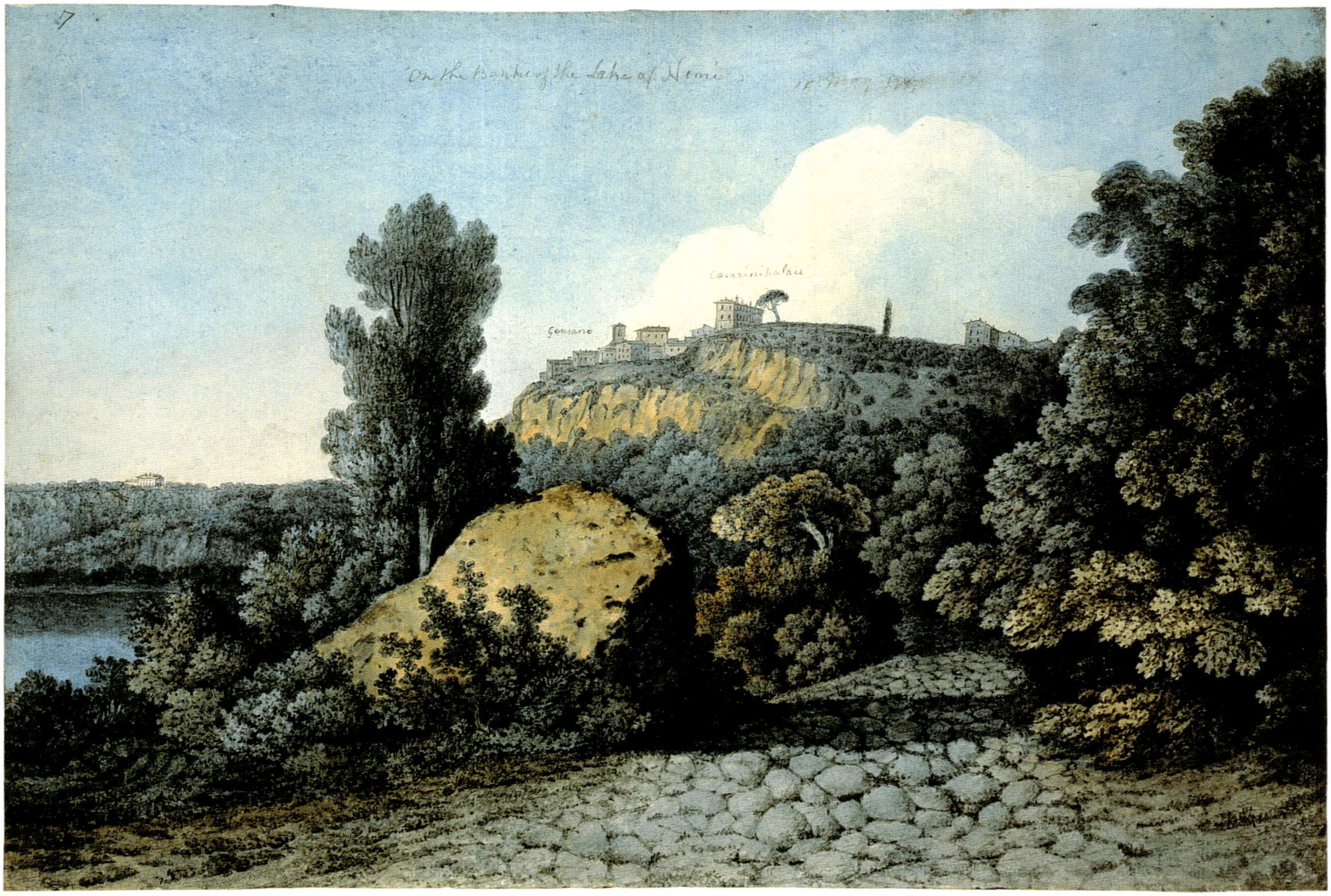

also used larger sheets of unbound paper. This drawing is the first dated use of a format that became standard over the next few years – *c.*27.9 × 40.6 cm, *c.*11 × 16 inches. Jones annotated the pencil drawing with various topographic details, as well as colour notes – the house to the right is marked with a 'w', presumably meaning white. This suggests that he did not initially intend to colour the work, and the washes were presumably added much later. The view of the south-west side of Nemi, with Genzano situated high above, was known to Jones from Richard Wilson's slightly closer view from the Capuchin Convent and he may have copied the composition in his studio. (GS)

79

THOMAS JONES (1742–1803)

Lake Nemi *c.*1777

Pencil, watercolour, gum arabic on Italian laid writing paper*, 28.6 × 42.8 (11¼ × 16⅞)

Ins.: '7' t.l.; 'On the Banks of the Lake of Nemi 15 May 1777 (indistinct)' t.c.; 'Genzano' and 'cesarini palace' on the drawing
Prov.: Captain John Dale, then by descent; Sotheby's, 26 July 1961, no. 60; Agnew's; Mrs Cecil Keith; Agnew's, 1984; purchased, 1984
Exh.: London, 1985, no. 40; Manchester, 1988, no. 67; Cleveland, 1991, no. 18

British Museum, London (1984-6-9-12)

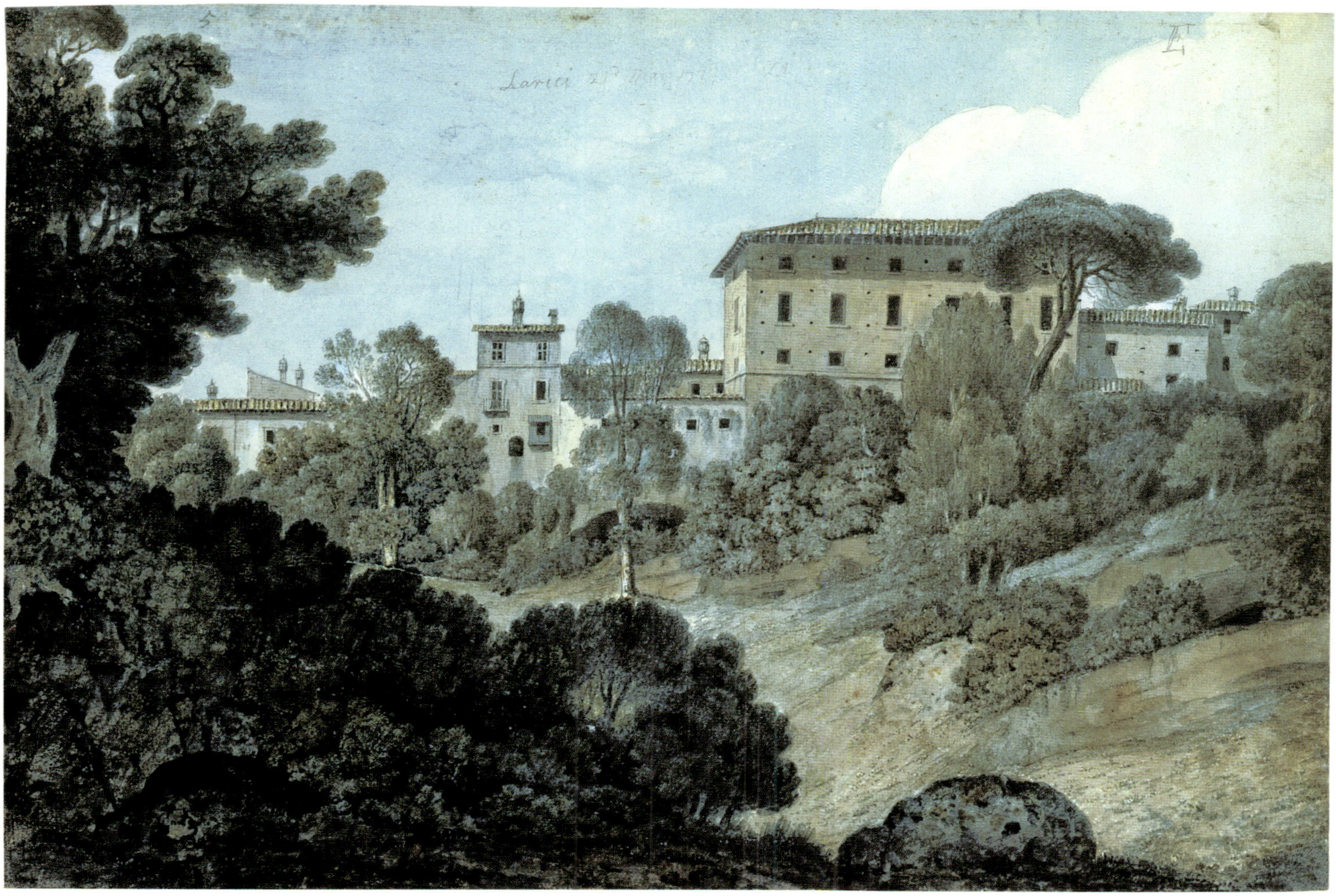

Jones moved further down the hill to draw a second view of Genzano, overlooking Lake Nemi. The pencil drawing, to which he later added further watercolour washes, dates from a week later than cat. no. 78. As Jones noted, the area around the volcanic lakes of Albano and Nemi was of interest to 'the Scholar, naturalist, Antiquarian and Artist' (*Memoirs*, p. 55). In the private medium of watercolour, however, Jones did not emphasize the classical associations of the site, certainly in comparison with oil paintings such as cat. no. 58, and the work lacks the poetic qualities which John Robert Cozens invested the same view (cat. no. 95). Instead, Jones demonstrates the same interest that led him to discuss the geology of the area and to speculate on its volcanic origins. This is one of the most elaborately worked of Jones's pencil drawings, with a rich range of blues, greens and warmer tones deepened with gum arabic. Jones returned to this work in the 1790s to make a copy (cat. no. 65). (GS)

80

THOMAS JONES (1742–1803)

Ariccia: Buildings on the Edge of the Town

1777

Pencil, watercolour on Italian laid writing paper (watermark: circled fleur-de-lys/CB monogram)*, 28.3 × 42.8 (11⅛ × 16⅞)

Ins.: '5' t.l.; 'Larici 22d May 1777 T J' t.c.; 'E' t.r.; 'Larici', 'Gardens of the Capuchin Convt at Albano', 's', 'Benedictine Convent of the Madona of the Galoro / near Larici' on the drawing; unfinished sketch inscribed 'continuation of the view marked "D"' verso
Prov.: Captain John Dale, then by descent; Christie's, 28 July 1955, no. 1; Colnaghi's; Paul Oppé; Armide Oppé; purchased 1996
Exh.: London, 1970, no. 25; London, 1997, no. 44

81

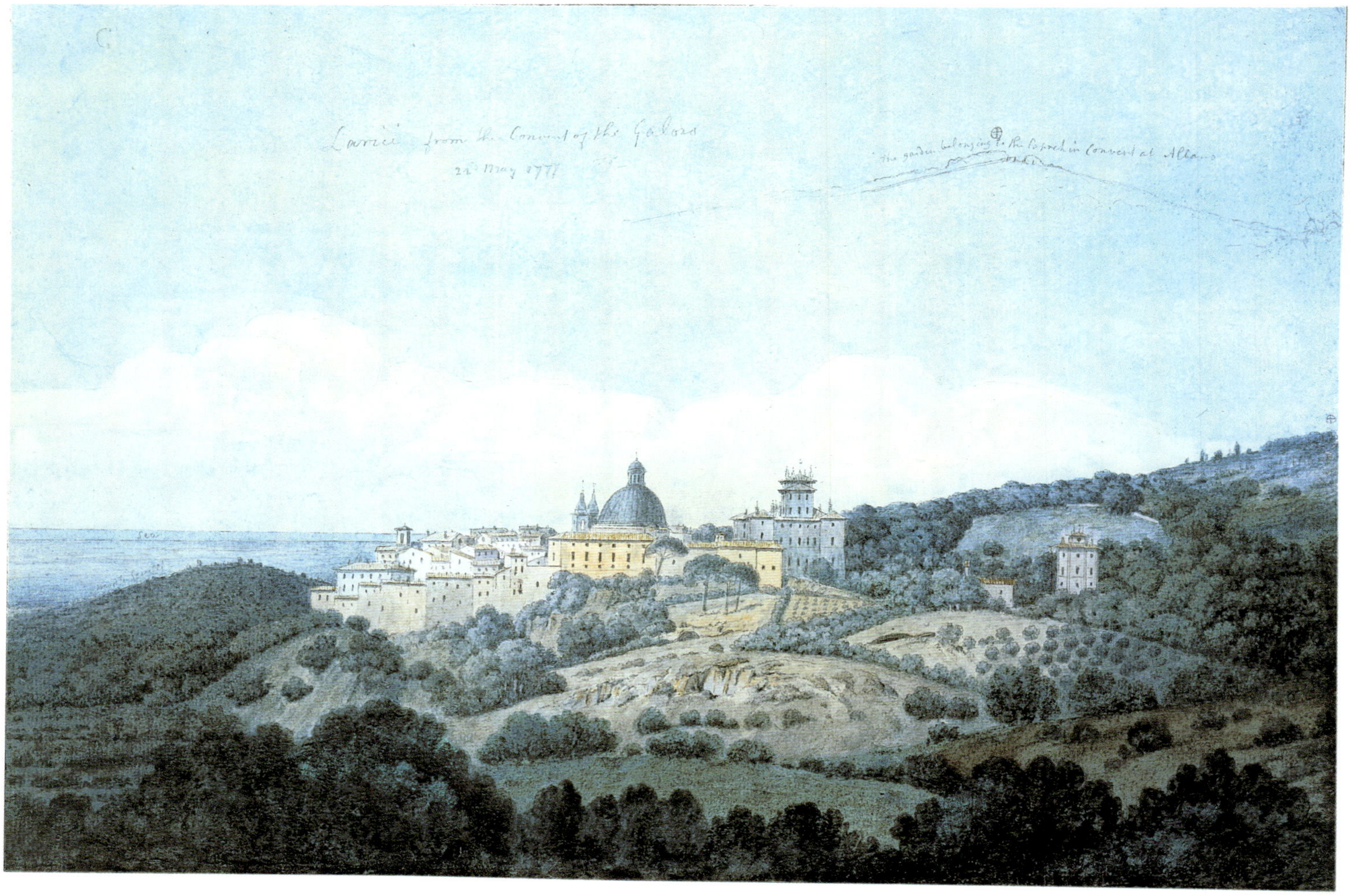

Tate. Purchased as part of the Oppé Collection with assistance from the National Lottery through the Heritage Lottery Fund 1996 (T08141)

Jones walked 'to *Galoro Larici* &c sketching' on 22 May 1777 (*Memoirs*, p. 60). The artist had time only to make pencil drawings, and he would have coloured this work later, changing a careful record into a finished watercolour. The subject is especially interesting because it shows a commonplace group of buildings on the town's edge, rather than the famous view of the Palazzo Chigi and Santa Maria dell'Assunzione depicted by Richard Wilson (cat. no. 17). In contrast to other, larger sketches which feature popular views, Jones indulged his interest in the appearance of flat walls, stained masonry and darkened windows. The artist acknowledged the unusual focus of his attention, noting that he had omitted to sketch in Chigi Park, the 'common Study of all landscape painters' (ibid., p. 61).

The unfinished drawing on the verso continues a view of Ariccia shown in another watercolour (private collection). That watercolour is marked 'D' – this is 'E' – indicating that this is the next in a sequence. Jones often extended compositions when his paper could not accommodate a view. (GS)

81

Thomas Jones (1742–1803)

Ariccia from the Convent of Galoro 1777

Pencil, watercolour, gum arabic on laid paper, 27 × 41 ($10\frac{5}{8} \times 16\frac{1}{8}$)

Ins.: 'C' t.l.; 'Larici from the Convent of the Galoro / 22 May 1777 TJ' t.c.; 'the garden belonging to the Capuchin Convent at Albano' t.r.

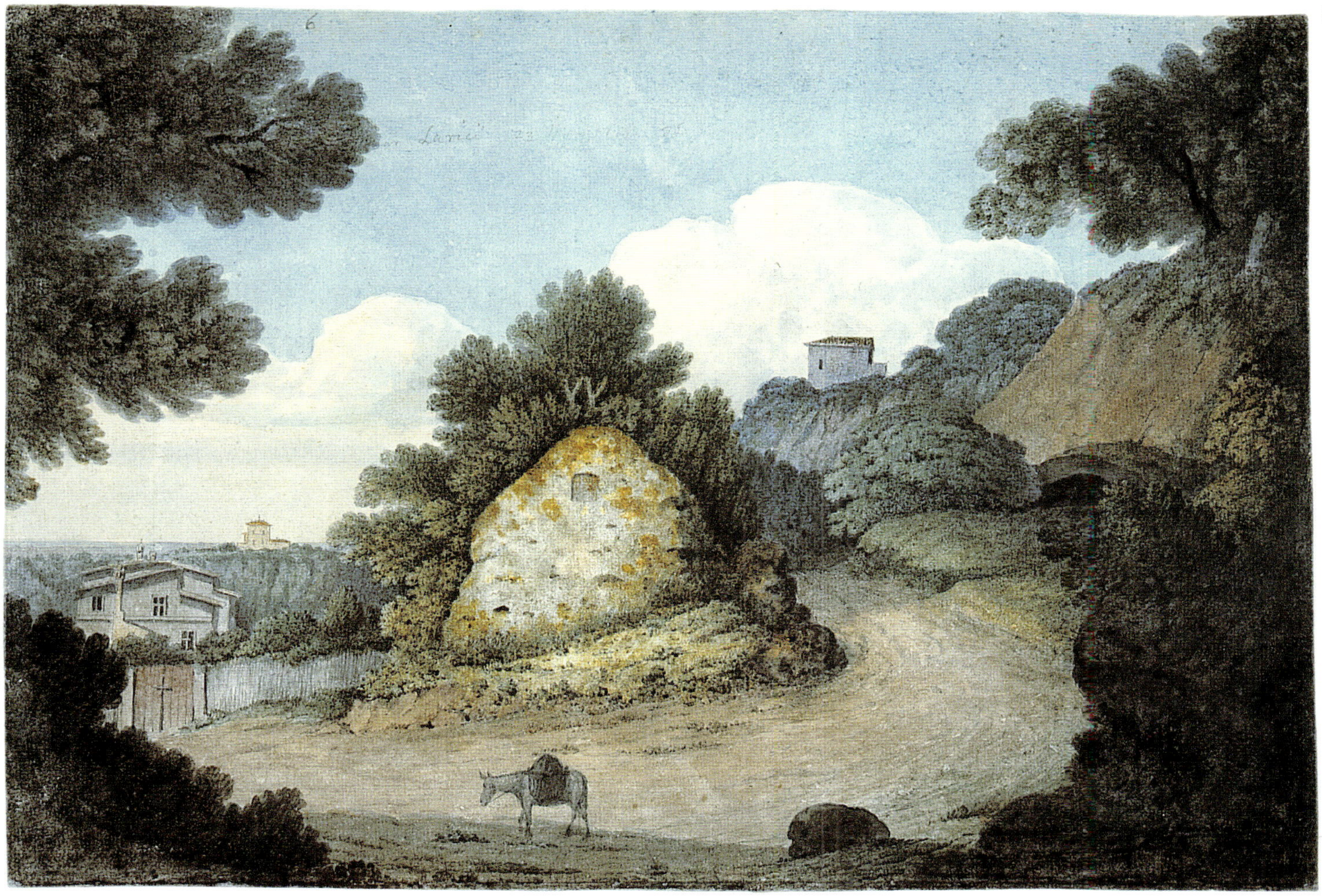

82

Prov.: Phillips, 15 April 1985, no. 139; Sotheby's, 31 March 1999, no. 152; Artemis; purchased 2002

National Gallery of Art, Washington

This work was begun on the same day as cat. no. 79, 22 May, though the fine watercolour washes were added later in the studio. The drawing offers fascinating evidence of the systematic manner in which Jones gathered topographical material in the field. There is, for instance, a rapid pencil sketch at the top right of the sheet which continues the view further to the right – it is marked by an encircled cross which marks the position of the continuation. The initial 'C' to the left also shows that this drawing it is part of a sequence of views of Ariccia. A more distant view of the town (private collection) is marked 'D', whilst cat. no. 80, showing buildings on the edge of the town, is 'E'. (GS)

82

THOMAS JONES (1742–1803)

Near Ariccia 1777

Pencil, watercolour on Italian laid writing paper*, 28 × 41.2 (11 × 16¼)

Ins.: 'Near Larici' t.c.; '6' t.l.; '23 May (unclear) 1777 (unclear) T J' verso; 'L'ariccia T Jones' verso
Prov.: Agnew's; purchased, 1959
Exh.: London, 1970, no. 29

National Museums & Galleries of Wales (NMW A 3652)

Jones walked from Genzano to Albano on 23 May, passing through Ariccia on the way (*Memoirs*, p. 60). The partially obscured date on this drawing is presumably 'May' and it was therefore begun on

83

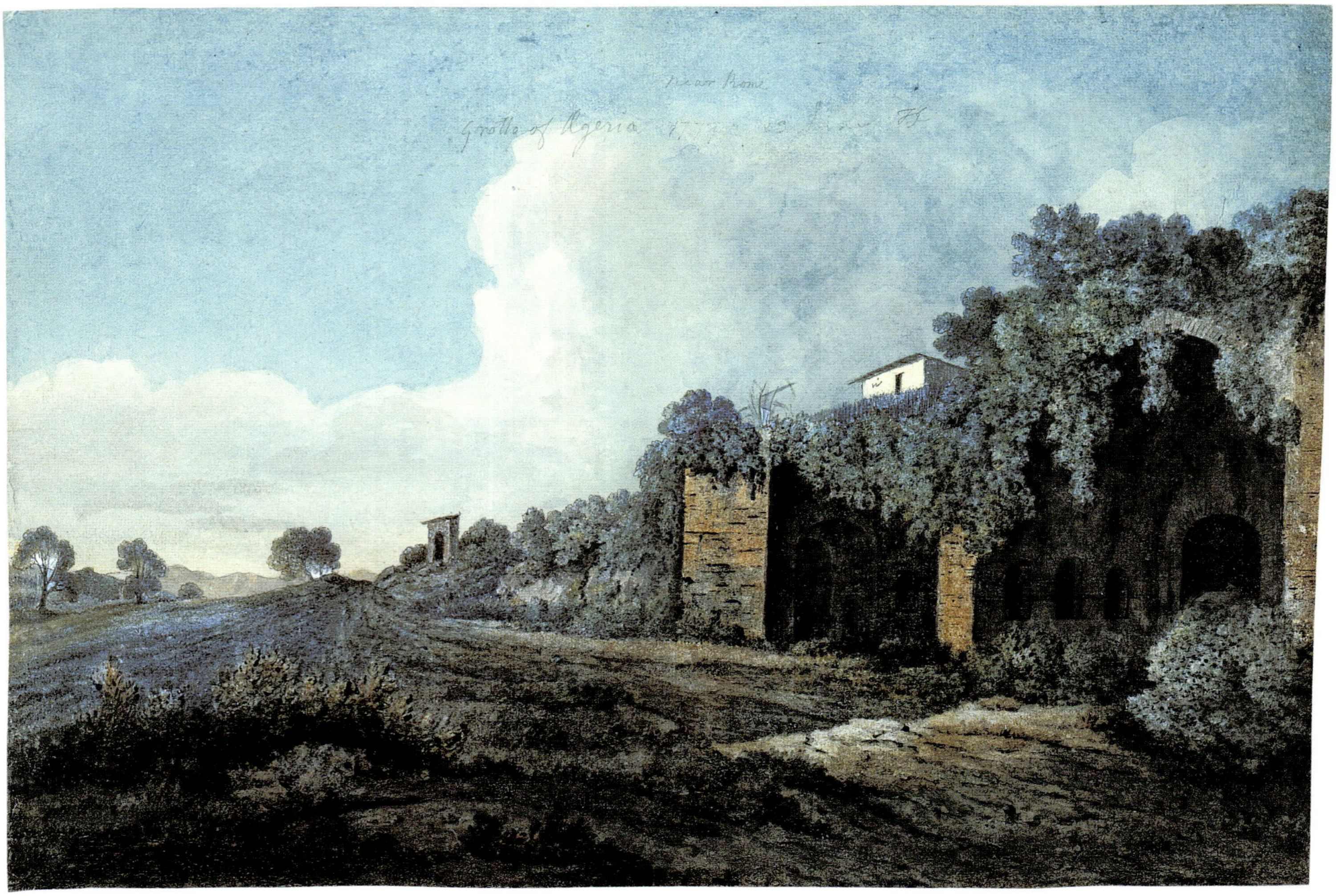

the day after cat. nos 80 and 81. The former is numbered '5', this is '6', and another of Lake Nemi from 30 April (private collection) is '2', suggesting that there was a sequence of views of the area and that there are other missing works. As with the other two drawings, this sheet has been elaborated in watercolours at a later date, and it may have been at this stage that the artist tried to bring order to his sketches by numbering them. (GS)

83

THOMAS JONES (1742–1803)

The Grotto of Egeria, near Rome 1777

Pencil, watercolour on paper, 27 × 41 ($10\frac{3}{4}$ × 16)

Ins.: 'near Rome / Grotto of Ageria 1777 23 June T. J.' t.c.

Prov.: Captain John Dale, then by descent to Canon J. H. Adams; Phillips, 3 November 1986, no. 12; Martyn Gregory

Private collection

Jones spent much of the summer of 1777 after his stay in the Campagna painting two important commissions and consequently there is only a handful of sketches from this period. The so-called grotto of the nymph Egeria – actually part of the remains of the Villa of Herodes Atticus – was a little way off the Via Appia, to the south-east of the city, and so it was only a short excursion for the artist. Jones shows no interest in the putative classical associations of the site, concentrating instead on the ruin's rather ordinary setting. There could not be a greater contrast with the tree-encrusted image produced by Giovanni Battista Piranesi for his *Vedute di Roma* which squeezes every last bit of dramatic potential from the site. (GS)

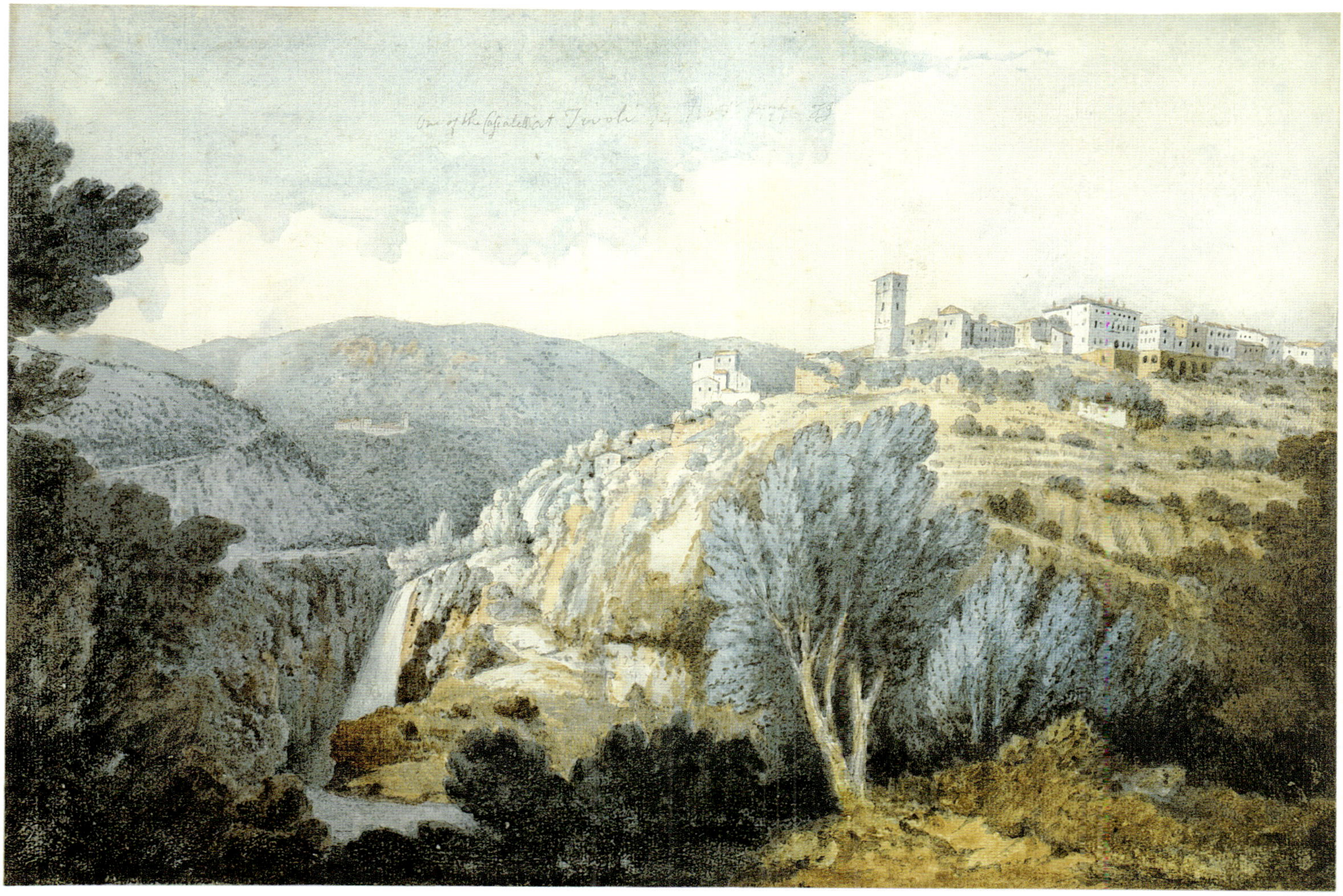
84

84

Thomas Jones (1742–1803)

The Grand Cascatelle at Tivoli 1777

Pencil, watercolour on laid paper, 27.2 × 41.2 ($10\frac{5}{8} \times 16\frac{1}{8}$)

Ins.: 'One of the Cascatelli at Tivoli 14 Novr. 1777 T.J.' t.c.
Prov.: Captain John Dale, then by descent; Sotheby's, 26 July 1961, no. 62; Agnew's; purchased 1961
Exh.: London, 1970, no. 34; Cambridge, 1982, no. 22; Manchester, 1988, no. 51; Cambridge, 1994, p. 42

Lent by the Syndics of the Fitzwilliam Museum, Cambridge (P.D.15–1961)

Cardiff and Manchester only

This watercolour was begun on a trip to Tivoli in November 1777. Jones hired a guide to show him the 'most remarkable Scenes' in the town and its environs and in the course of six days he conducted a systematic sketching campaign (*Memoirs*, p. 65). The number of drawings he produced means that he could not have completed such a carefully finished watercolour. Like cat. nos 80–3, therefore, this work was not substantially coloured on the spot, though it is unclear when it was reworked. Another view of the Grand Cascatelle (Yale Center for British Art) is inscribed 'for the painting' and it includes the sunset effect that featured in the finished painting (untraced). This suggests that the drawings were conceived, initially at least, as preparatory studies.

Jones took his view from the slopes of the northern bank of the Aniene, showing the Cascatelle and part of the town above. Looking south-east, the drawing includes a distant view of Mount Catillo that perfectly illustrates Jones's belief that Tivoli was 'situated in the most Romantic manner' (ibid., p. 66). (GS)

85

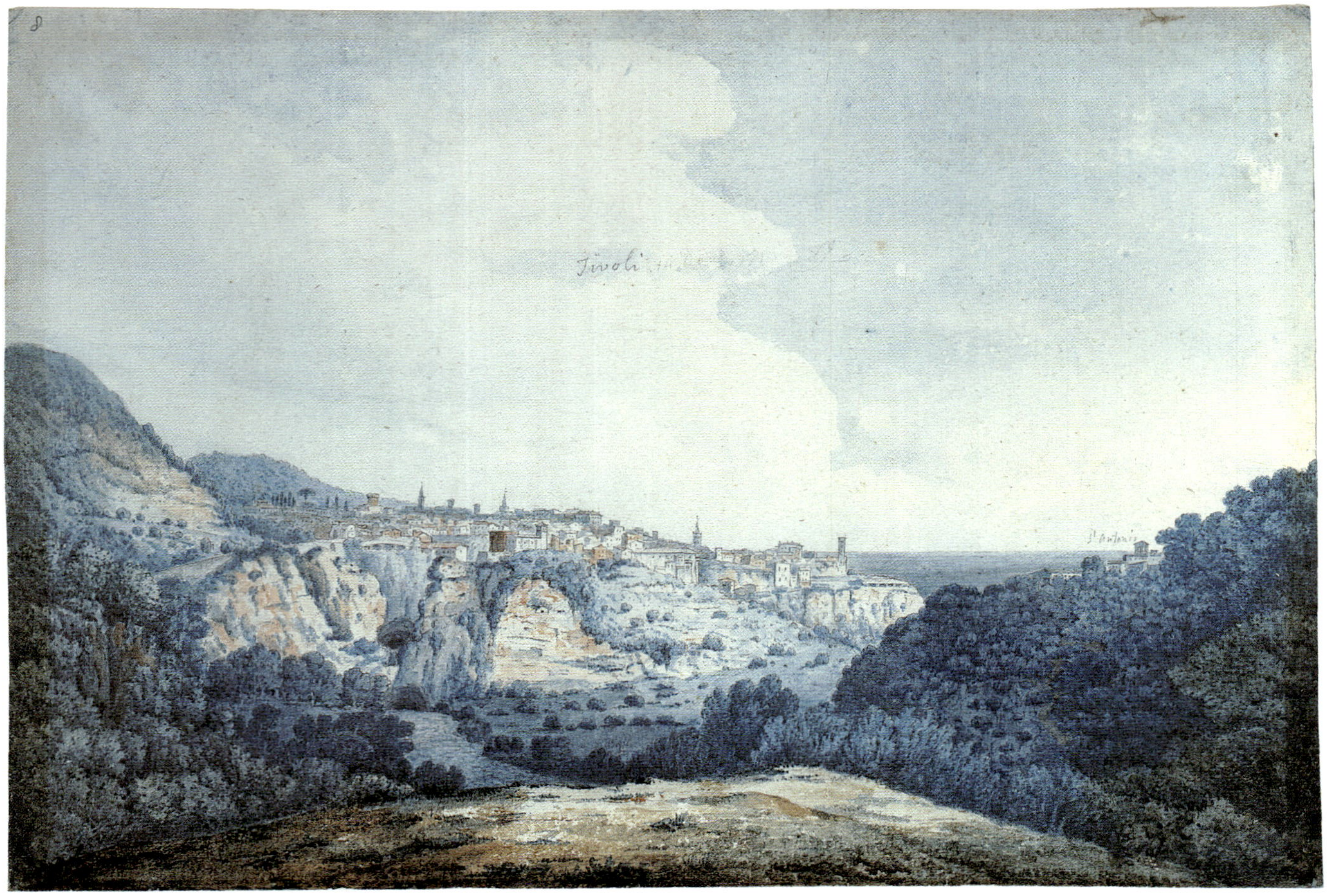

85

THOMAS JONES (1742–1803)

View of Tivoli with San Antonio 1777

Pencil, watercolour on laid paper, 28.5 × 42.5 (11¼ × 16¾)

Ins.: 'Tivoli 14 Novr 1777 T J' t.c.; 'S'antonio' l.r.; '8' (?) t.l.
Prov.: Captain John Dale, then by descent; Sotheby's, 27 November 1975, no. 87; Sotheby's, 17 November 1988, no. 75

Private collection

Like cat. no. 84, this watercolour was initially sketched on 14 November. Jones recorded that he was 'making Views near the Monasteries of St Antonio and S'Angelo' on that day and the former can be see to the right (*Memoirs*, pp. 65–6). The view takes in the same part of Tivoli shown in cat. no. 87, with the Temple of the Sibyl prominent in the centre and the Grotto of Neptune below, though from this distance the falls are not visible. Like another Tivoli view (Yale Center for British Art), the drawing is numbered – in this case '8'. This does not tally with the drawings in the sketchbook he used at Tivoli (cat. no. 76), however, and unless there are missing works, the numbers do not fit any logical sequence. Jones restricted himself to a limited palette of blues and greens relieved by a warmer earth colour similar to the other Tivoli subjects. The uniformity of the tints gives the impression that they were coloured in a single campaign. (GS)

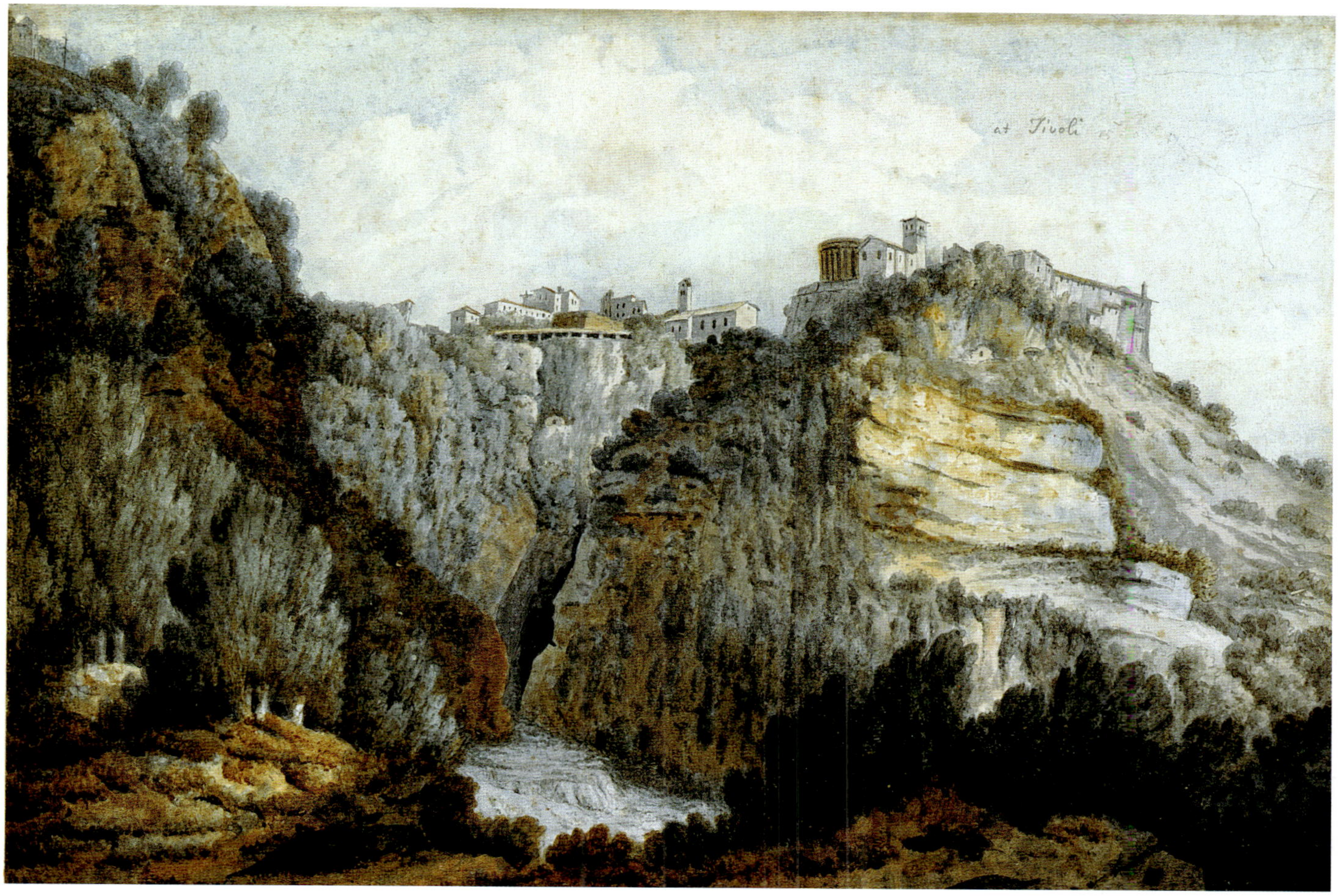

86

86

Thomas Jones (1742–1803)

The Grand Cascade at Tivoli 1777

Pencil, watercolour on Italian laid writing paper*, 27.5 × 40.5 (10¾ × 15⅞)

Ins.: 'At Tivoli 15 Nov (unclear) 177[?]' t.r.
Prov.: Captain John Dale, then by descent to Canon J. H. Adams; Phillips, 3 November 1986, no. 11; purchased by the National Museum of Wales, 1986
Exh.: London, 1970, no. 35; London, 1974a, no. 123; Manchester, 1988, no. 50

National Museums & Galleries of Wales (NMW A 3700)

On the day this work was begun, 15 November 1777, Jones noted that he was 'Mak'g Sketches above the great Cascade & about the Grotto Nettuno or Grotto of Neptune' (*Memoirs*, p. 66). In this work, Jones adopts a lower viewpoint than hitherto in order to capture the full impact of the town's dramatic setting on the towering cliffs above the River Aniene. From this position, one can see the famous rounded form of the Temple of the Sybil, as well as part of the Cascade below, though the Grotto of Neptune is hidden behind the prominent cleft of the gorge through which the river falls. The attraction of the view for Jones lay partly in the thickly forested slopes, but also in other areas where 'the perpendicular & hanging Sides admit of no vegetation [and] you discover the naked Rock' with all of its tantalizing colours. Rock, sky, water and vegetation together leave little room for signs of civilization.
(GS and BM)

87

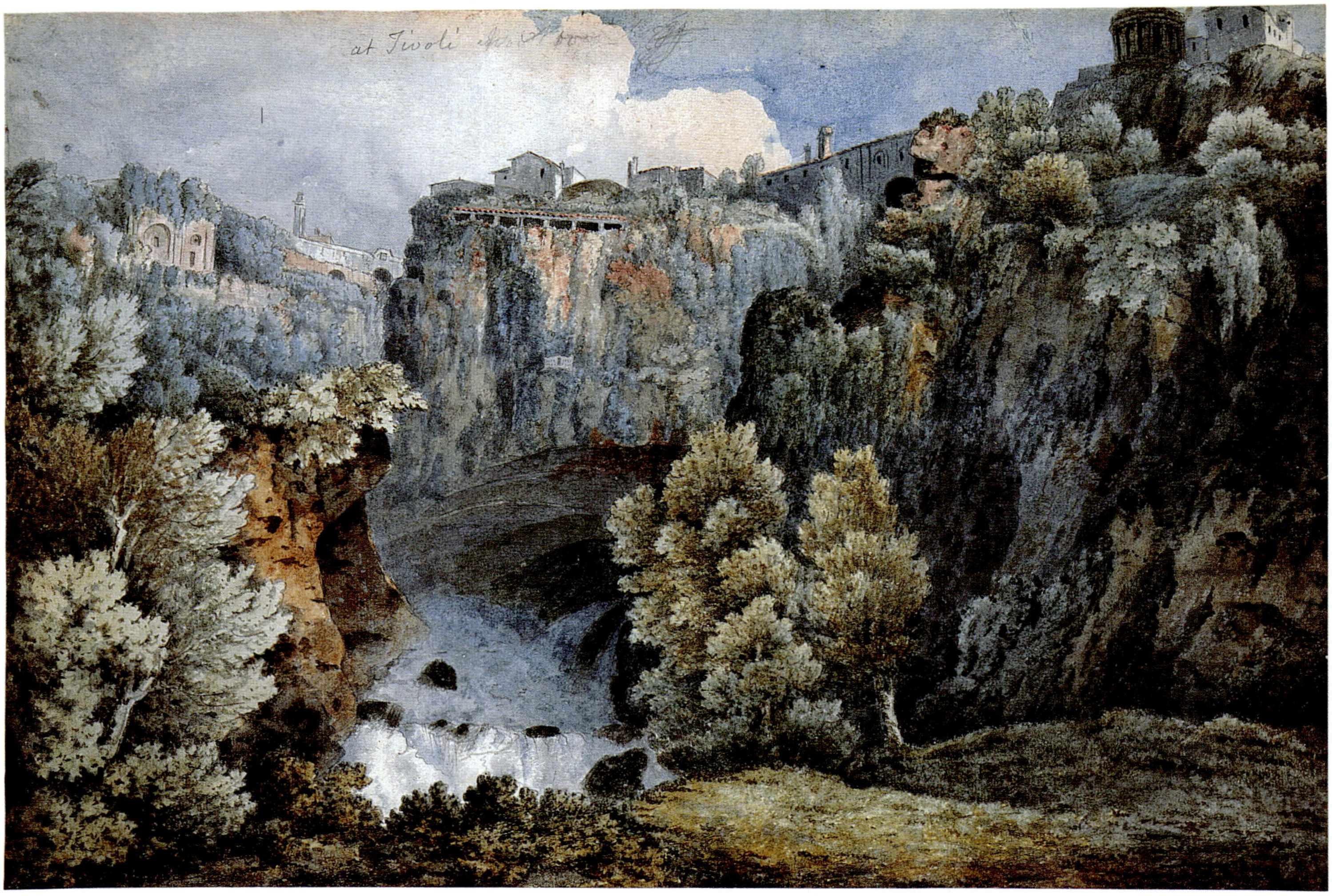

87

THOMAS JONES (1742–1803)

The Grotto of Neptune at Tivoli 1777

Pencil, watercolour on laid paper, 27 × 40.8 (10⅝ × 16)

Ins.: 'at Tivoli Above (unclear) TJ' t.c.; 'vinyd', 'ivy' on the drawing
Prov.: Captain John Dale, then by descent; Sotheby's, 26 July 1961, no. 63; Jane Evan-Thomas; given to present owner
Exh.: London, 1970, no. 36 as 'At Tivoli above'
Lit.: Gowing, 1985, p. 36, pl. 29

Private collection

Although this watercolour is undated, it was presumably begun on the same day as cat. no. 86, as it shows a similar view, though from closer to. As a result, more of the Cascade and the Grotto are visible and we are able to appreciate Jones's characterization of Tivoli's greatest thrill: the 'foaming Torrents [which] rush down the precipices into the deep Abyss with a fearful Noise and horrid Grandeur' (*Memoirs*, p. 66). A few of the inscriptions that are a feature of Jones's coloured pencil drawings are still visible, but this is one of the most highly finished examples and the hues are particularly vivid and redolent of an autumn scene. This reflects Jones's observation that when looking at this view 'the Eye is charmed with the most beautiful variegated Tints – White, Grey, Red & Yellow – opposing, or blending their different Dyes together' (ibid., p. 67). At the same time, the artist cropped one of Tivoli's most famous monuments – the Temple of the Sibyl – suggesting that the classical associations of the site were not foremost in his mind. (GS)

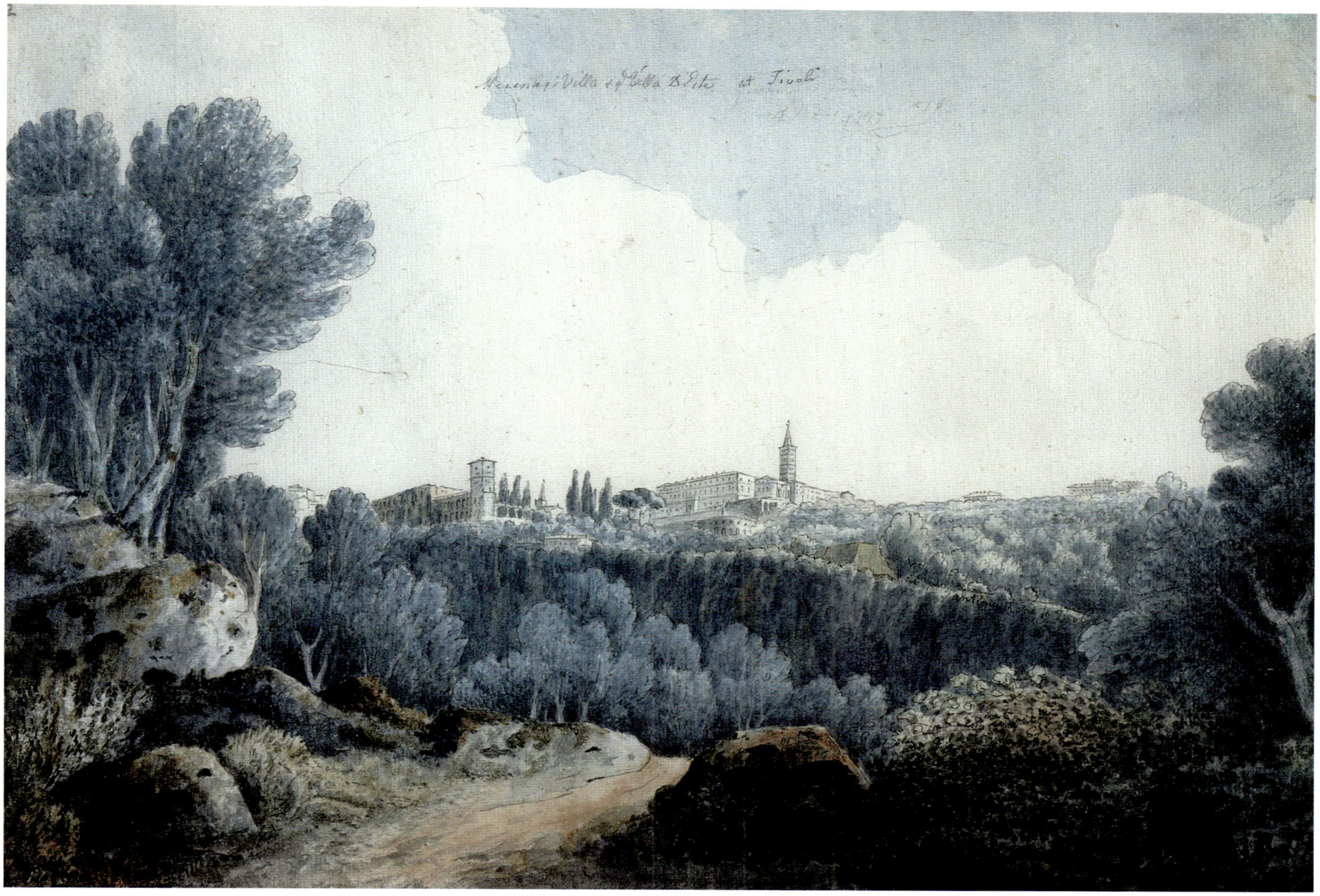

88

THOMAS JONES (1742–1803)

The Villa of Maecenas and the Villa D'Este, Tivoli

1777

Pencil, watercolour on laid paper, 27.5 × 42 (11 × 16½)

Ins.: 'Mecenas's Villa & y^e^ Villa D'Este at Tivoli' t.c.; '15 Novr 1777 T.J.' indistinct below
Prov.: Captain John Dale, then by descent; Sotheby's, 27 November 1975, no. 86; Sotheby's, 11 April 1991, no. 48; Sotheby's, 15 July 1993, no. 48

Private collection

Like cat. no. 86, this work was also begun on 15 November, though the watercolour washes were presumably added later, when Jones also strengthened many of the lines and introduced a title which is sharper than the date and signature below. The view shows two of the leading attractions of Tivoli, the Villa D'Este in the distance and the ruins of the so-called Villa of Maecenas. The latter was the home of the most renowned patron of Roman literature and it was partly through his support for writers that Tivoli gained a reputation for its scenic beauties. This, in turn, attracted the interest of generations of artists and British tourists. Jones may have had a commission for a view of Tivoli, since he repeated this composition from a slightly different angle from further along the road to the left (Pierpont Morgan Library, New York), as if he were trying out different options. (GS)

89

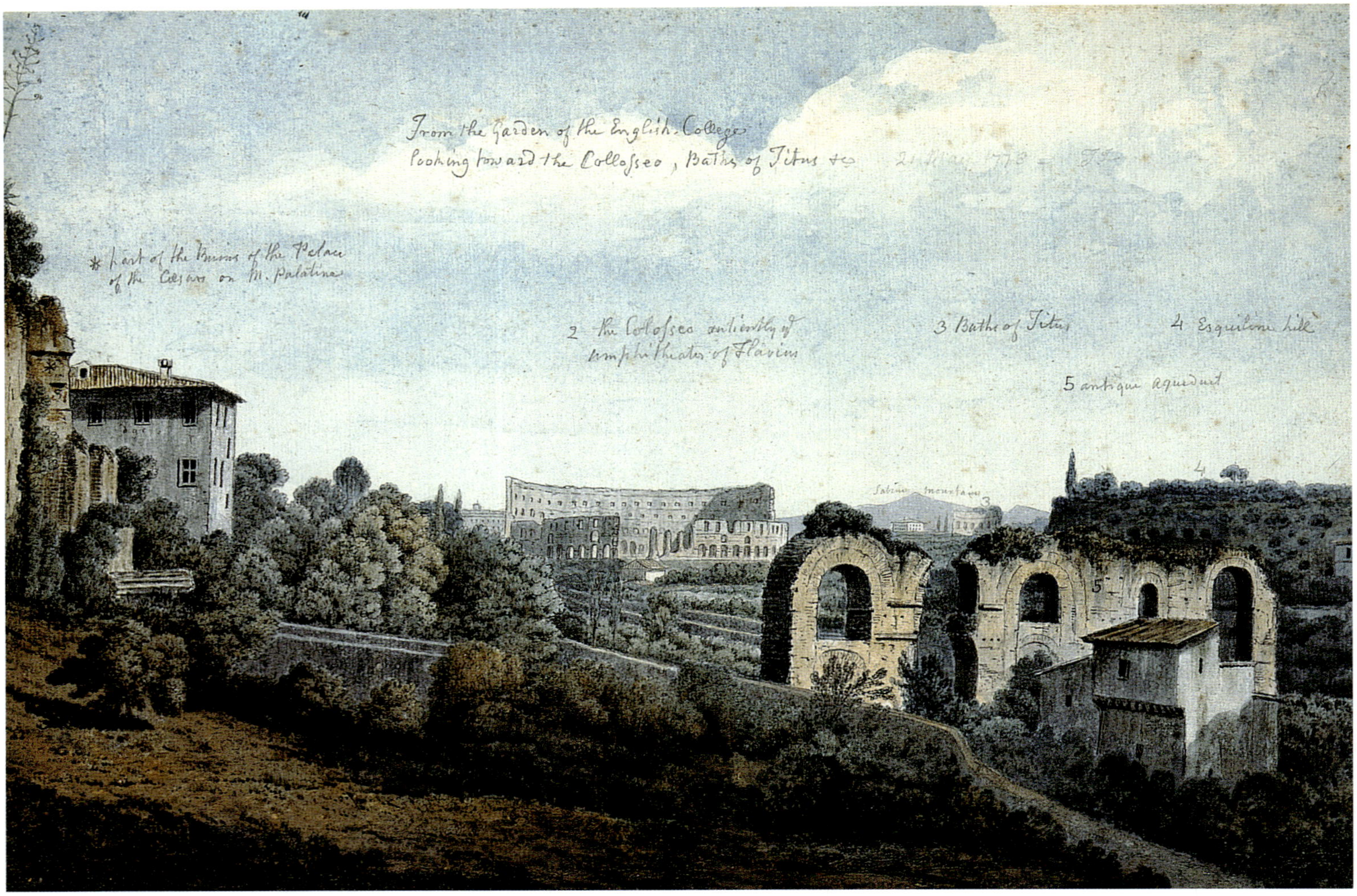

89

Thomas Jones (1742–1803)

From the Gardens of the English College Looking Towards the Colosseum and the Baths of Titus, Rome 1778

Pencil, watercolour, gum arabic on Italian laid writing paper*, 25.8 × 39.8 (10⅛ × 15¾)

Ins.: 'From the Garden of the English College / looking toward the Collosseo, Baths of Titus &c' t.c.; '21 May 1778 T J' t.c.; other extensive inscriptions keyed to the drawing
Prov.: Captain John Dale, then by descent
Exh.: London, 1970, no. 37; London, 1974a, no. 10

Private collection

Jones records that he made 'some Drawings in the Garden belonging to the English College upon Mount Palatine' on 21 May and inscriptions on this watercolour identify this as one of the results (*Memoirs*, p. 72). The use of the plural indicates that he was referring to detailed on-the-spot pencil drawings, since he would not have had time to work up the carefully finished effects seen here. These areas, which would have been executed in the studio, transcend the drawing's original function as a utilitarian record, though the inscriptions betray its origins.

In a charming passage in the *Memoirs*, Jones describes how he listened to his youthful compatriots making 'very free' comments, unaware that the artist sketching from their 'Play-ground' spoke English. On revealing his nationality, he was bombarded with 'Questions about England – how the war went on &c' from the homesick children (ibid.). (GS)

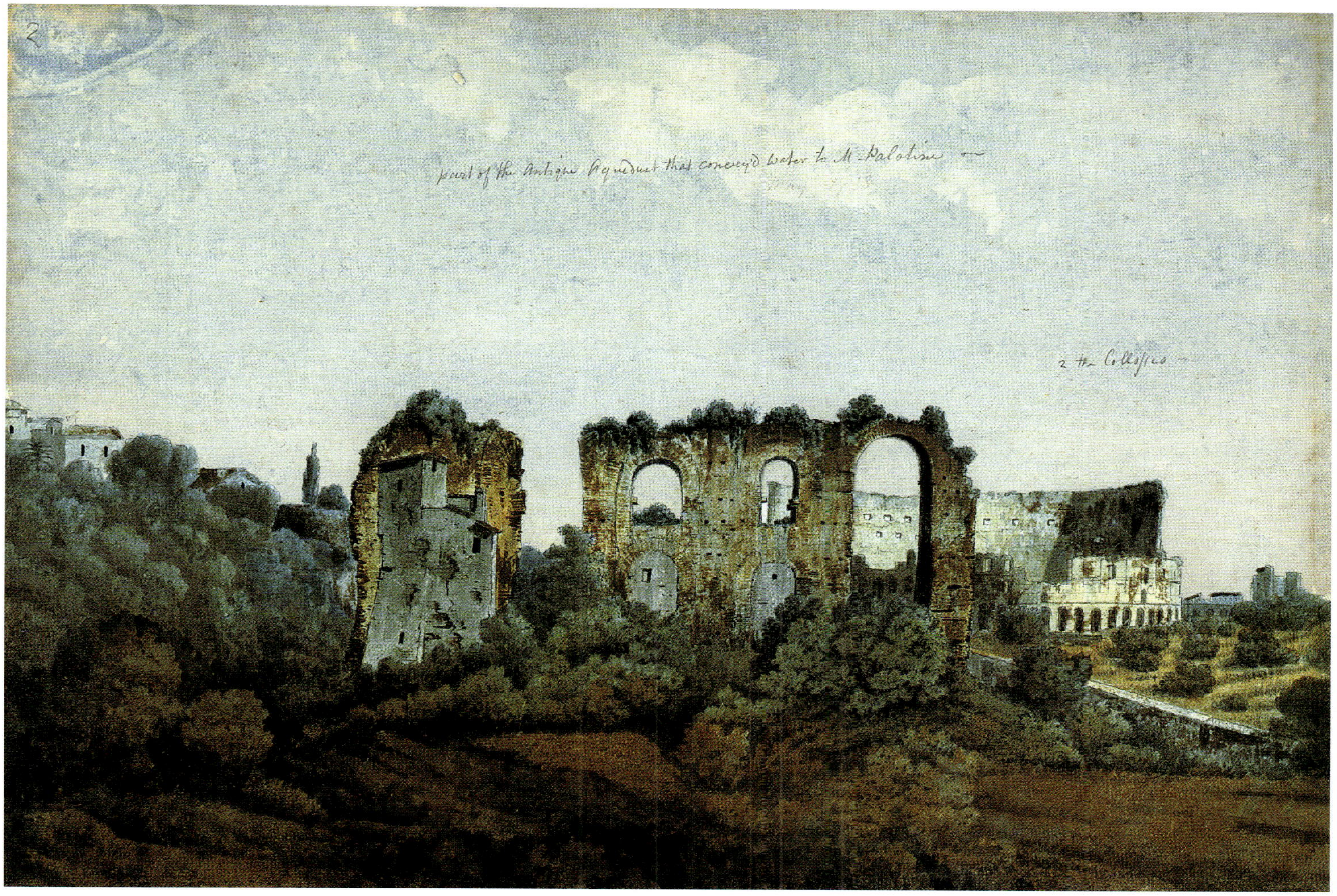

90

90

Thomas Jones (1742–1803)

The Claudian Aqueduct and Colosseum, Rome

1778

Pencil, watercolour on paper, 27.3 × 41.2 (10¾ × 16¼)

Ins.: 'part of the Antique Aqueduct that convey'd Water to M. Palatine / May 1778' t.c.; '2' t.l.; '2 the Collosseo-' c.r.; 'vinyard' l.r.
Prov.: Captain John Dale, then by descent; Sotheby's, 27 November 1975, no. 90; purchased by Paul Mellon; presented 1981
Exh.: London, 1970, no. 38; New Haven, 1981, no. 68; New Haven, 1982, no. III.14; New Haven, 2001, no. 101
Lit.: Gowing, 1985, p. 38, pl. 31

Yale Center for British Art, Paul Mellon Collection (B1981.25.2637)

Cardiff and Manchester only

The pencil drawing to which Jones later added watercolour washes may have been made on the same day – 21 May – as cat. no. 89, and it is taken from an adjacent viewpoint (*Memoirs*, p. 72). It, too, shows the Claudian Aqueduct in the foreground, but from a point to the right, so that the ruins partially block the view of the Colosseum. As the inscription notes, the aqueduct was constructed to bring water to the imperial palaces on Mount Palatine and it was largely built during the reign of Claudius (*c.*AD 40–50). The drawing exemplifies one of the characteristic features of the watercolours that Jones later reworked. Unlike the works he made in the studio from sketches, such as cat. no. 70, the scene contains no figures, since they would have been inappropriate to what was initially a simple utilitarian record. When this was converted into what purports to be a finished watercolour, however, the absence of people defies our expectations and creates a disconcerting quality in an otherwise familiar view. (GS)

91

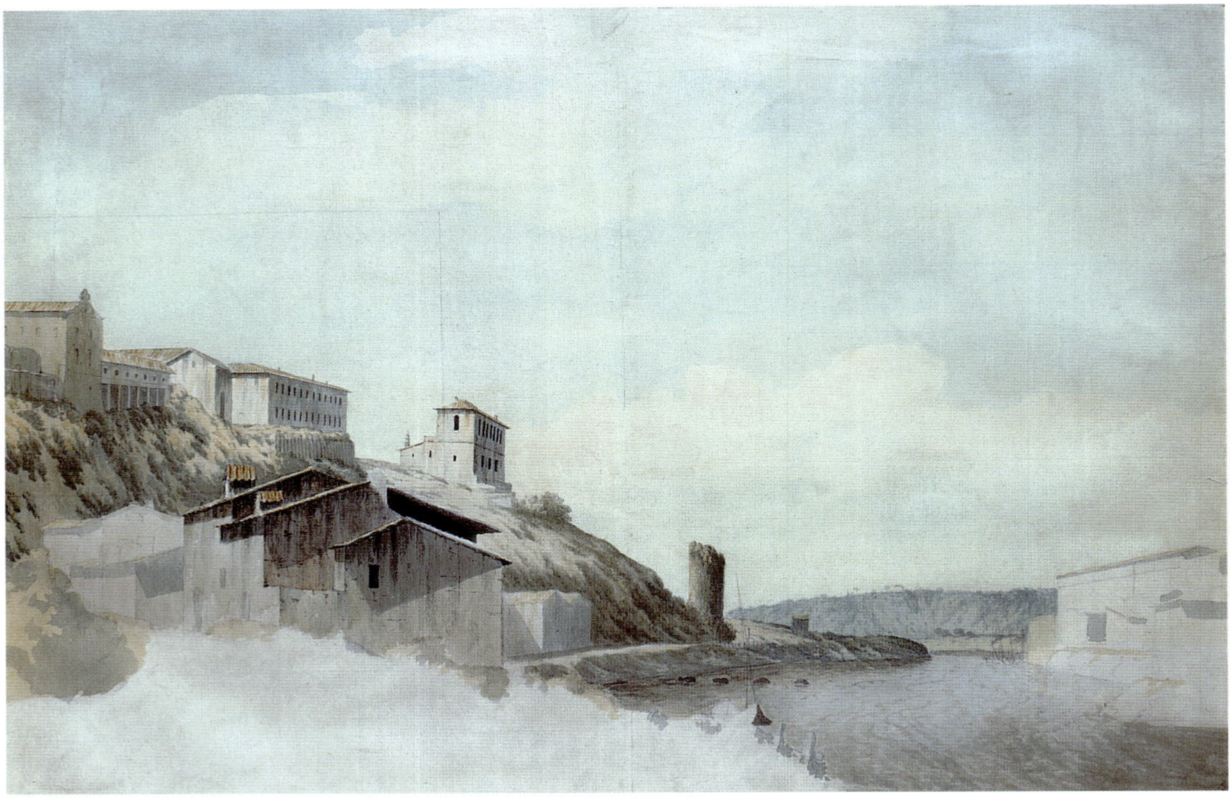

91

THOMAS JONES (1742–1803)

The Aventine Hill from the River Tiber, Rome

1780s

Pencil, watercolour on laid paper (Watermark: Strasbourg Lily / J. Whatman), 33.7 × 52 ($13\frac{1}{4} \times 20\frac{1}{2}$)

Prov.: Agnew's, 1959; W. A. Brandt, then by descent
Exh.: Agnew's, 1959, no. 2; London, 1970, no. 40 as 'Near Rome'
Lit.: Gowing, 1985, p. 38, pl. 30

Private collection

The lack of inscriptions would indicate that this watercolour was not executed on the spot, even if its source in two sketches in the larger Roman sketchbook had not been recognized (cat. no. 75, pp. 11–12). Inscriptions on the sketches, which are dated 22 March 1777, identify the view as a stretch of the River Tiber beneath the Aventine Hill, seen from near the Ponte Rotto. When sketching, Jones included in a separate box an extra detail of the distance which he could not fit onto the page (cat. no. 75, p. 12), and he included this in the watercolour, removing a building in the foreground. As a result, the river gains the prominence seen in the view on the previous sketchbook page.

It is not clear why Jones left the foreground unfinished – it would have included a broad stretch of road with space for figures, something he usually added last. Pencil lines to the left mark out a smaller area, so perhaps he contemplated an alternative composition. (GS)

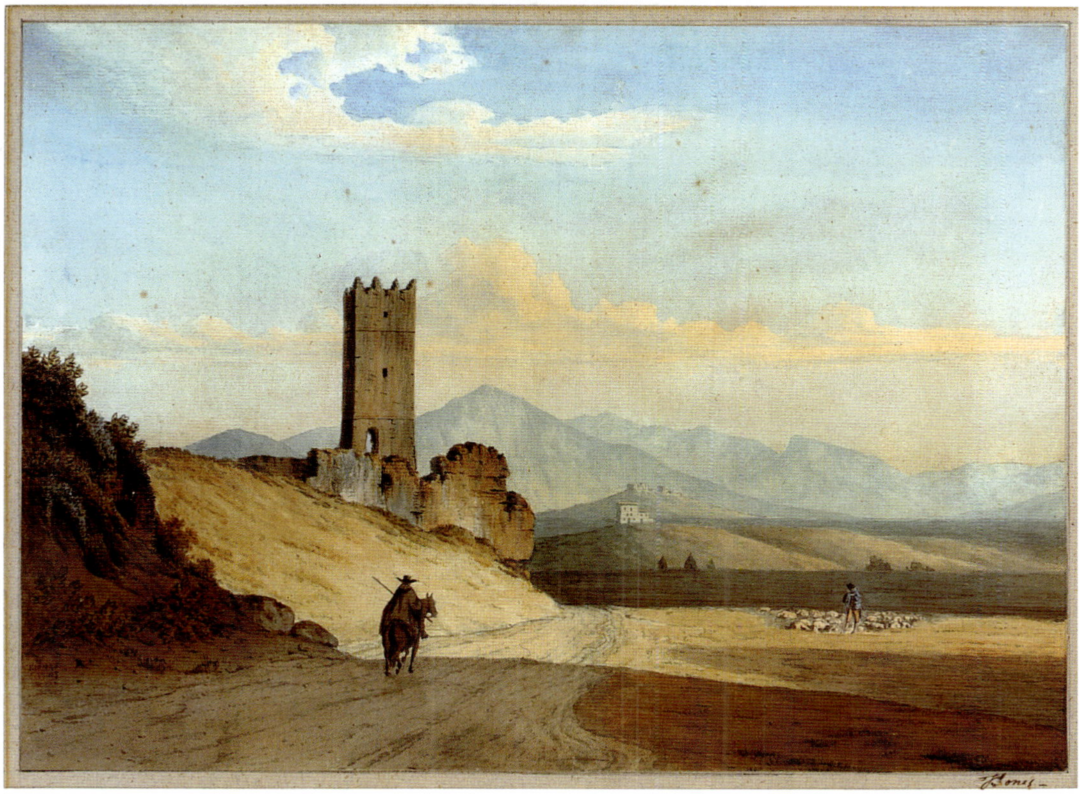

92

92

THOMAS JONES (1742–1803)

In the Campagna, near Rome 1783

Pencil, watercolour, pen and ink on Dutch writing paper on original mount*, 24.7 × 34.7 (9¾ × 13⅝)

Ins.: 'T Jones-' l.r. on original mount; 'In the Campagna, near Rome' l.c. on original mount; 'T. JONES / 1783' l.l.
Prov.: Thomas Thomas, then by descent
Exh.: London, 1970, no. 24

Private collection

This watercolour is based on a drawing in the smaller Roman sketchbook inscribed 'on ye road to Civita Castellana / above Ponte Mola near Ovids tomb / 15 Feb 1777' (cat. no. 74, p. 47). Jones made fourteen pencil drawings on that day, on an excursion that took him along the Tiber and on to the road to Civita Castellana. Three other studio works were subsequently produced from these studies: a small oil (cat. no. 71); another watercolour showing the same tower from another direction (cat. no. 149); and cat. no. 150. Cat. no. 149, *On the Road to Civita Castellana*, is dated 1785, after Jones left Italy, and, although the date here is given as 1783, it might have been a mistake, since the two views are clearly meant as a pair. They are on the same size of paper and have been mounted in a similar manner, with a signature in pen and ink to the right. Along with *Houses on the Road from Rome to Civita Castellana* (cat. no. 150), this work and cat. no. 149 form a distinct group which has much in common in terms of their presentation and function with the later Welsh watercolours such as cat. no. 159. (GS)

FOLLOWING PAGES Detail of cat. no. 103.

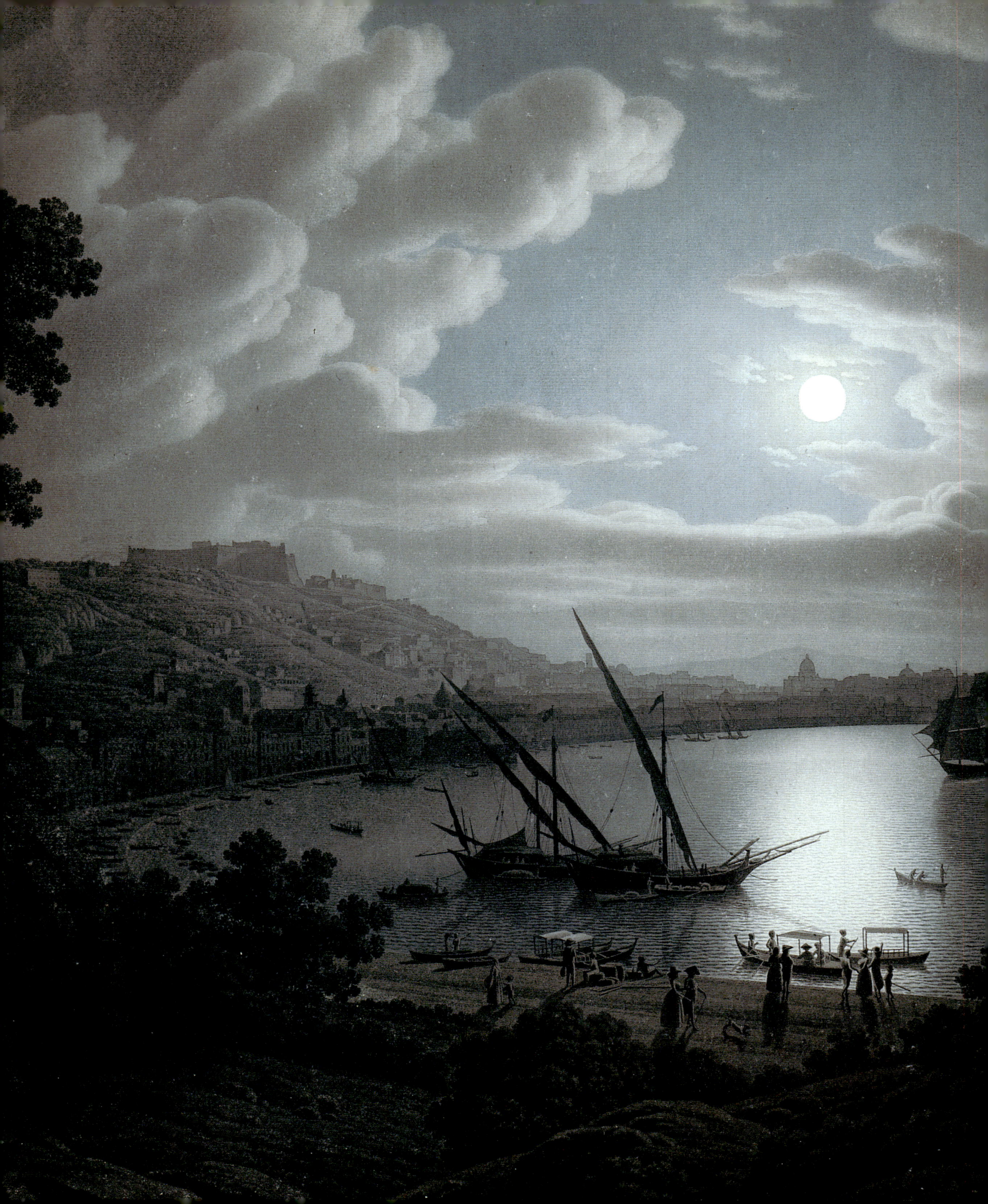

JONES'S CONTEMPORARIES IN ITALY

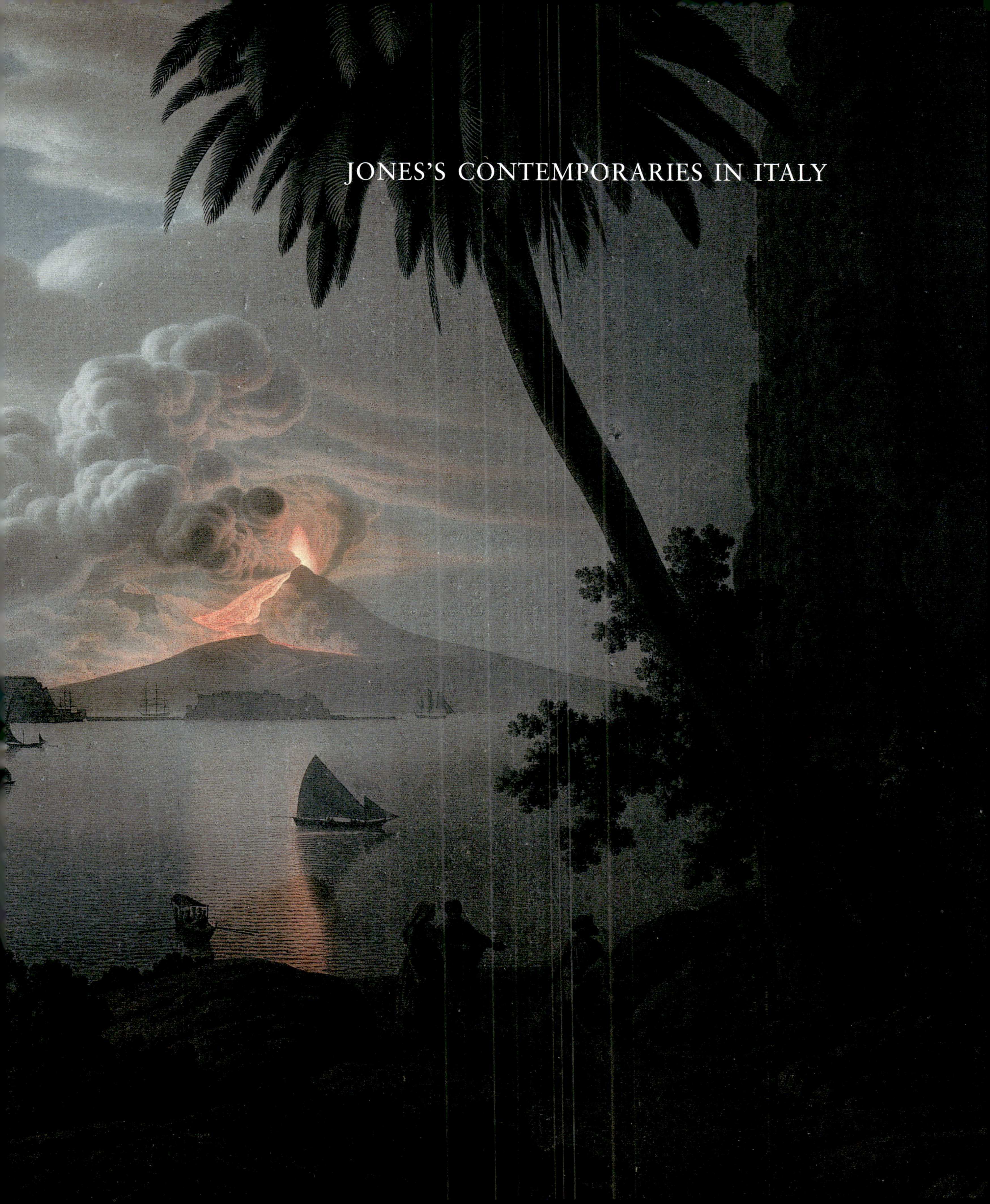

93

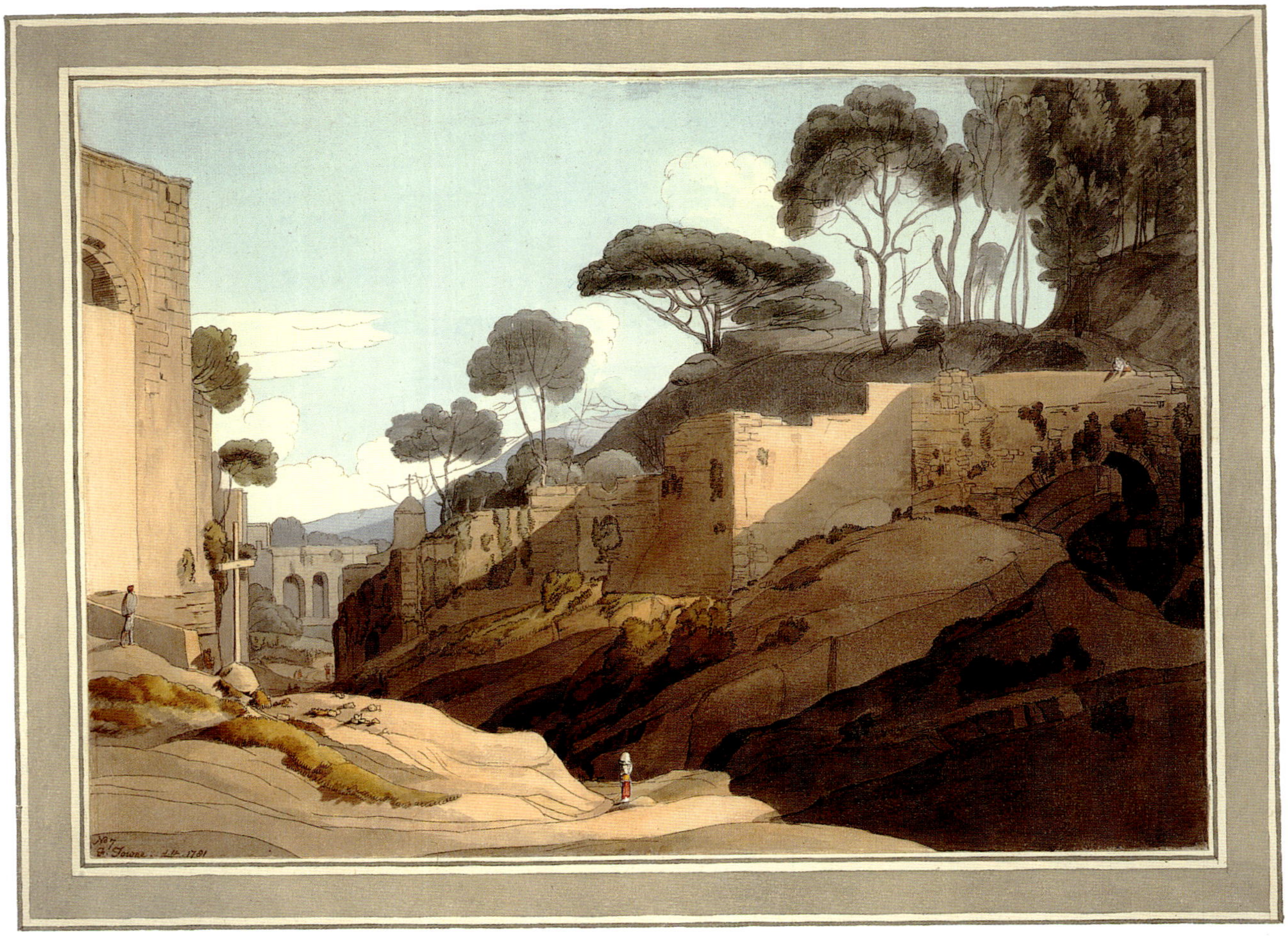

93

Francis Towne (1739–1816)

The Descent from Capodimonte 1781

Pencil, watercolour, pen and ink on laid paper with original mount, 32.2 × 46.6 (12⅝ × 18⅜)

Ins.: 'No 7 / F. Towne delt. 1781' l.l.; 'Naples / No 7 Coming down from Capa de Monta / drawn on the spot by Francis Towne / March, No. 7 – 1781.' on back of the mount
Prov.: Donated in accordance with the artist's wishes, by his executor, James White, 1816
Exh.: London, 1981 (no cat.); London, 1990, pp. 132–3
Lit.: Bury, 1962, p. 126

British Museum, London (1972.U.640)

Cardiff and Manchester only

Francis Towne arrived in Naples in March 1781 and Jones offered his services to his 'old Acquaintance' as a guide, revisiting for his benefit 'all the Curiosities of Art and Nature' in the city. These excursions took in the 'picturesque places' that Jones had discovered and this, he added, was 'rather favourable to Mr Towne, in his Profession' as an artist, since it saved him time and labour (*Memoirs*, p. 102). Although Jones is not known to have painted this scene, he may have introduced Towne to a subject that would have appealed to both artists as the embodiment of the gloomy 'romantick' landscapes favoured by Salvator Rosa (ibid., p. 104).

Towne carefully numbered the sketches he made during his three-week stay; this is number seven in a sequence that stretches to at least twenty-one. He returned to the sketches at some time after his return to England, adding watercolour washes and penned lines and mounting them in a uniform style; as with Jones's studies, therefore, the inscribed date noting when the work was begun tells only part of the story. (GS)

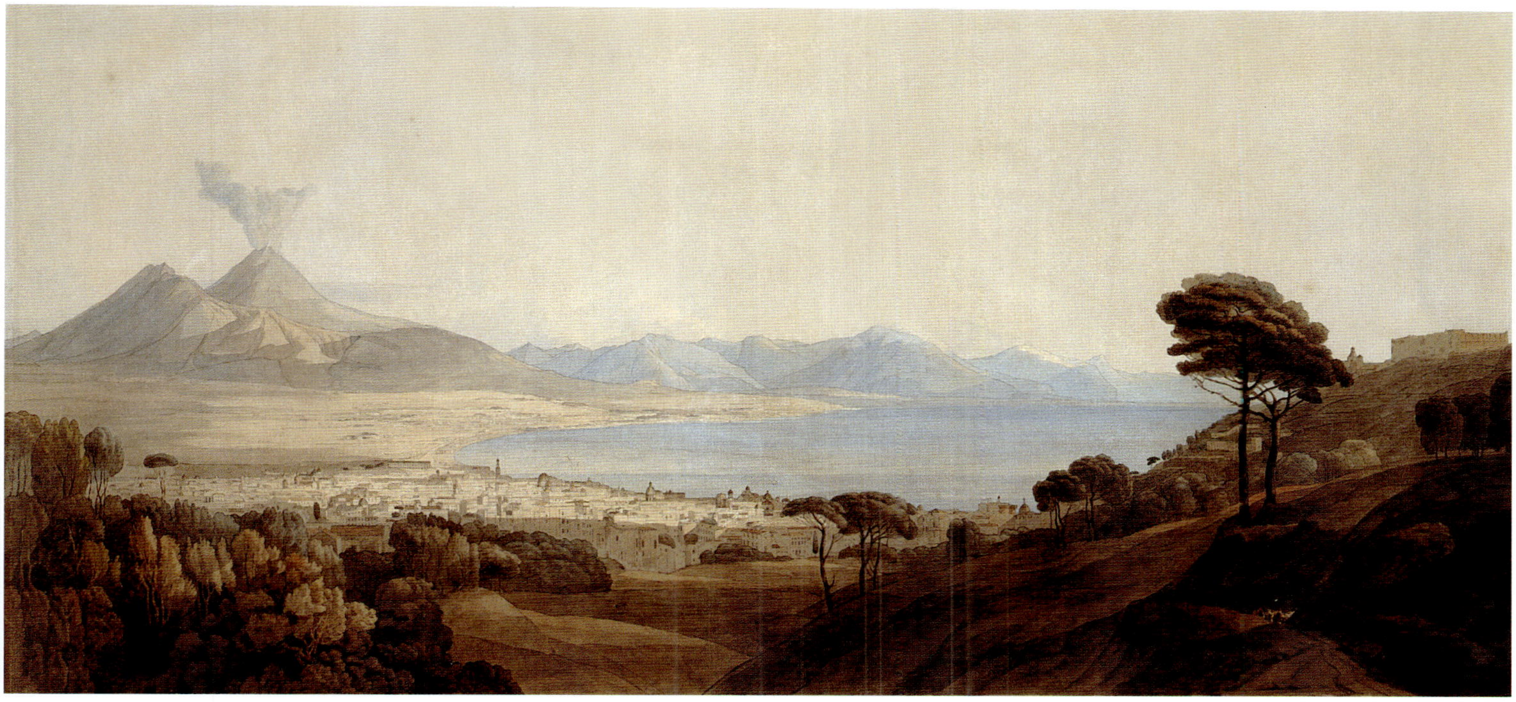

94

94

Francis Towne (1739–1816)

The Bay of Naples 1785

Pencil, watercolour, pen and ink on paper, 40.4 × 88.5 (15⅞ × 34⅞)

Ins.: 'F. Towne delt 1785' l.r.
Prov.: Mrs E. S. Abbott; purchased 1927
Exh.: Arts Council, 1960, no. 69; London, 1967, no. 17; London, 1968a, no. 97; Manchester, 1973a, no. 9; Brussels, 1973, no. 86; Manchester, 1988, no. 97; Manchester, 1993, no. 41
Lit.: Bury, 1962, p. 136

The Whitworth Art Gallery, The University of Manchester (D.1927.15)

Cardiff and Manchester only

This watercolour dates from after Towne's return to England and is a commissioned studio work. The provenance suggests that it might have been ordered by Towne's pupil, John White Abbott, who would have chosen the subject from the artist's sketches. Only the drawing for the right of the panoramic view survives, however (Fitzwilliam Museum, Cambridge). It is dated 'March 17th 1781' and is inscribed 'no 1' which presumably makes it the first view the artist took of the city. This would make sense if Jones introduced Towne to the stunning view on his arrival. It was from the same spot in the vicinity of Capodimonte that Jones made the lost study that became the basis for his oil painting *The Bay of Naples* (cat. no. 106). Although Jones introduced a more prominent foreground befitting an oil painting in the Claudian manner, one can recognize the same topographical features in Towne's view, framed by Castel Sant'Elmo to the right and Vesuvius to the left. (GS)

95

John Robert Cozens (1752–1797)

The Lake of Nemi Looking Towards Genzano c.1778

Pencil, watercolour on paper, 36 × 52.8 (14⅛ × 20¾)

Prov.: C. S. Bale; Dr J. Percy; John Edward Taylor; presented by him, 1892
Exh.: London, 1891, no. 27; Manchester, 1891, no. 7; Manchester, 1937, no. 48; London, 1954, no. 33; Manchester, 1956, no. 39; Arts Council, 1960, no. 25; Vienna, 1965, no. 31; London, 1967, no. 18; Paris, 1972, no. 83; Manchester, 1973b, no. 70; London, 1974a, no. 113; Bourdeaux, 1977, no. 3; Stockholm, 1982, no. 159;

95

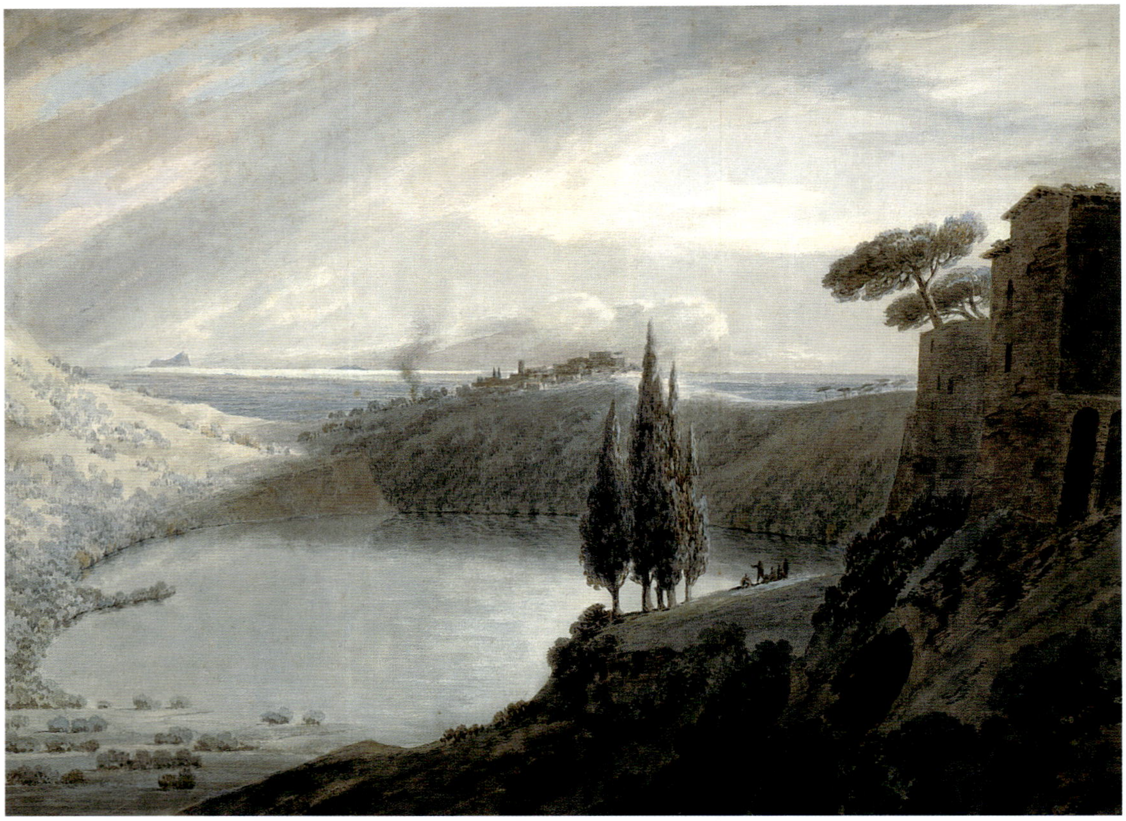

Manchester, 1983, no. 6; Manchester, 1988, no. 70; Manchester, 1993, no. 43
Lit.: Bell and Girtin, 1935, p. 44, no. 141; Herrmann, 1974, p. 87; Wilton, 1977, pp. 182–3

The Whitworth Art Gallery, The University of Manchester (D.1892.24)

Cardiff and Manchester only

John Robert Cozens's two Italian trips overlapped with Jones's stay, but they only met on a few occasions, and though the artists often sketched the same sites, it was only in June 1778 that they probably worked together. Cozens made the sketch on which this view is based in April 1777 (Sir John Soane's Museum, London), but, though the composition is almost identical to Jones's (cat. no. 78), they probably worked independently in this case, even though the latter was also sketching here. The similarity possibly derives from the two artists' interest in the work of Richard Wilson, who depicted the same view of Genzano from the Capuchin monastery (Rhode Island School of Design, Providence). There is, however, a significant difference between the watercolours by Jones and Cozens. The latter worked to a commission in the studio – one of seven, which says much about the market amongst tourists for views – whilst Jones sketched on the spot, though he added more considered washes of colour later. (GS)

96

JOHN ROBERT COZENS (1752–1797)

Cavern in the Campagna 1778

Pencil, watercolour bodycolour on laid paper on original mount, 45.3 × 60.7 ($17\frac{7}{8}$ × 24)

Ins.: 'John Cozens – 1778' on the mount l.l.; 'cavern in y^{e} campagna' on the mount l.r.
Prov.: Bequeathed by William Smith, 1876
Exh.: Trento, 1993, no. 4
Lit.: Bell and Girtin, 1935, p. 43, no. 134.I, plate IXb; Sloan, 1986, pp. 132–4; Parkinson, 1998, p. 30

Victoria and Albert Museum, London (3020–1876)

Cardiff and Manchester only

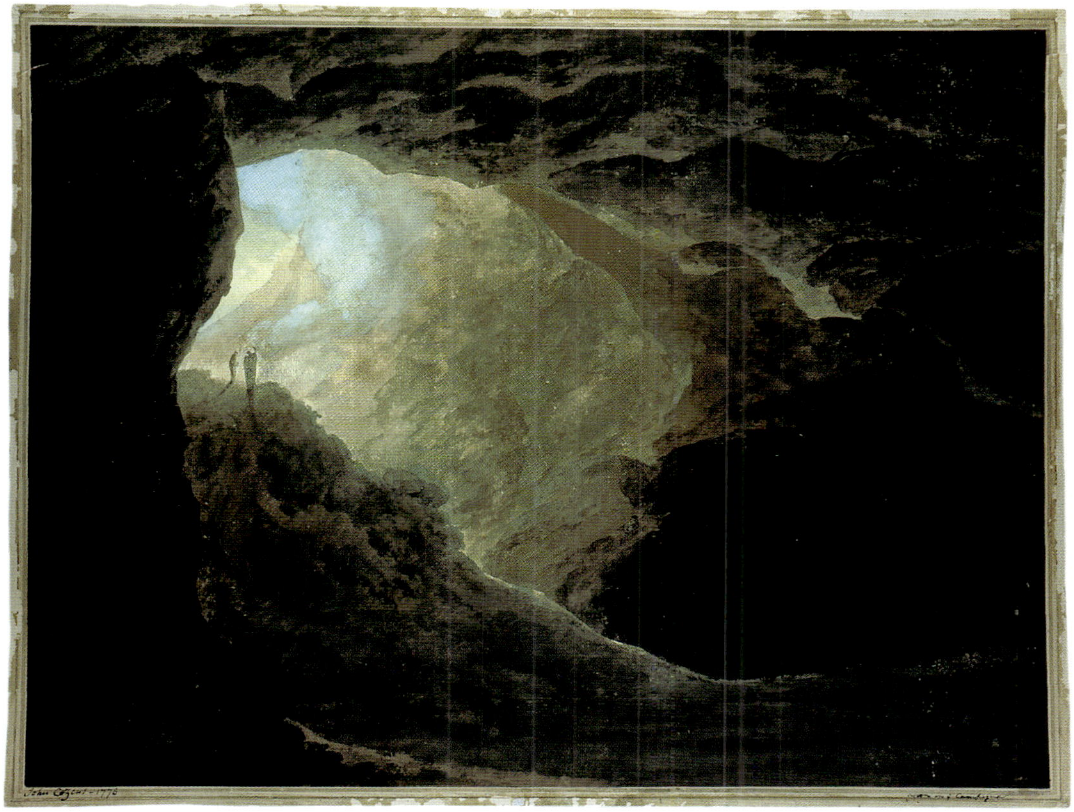

96

Jones's views of caverns near Rome (cat. nos 61 and 62) were probably sketched in oils on the spot in the summer of 1778. Similar views by Cozens in watercolours dating from the same year are more likely to have been made after drawings done on the spot and it is therefore possible that the two artists worked together, even if the end results were different. There is no evidence that Jones was interested in such scenes before this date, though the sublime character of caves was frequently explored by artists at this time, and so it may be that he followed Cozens's lead in this area, if not elsewhere.

Jones's views of caves lack the drama of Cozens's watercolours, even though they may have been painted on the spot. In this case, the smoke from the guide's torch creates an eerie effect which suggest a scene in the Underworld rather than the environs of Rome. Both artists, however, explored the site's potential for creating unconventional compositions. (GS)

97

WILLIAM PARS (1742–1782)

Rome: The Forum *c.*1775

Pencil, watercolour, pen and ink on laid paper, 40.2 × 58.8 (15⅞ × 23⅛)

Ins.: 'S. Lorenzo in miranda de Speciale / Tempio della Pace / Tempio de Giove Tonante / Sa. Francesca Romana / Colosseo / Sa Maria Liberatrice / Tempio de Antonio e Faustina / vasca antica di granito / S. S. Cosmo e Damiano' on the drawing
Prov.: Captain John Dale, then by descent to Marion Adams; presented by her, 1986
Exh.: Manchester, 1980, no. 45; London, 1997a, no. 107
Lit.: Tate, 1986, pp. 53–4; Brilli, 1987, pp. 264–5

Tate. Presented by Mrs Marion Adams in memory of her husband Canon J. H. Adams 1986 (T04852)

Cardiff and Manchester only

William Pars was an old friend of Jones and they were often in each other's company, lodging, sketching and socializing together.

97

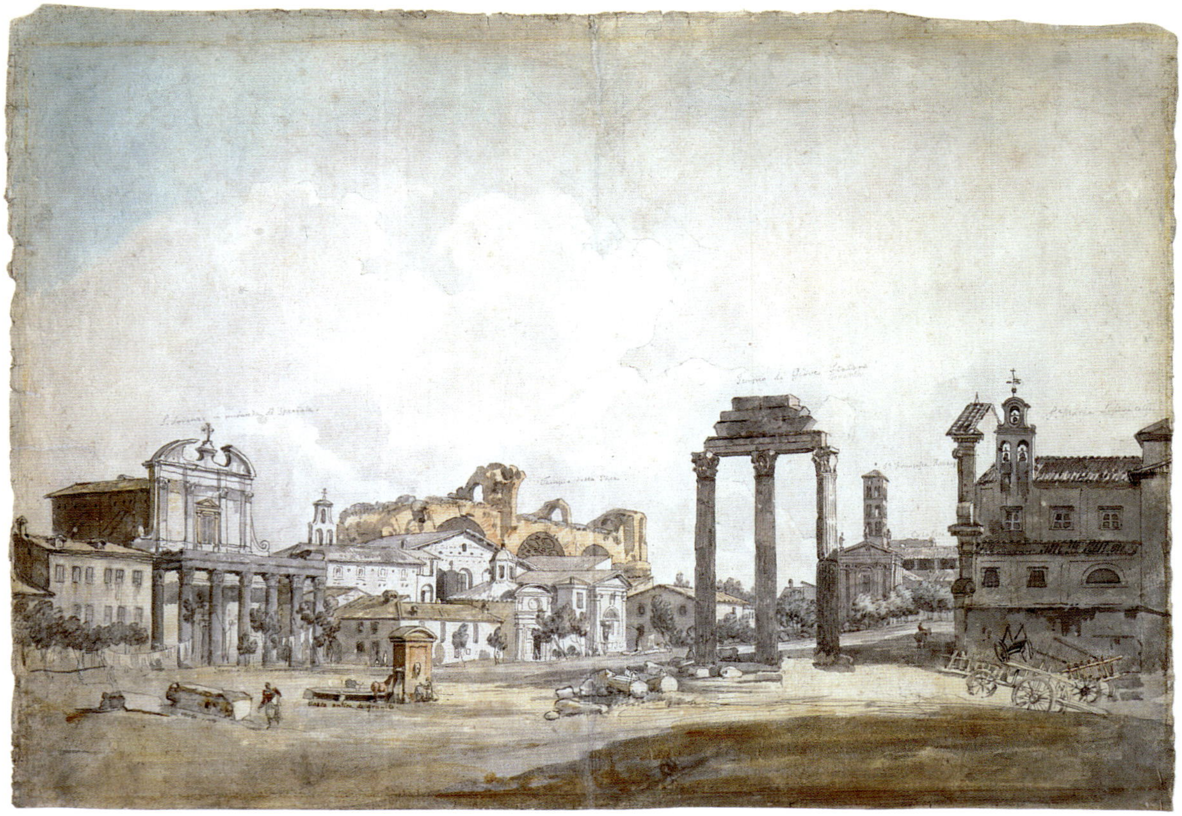

Pars arrived in Rome in 1775 and it was presumably early in his stay that he sketched the Forum. The drawing was coloured on the spot and Pars carefully annotated the main sites for future reference. He used it as the basis for at least four finished watercolours – one of which is dated 1778, and was possibly shown to patrons interested in commissioning works. Both Francis Towne and John 'Warwick' Smith made similar views in 1781, but there is no evidence that Pars sketched in company on this occasion. The drawing is linked to Jones, however, since he is known to have had it in his possession at some stage. This was presumably after Pars's death in 1782, since the artist would not have dispensed with a valuable working drawing, and Jones may have acquired it as a memento of his friend. (GS)

98

WILLIAM PARS (1742–1782)

The Grotto at Posillipo *c.*1781

Pencil, watercolour on laid paper on original mount, 39 × 51.5 (15⅜ × 20¼)

Ins.: 'THE GROTTO OF PUZZUOLI' on the mount
Prov.: J. Leslie Wright; bequeathed, 1953
Exh.: Birmingham, 1938, no. 56; London, 1949, no. 60; London, 1984b, no. 12; Birmingham, 1987, no. 9; Manchester, 1988, no. 135; Paris, 2001, no. 39

Birmingham Museums and Art Gallery, J. Leslie Wright Collection (1953P448)

Cardiff and Manchester only

Pars briefly visited Naples in October 1780 and made a longer stay in the summer of 1781, when he explored the city and its environs. Jones noted that he and Pars 'made daily excursions with our portfolios & pocketbooks', many of which would have taken them through the so-called grotto at Posillipo (*Memoirs*, p. 105). This

98

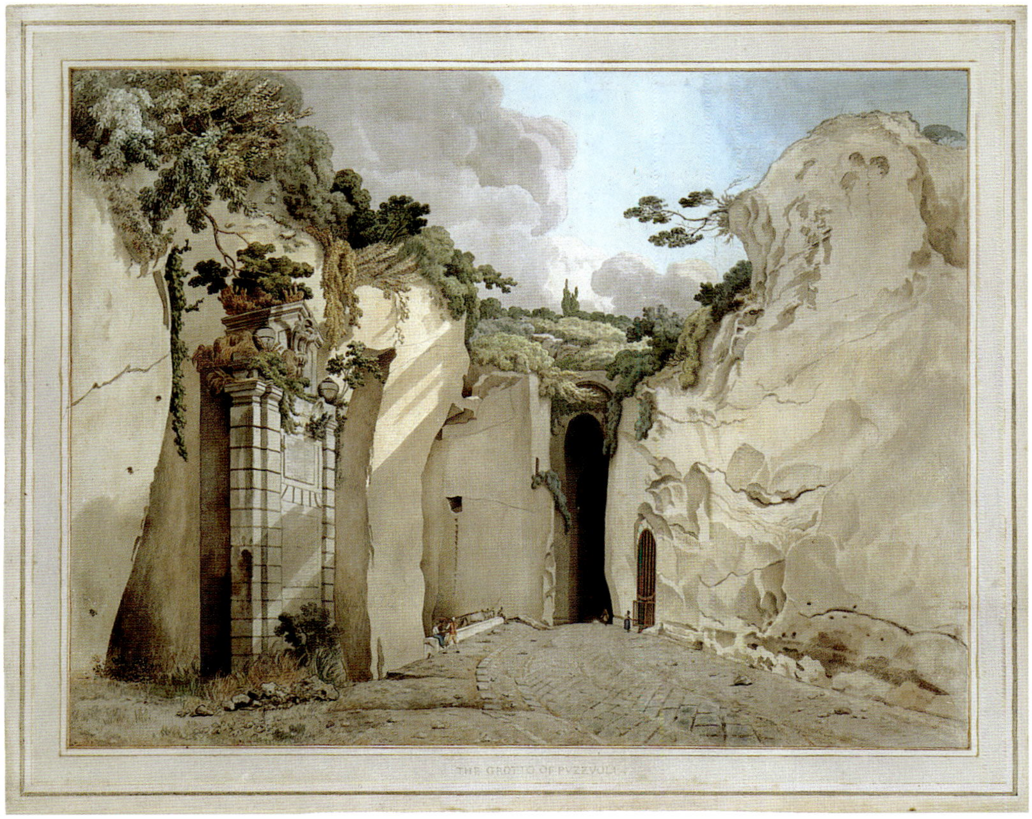
THE GROTTO OF PUZZUOLI.

99

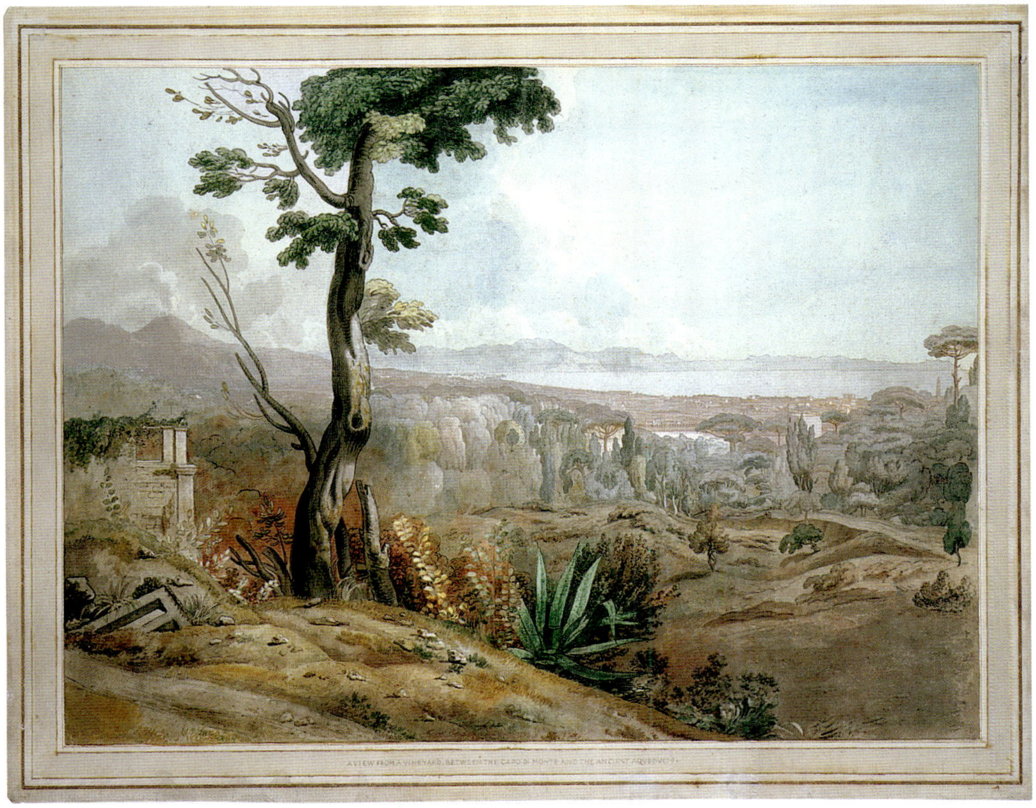
A VIEW FROM A VINEYARD, BETWEEN THE CAPO DI MONTE AND THE ANCIENT AQUEDUCTS.

finished watercolour was presumably made from one of those sketches and it is perhaps more than coincidental that Jones chose the same subject, viewed from a few metres away, for one of his rare studio drawings from this time (cat. no. 139). The slight difference of viewpoint means that Jones's work has a less conventional composition, in which the rock face and the dark recess of the 'grotto' are more prominent.

The status of this and cat. no. 99 as finished studio watercolours is underlined by the survival of their contemporary mounts. These are an integral part of the work and suggest that the watercolours were commissioned to be stored in portfolios rather than framed for display. (GS)

99

WILLIAM PARS (1742–1782)

The Bay of Naples from Capodimonte c.1781

Pencil, watercolour, pen and ink on laid paper on original mount, 42 × 57.6 (16½ × 22⅝)

Ins.: 'A VIEW FROM A VINEYARD, BETWEEN THE CAPO DI MONTE AND THE ANCIENT AQUEDUCTS.' on the mount
Prov.: J. Leslie Wright; bequeathed, 1953
Exh.: Birmingham, 1938, no. 46; London, 1949, no. 55; Birmingham, 1980, no. 49; Tokyo, 1991, no. 23

Birmingham Museums and Art Gallery, J. Leslie Wright Collection (1953P293)

Cardiff and Manchester only

Before moving in with Jones in Naples in 1781, Pars took lodgings in Capodimonte, and he therefore had ample opportunities to study the views over the city and bay that unfolded from its elevated position. However, it may be that Jones introduced him to this view, since, although the watercolour does not take in the full sweep shown in *The Bay of Naples* (cat. no. 106), it features many of the same elements. The differences are less to do with topography than with propriety, however. For whilst Jones felt compelled, in his large-scale oil painting, to stick to a traditional Claudian composition, with framing elements and a dark foreground, Pars dispensed with such conventions. A decrepit and unpicturesque tree is placed at the centre of a more detailed foreground than Jones generally employed. (GS)

100

JOHN 'WARWICK' SMITH (1749–1831)

The Villa Medici, Rome c.1779

Pencil, watercolour, pen and ink on laid paper on original mount, 33.5 × 52.8 (13⅛ × 20¾)

Ins.: 'The Villa Medici in Rome' on the mount; 'Villa Medici at Rome' on the verso of the mount
Prov.: The Earl of Warwick, acquired from the artist 1781; by descent; Sotheby's, June 1936; purchased
Exh.: London, 1981 (no cat.); Cleveland, 1991, no. 26; Paris, 2001, no. 28

British Museum, London (1936-7-4-29)

Cardiff and Manchester only

Jones records that his friend Smith had returned from Naples in July 1779 and had taken '*Apartments* at the *Monaco* . . . under the hill of the Trinida de Monti'. At the 'top of this house', he continued, 'was a delightful Loggia or Open Gallery where we spent many agreeable Evenings' (*Memoirs*, p. 90), and this view of the Villa Medici was presumably painted from this vantage point. Jones may have been inspired by Smith's example to develop this type of composition in Naples two years later when he, too, made a prominent feature of walls and roof-tops in the foreground. The complex web of relations between British artists in Rome and Naples means that such conclusions have to be treated with caution, especially as this watercolour is undated. It is safer to assume that interest in the elevated city view was shared, even if Jones explored it more fully. (GS)

101

JOHN 'WARWICK' SMITH (1749–1831)

Study of Part of the Interior of the Colosseum, Rome c.1780

Pencil, watercolour on laid paper on original mount, 39 × 53.3 (15⅜ × 21)

Ins.: 'in the Colloseo' on the mount; 'In the Collosseum / Rome / 176' verso
Prov.: The Earl of Warwick, acquired from the artist 1781; by descent; Sotheby's, June 1936; purchased
Exh.: London, 1981 (no cat.); London, 1985, no. 54; London, 1993a, no. 265

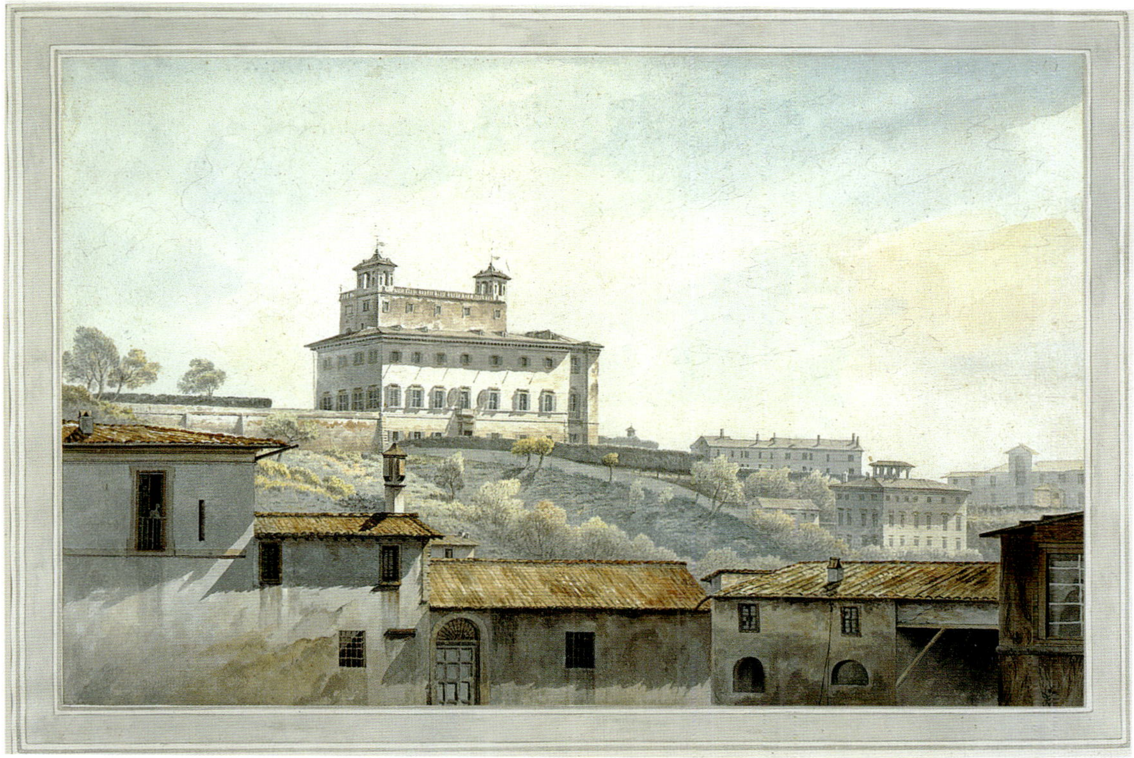

100

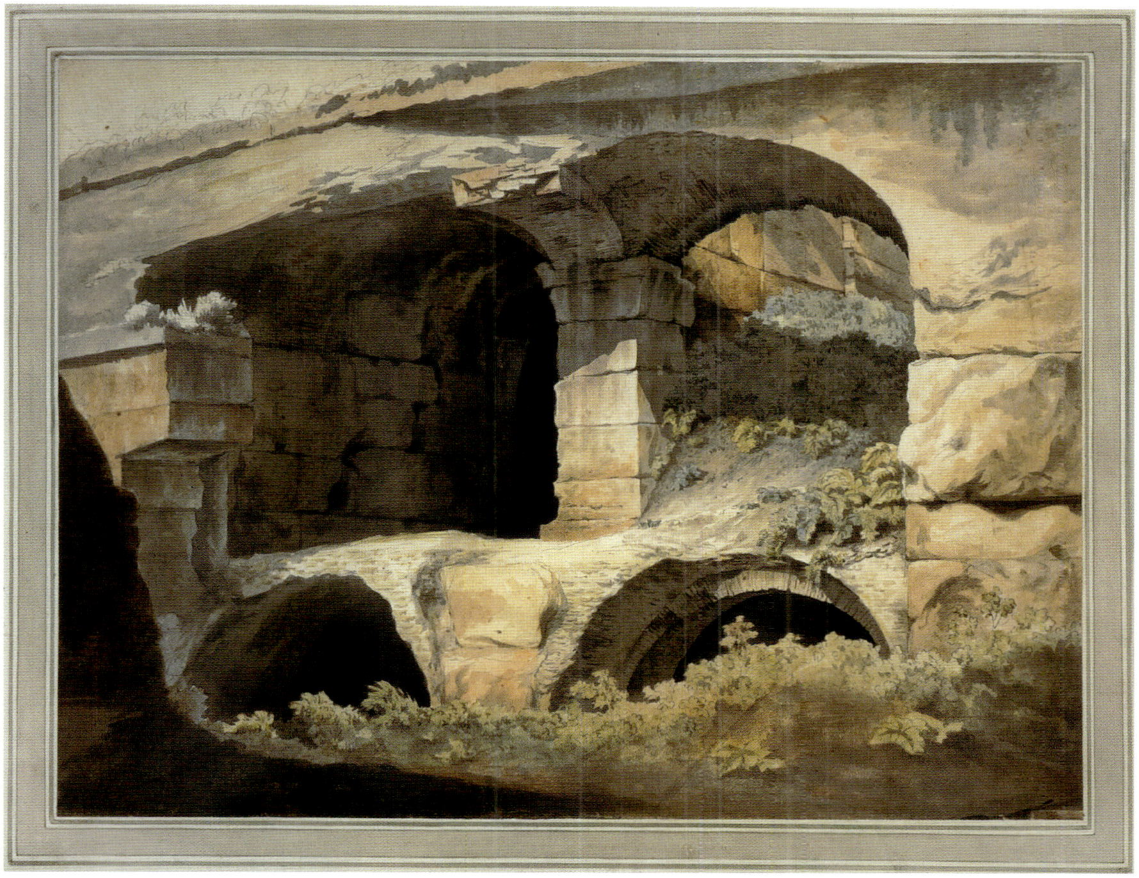

101

102

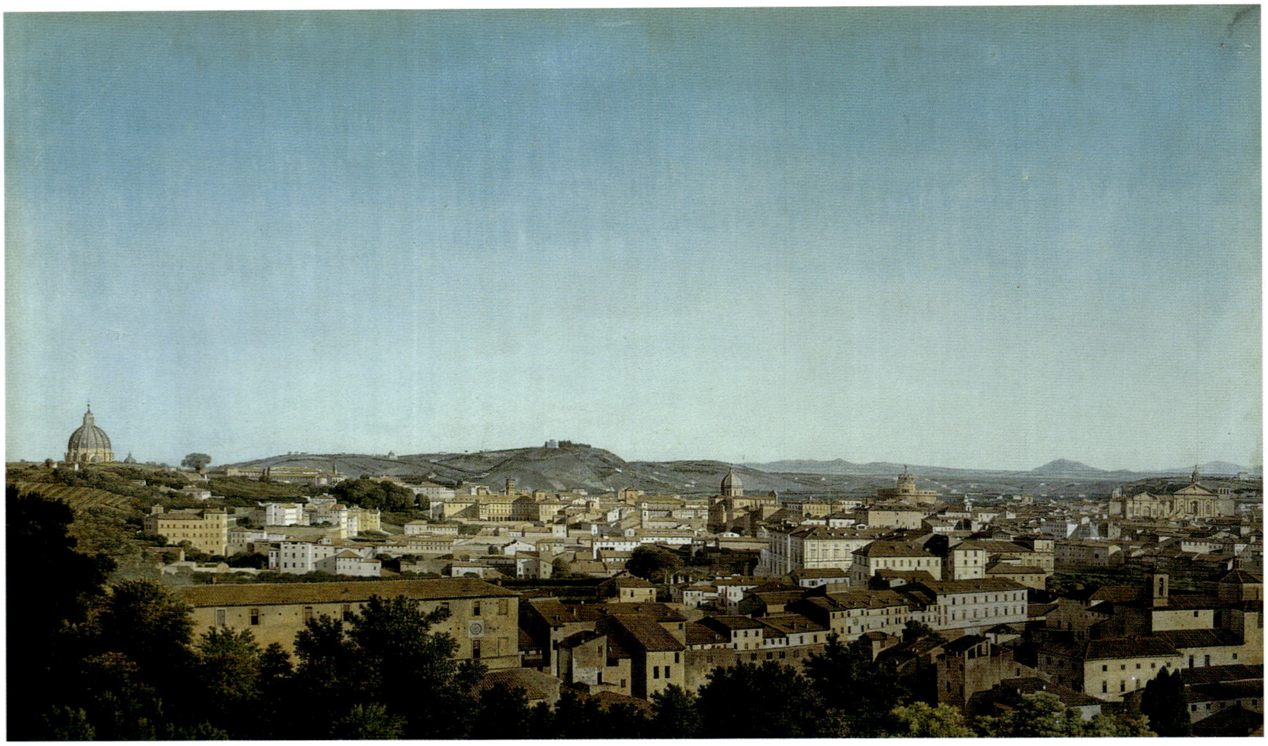

British Museum, London (1936-7-4-13)

Cardiff and Manchester only

This work is one of a series of large-scale colour sketches that Smith made of the Colosseum. Features such as the large blocks of colour and the way that pencil marks show through less worked areas suggest that he coloured it on the spot. The work is not dated, but the number on the back – towards the end of the sequence of Italian drawings – indicates that it was made late in his stay, which lasted from 1776 to 1781. In which case, it was probably produced after Jones's views of the Colosseum (cat. nos 59 and 60) and it is unlikely that the artists worked together. The two artists none the less shared an interest in the range of dark voids found in the ruins and they both produced close-up views which abandoned conventional compositional formulae. (GS)

102

GIOVANNI BATTISTA LUSIERI (*c*.1755–1821)

View of Rome, from the Janiculum *c*.1775–82

Watercolour on paper, 54.5 × 93.5 (21½ × 36¾)

Prov.: Possibly purchased by the 3rd Earl Somers, mid-nineteenth century, then by descent
Exh.: Manchester, 1988, no. 15, as 'Rome from the Aventine'

Private collection

Cardiff and Manchester only

Jones met Lusieri in June 1782, when he referred admiringly to his 'tinted Drawings' which are noted 'for their Correctness and strict attention to Nature' (*Memoirs*, p. 112). Finding a kindred spirit, the artists spent time together 'making Studies from Nature' (ibid., p. 113). The fact that they did not meet until this date effectively rules out the possibility that Lusieri influenced Jones's approach, even though he was the only foreign landscape artist that impressed Jones and with whom he worked. Lusieri may have depicted the panoramic sweep of Rome seen from a high viewpoint with a foreground dominated by the walls of humble buildings, but Jones had arrived at the same approach independently.

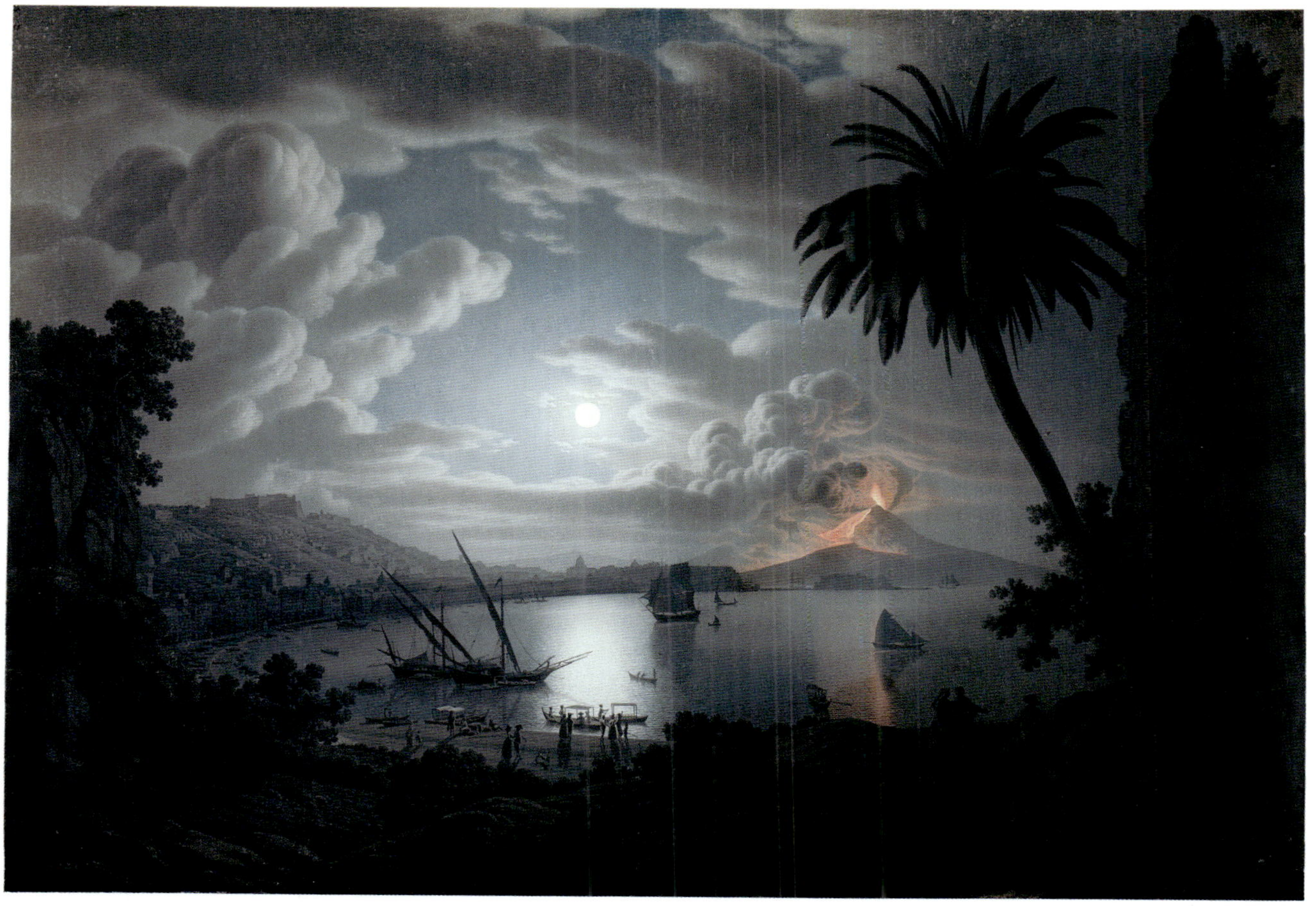

103

Lusieri's view from the Janiculum Hill near to S. Pietro in Montorio to the south of St Peter's shows the dome of that church appearing above the hill to the left, with Castel S. Angelo in the centre right and Monte Mario in the distance. (GS)

103

GIOVANNI BATTISTA LUSIERI (*c.*1755–1821)

Vesuvius from Posillipo by Night, during the Eruption of 1787 1797

Watercolour, pen and ink on paper, 64.2 × 94.3 (25¼ × 37⅛)

Ins.: 'Veduta di Napoli con l'Eruzzione del Vesuvio presa da Posilipo dipinta da Gio: Battista Lusieri 1797. / L'eruzzione e del 1787' on verso
Prov.: Sir William Hamilton?; Sir Richard Colt Hoare?; Christie's, 5 July 1983, no. 133
Exh.: Manchester, 1988, no. 93; London, 1996, no. 46
Lit.: Williams, 1982, p. 492

Private collection

Cardiff and Manchester only

Despite arriving in Naples in 1778 when Vesuvius was active and seeing the 'grand & wonderful Effect' of the mountain lighting up the night sky, Jones did not try to capture such effects, even though he made various ascents of the volcano (*Memoirs*, pp. 78–9). In contrast, this highly attractive and technically competent piece illustrates why Lusieri was so successful with grand-tour patrons, who readily appreciated the glorious evocation of moonlight and the tumultuous effect of a night-time eruption. Lusieri's greater commercial acumen meant that he was actually able to bring his older colleague to the attention of collectors in Naples, allowing Jones to 'emerge a little from that Cloud of Obscurity' under which he felt he 'had been so long enveloped' (ibid., p. 113). Just before leaving Naples, Jones visited Torre Annunziata to say farewell to Lusieri. It is telling that the larger oil on paper (cat. no. 122) that resulted lacks the drama that brought his friend remunerative commissions. (GS)

FOLLOWING PAGES Detail of cat. no. 125.

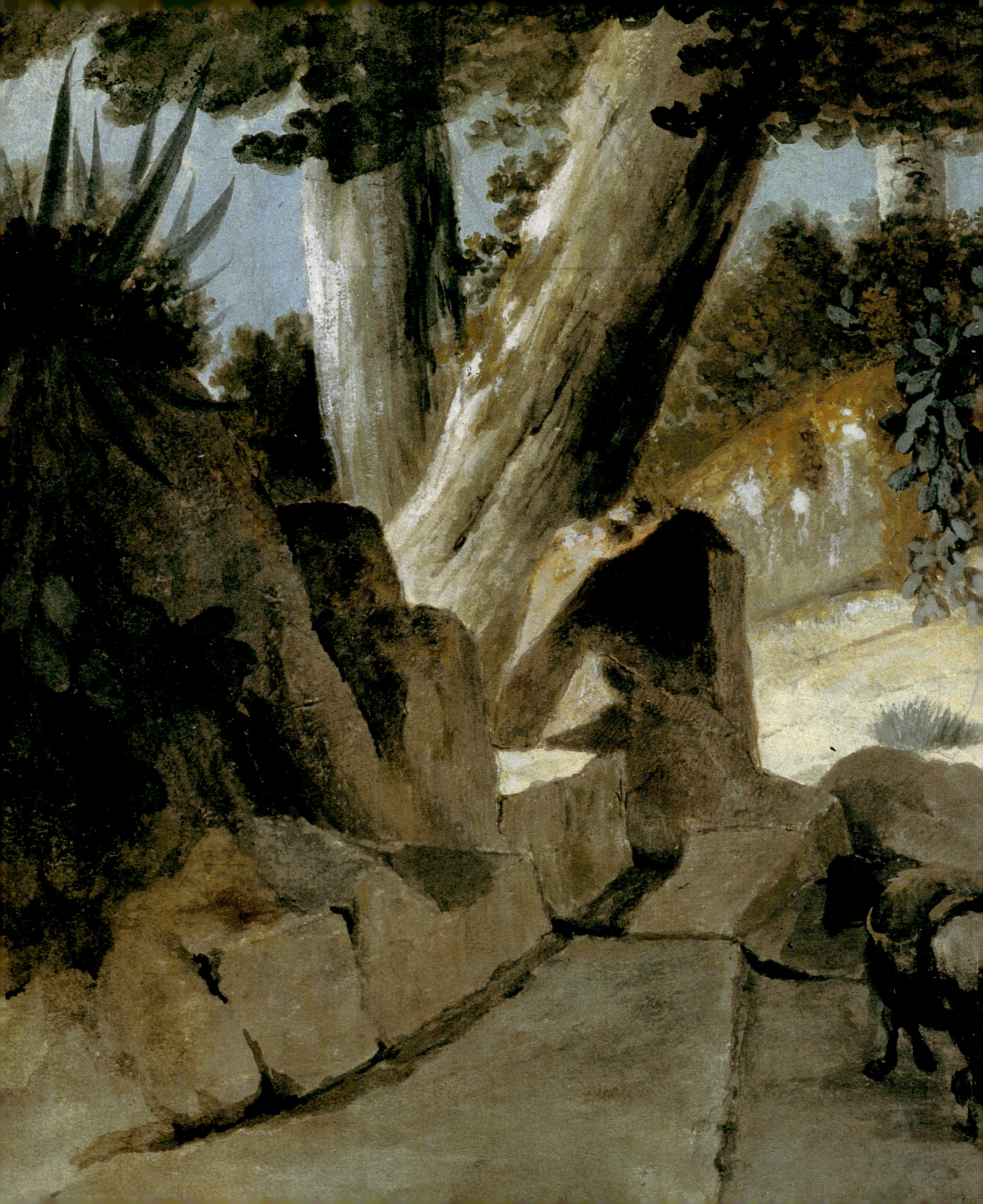

JONES IN ITALY II:
NAPLES AND ITS ENVIRONS

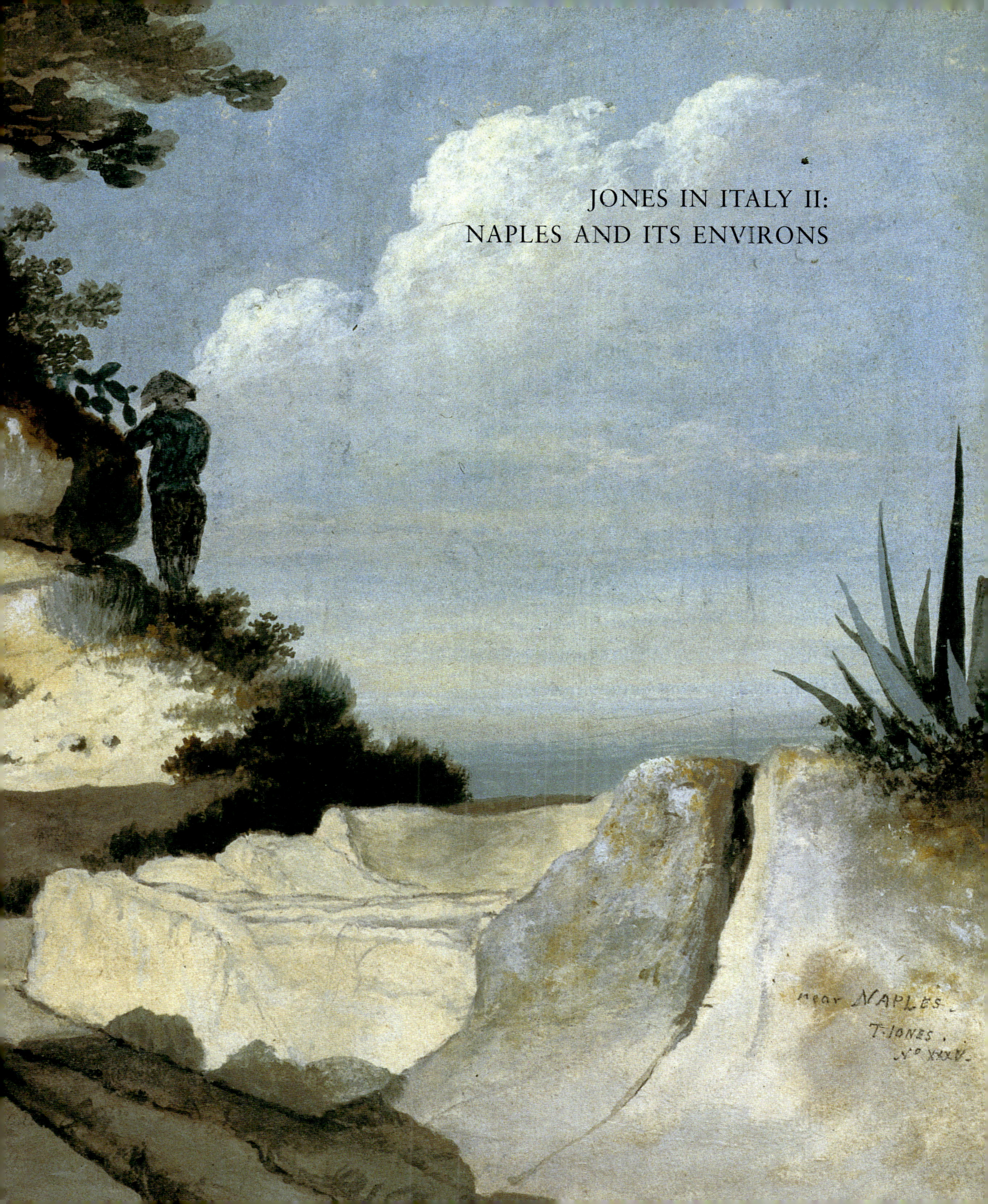

104

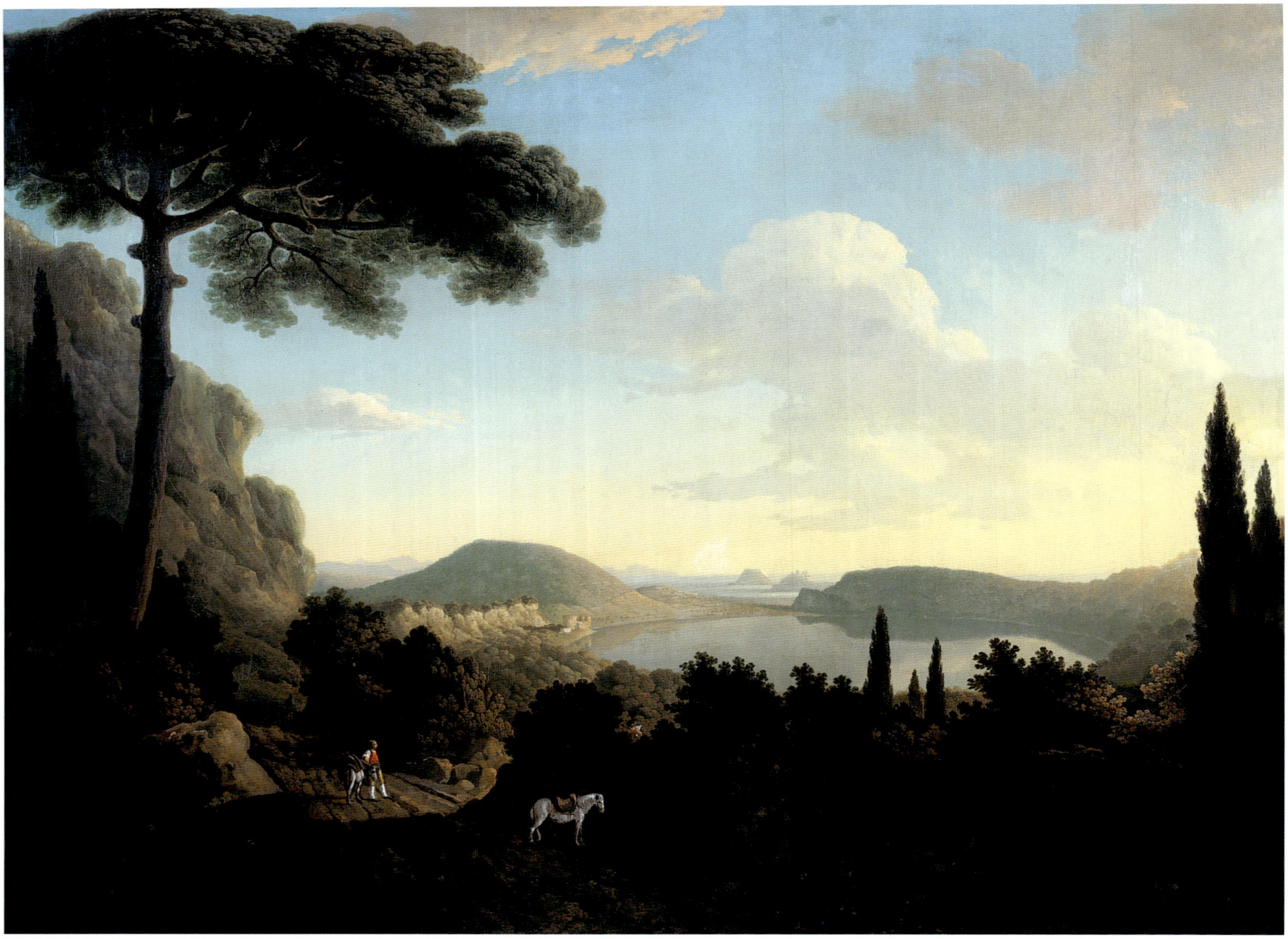

104

THOMAS JONES (1742–1803)

View of Lake Avernus *c.*1779

Oil on canvas, 121 × 170 (47½ × 67)

Prov.: Commissioned by Philip Yorke, later 3rd Earl of Hardwicke, then by descent; Sotheby's, 9 April 1997, no. 55

Private collection

Cardiff and Manchester only

Jones visited Avernus on 14 November 1778 on his first trip to Naples, making 'a drawing of the Lake looking toward Caprea' (*Memoirs*, p. 81). The outstanding beauty of Lake Avernus, one of the Phlegraean lakes, attracted many artists, especially as the volcanic area between Naples and Cuma was particularly rich in classical associations. This large oil, which includes a horse in the foreground, with an artist sketching, shows the view south to Capo Miseno. It is listed as 'A View of the Lake of Avernus on a Cloth 7 palms 5 Inches by 5P.4I. for D'o (Mr Yorke) 50.0.0' in a list of commissioned paintings Jones drew up in April 1779 (ibid., p. 88). Philip Yorke (1757–1834), later 3rd Earl of Hardwicke, was an important patron. The purchase did not go smoothly, however. Jones had a disagreement with James Byres and his agent Norton over the commission they claimed. Jones felt Byres had played no part in securing Yorke's patronage and his refusal to pay harmed his standing with these important middlemen in the Roman art world. (ABS)

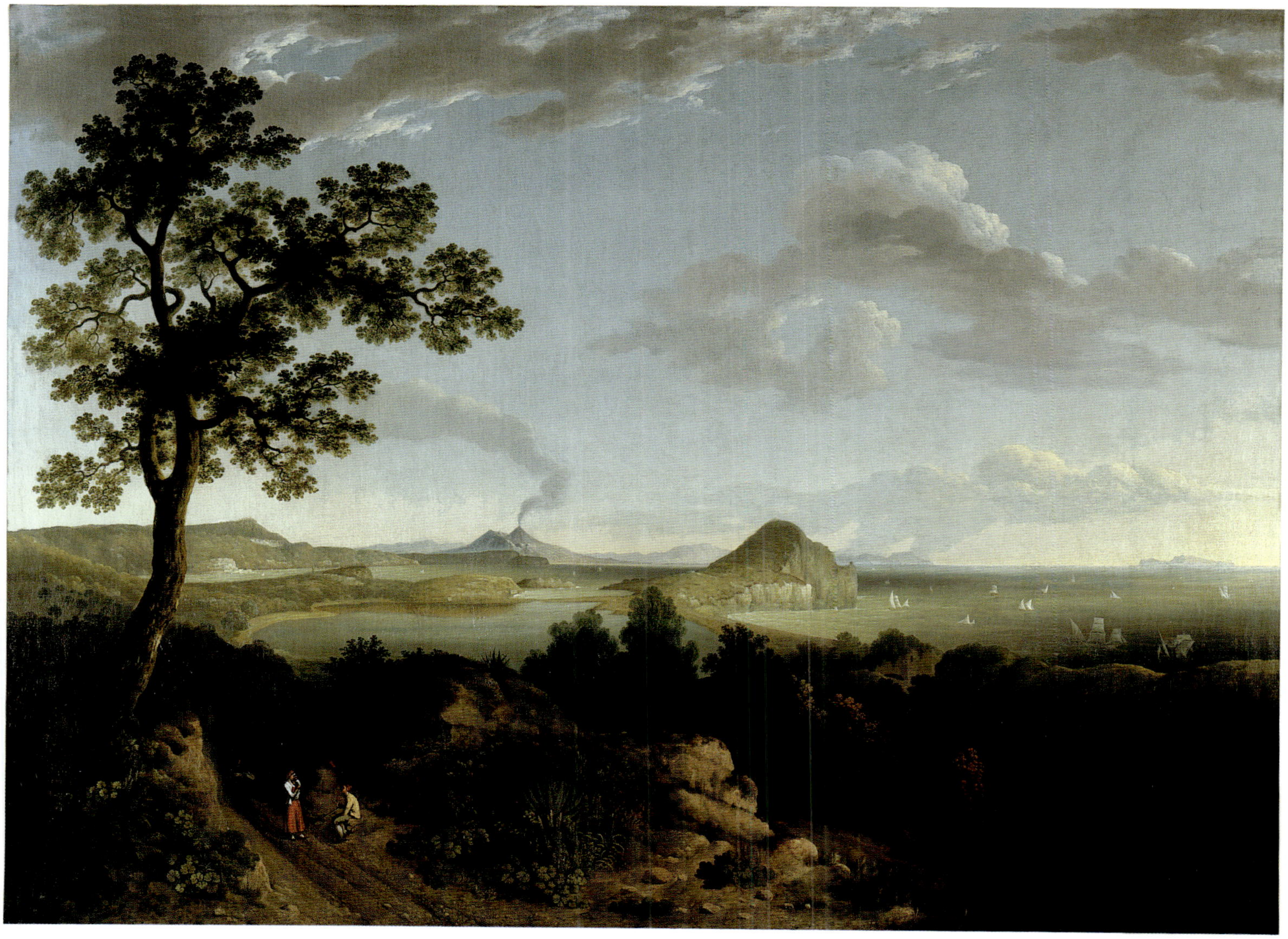

105

105

THOMAS JONES (1742–1803)

The Bay of Baia near Naples 1780

Oil on canvas, 139.7 × 198.1 (55 × 78)

Ins.: 'THO JONES / ROMA / MDCCLXXX' l.l.
Prov.: Possibly purchased by the 3rd Earl Somers, mid-nineteenth century, then by descent

Private collection

Cardiff and Manchester only

This painting has until recently been misattributed to Jakob Philipp Hackert, but Jones signed and dated it, albeit indisinctly, indicating that it was produced in Rome after his first trip to Naples. The view across the Bay of Baia, with Vesuvius in the distance and Pozzuoli to the left, also includes Capo Miseno and the Gulf of Gaeta to the right. A smaller version of the composition, also dated 1780 (fig. 32), shows differences in the figures, the form of the tree to the left and the shipping. Jones noted in 1779 that he was working on three paintings of Baia, including a view with 'M. Vesuvius & ye Islands &c . . . for the Bishop of Derry' (*Memoirs*, p. 87). The smaller work (fig. 32) may have been ordered by a Mr Burdon as it tallies with Jones's measurement of '5 Palms by 3', whilst this painting could be the larger version commissioned by Philip Yorke for £70 (ibid., p. 88). Unfortunately, it is not possible

106

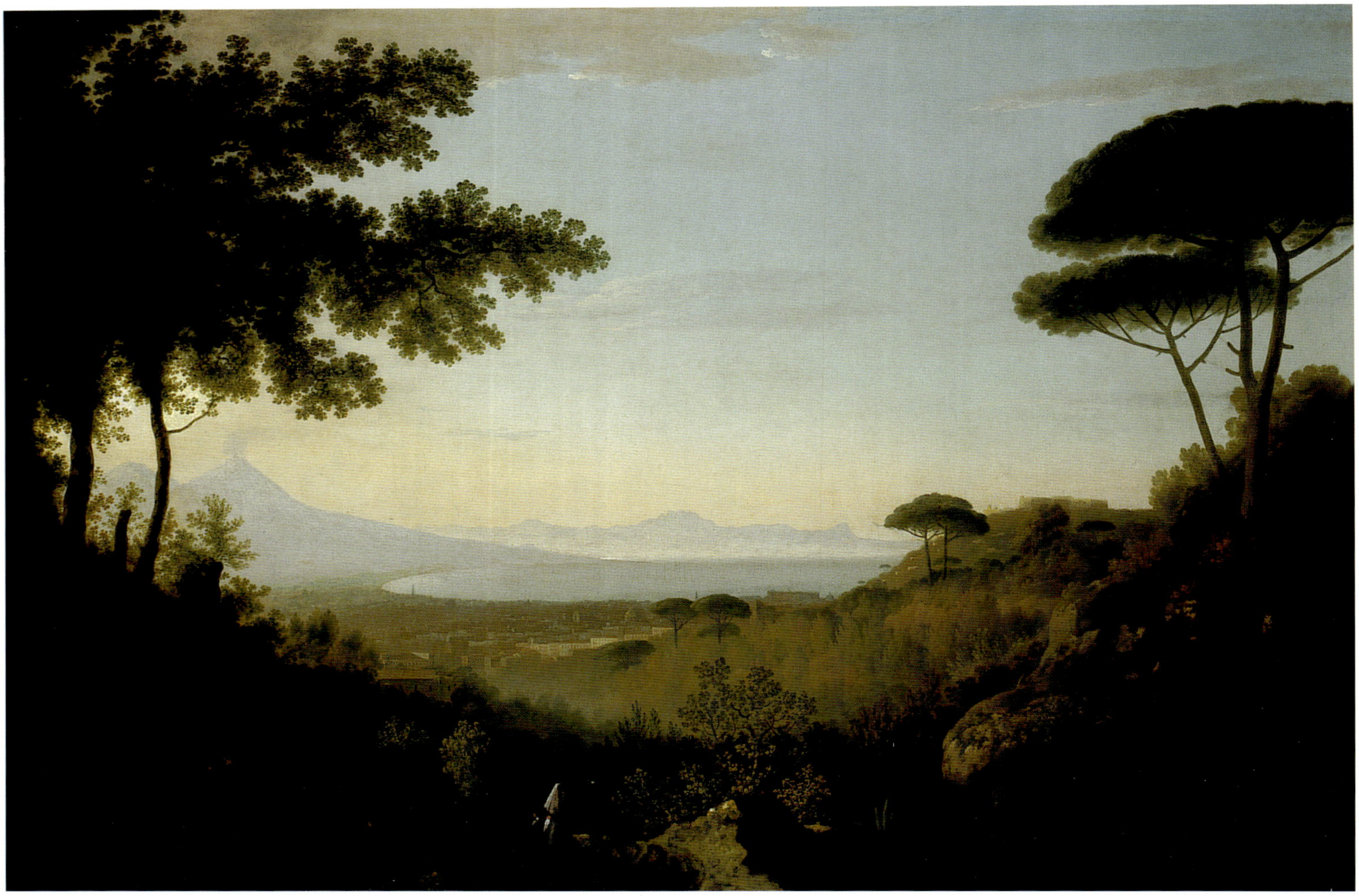

to confirm this as the painting's early provenance is unknown. None the less, this is clearly one of Jones's most important early Italian compositions and it is a significant and exciting addition to his oeuvre. (GS)

106

THOMAS JONES (1742–1803)

The Bay of Naples 1782

Oil on canvas, 103.2 × 156.8 ($40\frac{5}{8} \times 61\frac{3}{4}$)

Ins.: 'THO. JONES Napoli MDCCLXXXII' l.l.
Prov.: Thomas Thomas, then by descent to Jane Evan-Thomas; presented 1952
Exh.: Royal Academy, 1784, no. 232?, as 'Morning View of Naples'; London, 1970, no. 44; Manchester, 1988, no. 91; Seville, 1992; London, 1997a, no. 99
Lit.: Edwards, 1968, pp. 10–14; Causa, 1981, repr; Gowing, 1985, p. 56

National Museums & Galleries of Wales (NMW A 87)

Jones's large view of the Bay of Naples is taken from near Capodimonte, a popular vantage point favoured by artists. It shows the east end of the city, the great curve of the bay itself, with Vesuvius to the left and the Sorrentine peninsula faintly visible on the horizon. The composition, with its ubiquitous pine trees and luminous quality, is indebted both to Claude and Richard Wilson, though it has a more decorative quality, with particular attention paid to the foreground vegetation. There has been confusion about the inscribed date on this work and it has been suggested that it was painted in 1778 on Jones's first visit to Naples. Recent surface cleaning has confirmed the date as 1782, however. The present work and another adjacent view (cat. no. 107) remained in the artist's hands and it is likely that this picture is one of the paintings

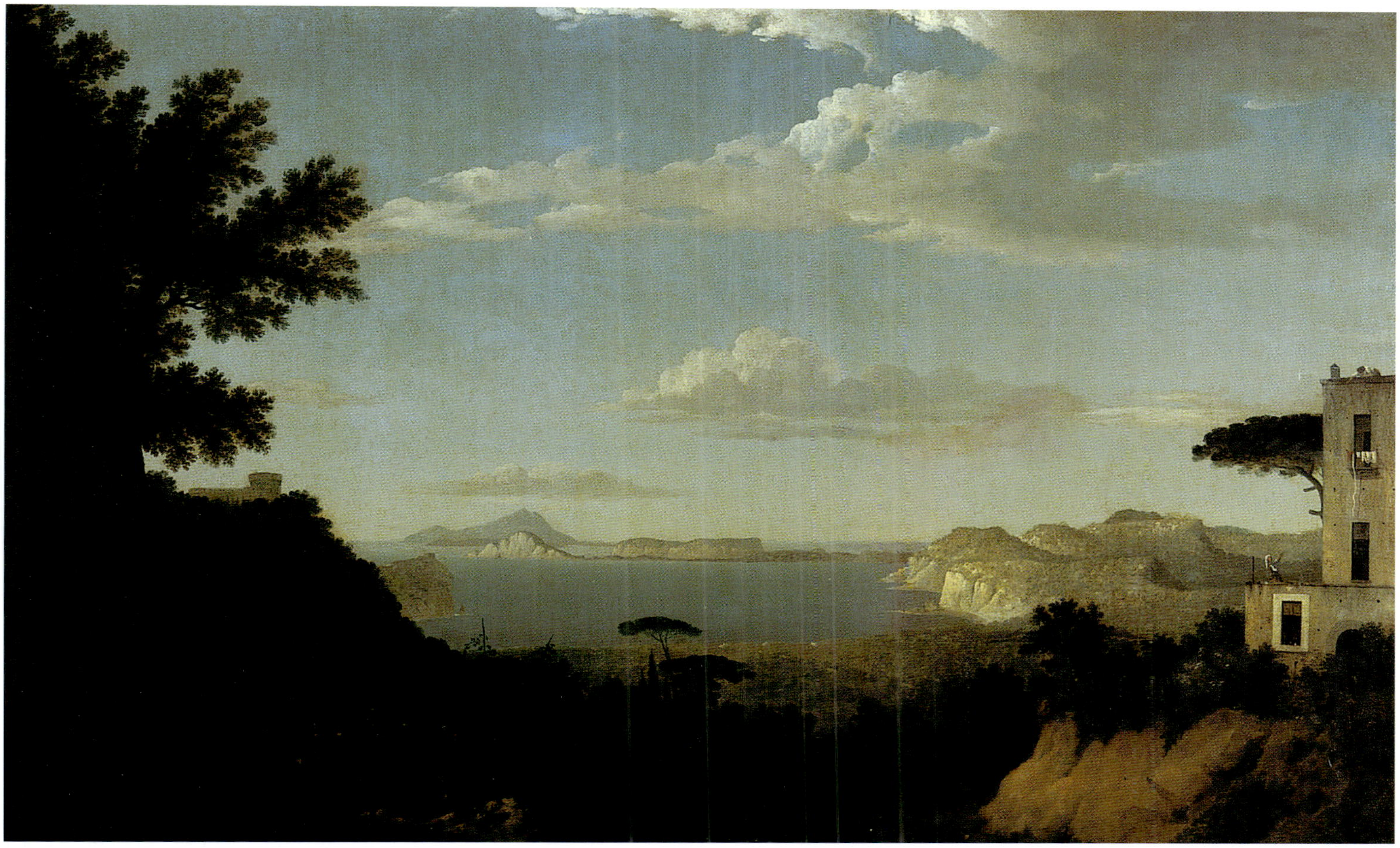

107

he referred to in September 1781, stating that 'it was about this time I began those two large Views of Naples which I have still by me' (*Memoirs*, p. 107) (see p. 72). (ABS)

107

THOMAS JONES (1742–1803)

The Bay of Naples 1786

Oil on canvas, 90 × 151 (35½ × 59½)

Ins.: 'THO. JON[ES] 1786' l.r.
Prov.: Thomas Thomas, then by descent
Exh.: London, 1970, no. 72
Lit.: Gowing, 1985, p. 54, pl. 48–9

Private collection (photographed before conservation)

Cardiff and Manchester only

This view, although traditionally titled *The Bay of Naples*, in fact shows a view from the Bay of Pozzuoli looking towards the island of Ischia with Capo Miseno to the right. Recent surface cleaning has revealed a signature and the date '1786' in the right lower corner, confirming that it was painted after Jones's return to Britain. Jones has also introduced the corner of a building to the right, which is reminiscent of the houses in his oil sketches of Naples. This is the only surviving example of him including the more intimate observations of architecture in his larger compositions on canvas. The washing hanging from the upper balcony includes a similar long white strip of material to that shown in *A Wall in Naples* (cat. no. 114). Despite this, Wilson's influence is still evident in the painting of the tree and the castle on the left of the composition. The domestic figures in the picture are unusually animated for Jones. A male figure on the roof gestures to a woman below, while an old man with a beard and red hat is just visible in the lower window. The fall of the shadows indicates that this is a mid-morning view (ABS)

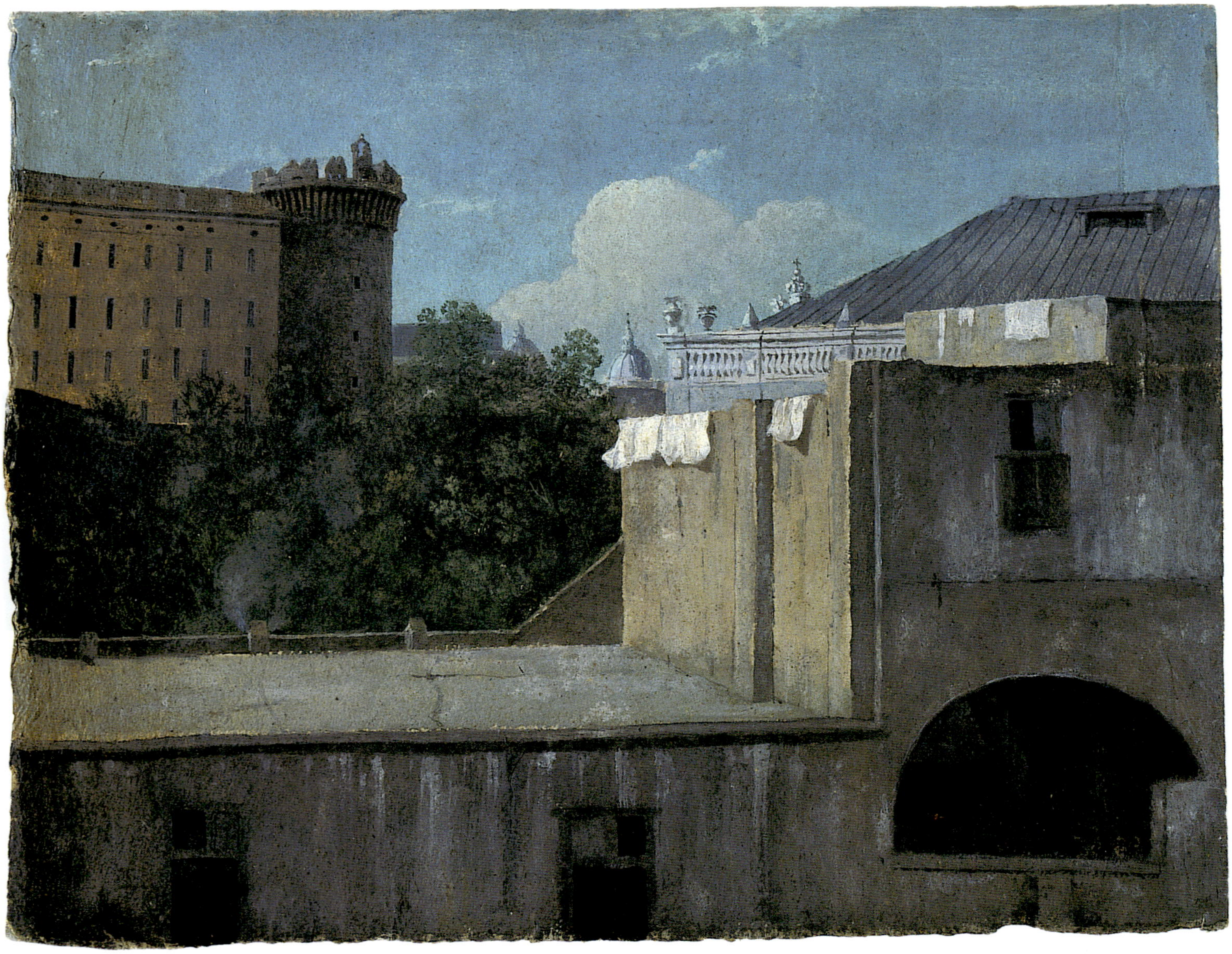

108

Thomas Jones (1742–1803)

Buildings in Naples, with the North-East Side of the Castel Nuovo 1782

Oil on Italian-made 'Dutch' laid writing paper*, 22.2 × 29.1 (8⅝ × 11¼)

Ins.: 'T. J. Naples, Jan 7 [9?] 1782' verso
Prov.: Captain John Dale, then by descent; Christie's, 2 July 1954, no. 212; purchased
Exh.: Naples, 1962, no. 52; London, 1970, no. 64; Aberystwyth, 1971, no. 26; Naples, 1979, no. 195; Detroit, 1981, no. 71; Manchester, 1988, no. 99; Paris, 2001, no. 32
Lit.: Edwards, 1968, p. 9; Blunt, 1973, pp. 498–500; Gowing, 1985, p. 48, pl. 41; Wollheim, 1987, p. 342; Wollheim, 1988; Ottani Cavina, 1994, p. 105; Smith, 1983, p. 145; De Seta, 1999, fig. 4; Egerton, 1999, pp. 128–31; Egerton, 2000, p. 189

National Museums & Galleries of Wales (NMW A 90)

This is the first of the Neapolitan studies with which, working on the roof terrace of his lodgings opposite the Dogana del Sale in early 1782, Jones made his most distinctive and deeply original

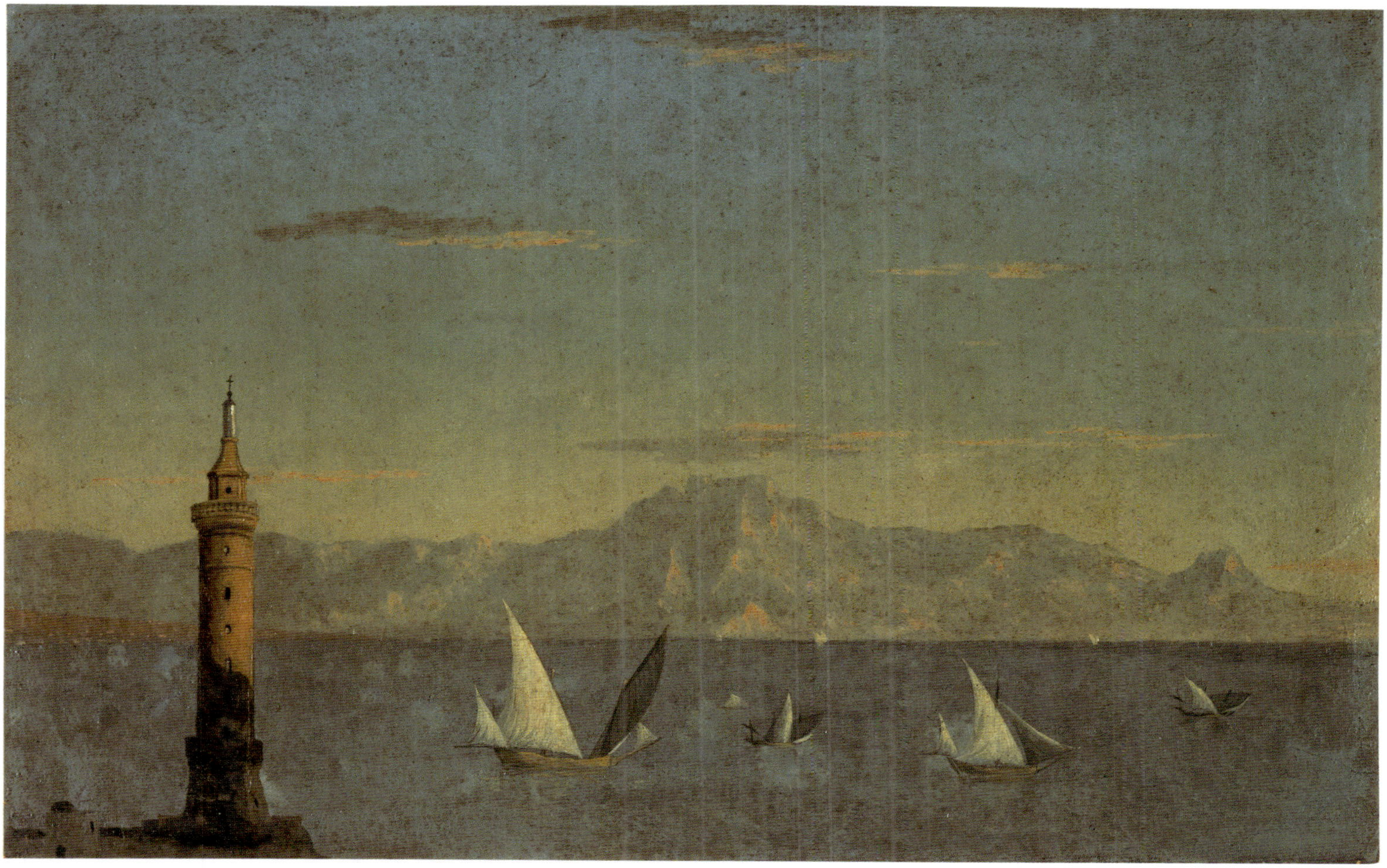

109

contribution to the oil sketch tradition. To the left is the north-east flank of the Castel Nuovo; to the right is the elegant, balustraded roofline of the Palazzo Reale. The trees of the Largo del Castello stand between them, and the domes of two churches and the lantern of a third animate the horizon. Examination with infra-red light has revealed the extensive pencil underdrawing with which Jones sketched in the principal architectural forms. (CR)

109

THOMAS JONES (1742–1803)

The Bay of Naples and the Mole Lighthouse

1782

Oil on Italian writing paper*, 24.3 × 39.6 ($9\frac{5}{8}$ × $15\frac{5}{8}$)

Ins.: 'T J / Naples – March 1782' verso
Prov.: Captain John Dale, then by descent; Christie's, 2 July 1954, no. 212; Colnaghi's; Paul Oppé; Armide Oppé; purchased 1996
Exh.: London, 1958, no. 294; Naples, 1962, no. 51; London, 1970, no. 59; Paris, 1972, no. 151; Manchester, 1988, no. 110; London, 1990, p. 63, p. 126; London, 1997, no. 45
Lit.: Spinosa, 1987, p. 161; Spinosa and Di Mauro, 1989, p. 198

Tate. Purchased as part of the Oppé Collection with assistance from the National Lottery through the Heritage Lottery Fund 1996 (T08246)

Jones lived near the Mole, on the Neapolitan waterfront, from 1780 to 1782. The lighthouse there, now destroyed, was a relatively recent addition to the skyline of Naples when Jones painted it in March 1782. It also figures prominently in views of the city made by many of Jones's contemporaries. Here, the artist looks south-east across the Bay of Naples, with Mount Faito and the hills of the Sorrentine peninsula in the distance. In this serene painting, he balances the vertical tower with the horizontal sweep of the placid water, the simple scene animated by the curving sails of fishing boats. (CR)

110

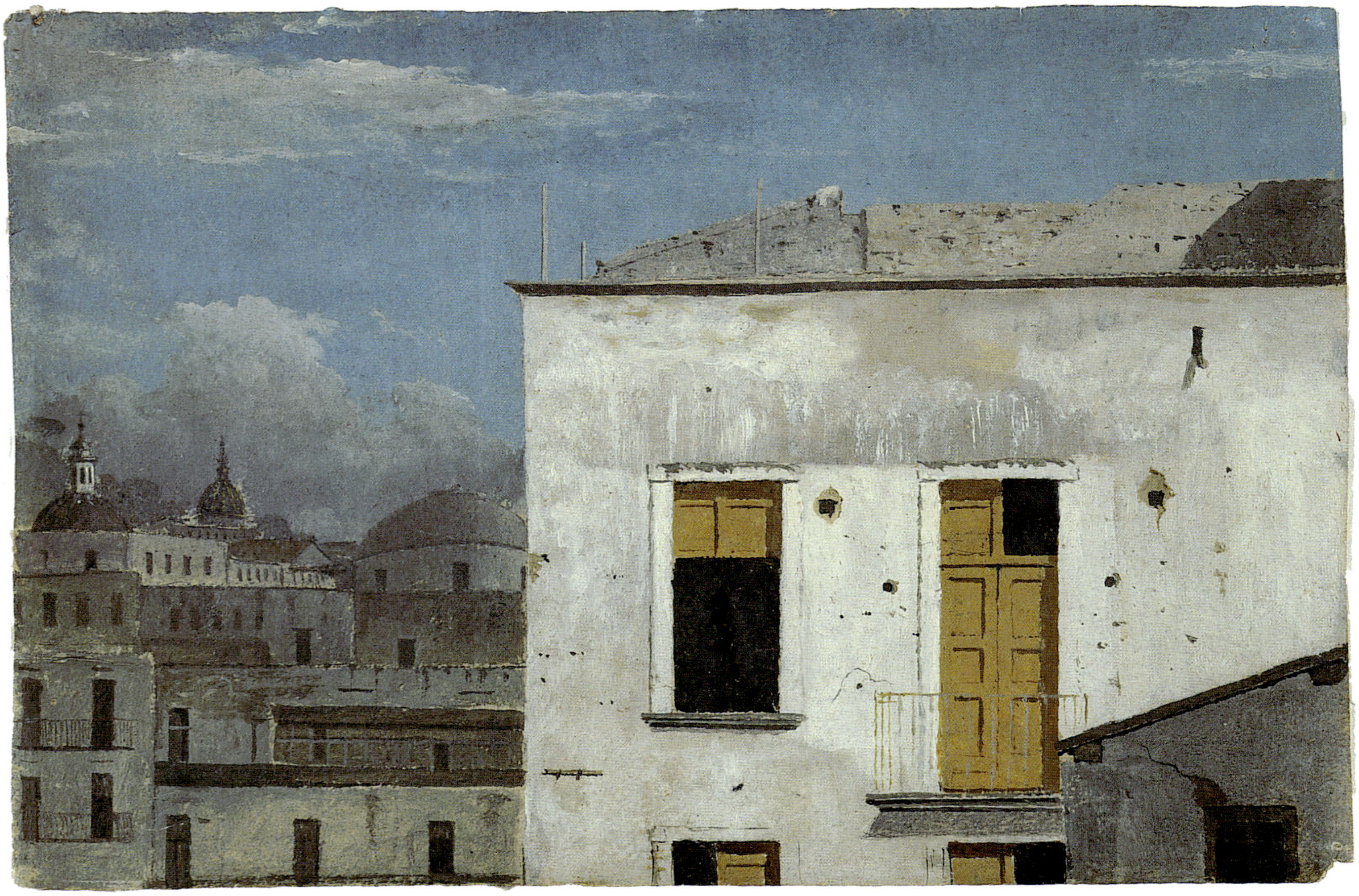

110

Thomas Jones (1742–1803)

Buildings in Naples 1782

Oil on Italian-made 'Dutch' writing paper*, 14.2 × 21.6 (5⅝ × 8⁹⁄₁₆)

Ins.: 'Thos Jones'; 'Naples April 1782' verso
Prov.: Captain John Dale, then by descent; Christie's, 2 July 1954, no. 212; purchased 1954
Exh.: Naples, 1962, no. 53; London, 1970, no. 61; Aberystwyth, 1971, no. 25; Paris, 1972, no. 150; Manchester, 1973a, no. 13; Munich, 1979, no. 111; Detroit, 1981, no. 72a; Japan, 1986, no. 11; Manchester, 1988, no. 101; Washington, 1996, no. 9
Lit.: Edwards, 1968, p. 9; Blunt, 1973, p. 500; Herrmann, 1974, p. 68; Smith, 1983, p. 145; Gowing, 1985, p. 44, pl. 38; Wollheim, 1987, p. 347; Wollheim, 1988; Galassi, 1991, p. 32; Egerton, 2000, p. 189; Lord, 2000, fig. 236

National Museums & Galleries of Wales (NMW A 89)

Like *Rooftops in Naples* (cat. no. 111), this sketch shows the humble house that lay directly opposite the roof terrace of Jones's quarters opposite the Dogana del Sale near the Castel Nuovo. The wall of the house, its windows partially shuttered, lies parallel to the picture plane. Its pitted surface, bathed in sunlight, is minutely detailed. In contrast, a view of the city opens out at the left and the domes of three churches are silhouetted against the sky. Here, the colours are more muted and the forms are not as sharply distinguished. In this, Jones was following, on a small scale, a convention of aerial perspective long observed by painters of cityscapes and panoramic views. (CR)

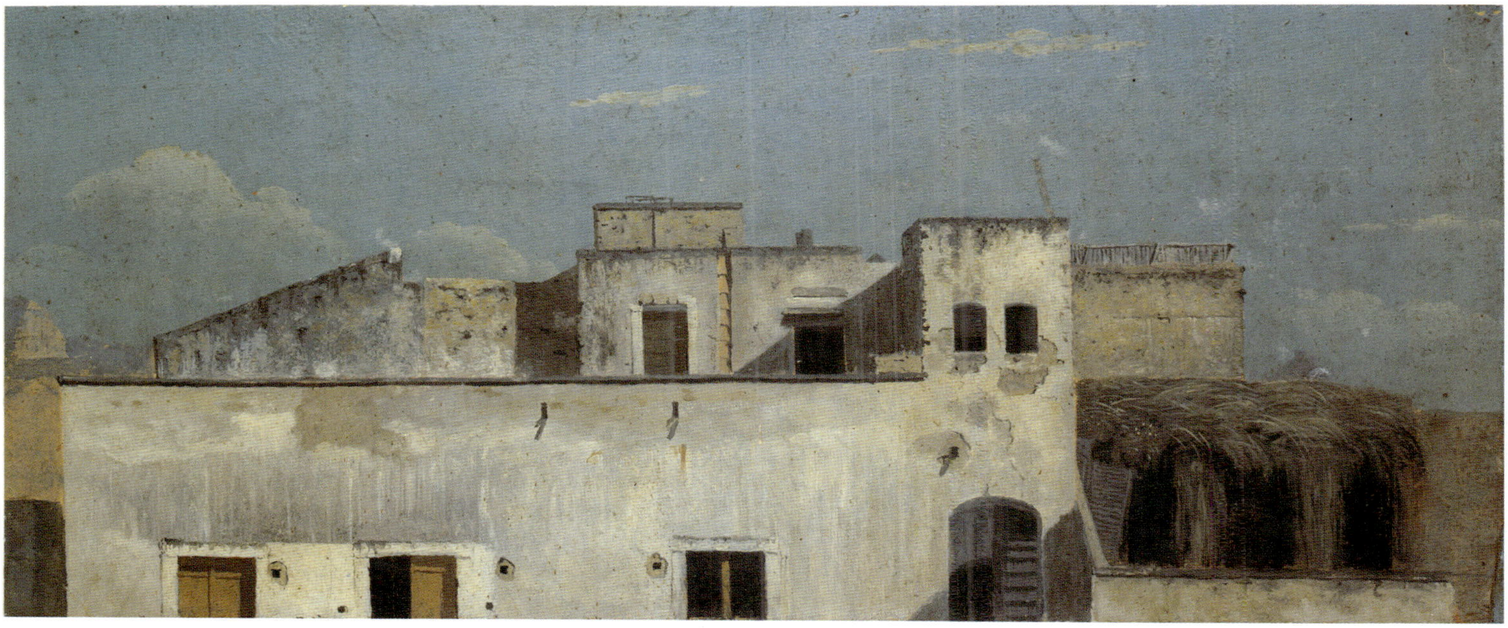

111

111

Thomas Jones (1742–1803)

Rooftops in Naples 1782

Oil on paper on laid paper, 14.3 × 35 (5¾ × 13¾)

Ins.: 'T. J. / Naples Aprile 1782' t.c. verso
Prov.: Captain John Dale, then by descent; Christie's, 2 July 1954, no. 213; Colnaghi's; purchased 1954
Exh.: Naples, 1962, no. 54; Detroit, 1968, no. 72; Norwich, 1969, no. 27; London, 1970, no. 60; Baltimore, 1979, no. 43; Detroit, 1981, no. 82b; Stockholm, 1982, no. 186; Oxford, 1983, no. 37; Manchester, 1988, no. 100; London, 1990, p. 63, p. 126; Washington, 1996, no. 8; Genoa, 2001, no. viii.43
Lit.: Herrmann, 1974, p. 68; Gowing, 1985, p. 44, pl. 37; Brown, 1982, no. 869; Wollheim, 1987, p. 344, pl. 347; Wollheim, 1988; Galassi, 1991, p. 32; Angelini, 1993, p. 19

Ashmolean Museum, Oxford (WA1954.81)

In May 1780, Jones rented rooms in Naples near the Castel Nuovo and opposite the Dogana del Sale, or salt customs house. It included a *lastricia* or roof terrace, from which, two years later as his lease was about to expire, he painted oil sketches of the surrounding flat-roofed vernacular buildings, including this sheet and cat. nos 108 and 110. Characteristically, the principal motif is a masonry wall occupying a surface parallel to the picture plane. The streaked, chipped and pitted surface of the wall dominates the composition, while block-like forms beyond echo it. (CR)

112

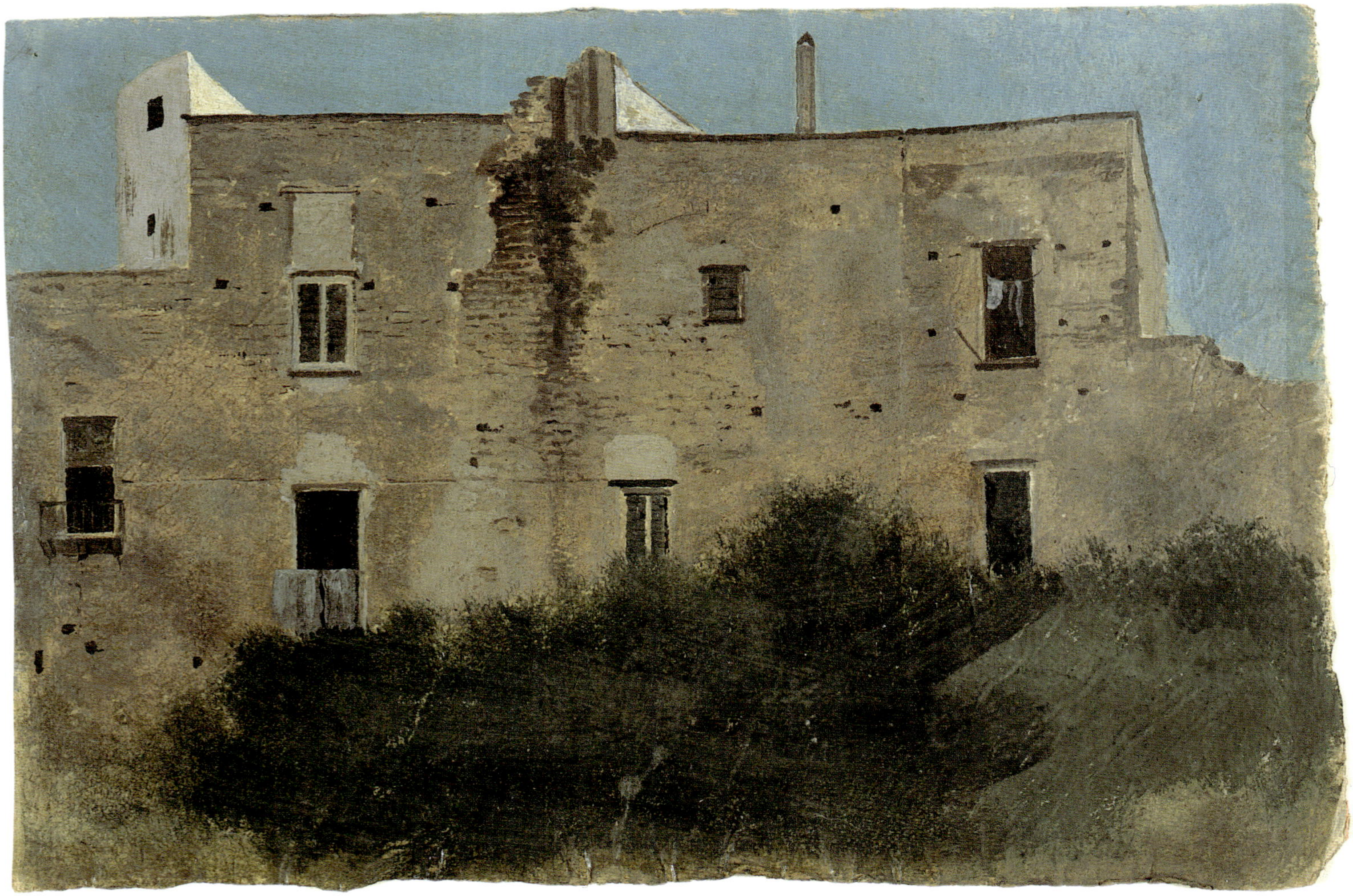

112

Thomas Jones (1742–1803)

Houses at Naples 1782

Oil on paper, 14.4 × 22 (5½ × 8⅝) (irreg.)

Ins.: 'TJ / Naples May 1782' t.r. verso
Prov.: Captain John Dale, then by descent; Christie's, 2 July 1954, no. 213; Colnaghi's; purchased by Paul Oppé, 1954; presented to Aydua Scott-Elliot; bequeathed 1999
Exh.: Manchester, 1988, no. 103

The Whitworth Art Gallery, The University of Manchester (0.1999.1)

This humble domestic building – drying laundry visible in an upper window – may have been one that Jones saw from the ground-floor studio he occupied for two weeks from 9 May 1782 in a convent in the Neapolitan suburb of Chiaja (*Memoirs*, p. 111). As in other oil sketches made there (see cat. no. 113), the point of view is from below, looking upwards, the object of study a masonry wall pitted and worn by time and the elements. Jones's studio was adjacent to a small garden. Here, he brushes in the greenery but does not otherwise detail it. This cursory manner of dealing with the foreground was common practice among artists who sketched in oils in the late eighteenth century. (CR)

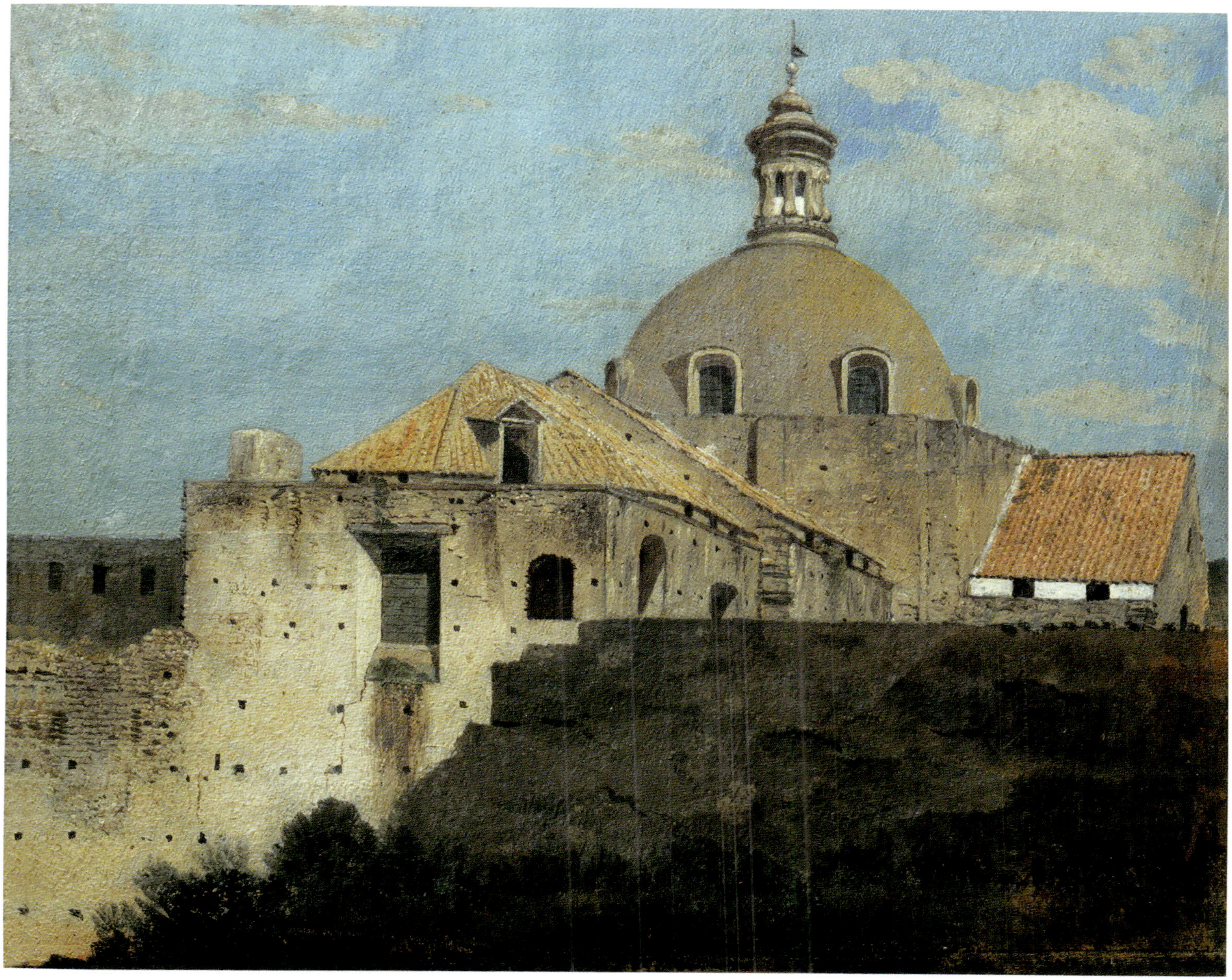

113

113

Thomas Jones (1742–1803)

The Capella Nuova Outside the Porta di Chiaia, Naples 1782

Oil on Italian writing paper*, 20 × 23.2 ($7\frac{3}{4} \times 9\frac{1}{8}$) (irreg.)

Ins.: 'The Capella nuova fuori della porta di – / Chiaja Napoli / May 1782 / T J' verso
Prov.: Captain John Dale, then by descent to Canon J. H. Adams; presented 1983
Exh.: London, 1970, no. 62; Cambridge, 1980, no. 21; Stockholm, 1982, no. 187; Manchester, 1988, no. 102; London, 1991, no. 3; London, 1997a, no. 135; Paris, 2001, no. 33
Lit.: Blunt, 1973, p. 500; Gowing, 1985, pp. 44–7, pl. 39; Wollheim, 1987, p. 344; Wollheim, 1988; De Seta, 1999, fig. 3; Hackney, 1999, pp. 190–5; Egerton, 1999, pp. 131–3; Egerton, 2000, p. 190

Tate. Presented by Canon J. H. Adams 1983 (T03545)

For a few weeks in May 1782, Jones acquired the use of a studio in the Convent of S. Maria a Capella Vecchia in the Borgo of Chiaja, just outside Naples. Cool and airy in the heat of spring,

114

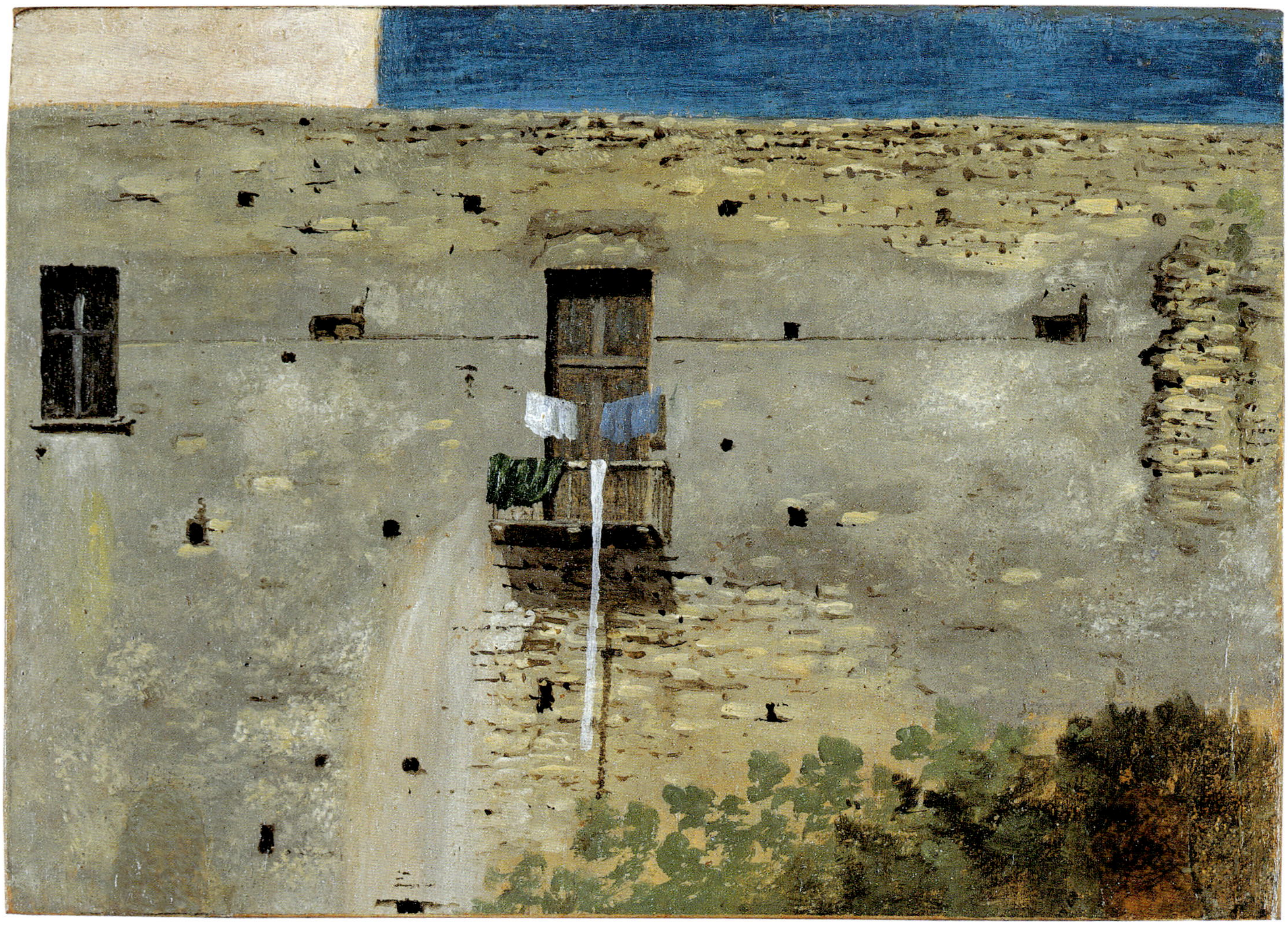

its single window looked on to a small garden and beyond to a second convent, the Capella Nuova, and other landmarks of the neighbourhood, 'all of which Objects, I did not omit making finished Studies of in Oil upon primed paper' (*Memoirs*, p. 111). This sketch shows the rough and unfinished rear wall of the Capella Nuova – exactly the kind of pitted surface Jones loved to paint in Naples – contrasting with the baroque dome beyond. Here, Jones drew the principal forms in pencil before adding colour (see Hackney, 1999). (CR)

114

THOMAS JONES (1742–1803)

A Wall in Naples *c.*1782

Oil on paper laid down on board, 11.2 × 15.8 ($4\frac{3}{8} \times 6\frac{1}{4}$)

Prov.: Captain John Dale, then by descent; Christie's, 28 July 1955, no. 6; Agnews; Lady Ashton; Christie's, 23 March 1979, no. 88; Jane Evan-Thomas; purchased 1993

Exh.: London, 1970, no. 65; New York, 1981, no. 27; Manchester, 1988, no. 105; Washington, 1996, no. 10; Paris, 2001, no. 35

Lit.: Gere, 1970, p. 470; Blunt, 1973, p. 498; Gowing, 1985, p. 47, p. 63, pl. 42; Morgan, 1984, pp. 51–76; Wollheim, 1987, p. 344; Wollheim, 1988; Galassi, 1991, pp. 33–4; Ottani Cavina, 1994, p. 104; Egerton, 2000, p. 190

National Gallery, London (N66544)

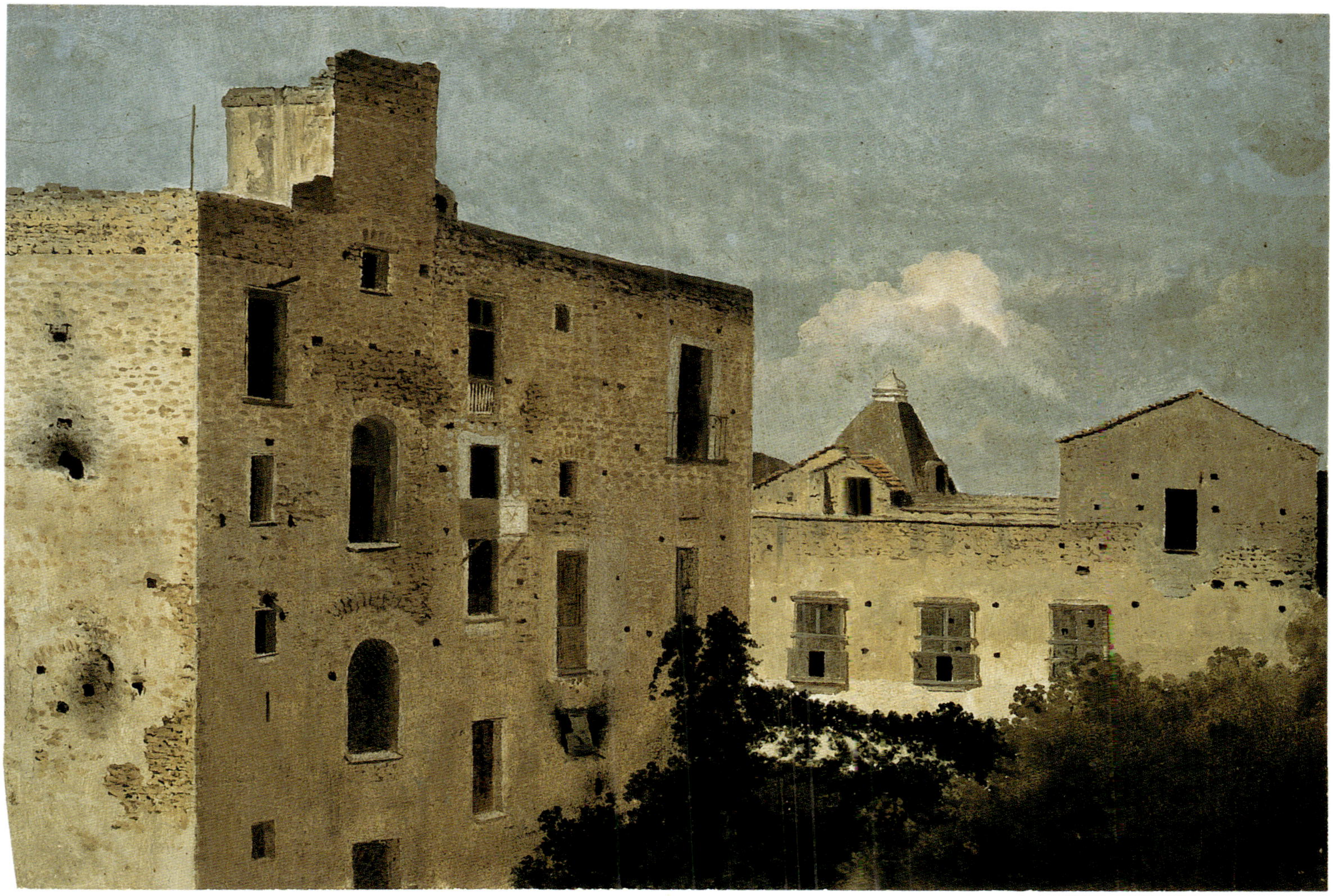

115

This depiction of the pitted wall of a humble Neapolitan house is among the most admired of Jones's oil sketches and a constant reference in any discussion of the oil sketch tradition. The location is unknown, but the sheet was probably painted in the summer of 1782. As casual as the image would seem to be, in fact, as has been pointed out by Gowing, it is carefully calculated in its effects, with the three colours that surround the wall, blue and white above, green below, subtly echoed in the laundry that hangs out to dry at the very centre of the sheet. (CR)

115

THOMAS JONES (1742–1803)

Houses in Naples 1782

Oil on Italian writing paper*, 25.4 × 38.1 (10 × 15)

Ins.: 'Naples August 1782 T J' verso
Prov.: Captain John Dale, then by descent; Christie's, 2 July 1954, no. 220; Colnaghi's; purchased 1954
Exh.: London, 1970, no. 67; Munich, 1979, no. 111; Cambridge, 1980, no. 22; Stockholm, 1982, no. 188; London, 1984a, no. 168; London, 1985, no. 41; Manchester, 1988, no. 104; London, 1990, p. 62, p. 126; Cleveland, 1991, no. 19; London, 1996, no. 19
Lit.: Gere, 1959, pp. 93–4; Blunt, 1973, p. 500; Gowing, 1985,

116

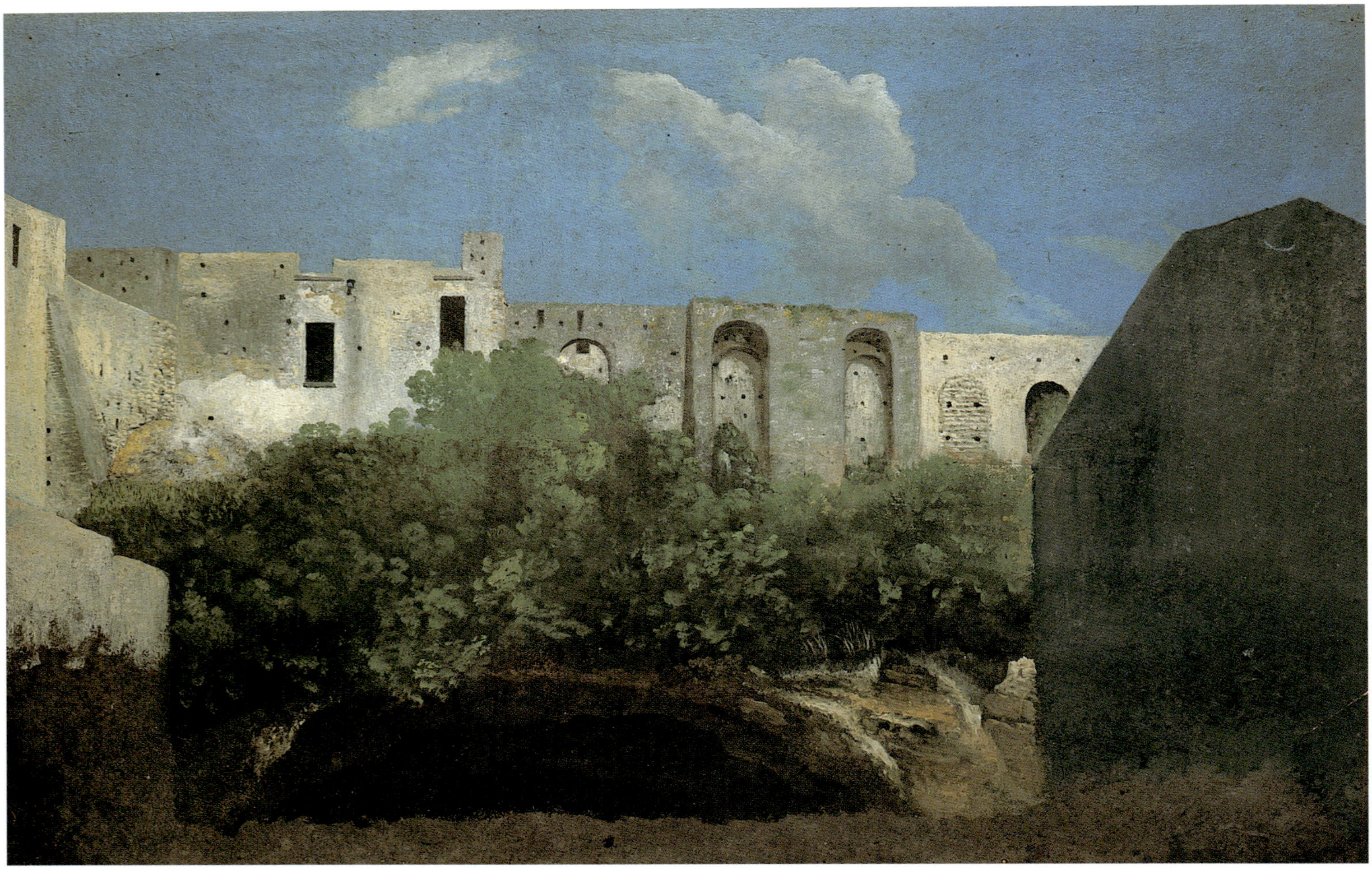

p. 49, pl. 43; Wollheim, 1987, p. 346; Wollheim, 1988; Spinosa and Di Mauro, 1989, p. 198; Egerton, 2000, p. 190

British Museum, London (1954-10-9-12)

The walls of these humble dwellings are marked by holes for scaffolding. The staccato pattern they set up across the sheet contrasts with the slower, more irregular rhythm of windows. Similarly, the shady darkness of the garden at bottom contrasts with the brilliant sky above. Jones delighted in such stark contrasts in his Neapolitan views of humble motifs. By the time Jones painted this view, in August 1782, he was living on the third floor of a residence near Capodimonte. (CR)

116

THOMAS JONES (1742–1803)

Ruined Buildings, Naples *c.*1782

Oil on paper, 24.7 × 39.3 (9¾ × 15½)

Ins.: 'Naples T. J.' verso
Prov.: Captain John Dale, then by descent; Christie's, 2 July 1954, no. 213; Colnaghi's; purchased 1954
Exh.: Naples, 1962, no. 56; London, 1970, no. 68; Manchester, 1988, no. 106; Washington, 1996, no. 7; Paris, 2001, no. 36
Lit.: Gere, 1970, p. 470; Blunt, 1973, p. 500; Gowing, 1985, p. 51, pl. 46; Spinosa and Di Mauro, 1989, p. 198; Egerton, 2000, p. 130

Glynn Vivian Art Gallery, Swansea (GV1954–1273)

The site has not been securely identified, though Conisbee points out the similarity to a drawing, also of 1782, in a sketchbook by Jones's friend, John Robert Cozens, inscribed 'a Range of Convents

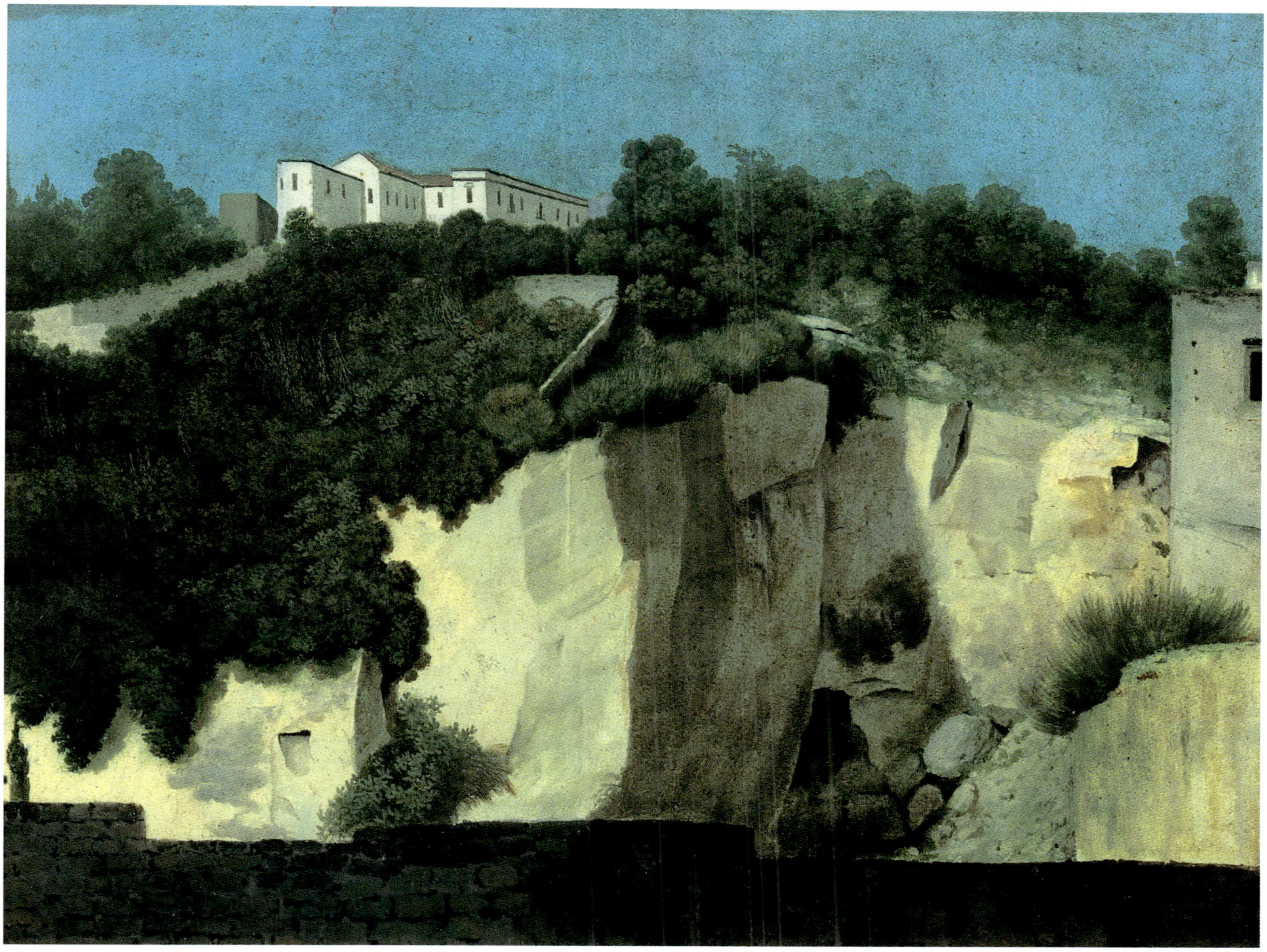

117

near Capo di Monte' (Washington, 1996, p. 120). The massive masonry substructures of ruined convents were indeed to be found on the slopes of Capodimonte. Here, Jones contrasts the rigorous architecture of the ramparts with lush, unruly foliage below and an echoing arch of clouds above. At about the same time in Rome, Valenciennes was advising oil sketch painters to ignore foreground elements and concentrate only on the middle ground. Similarly, the wall of a house rises up in the immediate foreground here, but Jones does not elaborate it. (CR)

117

THOMAS JONES (1742–1803)

Buildings on a Cliff-Top, Naples 1782

Oil on paper, 28.6 × 38.7 (11¼ × 15¼)

Ins.: 'Naples 1782 T J' verso
Prov.: Captain John Dale, then by descent to Canon J. H. Adams; Phillips, 3 November 1986, no. 18; purchased 1986
Exh.: London, 1970, no. 66; Trento, 1993, no. 5; London, 1997a, no. 136; Paris, 2001, no. 37
Lit.: Gowing, 1985, p. 50, pl. 44

Tate. Purchased 1986 (T04872)

118

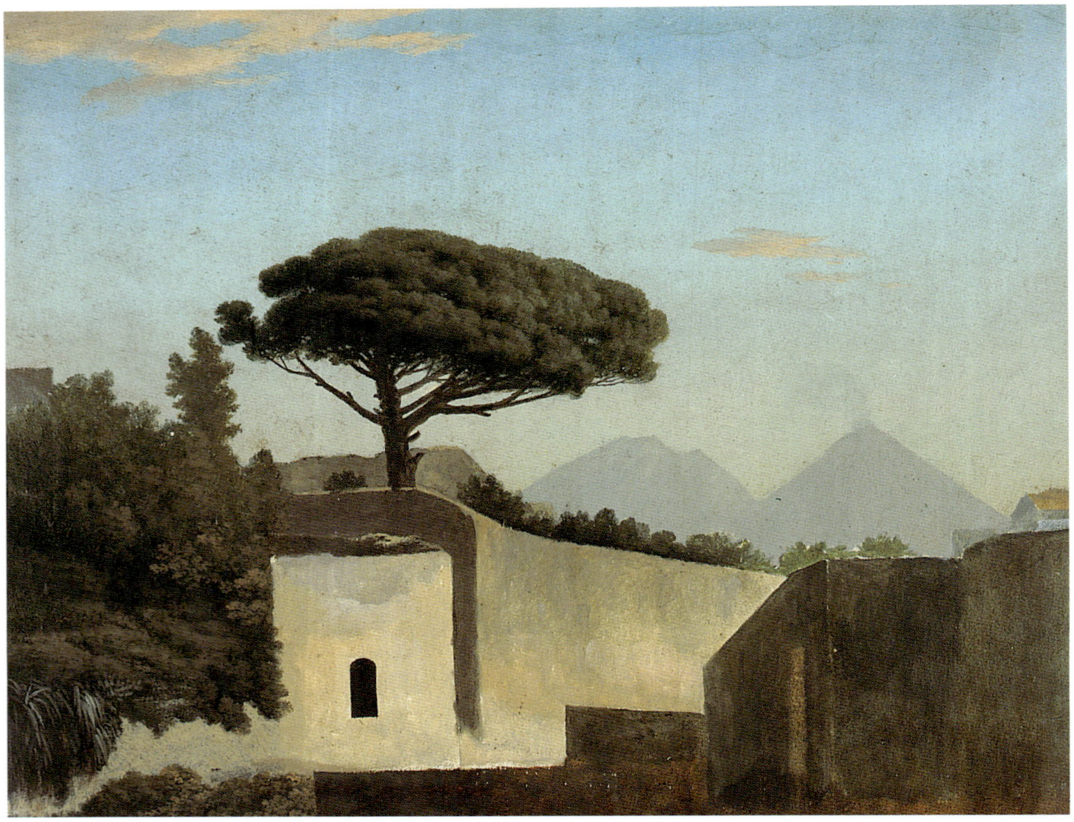

The site at Naples has not been identified. The subject of the sheet is a massive, angular wall of rock, partially bathed in sunlight, with all but its vertical surfaces covered in abundant foliage. Jones's vantage point must have been an upper floor of a nearby building which allowed him to look directly across at the naked rock face. On three sides, however, the natural outcropping is framed by relatively diminutive man-made structures. A wall, deep in shadow, runs across the foreground. The corner of a stone house can be seen at the right edge. Sunlit buildings atop the hill stand starkly against a brilliant blue sky untouched by clouds. (CR)

118

THOMAS JONES (1742–1803)

House and Tree with Vesuvius in the Background, Naples 1782

Oil on Italian writing paper*, 28.5 × 37 (11⅛ × 14⅝)

Ins.: 'Naples 1782 TJ' verso
Prov.: Captain John Dale, then by descent

Private collection

This rustic house, perched in the shade of a mighty plane tree, is also overshadowed by a more ominous, if distant, presence, Vesuvius. The sketch no doubt derives from one of Jones's many excursions into the Neapolitan countryside, such as one he succinctly described on 30 October 1780: 'Made some more Rambles & sketches' (*Memoirs*, p. 100). The sheet shows Jones's predilection for landscape motifs where timeless natural elements and time-worn man-made structures cohabit in harmony. As with several other Neapolitan sketches, Jones has left the foreground unfinished. (CR)

119

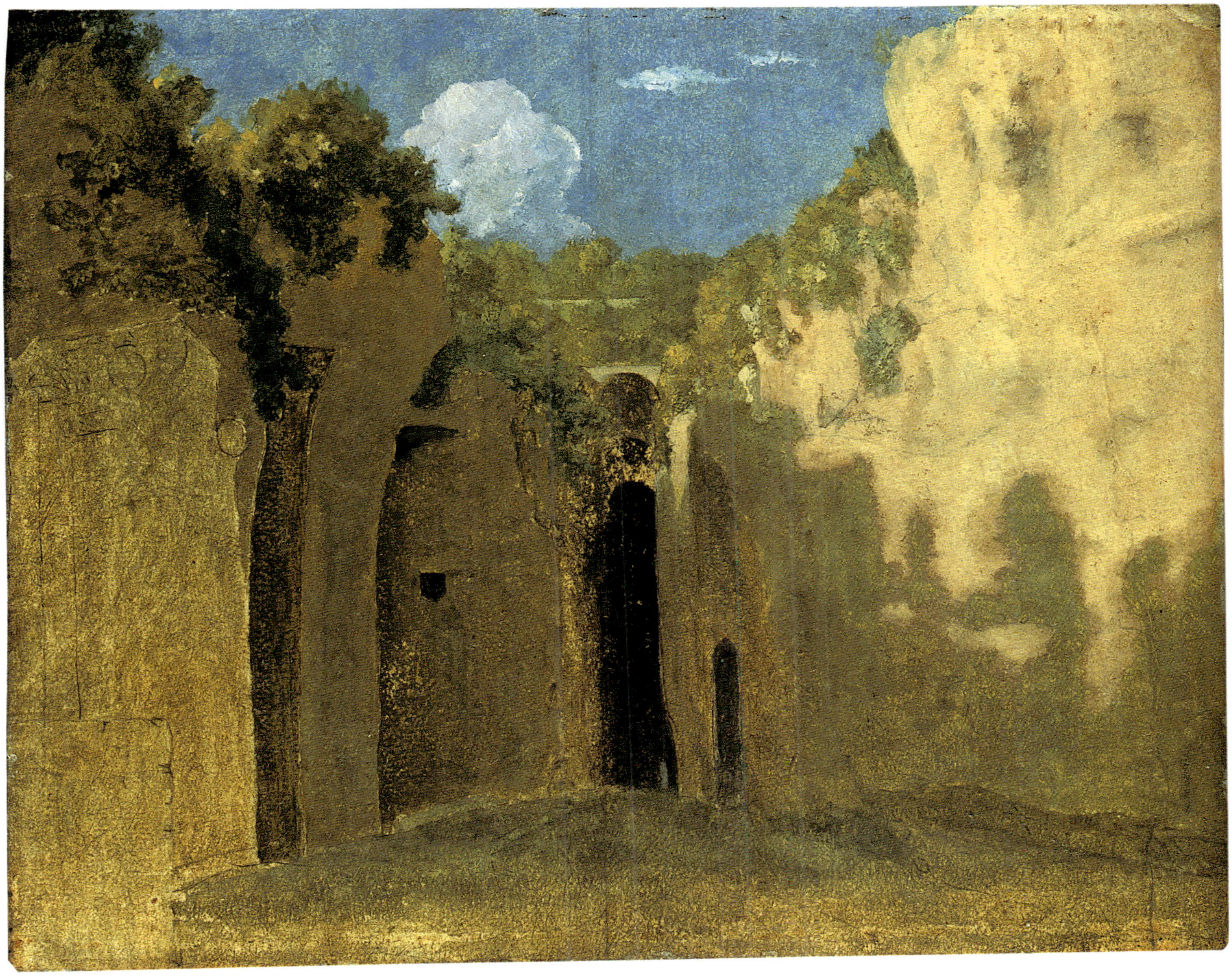

119

THOMAS JONES (1742–1803)

The Grotto at Posillipo 1782

Oil and pencil on paper laid on boad, 20.3 × 27.3 (8 × 10¾)

Ins.: 'T J Naples August 1782' verso
Prov.: Colnaghi's, 1956; John Gere; Charlotte Gere
Exh.: Naples, 1962, no. 55; London, 1970, no. 71; Manchester, 1988, no. 132; Washington, 1996, no. 12; London, 1999, no. 43; Paris, 2001, no. 38

Lit.: Gowing, 1985, p. 53, pl. 47; Galassi, 1991, pp. 34–5, pl. 36

The Gere Collection, on long-term loan to the National Gallery, London (L845)

The 'grotto', a popular landmark near Naples, is a tunnel cut by the ancient Romans to connect the city to Pozzuoli further along the coast. Jones used it on numerous occasions during his residencies in Naples. This sketch dates from August 1782, during his second and longer stay. The year before, his friends William Pars and Francis Towne had made more detailed watercolours of

120

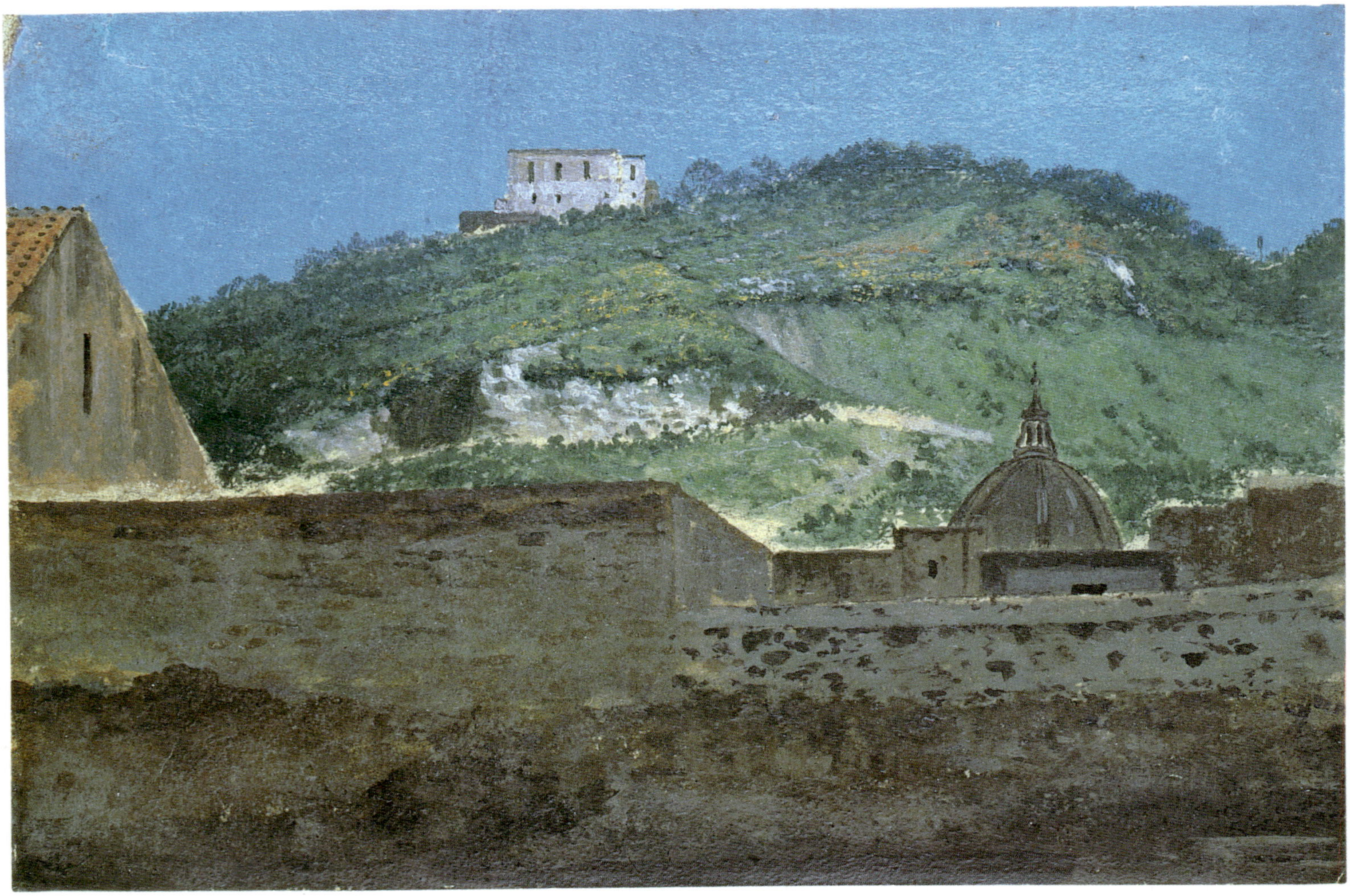

the same site (cat. no. 98 and British Museum) and Jones, too, depicted it in a watercolour of an unknown date (cat. no. 139). Working in oils on the spot, however, he reduces detail to focus attention on the stark contrast between sunlight falling on the rock face and the darkness of the tunnel entrance. (CR)

120

THOMAS JONES (1742–1803)

The Hill of Vomero and the Dome of S. Caterina, Naples 1782

Oil on paper, 14 × 21.5 ($5\frac{1}{2} \times 8\frac{1}{2}$)

Ins.: 'Naples 1782 T.J.' verso
Prov.: Captain John Dale, then by descent; Christie's, 2 July 1954, no. 215; Colnaghi's; purchased 1954
Exh.: London, 1970, no. 63; Cambridge, 1980, no. 23; London, 1990, p. 65, p. 127; Washington, 1996, no. 11; Paris, 2001, no. 34
Lit.: Blunt, 1973, p. 500; Gowing, 1985, p. 47, pl. 40; Spinosa and Di Mauro, 1989, p. 198; Galassi, 1991, p. 22

Birmingham Museums and Art Gallery (1954P55)

Like his view of the Capella Nuova (cat. no. 113), this sheet was painted in the studio at the Convent of S. Maria a Capella Vecchia, at Chiaja, a suburb of Naples, which Jones used for a few weeks in May 1782. Here, he looks up the hill of Vomero at a villa, starkly illuminated as it stands against the sky. The rounded shape of the hill is answered by the dome of the church of S. Caterina at lower left, sunlight glinting on its lantern. In his landscape oil sketches, Jones delighted in such echoes between the natural and the built environment. (CR)

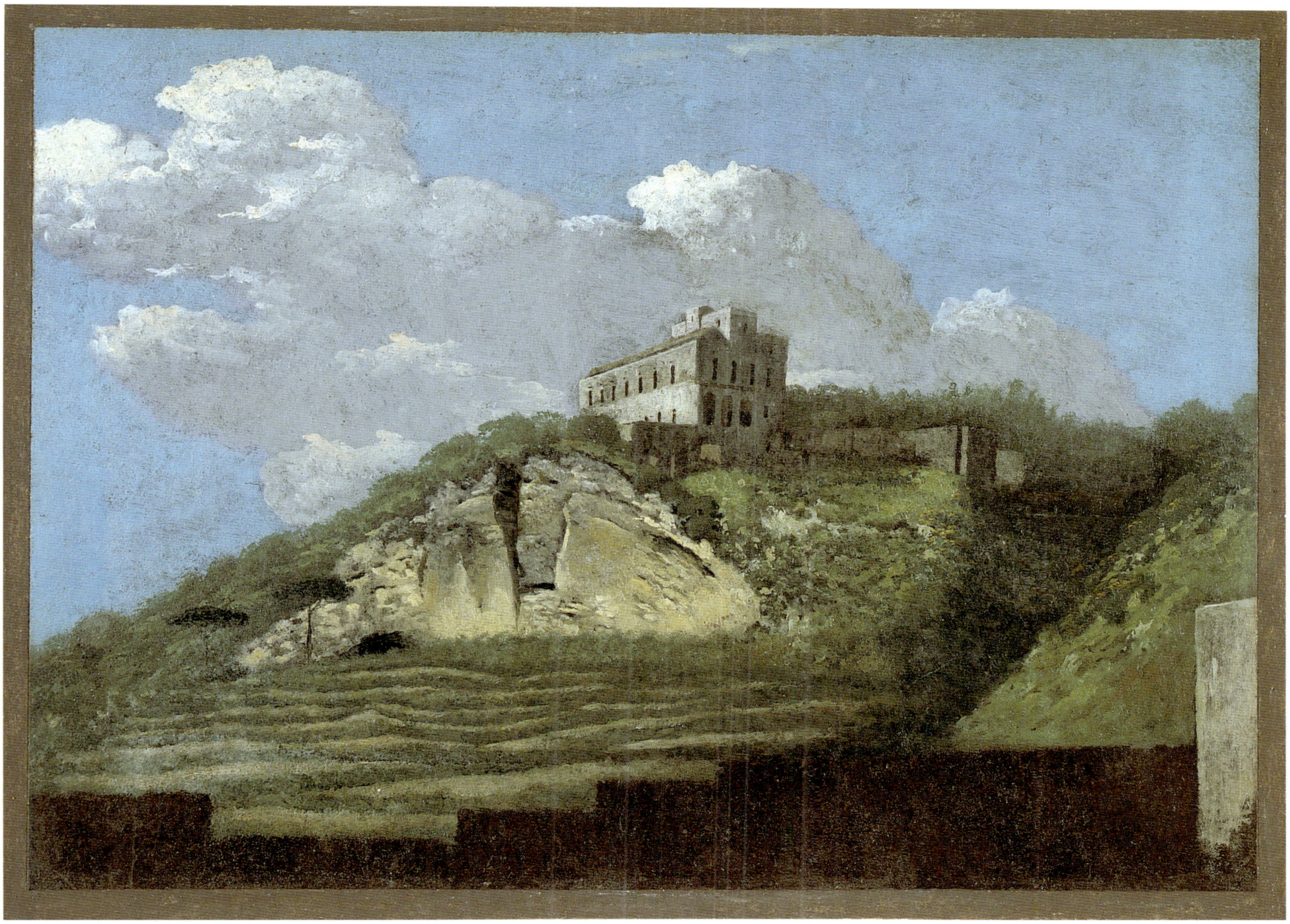

121

THOMAS JONES (1742–1803)

Scene near Naples 1783

Oil on paper, 24.1 × 34.2 (9½ × 13½)

Ins.: 'Naples Aprile 1783 TJ' verso
Prov.: Captain John Dale, then by descent; Christie's, 2 July 1954, no. 220; Colnaghi's; purchased 1954
Exh.: London, 1970, no. 73; London, 1974b, no. 31; Cambridge, 1980, no. 24; Washington, 1996, no. 13
Lit.: Blunt, 1973, p. 500; Gowing, 1985, p. 51, pl. 45; Egerton, 2000, p. 191

Lent by the Syndics of the Fitzwilliam Museum, Cambridge (PD.21–1954)

This sketch was painted in April 1783, not long before Jones's departure for Britain. The artist lived at Chiaja, a suburb of Naples, from December 1782 to May 1783, and the site was once identified as the Monastery of San Martino there, although the hilltop building appears to be too small. Could it perhaps be the same villa atop the hill of Vomero, though seen now from a different angle, that Jones had painted a year earlier when he had the use of a particularly pleasant studio at Chiaja in May 1782 (cat. no. 120)? In both sketches, a strong, simple architectonic form, caught in sunlight, is silhouetted against the sky. (CR)

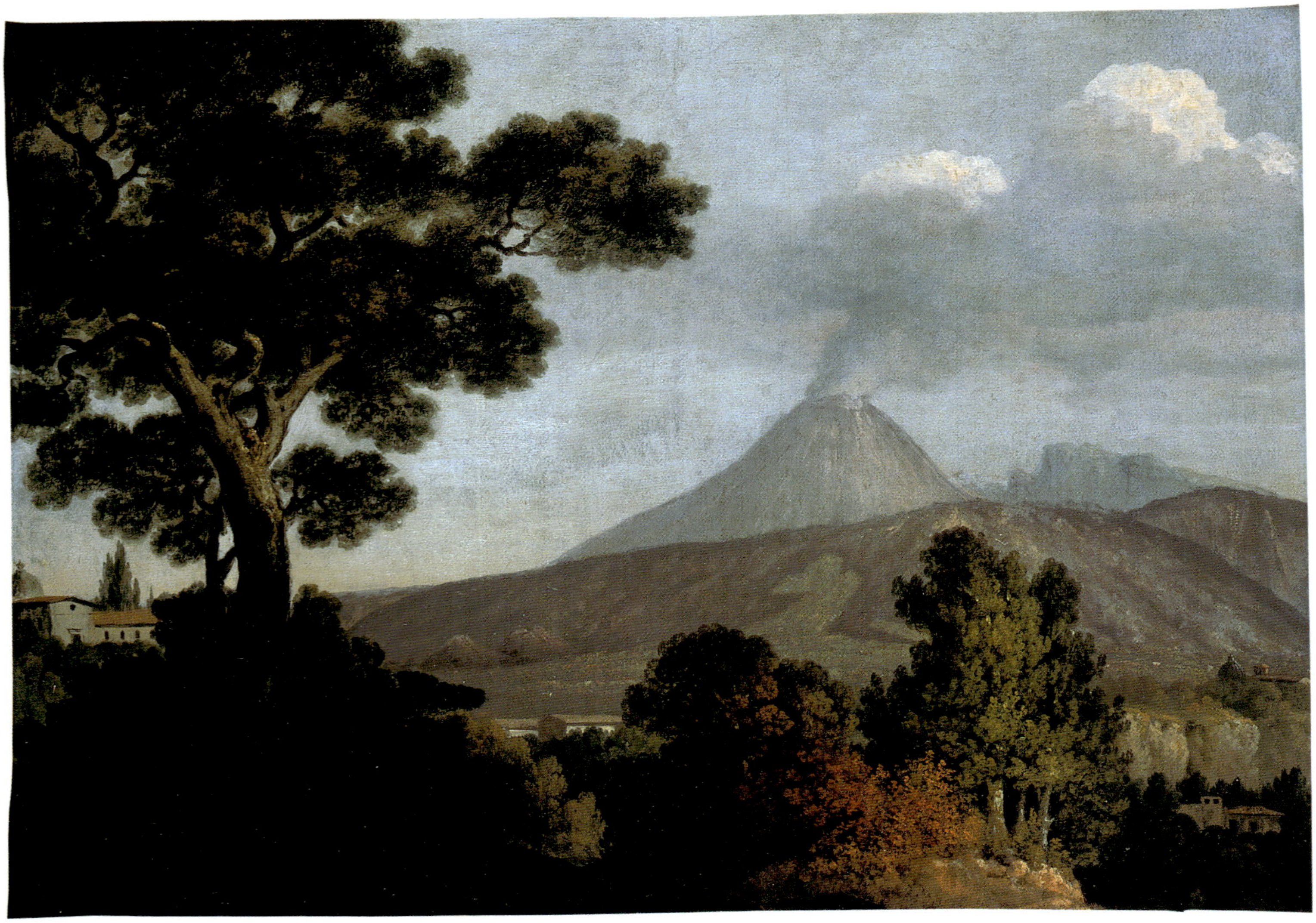

122

THOMAS JONES (1742–1803)

Mount Vesuvius from Torre Annunziata, near Naples 1780s

Oil on paper laid down on canvas*, 38 × 55.5 (15 × 22¾)

Ins.: 'N.3, Mount vesuvius from Torre dell'Annunziata / near Naples' on stretcher
Prov.: Thomas Thomas, then by descent to Jane Evan-Thomas; presented 1974
Exh.: London, 1970, no. 74; Manchester, 1988, no. 113
Lit.: Causa, 1981, repr.

Tate. Presented by Mrs Jane Evan-Thomas 1974 (T01844)

The most famous Neapolitan landmark is the volcano that towers over, and periodically threatens, the city. It was in eruption the first time Jones saw it, on 15 September 1778 (*Memoirs*, p. 77). He visited often after that, for the final time on 27 July 1783, when he ascended the crater from the town of Torre Annunziata, where he was staying with his friend, the Italian painter Giovanni Battista Lusieri (ibid., p. 124). This careful painting, showing a relatively benign Vesuvius surrounded by verdant fields, may derive from sketches made on that occasion. The large tree to the left is similar to ones that Jones often incorporated in his classically composed paintings to frame the principal motif and lead the eye into the landscape. (CR)

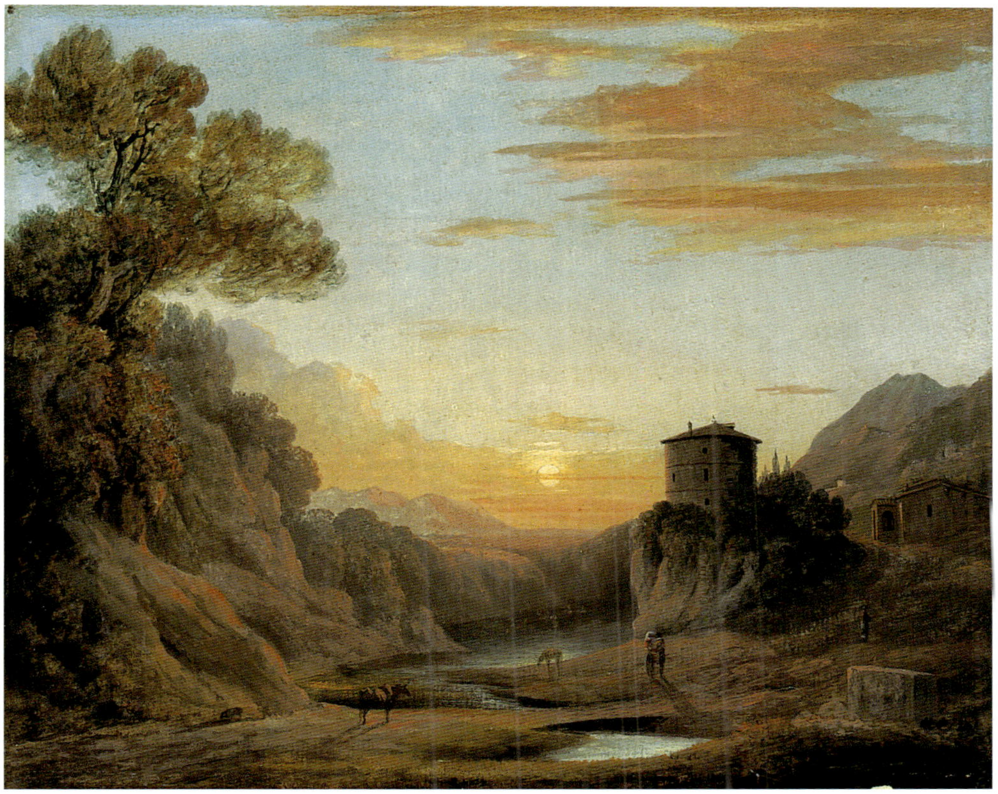

123

123

THOMAS JONES (1742–1803)

Italian Landscape at Sunset *c.*1775–6 or 1780s

Oil on blue paper later lined on canvas, 36 × 53 (14⅛ × 20⅞)

Prov.: Captain John Dale, then by descent to Canon J. H. Adams; Sotheby's, 27 November 1975, no. 94, as 'A Southern Landscape at Sunset'

Private collection

Cardiff and Manchester only

The sky and sunset in this work are poetically observed, but the figures are slight and the animals poorly painted, possibly suggesting an early or unfinished picture. It may be the work described by Jones as 'A Small Sun Set' in a list of works produced at Pencerrig in 1775–6 (*Memoirs*, p. 38). It also has similarities with an early painting (cat. no. 26). Technical analysis of the work has revealed extensive underdrawing, which is very free and is visible in some areas with the naked eye, for instance, around the central building, which shows that Jones initially intended it to be lower. The trees are also carefully sketched before painting. However, the dating of the present work remains problematic and the size and weight of paper used with oils for a small composition of this kind is consistent with a group including *Monte Compatri* (cat. no. 147) and *Temple of Diana at Nemi* (cat. no. 146) which were painted much later. (A3S)

124

THOMAS JONES (1742–1803)

Near Capodimonte, Naples 1780s

Oil on laid paper laid down on canvas, 33.5 × 49 (13⅛ × 19¼)

Ins.: 'near Capo di Monte / NAPLES' l.r.
Prov.: Thomas Thomas, then by descent to Jane Evan-Thomas; given to the present owner 1987
Exh.: London, 1970, no. 56; Manchester, 1983, no. 118
Lit.: Edwards, 1968, p. 10

Private collection

124

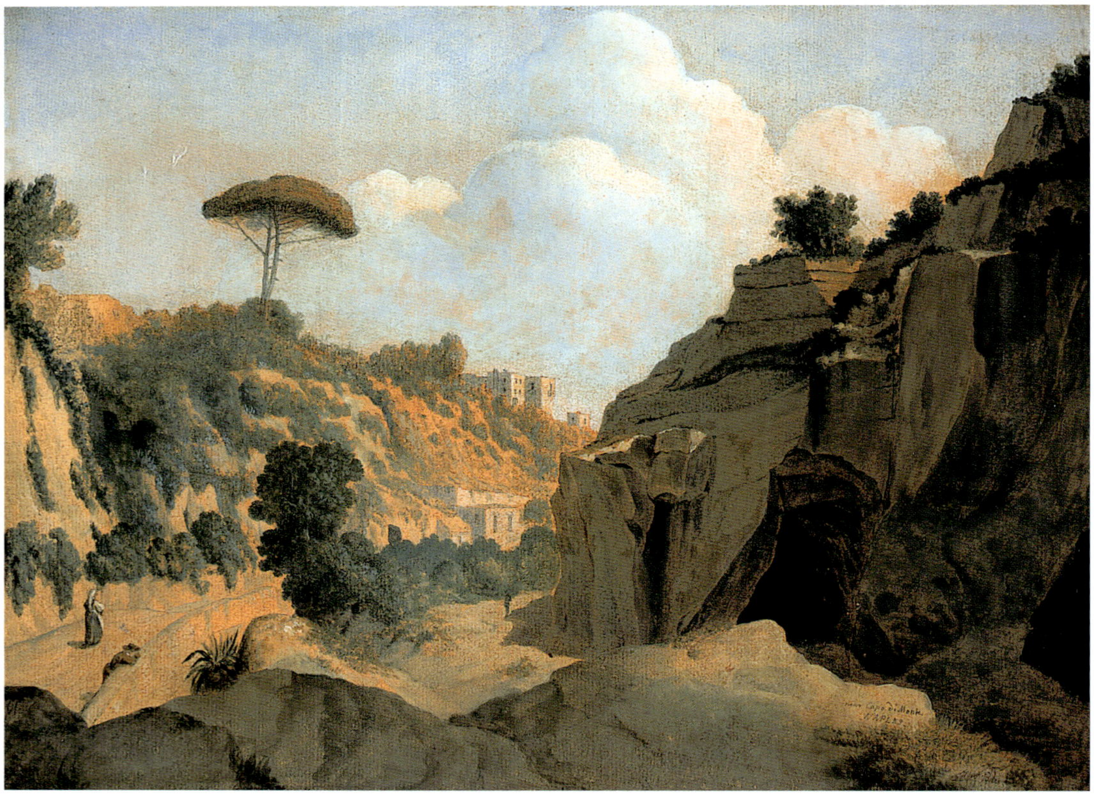

Although this work has previously been exhibited as part of the group of views Jones made on the road to Santa Maria dei Monti in the spring of 1781 (cat. nos 131–4), it probably shows a scene in the area of the Hospital of S. Gennaro, where he sketched a year later. The disposition of the rocks, buildings and vegetation is much closer to cat. nos 136 and 137 and the inscription is not specific about the location, unlike the views of the road to Santa Maria dei Monti. Uniquely for either group of Neapolitan subjects, it is worked in oils on paper, probably at a later date from a lost drawing. (GS)

125

THOMAS JONES (1742–1803)

Near Naples, with a Mule on a Track 1780s?

Oil on Italian writing paper*, 27 × 42 ($10\frac{3}{4} \times 16\frac{1}{2}$)

Ins.: 'near NAPLES / T. JONES / N°XXXV.' l.r.
Prov.: Thomas Thomas, then by descent
Exh.: London, 1970, no. 88

Private collection

Jones's *Memoirs* contain numerous descriptions of excursions into the countryside around Naples, where he and his companions sketched in pencil and oils. This sheet may derive from, or have been begun on, one such expedition. A rutted path, along which a donkey ambles, mounts a hillside. A solitary figure, seen from behind and silhouetted against the sky, gazes out over a landscape we cannot see. The 'staged' quality of that figure suggests that the painting was completed in the studio. Jones uses thin oil paint to depict the sharp break between areas of brilliant sunlight and deep shade. (CR)

126

THOMAS JONES (1742–1803)

Piperno 1780s?

Watercolour, oil on grey wrapping paper*, 23 × 32.8 ($9 \times 12\frac{7}{8}$)

Ins.: 'PIPERNO / XXIX / Ts. Jones' l.l.; 'starch'? l.c.
Prov.: Captain John Dale, then by descent; Christie's, 2 July 1954, no. 222; Colnaghi's; purchased by Tom Girtin, 1954; Sotheby's, 21 November 1984, no. 83; Martyn Gregory

125

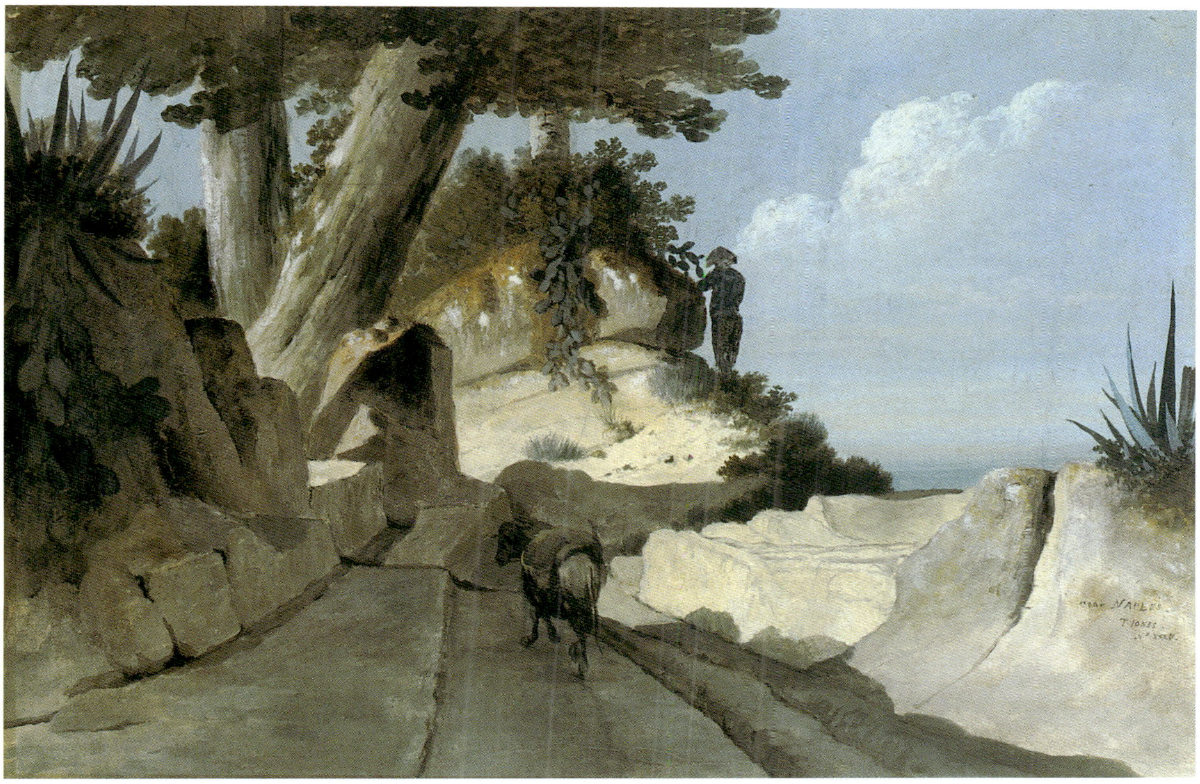

126

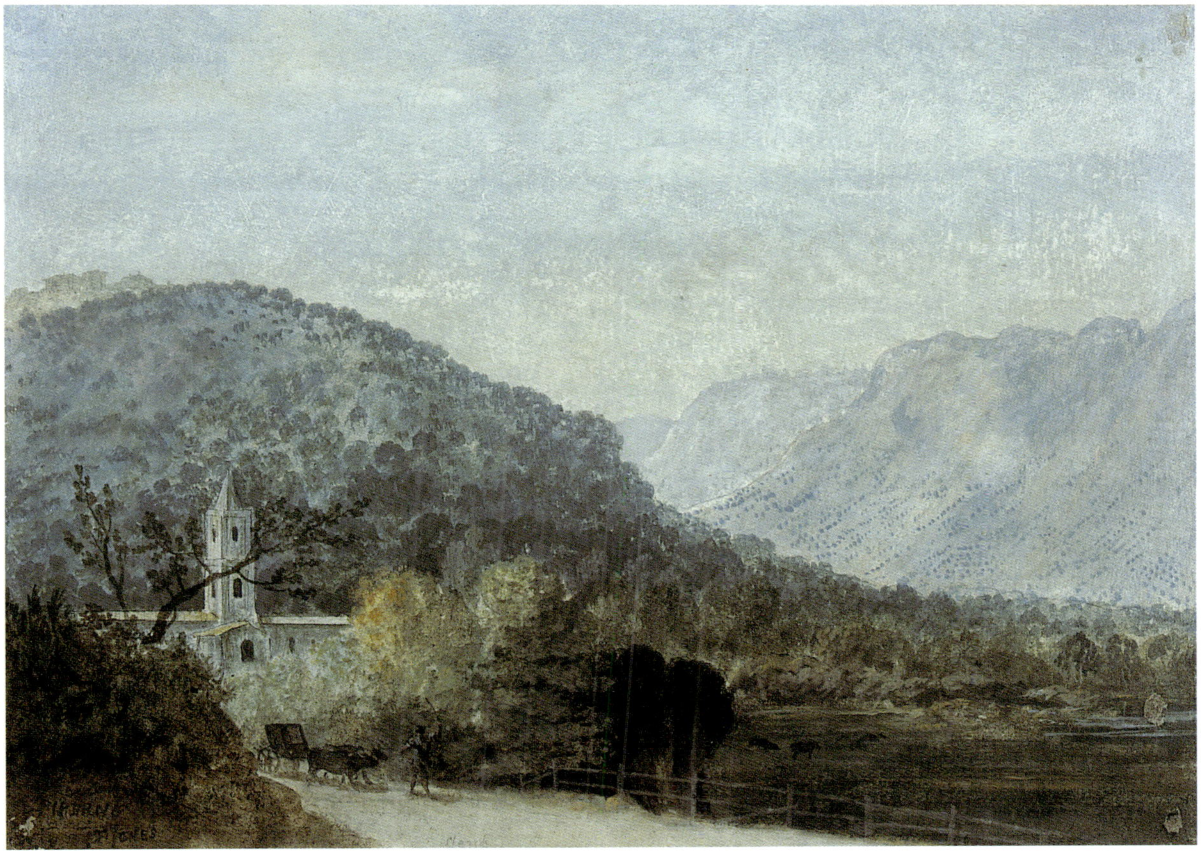

127

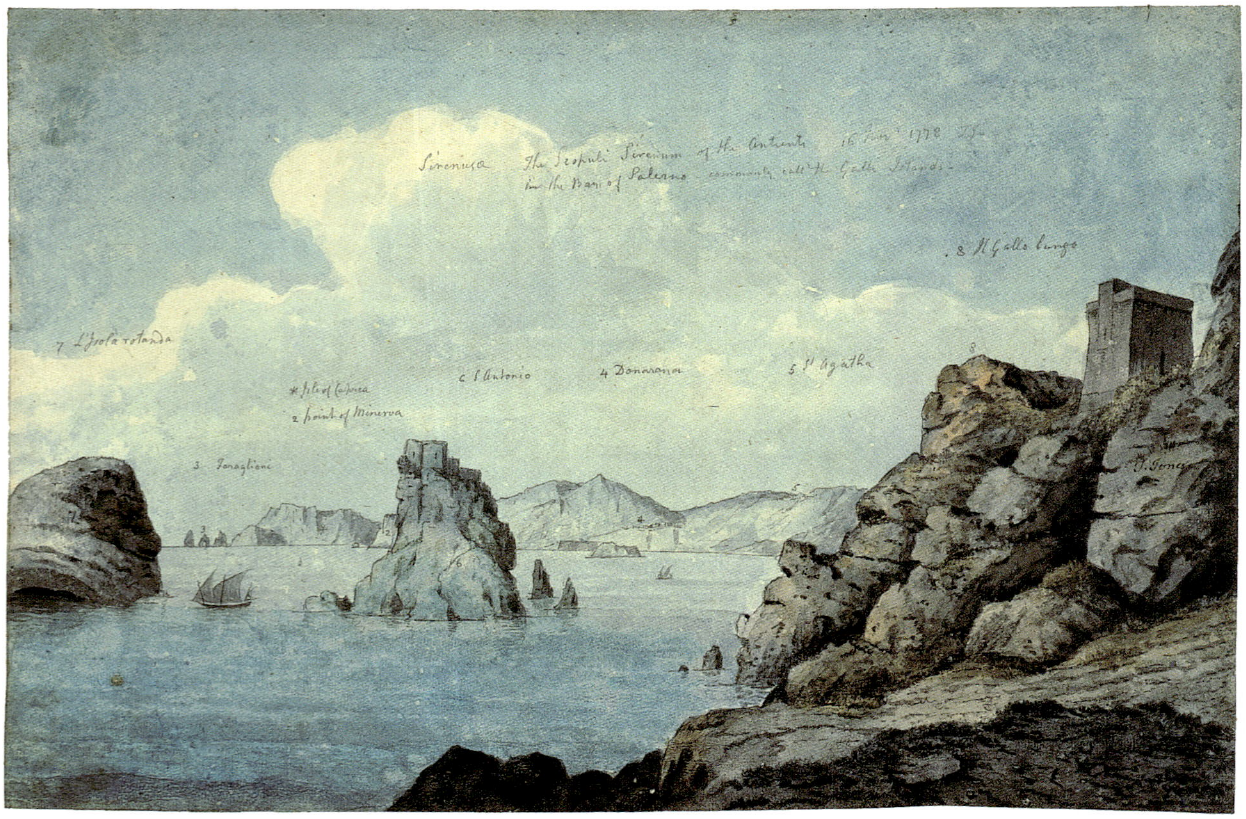

Exh.: London, 1970, no. 41
Lit.: Gowing, 1985, p. 39, pl. 32

Private collection

The approach to the town of Piperno, on the route from Rome to Naples, was a hilly road which experience soon taught Jones to avoid (*Memoirs*, p. 95). The first time he travelled to Naples, on Sunday, 13 September 1778, he recorded that guards and peasants with buffaloes were needed to drag the carriages in his party up the hill to the town (ibid, p. 77). This sheet may record that incident, although the unusual media, including starch and white chalk preparation, and the paper he used, suggest that it was completed in the studio, perhaps long afterwards, when Jones had returned to Wales (see. p. 83). (CR)

127

THOMAS JONES (1742–1803)

In the Bay of Salerno 1778

Pencil, watercolour on Italian writing paper*, 24.8 × 43.5 (9¾ × 17⅛)

Ins.: 'Sirenusa The Scopuli Sirenum of the Antients 16 Novr 1778 T.J. / in the Bay of Salerno – commonly call^{d} the Galli Islands' t.c.; 'T. Jones' r.c.; extensive annotations with a numerical key
Prov.: Colnaghi's; purchased 1960
Exh.: London, 1970, no. 43; Manchester, 1988, no. 124; London, 1990, p. 64, p. 126

British Museum, London (1960-12-5-1)

Cardiff and Manchester only

Jones began this watercolour on an excursion to Sorrento in November 1778, during his first visit to Naples, and he made another drawing of the Galli Islands on the same day in his sketchbook (cat. no. 76, pp. 142–3). Jones was therefore sketching in two formats at the same time. He used the small book for less

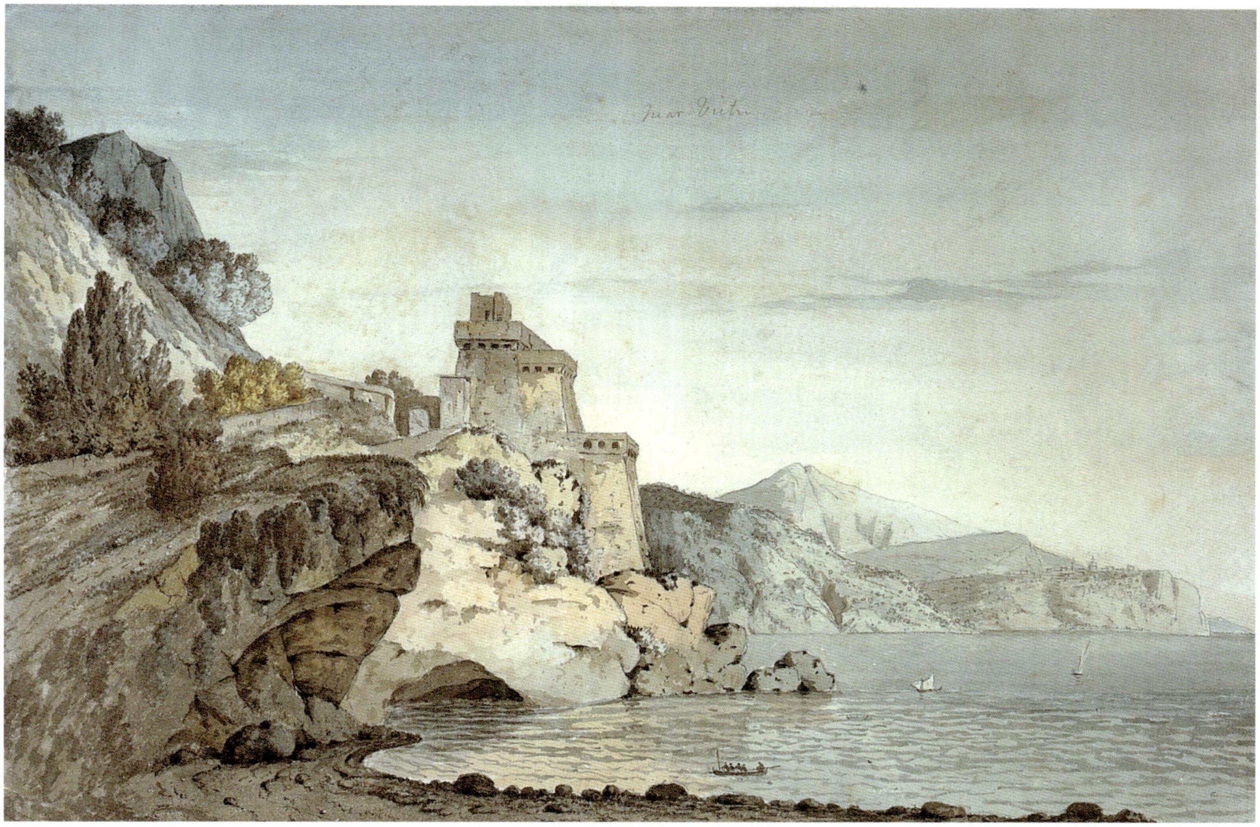
128

detailed work, and a larger sheet, as here, for a more complex outline which might be subsequently coloured. The signature in pen and ink to the right suggests that the colouring might have occurred some time later. Jones visited the islands the following day. As he noted on this drawing and in his *Memoirs*, they were known to Virgil as the 'Scopuli Sirenum of the Ancients' – the islands of the Sirens (p. 82). In such peaceful weather, however, they offered no threat to Jones and his party as they explored the bay in their hired boat. (GS)

128

THOMAS JONES (1742–1803)

The Coast near Vietri *c.*1778

Pencil, watercolour on Dutch writing paper (watermark: posthorn on a shield/L V GERREVINCK)*, 25 × 38.5 ($9\frac{7}{8} \times 15\frac{1}{8}$)

Ins.: 'near Vietri' t.c.; 'wall' l.c.; 'vietri' l.r.
Prov.: Captain John Dale, then by descent; Christie's, 28 July 1955, no. 2; Colnaghi's; Mr and Mrs W. W. Spooner; bequeathed 1967
Exh.: London, 1968b, no. 14; Bath, 1969, no. 42; Bristol, 1973, no. 34; Wellington, 1976, no. 7; New York, 1986, no. 96; Manchester, 1988, no. 125

Courtauld Institute Gallery, London (S.57)

Cardiff and Manchester only

Jones made trips along the coast to Salerno in 1778 and 1780. The artist had a commission for an oil of a 'View of Vietri in the bay of Salerno (Morning)' in 1779 and it is possible that this drawing was related to it, in which case it must have been begun in 1778 (*Memoirs*, p. 88). Only one of the larger drawings made on the Neapolitan coast is dated (cat. no. 127), but the uniformity of the works suggest that they form a group dating from 1778, though it is not clear when they were coloured.

This view, like cat. nos 127 and 141, includes one of the boldly situated castles and defensive towers that litter the area. In this case, the Torre della Marina di Albori is shown in the foreground, with Vietri further along the coast. John Robert Cozens drew the same view in 1782 (Whitworth Art Gallery), though, in a telling contrast, he characteristically shows it in stormy conditions. Jones's view recalls a pleasant excursion, perhaps in the sort of boat shown in the foreground. (GS)

129

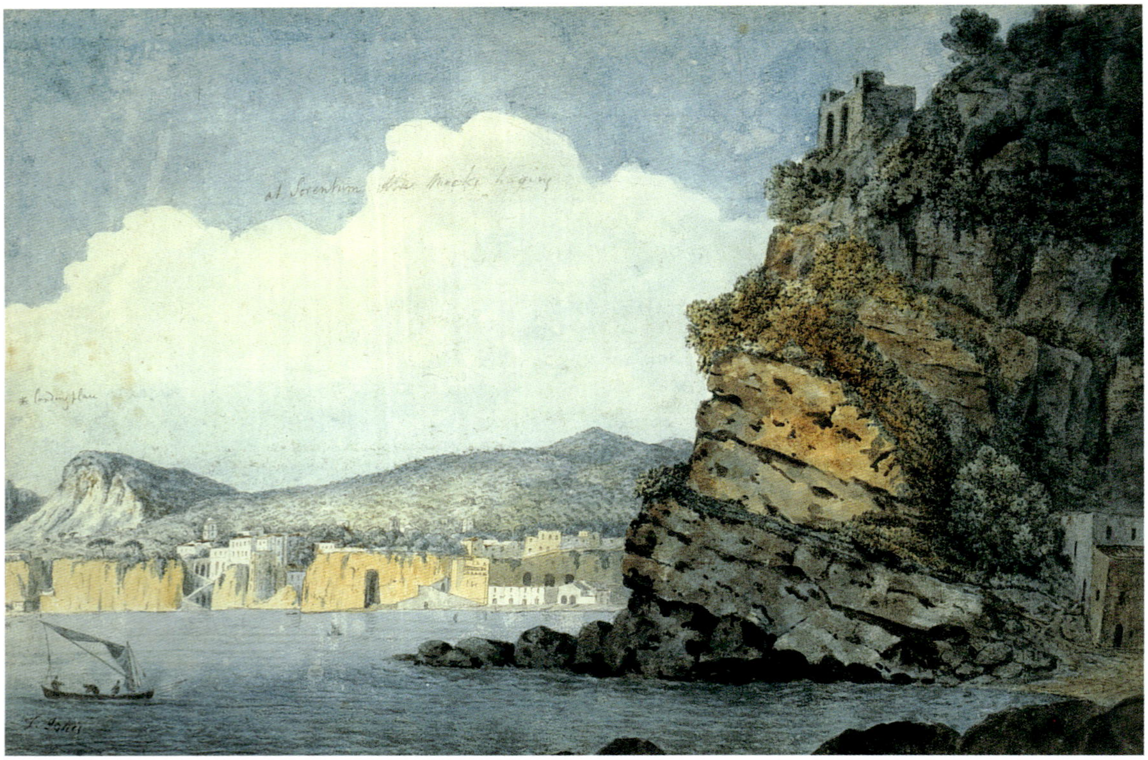

129

THOMAS JONES (1742–1803)

At Sorrento, the Rocks *c.*1778

Pencil, watercolour on Italian writing paper*, 29 × 43 ($11\frac{3}{8} \times 16\frac{7}{8}$)

Ins.: 'T. Jones' l.l.; 'at Sorentum off the Rocks Morning' t.c.; 'landing place' l.c.
Prov.: Captain John Dale, then by descent to Canon J. H. Adams; Sotheby's, 27 November 1975, no. 89; Agnew's; purchased 1976
Exh.: Manchester, 1988, no. 123
Lit.: Parkinson, 1998, p. 31

Victoria and Albert Museum, London (P1-1976)

Cardiff and Manchester only

Jones visited Sorrento for a second time in 1780, but it seems more likely that this watercolour was begun on the same excursion as cat. no. 127 in 1778. This is supported by the fact that the small boat to the left is adapted from a pencil drawing in a sketchbook which is inscribed 'Naples Novr 1778' and 'passage boat to Sorrentum Portici &c' (cat. no. 76, p. 141). Jones presumably added this autobiographical detail when he came to colour his original annotated drawing, though when this occurred is unclear. (GS)

130

THOMAS JONES (1742–1803)

Mare Chiara in the Vicinity of Virgil's School, Naples 1780

Black chalk on paper on original mount, 24.6 × 39.4 ($9\frac{5}{8} \times 15\frac{3}{8}$)

Ins.: 'T J 1780' l.l.; 'Jones Esq'; 'Mare Chiara vicina alla Scuola di Vergilio. Napoli – Punto di Pausilipo' on original mount in Soane's hand
Prov.: Sir John Soane

Trustees of the Sir John Soane's Museum, London

Jones mentions meeting John Soane on a number of occasions during the young architect's stay in Italy. There is no record of him providing a commission, however, and Soane probably acquired this work later in England, since he lost most of his Italian purchases on his return trip. One of Jones's descendants records that Soane had a 'small Painting' by Jones 'which he prizes highly' (MS, private collection). It may have been this drawing, which is inscribed in Soane's hand on the mount.

This carefully finished work is the artist's only known presentation drawing. It is based on two studies in a sketchbook he

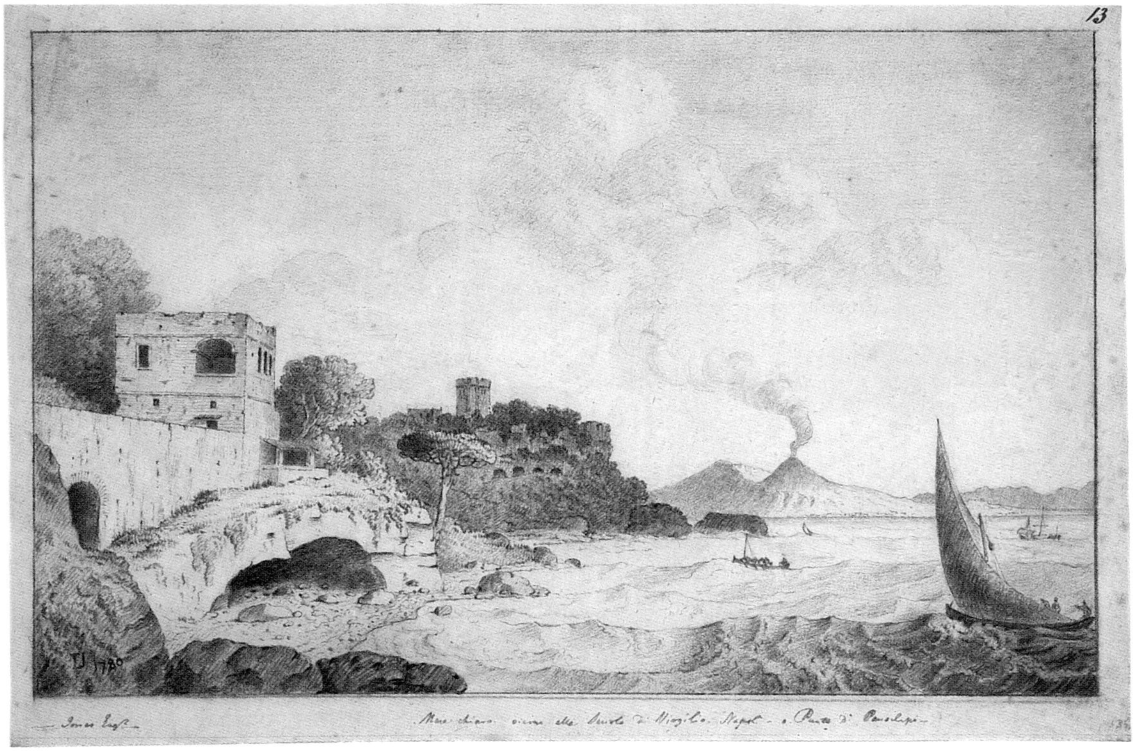

130

used in Naples in 1778 (cat. no. 76). One is dated 29 September and the other 24 October (pp. 82–3). The former drawing is marked with a symbol to the right, which is repeated at the centre of the other drawing to signify the continuation of the scene. The finished work therefore combines two different sketches into a broad sweep of the coast. The 'Scuola di Vergilio' was actually a ruined temple of Fortune, near Posillipo. (GS)

131

THOMAS JONES (1742–1803)

Santa Maria dei Monti, near Naples 1781

Pencil, watercolour, pen and ink on laid paper, 19.3 × 27.2 (7⅝ × 10¾)

Ins.: 'S[a] M[a] de' Monti by Naples 6 Oct 1781' ('Oct' written over 'May'); rays of sun and 'Evg-' t.l.; 'sandy bank'. Slight sketch inscribed 'S Effremo vecchio near Naples / 31 March 1781' verso
Prov.: Sotheby's, 26 July 1961, no. 69; Colnaghi's; presented by Lady Chorley through the Friends of the Whitworth, 1961
Exh.: Vienna, 1965, no. 73; London, 1967, no. 8; London, 1970, no. 57; Manchester, 1973a, no. 14; Nottingham, 1981, no. 68; Manchester, 1988, no. 119; Manchester, 1993, no. 46
Lit.: Egerton, 1979, p. 8, p. 15

The Whitworth Art Gallery, The University of Manchester (D.1962.3)

Cardiff and Manchester only

Jones was fascinated by the rugged scenery on the road to Santa Maria dei Monti, a monastery on a ridge to the east of Naples, and made perhaps as many as sixteen drawings there, mostly on larger pieces of paper. As ever, Jones was conditioned in his response to the location by his knowledge of painters before him, in particular Salvator Rosa, whose paintings of bandits in gloomy rocky landscapes were much admired in the eighteenth century. The altered date is confusing and also occurs on another drawing (cat. no. 132). It probably means that it was originally executed in monochrome and then coloured at a later date. Two other Santa Maria dei Monti drawings are dated 6 May, one of which is in monochrome and is the same size as this drawing (also in the Whitworth Art Gallery). It gives an idea, therefore, of what this drawing would have looked like before Jones added the extra washes of colour. The slight sketch of San Eframo on the verso was begun on the same day as a view by Francis Towne (Victoria and Albert Museum) – 31 March. (CN)

131

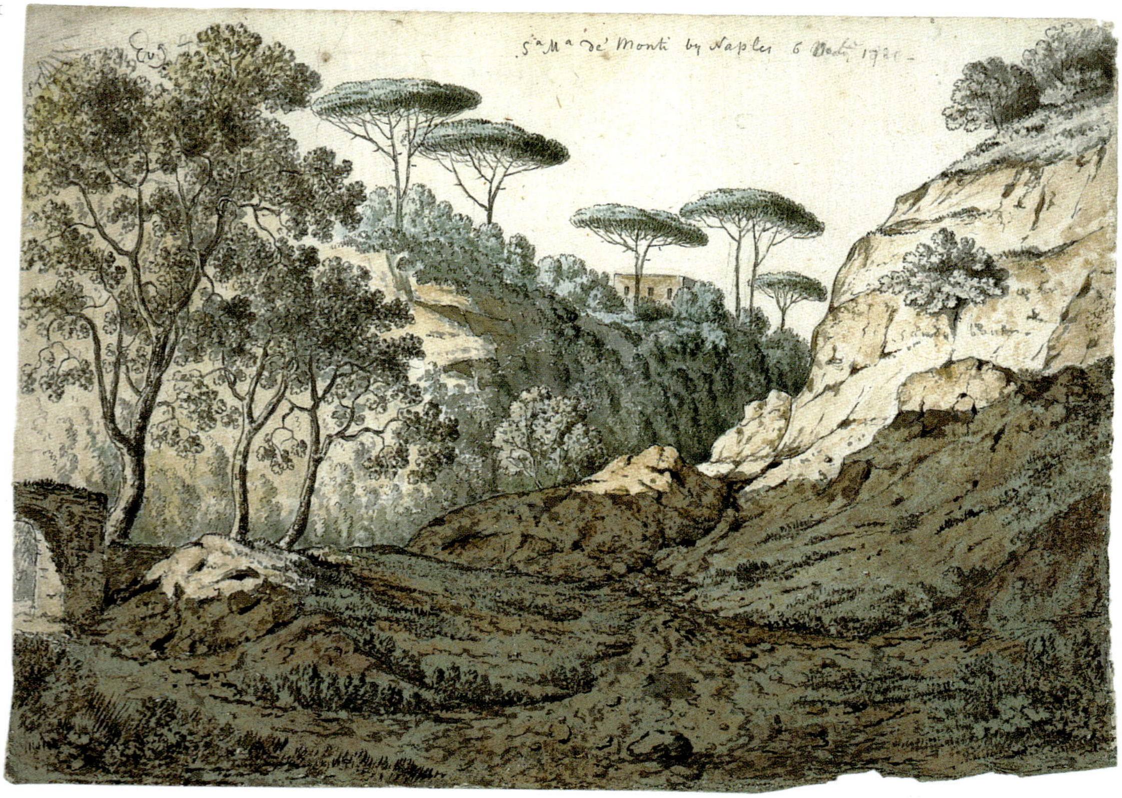

132

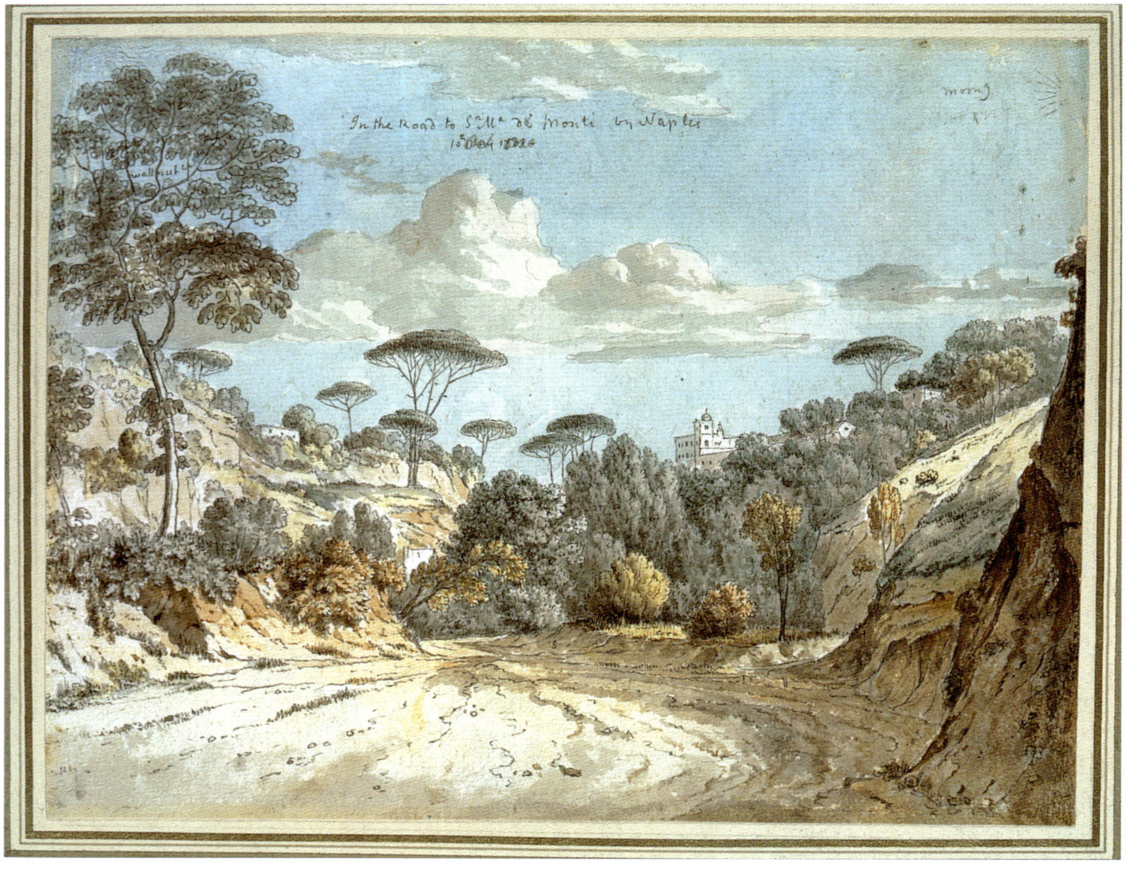

133

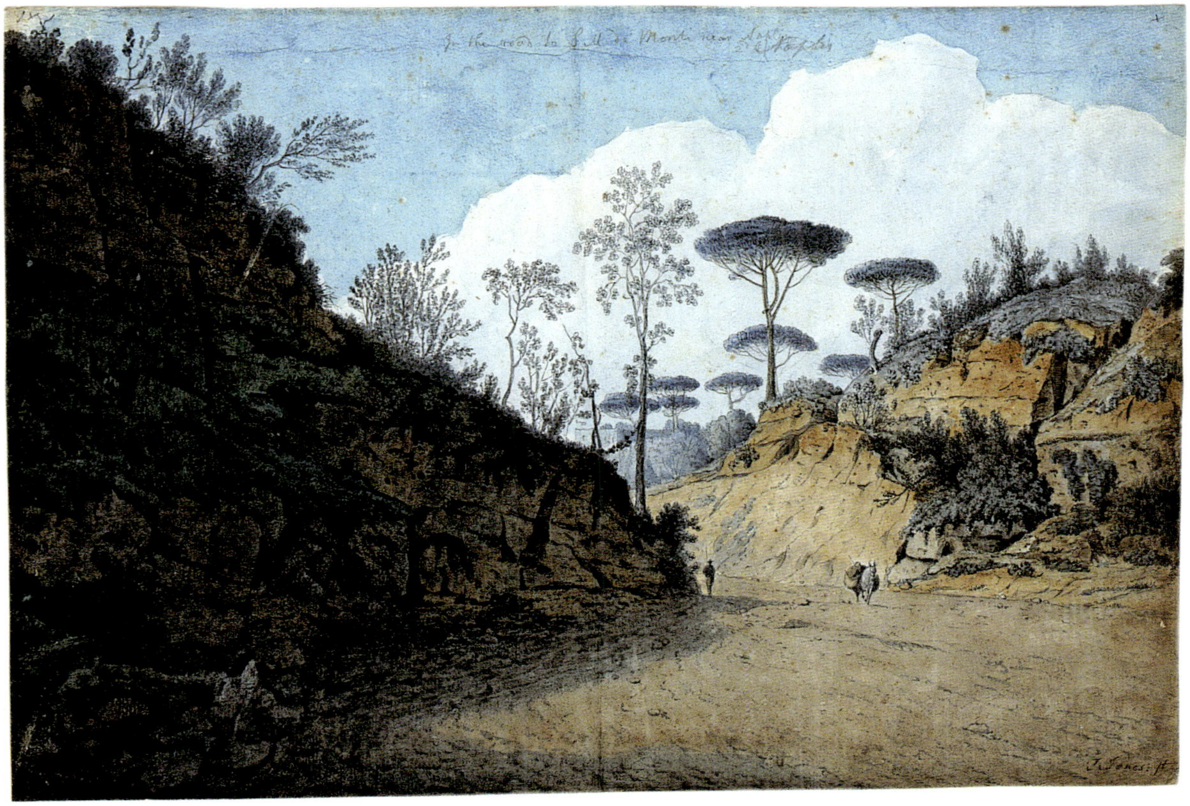

134

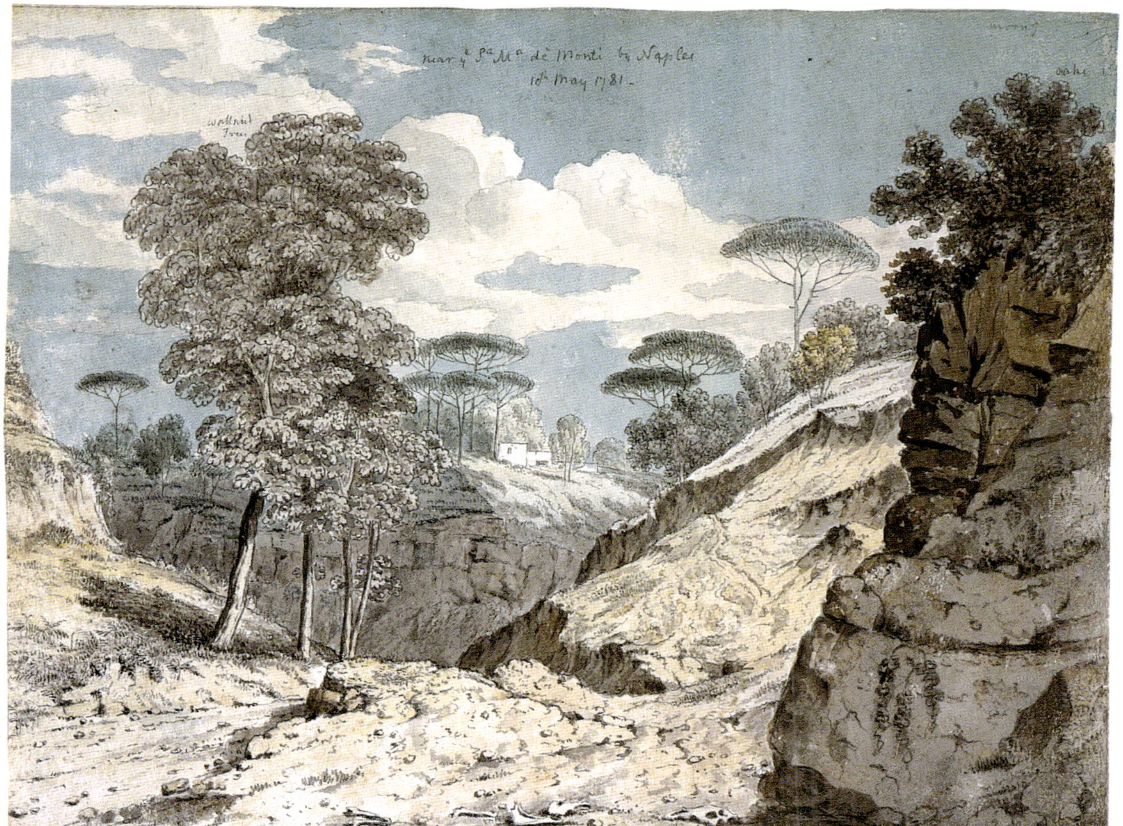

132

Thomas Jones (1742–1803)

In the Road to Santa Maria dei Monti, near Naples: Morning 1781

Pencil, watercolour on Italian writing paper*, 21.1 × 27.8 (8¼ × 11)

Ins.: 'In the Road to S^a^ M^a^ de' Monti by Naples / 10th Oct 1781' ('Oct' written over 'May') t.c.; rays of sun and 'morng' t.r.; 'wallnut' t.l.
Prov.: Captain John Dale, then by descent; Fine Arts Society; J. Hawkesley-Elliot; Mrs O. M. Morgan; Christie's, 14 March 1978, no. 101; Spink's; Morton Morris and Co; purchased 1982
Exh.: Spink's, 1979, no. 5; Manchester, 1988, no. 120
Lit.: Egerton, 1986, p. 11

Tate. Purchased 1982 (T03367)

Cardiff and Manchester only

Like the Whitworth drawing, this work has had the date altered to October, presumably when it was coloured. It must originally have read May, since there are at least eight other drawings where the inscription '10 May' has not been changed. Jones would not have had time to colour the drawings on one day and the later date presumably means that he returned to the work, if not the site. This was clearly a busy month for the artist. He began at least thirteen views along the road to Santa Maria dei Monti. Beginning at the end of March, he made a survey of the distinctive scenery that was unprecedented in its thoroughness. As with many of his drawings, Jones notes the time of day – morning – and uses a symbol to indicate the direction of the sun. (CN)

133

Thomas Jones (1742–1803)

In the Road to Santa Maria dei Monti, near Naples 1781

Pencil, watercolour on Italian writing paper*, 29.1 × 43 (11½ × 16⅞)

Ins.: 'In the road to S M de' Monti near Naples / 2d April 1781' t.c. (the latter crossed out and 'Naples' over the top); 'T J' t.c.; 'T Jones ft' l.r.
Prov.: Captain John Dale, then by descent
Exh.: London, 1970, no. 49

Private collection

Cardiff and Manchester only

Francis Towne, an old friend of Jones, arrived in Naples on 8 March 1781. Jones recorded that 'I gladly offered my Services to be his Cicerone . . . a Circumstance rather favourable to Mr Towne, in his Profession, as I was able to conduct him to many picturesque Scenes of my Own discovery, entirely out of the common road of occasional Visiters' (*Memoirs*, p. 102). One such 'Scene' was undoubtedly the road to Santa Maria dei Monti, since Towne made a drawing of the subject on 31 March 1781 (Christie's, 6 June 2002, no. 10). This drawing by Jones was also probably begun in company with Towne, who returned to Rome the following day. Its high level of finish, however, indicates that Jones also worked on it at a later date. (CN)

134

Thomas Jones (1742–1803)

Near Santa Maria dei Monti, near Naples 1781

Pencil, watercolour on laid paper, 20.8 × 27.8 (8½ × 11)

Ins.: 'near ye Sa Ma de' Monti by Naples / 10th May 1781-' t.c.; 'wallnut Trees' t.l.; 'oak' t.r.; 'morng' t.r.
Prov.: Captain John Dale, then by descent
Exh.: London, 1970, no. 51b

Private collection

Cardiff and Manchester only

In his *Memoirs*, Jones described a journey along the road to Santa Maria dei Monti with Francis Towne: 'Proceeding up the valley whose boundaries contracted more and more as we advanced, increasing in proportion the Gloominess of the Scene; We arrived at a Spot, which might very properly have been termed *the Land of Darkness & the Shadow of Death* . . . Here, says I, Mr Towne, is Salvator Rosa in perfection we only want *Banditti* to compleat the Picture – I had scarcely uttered the words, when turning round a Projection of the Rocks, we all-at once pop'd upon three ugly-looking fellows . . . with long knives, cutting up a dead jackAss . . . *Towne* started back . . . "I'll go no farther" says he . . . adding . . . that however he might admire such Scenes in a Picture – he did not relish them in Nature' (pp. 104–5). Jones goes on to record that

135

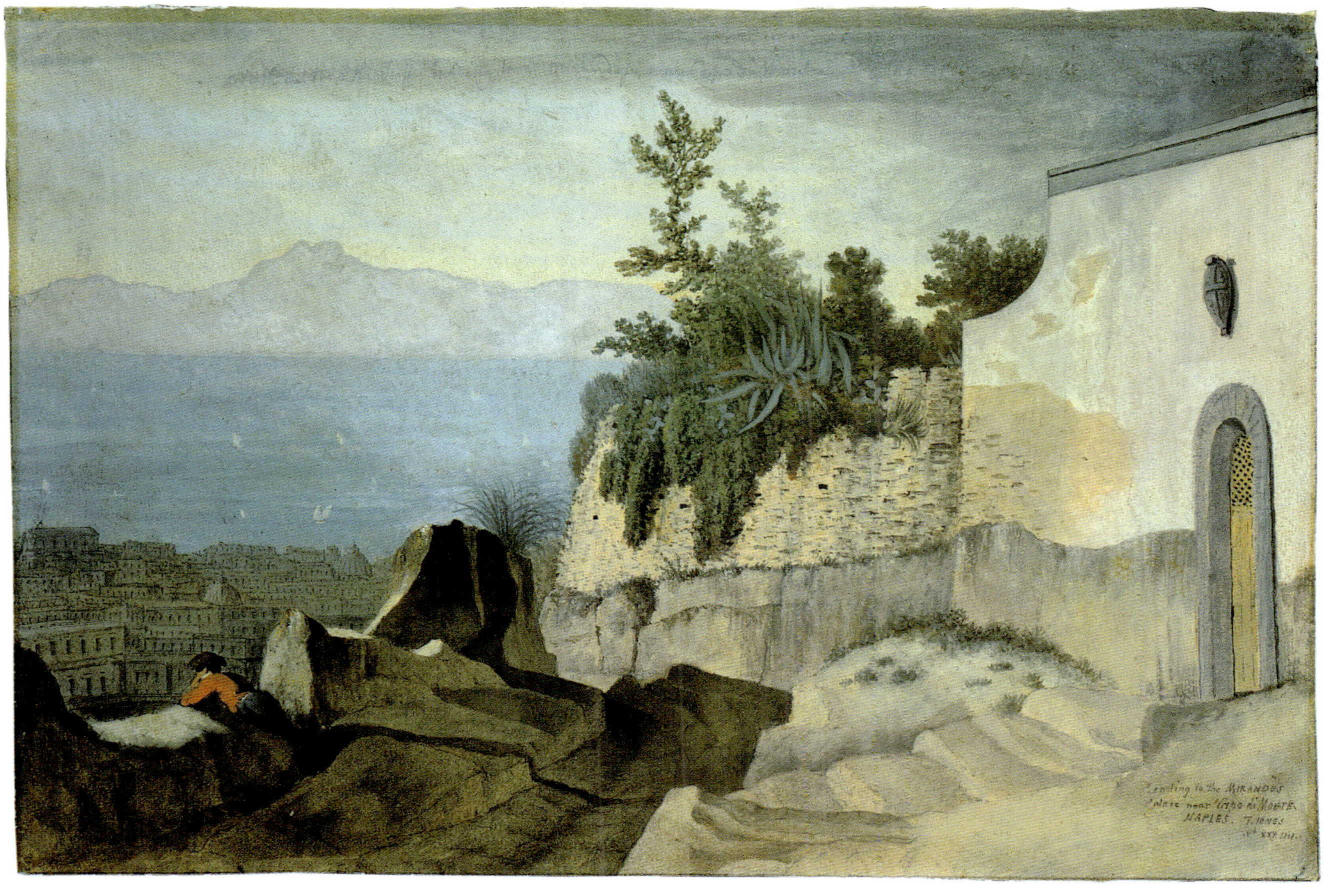

on later visits to the spot he used to see the bleached bones of the animal. Those in the foreground of this drawing are presumably a joking reference to the incident. (CN)

135

THOMAS JONES (1742–1803)

View over Naples on the Salita della Riccia, near Capodimonte *c.*1782

Watercolour, oil on paper, 28 × 42 (11 × 16½)

Ins.: 'Leading to the MIRANDUS / Palace near Capo di MONTE / NAPLES. T.JONES / No XXXIIII' l.r.; 'a Path cut thro' the Tuffa leading to the mirandose near Capo di Monte Naples august 17th' t.c.

Prov.: Sotheby's, 14 July 1994, no. 128

James Mackinnon

Cardiff and Manchester only

This work shows a view from the 'rocky Passage to the *Miradose* a Villa belonging to the Prince *L'Arriccia*', near Capodimonte (*Memoirs*, p. 116). Jones lived nearby from June 1782 to May 1783, and so the '17 August' inscribed on the drawing probably refers to 1782. Jones used a mixture of oil and watercolour and the drawing is a hybrid in another respect. The pencilled inscription in the sky is typical of those found on drawings sketched on the spot and then coloured later; the other, to the lower right, is characteristic of the larger oils on paper. Perhaps Jones took a pencil drawing with later watercolour washes and subsequently continued it in oils.

The work is closely related to cat. no. 125, which apparently shows the same road cut through the tufa. It has the next number in the sequence, '35', is the same size and contains a similarly dressed figure. These works may form a pair, but *Solfatara*, number '36' (cat. no. 140), bears no discernible relationship to either. (GS)

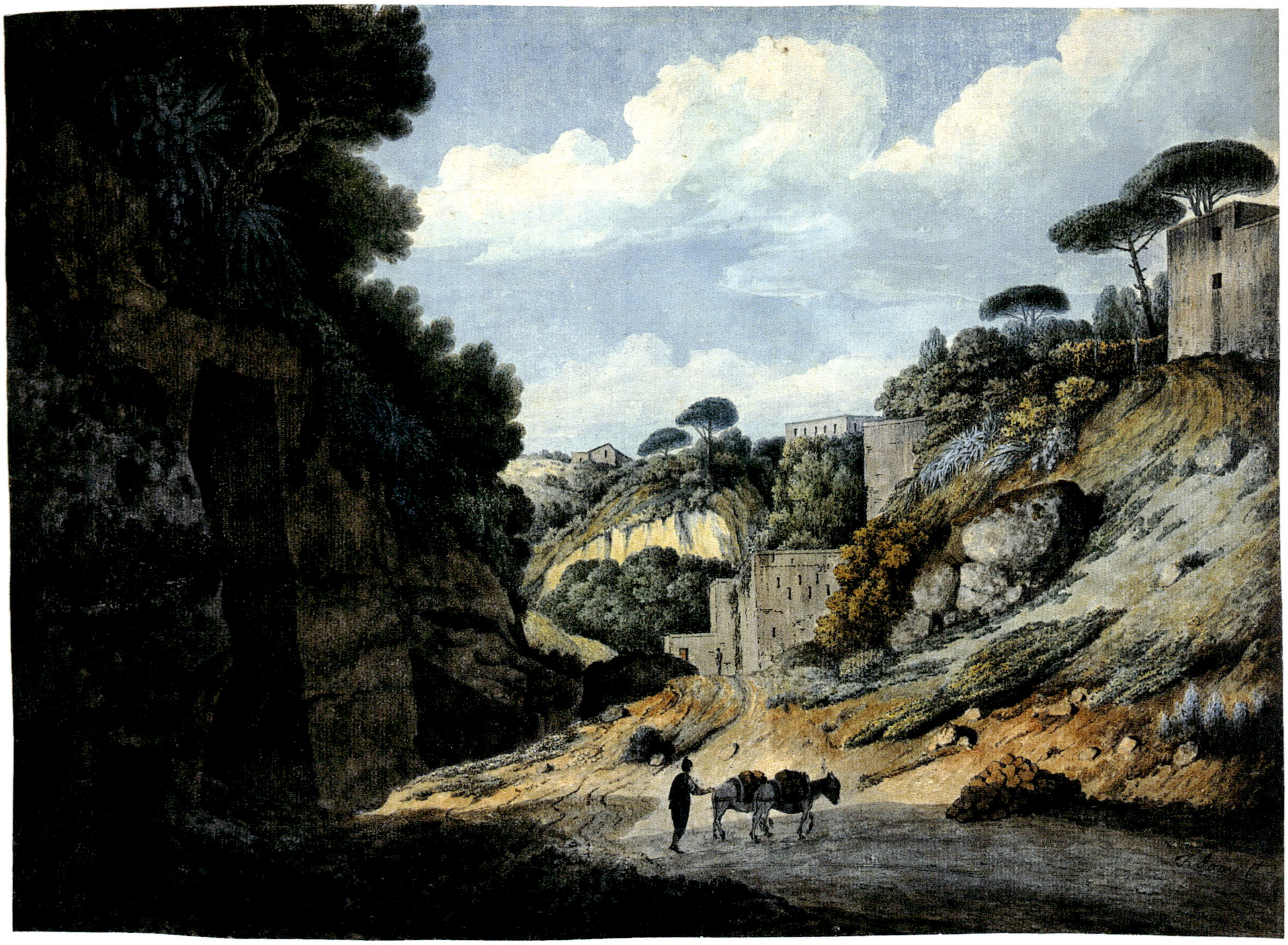

136

THOMAS JONES (1742–1803)

In the Suburbs of Naples *c.*1782

Pencil, watercolour, pen and ink and gum arabic on Italian writing paper*, 35.5 × 48.7 (13⅞ × 19⅛)

Ins.: 'T Jones' l.l.; 'No 3 Suburbs of Naples / T Jones' verso
Prov.: Phillips, 24 April 1989, no. 37; Agnew's; purchased 1989

National Museums & Galleries of Wales (NMW A 1860)

Jones explored the scenes along the road near the Hospital of S. Gennaro in 1782, completing a further watercolour (cat. no. 137), an oil on paper inscribed 'near Capodimonte' (cat. no. 124), and another titled *Suburbs of Naples with Figures and Bridge* (private collection). Jones noted that he and his friend Giovanni Battista Lusieri 'spent a great part of our time together in such kind of Scenery, making Studies from Nature' (*Memoirs*, p. 113). Jones was not able to capture in his sketches one of the things that most attracted him to the scene, however. 'What added much to the Solemnity of the Scene', he stated, 'were the hollow reverberations of Sound, proceeding from the Strokes of the Hammers and other Instruments of the Workmen' involved in the quarrying of stone that helped to fashion the landscape. (GS)

137

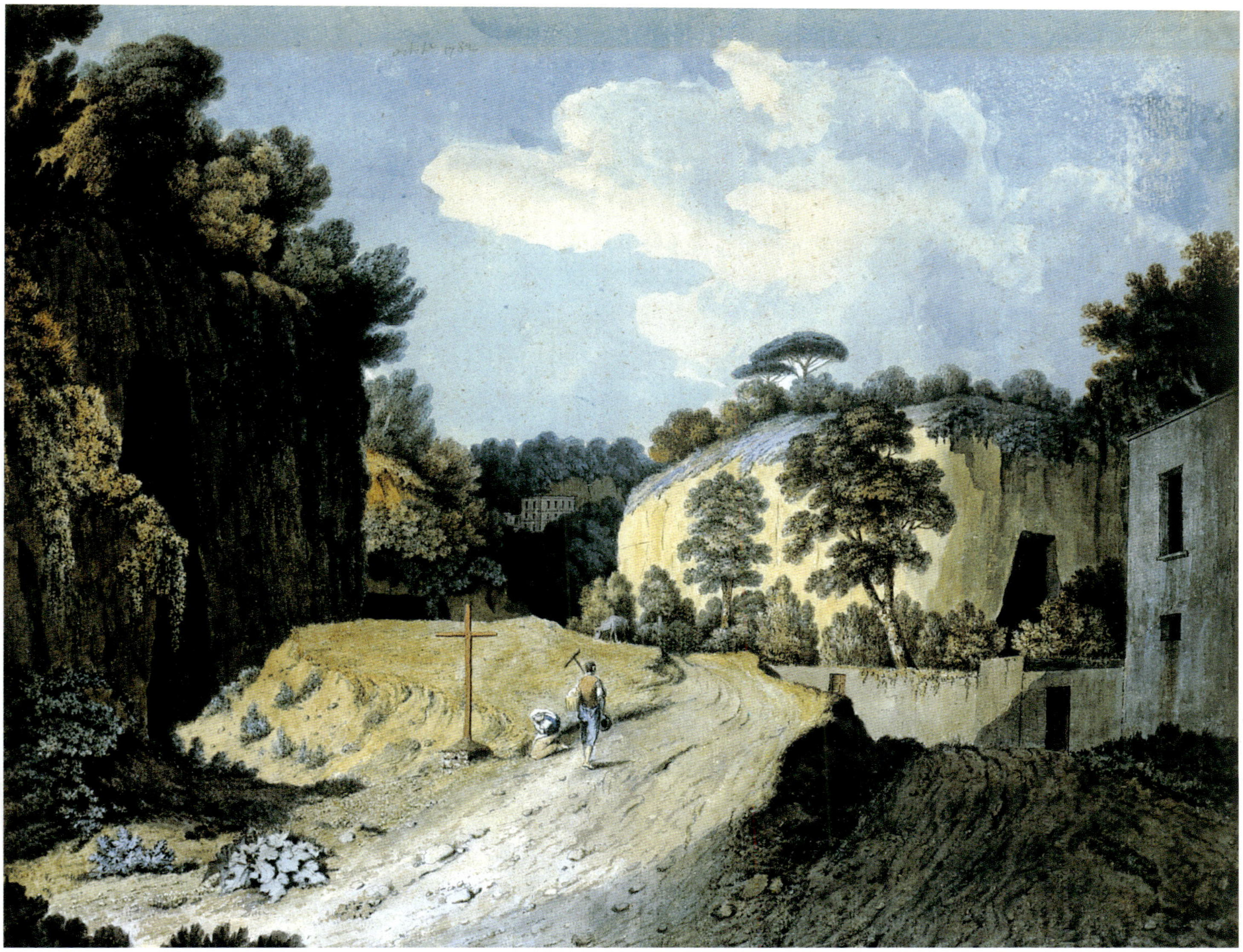

137

THOMAS JONES (1742–1803)

A Road in a Gorge near Naples 1782

Pencil, watercolour, pen and ink and gum arabic on Italian writing paper*, 37.3 × 48 (14⅝ × 18⅞)

Ins.: 'T. Jones' l.r.; 'Octob[r] 1782' t.c.
Prov.: Thomas Thomas, then by descent
Exh.: London, 1970, no. 48

Private collection

In October 1782, Jones noted that 'I spent [time] in those picturesque roads which I had discovered in the Environs of the City', referring to an area behind the 'Hospital of S. Gennaro', near Capodimonte (*Memoirs*, pp. 115–16, p. 113). Jones was excited by the location's pictorial possibilities and his description tallies so closely with this and cat. no. 136 that there is little doubt that this is the scene depicted. The road, he said, was flanked with 'immense Masses of Tuffa, finely fringed with Shrubs of various hues and Shades, intermixed with large overgrown Alloes and Indian figs'. Even more important, given Jones's interest in the effect of dark voids, the rocks were interspersed with 'Grottoes or Caverns, from whence Stones for the purpose of building were excavated' (ibid., p. 113). This work, which possibly shows the view from further up the road than cat. no. 136, is one of Jones's most carefully worked-up watercolours, with dense washes of colour, retouched with additional gum arabic to increase their richness. (GS)

138

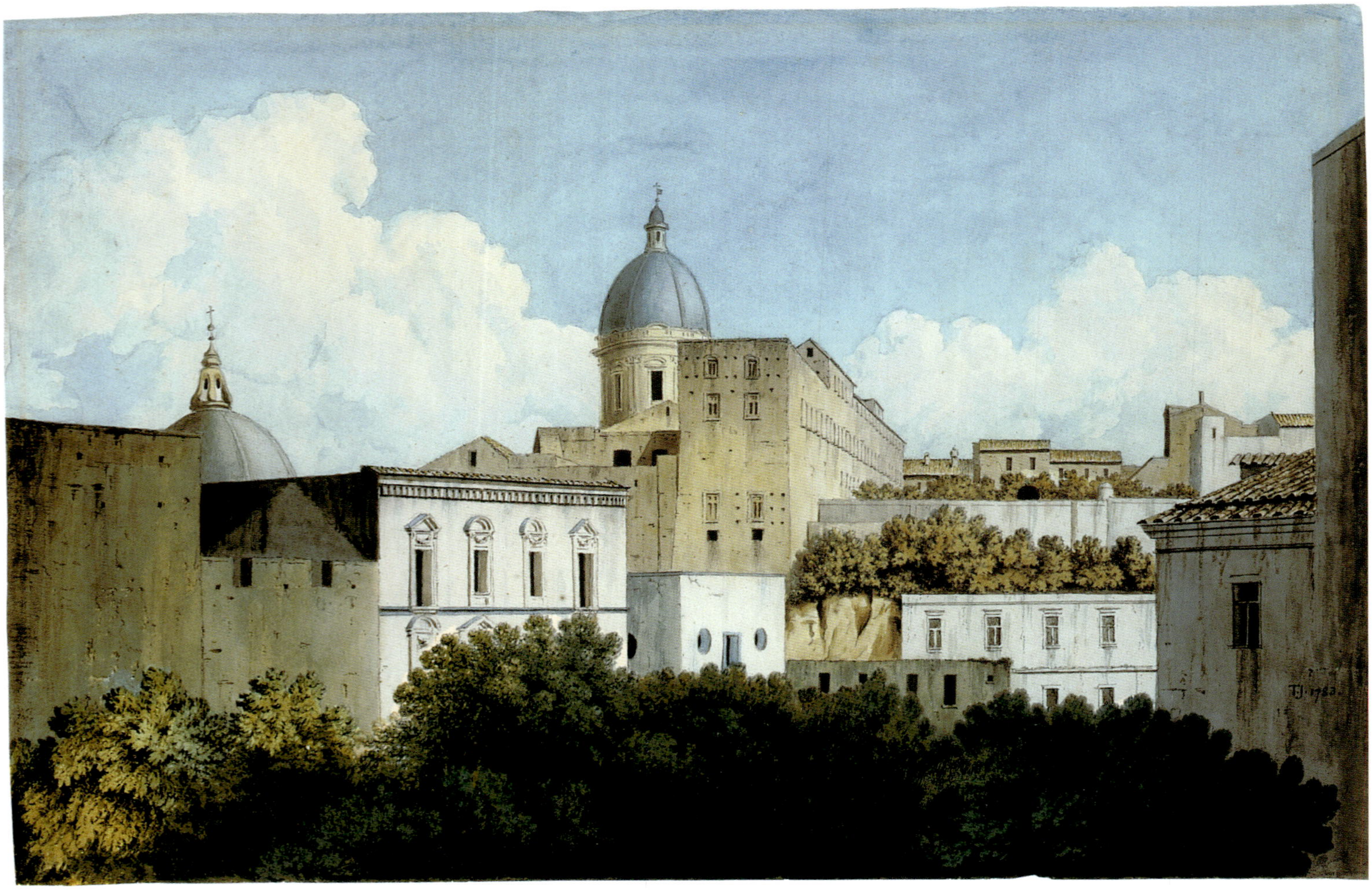

138

Thomas Jones (1742–1803)

View from Chiaja to Pizzofalcone, Naples 1783

Pencil, watercolour on Dutch writing paper*, 26.5 × 42.1 (10 3/8 × 16 5/8)

Ins.: 'T. J. 1783' l.r.
Prov.: Thomas Thomas, then by descent
Exh.: London, 1970, no. 70 as 'A group of Villas with Domes and Churches Beyond'
Lit.: Blunt, 1973, p. 500

Private collection

This watercolour was painted from the studio that Jones took in December 1782 at the '*Court End* of the Town'. The move was made in order that 'I might paint, and exhibit my Pictures within the *Reach* of Visiters'. The apartment at the 'back of the Chaja', the most fashionable street in the city, 'looked over fruitful Gardens, and commanded a View of many Churches, Convents, Villas and the greatest Part of the hill of Pusilippo' (*Memoirs*, p. 118). From here, he continued, 'I began several Studies of the different Scenes & Objects seen from the Windows on both Sides, some of which were painted in Oil, & some in Water Colors' (ibid., p. 119). This view, which looks eastwards to Pizzofalcone, shows the dome of S. Caterina in the distance, with S. Maria degli Angeli rising above the Theatine monastery. It is the only watercolour that survives of a subject that the artist normally painted in oils on paper. (GS)

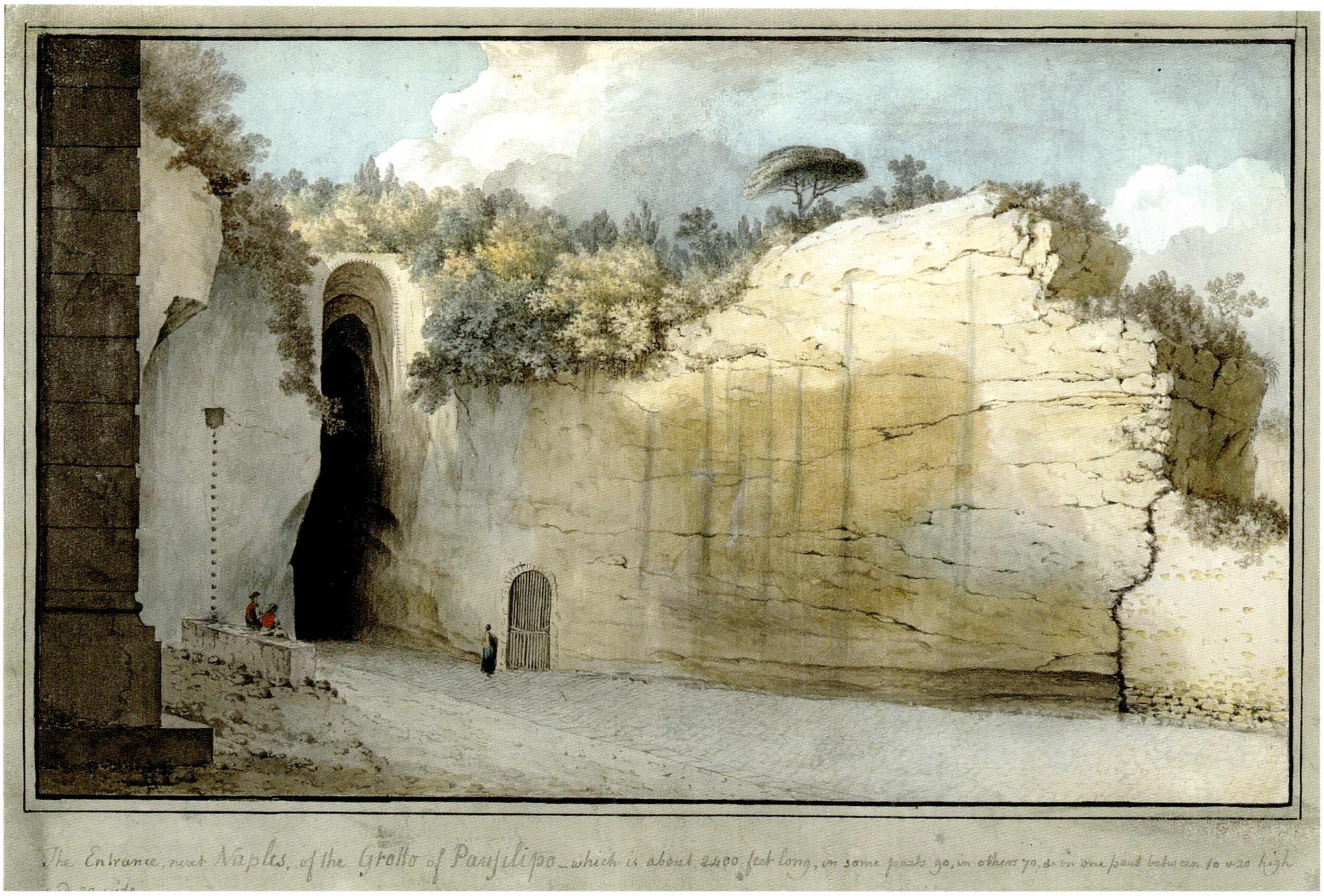

139

139

Thomas Jones (1742–1803)

The Entrance of the Grotto of Posillipo 1780s

Pencil, watercolour, bodycolour with original wash border on laid paper, 24.1 × 39.4 (9½ × 15½)

Ins.: 'The Entrance, next Naples, of the Grotto of Pausilipo – which is about 2400 feet long, in some parts 90 & in others 70, & in one part between 10 & 20 high / and 22 wide-' on the border
Prov.: Captain John Dale, then by descent; Christie's, 2 July 1954, no. 221; Agnew's, 1954; Maas Gallery; Dudley Snelgrove; Sotheby's, 19 November 1992, no. 196
Exh.: London, 1970, no. 42: Manchester, 1988, no. 133
Lit.: Mallalieu, 1979, vol. ii, p. 429

Yale Center for British Art, Paul Mellon Collection (B1993.9)

Jones made numerous trips to Posillipo to the south-west of Naples, making use of the tunnel cut under the hills. This famous feat of Roman engineering, known as the Grotto of Posillipo, was painted by many artists, including William Pars (cat. no. 98) and Francis Towne (British Museum). Jones sketched with both artists in Naples in 1781 and there are similarities between their views of the entrance of the 'grotto' from the Neapolitan side. They may have sketched together, but Jones's oil sketch, which was taken from a slightly different angle in 1782 (cat. no. 119), and this studio work were produced on different occasions. The absence of inscriptions on this watercolour, its careful finish and its presentation in a mount with a title suggest that it was produced in the studio, possibly at a later date. (GS)

140

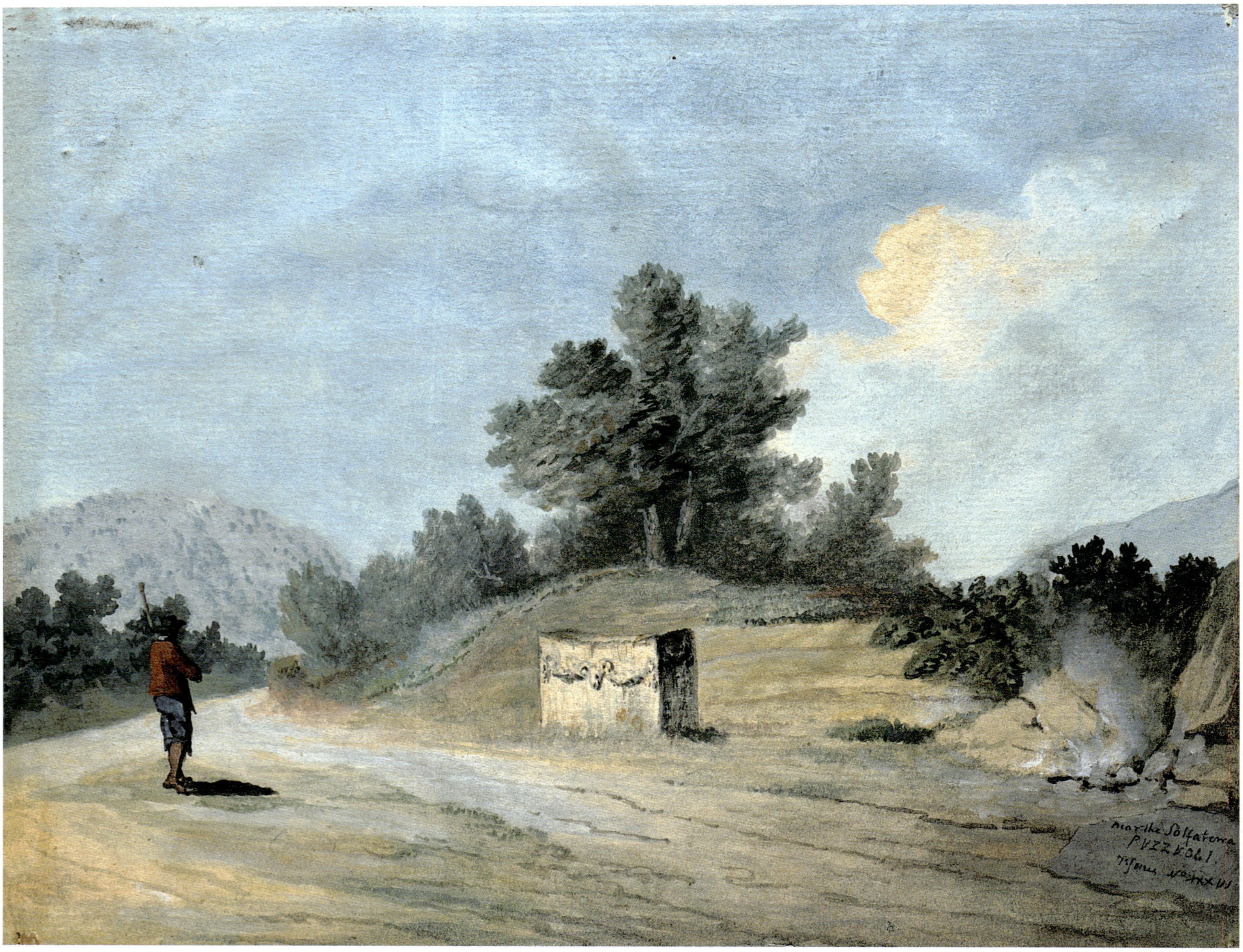

140

THOMAS JONES (1742–1803)

Near Solfatara, Pozzuoli 1780s

Pencil, watercolour, oil on laid paper, 23 × 28 (9 × 11¾)

Ins.: 'near the Solfaterra / PUZZUOLI / Ts. Jones N°·XXXVI' l.r.
Prov.: Colnaghi's, 1961; W. A. Brandt, then by descent
Exh.: London, 1970, no. 47

Private collection

Cardiff and Manchester only

Solfatara is the site of an extinct volcano north of Pozzuoli, though the ground is still disturbed by wisps of sulphurous steam and bubbling mud and the smoke to the left is presumably a manifestation of the former. Jones frequently visited this area in 1782, when he produced studies for his painting of the Campi Flegrei – the 'burning fields' (see p. 71). The lost sketch on which this studio work was based was probably made earlier, however. In October 1780, Jones records taking the road 'call'd by the Inhabitants Troja, which is lined on each side by Antique Sepulchral Monuments' (*Memoirs*, p. 98). The final element of the composition, the solitary peasant observing the antique sarcophagus, confirms that this is a carefully planned studio work where the figure adds another layer of meaning. Like the figures in Nicolas

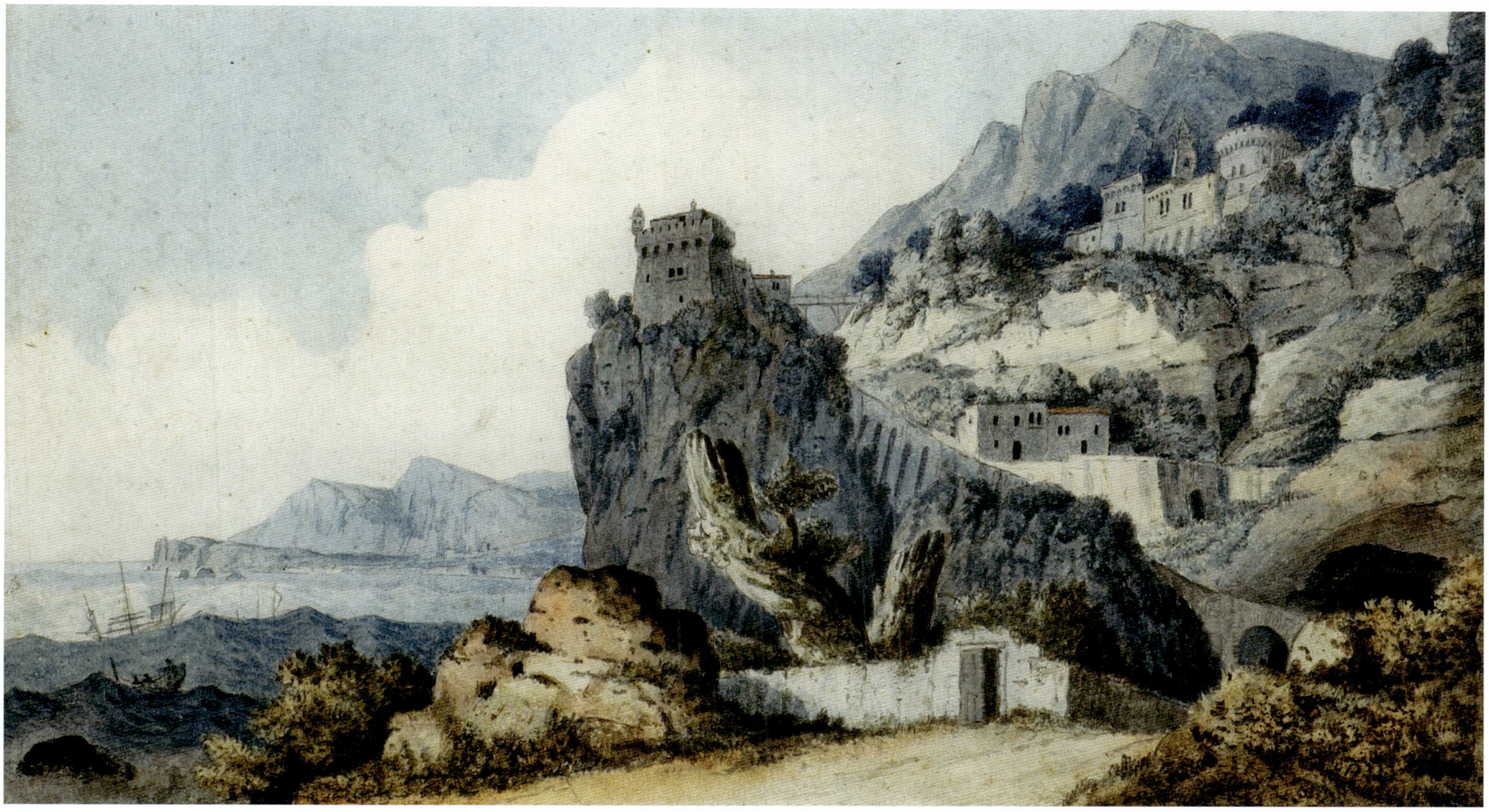

141

Poussin's *The Arcadian Shepherds* (The Louvre, Paris), the peasant is confronted with a reminder of mortality in keeping with the fire and its sacrificial associations. (GS)

141

THOMAS JONES (1742–1803)

A View of the Gulf of Salerno 1780s?

Watercolour, pen and ink on paper, 23 × 43 (9 × 16⅞)

Ins.: 'T. Jones' l.c.
Prov.: Clonterbrook Trustees; John Baskett Ltd; purchased 1981
Exh.: Manchester, 1988, no. 126; Paderborn, 1996

Bolton Museum & Art Gallery, Bolton MBC (BOLMG:1982.11)

Cardiff and Manchester only

Unusually for Jones, there are no inscriptions to help identify the subject of this watercolour. The disposition of the rocks and the form of the castle suggest that we are looking at a scene on the Gulf of Salerno, but it has not been possible to identify it. The problem may be that the work is actually a composite of a number of views, and the assemblage, as well as the individual architectural elements, has an unreal air. Jones also uncharacteristically depicts a stormy sea, though the effect is far from convincing. The lack of inscriptions, the unconventional panoramic proportions of the work and the attempt at a complex natural effect all suggest that this watercolour, like *At Terracina* (cat. no. 166), may have been executed after Jones's return from Italy. (GS)

FOLLOWING PAGES Detail of cat. no. 162.

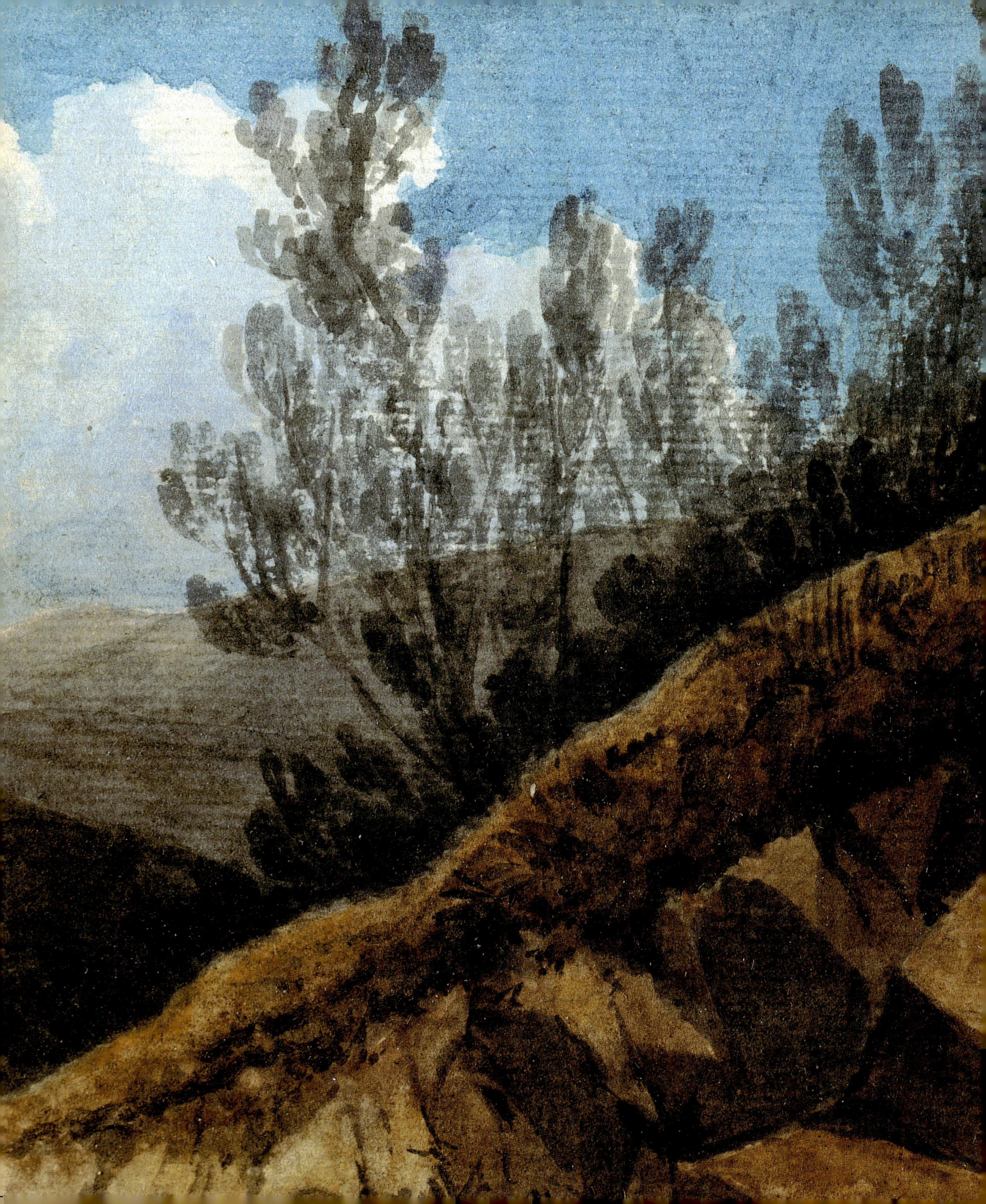

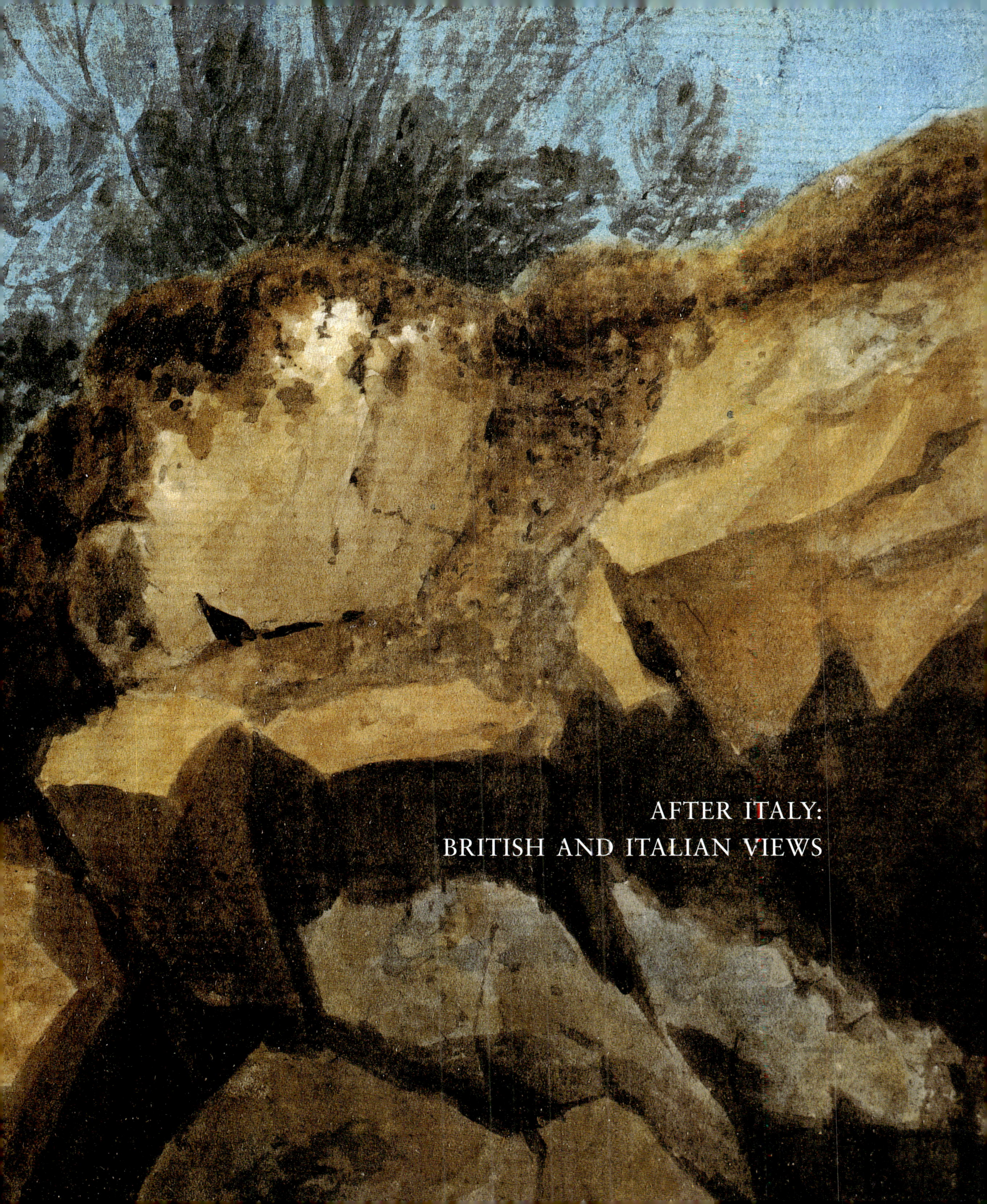

AFTER ITALY:
BRITISH AND ITALIAN VIEWS

142

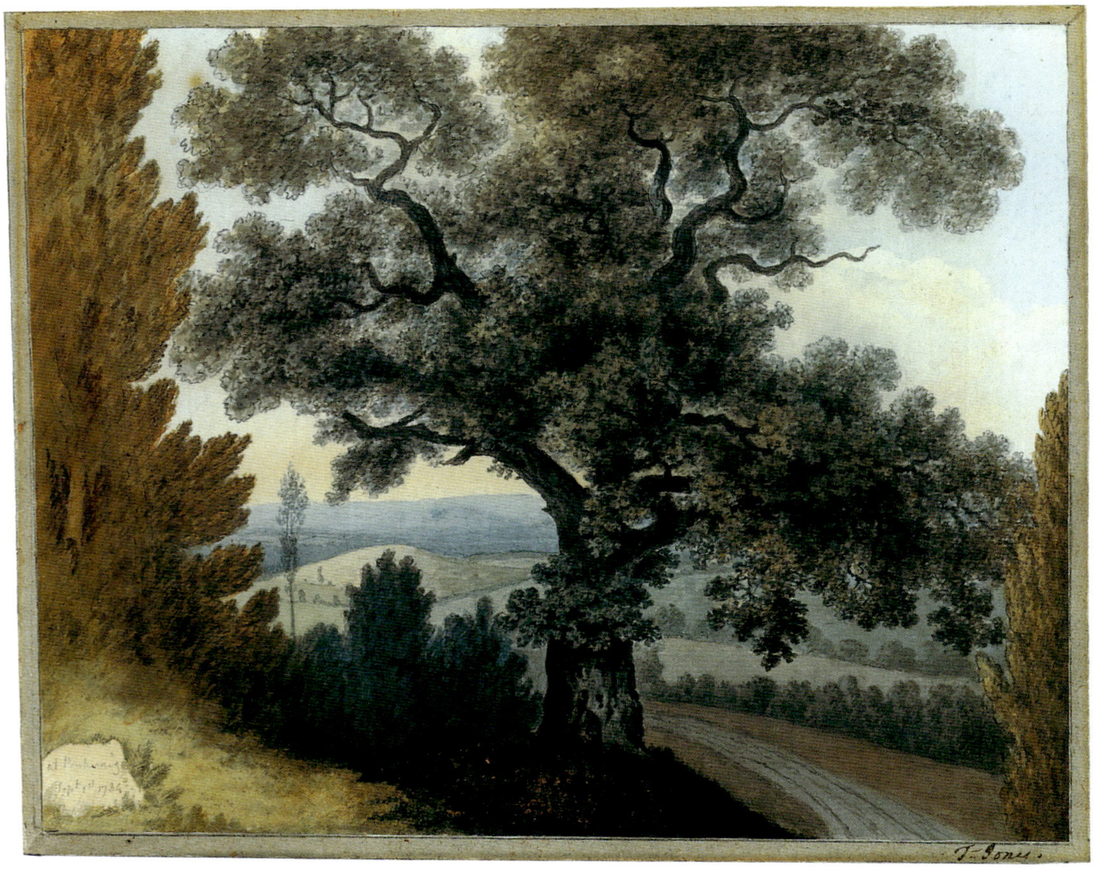

142

THOMAS JONES (1742–1803)

An Oak Tree with a Distant View near Pencerrig

1784

Pencil, watercolour on an English writing paper on an original two-ply mount made from sheets of wrapping and cartridge paper*, 20.7 × 26.7 ($8^{1}/_{4}$ × $10^{1}/_{2}$)

Ins.: 'at Pencerrig / Sept 1st 1784 / Thos Jones' l.l. on rock;
'T. – Jones.' l.r. on original mount
Prov.: Thomas Thomas, then by descent
Exh.: London, 1970, no. 79 as 'Pencerrig'

Private collection

Cardiff and Manchester only

Jones delayed returning to Wales until August 1784. During his short stay, he made a number of watercolours which record aspects of the family estates and nearby views such as this. In contrast to the oil sketches of 1772 and 1776, the main focus is now on the trees, rocks and buildings in the foreground. In this example, a picturesque oak bursts out of the confines of the composition. In his poem 'Petraeia', Jones expressed his love for the 'native forests' and the 'sturdy knotted oak' in particular. Examples such as this had a special significance because of the desecrations that had been visited on the trees at Pencerrig. As he noted, the value of an aged tree was enhanced by its survival:

> With pious awe the axe withdrew,
> And sav'd the consecrated few;
> The hoary parents of the wood,
> Who long the furious western gales have stood
> (Baker, 1795, p. 225).

The tree seen in this watercolour, however, was probably not on the estate, as the view in the distance shows Garth Bank and in the middle ground another small hill, both of which are visible from the old Builth to Llandrindod Wells road. (GS)

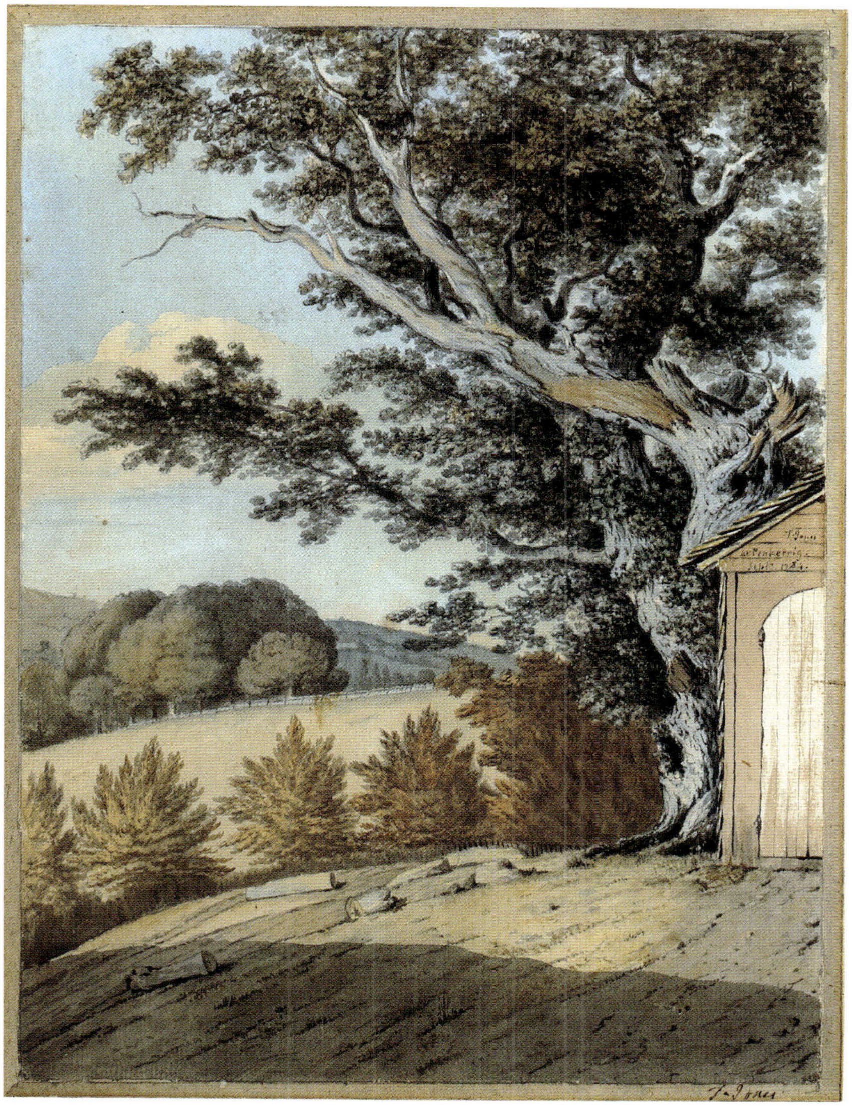

143

143

THOMAS JONES (1742–1803)

A Shed with an Oak Tree at Pencerrig 1784

Watercolour on English writing paper on an original two-ply mount made from sheets of grey wrapping paper and cartridge*, 27.8 × 21 (11 × 8¼)

Ins.: 'T. Jones / at Penkerrig. / Sept. 1784.' c.r. on the shed; 'T. Jones' l.r. on the original mount
Prov.: Thomas Thomas, then by descent
Exh.: London, 1970, no. 80 as 'at Pencerrig'

Private collection

Cardiff and Manchester only

This watercolour, together with other Welsh views such as cat. nos 142 and 144, are mounted in a similar manner and Jones signed each in the same place on the grey wash surround. The presentation of his watercolours in this way was a new departure for Jones and it reflects the fact that he had begun to use the medium to create finished studio works, rather than to add colour to a drawing begun in the field. The presentation of drawings in a consistent format also suggests that he was using watercolour to produce systematic records for his own personal interest. In this case, the motive was presumably pride in a well-run family estate in which new plantations, fences and buildings are balanced by ancient trees and reminders of ages past. The view is probably at Pencerrig, looking from the mound of oak trees south-east of the drive. (GS)

144

Thomas Jones (1742–1803)

A Barn at Pencerrig 1784

Pencil, watercolour, pen and ink on an English writing paper on an original mount of grey flecked wrapping paper*, 23 × 29.8 (9⅛ × 11¾)

Ins.: 'at Penkerrig / 1784' l.r.; 'T. Jones' l.r. on original mount
Prov.: Thomas Thomas, then by descent
Exh.: London, 1970, no. 89 as 'at Penkerrig'

Private collection

Cardiff and Manchester only

Illustrated on p. 77, fig. 36

The juxtaposition of bare rocks and the buildings of a well-ordered working estate is typical of the dual focus in Jones's 1784 watercolours of Pencerrig. Here, the rocky outcrop, with its echoes of the hills above Naples, is balanced by a barn and a hay rick as well as new plantations in the distance. This reflects the double significance of Pencerrig. The landscape of rocks, hills and ancient trees was a source of artistic inspiration – nature as a teacher – whilst the barn signifies another image of nature as a provider and guarantee of financial wealth. In fact, even the rocky outcrops (dolerite) on the Pencerrig estate had an economic return: they were quarried for building stone.

Jones's inexperience with the watercolour medium is evident in these works; the distances, for instance, lack the subtle gradations typical of the best contemporary work, and his foregrounds, as here, are often crudely painted. The hay rick to the left, however, is effective, with the artist using a dry brush to drag colour across the underlying wash to replicate the texture of straw. (GS)

145

James Peak (*c.*1730–*c.*1782) after Thomas Jones (1742–1803)

The Travellers' Repose 1784

Engraving and etching, 38.1 × 53.2 (15 × 21)

Ins.: 'Thos Jones Pinxit' l.l.; 'John Boydell exudit. London 1784' l.c.; 'Published Jany 1st, 1784 by John Boydell Engraver in Cheapside London' l.c.; 'James Peak sculpsit' l.r.

National Museums & Galleries of Wales (NMW A 16334)

Cardiff and Manchester only

Published by John Boydell in 1784, this engraving was perhaps conceived in an attempt by Jones to reintroduce himself to the British public after his return to the country. The 1970 Thomas Jones exhibition catalogue suggests that the source for this print is *Classical Landscape* (cat. no. 24). However, the composition is quite different and it appears to be after a painting, perhaps of an Italian landscape, which is now lost. James Peak had also been employed by Boydell to engrave landscapes after Richard Wilson and Claude. This impression is probably a working proof and there is another later state in the British Museum which has further engraved inscriptions, including the title. (BM)

145

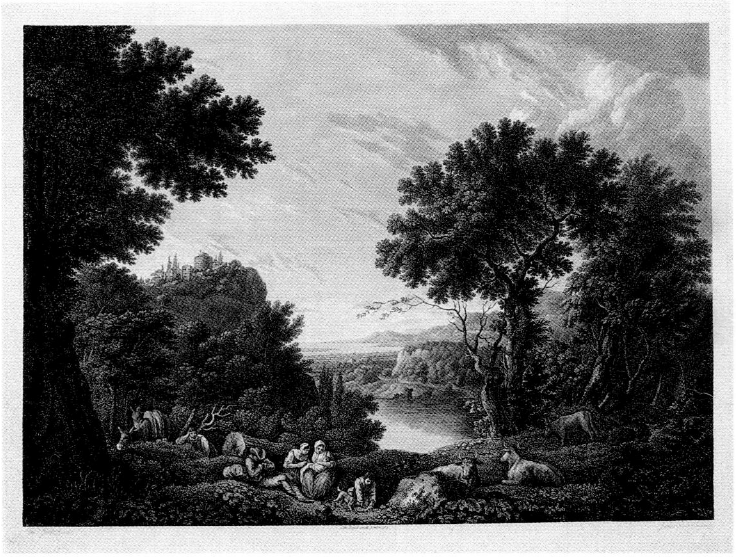

146

Thomas Jones (1742–1803)

View of the Temple of Diana at Nemi 1785

Oil on paper, 36.2 × 52 (14¼ × 20½)

Ins.: 'TEMPLUM DIANAE / NEMI / JONES 1785 No 29' l.l.
Prov.: Thomas Thomas, then by descent to Jane Evan-Thomas; given to the present owner
Exh.: London, 1970, no. 81

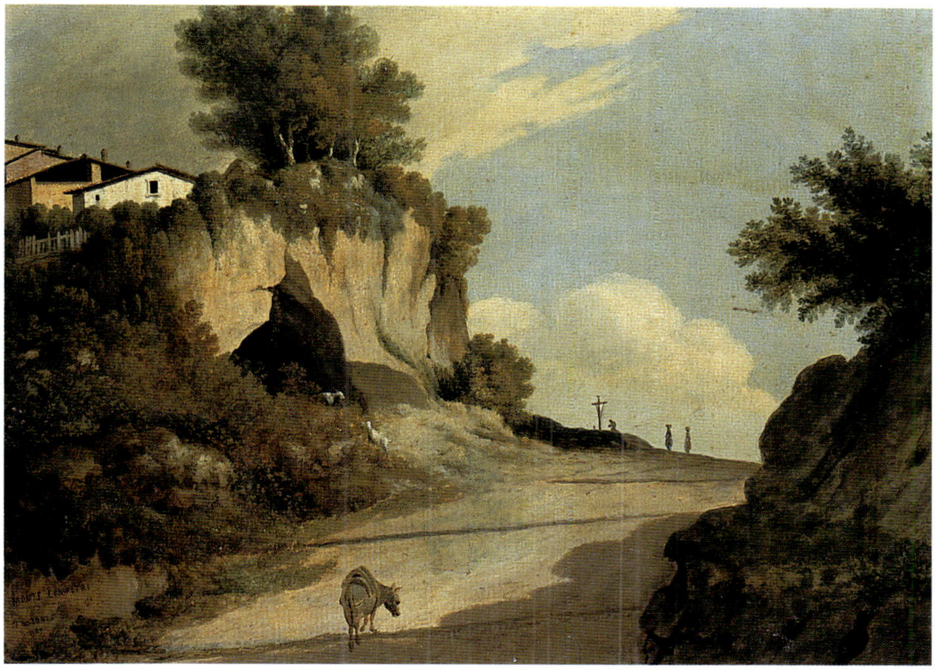

147

Lit.: Edwards, 1968, p. 11

Private collection

Cardiff and Manchester only

Illustrated on p. 82, fig. 41

The village of Nemi is situated above the north-east side of the lake. This view is taken from the area below, known as I Giardini, the site of the partly excavated Temple of Diana. The lake – out of view to the right – took the name of the Speculum Dianae (the mirror of Diana) in reference to its circular shape and smooth surface, and the site was sought out by tourists as the centre of her cult.

The date inscribed on this work indicates that it was painted back in England and this is crucial, since it confirms that Jones produced a category of oil painting on paper that was not only not painted on the spot, but was produced years later as a memento of his trip. Characteristics of this and other dated works, such as the prominent inscription consisting of a title, signature and number in capitals, the size of paper, the degree of finish and the important role played by the staffage, help to identify other later oils. (GS)

147

THOMAS JONES (1742–1803)

Monte Compatri, near Frascati 1785

Pencil, oil on blue wrapping paper, varnished*, 33.5 × 48 ($13\frac{1}{4} \times 18\frac{7}{8}$)

Ins.: 'MONTE COMPETRI / THO: JONES / 1785' l.l.
Prov.: Captain John Dale, then by descent

Private collection

Jones records that he hired a 'Man & his 4 Asses' at Frascati on 22 April 1777 to undertake an excursion to Rocca di Papa and on to Monte Cava. The party enjoyed the views from the highest point in the Alban Hills and returned via the small hilltop town of Monte Compatri, 'where we refreshed ourselves with very good wine in a large Vault with a great many of the Inhabitants' (*Memoirs*, pp. 57–8). This oil, which is dated after Jones's return from Italy, was presumably based on a lost sketch. As with many of the views that Jones worked up later, it has the air of being a memento of his travels. Roads and the people and animals who frequent them are a consistent theme and they commonly feature sites which could only have interest for the traveller himself. Typically, this work has remained in the family and it was clearly painted by Jones 'for my own Amusement' (ibid., p. 141). (GS)

148

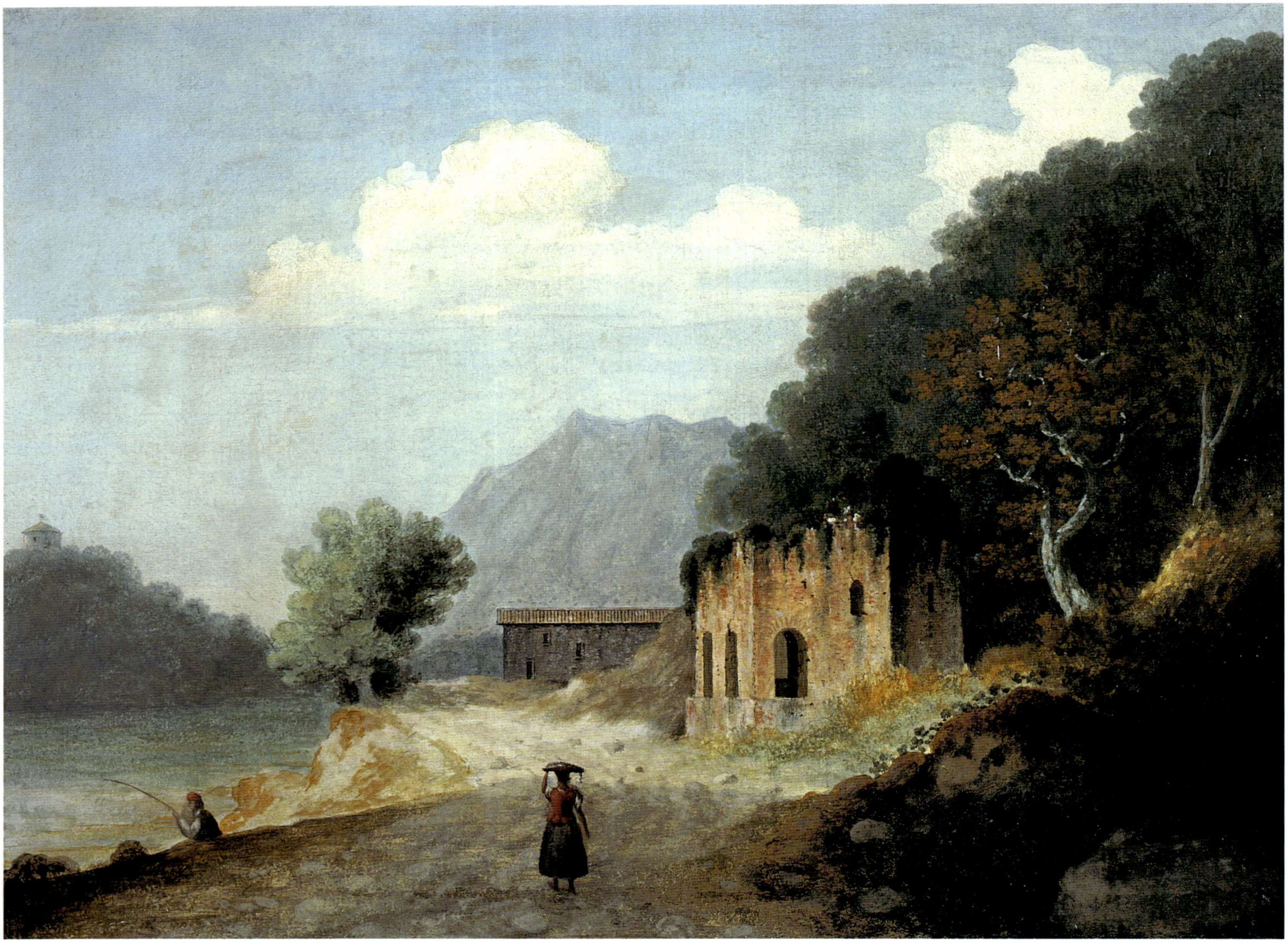

148

THOMAS JONES (1742–1803)

Italian River Scene with a Man Fishing 1785

Oil on paper, 34.8 × 46.4 (13½ × 18¼)

Ins.: 'T. Jones 1785' verso
Prov.: Thomas Thomas, then by descent to Jane Evan-Thomas; given to present owner

Private collection

Cardiff and Manchester only

It has not been possible to identify the subject of this work, but it is clear that although it is dated 1785, and from after Jones's return from Italy, it does not show a British scene. The ruined building and the costumes of the figures clearly indicate an Italian location. The fact that this is a later reworking of an Italian sketch is confirmed by the use of oil on a larger piece of paper than Jones commonly used for sketches made on the spot and by the carefully worked-out figures. This places it in a group of works such as *View of the Temple of Diana at Nemi* (cat. no. 146) – also dated 1785 – which were presumably made for the artist's own amusement and therefore remained in the family's possession. (GS)

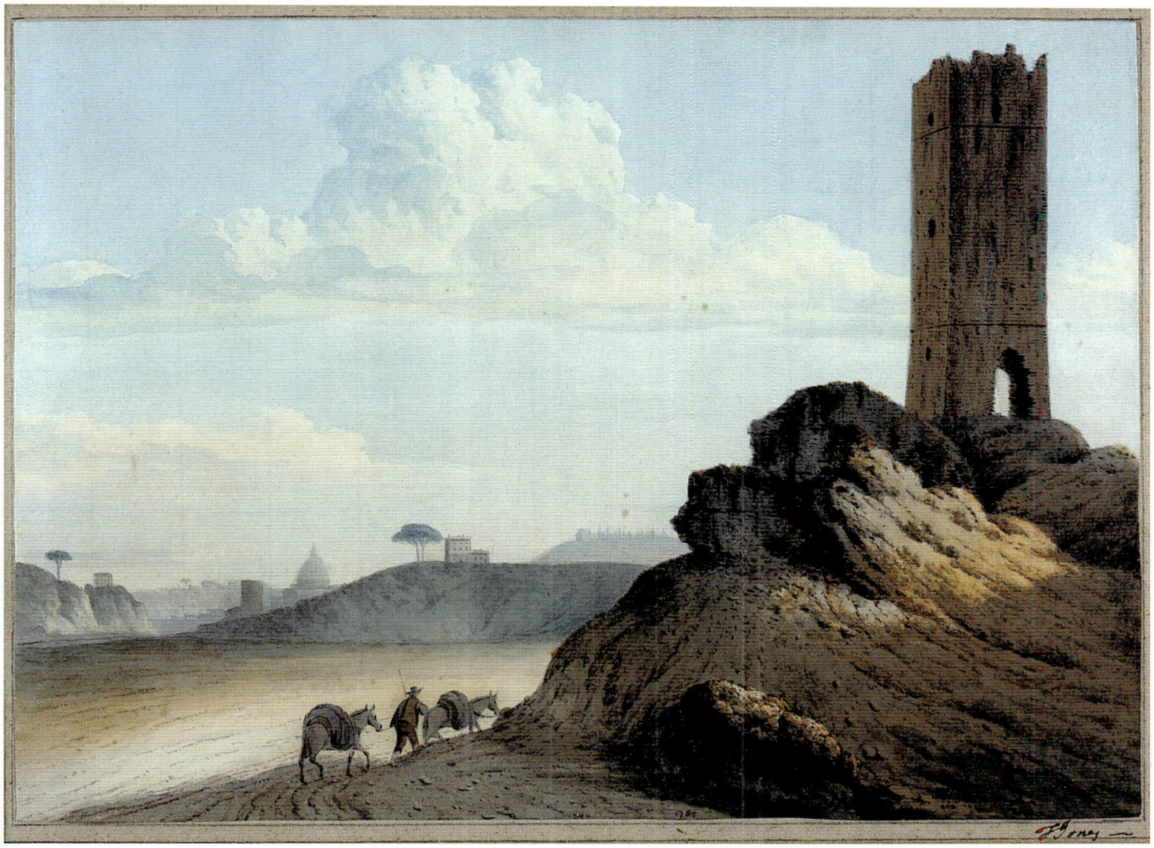

149

149

Thomas Jones (1742–1803)

On the Road to Civita Castellana, near Rome

1785

Pencil, watercolour on laid paper on original mount, 24.7 × 34.7 (9¾ × 13⅝)

Ins.: 'T Jones' l.r. on original mount; 'T. JONES' on a rock l.r.; '1785' l.c.
Prov.: Thomas Thomas, then by descent

Private collection

Cardiff and Manchester only

This watercolour derives from a pencil sketch in the smaller of the Roman sketchbooks, inscribed 'on ye road to Civita Castellana / 15 Feb 1777 ye same as page 47 / looking towards Rome' (cat. no. 74, p. 53). The inscription underlines the fact that it is a pair to cat. no. 92 and that here we look south towards St Peter's, with the Villa Mellini on the horizon to the right. Jones made this watercolour in London, probably at the same time as cat. no. 150. As he noted, he was mainly working 'for my own Amusement' at this date and the group has remained with his family ever since. One of the characteristic features of these drawings is the carefully placed figures, which are largely absent from studies made on the spot. The Cardiff sketchbook (cat. no. 76) contains a number of drawings of peasant figures made from life and such studies were presumably the basis for the travellers that populate these finished views. (GS)

150

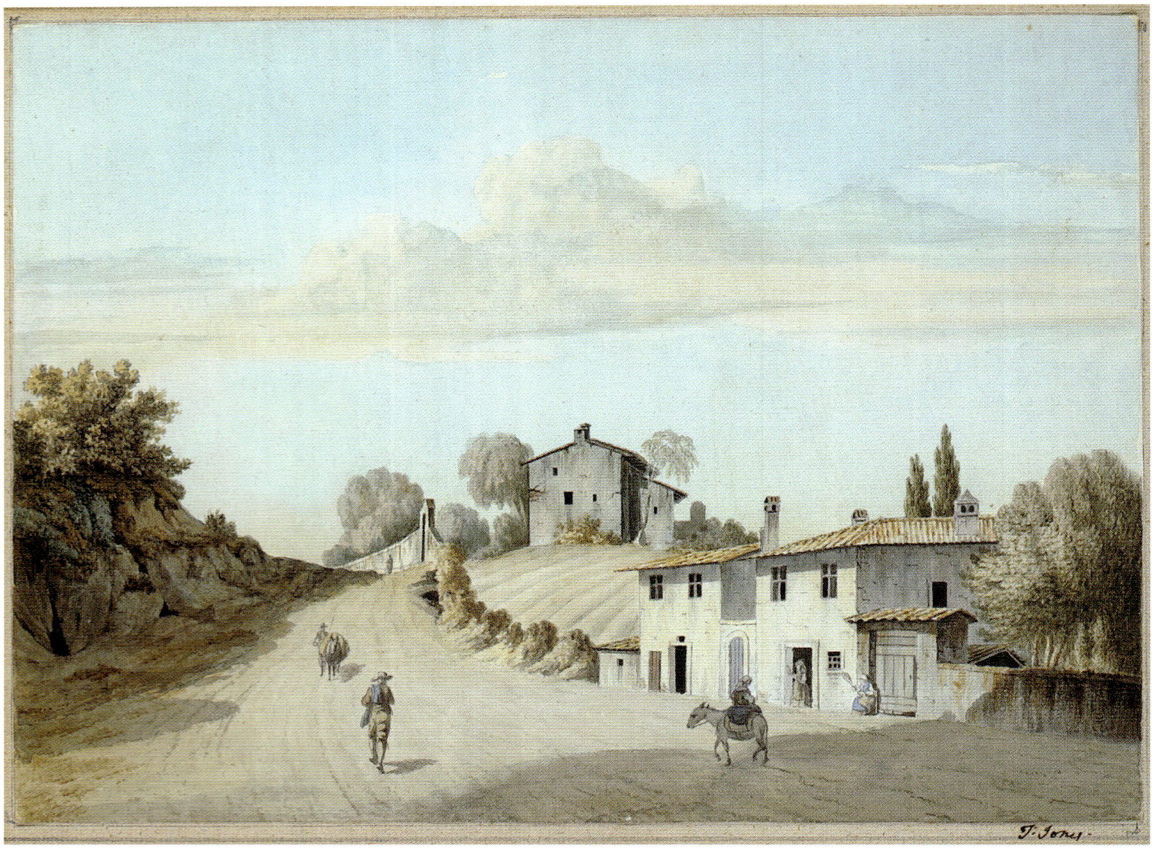

150

THOMAS JONES (1742–1803)

Houses on the Road from Rome to Civita Castellana 1780s

Pencil, watercolour on Dutch writing paper on original mount of blue-grey wrapping paper*, 24.7 × 34.7 ($9\frac{3}{4} \times 13\frac{5}{8}$)

Ins.: 'T. Jones' l.r.; inscription on the mount (obscured)
Prov.: Thomas Thomas, then by descent
Exh.: London, 1970, no. 75 as 'Near Rome on the Road to Florence'

Private collection

This watercolour is based on a drawing in the smaller of the sketchbooks, dated 15 February 1777 (cat. no. 74, p. 45). The sketch is inscribed 'beyond ye Ponte Mola' and 'Road from Rome to Civita Castellana & Loretto' and immediately precedes two others made along the same road, both of which Jones subsequently worked up as watercolours (cat. nos 92 and 149). The size of the sheet and the form of the mount also connect it to those works, and there is little doubt that it, too, dates from *c.*1785 and Jones's return to Britain. As with all three works, the artist adopts a close viewpoint which emphasizes the breadth of the road in which the carefully placed figures express the theme of travel. (GS)

151

THOMAS JONES (1742–1803)

The Ponte Loreto Close to Lake Nemi 1780s?

Pencil, oil on paper laid down on canvas, 34 × 53 ($13\frac{3}{8} \times 20\frac{7}{8}$)

Ins.: 'PONTE LORETO / near / Nettuno' l.r. on rock; 'T. Jones / N°. 42' l.r.
Prov.: Captain John Dale, then by descent; Sotheby's, 27 November 1975, no. 92; Colnaghi's; Galerie Bruno Meissner, Zollikon, Switzerland, 1976; Pierre Boissonnas, Zurich; Christie's, 10 June 1999, no. 14; Artemis Fine Arts
Exh.: Royal Academy, 1787 (no. 58) as 'Ponte Loreto near

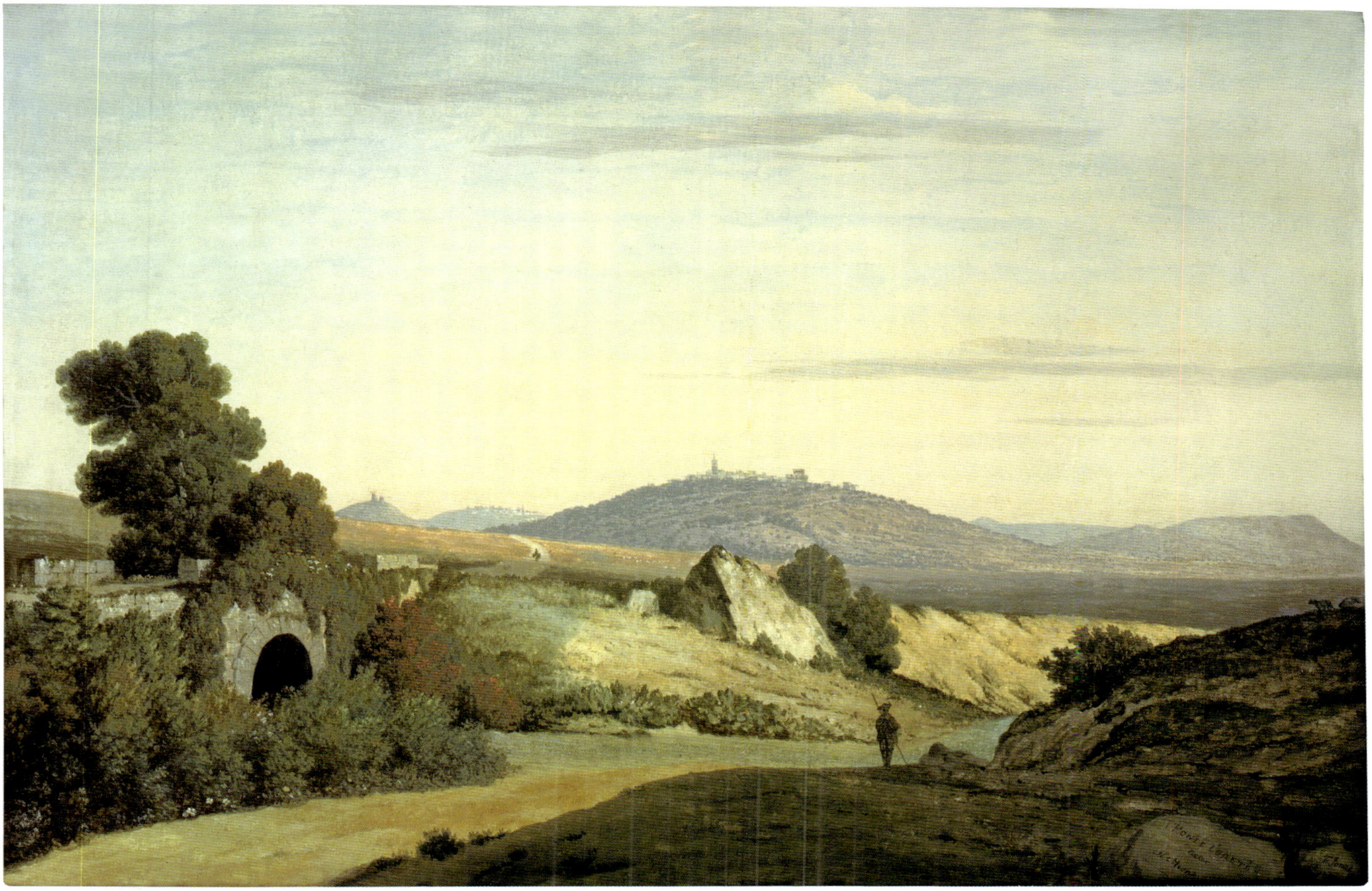

151

Nettuno'; Bremen, 1977, no. 218; Paris, 2001, no. 31; New York, 2002, no. 64

Thaw Collection, The Pierpont Morgan Library, New York

On his first trip out into the Campagna since arriving in Rome, Jones, his friend William Pars, and other sketching companions came upon this ancient Roman bridge on the way to Ostia on 1 May 1777. 'As we found nothing else worthy of Observation in this dreary Plain', Jones recorded, they measured and made sketches of the single-arch structure, overgrown with foliage (*Memoirs*, p. 59). The present, heavily worked and carefully composed sheet was painted afterwards, based on the sketches made that day. On his return to London, Jones exhibited this painting at the Royal Academy in 1787 (see p. 72). (CR)

152

THOMAS JONES (1742–1803)

The Villa of Maecenas, Tivoli 1780s?

Oil on Italian writing paper*, 33 × 54.5 (13 × 21½)

Ins.: 'T. JONES' l.r.; 'A View near Tivoli / T. Jones' verso
Prov.: Captain John Dale, then by descent
Exh.: London, 1970, no. 27 as 'A View near Tivoli'
Lit.: Gowing, 1985, p. 33, pl. 25

Private collection

Jones records that he 'went to see Mecaenas's Villa' on 12 November 1777 (*Memoirs*, p. 65) and this is the date recorded on a watercolour of this view (Art Institute of Chicago), which looks towards Mount Celli, with the Temple of Tossa to the left. Jones's hectic schedule whilst he was in Tivoli would not have allowed time

152

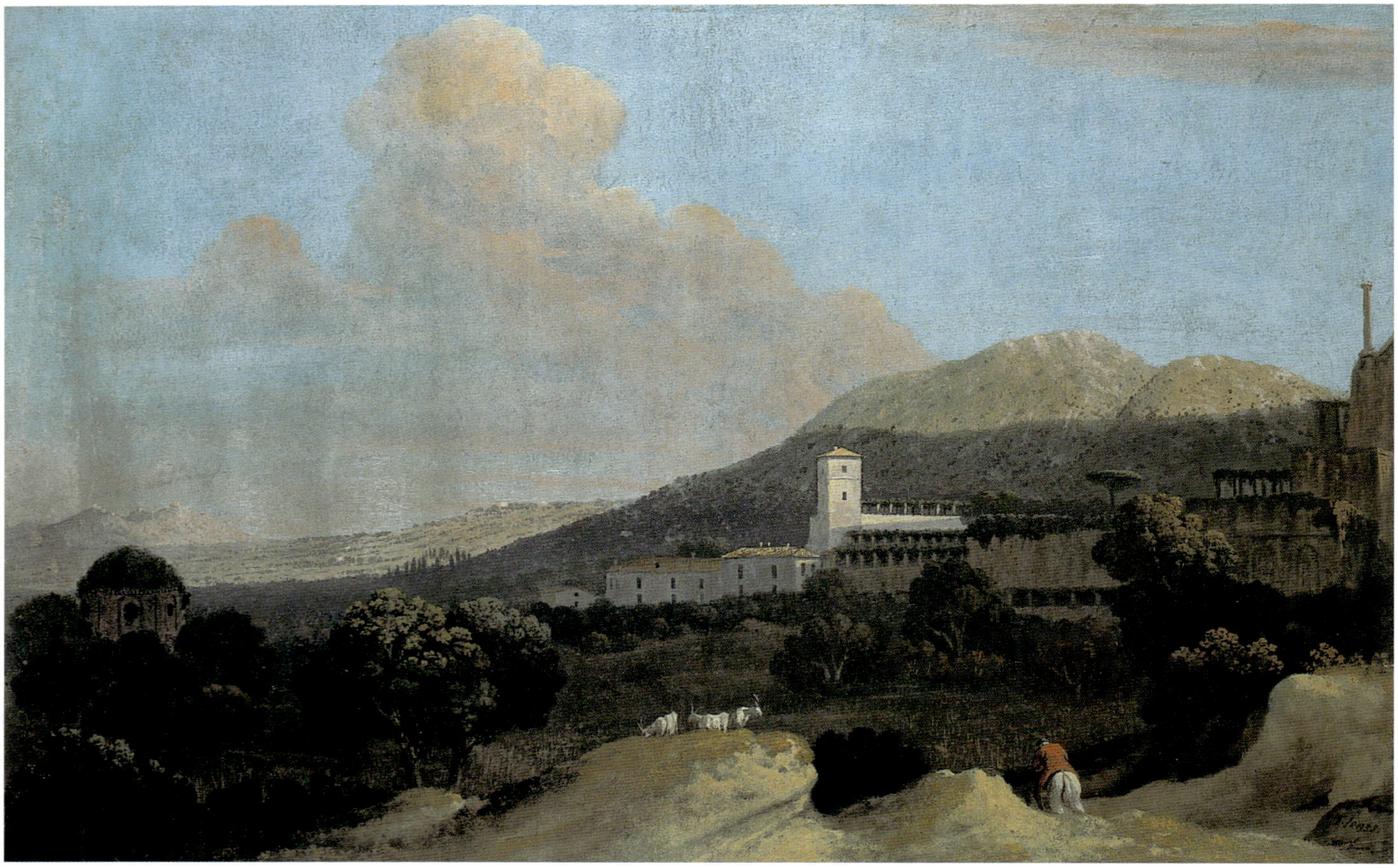

to paint such a complex work as this on the spot, however. It is also clear that this is not a commission, since it remained in the family, and this is confirmed by its relatively small size and the fact that it is not on canvas. Instead, the addition of figures and the use of oil on paper of a characteristic size – 13 × 21½ inches (see pp. 81–2) – suggests that it may be one of those works Jones produced back in England for his own amusement and that, unusually for the artist, he used a watercolour as his source. (GS)

153

THOMAS JONES (1742–1803)

The Outskirts of London: A View Looking Towards Queen Square 1785

Oil on paper*, 24 × 33 (9½ × 13)

Ins.: 'varnish.[d] with Sizes / 16 Dec[r]. 1785' verso
Prov.: Captain John Dale, then by descent; Christie's, 2 July 1954, no. 222; Colnaghi's; purchased by Ian Fleming-Williams, October 1954; purchased 1974
Exh.: London, 1970, no. 77
Lit.: Gowing, 1985, pp. 56–7, pl. 50; Tate, 1986, pp. 30–1

Tate. Purchased 1974. (T.1929)

Cardiff and Manchester only

Jones noted that he 'took a little, neat house in London Street Tottenham Court Road' in January 1785, living there for two years (*Memoirs*, p. 141). This, the only surviving on-the-spot oil sketch

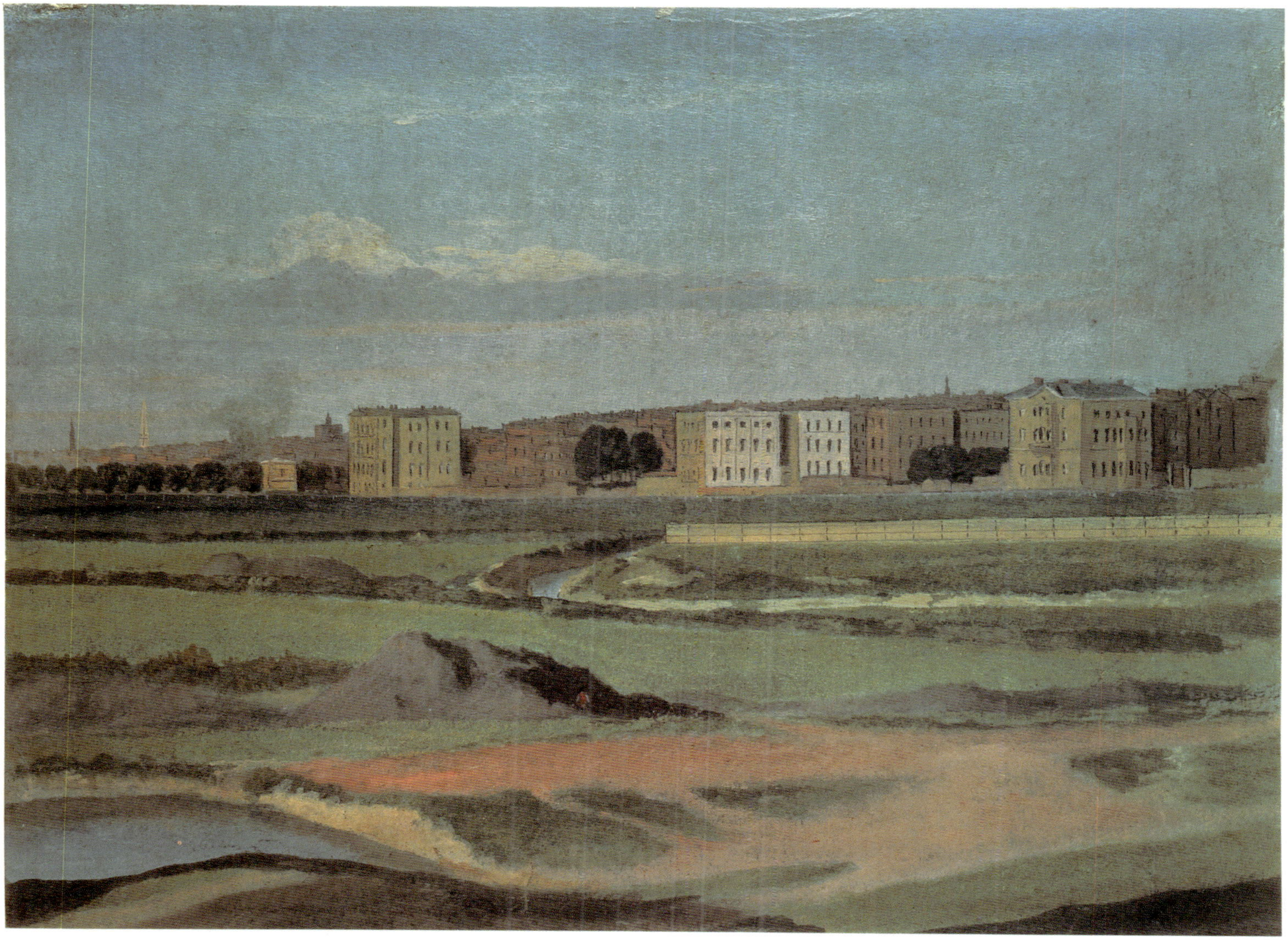

153

dating from after his return from Italy, was painted nearby. The unconventional view was taken from the vicinity of Bedford Way, Russell Square, looking across open ground towards the north end of Queen Square, Bloomsbury, which at this date was still incomplete. The avenue of trees to the left leads to the Foundling Hospital – out of sight – whilst the spires and towers of St Leonard, Shoreditch and St Luke, Old Street can be identified, along with St James, Clerkenwell. What is more unusual is the featureless foreground, for this was still the edge of London in 1785. The views from here up to the villages of Hampstead and Highgate were soon to be lost, however. Local residents protested, but the expansion of London into the surrounding countryside continued its inexorable progress. The workmen in the foreground hint at the impending changes. (GS)

154

THOMAS JONES (1742–1803)

Sketchbook, Showing 'View Towards Garth from Llanelwedd Rocks' 1786–92

Pencil, pen and ink (77 sheets), 16 × 13 (6¼ × 5⅛)

Ins.: 'Book of Tree and Landscape Sketches' on cover; 'Lanelved rocks Radnorshire / 13 Octr 1786' t.c.; '54' t.r. on the exhibited page (p. 54)
Prov.: Thomas Thomas, by descent to Jane Evan-Thomas; bequeathed 2000
Lit.: Hallett, 1991, pp. 4–10; Ledger et al., 1992, pp. 13–14; Cumberland, 1996, seven illustrations; Lord, 2000, p. 151, fig. 234

155

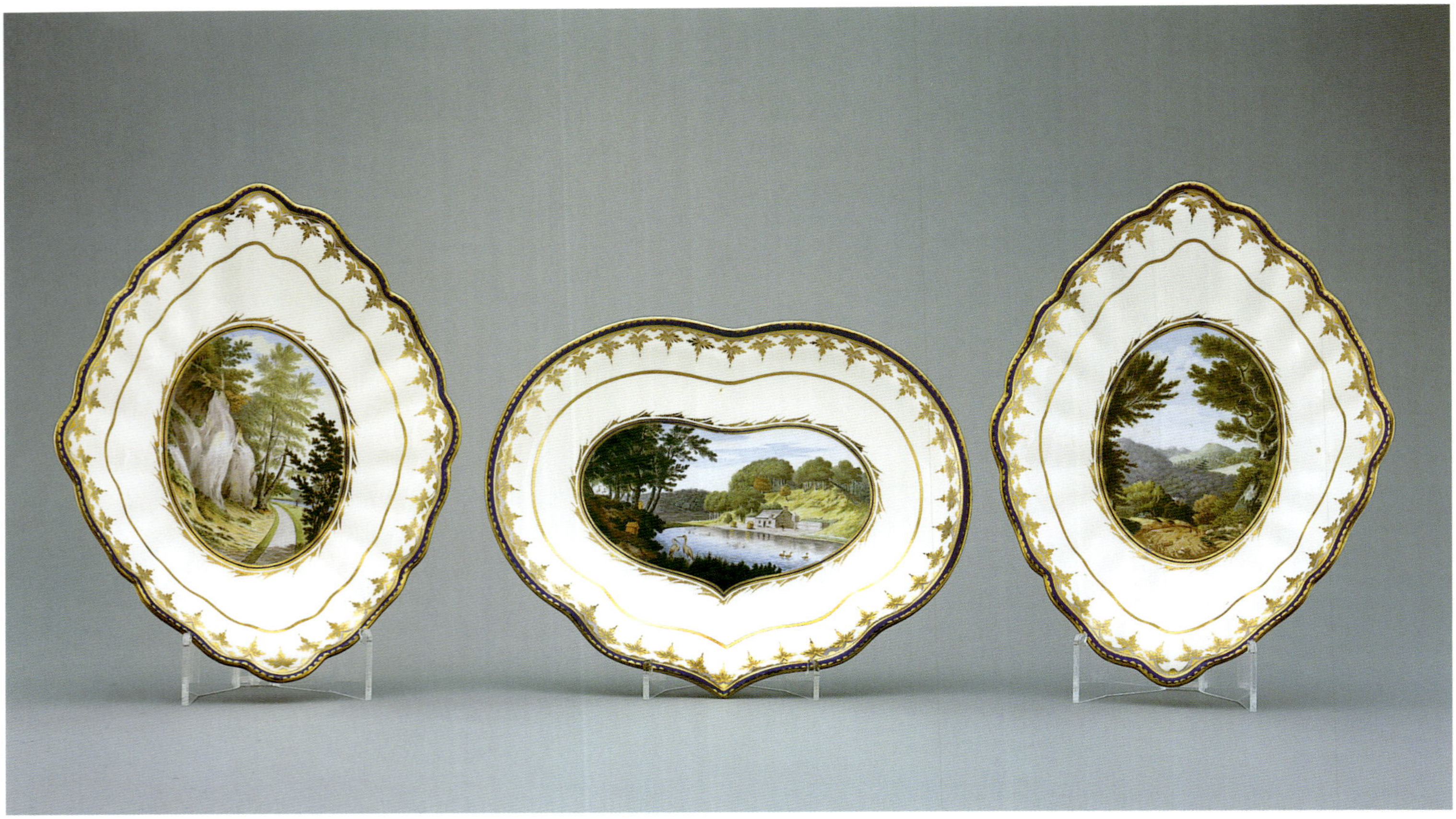

Llyfrgell Genedlaethol Cymru, The National Library of Wales (0200108440)

Cardiff and Manchester only

Pages illustrated on p. 73, fig. 33, and p. 78, fig. 38

Jones first used this book on a trip to Hafod, the estate of Thomas Johnes, in September 1786. On the way, he sketched the Devil's Bridge, and he made studies along the River Rheidol on his return. Jones made about twenty-five drawings of the grounds during his week's stay. These may have been used as the basis for finished compositions, though none are known (see pp. 73–4). Jones made a second trip to Hafod in early October and in the same month he sketched on local excursions from Pencerrig to Llwynmadoc, the River Wye near Builth and Llanelwedd Rocks. Jones also used the book for studying the aftermath of a 'remarkable Storm' at Pencerrig and he returned to it six years later when he made further views on or near his estate. The book is opened at a view looking towards Garth from Llanelwedd Rocks, dated 13 October 1786 (p. 54). (GS)

155

Derby Porcelain Factory

Three Dessert Dishes from the 'Hafod' Service

1787

Soft-paste porcelain, painted in enamels and gilded, i) 5.1 × 26.5 × 21 ($2 \times 10\frac{7}{16} \times 8\frac{1}{4}$), ii) 4.8 × 27.1 × 20.9 ($1\frac{7}{8} \times 10\frac{5}{8} \times 8\frac{1}{4}$), iii) 3.7 × 25.5 × 20.7 ($1\frac{3}{8} \times 10 \times 8\frac{1}{8}$)

Ins.: i) 'Ladies Walk / Hafod', ii) 'Cold Bath / Hafod', iii) 'The Menagerie / Hafod', in blue enamel on the reverse, painted factory mark, pattern number 67, numerical marks of the ground layer, Jno Yates, and the gilder Thomas Soar
Prov.: Thomas Johnes (1748–1816), MP; given to the 1st Lord Thurlow before December 1788; by descent, dispersed by 1876; i) purchased 1991, ii) given by Nicholas S. Harris, 1996, iii) purchased 1998
Exh.: Derby Warehouse, London, 1787
Lit.: Kerkham and Briggs, 1990, pp. 190–210; Hallett et al., 1992a, pp. 7–14; Hallett et al., 1992b, pp. 15–21; Cumberland, 1996

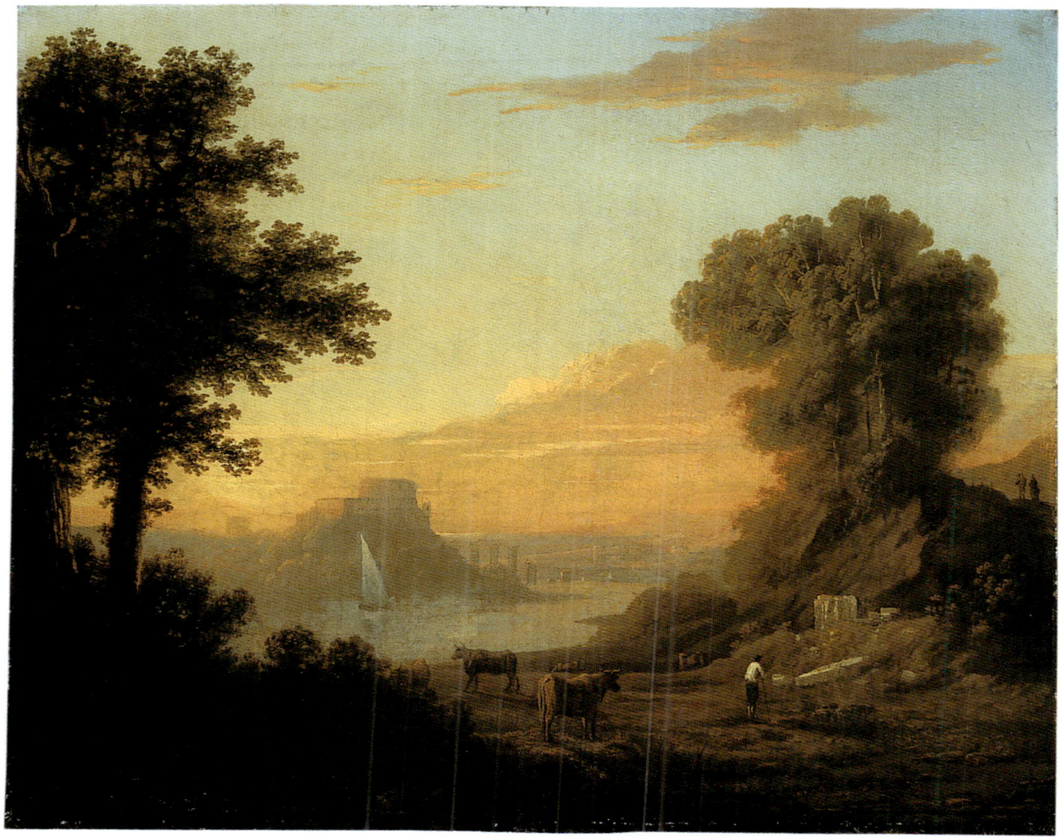

156

National Museums & Galleries of Wales (NMW A 30,224, NMW A 32,653 and NMW A 33,791)

Cardiff and Manchester only

In 1787, Thomas Johnes commissioned a dessert service from the Derby factory to be painted with views of Hafod. This was to become one of the most celebrated picturesque landscapes in Britain, though in 1787 the mansion was unfinished and the planting and landscaping schemes incomplete. As this was an important and valuable commission (the service cost £63), the factory's proprietor, William Duesbury II, called on Johnes to collect images of the estate to be used as source material by the enamel painter, probably Zachariah Boreman. At least some of these views were presumably by Thomas Jones, who visited Hafod on a number of occasions. William Gilpin saw 'a large port-folio, full of paintings (on paper) of a variety of views round' Hafod by Jones in April 1787 – now lost – and these may have been used by the factory (Barbier, 1963; pp. 71–2).

Although the service is now dispersed, eleven pieces are in the collection at Cardiff. Of the three shown here, one oval dish depicts the Ladies' Walk, a path running beside the bank of the River Ystwyth. The other oval dish and the heart-shaped dish include buildings that Jones sketched in 1786 (cat. no. 154): the Cold Bath, a small Gothic tower, and the Menagerie. (ONF)

156

THOMAS JONES (1742–1803)

Classical Landscape with a River 1794

Oil on canvas, 48.3 × 61 (19 × 24)

Ins.: 'Tho. Jones 1794' l.l.
Prov.: Sir John Leach; bequeathed to Caroline Eden; A. Polwhele-Godfrey; S. Rees Jones; allocated by H. M. Government in lieu of inheritance tax, 2000
Exh.: London, 1969, no. 139; London, 1970, no. 82

National Museums & Galleries of Wales (NMW A 17686)

Cardiff and Manchester only

157

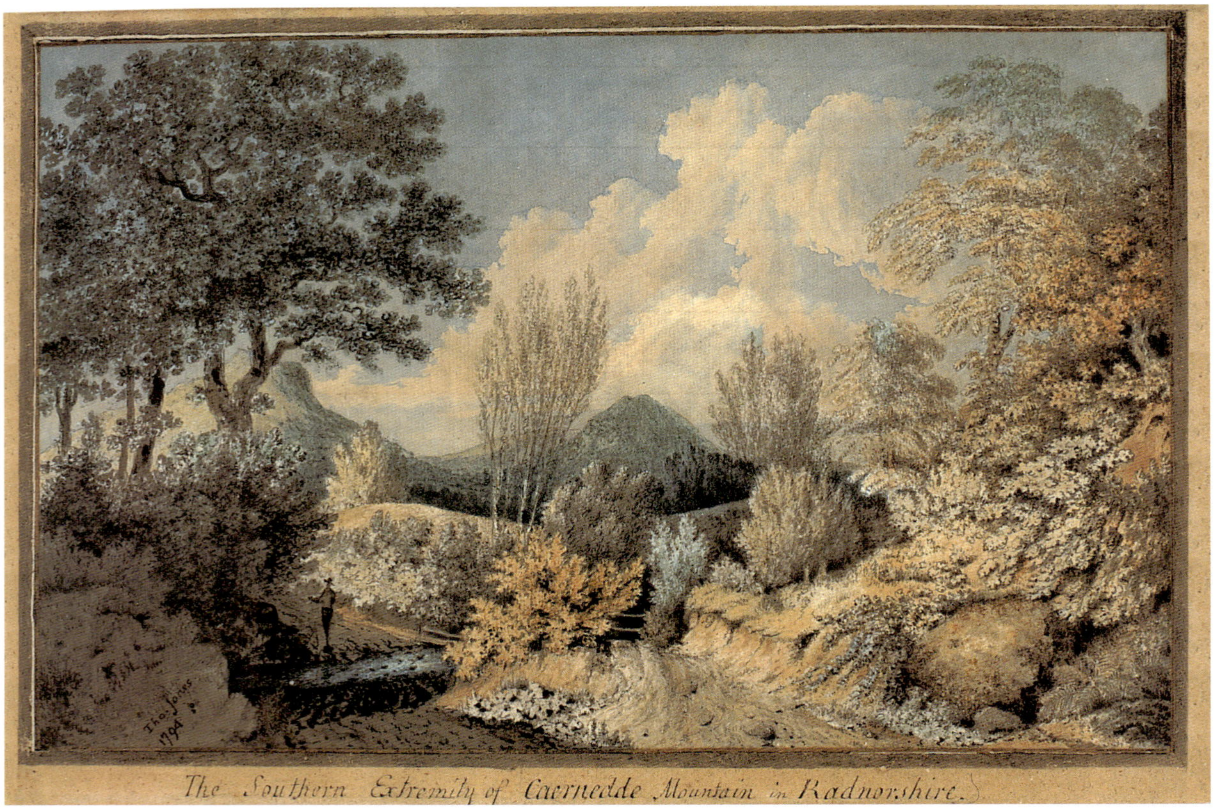
The Southern Extremity of Caernedde Mountain in Radnorshire

158

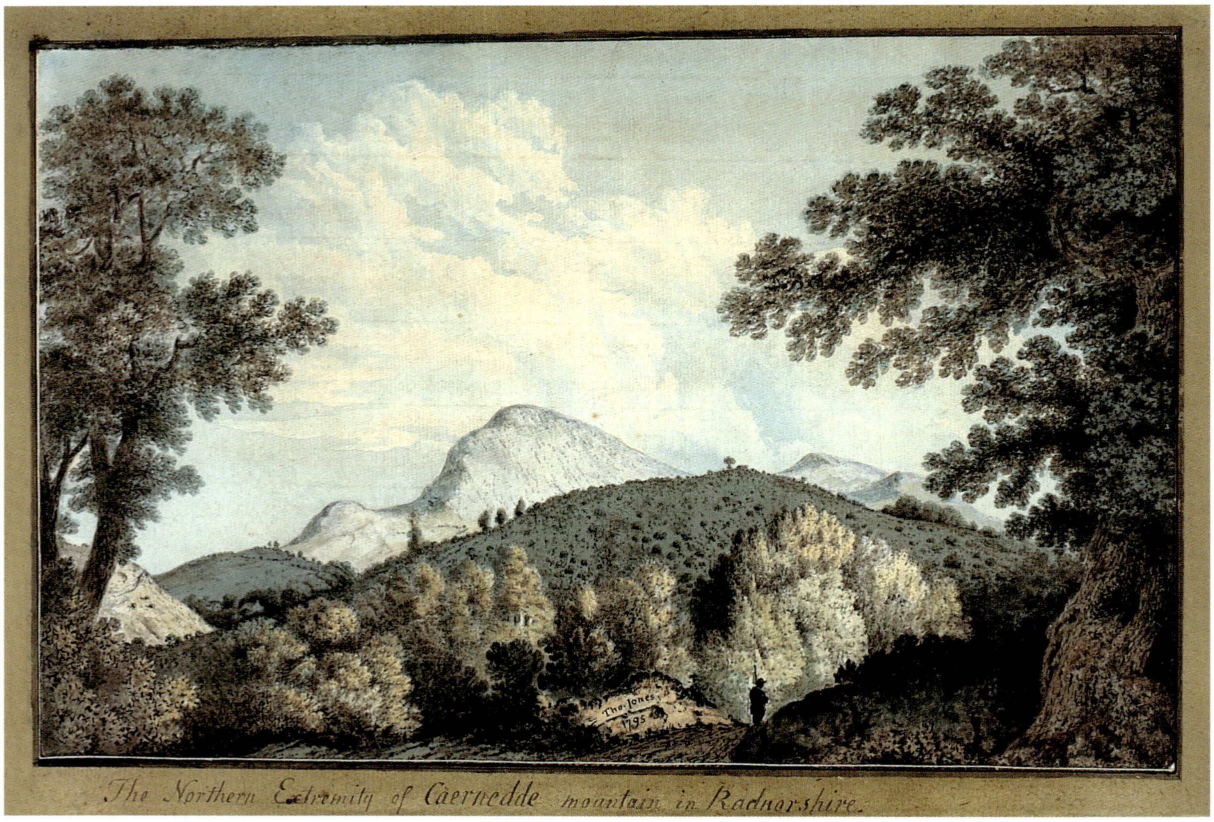
The Northern Extremity of Caernedde mountain in Radnorshire

Although Jones does not record working on any oils in the diary entries found in the Account Book, this signed and dated work is evidence that he was still painting at this date. It is a conscious essay in the manner of Claude, showing a luminous sunset with a distant castle, wide river and sailing boat. The centre of the canvas has suffered abrasion, which has altered the reading of the composition and made certain structural features unidentifiable. This painting belonged to Sir John Leach (1760–1834), who studied architecture under Sir Robert Taylor before being called to the Bar in 1790. As Jones was active as a magistrate from 1792, it is likely that his involvement in the legal profession brought him into contact with Leach, a future Master of the Rolls. (ABS)

157

THOMAS JONES (1742–1803)

The Southern Extremity of the Carneddau 1794

Pencil, watercolour, pen and ink on laid paper on original mount, 24.4 × 39 ($9\frac{5}{8} \times 15\frac{3}{8}$)

Ins.: 'Tho. Jones / 1794' l.l.; 'The Southern Extremity of Caernedde Mountain in Radnorshire' on original mount
Prov.: Thomas Thomas, then by descent to Jane Evan-Thomas; bequeathed 2000

Llyfrgell Genedlaethol Cymru, The National Library of Wales (0200108450)

Cardiff and Manchester only

From 1794–5, Jones produced a group of seven highly finished watercolours, all of roughly similar size and presented in the same mounts, with their long descriptive titles added in a fine hand at the bottom. The group appears to have hung on the walls of Pencerrig for much of its existence and it may be that the watercolours were designed by Jones for that purpose. All of the watercolours show the Carneddau, a few miles to the east of Pencerrig, though the topography is somewhat exaggerated. The one exception, which shows Jones's birthplace at Trefonnen (cat. no. 8), gives an insight into the artist's motivation in producing the works. For it was surely Jones's feeling for views which he had known throughout his life, as much as the beauties of the area itself, that are celebrated here. (GS)

158

THOMAS JONES (1742–1803)

The Northern Extremity of the Carneddau 1795

Pencil, watercolour, pen and ink on laid paper on original mount, 24.7 × 38.7 ($9\frac{3}{4} \times 15\frac{1}{4}$)

Ins.: 'Tho. Jones / 1795' l.c.; 'The Northern Extremity of Caernedde mountain in Radnorshire' on the original mount
Prov.: Thomas Thomas, then by descent to Jane Evan-Thomas; bequeathed 2000

Llyfrgell Genedlaethol Cymru, The National Library of Wales (0200108460)

Cardiff and Manchester only

The compositions of the watercolours in this group, including cat. nos 157 and 159, help to create a sense of unity beyond what is ensured by their common presentation. All of the views are flanked with trees that extend beyond the height of the sheet, each is organized around a road which, though it leads into the picture, is blocked in some way, either by trees or rocks; finally, the central focus on the distant mountain is consistently obscured. As James Baker noted in relation to the nearby stretch of the Wye that Jones portrayed so often, this part of Wales may have been 'worthy of the pencil of Poussin, or Salvator Rosa', but because the region was 'a little out of the main road . . . this British Tivoli passed by unnoticed and unknown' (Baker, 1795, p. 228). The point is not just that this scenery had not been painted before, but there were no ready precedents to fall back on. (GS)

159

THOMAS JONES (1742–1803)

Carneddau Mountains 1795

Pencil, watercolour, pen and ink on laid paper on original mount, 24.3 × 38.7 ($9\frac{5}{8} \times 15\frac{1}{4}$)

Ins.: 'Tho. Jones / 1795' l.l. over pencil inscription
Prov.: Thomas Thomas, then by descent to Jane Evan-Thomas; bequeathed 2000
Exh.: London, 1970, no. 86

Llyfrgell Genedlaethol Cymru, The National Library of Wales (0200108448)

Cardiff and Manchester only

159

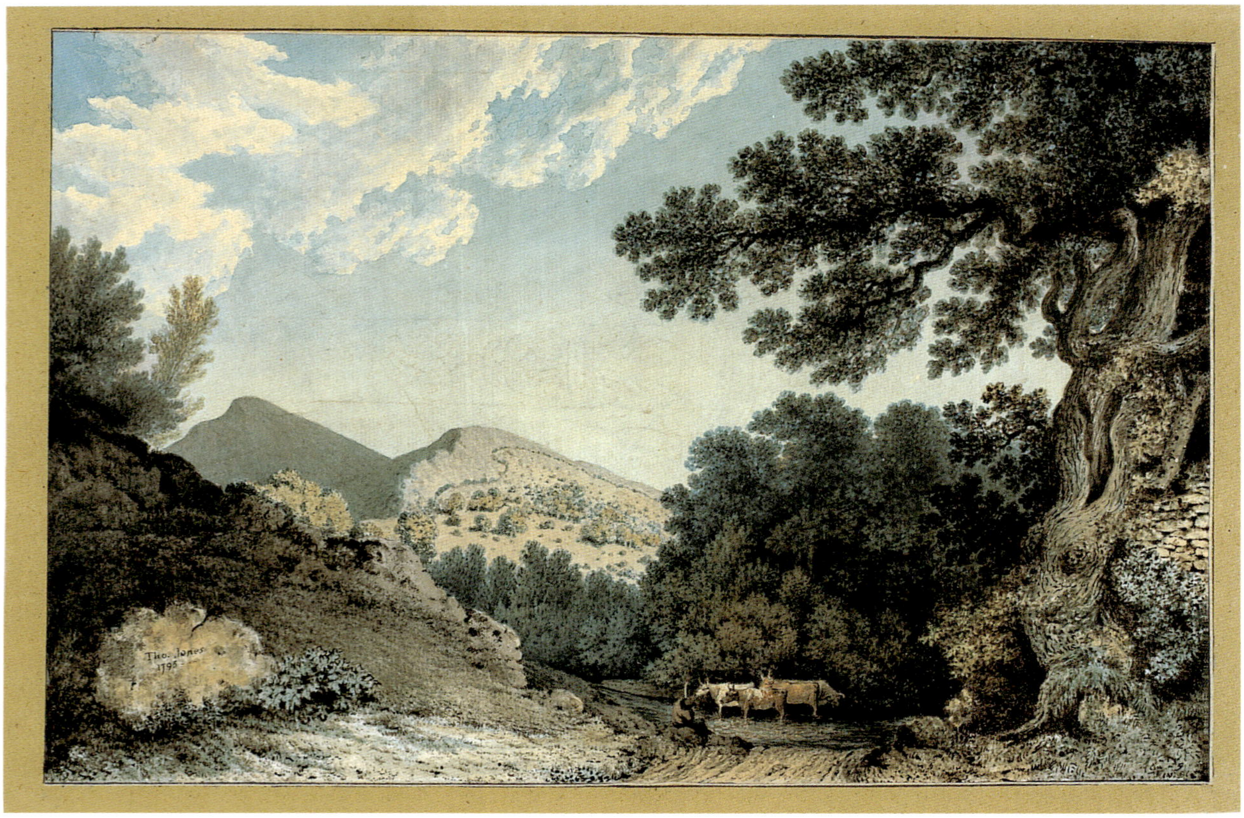

According to James Baker, the Carneddau were 'so called from the various mounds of raised earth or tumuli thereon . . . the burial places of the ancients', but there are no ancient or supernatural associations in Jones's views of the mountains. Jones mentioned the Carneddau in his ode to the beauties of the local landscape, 'Petraeia'. The 'distant mountains melting into air' was one of the lessons that nature imparted to the artist as a youth and he also talked of the glorious way in which 'high Carnedda's top reflects the ling'ring rays' as the sun declines in the west (Baker, 1795, p. 227). Jones's interest as an artist was not primarily in the depiction of such natural effects, however, and the degree to which a penned outline is still prominent in views such as this indicates how conservative they are in comparison with the work of a rising generation of watercolourists who were making an impact with a different type of landscape vision. (GS)

160

THOMAS JONES (1742–1803)

Old Oak Tree at Pencerrig 1795

Pencil, pen and ink, watercolour on laid paper on original mount*, 30.2 × 22.9 (12 × 9)

Ins.: 'Tho. Jones / 1795' l.l.
Prov.: Thomas Thomas, then by descent to Jane Evan-Thomas; given to Joy Ashton; presented by her, 2000
Exh.: London, 1970, no. 83

Radnorshire Museum, Powys County Council (2000.22)

Cardiff and Manchester only

Solitary oak trees were often painted during this period, and though some specimens were appreciated simply for their picturesque lines, others had historical and even nationalistic associations. James Baker talked of the glorious 'native oak groves' of Pencerrig, and in a Welsh context this conjures up associations with the Druids, since it was sacred as the refuge of mistletoe. The fact that a solitary tree on an exposed rocky eminence has suffered

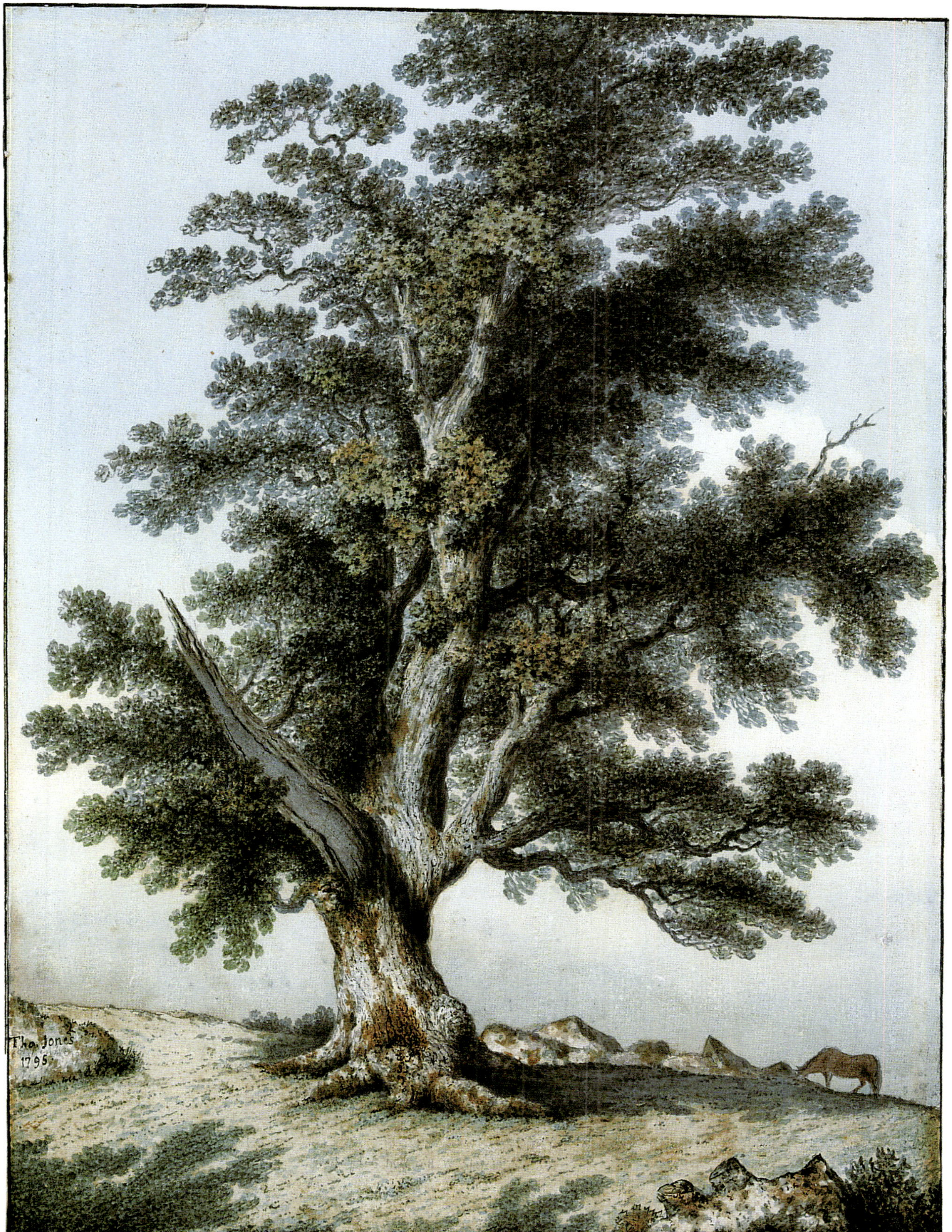
Tho. Jones
1795

161

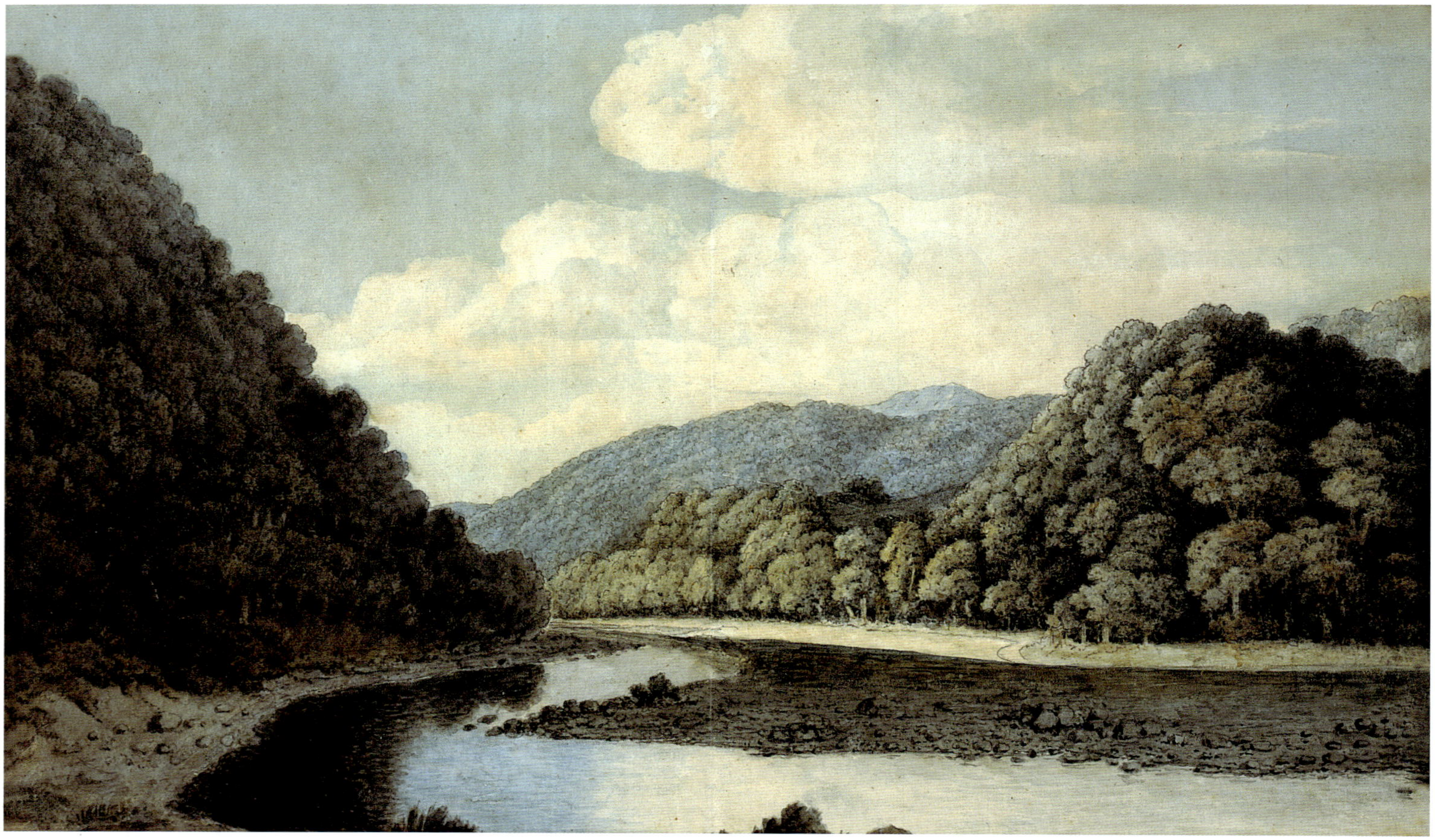

during its lifetime is more relevant in this case, however. The blasted oak bears the marks of its struggles over time against tumultuous storms, or, as Jones described it, 'who long the furious western gales have stood' (Baker, 1795, p. 225). A group of oak trees growing in front of the house at Pencerrig has been identified with this work, but no specimen now tallies with this tree and its surrounding rocks. (GS)

161

THOMAS JONES (1742–1803)

The River Wye 1790s?

Pencil, watercolour, pen and ink on wove paper, 21.8 × 37.5 ($8\frac{1}{2} \times 14\frac{3}{4}$)

Prov.: Captain John Dale, then by descent; Christie's, 28 July 1955, no. 4; Agnew's; purchased 1956
Exh.: Arts Council, 1960, no. 44; London, 1962, no. 44; Vienna, 1965, no. 72; London, 1970, no. 15; Brussels, 1973, no. 58; Leningrad, 1974–5, no. 28; Manchester, 1993, no. 141
Lit.: Gowing, 1985, p. 29, pl. 19

The Whitworth Art Gallery, The University of Manchester (D.1956.2)

Cardiff and Manchester only

This work has always been dated to the sketching campaign Jones undertook on the Wye and around Pencerrig in 1775–6. However, a number of factors point to a later date. Firstly, wove paper was

162

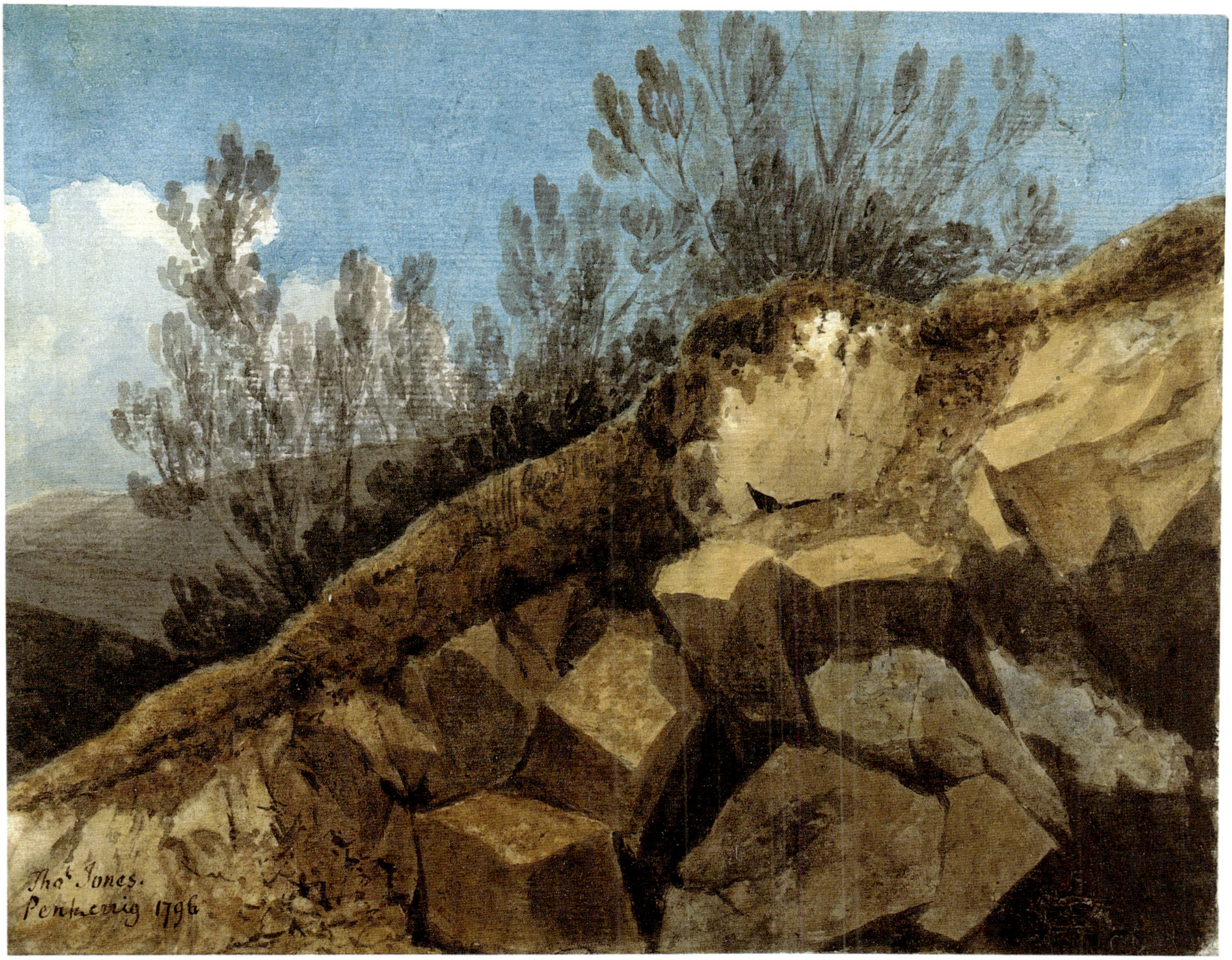

more generally available in the 1780s and the dated works by Jones on this type of support are primarily from after his return from Italy. Secondly, there is the size and format of the drawing. Jones only rarely used watercolour for more finished pieces on a larger scale prior to his stay in Italy. Finally, there is nothing in the handling of the medium and his use of pen and ink which is inconsistent with dated works of the mid-1790s such as the Welsh views (cat. nos 157–9) or *Terracina* (cat. no. 166). If the work had retained its original mount, the similarities would no doubt have been even more pronounced. This view on the Wye can be located near Builth, though recent quarrying has destroyed the hill to the right. (GS)

162

THOMAS JONES (1742–1803)

Study of Rocks near Pencerrig 1796

Watercolour on laid paper, 15.6 × 20 ($6\frac{1}{8} \times 7\frac{7}{8}$)

Ins.: 'Thos Jones. / Penkerrig 1796' l.l.
Prov.: Captain John Dale, then by descent; Christie's, 2 July 1954, no. 218; L. G. Duke; Colnaghi's, 1961
Exh.: New Haven, 1977, no. 49; New Haven, 1986, no. 36

Yale Center for British Art, Paul Mellon Collection (1977.14.4665)

Cardiff and Manchester only

This drawing illustrates a small quarried exposure of a hard igneous rock (dolerite) which shows columnar jointing of the type seen at the Giant's Causeway, albeit less spectacularly developed. The scene is painted at Pencerrig close to the house with the Carneddau represented in the distance. Together with cat. no. 163 they are the last known dated works by Jones. Both measure the same size and their small scale suggests that they came from a lost sketchbook. The drawings represent something of a departure for Jones, even at this late stage of his career. Instead of beginning with a pencil drawing, and then adding washes of colour, the artist worked solely in watercolour. This was increasingly common in the 1790s, but there is nothing in Jones's later works to suggest that he might have been influenced by the innovations of his contemporaries. The result is a direct response to nature that has no precedent in his use of the watercolour medium and is closer in spirit to his use of oils for sketching in Italy ten years previously. (GS)

163

THOMAS JONES (1742–1803)

A Rocky Outcrop at Pencerrig 1796

Watercolour on laid paper, 15.8 × 20.2 ($6\frac{1}{8}$ × 8)

Ins.: 'Tho[s] Jones. / penkerrig. 1796.' l.r.
Prov.: Brinsley Ford, then by descent
Exh.: London, 1970, no. 90 as 'Penkerrig'
Lit.: Gowing, 1985, p. 58, pl. 52

Private collection

Cardiff and Manchester only

Illustrated on p. 80, fig. 39

Jones's recurrent interest in rocks is given a new twist in this late work. Both the small scale of the sketch and the use of pure watercolour without any outline creates a less artful vision of nature. In contrast to earlier views in Wales, where the view tends to be more open, the focus on the foreground, with just a glimpse of the distance, creates a monumental form from a relatively small motif. In a slightly disconcerting juxtaposition, the closer rock almost eclipses the distant hill. This is just the sort of sketch that one cannot imagine being done in relation to a finished work: it certainly would not fit into any conventional compositional structure. One can only imagine it as an exercise done by the artist 'for my own Amusement' (*Memoirs*, p. 141). (GS)

164

THOMAS JONES (1742–1803)

Gaiola on the Coast of Posillipo, near Naples

1796

Pencil, watercolour on a Whatman white wove writing paper*, 19.9 × 50.5 ($7\frac{7}{8}$ × $19\frac{7}{8}$)

Ins.: 'Gajola on the Coast of Pusilipo near Naples T.J. / 1796' t.r.; '1778' very faintly beneath; faint pencil sketch of a landscape in a box marked '18' and '13' verso
Prov.: Captain John Dale, then by descent; Christie's, 2 July 1954, no. 221; Agnew's; Colnaghi's, 1965; purchased
Exh.: London, 1970, no. 87; London, 1990, p. 64 and p. 126
Lit.: Spinosa and Di Mauro, 1989, p. 198

National Museums & Galleries of Wales (NMW A 1861)

Cardiff and Manchester only

Illustrated on p. 81, fig. 40

This work dates from Jones's return to Wales and was painted at the same time as the *Memoirs* were written. This late date is confirmed by Jones's choice of a wove Whatman paper, probably produced in the 1790s. The sheet has a second fainter date, 1778, and this presumably refers to Jones's visit to Gaiola and the lost drawing on which this watercolour is based. Jones recorded an excursion by boat to Baia, south of Naples, in September 1778 and he shows just such a party of sightseers in the foreground.

The mottled effect in the sky and sea is caused by the breakdown in the paper's sizing. This would not have been so noticeable when Jones painted the work. Another unusual aspect is the use of a panoramic format. The artist sometimes carried on a composition across two pages of a sketchbook and this proportion is preserved here. (GS)

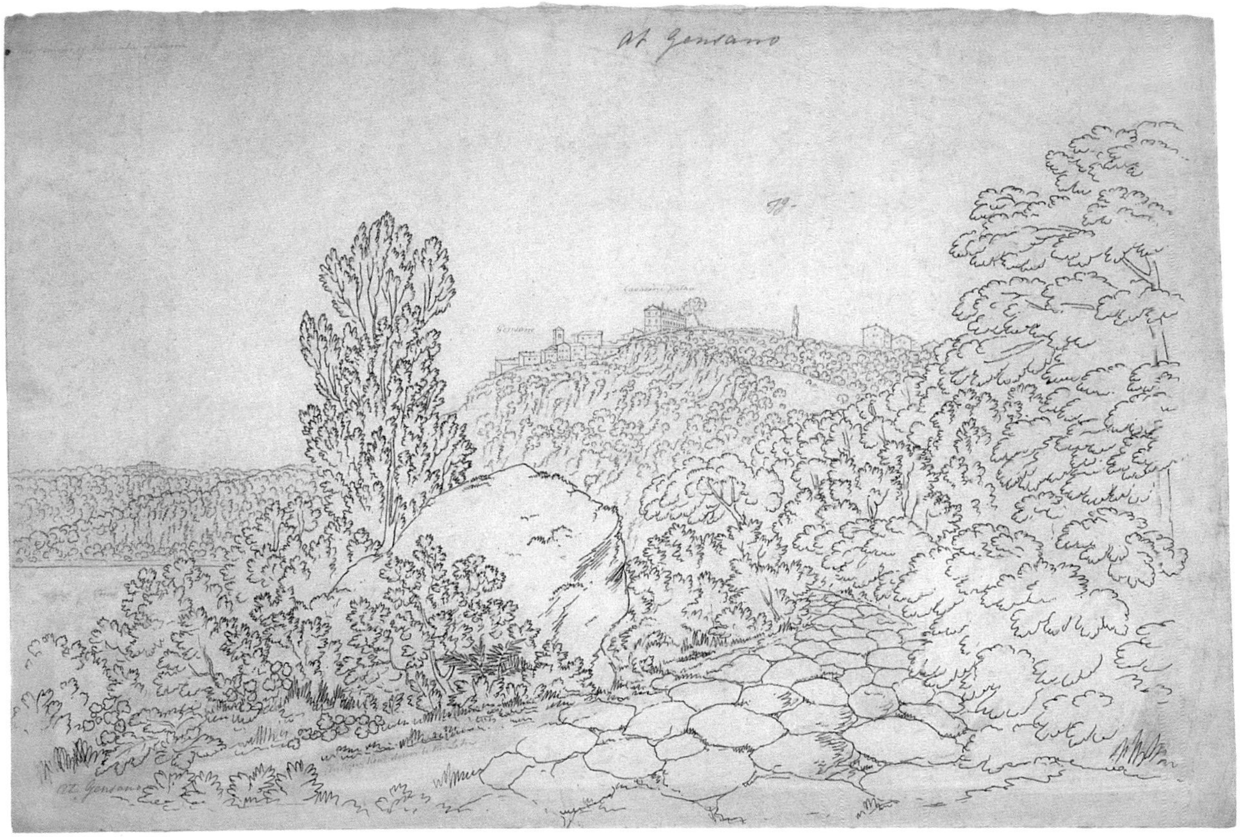

165

165

THOMAS JONES (1742–1803)

Lake Nemi early 1790s

Pencil, pen and ink on Whatman white wove writing paper (watermark: J WHATMAN)*, 30 × 44.8 (11⅞ × 17¾)

Ins.: 'The Banks of the Lake of Nemi' t.l.; 'at Gensano' t.c.; 'TJ-' t.c.; 'Gensano', Cesarini Palace', 'Lake of nemi', 'Antique road down the Lake' inscribed on the drawing
Prov.: John Manning, 1964; purchased

National Museums & Galleries of Wales (NMW A 16767)

The relationship between this drawing and a watercolour in the British Museum (cat. no. 79) of an identical composition is a curious one. Initially, the sheet appears to be the sort of large-scale pencil drawing with inscriptions that Jones executed on the spot and which he subsequently coloured, though in this case the outlines are reinforced in pen and ink. However, the work is on a wove paper that dates from after his return from Italy. It is possible that Jones copied or traced his own drawing with the intention of producing a second watercolour, just as in the case of *Gaiola* (cat. no. 164) where he made a version in 1796 of a composition dating from 1778, though why he added inscriptions which do not tally with cat. no. 79 is unclear. (GS and BM)

166

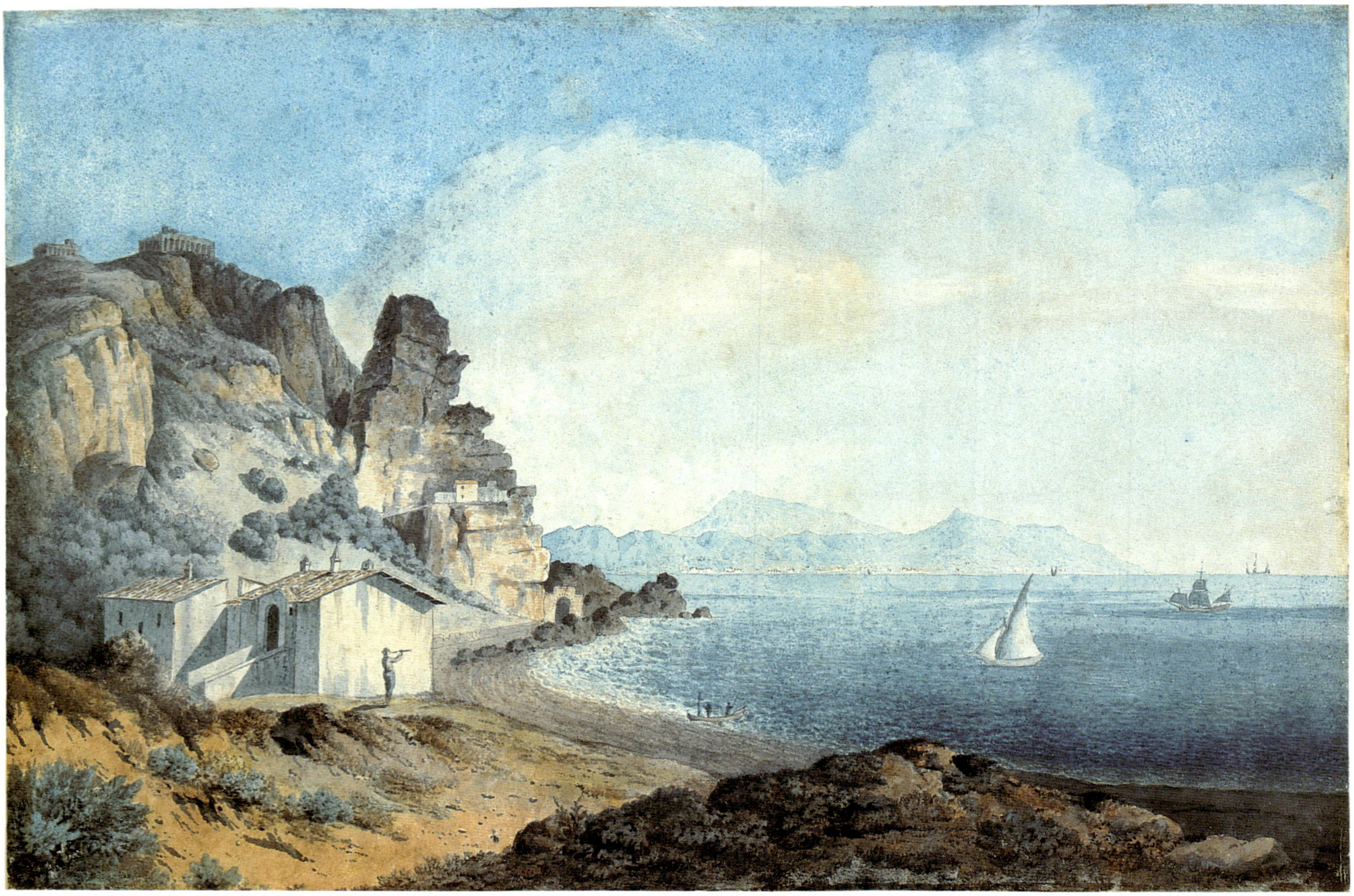

166

Thomas Jones (1742–1803)

At Terracina 1790s

Pencil, watercolour on Whatman white wove writing paper*, 26.7 × 40.2 (10½ × 15⅞) (sight)

Ins.: 'Gate divide the King of Naples & (indistinct) / At Terracina No16 1779' verso
Prov.: Captain John Dale, then by descent; Christie's, 28 July 1955, no. 3; Jane Evan-Thomas; given to Ralph Edwards; then by descent to present owner
Exh.: London, 1970, no. 45

Private collection

Cardiff and Manchester only

Jones passed through Terracina in 1778 and 1780, but the sketch on which this work is based (untraced) was made on his return from Naples to Rome in 1779. On 25 January he recorded that he had 'made some Sketches & dined there', and this is confirmed by the inscription (*Memoirs*, p. 85). This watercolour was painted much later, however. The paper is a Whatman wove, probably dating from the early 1790s – like cat. no. 164, the mottled effect in the sky is caused by a failure of the sizing – and so it was probably painted while he was writing his *Memoirs*.

The inscription notes that the gate at the base of the cliffs marked the border between the kingdom of Naples and the papal states. Crossing such boundaries was fraught with difficulties and in 1780 Jones complained bitterly about the 'Impositions of the Customhouse underlings who exorted Money from me' (ibid., p. 95). The prominent building in the foreground, as well as the man looking through a telescope, possibly had a significance for Jones, perhaps as a reminder of the frustrations of Italian travel. (GS)

BIBLIOGRAPHY

Exhibitions

The Old Masters, Including Water Colour Drawings, Royal Academy of Arts, London, 1891 (London, 1891)

Watercolour Drawings, Whitworth Art Gallery, Manchester, 1891 (Manchester, 1891)

Richard Wilson and John Constable, Oxford Arts Club, 1937 (Oxford, 1937)

Water-Colour Drawings by J. R. Cozens and J. S. Cotman, Whitworth Art Gallery, Manchester, 1937 (Manchester, 1937)

Exhibition of Early English Water-Colours from the Collections of J. Leslie Wright, Esq. and Walter Turner Esq., Birmingham Museum and Art Gallery, 1938 (Birmingham, 1938)

Richard Wilson and his Circle, Birmingham Museum and Art Gallery, 1948 (Birmingham, 1948)

Masters of British Water-Colour (17th–19th Centuries), Royal Academy of Arts, London, 1949 (London, 1949)

Early English Drawings and Watercolours from the Collection of Paul Oppé Esq., Graves Art Gallery, Sheffield, 1952 (Sheffield, 1952)

Water Colour Drawings from the Whitworth Art Gallery, Manchester, Agnew and Sons, London, 1954 (London, 1954)

Watercolours and Drawings by Alexander Cozens and John Robert Cozens, Whitworth Art Gallery, Manchester, 1956 (Manchester, 1956)

Italy and the Grand Tour, Norwich Castle Museum, 1958 (Norwich, 1958)

The Paul Oppé Collection, Royal Academy of Arts, London, 1958 (London, 1958)

Il Settecento a Roma, Rome, 1959 (Rome, 1959)

Drawings and Watercolours from the Whitworth Art Gallery, Arts Council, 1960 (Arts Council, 1960)

Il Paesaggio Napoletano nella Pittura Straniera, Naples, 1962 (Naples, 1962)

Primitives to Picasso, Royal Academy of Arts, London, 1962 (London, 1962)

Mr. and Mrs. Paul Mellon Collection, Virginia Museum of Fine Arts, Richmond, Virginia, 1963 (Richmond, 1963)

Art in Wales, Swansea, 1964 (Swansea, 1964)

Englische Aquarelle des 18. Jahrhunderts von Cozens bis Turner, Albertina, Vienna, 1965 (Vienna, 1965)

A Loan Exhibition of English Drawings from the Whitworth Art Gallery, Colnaghi's, London, 1967 (London, 1967)

Romantic Art in Britain: Paintings and Drawings 1760–1860, Detroit Institute of Arts, 1968 (Detroit, 1968)

Englishmen in Italy, Victoria and Albert Museum, London, 1968 (London, 1968a)

The William Spooner Collection, Courtauld Institute Galleries, London, 1968 (London, 1968b)

A Decade of English Naturalism: 1810–1820, Norwich Castle Museum, 1969 (Norwich, 1969)

Masters of the Watercolour: Watercolours from the Spooner Collection, Holburne of Menstrie Museum, Bath, 1969 (Bath, 1969)

British Neo-Classical Art, Ickworth, National Trust, 1969 (Ickworth, 1969)

The Art of Claude Lorraine, Hayward Gallery, London, 1969 (London, 1969)

Richard Wilson, Painter, Welsh Arts Council, 1969 (Cardiff, 1969)

Thomas Jones (1742–1803), Marble Hill House, London, 1970 (London, 1970)

Paintings by British Artists from the National Museum of Wales, Aberystwyth, 1971 (Aberystwyth, 1971)

La Peinture Romantique Anglaise, Petit Palais, Paris, 1972 (Paris, 1972)

English Drawings and Watercolours 1550–1850 in the Collection of Mr and Mrs Paul Mellon, Pierpont Morgan Library, New York, 1972 (New York, 1972)

British Artists in Europe, Whitworth Art Gallery, Manchester, 1973 (Manchester, 1973a)

British Watercolours from the John Edward Taylor Collection in the Whitworth Art Gallery, Whitworth Art Gallery, Manchester, 1973 (Manchester, 1973b)

Landscape in Britain, c.1750–1850, Tate Gallery, London, 1973 (London, 1973)

English Watercolours of the 18th and 19th Centuries from the Whitworth Art Gallery, Musée d'Arte Moderne, Brussels, 1973 (Brussels, 1973)

English Watercolours, the Spooner Collection, Bristol City Art Gallery, 1973 (Bristol, 1973)

British Artists in Rome 1700–1800, Kenwood House, London, 1974 (London, 1974a)

Landscapes from the Fitzwilliam, Hazlitt, Gooden & Fox, London, 1974 (London, 1974b)

English Watercolours of the 18th and 19th Centuries from the Whitworth Art Gallery, State Hermitage Museum, Leningrad, 1974 (Leningrad, 1974)

Pittura Inglese 1660–1840, Milan, 1975 (Milan, 1975)

Exhibition of Drawings and Watercolours from the Spooner and Witt Collections, National Art Gallery of New Zealand, Wellington, 1976 (Wellington, 1976)

English Landscape 1630–1850 – Drawings, Prints & Books from the Paul Mellon Collection, Yale Center for British Art, New Haven, 1977 (New Haven, 1977)

Zuruck zu Natur, Die Kunstlerkolonie von Barbizon, Kunsthalle, Bremen, 1977 (Bremen, 1977)

La Peinture Britannique de Gainsborough á Bacon, Galerie des Beaux Arts, Bordeaux, 1977 (Bordeaux, 1977)

Joseph Farington: Watercolours and Drawings, Bolton Museum and Art Gallery, 1977 (Bolton, 1977)

Eighteenth Century Master Drawings from the Ashmolean, Baltimore Museum of Art, 1979 (Baltimore, 1979)

Zwei Jahrhunderts Englische Malerei: Britische Kunst und Europe 1680 bis 1880, Haus der Kunst, Munich, 1979 (Munich, 1979)

Civilità del Settecento a Napoli, 1734–1799, Naples, 1979 (Naples, 1979)

Painting from Nature. The Tradition of Open-Air Oil Sketching from the 17th to 19th Centuries, Fitzwilliam Museum, Cambridge, 1980 (Cambridge, 1980)

British Watercolours 1760–1930 from the Birmingham Museum and Art Gallery, Arts Council, 1980 (Birmingham, 1980)

Before Photography: Painting and the Invention of Photography, Museum of Modern Art, New York, 1981 (New York, 1981)

The Golden Age of Naples, Detroit Institute of Arts, 1981 (Detroit, 1981)

Classic Ground. British Artists and the Landscape of Italy, 1740–1830, Yale Center for British Art, New Haven, 1981 (New Haven, 1981)

John 'Warwick' Smith and Francis Towne, British Museum London (no catalogue), 1981 (London, 1981)

Great British Watercolours, Castle Museum, Nottingham, 1981 (Nottingham, 1981)

På Klassisk Mark Målane i Rom på 1780–1982, Nationalmuseum, Stockholm, 1982 (Stockholm, 1982)

Richard Wilson: The Landscape of Reaction, Tate Gallery, London, 1982 (London, 1982)

Presences of Nature. British Landscape 1780–1830, Yale Center for British Art, New Haven, 1982 (New Haven, 1982)

Town, Country, Shore and Sea, British Drawings and Watercolours from Anthony Van Dyck to Paul Nash, Fitzwilliam Museum, Cambridge, 1982 (Cambridge, 1982)

'The most beautiful art of England': Fifty Watercolours, 1750–1850, Whitworth Art Gallery, Manchester, 1983 (Manchester, 1983)

English Drawings from the Ashmolean Museum, Ashmolean Museum, Oxford, 1983 (Oxford, 1983)

Master Drawings and Watercolours in the British Museum, British Museum, London, 1984 (London, 1984a)

The Watercolour Collection Formed by Mrs Cecil Keith, Thos Agnew & Sons, London, 1984 (London, 1984b)

British Landscape Watercolours 1600–1860, British Museum, London, 1985 (London, 1985)

British Watercolours. Drawings of the 18th and 19th Centuries from the Yale Center for British Art, Yale Center for British Art, New Haven, 1985 (New Haven, 1985)

The Northern Landscape, The Drawing Center, New York, 1986 (New York, 1986)

Masterpieces from the National Museum of Wales, Japanese tour, 1986 (Japan, 1986)

Oil on Water. Oil Sketches by British Watercolourists, Yale Center for British Art, New Haven, 1986 (New Haven, 1986)

The Blasted Oak. The Oak Tree: Natural History, Art and Myth in European Culture, Herbert Art Gallery and Museum, Coventry, 1987 (Coventry, 1987)

Fifty Watercolours from Birmingham, Birmingham Museum and Art Gallery, 1987 (Birmingham, 1987)

Visions of Stonehenge, Southampton Art Gallery, 1987 (Southampton, 1987)

Travels in Italy, 1776–1783, Based on the Memoirs of Thomas Jones, Whitworth Art Gallery, Manchester, 1988 (Manchester, 1988)

In the Shadow of Vesuvius. Views of Naples from Baroque to Romanticism 1631–1830, Accademia Italiana delle Arti, London, 1990 (London, 1990)

Nature into Art. English Landscape Watercolours, Cleveland Museum of Art, 1991 (Cleveland, 1991)

British Watercolours from Birmingham, Station Gallery, Tokyo, 1991 (Tokyo, 1991)

From Gainsborough to Constable. The Emergence of Naturalism in British Landscape Painting 1750–1810, Gainsborough's House, Sudbury, 1991 (Sudbury, 1991)

Oil Sketches from Nature: Turner and his Contemporaries, Tate Gallery, London, 1991 (London, 1991)

Pintura Britanica de Hogarth a Turner, Prado, Madrid, 1992 (Madrid, 1992)

El Paisage Mediterraneo, Expo '92, Seville, 1992 (Seville, 1992)

Romanticismo: Il Nuovo Sentimento della Natura, Palazzo delle Albere, Trento, 1993 (Trento, 1993)

From View to Vision. British Watercolours from Sandby to Turner in the Whitworth Art Gallery, Whitworth Art Gallery, Manchester, 1993 (Manchester, 1993)

The Great Age of British Watercolours 1750–1880, Royal Academy of Arts, London, 1993 (London, 1993a)

Anton Raphael Mengs 1728–1779 and his British Patrons, Kenwood House, London, 1993 (London, 1993b)

British Landscape Watercolours 1750–1850, Fitzwilliam Museum, Cambridge, 1994 (Cambridge, 1994)

British Landscape Painting, The Leger Galleries, London, 1994 (London, 1994)

Gainsborough to Ruskin. British Landscape Drawings & Watercolours from the Morgan Library, Musée Communal d'Ixelles, Brussels, 1995 (Brussels, 1995)

In the Light of Italy: Corot and Early Open-Air Painting, National Gallery of Art, Washington, 1996 (Washington, 1996)

British Art Treasures from Russian Imperial Collections in the Hermitage, Yale Center for British Art, New Haven, 1996 (New Haven, 1996)

British Watercolours, Paderborn, 1996 (Paderborn, 1996)

Vases & Volcanoes. Sir William Hamilton and his Collection, British Museum, London, 1996 (London, 1996)

British Watercolours from the Oppé Collection, Tate Gallery, London, 1997 (London, 1997)

Grand Tour. The Lure of Italy in the Eighteenth Century, Tate Gallery, London, 1997 (London, 1997a)

A Brush with Nature. The Gere Collection of Landscape Oil Sketches, National Gallery, London, 1999 (London, 1999)

Mehr Licht. Europa um 1770, Die Bildende Kunst der Aufklarung, Frankfurt am Main, 1999–2000 (Frankfurt, 1999)

Art in Rome in the Eighteenth Century, Philadelphia Museum of Art, 2000 (Philadelphia, 2000)

Paysages d'Italie. Les Peintres du Plein Air (1780–1830), Grand Palais, Paris, 2001 (Paris, 2001)

Viaggio in Italia. Un Corteo Magico dal Cinquecento al Novecento, Palazzo Ducale, Genoa, 2001 (Genoa, 2001)

An Exhibition of Artefacts, Paintings, Manuscripts, Text, Illustrations and Maps Outlining the Lives of Five Men from Brecknock in the East India Company During the Second Half of the Eighteenth Century, Brecknock Museum and Art Gallery, Brecon, 2001 (Brecon, 2001)

The Line of Beauty. British Drawings and Watercolours of the Eighteenth Century, Yale Center for British Art, New Haven, 2001 (New Haven, 2001)

Il Neoclassicismo in Italia. Da Tiepolo a Canova, Palazzo Reale, Milan, 2002 (Milan, 2002)

The Thaw Collection: Master Drawings and Oil Sketches Acquisitions Since 1994, The Pierpont Morgan Library, New York, 2002 (New York, 2002)

Literature

Allan, D. G. C., *William Shipley, Founder of the Royal Society of Arts*, London, 1968 (Allan, 1968)

Andrew, Patricia R., 'Jacob More, Biography and a Checklist of Works', *The Fifty-Fifth Volume of the Walpole Society*, 1989 (Andrew, 1989)

Angelini, M. (ed.), *Gionache dell'Arte Italiana dell'Ottocento*, Milan, 1993 (Angelini, 1993)

Ashton, Joy, 'The "Discovering" of Thomas Jones 1742–1803', *Transactions of the Radnorshire Society*, vol. LXX, 2000 (Ashton, 2000)

Baker, James, *A Picturesque Guide Through Wales and the Marches*, 2nd edn, Worcester, 1795 (Baker, 1795)

Barbier, Carl Paul, *William Gilpin. His Drawings, Teaching, and Theory of the Picturesque*, Oxford, 1963 (Barbier, 1963)

Baxter, Ann, *The Landscape Painting Technique of Richard Wilson*, Post Graduate Diploma Thesis, Easel Painting Conservation, Courtauld Institute of Art, London, 1986 (Baxter, 1986)

Bell, C. F. and Girtin, Thomas, 'The Drawings and Sketches of John Robert Cozens', *The Twenty-Third Volume of the Walpole Society*, 1935 (Bell and Girtin, 1935)

Bignamini, Ilaria, 'Art Institutions in London, 1689–1768: A Story of Clubs and Academies', *The Fifty-Fourth Volume of the Walpole Society*, 1988 (Bignamini, 1988)

Blunt, Anthony, 'Recorders of Vanished Naples – I: Thomas Jones', *Country Life*, 23 August 1973 (Blunt, 1973)

Bowen Hamer, W., *Radnorshire in History, Topography and Romance*, Llandridnod Wells, 1914 (Bowen Hamer, 1914)

Bower, Peter, 'The Papers Used by John Downman', *The Quarterly. The Journal of the British Association of Paper Historians*, no. XX, October 1996 (Bower, 1996)

——, 'Tone, Texture and Strength: Girtin's Use of Paper' in Greg Smith, *Thomas Girtin: The Art of Watercolour*, London, 2002 (Bower, 2002)

Brilli, Attilio, *Il Viaggio in Italia*, Milan, 1987 (Brilli, 1987)

Brown, David Blayney, *Catalogue of the Collection of Drawings in the Ashmolean Museum. Vol. 4. The Earlier British Drawings*, Oxford, 1982 (Brown, 1982)

Bury, Adrian, *Francis Towne: Lone Star of Water-Colour Painting*, Exeter, 1962 (Bury, 1962)

Causa, Raffaello, 'Un Pittore Inglese nella Napoli di Ferdinand IV', *Campania*, no. 3, 1981 (Causa, 1981)

Conisbee, Philip, 'Pre-Romantic Plein-Air Painting', *Art History*, vol. II, no. iv, 1979 (Conisbee, 1979)

Constable, W. G., *Richard Wilson*, London, 1953 (Constable, 1953)

——, 'Richard Wilson: some Pentimenti', *The Burlington Magazine*, vol. XCVI, May 1954 (Constable, 1954)

Cormack, Malcolm, *A Concise Catalogue of Paintings in the Yale Center for British Art*, New Haven, 1985 (Cormack, 1985)

Cozens, Alexander, *A New Method of Assisting the Invention in Drawing Original Compositions of Landscape*, London, 1786 (Cozens, 1786)

Cumberland, George, *An Attempt to Describe Hafod*, Aberystwyth, 1996 (Cumberland, 1996)

De Seta, C., 'Thomas Jones e i suoi Memoirs', in *Vedutisti e Viaggiatori in Italia tra Settecento e Ottocento*, Turin, 1999 (De Seta, 1999)

Edmunds, M., 'History of the Brecknockshire Agricultural Society, 1755–1955', *Brycheiniog*, vol. II, 1956 (Edmunds, 1956)

Edwards, Ralph, 'Richard Wilson and his Pupil. Fresh Light from the Diary of Thomas Jones', *Country Life*, 16 November 1945 (Edwards, 1945)

——, 'Thomas Jones, 1742–1803: a reappraisal of his art', *Connoisseur*, May 1968 (Edwards, 1968)

Egerton, Judy, *English Watercolour Painting*, London, 1979 (Egerton, 1979)

——, *British Watercolours*, London, 1986 (Egerton, 1986)

——, 'Thomas Jones', *The World of Interiors*, April 1999 (Egerton, 1999)

——, *National Gallery Catalogues. The British School*, London, 2000 (Egerton, 2000)

Everett, Nigel, *The Tory View of Landscape*, New Haven and London, 1994 (Everett, 1994)

Fenton, James, 'Who was Thomas Jones?', *The New York Review of Books*, vol. XLIV, no. iv, 6 March 1997 (Fenton, 1997)

Ford, Brinsley, *The Drawings of Richard Wilson*, London, 1951 (Ford, 1951)

Galassi, Peter, *Corot in Italy: Open-Air Painting and the Classical Landscape Tradition*, New Haven and London, 1991 (Galassi, 1991)

Garlick, Kenneth, Mackintyre, Angus, Cave, Kathryn, and Newby, Evelyn, eds, *The Diary of Joseph Farington*, New Haven and London, 17 vols, 1978–98 (Farington, *Diary*)

Gere, John, 'An Oil-Sketch by Thomas Jones', *British Museum Quarterly*, vol. XXI, no. iv, 1959, (Gere, 1959)

——, 'Thomas Jones: An Eighteenth-century Conundrum', *Apollo*, June 1970 (Gere, 1970)

Gowing, Lawrence, *The Originality of Thomas Jones*, London, 1985 (Gowing, 1985)

Granville, H., 'A Portrait of Richard Wilson', *Connoisseur*, vol. CXXII, March 1948 (Granville, 1948)

Hackney, Stephen et al., ed., *Paint and Purpose. A Study of Technique in British Art*, London, 1999 (Hackney, 1999)

Hallett, Roger, 'The "Hafod" Sketchbook of Thomas Jones', *Friends of Hafod, Newsletter*, no. 5, Spring 1991 (Hallett, 1991)

——, 'The "Hafod" Sketchbook of Thomas Jones', *Welsh Historic Gardens Trust Newsletter*, no. VI, August 1992 (Hallett et al., 1992a)

——, Ledger, A. P., Pendred, G. L., 'Scenes from Hafod on Derby Porcelain', *Welsh Historic Gardens Trust Newsletter*, no. VI, August 1992 (Hallett et al., 1992b)

Herrmann, Luke, *British Landscape Painting of the 18th Century*, Oxford, 1974 (Herrmann, 1974)

Hinnant, C. H., 'Changing Perspectives on the Past. The Reception of Thomas Gray's *The Bard*', *Clio 3*, no. III, 1974 (Hinnant, 1974)

Ingamells, John, *A Dictionary of British and Irish Travellers in Italy 1701–1800*, New Haven and London, 1997 (Ingamells, 1997)

Joyner, Paul, *Artists in Wales: A Handlist of Artists Living and Working in Wales*, c.*1740*–c.*1851*, Aberystwyth, 1997 (Joyner, 1997)

Kerkham, Caroline, and Briggs, Stephen, 'A Review of the Archaeological Potential of the Hafod Landscape', *Ceredigion*, vol. XI, 1990 (Kerkham and Briggs, 1990)

Kitson, Sydney M., *The Life of John Sell Cotman*, London, 1937 (Kitson, 1937)

Kroll, A., *English Painting of the XVI–XIXth Centuries at the Hermitage Museum*, Leningrad, 1961 (Kroll, 1961)

Lacambre, Genevieve, 'Une Lettre de Pierre Henri de Valenciennes a une Jeune Elève', *Archives de l'Art Français*, nouv. per., vol. XXVIII, 1986 (Lacambre, 1986)

Ledger, A. P., Pendred, G. L. and Hallett, Roger, 'The "Hafod" Service', *Derby International Porcelain Society Newsletter*, no. XXVII, December 1992 (Ledger et al., 1992)

Lord, Peter, *Gwenllian: Essays on Visual Culture*, Llandysul, Gomer, 1994 (Lord, 1994)

——, *The Visual Culture of Wales. Imaging the Nation*, Cardiff, 2000 (Lord, 2000)

Malkin, Benjamin H., *The Scenery, Antiquities, and Biography, of South Wales*, London, 1804 (Malkin, 1804)

Mallalieu, H. L., *The Dictionary of British Watercolour Artists up to 1920*, Woodbridge, 1979 (Mallalieu, 1979)

Marrozzi, Ivo, 'Le Filigrane e la Questione della Qualita della Carta nella Republica Veneta della Fine del'700', in Castagnari, Giancarlo, ed., *Produzione e Uso della Carta Filigranata in Europa (Secoli XIII–XX)*, Fabriano, 1996 (Marrozzi, 1996)

Morgan, Prys, 'Thomas Jones of Pencerrig', *Transactions of the Honourable Society of Cymmrodorion*, 1984 (Morgan, 1984)

——, 'Thomas Jones of Pencerrig', *Transactions of the Radnorshire Society*, vol. LVII, 1987 (Morgan, 1987)

Mulvany, T. (ed.), *The Life of James Gandon*, Dublin, 1846 (Mulvany, 1846)

Northcote, James, *The Life of Sir Joshua Reynolds*, 2 vols, London, 1818 (Northcote, 1818)

Oliver, R. C. B., 'Pencerrig: House at the top of the Rocks', *Transactions of the Radnorshire Society*, vol. XXXIX, 1969 (Oliver, 1969)

——, *The Family History of Thomas Jones the Artist of Pencerrig, Radnorshire*, Llandrindod Wells, 1970 (Oliver, 1970)

——, 'The Jones Family of Pencerrig, Radnorshire', *Brecon & Radnor Express*, 23 and 30 July, 6, 13 and 20 August, 1970 (Oliver, 1970a)

——, 'The Diary of Captain Frederick Jones', *Transactions of the Radnorshire Society*, vols LIII–IV, 1983–4 (Oliver, 1983–4)

Oppé, Paul, ed., 'Memoirs of Thomas Jones, Penkerrig, Radnorshire, 1803', *The Thirty-Second Volume of the Walpole Society*, 1946–8 (*Memoirs*)

Ottani Cavina, Anna, *I Paesaggi della Ragione. La Città Neoclassica da David a Humbert de Superville*, Turin, 1994 (Ottani Cavina, 1994)

——, 'Landscapes of Reason: The Quest for Basic Geometric Forms in Landscape Painting from David to Corot', in Stuffmann, Hersog, von Margaret and Busch, Werner (eds), *Zeichnen in Rom 1790–1830*, Cologne, 2001 (Ottani Cavina, 2001)

Owen, Felicity, and Brown, David Blayney, *Collector of Genius. A Life of Sir George Beaumont*, New Haven and London, 1988 (Owen, 1988)

Parkinson, Ronald, *British Watercolours at the Victoria and Albert Museum*, London, 1998 (Parkinson, 1998)

Payne, Ffransis G., 'Thomas Jones, Yr Arlunydd', *Y Llenor*, vols XXIII–IV, 1944–5 (Payne, 1944–5)

——, *Crwydro Sir Faesyfed*, Llandybie, 1966 (Payne, 1966)

Pemberton, William Shakespear Childe, *The Earl Bishop. The Life of Frederick Hervey, Bishop of Derry, Earl of Bristol*, London, 1925 (Pemberton, 1925)

Price, Cecil, 'Unpublished Letters of Evan Lloyd', *The National Library of Wales Journal*, vol. VIII, 1953–4 (Price, 1953–4)

Probyn, Callista, *A Short History of Pencerrig*, n.d. (Probyn)

Radisich, Paula, 'Eighteenth-Century Plein-Air Painting and the Sketches of Pierre Henri de Valenciennes', *Art Bulletin*, vol. LXIV, March 1982 (Radisich, 1982)

Rees, T. Mardy, *Welsh Painters, Engravers, Sculptors 1527–1911*, Carnarvon, 1911 (Rees, 1911)

Rees, Thomas, and Thomas, J., *Hanes Eglwysi Annibynol Cymru*, Liverpool, 1872 (Rees, 1872)

Reynolds, Graham, *A Concise History of Watercolours*, London, 1971 (Reynolds, 1971)

Seta, Cesare de, 'Thomas Jones e i suoi Memoirs', in *Grand Tour: Viaggi narrati e dipinti, a cura di Cesare de Seta*, Naples, 2001, pp. 83–105 (Seta, 2001)

Sloan, Kim, *Alexander and John Robert Cozens. The Poetry of Landscape*, New Haven and London, 1986 (Sloan, 1986)

Smiles, Sam, *The Image of Antiquity. Ancient Britain and the Romantic Imagination*, New Haven and London, 1994 (Smiles, 1994)

Smith, Bernard, 'William Hodges and English Plein-Air Painting', *Art History*, vol. VI, no. II, 1983 (Smith, 1983)

Smith, Greg, *The Emergence of the Professional Watercolourist. Contentions and Alliances in the Artistic Domain, 1760–1824*, Aldershot, 2002 (Smith, 2002)

Solkin, David H., 'Some Variations by Richard Wilson on a Theme by Gaspard Dughet', *Burlington Magazine*, vol. CXXIII, July 1981 (Solkin, 1981)

Spinosa, Nicola, *Pitturi Napoletani del Secondo Settecento. Dal Roco al Classicismo*, Naples, 1987 (Spinosa, 1987)

——, and Di Mauro, Leonardo, *Vedute Napoletane del Settecento*, Milan, 1989 (Spinosa and Di Mauro, 1989)

Stedman Davies, D., 'Extracts from the Diaries and Account Book of Thomas Jones, Pencerrig', *Transactions of the Radnorshire Society*, vol. XII, 1942 (Stedman Davies, 1942)

Strattam, J. A., *A Short Guide to Caebach Chapel*, Llandrindod Wells, n.d. (Strattam)

Stuebe, Isabel Combs, *The Life and Works of William Hodges*, New York, 1979 (Stuebe, 1979)

Sunderland, John, 'John Hamilton Mortimer: His Life and Works', *The Fifty-Second Volume of the Walpole Society*, 1986 (Sunderland, 1986)

Sutton, Denys, and Clements, Ann, *An Italian Sketchbook by Richard Wilson RA*, London, 1968 (Sutton and Clements, 1968)

Tate Gallery, London, *The Tate Gallery 1982–84: Illustrated Catalogue of Acquisitions*, London, 1986 (Tate, 1986)

Wark, Robert R. (ed.), *Sir Joshua Reynolds Discourses on Art*, New Haven and London, 1975 (Wark, 1975)

Waterhouse, Ellis, *The Dictionary of British 18th Century Painters*, London, 1981 (Waterhouse, 1981)

Wilcox, Timothy, *Francis Towne*, London, 1997 (Wilcox, 1997)

Williams, C. I. M., 'Lusieri's Surviving Works', *The Burlington Magazine*, vol. CXXIV, August 1982 (Williams, 1982)

Williams, Jonathan, 'The History of Radnorshire', *Archaeologia Cambrensis*, 1859 (Williams, 1859)

Wilton, Andrew, *British Watercolours, 1750–1850*, Oxford, 1977 (Wilton, 1977)

Wollheim, Richard, *Painting as an Art*, London, 1987 (Wollheim, 1987)

——, 'Thomas Jones in Naples', *FMR*, August 1988 (Wollheim, 1988)

Wright, T., *Some Account of the Life of Richard Wilson, Esq. R.A.*, London, 1824 (Wright, 1824)

Yerburgh, David S., *An Attempt to Depict Hafod: An Artistic Impression*, Salisbury, 2000 (Yerburgh, 2000)

Ziff, Jerrold, '"Backgrounds, Introduction of Architecture and Landscape": A Lecture by J. M. W. Turner', *Journal of the Warburg and Courtauld Institutes*, vol. XXVI, 1963 (Ziff, 1963)

PHOTOGRAPHIC CREDITS

Catalogue

Ashmolean Museum, Oxford, 111; Birmingham Museum and Art Gallery, 40, 98, 99, 120; Bolton Museum and Art Gallery, Bolton MBC, 141; Brecknock Museum & Art Gallery, 35; Bristol Museum and Art Gallery, 16; © The British Museum, 74, 75, 79, 93, 100, 101, 115, 127; Courtauld Institute Gallery, London, 128; Fitzwilliam Museum, Cambridge, 84, 121; City & County of Swansea: Glynn Vivian Art Gallery, 116; by courtesy of the Trustees of Sir John Soane's Museum, 130; Museo di Roma, 69; © National Gallery, London, 63, 114, 119; National Gallery of Art, Washington, 81; National Museums & Galleries of Wales, 1, 6, 9, 14, 21, 24, 31, 42, 45, 49, 57, 61, 76, 82, 86, 106, 108, 110, 136, 145, 155, 156, 164, 165; Llyfrgell Genedlaethol Cymru/National Library of Wales, 8, 10, 55, 154, 157, 158, 159; Pierpont Morgan Library, 151; Radnorshire Museum, 73, 160; The State Hermitage, St Petersburg 2003, 20; Southampton City Art Gallery/ Bridgeman Art Library, 32; © Tate, London, 2002, 15, 17, 41, 44, 59, 65, 80, 97, 109, 113, 117, 122, 132, 153; Towner Art Gallery, Eastbourne, 23; © Photo V&A Picture Library, 11, 12, 18, 96, 129; The Whitworth Art Gallery, The University of Manchester, 51, 52, 53, 78, 94, 95, 112, 131, 161; Yale Center for British Art, New Haven, 13, 19, 22, 28, 29, 43, 56, 90, 139, 162; by courtesy of the owner, 33, 46, 67, 135; by courtesy of the owner, photograph Christie's Images, 30; by courtesy of the owner, Photographic Survey, Courtauld Institute of Art, 102; by courtesy of the owner, photograph National Gallery, London, 36, 38, 48, 60, 66, 71, 72, 83, 85, 88, 91, 103, 104, 140, 148, 149, 163; by courtesy of the owner, photograph National Museums & Galleries of Wales, 2, 3, 4, 5, 7, 25, 26, 27, 34, 37, 39, 47, 50, 54, 64, 68, 77, 87, 89, 107, 118, 123, 124, 126, 133, 146, 147, 152, 166; by courtesy of the owner, photograph Prudence Cuming Associates Limited, 70, 92, 105, 125, 137, 138, 142, 143, 144, 150; by courtesy of the owner: Photographic Department, Whitworth Art Gallery, University of Manchester, 62, 134.

Figures

By courtesy of APOLLO Magazine, 9; Collection of Bayerische Hypo- und Vereinsbank AG in the Alter Pinakothek Munich and Kunstdia-Archiv ARTOTHEK, D-Weilheim, 18; courtesy of Bonhams Auctioneers, 14, 15; by permission of the British Library, London, 31; Country Life Picture Library, 19; Derby Museums and Art Gallery, 24; © The J. Paul Getty Museum, 29; © National Gallery, London, 10, 21; Ailsa Mellon Bruce Collection, Photograph © Board of Trustees, National Gallery of Art, Washington, 27; Llyfrgell Genedlaethol Cymru/The National Library of Wales, 20, 22, 33, 38; National Museums & Galleries of Wales, 1, 2, 4, 5, 7, 8, 13, 17, 34, 35, 39, 56, 57, 58, 59, 60, 61, 62; by courtesy of the National Portrait Gallery, London, 11; Palazzo Reale, Caserta, 30; RSA, London, 12; © Photo RMN – C. Jean, 23; © Photo RMN – Gérard Blot, 25; Private collection, Rome, 32; © Tate, London 2002, 28; The Whitworth Art Gallery, The University of Manchester, 26; Yale Center for British Art, New Haven, 16; by courtesy of the owner, photograph National Museums & Galleries of Wales, 3, 6, 36, 37, 40, 41, 42, 43, 44, 45, 46, 47, 48, 49, 50, 51, 52, 53, 54, 55.

Copyright

Andrew Motion, *A Wall in Naples* is reprinted from the *Guardian* by permission of PFD on behalf of Andrew Motion.

LIST OF LENDERS

Public Institutions

Ashmolean Museum, Oxford; Birmingham Museums & Art Gallery; Bolton Museum and Art Gallery, MBC; Brecknock Museum and Art Gallery, Brecon; Bristol Museum and Art Gallery; British Museum, London; Courtauld Institute Gallery, London; Fitzwilliam Museum, Cambridge; City & County of Swansea: Glynn Vivian Art Gallery; Sir John Soane's Museum, London; Museo di Roma, Rome; National Gallery, London; National Gallery of Art, Washington; National Library of Wales, Aberystwyth; National Museums & Galleries of Wales; Thaw Collection, Pierpont Morgan Library, New York; The Radnorshire Museum, Powys County Council; The State Hermitage Museum, St Petersburg; Southampton City Art Gallery; Tate, London; Towner Art Gallery and Museum, Eastbourne; Victoria & Albert Museum, London; Whitworth Art Gallery, University of Manchester; Yale Center for British Art, New Haven.

Private Lenders

Joy Ashton on behalf of the Radnorshire Society; Lady Ginette Darwin; Judy Egerton; Mrs George Lindsay; David W. Posnett; and other generous lenders who wish to remain anonymous.

INDEX